"FIRST WITH THE MOST" FORREST

By Robert Selph Henry

The Story of the Confederacy
The Story of Reconstruction
Trains
This Fascinating Railroad Business

FORREST IN ACTION
By Colonel John W. Thomason, Jr., U.S.M.C.

"First With the Most"
Forrest

by

Robert Selph Henry

THE BOBBS-MERRILL COMPANY

PUBLISHERS

INDIANAPOLIS   NEW YORK

To

THREE LONG-SUFFERING LADIES

CONTENTS

LIST OF ILLUSTRATIONS

LIST OF MAPS

CHAPTER I

A MEASURE OF THE MAN

"Ever greater than his opportunities . . .
The greatest soldier of his time."

ON THE fourteenth day of June 1861, one month before his fortieth birthday, Nathan Bedford Forrest quietly walked into a Memphis recruiting office to enlist as a private in the service of the Confederate States of America.

In age, in appearance, in his air of successful management of affairs, the new trooper in Captain Josiah White's company of Tennessee Mounted Rangers stood out from the general run of eager youth crowding to enlist in the Confederate cause. There was six feet two of him, lithe and powerful of build, with steady eyes of deep gray-blue set wide in a lean, high-cheeked, swarthy face crowned with thick, wavy, iron-gray hair and set off with a short black chin beard—altogether a man of striking and commanding presence.

But he was no *beau sabreur* of the sort in whom the South delighted. Rather, he was a middle-aged, quiet-spoken businessman who, by the time he was forty, had earned from nothing a fortune, according to his own estimate, of more than a million dollars,[1] and who was going to war in no mood of youthful and romantic adventure, but in cold and sober earnest, wholly and without reservation. "I went into the war because my vote had been unable to preserve the peace," he said in an interview published in the New York *Times* of June 22, 1868. But he added, "I took a through ticket, and I fought and lost as much as any one else; certainly as much as I could."

This one private soldier of all the armies of that war who was to rise to the rank of lieutenant general,[2] and whose operations, long after he was dead, were to receive the respectful study of commanders of armies in the United States and in Europe, had no military education whatsoever.

His formal education of any sort, indeed, is supposed to have consisted of no more than three months of schooling in the village of Chapel Hill, in Middle Tennessee, where he was born in 1821, and about as much more between his thirteenth year, when the family removed to Tippah County, in northern Mississippi, and his sixteenth year, when the

13

death of his pioneer blacksmith father threw upon young Bedford, as the eldest son, much of the care and support of a widowed mother and nine younger children.

But though he lacked formal education, Forrest was by no means the illiterate ignoramus. His surviving writing is clear, direct and distinctly to the point, despite unconventional spelling. He would not be bothered with such extra and entirely unnecessary letters as the "a" in "hedquarters," nor did he pay attention to such letters as the silent "gh" in so simple a word as "fite," for example. He spelled as he fought, by ear, but there would have been no room to doubt his meaning when he wrote across the face of a three-times persistently repeated application for a furlough, "I have tole you twict goddamit No!"[3] In this story, as usually told, Forrest is represented as having expanded "no" into a four-letter word. His actual practice, however, to judge from at least three of his surviving letters, was just the reverse: to cut "know" down to a two-letter word by discarding its superfluous and meaningless beginning and ending.

To the handicap of lack of education there was added another—the nature of the business in which Forrest made his fortune. Along with trading in lands and livestock and cotton planting, he had engaged in a large and conspicuous way in the buying and selling of slaves. It was a business entirely lawful at the time and place, but it is a commentary upon the South's "peculiar institution" that even among those who owned them, and who upon occasion bought and sold them, there attached to the commercial traffic in slaves a certain social stain. And this was true even where, as in the case of Forrest, the dealer was more than usually kind to his human stock in trade. "There were men in Memphis," Lafcadio Hearn reported, "to whom Forrest would never sell a slave because they had the reputation of being cruel masters."[4]

Forty-five of Forrest's own slaves, indeed, served through the war with him as teamsters. "I said to forty-five colored fellows on my plantation . . ." Forrest told a Congressional committee after the war, "that I was going into the army; and that if they would go with me, if we got whipped they would be free anyhow, and that if we succeeded and slavery was perpetuated, if they would act faithfully with me to the end of the war, I would set them free. Eighteen months before the war closed I was satisfied that we were going to be defeated, and I gave those forty-five men, or forty-four of them, their free papers, for fear I might get killed."[5]

The rest of the story of these forty-five slaves—or of those of them who stuck to the end—comes from a very young and then totally unknown Confederate soldier, George W. Cable of New Orleans, who, wounded, lost his horse and under the Confederate system of mounting troops could not continue as a cavalryman until he could get himself another. In the interim he served for a time as a clerk in Forrest's headquarters, where one of his tasks was to help make out some of these manumission papers.[6]

Forrest's fame was all before him when he enlisted as a forty-year-old private soldier, but locally, in the rising river port of Memphis, he had already come to be known as a man of substance and standing in the commercial world. By some he is remembered as "arbitrary, imperious, and determined," a man "fierce and terrible."[7] It is agreed that "his temper when aroused was terrific," and his "language was often violent and profane, but never vulgar or obscene."[8] In a society which took its liquor hard and treated tobacco as a staple of life, he drank not at all, never smoked and did not even "chew." Despite his outbursts of temper, there was about him at other times a grave dignity.

Life for him had been a struggle and combat in a harsh and hard-bitten world but it had not driven from him that touch of sentiment which led him to do such things as leave a lock of hair for Emma Sanson, the sixteen-year-old girl who risked her life to guide him to the lost ford by which he crossed the Big Black to come up with Streight's raiders, or weep with Lieutenant Gould, dying of the wound which Forrest himself had implacably inflicted. And always, he would leave the company of grownups to talk gravely and interestedly with children—one of whom remembered him in the days before the war as "a stalwart man, who habitually went in his shirt sleeves and spoke kindly to children."[9]

He was, indeed, a man of mixed nature, compounded of violence and of gentleness. But through all the contradictions of a contradictory character, in one thing there was never a variation, never a contradiction. Always and everywhere, whenever and wherever there was fighting to be done, he fought.

Nor was that all, for as he stood there in Captain White's recruiting office, quietly taking the oath which made of him a soldier in the Confederate service, there was latent in him the power to create and to command armies. "His commission as General," one of his soldiers, Sergeant Frank T. Reid, wrote, "was signed not only by Mr. Jefferson Davis, but by the Almighty as well."[10]

"And," Sergeant Reid added, "his soldiers knew it." They were, indeed, the first to discover it. "It cost something to ride with Forrest,"[11] another one of them wrote afterward, but for what it cost they got victory. His men "he ruled so that they feared him more than the enemy," Lafcadio Hearn concluded from what was told him by old soldiers and citizens of Memphis, "and yet they confided in him as though he were

15

incapable of an error or a fault."[12] They recognized in him the qualities of sagacity and energy, of courage and constancy in his chosen course, and that rare and most uncommon quality called common sense, and so they gave him, as men and soldiers, an immense confidence. They went where he told them to go, and they did what he told them to do, because they believed in Old Bedford, and when Old Bedford led, they believed in themselves.

These soldiers of Forrest's were not a selected *corps d'élite* of scions of the white-columned mansions of the South. They were very much run-of-the-mine young fellows, many of whom were secured during the latter stages of the war by vigorous and even ruthless application of the conscript law. From such average material, the magic hand of Forrest made a sort of early model of today's Commandos or Rangers. Under him, wrote Lieutenant Colonel George T. Denison of the British army in his standard *History of Cavalry*, horse troops "could perform outpost duty with wonderful ability; they could dismount and fight in line of battle against infantry, cavalry or artillery; they could attack fortifications, capture gunboats, storm stockades, in fact, do anything that could be expected of soldiers."[13]

And so, as a veteran of Forrest's Old Brigade said, "as long as we followed him we enjoyed the respect of the army. If we passed a regiment of infantry they would heap on us the customary contempt for cavalry but when they learned that we belonged to Forrest's people they would change tune and fraternize with us as real soldiers. . . . We were heroes, even to the infantry."[14] Which is praise as high as could be won by any body of troops.

Those against whom Forrest fought came, too, to an early realization that this was no common soldier and no ordinary commander. General Grant, reflecting upon the whole course of the Confederate War, rated Forrest as "about the ablest cavalry general in the South."[15] To General Sherman, during the heat of the war, he was "that devil Forrest," who must be "hunted down and killed if it costs ten thousand lives and bankrupts the Federal treasury."[16] Hardly could a soldier have won more sincere recognition from those against whom he fought.

Forrest's gift for strategy was a constant wonder and delight to the young men who served under him, many of them men of wide education and some of them capable professional soldiers. Logistics, probably, wasn't even a word to him, but he was "a good quartermaster and commissary as well as soldier,"[17] with an instinctive perception of the importance of the care, feeding and supply of men and horses, and a vast practical talent in seeing that *his* men and *his* horses were looked after, down to the infinity of detail which makes or mars a command. "In Forrest's command, a sore-backed horse was a felony."[18]

16

More than this, he infused into his whole command his own spirit and purpose, his own energy and vitality. For him men, and even horses, marched impossible marches to fight impossible fights and win incredible victories. His men remembered the "electrical effect" of his passage from rear to front along columns of "men and beasts worn out with loss of sleep and with work and hunger," as they struggled through swamps in the darkness of night and torrents of rain. They remembered how, "at the sound of that strange, shrill voice, and at the sight of that dark form . . . riding by on his big gray war-steed" men were "invigorated as by the first fresh breath of early dawn" and "the very horses recovered their strength."[19] Another soldier, an infantryman who served under Forrest only during the dreadful midwinter retreat of the rear guard of Hood's broken army after the battle of Nashville, remembered how the General gave up his own horse to help along men of the bleeding "barefoot brigade"—and how, too, the gloom of that most gloomy Christmas season was lightened by the presence of Forrest "as he rode the lines, the light of battle in his eye and the thunderous 'Charge!' upon his lips." On that day, the soldier wrote thirty-five years later, "he rode into my heart as well . . . and rides there still."[20]

He was not only a commander but himself a trooper in the very midst of combat, wounded four times, with horses shot under him twenty-nine times, with no fewer than thirty enemy soldiers accounted for in hand-to-hand fighting in the almost innumerable affairs at arms in which he was engaged.

But he was not an "educated soldier" in the understanding of a day which laid large store by the elaborate ritual of parade-ground "tactics" and the counts or motions of the manual of arms. For all such he had something of disdain—"fifteen minutes of *bulge*," he said to a Union officer, "is worth a week of tactics"[21]—but these things occupied a place of importance in the military world of that day which in the light of the more flexible handling of troops now can scarcely be imagined.

In that world, Forrest did not "belong," nor did he conform. And so while the war went on, this unknown in the West who raised regiments, brigades and divisions, and armed and equipped them mostly at the expense of the enemy, was rated at Richmond as little more than a "bold and enterprising raider and rider,"[22] a sort of glorified guerrilla whose habit of winning battles in an unorthodox fashion could not make up for his lack of familiarity with the minutiae of army regulations and the fine print of the drill books.

And so Forrest was, until almost the very last of the war, held to be incapable of military command in the large. What he could have accomplished with larger forces, no one can say for sure. What he did was to make the most of what he had in every situation. "He continually grew

17

in power to the last," as one scholarly Virginian under whom he served for a season wrote of him, "and was ever greater than his opportunities."[23]

For a long generation after the war of the sixties, its veterans talked. They talked of its camps and marches, its battles and campaigns, its supplies and the lack thereof, of anything and everything connected with that experience of their youth which, to them, remained always and simply The War.

But most of all they talked about men, the qualities and abilities of the men under whose leadership they had lived and marched and fought. The men of whom they talked fought in a war whose last shot was fired nearly fourscore years ago. The tactics of that war are as outmoded today as are the weapons with which it was fought. Its strategy, limited by means of communication and transportation then available, was that of a local, not a global, struggle. It was fought in two dimensions instead of three. But granting all this, still it was fought by men—and men, and the leading of men, remain the unchanging elements in war.

Forrest's men never tired of talking of his courage and sagacity, and of his care for his men and horses, as well as the demands he made upon them. They talked of the flash of his eye, the brassy clangor of his voice in the charge, so unlike his quiet and low speech at other times. They talked of his way with men, of his exploding and consuming wrath, of his unexpected touches of gentleness and sentiment. They talked of his unwearying vitality and his unyielding will, and, above all, of the strategy, bold and wily, by which he won his, and their, fights—a strategy which Sherman described as "original and to me incomprehensible,"[24] which met attack by attacking, and never, until the failing days at the very last, stood to receive an attack of the enemy.

These men, whose point of pride ever after was that in the days of their youth they, too, "rode with Old Bedford," talked of him as the men of the Hellenic main and the islands of the Aegean might have talked of Ajax or Achilles—for Forrest was a figure about whom, even while he lived, legend began to gather.

Legend has had its way the more with the story of Forrest because so much of his fame is folk-fame. Among the Southern people, or at least that portion of them to whom Shiloh and Chickamauga are more than vaguely familiar names of fields of battle, it rests quite as much upon the remembered talk of the veterans as it does upon the records. By most of the rest of the world he is remembered chiefly, especially in these latter days when the world's attention is focused on war of swift movement and sudden surprise, not so much by what he did as by what he is supposed to have said—"Git thar fustest with the mostest men."

18

Of course that wasn't just what he said. Forrest would have been totally incapable of so obvious and self-conscious a piece of literary carpentry. What he said, he said simply and directly—"Get there first with the most men," although doubtless his pronunciation was "git thar fust," that being the idiom of the time and place. Such a phrase, compacting about as much of the art of war as has ever been put into so few words, had no need of the artificial embellishment of double superlatives.

The first man who heard the phrase and wrote about it, though the writing was not until long afterward, was Basil Duke, brother-in-law and second in command to General John Hunt Morgan. Both Morgan and Forrest were serving under General Bragg at the time. Both of them had recently carried out brilliant little operations, Morgan in Kentucky and Forrest in Middle Tennessee. The two were comparing notes at Murfreesborough, Tennessee, each more interested in finding out what the other had done and how he had done it than in telling his own exploits, when Forrest explained his success with the impatient exclamation, "I just . . . got there first with the most men."[25] The phrase is given in the same form in perhaps the earliest printed reference to it, in Lieutenant General Dick Taylor's informative and delightful memoirs.[26] To Federal officers whom Forrest met under flag of truce in Mississippi, in the dying days of the war, he "reflectively declared that he had not the advantage of a military education, and knew but little as to the art of war, but he always made it his rule 'to get there first with the most men.' "[27]

And so Forrest's phrase gradually gained currency but it was not until he himself had long been dead that its embellishers began to transmute his simple and direct words into the jargon of superlatives in which it is now most often quoted. The "mostest" seems to have appeared first, with the "fustest" as a natural corollary once someone started the thing.[28]

By the time of the First World War, these weird terminations had become so thoroughly established that when Sir Frederick Maurice quoted Forrest correctly and without them, in one of his 1918 war dispatches from Great Britain, the New York *Tribune* promptly took him to task for being "unjust to Forrest." Forrest, said the *Tribune*, was a "unique and incomparably racy genius . . . the most extraordinary cavalry leader produced by our Civil War," but he "talked what might be called 'cracker' Southern dialect," and "no one would have been more astonished than he at the unimpeachably academic form given by a cultivated British brother-in-arms to one of his pithiest and most characteristic sayings."[29] To which the New York *Times* responded on the next day, agreeing with the *Tribune's* estimate of Forrest's military stature, but

19

pointing out truly that no uneducated man, whether Southern cracker or not, would ever have thought of casting the phrase in so purely artificial a form as that insisted upon by the *Tribune*.[30] Sir Frederick himself, however, must have accepted the *Tribune's* version, for when he had occasion once more to use the phrase in his *Lee, the Soldier*, he quoted it with the extra terminations. "There we have in eight words," the British commentator added, "the gist of many volumes of Jomini and Clausewitz."[31]

So widely have these terminations passed into the folklore of American sayings, however, that, as the Baltimore *Sun* remarked, we probably shall never hear the "lastest" of them, and there is no real use now to try to lop them off. They have become part of the traditional Forrest—and Forrest has become part of the American fighting tradition.

Forrest coined the phrase but in his own operations he almost never applied it literally. He was prompt, very prompt, in his movements, and usually "got there first," coming in fast and hitting hard, but rarely did he have the "most men." He did have, though, the great gift of using such men as he had, almost always inferior in number in the whole field of action, so as to have the superior force at the decisive place—"there"—and the critical time—"first." Or if, perchance, he did not manage that, he usually was able, as one of Joel Chandler Harris' characters put it, to "git thar ahead of" the enemy and to "make him believe he had the most men."[32]

At the heart of the story of Forrest the soldier there is an ample core of recorded fact—much of it more remarkable, indeed, than the overlay of legend. His second public career, in the days after the war, however, rests entirely upon tradition and legend, for most of what he did in those desperate days of struggle was never written down, and some of it, no doubt, never even told. Secrecy surrounded, and to a large extent still surrounds, the original Ku Klux Klan. Mysterious in its birth, its life and its dissolution, the Klan left almost no records, and even tradition deals more with the methods by which it sought to interpose the shield of its ghostly terrors between the South and the more vengeful features of Reconstruction, than it does with the individuals who composed the organization. No man who could have known the fact of his own knowledge ever wrote it down and published it, but it is universally believed in the South, nevertheless, that the Grand Wizard who was called to head the Invisible Empire, and who under the absolute powers granted him disbanded the organization forever when he felt that it had done all it could do, was General Forrest. In this work—hard, dangerous, desperate—he was engaged while more than one of the more prominent generals of the losing side in the war were withdrawn from the world, perhaps pondering the writing of memoirs of self-justification.

Through fact and through legend, there stands out the man and the soldier of whom it was to be truly written, on the day of his funeral, that "he was fairly worshipped" by his old soldiers;[33] and who fifteen years later was to be held up by the General in Chief of the British Imperial forces as the ideal of a leader for the mounted forces of his country;[34] who was to be adjudged by one commander under whom he served "the greatest soldier the war produced" on either side; and by another, "the greatest soldier of his time."[35] Through the years he has grown in stature until in our time his fundamental rule of victory, to "get there first with the most," has come to be accepted all over the world as the very antithesis of "too little, too late."

CHAPTER II

THE FIRST FORTY YEARS

1821-1861

NATHAN BEDFORD FORREST was born on July 13, 1821, in the Duck River country of Middle Tennessee, at the hamlet of Chapel Hill, in what now is Marshall County but then was Bedford—hence the middle name. He was the first son of William Forrest, pioneer blacksmith, and his wife, Mariam Beck. Of his ancestors little is known beyond the fact that they were of English, Scottish and Irish stock, and that they constituted part of that vast migration of obscure people who, generation after generation, pushed westward the frontier of America.

In the days of General Forrest's fame, and in efforts to explain his military genius, writers undertook to construct a genealogy, largely conjectural, which traveled back through Sir Thomas Forrest, early settler at Jamestown, to titled families and knights of old in Britain.[1] But the clear line of his ancestry runs back, on his father's side, no farther than to his great-grandfather Shadrach Forrest, who removed from western Virginia to Orange County, North Carolina, about 1730. Shadrach's son, Nathan, born in North Carolina, there married a Miss Baugh and, early in the new century, emigrated with his family, including the ancient Shadrach, to Tennessee, to settle first in the county of Sumner and then in Bedford.

Of the family of General Forrest's mother, Mariam Beck, still less is known.[2] But one seeking the source of her son's power hardly need go beyond Mariam Beck herself. Scotch-Irish by blood, of a family which had moved from upcountry South Carolina to Tennessee, inflexibly Presbyterian in faith, tall and powerful of frame, with level gray eyes under level black brows, dauntless of heart, that masterful woman bore to William Forrest, and raised to maturity, six sons, and after six years of widowhood bore three more sons and a daughter to a second husband, Joseph Luxton.

Of her sons, Nathan Bedford became a lieutenant general of the Confederate army. Jeffrey, the youngest Forrest, was commissioned a brigadier general at the age of twenty-six but was killed in a charge at the head of his brigade at Okolona, before his commission reached him. Aaron, commanding a regiment, died of pneumonia near Dresden on

22

the hard winter campaigns of 1864 in West Tennessee. Jesse, also lieutenant colonel of a regiment, was disabled for further service by wounds in battle. William, captain of daredevil scouts, suffered a shattered leg in a desperate charge but recovered to finish the war. Still another Forrest son, John, next in age to Bedford, was partially paralyzed and permanently disabled by wounds received in the War with Mexico. Two of the younger Luxton sons of Mariam Beck—boys still in their teens—became soldiers in the Confederate service, while, at the very last, the third and youngest of the Luxton boys, not yet sixteen, left his mother's farm and passed through the lines to join the failing forces of the Confederacy.[3]

From 1821 when young Bedford and his twin sister Fanny were born, the Forrest family remained at Chapel Hill and grew in numbers until 1834, when William, the blacksmith, disposed of small belongings which could not be moved, packed up those which could be, and set out, following the frontier to Tippah County in northern Mississippi, just below the Tennessee line, to settle on lands only recently made available by the removal of the Chickasaw Nation to the new Indian Territory.

In Tippah County, in 1837, William Forrest died. His oldest son, Bedford, not yet sixteen, became the "man" of the family, consisting then of five brothers and three sisters—and the dauntless Mariam. Their home was a cabin in a clearing in the wilderness, Salem being the nearest hamlet. Like that other and more famous early American Salem, in Illinois, the hamlet has since disappeared, leaving no trace of a town, and the site is now known locally as Old Salem. It is located not far from Ashland in that part of Tippah County which in 1870 became Benton County.[4]

This boy who, with his mother, faced the responsibility of making a home in the wilderness, infested by panthers and other "varmints,"[5] and of bringing up a family, is supposed to have had three months of schooling in Tennessee before his thirteenth year, and a like period in Mississippi before his father's death.[6]

The family was soon to be enlarged by the posthumous birth of another boy, Jeffrey, but the pestilential fevers of the newly cleared forest lands took their toll in the death of two boys and all three girls, including Bedford's twin sister Fanny.

It was a life of "poverty, toil and responsibility,"[7] work in field or forest clearing as long as there was light to see, work late in the house by the flickering firelight, making buckskin moccasins, leggings and shirts, or coonskin caps for the younger children. "Store-bought" goods were all but unknown. But hard work, frugality and good management counted, and within three years after the death of William Forrest, the family was

23

established on a more secure footing than it had ever known before.

In his twentieth year Bedford showed his first inclination to the military, and the only one until the outbreak of the war in the sixties, two decades later. The five-year-old Republic of Texas was in conflict with Mexico. An invasion from below the Rio Grande was rumored and feared. Texas had been settled and its independence won largely by Southern men. Here and there throughout the South, military companies were organized to go to the aid of Texas. Bedford Forrest, a "tall, black-haired, gray-eyed athletic youth,"[8] joined such a company formed at Holly Springs, Mississippi.

The company proceeded to New Orleans, found that steamer transportation to Galveston could not be arranged, disbanded and turned back—but not young Forrest. He and a few others pushed on to Houston, to find when they got there that there was no invasion, no war and no demand for their soldierly services. Forrest's first step toward a military career ended then and there, in a job on a plantation splitting rails at fifty cents a hundred, and saving his money to get back home, which he did after an absence of more than four months.

In 1842, shortly after Bedford reached his majority, he entered the livestock and livery-stable business with his uncle, Jonathan Forrest, in the town of Hernando, Mississippi, twenty miles south of Memphis, Tennessee. The new scene of young Forrest's endeavors is described in the gazetteers of the time as a "post village, capital of De Soto County, situated 18 miles East of the Mississippi River, in a fertile region, and containing a court house, several stores, and 400 inhabitants"—in contrast with Salem, which is credited with no more than a post office.

The partnership with his uncle ended on March 20, 1845, when the elder Forrest was killed in one of the fights which seem to have been part of the life of that gun-toting frontier era. The old gentleman was set upon on the Public Square at Hernando by four men, three Matlocks and their overseer, Bean, and was killed at almost the first fire. But young Bedford immediately declared himself in the fight—one against four—and to such good effect that one Matlock was killed, the others wounded and driven off, and Bean was captured. Bedford, the surviving Forrest, was not indicted, while the other participants were tried and punished by the courts, in itself an unusual circumstance since in those days the law did not concern itself, usually, with the fighting quarrels of the quick-tempered and quick-triggered men of northern Mississippi.

This year of 1845, the twenty-fourth of Forrest's life, was eventful for him. Riding out on a Sunday morning that summer, he found a carriage stuck in the mud of a creek crossing near Hernando. In the carriage were Miss Mary Ann Montgomery and her widowed mother, ladies

24

of a Middle Tennessee family recently come to De Soto County. The Montgomery family traced descent from General Richard Montgomery, killed in the attack on Quebec in 1775, while Mrs. Montgomery was of the Cowan family from whom the rail junction of Cowan, Tennessee, takes its name. Near by sat two of the local gallants, watching the vain efforts of the Negro driver to get the carriage started.

Up rode young Forrest, brave in his Sunday best. To rescue the ladies in distress and carry them to the bank; to return, wade into the mud and extricate the stuck carriage with a heave of his powerful frame; to chase away with threats of bodily violence the two gallants who had watched the scene with interest but without action—all this was preliminary to introducing himself to Mrs. Montgomery and her gentle nineteen-year-old daughter.

The mud-splattered Forrest asked and was granted permission to call—which he did forthwith. On the porch of the Montgomery home he found the same two young men whom he had so fiercely chased away from the mudhole. His feelings toward them had changed not one bit, nor his actions. He unceremoniously chased them again, even though one was in training for the ministry, a circumstance which in that day and place was claim to more than usual respect and consideration.

That day he proposed marriage to Mary Ann. On his next visit—their third meeting—he was accepted. He had yet, however, to win the consent of her uncle and foster father, the Reverend Samuel Montgomery Cowan, of the Cumberland Presbyterian Church and a mighty man of God in those parts. The story, as it comes down through Miss Sarah Hall, who had attended Dr. Elliott's famous Nashville Female Academy with Mary Ann, is that when young Bedford approached the sometimes fierce Reverend Cowan, he was met with refusal.

"Why, Bedford, I couldn't consent. You cuss and gamble and Mary Ann is a Christian girl."

"I know it, and that's just why I want her," was the reply.[9]

Persistence won and within the month, in September 1845, the Hernando paper announced:

> MARRIED—On Thursday evening, the 25th inst., by the Rev. S. M. Cowan, Mr. N. B. Forrest to Miss Mary Ann Montgomery, all of this county:
> The above came to hand accompanied by a good sweet morsel of cake and a bottle of the best wine. May the happy couple live long to enjoy the felicity of this world is our sentiment, and we heartily thank them for remembering us in the midst of their hymeneal joy.[10]

25

The cottage in which the young couple set up housekeeping has disappeared, but a photograph, made a half a century later when it was becoming ruinous, shows what manner of place it was—a double log house, clapboard covered, wide rooms on either side of a central hall, a half-story above, a covered gallery across the front, brick chimneys at either end. It was a small house of simple dignity in line and proportion, undistinguished among the thousands of like houses whose very number surviving even to this day is enough to tell anyone with eyes to see that the population of the ante-bellum South included those who were neither "planter aristocracy" nor "poor whites."[11] There, a year later, their son William was born, and two years after that a daughter, Fanny, who lived to be but five years old.

In 1851, the scope of his business having outgrown Hernando, Forrest moved to the bustling, booming river port of Memphis. There he dealt in cotton, in plantations, in livestock and in slaves. His slave yard, surrounded by a high brick wall, was near the corner of Adams and Third Streets. The place was pointed out in 1877 to Lafcadio Hearn, who described it as a "square, old fashioned four-story building, with a brick piazza of four arches, painted yellow. This is now called the Central Hotel. It used to be Forrest's slave market. . . ." Describing the operations of the business there conducted, as it was told him by witnesses, some of whom he said had "feared and disliked him [Forrest] about evenly," Hearn continued:

"It is said Forrest was kind to his negroes; that he never separated members of a family, and that he always told his slaves to go out in the city and choose their own masters. There is no instance of any slave taking advantage of the permission to run away. Forrest taught them that it was to their own interest not to abuse the privilege; and, as he also taught them to fear him exceedingly, I can believe the story. There were some men in the town to whom he would never sell a slave, because they had the reputation of being cruel masters."[12]

Testimony is unanimous that besides the ordinary good business practice of looking after the physical well-being of the slaves he bought and sold, he went to lengths to keep families together, and even to reunite them, so as to avoid the painful separations that were too common in the days of the rapid expansion of cotton planting in the lower Mississippi River region; and that frequently he was besought by slaves to purchase them, because of his reputation for kindness and fair treatment.

There is a glimpse of Forrest as he appeared in these days, "on one of his trading expeditions," encamped in front of the Mississippi home of a lad with an aching tooth, into which Forrest put creosote, the first the boy had ever seen. Writing sixty years later, the boy recalled the incident and the "image which I should have carried in my mind to this day even if there had never been a war," that of "a man of commanding but pleasing personality . . ."[13]

Forrest was thirty years old when he and his young family moved to Memphis. There he first attracted public attention outside the circle of his business in 1857, when, as a private citizen with no special responsibility for the upholding of law, he risked his life twice in one evening to rescue from the hands of a mob intent on lynching him a man whom Forrest did not even know. The quick boldness with which Forrest cut the rope already around the prisoner's neck, the fast thinking by which he got him from the Navy Yard, where the hanging was to have been, to the comparative safety of the jail, and the calm courage with which he there outfaced the mob, all combined to make him a man of mark in the Memphis of the day.[14]

Members of the mob which he had outwitted and outfaced doubtless were among those who elected him an alderman of the city of Memphis—the only political office he ever held—in 1858 and re-elected him in 1859. By that time, however, Forrest's attention was turned more and more from his business as a trader to the raising of cotton on his three-thousand-acre plantation in Coahoma County, Mississippi, and a smaller one in Tunica County. Early in 1859 the real-estate, livestock and slave business was closed out in Memphis, and Alderman Forrest resigned to settle on his plantation in Mississippi. Before the end of the year, however, he returned to make his residence in Memphis, where he was promptly re-elected as Alderman, to serve his unexpired term until 1860.

One characteristic story told of Alderman Forrest is that when it was proposed that the city sell the stock it owned in the Memphis and Charleston Railroad, he protested and fought the sale because he believed the price too low. Having failed in his effort to prevent the sale, he backed his judgment by buying some of the stock and turning a neat profit on its resale.[15]

But the affairs of the Board of Aldermen of Memphis must have seemed small game by 1860. In the national election of that year there was, for the first time, a complete cleavage between the states, along sectional lines. Before the end of the year, secession of states began, South Carolina leading off in December. Mississippi, the state in which Forrest passed his young manhood and in which, after 1859, his principal property lay, acted on January 9, 1861. By February, seven states had seceded and their representatives met in Montgomery to organize a provisional government for the Confederate States.

27

While that convention was in session, and on the same day on which Jefferson Davis of Mississippi was elected President of the Confederate States, Tennessee voted on the question of secession—and voted nearly four to one against it. "Our Federal Union: it must be preserved!" Andrew Jackson had said nearly thirty years before, and the memory and spirit of Jackson were potent in his state.

But with April came the guns at Fort Sumter, Lincoln's call for the militia of the states to invade the South. War had come. For Tennessee, neutrality was impossible. The formation of a Tennessee Provisional Army began. In May, Governor Isham G. Harris and the legislature, secessionist in sentiment, entered into a military alliance with the Confederate government at Montgomery. A new election on the question of secession was called for June eighth.

Recruiting for the Southern armies began in Memphis long before the election. With the blithe and confident ignorance with which the unprepared go about getting ready for war, the town was aboil with military preparation. "The Southern Military Drum Manufactury" was in operation; C. Wolmer and others were "manufacturing Flags of the Southern Confederacy of all sizes"; printing houses were advertising "Confederate States Flag Envelopes," of which, so the public was assured, "every merchant should order one or two thousand; Hotel Keepers twice as many; Steamboatmen a bushel of them."

One enterprising firm advertised:

WAR! WAR! WAR!
We will in a few days have a full supply of brass buttons.

To so many of the lighthearted youngsters who accepted the statement of their newspapers that the new Southern armies were "worth double their number of onion eating Yankees,"[16] or that one Texas Ranger could easily whip three New York Zouaves, that was what war then was—a matter of brass buttons, flags and drums.

One Tennessee lad, writing long afterward his recollections of those days, recalled the question raised in his young mind by a fire-eating orator's declaration that the women of the South could lick the Yankees with their brooms—a question not as to the fact of the licking but only as to which end of the brooms would be used to accomplish it.[17]

In the sixty days between the call of President Lincoln following the firing on Fort Sumter, and the final election on secession in Tennessee, some might labor for peace, but not the eager youngsters who were coming into the towns to join up with the new military companies forming and drilling everywhere. There were, in and about Memphis, various

28

companies of Grays—the Shelby, the Bluff City and the Dixie—and at least one company of Blues. There were the Hickory Rifles, who, it appears from the press of the time, were without rifles, and the Washington Rifles, who may or may not have had them for all that now appears. There were Southrons and Sons of Liberty, the Memphis Light Dragoons and the Rangers, Invincibles of various descriptions, and Rough and Readys, in memory of old Zach Taylor and Mexico, and, in recognition of Sumter, the Beauregards.

There were, in fact, so many of them, and so many calls and announcements and notices by them and about them, that the newspapers of the city carried the following:

Military Notice!

By special agreement between the papers of the city it is arranged that all calls for, or proceedings of, military meetings shall be charged ten cents per line in our local columns—which is but half our regular rates—and to be paid for invariably in advance.[18]

The concluding clause of the agreed-upon announcement would indicate that at least some of the organizers were showing more military ardor than financial responsibility.

As the date of the election on the ratification of secession by Tennessee approached, excitement became more intense. Trains were delayed by people at the country stations crowding around to buy papers of the news agents until, by public notice, such crowds were requested to speed up matters by pooling their purchase money in the hands of one man who could promptly get papers for all.[19]

Through it all, Forrest remained quiet. He was no fire-eater. Mississippi had acted, and he had large interests and close ties in that state, but he was a citizen of Tennessee, and it was Tennessee's action which he awaited. So little active was he in the agitation of the secession question that no contemporary record of his position has come down, although afterward he was described as having been a "strong Union man," and some of his postwar statements so indicate.[20]

On June eighth, Tennessee acted. The state which in February had voted to stay in the Union voted by a majority of more than two to one to become one of the Confederate states.

The Tennessee Provisional Army was transferred from state to Confederate command, although so complicated were the processes of trans-

29

fer and so complete the confusion in the organization of the new government that it was not until well into the autumn of 1861, and after the state had spent $4,000,000 and owed another $1,000,000, that the Tennessee troops were picked up on the Confederate pay rolls.[21]

During the last two weeks of the ratification campaign there appeared in the Memphis newspapers, among the other military notices, one calling for twelve-month volunteers for the "Tennessee Mounted Rifles," to be commanded by J. S. White, captain. Recruits were "expected to furnish themselves with a good horse, saddle and the arms, so far as practical; if not they will be furnished by the State." Captain White added that he wished "good active horsemen who have the health and the constitution to stand an exposed campaign." On June fourteenth, six days after the election, Forrest enlisted in Captain White's company.

By the time such men as Forrest began joining up, the preparations for war in Memphis had got somewhat beyond the drum and brass-button stage. Cannon were being cast at a foundry on the river front and cannon balls at the Charleston Railroad shops. The new government organized a factory there to make gun carriages, and one for cartridges, where fifty-five men and two hundred and thirty "females"— women who were paid $4.50 a week or girls whose wage was $3.00—were at work. A bonus was offered for production and the mill got up to 75,000 paper cartridges daily, while the men molded 2,000 pounds of lead into ball and bullet each day.

But in the main, Memphis was going to war in the good old traditional, hip-hooray American way. The Southron Gallery advertised its services in the making of likenesses of departing soldiers, for some soldiers were beginning to depart. In fact, enough were going to cause resentment among those left behind. The captains of companies in the 2nd Tennessee Regiment conducted an investigation of the alleged conduct of their colonel in holding them back when other regiments were going to the front, and publicly exonerated him.[22]

There were soldiers from the far South in the town, too, on their way north, and there were, of course, the usual and apparently inevitable fights between different outfits. One Louisiana command, quartered in a cotton shed, was reported as having engaged in a fair-sized riot with other troops in town. News of the riot was featured along with other disorders of the day, such as buggy-racing and fast driving of drays, the latter an offense for which a free man was usually fined $5.00, a slave whipped.[23]

"Bust-head" whisky (not yet called "Confederate pop-skull") was given in the newspapers as the cause of a more serious riot of troops traveling north from Louisiana by boxcar, at Grand Junction, fifty miles

FORREST THE CIVILIAN

From a photograph made at about age forty shortly before his
enlistment as a soldier.

From J. Harvey Mathes' *General For*

HOME IN HERNANDO

The house in which the Forrests were married, from a photograph made half a century later af
the house had become ruinous. It is no longer standing.

east of Memphis, wherein, it was reported, one man was thrown from the train and killed, the town was sacked, and fourteen soldiers were killed or wounded when the commanding officer had to open fire on the rioters.[24]

In contrast to these exhibitions of ebullient indiscipline, "Virginius," correspondent of the Memphis *Appeal* with the Tennessee troops which had already reached Virginia, entered public protest against what he considered the apparent intent of the Richmond government to "regularize our gallant little army" by lengthening the terms of enlistment, appointing field officers instead of leaving that to election, and enforcing a rigid discipline "irksome and unprofitable if applied to our volunteers."[25]

"Virginius" was by no means alone in his feeling, then or afterward. Irvin Cobb tells the story of the Georgia officer who lined up his command, doffed his hat in sweeping salute to them and gave the order, "Gentlemen of the Liberty County Guards, kindly come to attention!"[26] His spiritual fellows were to be found among the commanders of some of the new companies being formed in Memphis, who as late as August were publishing notices in the newspapers, "requesting" their soldiers to show up for drill.

The company of Private Forrest—or rather the three Privates Forrest, for his "baby" brother Jeffrey, whom he had raised as a son, and his fifteen-year-old son William joined up along with Bedford—did not remain in Memphis but went sixty-five miles up the river to the camp of instruction at Randolph, known to the soldiers as Camp Yellowjacket because of the size and number of those vicious insects which infested the site.

There Captain White's troop became Company D of a regiment which was to win fame as the Seventh Tennessee Cavalry, and was to end its career only with the final surrender of Forrest's corps in 1865.[27] John Milton Hubbard, private in the Hardeman Avengers, which became Company E of the same regiment, relates that "one day I met a soldier speeding a magnificent black horse along a country road as if for exercise, and the pleasure of being astride of so fine an animal. On closer inspection I saw it was Bedford Forrest, only a private like myself, whom I had known ten years before down in Mississippi."[28]

But Bedford Forrest did not long remain a member of Company D, nor a private. About July tenth, Governor Isham G. Harris of Tennessee, "knowing Forrest well and having a high regard for the man, telegraphed him to come to Memphis" for a meeting which resulted in the discharge of Private Forrest, to recruit a battalion of Mounted Rangers, under the authority of the Confederate States.[29]

31

CHAPTER III

THE FIRST COMMAND AND THE FIRST FIGHT

July 10, 1861-December 28, 1861

PURSUING the practice of personally raising troops, common in all American wars, even into the early stages of the First World War, Forrest opened his recruiting headquarters at the Gayoso Hotel in Memphis, and began to publish in the newspapers his call for 500 men for "mounted ranger service," the men to furnish their own mounts and arms, "shot guns and pistols preferable."

But the future commander of the battalion (if he should succeed in raising one) had no intention of depending on such casual and uncertain sources of supply, nor yet on the scant resources of the new Confederate government. He started then the practice which he followed all the way through. He went out and supplied himself.

Within a week after his designation to raise troops he was in the officially neutral state of Kentucky, seeking both recruits and equipment. The equipment he bought and paid for with his own funds but buying and paying for it was but the beginning. Five hundred pistols—no sabers—and one hundred sets of horse equipment, with other needed supplies, were gathered and stored in a Louisville livery stable. Thence some of the supplies moved into the country as "potatoes," others moved to a tanyard in the suburbs as "leather," and still others, stowed in coffee sacks, were carried by Forrest himself and a handful of enthusiastic young Southern sympathizers to be loaded on a little train of ordinary farm wagons, which quietly started south that night. "Potatoes," "leather" and "coffee" all reached the Confederate lines in Tennessee safely.[1]

During the July weeks in which Forrest was in Kentucky, the war, which since January had been a vast and vague confusion of organizing, began to take shape. First Manassas was fought in Virginia that month, and in Missouri there were small engagements between Missouri state troops and the Union Army contending for the possession of that state.

But in the central stretch of the South, between the Appalachians and the Mississippi, there was as yet no armed conflict, with Union and Confederate forces kept apart by regard for the officially proclaimed neutrality of Kentucky, which state both sides were courting. But since this

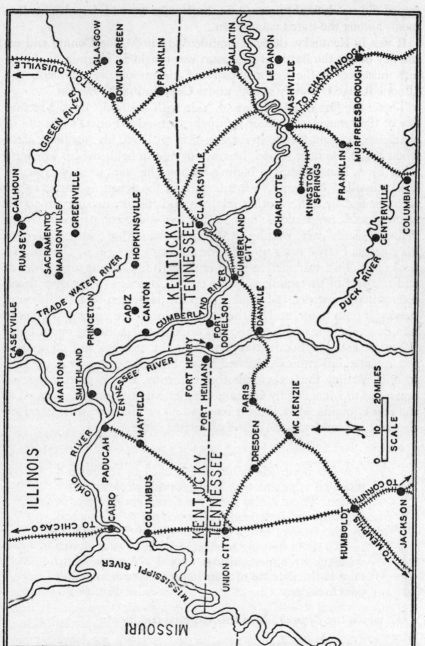

NORTHERN TENNESSEE AND SOUTHERN KENTUCKY

regard did not extend to recruiting, both sides were busy seeking enlistments among the state's young men.

It was in Kentucky, then, at Brandenburg in Meade County and on the day before the Battle of Manassas was fought in Virginia, that Forrest mustered in the first company of his prospective regiment, the "Boone Rangers," ninety strong, under Captain Frank Overton.

These, the first of all soldiers to "ride with Bedford," on the second day of their movement out of Kentucky, witnessed Forrest's first use of characteristic fight-saving stratagem—for with all his headlong dash when battle was once joined, he was not one to fight just for fighting's sake. From Brandenburg to Nolin's Station, the point of rendezvous on the Louisville & Nashville Railroad, many of the departing Rangers were accompanied by fathers, other relatives and friends, making altogether a considerable cavalcade. Informed that two strong companies of Union "Home Guards" were waiting at Munfordville, farther South, to dispute his passage, Forrest drew up his little company in sight of the railroad tracks at Nolin's, extended its short ranks with the accompanying friends and relatives of its members, broke out a Confederate flag over them, ostentatiously paraded the whole group for passengers on a southbound passenger train to see, and let the report of his seeming strength precede him down the line to discourage and disperse the gathering opposition.[2]

Forrest and the Boone Rangers, with the supplies and equipment accumulated in Kentucky, reached Memphis in the first week of August, to find awaiting them there another company, the "Forrest Rangers," organized in Memphis by Captain Charles May. Camp was formed at the Fair Grounds, while Forrest renewed his call for men with an advertisement in the Memphis *Appeal* of August 29th:

FOR ACTIVE SERVICE!
A few more companies are needed to complete a mounted regiment now being formed here for active service. There is also room for a few more recruits in a company of Independent Rangers not to be attached to any regiment unless on the option of the members. . . . To those desiring to engage in the cavalry service an excellent opportunity is offered. Now, freemen, rally to the defense of your liberties, your homes and your firesides.   N. B. FORREST.

To which the *Appeal* added this editorial comment:

To Arms! We invite attention to the call of Col. N. B. Forrest in today's paper. There are still hundreds of young men in the country anxious to engage in the military service. Those whose fancy inclines them to the cavalry service will find no better opportunity to enlist under a bold, capable and efficient commander. Now is the time.

Congregated in Memphis at this season were several independent companies of cavalry, keenly competing to get their requisitions for equipment through the crowded confusion of the Confederate supply arrangements. The ambitious officers who had raised these companies in their home towns, and who had mounted them, too, on the usual Confederate principle of each soldier furnishing his own horse, were in no great hurry to attach themselves to an untried command. Among them was Captain D. C. Kelley, a young Methodist minister of burning zeal in the faith or in a fight, commanding a company raised at Huntsville in Alabama. Captain Kelley, noticing that "persistent watchfulness" would get his requisitions filled except when he "came in contact with the requisitions of N. B. Forrest,"[3] decided to join the battalion which Forrest was trying to form, and thereby started a movement for other independent Alabama companies to do likewise.

Captain Kelley, then and throughout the war, combined the soldierly duty with the ministerial, conducting services in the camps as opportunity offered. To one of these services, early in his association with Forrest, there came the matriarch of the Forrest clan, to "sit side by side with her son at the service held in the woods nearby." Later, Kelley found in Forrest's tent the well-worn Testament, bearing the name of his mother, which she had left for him.[4]

Meanwhile, war was beginning to nibble at the edges of Kentucky, despite official solicitude for its precarious neutrality. On August twenty-second the Union gunboat *Lexington*, operating from Cairo in Illinois, seized "the little steamer W. B. *Terry*" at the wharf at Paducah, Kentucky, alleging that the vessel was "employed in the rebel trade and carrying their flag."[5] Later in the same day, by way of reprisal, the late commander of the *Terry* and other Paducah citizens seized the Evansville mail steamer *Samuel Orr* and ran it up the Tennessee River.

The unreal neutrality status of Kentucky was maintained, however, for a fortnight longer, even though for weeks a force of Union recruits had been gathered, armed and drilled at Camp Dick Robinson, between Lexington and Danville. Finally, however, "neutrality" was cracked wide open when on September third the Confederate forces in northwestern Tennessee advanced and occupied the village of Columbus, the northern terminus of the Mobile & Ohio Railroad, situated on a commanding bluff on the Mississippi River a few miles below the mouth of the Ohio—and in Kentucky.

General Pillow had wanted to make the move as early as May, when he was commanding the troops of the state of Tennessee, which had not yet become one of the Confederate States, but had been restrained then by the politic Governor Harris.[6] When the move was made, finally, it was justified in the Confederate mind by the belief that the movements of Union forces at Cairo, in Illinois, and down the Missouri shore of the river, were directed toward the same occupation—as, in fact, they were. As early as August twenty-eighth, Major General John C. Frémont, commanding for the Union at St. Louis, had told his subordinate, Brigadier General U. S. Grant, that "it is intended . . . to occupy Columbus, Ky., as soon as possible," and had ordered dispositions and movements to that end.[7]

The Confederate occupation had the military value of forestalling like action on the part of the impetuous Frémont but from every other respect it was an act of impolicy on the order of firing on Fort Sumter. In a game which was being played by indirection, it was an overt and direct act, to be seized upon and exploited as an attack by the South upon the sovereignty of Kentucky.

Governor Isham Harris of Tennessee, with whom Simon Bolivar Buckner, Inspector General of the Kentucky State Guards, had entered into a sort of nonaggression pact, following a similar arrangement with Major General George B. McClellan who commanded for the Union at Cincinnati,[8] recognized the inexpediency of the occupation of Columbus and protested to the Richmond government. So, too, did Buckner himself, who had resigned his military post in Kentucky on July twentieth, but who still was working to avoid hostilities along the state's southern border. Both Harris and Buckner wired protests to Richmond, demanding that the "unfortunate move" of Generals Polk and Pillow be undone. L. P. Walker, Confederate Secretary of War, did order Polk back from Columbus, on September fifth, and sent word to Governor Beriah Magoffin of Kentucky that the advance was "wholly unauthorized," the Secretary of War not having been advised, apparently, that already, on the day before, President Jefferson Davis had approved it as "justified by necessity."[9]

But whether forced by necessity or not, the movement to Columbus brought the neutrality policy to its end, and to the end which, in the long run, would be most helpful to the Union cause. Before midnight of September fifth, Brigadier General U. S. Grant, with 1,800 men and sixteen guns, pulled out from the Cairo wharf, steamed fifty miles up the Ohio to Paducah, at the mouth of the Tennessee, and on the morning of the sixth quietly and without opposition took possession of that Kentucky town for the Union.[10]

On the next day Brigadier General Robert Anderson, the Union "Hero of Fort Sumter," moved the headquarters of the Department of the Cumberland from Cincinnati to Louisville, and immediately ordered Brigadier General George H. Thomas to take command of the Union recruits gathered at Camp Dick Robinson.[11] By mid-September, the Union forces held the mouths of the Tennessee and the Cumberland, and all the south bank of the Ohio, and had forces well down into the state, while the Confederates held only Columbus, at the western extremity, and a small segment of Kentucky territory away to the east on the far upper Cumberland, into which Brigadier General Felix K. Zollicoffer marched with three Tennessee regiments on September tenth.

On that day, also, the government at Richmond ordered out to take command of the scattered Confederate forces in "the West" the highest-ranking general of the Confederate armies available for field service— Albert Sidney Johnston.[12]

A Kentuckian by birth, Johnston had preceded Jefferson Davis at Transylvania University at Lexington, and had been a cadet at West Point two classes above the future President of the Confederate States. There, too, he had been the roommate of Leonidas Polk, who at Davis' request laid aside his episcopal vestments as Bishop of Louisiana to accept the command of the Confederate forces along the Mississippi. After nearly ten years' service in the army, Johnston resigned the profession of arms in 1835, to take it up again the following year in the service of the new Republic of Texas, where he became commander in chief of the army and later secretary of war. Resigning again in 1840, he spent six years as a Texas planter, returning to the United States Army in 1846 for service in the war with Mexico. In 1855, when Jefferson Davis was Secretary of War, Johnston became colonel of the new Second Cavalry, with Robert E. Lee as his lieutenant colonel, and a list of officers whose after-careers were to make the Second the most famous of all American regiments. By 1860 Johnston had received the brevet rank of brigadier general and the command of the Pacific Coast.

As soon as news of the secession of his state of Texas reached California, he resigned, but kept the resignation secret and punctiliously remained on duty until he could turn over everything in good shape to his successor in command, and then, in midsummer, crossed the continent on horseback to join the Confederacy; "without pretension or claim to high rank . . . he simply offered himself to the cause." By President Davis and by all ranks of the people his coming was looked upon as a "great support added to the Confederate cause." The Presi-

37

dent, indeed, as he afterward told representatives of the postwar Association of the Army of Tennessee, regarded his friend of West Point days as "the greatest soldier, the ablest man, civil or military, Confederate or Federal, then living."[13]

What his strictly military ability may have been will never be known. He had the misfortune to come early to high command, and to find himself, in an America where no soldier had ever seen as many as 15,000 men in one body, called upon to organize, equip, train and handle armies totally insufficient to defend a "frontier" stretching 300 miles across Kentucky from the gaps of the Cumberlands to the banks of the Mississippi, and nearly as far beyond the Mississippi to the Indian Territory. In this, his first great military problem, he failed, but the problem itself, as will appear, was impossible of successful solution. And in the first great battle of the war in the West, at Shiloh, he met his death.

But whatever his strictly military merits may have been, his personal presence, his largeness of spirit, his qualities as a man, were such that the whole western South settled back when he arrived in Nashville on September fourteenth to take over his vast spread of command, in the comfortable conviction that with Albert Sidney Johnston on guard no harm could befall.

Johnston himself, despite the grand confidence of his outer bearing, did not share the conviction. He knew too much of the situation but he knew, also, that it would never do for the enemy forces strung out south of the Ohio River to know what he knew. To guard his 300-mile frontier he had about 11,000 men under Polk at the western end, about 4,000 under Zollicoffer at the eastern, and in between, at camps of instruction near the northern border of Tennessee, about 5,000 more. And nowhere did he have, nor could he get, the arms, equipment and ammunition for even these meager forces.

The 5,000 men in camp in northern Tennessee he sent forward at once, under command of Buckner, to occupy Bowling Green, in southern Kentucky, where the railroad from Louisville forks, with one line running to Nashville, one to Memphis. He reported to President Davis that he had not more than half the number of *armed* men needed to avert disaster;[14] he called upon the governors of the states behind him for more men, and began to call upon whomsoever in authority he could reach for arms.[15] To Judah P. Benjamin, the new Secretary of War, he reported that he could not buy supplies locally in Kentucky, because the farmers would sell only for gold or Kentucky paper money while the army had nothing but Confederate and Tennessee paper, and asked that he be allowed to draw upon the huge stores of supplies accumulated by the Confederate Commissary at Nashville. Denied access to these,

38

which had been collected for the Virginia armies but were held at Nashville "on account of the embarrassments in transportation on the railroads," he went about setting up his own independent commissary at Nashville.[16]

But always he maintained to the enemy the bold front, and never until disaster overcame him, did the people of the South realize how thin and fragile was the shield which Sidney Johnston held before them in southern Kentucky.

It was to the center of this shield that the new battalion of Forrest's cavalry was ordered from Memphis upon the completion of its organization during the second week in October 1861. In the battalion there were eight companies, two from Kentucky, three from northern Alabama, one from the southern part of that state, one from Texas and one raised in Memphis itself—altogether 650 men. Upon organization, N. B. Forrest was elected Lieutenant Colonel and D. C. Kelley, the Methodist minister, Major. The day after organization was completed the first squadron, under Major Kelley, took the road under orders to report to Colonel Adolphus Heiman, commanding the Tenth Tennessee (Irish) Regiment, then stationed at Fort Henry, on the Tennessee River. Before the end of the month the whole battalion, including a compact wagon train driven by Forrest's slaves, was on the way.

The center of the Confederate line, to which the Forrest battalion was ordered for its first duty in the field, was pierced by two navigable rivers, the Tennessee and the Cumberland, flowing northward to the Ohio on parallel courses which, at a point just before they pass from Tennessee into Kentucky, are only twelve miles apart. The importance of these rivers as a weak point in the defense of Tennessee had been recognized by the indefatigable Governor Harris even before that state became a member of the Confederacy, and officers of the Tennessee Provisional Army, under his direction, had located forts for their defense—Fort Henry on the Tennessee and Fort Donelson on the Cumberland.

The ideal point for such defensive works, probably, was farther north, or down the rivers, where they are but three miles apart and one strongly held work could block both. This location was in Kentucky, however, and therefore not available when work started on the forts in May. By September, when Kentucky neutrality was abandoned, everyone seemed tacitly to accept the idea that work on the forts was too far along to be abandoned, although, to judge from the reports of the succession of officers who inspected them during the desultory progress of their construction, no one was entirely satisfied with anything about them.

39

In October Colonel Heiman reported to his superior officer, General Polk at Columbus, that his position at Fort Henry was commanded by higher hills on the left, or Kentucky, bank of the river, while the lower parts of the works were subject to overflow in high water. As for the defenses of the Cumberland, they "had so far been almost entirely overlooked" except for a little fort which Heiman's regiment had built but which he esteemed "entirely worthless," and which was garrisoned by only three companies of almost unarmed men. For scouting and outpost work, and for communication with Fort Donelson and the telegraph office at Danville, where the railroad which afforded the connection between the Confederate wings at Columbus and Bowling Green crossed the Tennessee River, he asked for a "company of cavalry."[17]

He got more than he asked for with the arrival, a week later, of Forrest's advance squadron under Kelley, which was immediately put to work, leaving Fort Donelson on October twenty-fifth, to accompany an expedition down the Cumberland some thirty-five miles into Kentucky. Kelley's men were to scout and guard the working parties attempting to block navigation by sinking bargeloads of stone at Ingram's Shoals—a procedure which proved to be of small account in a river that occasionally rises as much as fifty feet. No enemy appearing during the five days in which the work went on, the squadron returned to Fort Donelson by the end of the month, to find that the rest of the battalion had marched in from Memphis.[18]

The "frontier" at that stage of the war was fifty miles farther north, along the line of Green River, which flows northwesterly across Kentucky to fall into the Ohio near Henderson. From this line Brigadier General William Tecumseh Sherman, who had taken over the Union command in Kentucky when Anderson of Fort Sumter retired for reasons of health, ordered small scouting expeditions in the direction of Hopkinsville in Christian County, both to hearten the Union sympathizers in southern Kentucky and to "disturb Buckner," commanding for the South in that region.[19]

The principal post in the area, Hopkinsville, was held by a brigade of Mississippi state troops who, at the very last of October and just as Forrest came into the field, were finally mustered into Confederate service. But while the men were taken into the service, their commander, Brigadier General James L. Alcorn, of the Mississippi state forces, was not. To the harried Buckner, Alcorn wrote feelingly that while his command would complain at his leaving them, "this will soon be hushed for now they are bound" in the Confederate service. As for himself, he declared that he "had about as soon be shot as to leave here, but would rather be shot than remain a hermaphrodite in the service."[20]

The state of the garrison at Hopkinsville, the post toward which events were leading Forrest and his cavalry for their first active assignment, appears both from the dispatches of General Alcorn and those of his successor, Brigadier General Lloyd Tilghman. The state of discipline is indicated by the former's report that he "had a young man now under arrest for making or using threatening and abusive language on the streets toward myself and the army; among other things that he intended to shoot myself," which might be dismissed as an isolated situation but for the General's threat to "make some examples of severity that will be sufficient to suppress" such language.[21]

As to the health of the command, General Tilghman reported when he took over that the troops were down with the measles in a "camp which was merely one large hospital with scarce enough men on duty to care for the sick and maintain a feeble guard around them." Union scouting parties from across Green River, he added, were "drawing heavily daily" on the supplies of wheat, flour, corn and hogs in the country between the Green and the Cumberland. The Union parties were aided by the gunboat *Conestoga*, which, sometimes accompanied by transports, was working up and down the latter river. To meet all this, he asked, among other things, for cavalry—"500 good men."[22]

From headquarters at Bowling Green Tilghman was advised on November first to get in touch with a "regiment of cavalry (Forrest's)," which was "understood to be on the north side of the Cumberland."[23] Forrest was still south of the Cumberland at the time,[24] but crossed over early in the month and, from Hopkinsville on November fourteenth, reported his movement to Johnston's Assistant Adjutant General:

"I have been operating with my command of eight companies of cavalry near Fort Henry and Fort Donelson, by order of General Polk. Finding the country impracticable for cavalry, and with scant subsistence, I moved a part of my command to Canton, north side of Cumberland River, leaving two companies at Dover. I am of no use south of Cumberland; desire my command united, and can do vast service with General Tilghman. Will you so order?"[25]

In this earliest dispatch from Forrest to appear in the *Official Records*,[26] there appear some of the qualities which made him. He saw where there was work to be done and subsistence to be had, and he moved in the direction of the enemy, without waiting to be told.

Even before their presence was reported by their commander, Forrest's troops had gone to work, as appears from Tilghman's dispatch of November thirteenth. Major Kelley's battalion, he reported, had arrived at

Hopkinsville "in good order" on the evening of November eleventh, and on the thirteenth had departed for the lower reaches of the Cumberland to intercept a Union raiding party reported to be coming after a drove of the Confederate commissary's hogs.[27] There is no further reference to this expedition in the *Official Records* but from later accounts, it appears that Forrest moved forward with the main body of the regiment to Princeton, some thirty miles northwest of Hopkinsville, whence Major Kelley and his squadron scouted forward to the banks of the Ohio. There they waylaid and captured a Union transport steamer, and relieved it of its freight of sugar, coffee, blankets and other desirable supplies. The fact that the steamer was "expected" by the Confederate raiders, and that it "was speedily brought to without resistance," would indicate that in this first contact of Forrest's men with the enemy there was more of stratagem and connivance than there was of fighting.

As Kelley and his men returned to Princeton, a citizen of Smithland, the village at the mouth of the Cumberland, galloped in on November nineteenth to report to Forrest that the gunboat *Conestoga* had gone up the Cumberland to seize Confederate clothing and other stores at Canton, thirty-two miles to the west. Covering the distance in an eight-hour night march, the command reached the Cumberland ahead of the gunboat, disposed themselves in ambush above and below Canton landing, leaving a few men in sight to tempt the boat to put ashore a landing party, and waited. Soon the gunboat steamed up, sensed a ruse, anchored in the stream and prepared for action.

Action opened with a couple of rounds from a brass four-pounder, attached to Forrest's command for the expedition. The four-pounder popgun was driven off in short order by the *Conestoga's* heavier metal, but Forrest's men, sheltering behind trees and rocks along the bank, fired at the open portholes of the gunboat with such effect that she was compelled, after a few hours, to close them, up-anchor and steam back down the Cumberland—amid the jubilant elation of Forrest's men. They had fought their first fight, and in it had worsted a gunboat, "a species of adversary that hitherto had been regarded with actual terror by the raw troops of the Confederate service, on account of the large calibres of their armament and their comparative invulnerability."[28]

The Canton affair was not only a forerunner of fighting gunboats but, even more characteristically, a foretaste of the marches which were to be made by men who followed Forrest. The new regiment, which had reached Canton after an all-night march and had fought all day, marched again that night to reach Hopkinsville, twenty-five miles away, on the morning of November twenty-first.

Three days later away they went again on a reconnaisance in force ordered by Brigadier General Charles Clark, who had succeeded Tilghman when the latter was sent to take command of the unfinished works at Fort Henry and Fort Donelson. Northeast they marched, to Greenville, and thence in a wide sweep to the north and west, to Providence and Morganfield and on to Caseyville, on the Ohio at the mouth of the Tradewater, where they spent the last day of November.[29]

On the next day two steamboat loads of Federal troops escorted by the ubiquitous *Conestoga* came up from Paducah to Caseyville, to find Forrest "at least 20 miles distant and pushing southward." So far the accounts agree. As to what happened during the day which the Union troops spent at Caseyville there is no agreement. The Union commander reported that his men captured sixty Confederate hogs. Forrest agreed with that much, although he figured the hogs at eighty head instead of sixty, but added that the Federal soldiers also "became intoxicated on stolen whisky and left in a row."[30]

Although this was the closest that Forrest's men came to seeing enemy soldiers on this sweep through the country, it was on that same first of December that the command suffered its first death from hostile fire, as a result of the peculiar bitterness between the sympathizers of the two sides which plagued all border sections. Arriving at Marion, Forrest was appealed to for help by the wife and family of a Southern sympathizer who had been arrested, arbitrarily and oppressively it was claimed, by one Jonathan Bells. As Forrest and his regimental surgeon, Dr. Van Wyck, rode toward Bells's home, with intent to arrest him in turn, a shot was fired from the house, with deadly aim, at the surgeon, whose impressive uniform no doubt caused him to be mistaken for the commander by whose side he rode.[31]

Back in Hopkinsville after their twelve-day swing, the Forrest regiment set to work building winter huts, battling the while with that scourge of new armies—the measles. When Adam Johnson, who was to serve as one of Forrest's scouts before becoming a Colonel under Morgan and, finally, a Brigadier General, rode in from Texas to join up just before Christmas, he found "the whole command very comfortably fixed with good floored tents and good beds," the "commissary department most abundantly supplied" and the commander himself established "in his private tent with his wife" and son, Private Willie Forrest.[32]

On the day after Christmas, however, they were on the road again, to reconnoiter a reported advance across the Green River.[33] The first day's march took them to Greenville, where the column was joined by detachments of Tennessee cavalry, under Lieutenant Colonel J. W. Starnes, who had been surgeon of the First Tennessee in the War with Mexico.

On the twenty-eighth the column of 300 moved out from Greenville

43

toward Rumsey, on the south bank of the Green, with scouts far ahead and an advance guard under Captains Meriwether and McLemore well out to the front. At the head of the main body rode Forrest himself, with the center of the little column under Major Kelley and the rear under Lieutenant Colonel Starnes. And so, in a formation prescribed by regulations and approved by common sense, Forrest's regiment of cavalry advanced to its first land fight.

Eight miles out from Greenville, scouts came back on the run with the report that the "enemy 500 strong" was ahead, also moving toward Rumsey. Forrest ordered his men forward "at a rapid pace" which soon became an exhilarating gallop, with the men giving voice to irrepressible "jubilant and defiant shouts, which reached the height of enthusiasm as the women from the houses waved us forward." The commander himself was not insensible to the same influences, when "a beautiful young lady, smiling, with untied tresses floating in the breeze, on horseback, met the column just before our advance guard came up with the rear of the enemy," and informed the Confederates that she had seen and passed through the Union troopers at the village of Sacramento. She did even more. In her enthusiasm she galloped forward with the troops until she was ordered out of line before the fighting began, thereby, in the language of Forrest's official report, "infusing nerve into my arm and kindling knightly chivalry within my heart."[34]

A mile south of Sacramento, after an hour's hard gallop, the advance guard came up with the rear of the Union scouting expedition. When Forrest opened on them, firing the first shot himself, off they rode up a long slope, to form line of battle across the road along the brow of a low ridge. Forrest's men pressed on under fire but under orders to hold their own fire until within good range. Three rounds fired at eighty yards indicated to the commander that his men, strung out along the road by the hard gallop, were not up in sufficient numbers to make the fight with success.

Whereupon, with instinctive generalship, Forrest sent Kelley and a party around through the woods to the right and Starnes with another party to the left, and drew back his center, at the same time dismounting some of his best-armed men to act as sharpshooters. The enemy, as was intended, mistook the movement for the beginning of a retreat, and themselves advanced. Forrest sat his horse narrowly watching the enemy, while those of his own men who were mounted on slower horses continued to gallop in from the south to the sound of firing.

With about half his column up, he saw the signs which told him that Kelley and Starnes were in position on the flanks, ready to begin their attack. Forrest had made his dispositions with skill and cunning, and

44

now the time had come for fighting. Into the fight he went, a giant of a man standing high in his stirrups, his skin dark with the congestion of blood beneath the surface, his eyes ablaze, his ordinarily quiet voice raised to a harsh and brassy roar of "Charge! Charge!"[35]

Charged from flanks and front, the Union forces broke into retreat,[36] covered by a handful of determined fighters at the rear. Into them Forrest rode, headlong, in the very forefront of the fight, slashing and shooting a pathway among the demoralized Union troopers until he struck determined resistance from a soldier and two officers. When the private put a bullet through his coat collar, Forrest "quieted him with a pistol shot,"[37] just in time to whirl and engage the two officers riding at him with sabers swinging. One he shot; the other he sabered. A third officer coming into the fight Forrest charged head on and knocked from his horse, dislocating his shoulder, just before Forrest's own horse careened on into two riderless horses who were down, went down himself in the struggling and kicking mass, and threw his rider twenty feet beyond.

The fight and pursuit lasted to, through and beyond Sacramento, altogether about three miles, before the exhaustion of the Confederate mounts which that day had made twenty-five miles, with the last one-third of it at the gallop or full canter, brought to an end what Forrest's superior officer, General Clark, described in dispatches as "one of the most brilliant and successful cavalry engagements which the present war has witnessed."[38]

Confederate losses reported were Captain C. E. Meriwether, commanding the advance, and Private W. H. Terry, who went down fighting alongside Forrest in the melee, both killed, and three soldiers wounded. General Crittenden reported that the Union forces engaged, a detachment of 168 men of Jackson's cavalry regiment, lost two officers and eight soldiers killed, and one officer and "8, perhaps 13 soldiers" captured. Forrest reported Union casualties as far heavier, about 100 altogether, including thirty-five prisoners.

No matter what the exact number and losses may have been on either side, Sacramento was a small affair, following weeks of small operations. But in those operations and this small affair at arms, there began to appear a certain pattern of action which was to become characteristic of Forrest and the men he led.

In the marches and bivouacs of two months through the wintry Kentucky countryside Forrest's men learned, as Colonel Kelley afterward put it, "that it was his single will . . . which was ever to be the governing impulse in their movements."[39] And they began to learn, too, confidence in him and in themselves.

This confidence, the "brilliant and dashing affair at Sacramento"

45

cemented. In the vigilant and wary advance, the skillful disposition of slender forces to the best advantage, the timing of simulated retreat in the front and surprise attack upon the flanks and, at the last, the thunderbolt charge with everything hurled into a never-let-up, never-slow-down, driving fight, Forrest's men saw him demonstrate an instinctive mastery of military principles of which, in all probability, he had never heard.

And so there began to grow that great pride of men who could say that they "rode with Old Bedford."

CHAPTER IV

OUT OF THE FALL OF FORT DONELSON

December 28, 1861-February 16, 1862

FROM their "brilliant little victory" at Sacramento, Forrest and his men were to go within six weeks to meet sterner tests in the bitterness of the first great Confederate defeat at Fort Donelson. From it they emerged with the beginnings of recognition for command and commander, and with the ties of pride and confidence which bound them together fire-welded.

The fall of the river forts—Henry on the Tennessee and Donelson on the Cumberland—was the critical event of the whole war. When the writer of the editorial on the fall of Fort Donelson in the March 1, 1862, issue of *Harper's Weekly* headed it "The Beginning of the End," he was a better prophet than he knew. For it was, indeed, the beginning of that succession of great splitting movements, cutting the Confederacy into smaller and smaller segments, which was to end only in April three years later, with the surrender first of the Army of Northern Virginia and then of the Army of Tennessee.

The chain of events which led up to the fall of Fort Henry and Fort Donelson, and on to the final fall of the Confederacy, began back in November of 1861, about the time that Forrest and his men were reporting for service in Kentucky. Major General Don Carlos Buell, at Louisville, commanding for the Union in Kentucky east of the lower Cumberland River, then first proposed to his colleague, Major General Henry W. Halleck at St. Louis, commanding in the western part of the state, that they join forces in a concerted move southward. The suggestion was that Buell should follow down the railroad against the Confederate position at Bowling Green, while Halleck's forces should work up the rivers to strike "the center where the railroads cross the Cumberland and the Tennessee." There, as Buell urged with true strategic insight, was at once the most critical and the most vulnerable point in the whole long line of the Confederacy from the mountains to the Mississippi.

Since the rivers were in the geographical limits of Halleck's command, however, there followed a long triangular correspondence, weeks of it, between Buell, Halleck and the new generalissimo at Washington,

47

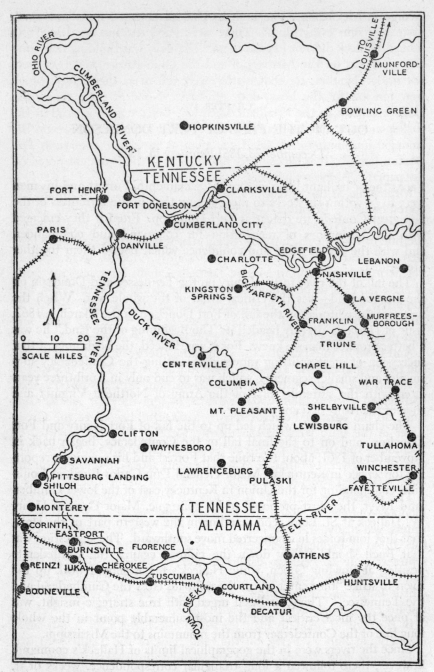

THE LOWER CUMBERLAND AND TENNESSEE RIVERS

George B. McClellan. The hesitant Halleck objected that "too much haste will ruin everything." There were good reasons for delay, too, though Halleck did not express them. The navy was building new ironclad gunboats on the Mississippi and the Ohio Rivers, and they were not ready. Neither, for that matter, were the rivers themselves, which were too low for the heavy-draft gunboats. None of these things did Halleck explain to the President when Mr. Lincoln took a hand in the correspondence. He contented himself with a pedantic lecture on the strategic unsoundness of the Buell plan as involving operations "on exterior lines." "It is exceedingly discouraging," the President noted on the papers. "As everywhere else, nothing can be done."[1]

Meanwhile, at the forts which were the object of all the planning and correspondence, Brigadier General Lloyd Tilghman was trying to get some real fortifying done. Local plantation owners were appealed to for the hire of their slaves, but with small success—partly because the forts were not located in a large plantation country. Appeals were made in northern Alabama, and in Middle Tennessee about Nashville, for drafts of slave laborers to be brought down to the works on steamboats, and some few were sent, but never enough to do a great deal. As late as January, Tilghman could only report that he was "fortifying hard" and that granted enough time he hoped to make the posts strong.[2]

And then, in mid-January, the rains came. Between the fifteenth and the twenty-second, the Tennessee rose fourteen feet. The Cumberland went up until the obstructions to navigation, which Forrest's men had helped place as their first active duty, became useless.[3] At the same time, on the basis of Forrest's report made after a scout to the Green River in the third week of the month, General Johnston reported to Richmond that Brigadier General T. L. Crittenden's Union forces had crossed that river, and that he expected enemy action at any time on the now "well-filled rivers of the Ohio, Cumberland and Tennessee."[4]

The rivers were ready, the new ironclad gunboats were ready, Commodore Andrew H. Foote, commanding the navy on the Western waters, was ready, and Brigadier General U. S. Grant, commanding for the Union at Paducah, was ready. Grant and Foote joined in earnest representations to Halleck just to be allowed to go up the Tennessee and take Fort Henry, as a base for further operations. Halleck hesitated a little longer and then, at the last of January, suddenly decided to permit his eager subordinates to go ahead.[5]

By the night of February fifth, the steamboats had landed twenty-three regiments at Bailey's Ferry, on the right bank of the Tennessee three miles below Fort Henry. There the soldiers bivouacked in the rain, while out in the wide river, booming on the rise, the seven gunboats lay

49

ready for their work. About noon of February sixth the boats stood up the river, bow-on, the four ironclads in front, the three "tinclads" behind, firing overhead with "curvated" shot—altogether fifty-four guns against the dozen which the fort could bring to bear on the river.

Inside the fort Tilghman, watching the movements of the boats and the troops downstream, watching the implacable rise of the river first into his lower batteries and then into his magazines, wondering whether he would be flooded out of the fort before he was shelled out, early despaired of saving the work and decided to save the garrison, whose outlying camps were already cut off from the fort proper by rising backwaters. Ordering Colonel Adolphus Heiman and some 2,500 of his men away to Dover or Fort Donelson, he himself remained in the fort with a forlorn hope of fewer than 100 artillerists—mostly green at the guns.

Such a fight could not last long. By two o'clock in the afternoon it was over, and the fort surrendered. Grant's troops, hampered by rain, mud and backwater, failed to come up in time to head off Heiman's escaping Confederates but despite this mischance, the Union commanders were jubilant, and justly so, over the first major victory of the whole war.[6]

The most immediate result of the victory was the breaking of the railroad which held together the long Confederate line of defense, where it crossed the Tennessee at Danville, twenty miles above Fort Henry. This was accomplished by the navy's "tinclads" at dusk of the same evening on which the fort surrendered. By dark that day, the tinclads were away up the river, destroying Confederate steamers as they found them, including the gunboat *Eastport* under construction, and in a couple of days carrying the war clear across the state of Tennessee and into the corners of Mississippi and Alabama.[7]

It was recognized at once that the whole Confederate line across Kentucky had become untenable. Grant dispatched Halleck on the evening of the sixth, ". . . I shall take and destroy Fort Donelson on the 8th,"[8] and his confidence in its quick and easy capture was no more complete than was the Confederate conviction that it could not be held.[9]

On the morning of the seventh, at a conference held in Bowling Green, the immediate abandonment of Kentucky, and the probable abandonment of Middle and West Tennessee, was decided upon. Present at the conference besides Johnston, the commander, were his lieutenant Hardee, and General Pierre Gustav Toutant Beauregard, just out from Richmond to lend to the cause in the West the benefit of his counsel and the luster of his name as the conqueror of Fort Sumter and the "Hero of Manassas." The plan quickly agreed upon was for Hardee's troops at Bowling Green to fall back along the railroad to Nashville, and possibly even to Stevenson in Alabama; for Polk's troops about Columbus likewise to fall back along the railroad as far as Humboldt and possibly on into Mississippi, leaving behind garrisons to defend the chain of fortifications along the river from Columbus down; and for other troops to be concentrated on the Cumberland River, the idea being to "defend Nashville at Donelson"—despite the view which Johnston communicated to Secretary of War Benjamin that the Federal forces could "probably take Donelson with gunboats alone."[10]

Forrest, again out on scout above Hopkinsville, was caught in this stream of events moving toward Fort Donelson when, on the sixth, General Clark's force was ordered to fall back to Clarksville, on the way to reinforce the forts while Forrest and his cavalry covered the withdrawal.[11]

Other troops were moving on Donelson by train, by steamboat and by marching, from posts in Tennessee and southern Kentucky. With them went an assortment of commanding officers whose divisions of counsel, antagonisms of personality and uncertainties of action were to cancel out whatever dim hope there may have been that Johnston could "defend Nashville at Donelson" against Grant and Foote advancing from the northwest, and at the same time against Buell, coming down the railroad from the northeast. Johnston probably erred in dividing his force in the face of these two advancing armies, either one equal to all that he had, and most certainly he erred in neither going to Donelson himself nor sending there a commander with the rank and prestige necessary to secure promptness in decision and unity of action—Beauregard, say, or Hardee. Instead he sent three commanders of nearly equal rank to make up what became a divided and ineffective triumvirate of command.

First to arrive, on the night of the ninth, was Brigadier General Gideon J. Pillow, lawyer, planter, Major General of Volunteers in the War with Mexico, and Major General of the Provisional Army of Tennessee in 1861. Things at the fort appeared to him, upon arrival, to be in a state of "deep gloom, depression and demoralization," which he undertook to correct by the immediate issue of a special order announcing "our battle cry, 'Liberty or Death,'" and by putting his fiery energy behind the work on the three and-one-half-mile line of rifle pits and abatis which had been started as a protection of the Donelson-Dover area on the landward side.[12]

The original Fort Donelson was no more than a small enclosed work of about fifteen acres, on a commanding bluff just at the head of a reach of river running almost straight north for a mile and a half. Down

51

the side of the bluff, but still well above the level of the river even in flood, was a small water battery, with its guns bearing on the river. Falling into the river just north of the fort is Hickman Creek; just south of the fort, and between it and the little county town of Dover, Indian Creek. The lower reaches of the two creeks were deep-filled with backwater and impassable. Their upper reaches and little tributaries, spreading fanwise, cut the high ridge paralleling the river on the west into a maze of spurs and ravines. The new rifle pits, starting at the fort proper, extended in an irregular trace along these ridges, first to the west, at right angles to the river, and then southward as far as a small stream falling into the river south of, or upstream from, Dover. Besides the slight trenches, the thick growth of scrub oak or blackjack which clothed the ridges was cut, with the trees falling outward, to form with their interlacing boughs a sort of abatis.

On the evening of Monday, February tenth, Forrest's cavalry rode up to the right bank of the river, opposite Dover, and began to cross over. The crossing was completed on the morning of the eleventh, the same day on which General Grant started his delayed movement from Fort Henry across the neck of land toward Donelson. Forrest's men, sent out to reconnoiter, met the Union cavalry three miles west of the fort, and drove them back in a running fight—the beginning of the fighting about Donelson.[13]

That night Forrest was put in command of all the cavalry of the garrison—his own regiment, Gantt's Tennessee battalion and three separate companies of Kentuckians.[14]

On the same night there arrived at Donelson the junior of the triumvirate of brigadier generals, Simon Bolivar Buckner, veteran of the Mexican War—where he had been in sharp personal disagreement and conflict with Pillow—and commander of the Kentucky State Guards during the period of neutrality. Buckner came in ahead of his troops, which had been left at Cumberland City, fourteen miles up the river, where the railroad and the river diverge. Besides Buckner's troops, the small Virginia and Mississippi brigade of Brigadier General John B. Floyd was also being held at Cumberland City, while Floyd, senior of the triumvirate of brigadiers, sent Buckner down to Donelson with orders to Pillow to leave in that post no more than a rear-guard garrison and to fall back with the rest of the troops to a concentration at Cumberland City.[15]

There was merit in the idea, too—for only four days later the Confederate garrison at Donelson was to do battle in an unsuccessful effort to get back to some such place, where there would be open communications and room to maneuver, and a chance to fall back for a further concentration with Johnston at Nashville.

Pillow, however, declined to obey the order sent down by Buckner until he had had a chance to talk it over with Floyd, who had been vested by Johnston with "authority to make any disposition of the troops which in my [his] judgment was best."[16] Early on the morning of Wednesday the twelfth, therefore, Pillow took steamer for a hurried trip up the river, after having directed the commander of his new provisional brigade of cavalry to make reconnaissance again toward Fort Henry, but "in no event to bring on an engagement should the enemy approach in force."[17]

While Pillow was up the river, Forrest marched five miles out toward Fort Henry, where he found that Grant was indeed "advancing in force," with everything he had. From nine in the morning until two in the afternoon there was skirmishing and maneuvering, with Forrest, characteristically, fighting one squadron dismounted as skirmishers, while the remainder of the command, under Kelley, sought to flank the Federal advance. The affair ended, according to the commander of the Federal advance guard, when Forrest's men ran into shellfire and "fled in confusion"; according to Forrest, when his men "drew off in good order" and fell back, in accordance with their orders, into the entrenchments. "The enemy advanced no more that day," he reported, "but planted a few cannon and opened fire at long range."[18]

Early in the afternoon of Wednesday the twelfth General Pillow returned, having persuaded General Floyd to abandon his plan for a concentration at Cumberland City and to order everything he had down the river to Donelson. Through the afternoon and night of the twelfth the steamboats were busy bringing down the troops of Buckner and Floyd, with Floyd himself getting in before daylight of Thursday the thirteenth.

That afternoon, while the first of Foote's gunboats to come up the Cumberland was driven off by the fort's one big gun, and while there were smart brushes along the land side of the fortifications, the deceptive mildness of the weather changed. The wind whipped around into the north, a mild rain turned to a blizzard of sleet and snow, and the temperature dropped twenty degrees below freezing. The night was one of most intense suffering for men on both sides, many of whom had relieved themselves of their blankets during the spell of springlike weather. They were too close together to light fires, while those wounded in the actions of the afternoon lay between the lines, suffering the tortures of freezing and, in some cases, the tortures of fire as the dead winter underbrush burned up to and over them.

Having completed the assemblage of the garrison in the fort area only on the morning of the thirteenth, the Confederate commanders decided at a council of war twenty-four hours later to evacuate the post and fall back up the river, whence they had come. The task of opening the road to Charlotte was entrusted to Pillow, whose troops held the left of the Confederate line, south of Indian Creek. Pillow accordingly began to draw his division out of the trenches and form them for the attack, while Forrest provided sharpshooters to dislodge those of the enemy who, perched in the branches of trees, were annoying the infantry. In the early afternoon, however, Pillow decided that it was too late in the day to attempt the sortie, and canceled the movement.

About the same time, Foote's flotilla of gunboats came into full action against the fort proper—half a hundred guns in the river against one heavy piece and a dozen light guns on the land. Forrest, along with many another Confederate, went over to watch the novel sight. While the fight lasted, his excitement was extreme, according to the recollection of those who saw him there. His own report notes that "more determination could not have been displayed by the attacking party, while more coolness and bravery never was manifested than was seen in our artillerists." He did not fail to note, either, that well-placed and well-served land artillery, even when scant in numbers, could hold its own with the new ironclads—for this was to be no repetition of Fort Henry. From its height above the water the one Confederate heavy gun in action scored hit after hit on the ships, which finally drew off battered and disabled, while not a man nor a gun on the Confederate side was hurt. The outcome, Forrest observed, "relieved [the Confederates] of their greatest terror" and left them feeling that they could "whip any land force that could be brought against them."[19]

That night, Friday the fourteenth, the generals met again in council of war, and again decided that Pillow should sally forth on the left and open the way for retreat toward Charlotte and Nashville. "In the early gray of the morning" of Saturday, the weather still being bitter, blizzardy cold, Forrest's men led out, "moving to the attack, the cavalry on the left and in the advance." Finding the enemy "prepared to receive us," Forrest's men "again engaged with the sharpshooters till our infantry were formed for the attack."

So began, about 5:30 A.M., the Confederate attempt to drive back McClernand's division, then holding Grant's right. As seen from Forrest's position, there was first "an obstinate fight of two hours," through "undergrowth so thick horses could scarcely press through it," ending with the retreat of the enemy. In the retreat the enemy flank was exposed across an open field which, however, proved to be a marsh impracticable for cavalry to cross. But between pressure from the advancing infantry and threats of a flank attack from the Confederate cavalry, the enemy retired again, and then once more, stubbornly falling back through the blackjack scrub and underbrush, firing and fighting as they went.[20]

At this stage of the fight, well into the morning, Forrest, acting very much on his own and without orders, moved his command across behind the line of Pillow's infantry to charge a battery of six guns, which was holding up the advance some two miles north of the starting point.[21] The battery, four brass pieces and two 24-pounder iron pieces, was captured in the charge—the first of the more than 100 guns which were to be captured by Forrest's men before the war ended. In the same charge, Forrest's horse was struck—the first of the more than a score of horses to be shot under him—while his brother Jeffrey, by this time a lieutenant, was painfully injured by the fall when his horse was killed.[22]

Coming under Pillow's personal orders, Forrest was sent on to the right, to charge a line of the enemy in one of the numerous ravines. Seeing a battery still farther to the right "about to turn on us," he charged it also and, in conjunction with Roger Hanson's Second Kentucky, of Buckner's division, captured three of its guns. In this charge Captain Charles May, organizer of the Forrest Rangers, the second company to come into the command, was shot dead, while Forrest's horse, struck again, fell dead under him.

As Forrest's horse fell, Lansing Burrows, a "young Baptist preacher who had been with him all day in the battle," turned over another to the Lieutenant Colonel, who mounted and, with a couple of scouts, rode still farther to the right front, on reconnaissance. A few minutes later, an artillery shell tore through the body of young Burrows' horse, just back of the saddle skirt.[23] In that war, it would seem that nothing was quite so unsafe as a horse carrying Old Bedford.

On foot again—the time being about two o'clock in the afternoon— Forrest ran back to join his command where he had left them, near the point of junction between the troops of Pillow and those of Buckner.

"We had driven the enemy back without a reverse from the left of our intrenchments to the center," Forrest reported, "having opened three different roads by which we might have retired if the generals had, as was deemed best in the council of the night before, ordered the retreat of the army."

But the generals, or one of them at least, had again changed their minds. What the soldiers had set out to do in the morning had been done. McClernand, commanding Grant's right division, had been driven back against Lew Wallace, commanding the center. Wallace had begun to give way. Grant himself was away, down the river to see Foote, who had been wounded in the gunboat action of the day before.

At this stage of the action Pillow, for reasons which afterward became the subject of extended controversy, "called off further pursuit" and ordered both his own troops and those of Buckner to "retire to their original position in the intrenchments."[24] Afterward he explained that "the object of opening the way had been accomplished" but that it had "taken all day, and before we could leave the enemy reinvested."

Buckner disagreed sharply with Pillow's order. When Pillow sent him "reiterated orders to return" to the intrenchments, he hunted up Floyd, senior in command, to protest and appeal. Floyd, astonished at the change in plans, halted the movement of Buckner's troops "until he should have conversed with General Pillow." When he did so, Pillow changed Floyd's mind once more, and orders went on to Buckner's men to return to their part of the entrenched line—a march of some two miles, on account of the encroaching backwaters. And then, to crown the day's misfortunes, C. F. Smith's Union division, holding the left of Grant's line, struck the one regiment left to guard Buckner's original position, drove them out and, before dark, made good a lodgment within the Confederate works from which they could not be pried loose.[25]

Forrest, meanwhile, was left on the field with orders to gather up and bring in the wounded, the thousands of abandoned shoulder arms and the other military equipment scattered over the three miles of woodland and field over which the fight had swung. Darkness—the darkness of another night of freezing cold and knifelike winds—found him and his men still at work, having brought in nine guns and 4,000 small arms.

Throughout Saturday's fight, by a minor miracle of journalistic enterprise, the people of Nashville, seventy-five miles up the river, were informed of its progress through a series of glowing dispatches published in extras of the *Union & American*, which quite counteracted the depressing effect of the news that the Bowling Green army was falling back.

"Glorious News—Rush to the Battle—Our Troops Now Triumphing," read a 10:30 A.M. dispatch, telling of "one of the fiercest fights on record" on the left wing. In a "Second Dispatch—Still Later and More Glorious," dated at 12:50 P.M., the anonymous correspondent of the *Union & American* telegraphed, "I think I can safely say the day is ours," while the "Third Dispatch," only ten minutes later, added that "we have whipped them by land and water."

The "Fourth Dispatch—The Latest and Most Glorious," told how the enemy were driven "inch by inch from every point in the field," but added that "They are largely reinforced and may attack us again." The "Fifth Dispatch—Latest from Fort Donelson—Some Details of the Fight," dated at 7:00 P.M., acclaimed the victory but closed on the ominous note that "late in the afternoon they . . . attacked our right wing with fresh troops, before our men returned to position. . . ."

56

The citizenry of Nashville, not noting this last ominous statement, retired on Saturday night with visions of victory. Even General Johnston, who by this time had fallen back to Edgefield, the village across the river from Nashville, dispatched Secretary Benjamin at Richmond, at 5:15 P.M., that the Confederate "arms were successful," and again at midnight, that they had "won a brilliant victory." The latter report was based on a dispatch from General Floyd, sent at 11:00 P.M.,[26] but even as it was on its way, there came another change of minds and plans on the part of the three brigadiers at Donelson.

Toward midnight another of the fateful councils of war met, this time in the old Dover Inn, Pillow's headquarters hard by the steamboat landing. About one o'clock on the morning of Sunday the sixteenth, the commander of cavalry was sent for, and told that word had been received that the enemy had landed eleven boatloads of reinforcements down the river, and that the ground from which the Federal right had been driven during the day's hard battle had been reoccupied by them.

"I told him I did not believe it," Forrest reported, "as I had left that part of the field, on our left, late the evening before." Scouts were sent out—Adam Johnson and Bob Martin, one of whom was to become a brigadier before the war ended, and the other to command one of Morgan's regiments—who crawled on their bellies through freezing backwaters to approach what they took to be Federal picket fires, and who also reconnoitered a fordable passage across the flooded creek south of the town. To their colonel they reported "that they saw no enemy, but could see their fires in the same place where they were Friday night." As to the road up the river, they had found "the water about to the saddle skirts, and the mud about half-leg deep in the bottom where it had been overflowed"—the bottom being about a quarter of a mile wide and the stream itself about 100 yards wide.[27]

While Johnson and Martin, half-frozen from their crawl in mud and water and their wild gallop back to headquarters with their news, hugged the potbellied iron stove in the headquarters, and while staff officers came and went, the generals kept on with their talk.

General Floyd, according to his own report, thought that the situation was hopeless, and that "the general sentiment was averse to the proposition" of further fighting. To Johnston at Edgefield he reported that eleven transports had arrived with Union reinforcements, that the fort had been reinvested by "an army many times our own numbers," and that it was the "unanimous opinion of the officers . . . that we cannot maintain ourselves against these forces." His decision, therefore, was to devolve the command upon his junior brigadiers, "and to make an effort for my own extrication by any and every means that might present

57

themselves to me. I therefore directed Colonel Forrest, a daring and determined officer, at the head of an efficient regiment of cavalry, to be present for the purpose of accompanying me in what I supposed would be an effort to pass through the enemy's lines."[28]

General Floyd, former Governor of Virginia, had been Secretary of War in the Cabinet of President Buchanan. He was execrated in the North as were few men, it being believed then—though long since disproved by the records—that while Secretary of War he had stocked the Southern arsenals with war matériel for the purpose of having it seized and used by the seceding states. He had, too, been indicted after his resignation in January 1861 by a partisan grand jury on charges of malfeasance in office in connection with bonds deposited by subsistence contractors of the army. Hearing of the indictment, Floyd had returned to Washington, given bail and demanded trial. The indictments, however, were nolleprossed in March 1861, even in the height of increasing tension between North and South, and after the accession to office of the Lincoln administration, "there being no proof to sustain the charge."[29]

General Floyd, agreeing with General Buckner as to the demoralization of the Confederate force, and the probable loss of three-fourths of their strength in any effort to cut their way out, conceded the necessity of surrender but announced that he would not surrender himself but would "die first."[30]

General Pillow did not agree with Buckner as to the necessity of surrender. He insisted that the position could be held another day until the boats, which had gone upriver Saturday night with the wounded, might return with ammunition, supplies and reinforcements, and in any event he urged that the army attempt to cut its way out. He did agree, however, with Floyd on the matter of not surrendering his person, remarking "that he thought there were no two persons in the Confederacy whom the Yankees would prefer to capture than himself and General Floyd."[31]

Forrest, believing neither that surrender was inevitable nor escape impossible, offered to take his cavalry to any point in the lines so as to cover the withdrawal, or to cut his way at any point which the general might designate, and agreed, if the attempt were made, to keep the Union cavalry off the backs of the retreating column. His propositions receiving scant attention, he stepped from the room for a while, returning in time to hear Floyd's final announcement "that he could not and would not surrender himself."[32]

And then began the strange performance of the transfer of command. Having been assured by Buckner that he would surrender the post if he were placed in command, but would permit Floyd to take out himself and as much of his brigade as he could before the actual capitulation, the senior brigadier turned to Pillow and said: "I turn the command over, sir."

"I pass it," was Pillow's prompt reply.

"I assume it," said Buckner. "Give me pen, ink and paper, and send for a bugler."

Whereupon, up spoke the undaunted Lieutenant Colonel of cavalry: "I did not come here for the purpose of surrendering my command, and I will not do it if they will follow me out. General Pillow, what shall I do?"

"Cut your way out," was the reply.[33]

"I immediately left the house," Forrest said in his statement to the committee of the Confederate Congress which investigated affairs at Donelson, "and sent for all the officers under my command, and stated to them the facts that had occurred and stated my determination to leave, and remarked that all who wanted to go could follow me, and those who wished to stay and take the consequences might remain in camp. All of my own regiment and Captain Williams, of Helm's Kentucky regiment, said they would go with me if the last man fell.[34] Colonel Gantt[35] was sent for and urged to get his battalion as often as three times, but he and two Kentucky companies (Captains Wilcox and Huey) refused to come. I marched out with the remainder of my command, with Captain Porter's artillery horses, and about 200 men of different commands up the river road. . . ."[36]

Three-quarters of a mile out on the road, the column was halted by reports from a reconnoitering party that the enemy was ahead and to the right, in line of battle. Forrest turned the command over to Kelley, with orders to keep on the way, called Lieutenant Jeffrey Forrest to accompany him, and set out to see for himself. Stopping at the point from which the previous scouts had returned with news of the presence of the enemy, they saw or heard nothing. Riding on in the direction in which the enemy was reported, they came across a stake-and-rider fence which, in the dim gray light of the dawning, had some resemblance to a line of infantry. Riding still farther out to the right, they found fires around which Federal wounded, left on the field after the fight of Saturday, were huddled, shivering. It was this fence and these fires, Forrest always believed, which had misled the scouts sent out before midnight and caused them to report that the Union troops had reoccupied the ground from which they had been driven on Saturday.

Returning, the Forrests reached the head of the column just as it came to the deep, icy slough. When no one came forward promptly to

59

test its depth and bottom, the commander himself led the way across.[37]

"When about a mile out crossed a deep slough from the river, saddle-skirt deep," Forrest reported, "and filed into the road to Cumberland Iron Works. I ordered Major Kelley and Adjutant Schuyler to remain at the point where we entered this road with one company, where the enemy's cavalry would attack if they attempted to follow us. They remained until day was dawning. . . . More than two hours had been occupied in passing. Not a gun had been fired at us. Not an enemy had been seen or heard."[38]

Generals Floyd and Pillow, having first planned to go out with the cavalry, made other plans. The latter was ferried across the river on a small hand ferry, his horses and servant being brought over later by one of the two steamboats which had gone up the river with wounded the night before and which came in about four in the morning with supplies, ammunition and 400 reinforcements, who disembarked just in time to be surrendered. The boats were taken over by Floyd for the transportation to Nashville of himself and as much of his brigade as could be embarked upon them. The four Virginia regiments went aboard, while the one Mississippi regiment guarded the embarkation. It was planned to take it aboard as well, but since the boats became overloaded and were threatened with a rush which might have swamped them, the captains backed them into the stream, parting the lines and leaving the yelling and cursing Mississippians on the bank.[39]

Forrest, in his original report on Fort Donelson, made in the same month as the surrender, expressed the opinion that the enemy had not reinvested their former position on the Confederate left—the fires seen were probably old ones whipped into blaze by the howling wind that night, or rekindled by the hapless wounded lying on the field. He added: "I am clearly of the opinion that two-thirds of our army could have marched out without loss, and that, had we continued the fight the next day, we should have gained a glorious victory, as our troops were in fine spirits, believing we had whipped them. . . ."[40]

A month later, after the affair at Donelson had become the subject of investigation by the Confederate Congress and of furious crimination and recrimination within the army, Forrest modified his conclusions to the extent of conceding that "the weather was intensely cold; a great many of the men were already frost-bitten, and it was the opinion of the generals that the infantry could not have passed through the water and survived it."[41]

Six months later, in another statement made at the request of General Pillow, and after the filing of scores of reports (General Pillow alone had filed ten by that time, and was to file two more), Forrest further modified his comment to say, as to the events of Saturday afternoon, that the retreat could not then have been made from the field with any hope of success, because of the scattering and mixing of commands "in fragments" as a result of the day's hard fight, and that "the pursuit of the enemy could not have been continued longer without coming in contact with a large, fresh force, which, in the scattered and exhausted condition of our troops, we could not have withstood." As to the midnight decisions, in his supplemental statement he said merely that "the character of the country over which we would have had to retreat from Donelson to Charlotte was excessively poor and broken, and at that time covered with snow and sleet, and could not have furnished a half-day's ration for our force."[42] But, it will be noted, he never did say that a larger part of the troops could not have marched out from the lines at Fort Donelson and made the attempt to reach Nashville.

His original estimate of possible escapes probably was high, although something like one-fourth of the whole command did actually go out, either in organized bodies such as Floyd's and Forrest's, or as individuals. One brigadier general even, Bushrod R. Johnson, having stayed with his command through the surrender and until it was separated from him and sent aboard the transports which were to take the men to Northern prisons, but not having been himself listed or enrolled as a prisoner, simply walked away from the post as late as sunset of Tuesday, February eighteenth. On Sunday, Johnson said, "hundreds" of men escaped, and "I have not learned that a single one who attempted it met with any obstacle."[43]

But marching out small commands, or the escape of individuals, was a different matter from marching out the army. Buckner, whose sense of soldierly duty was as high as that of any man, felt that to attempt the latter would involve an unjustifiable loss of life, either in the fighting which would ensue or as a result of the exposure which, the medical officers assured him, would mean death to a large proportion of the command. Neither generals nor medical officers had yet had a chance to learn how tough an animal the Confederate soldier could be.

Buckner had every personal reason not to surrender. He realized the state of feeling against him in Kentucky, where the vengeful Union leaders were to seek his trial for treason. But he felt a soldierly obligation to do what he considered best for his command, and to take the consequences. And so he sent forth his bugler to sound the parley, in the dark, and asked Grant, his old friend of Mexican War and West Point days, for terms of surrender. Grant, who was under deep personal obligation to Buckner for an act of disinterested friendship during his own darkest days after his resignation from the army, did not let that fact

61

affect the performance of his duty, and exacted the terms of "Unconditional Surrender." Buckner, by that time having no choice, accepted them.

In the first shocked reaction the South turned a storm of abuse on Buckner as the man guilty of surrendering a fine fort and a fine army. As investigation was made, and the details of the affair became known, most of the obloquy was turned on Floyd, or Pillow, or Albert Sidney Johnston.

Fort Donelson is a study in command. On one side there was a single commander, not of high technical competence at that stage of his career, but of a singularly simple, direct and tenacious mind. On the other side, there was little more than a perpetually divided council of war. Given anything like equality of forces, under such conditions of command, there could have been little doubt of the result—and Grant had something like twice the force of the Confederates.

The Union commander's uncompromising firmness in near-defeat as well as in final victory, plus the happy accident of the erroneous listing of his initials at West Point, were to bring him fame as "Unconditional Surrender" Grant, and to carry him on to the highest command and honors. On the Confederate side, too, there emerged a soldier of an equally single mind and tenacious will, a soldier touched with genius— Forrest, who was for fighting and who would surrender neither himself nor his men.

CHAPTER V

PURPOSE IN THE MIDST OF PANIC*

February 17, 1862-March 16, 1862

FROM Fort Donelson Forrest led his weary but grimly exultant column southeastward to Nashville, over eighty miles of rutted, frozen roads. Twenty-five miles they made the first day, past the Cumberland Iron Works, engaged in making armor plate for Confederate gunboats which would never be finished, past Cumberland City, where they turned southward from the river, and on nearly to Charlotte.

Reaching Charlotte early Monday morning, they found the little county town in a "state of wild alarm and agitation" over the report, brought by a local member of the legislature after a hard forty-odd-mile ride, that Nashville had been taken by the Federals. Threatening the alarmist bearer of bad tidings with arrest and punishment for the circulation of false intelligence, Forrest devoted himself to quieting the populace, while the local blacksmiths and his own farriers worked at shoeing the horses most in need.

In keeping with his policy of readiness for combat, Forrest halted his men when they were about a mile out of Charlotte, on the way to Nashville, and had them discharge their pieces and reload. Another Confederate cavalry regiment which had turned back from its march to Donelson upon meeting the news of the fall of the forts and the rumor of the fall of Nashville, heard the firing, took it to be that of pursuing Federals, and gave way to disordered panic flight. Forrest's men, coming upon their wagons and supplies abandoned along the roadside, nearly replenished the stores which they had had to leave behind them in the before-dawn march out of the fort.[1]

The panic which the Charlotte legislator was helping to spread had its start in Nashville on Sunday morning, the sixteenth. Before that Sunday morning the fighting part of the war had seemed to the people of the city something far off—away over in Virginia, or across in Missouri, or at the closest, a hundred or more miles away up in Kentucky. The city had been too busy, or too proudly confident, or just too indifferent to fortify.

---

* The field of operations covered in this chapter is shown on the map on page 48.

63

When Johnston's chief engineer, Major Jeremy F. Gilmer, had sought hands to work on the batteries, he had got virtually no labor from the local officials and citizenry—seven had responded to one call for 300[2]—but had received from the local wags the derisive name of "Johnston's dirt digger."

From this state of mind, strengthened by the glowing succession of more and more "glorious" dispatches from Donelson on Saturday, the Nashvillians awoke on Sunday morning to a rising rumor. Not only had the fort fallen and its defenders been surrendered, the rumors ran, but already a fleet of swift gunboats was above Clarksville, Buell's army of 35,000 men was at Springfield, less than thirty miles away, and the two forces were to join in a bombardment of defenseless Nashville at three o'clock in the afternoon, no later.[3]

By mid-morning, stark panic struck. Before noon the flight from the city was under way. People hastened to the depots, carrying odd assortments of valuables. From the stations "the trains went off crowded to their utmost, even the tops of the cars being literally covered with human beings"[4]—and that in a pelting winter rain. For those who could not take the trains, "the hire of private conveyances was put up to fabulous prices," approaching the full value of the rigs hired. The mad exodus was driven on by still another rumor to the effect that Governor Harris had declared that "the women and children must be removed from the city within three hours, as at the expiration of that time the enemy would shell the place and destroy it"[5]—which, of course, he had not said.

The state government, however, was in fact evacuating the capital city. Members of the legislature, routed out of their several places of abode and resort, were rounded up for a special session at the Capitol, whence they and their baggage adjourned to the depot. During the afternoon the archives of the state and the officers of the state government took train via Stevenson, Alabama, for Memphis, which previously had been decided upon as a city of refuge and temporary capital.[6]

The 300 young ladies boarding at the Nashville Female Academy, which Mrs. Forrest had attended nearly twenty years before, were sent off on the trains that day to their homes, or to places of greater safety.[7]

Throughout the gloomy murk of the short February day Hardee's soldiers on their long retreat from Bowling Green tramped through the city, passing out to the southeast toward Murfreesborough. The people of Nashville, by this time, were in a perfect frenzy of fear and uncertainty as to whether the city was to be defended or surrendered without a fight—there being partisans of both plans.

Mayor R. B. Cheatham and State Senator Barrow went across the river to Edgefield to see General Johnston, found out that there was

NASHVILLE, scene of the "Great Panic" after the fall of Fort Donelson, where Forrest brought up the rear.

THE DOVER INN, where in 1862 Forrest refused to allow his men to be included in the surrender at Fort Donelson—and whence he stamped forth to his first fame.

THE HOUSE AT GAINESVILLE, ALABAMA, where on May 9, 1865, Forrest finally surrendered the last Confederate command in arms east of the Mississippi.

neither hope nor intention of making a stand at Nashville, and came back to reassure the crowds milling about the Public Square. At the same time, the civil officials announced that such Confederate commissary and quartermaster supplies as could not be shipped away would be distributed among the people to alleviate suffering.[8] Since Nashville was at that time an immense depot of supplies, and since Major V. K. Stevenson, the Confederate quartermaster, left the city by train that day without arranging for their shipment southward,[9] there seemed to be every likelihood of a considerable distribution.

The hour of the anticipated shelling passed without sight or sound of a bluecoat—none was to be seen, indeed, for another week—but nightfall brought out a new crop of rumors of incendiarism and a fresh wave of panic. The First Missouri Infantry and a company of Kentucky cavalry, commanded by a rising Captain John Hunt Morgan, were detailed to preserve order, however, and the night passed with a "degree of quiet which was surprising."[10]

By seven o'clock Monday morning, the boats from Fort Donelson came in with General Floyd and his troops, and also with General Pillow, who had been picked up at Clarksville.[11] At the landing Floyd was shocked to observe "the rabble on the wharf in possession of boats loaded with Government bacon," which they were pitching ashore; they were carrying off what was not lost by falling into the water. The meat had been given them, they said, by the city council.[12] Any further distribution of stores was soon stopped on orders from Floyd, whom Johnston put in command of the city. The military took over the railroad trains, impressed wagons to haul supplies to the depots of the two lines running southward, and undertook to ship away stores.

Meanwhile, most of the men brought by Floyd from Fort Donelson followed Johnston's troops from Bowling Green, tramping through the muddy streets and out to the southeast. The city through which they passed was prey to rumor and panic. The newspapers had suspended publication, the post office was removed to Murfreesborough, the banks and business houses were closed, people were gathered in knots on the corners listening to the bloodcurdling stories of straggling soldiers. That evening, notified by handbill that General Pillow would address them on the Public Square, the people gathered to hear his assurance that "the Federals will be with you only for a time, and I pledge you my honor that the war will not end until they are driven across the Ohio River." To neither the General nor his hearers was it given that night to know that it still was to be nearly a week before the Yankees came, but that when they did come it would be to stay until the war's end, and afterward.

65

Not content with hearing from Pillow, the crowd surged around to the house where Floyd was quartered, called for a speech and were promised by him "that the Confederates would be sure to whip the Federals when they got them back into the mountain gorges, away from their gunboats"—an opinion colored by the fact that General Floyd was himself a mountain man from southwestern Virginia.[13]

Panic started all over again during Monday night when, with great clangor of fire bells and glare on the sky, the hulls of two gunboats being fitted out at the boat yard were burned by order of the authorities.[14]

Through this second day of the panic, which by this time had spread as fast and as far as horses could go, Forrest and his men continued their march to Nashville. Late that afternoon they came down the long slope of the Highland Rim to make camp for the night in the hospitable valley of the Harpeth, eighteen miles from Nashville. Characteristically, Forrest approached Nashville with caution, sending scouts ahead to make sure that he was not running into a Federal occupying force.[15] Before noon of Tuesday the eighteenth, they reached the State Penitentiary, then located just on the western edge of the little city, and there they camped.

Four days Forrest's men had marched as the rear guard of the retirement from the Green River to the Cumberland. Five days—and most of the nights, too—they had scouted, worked on fortifications, shivered and fought at Fort Donelson. And then they had marched to Nashville, eighty mighty mean miles, in less than two and one-half days. Their commander referred to it in his report as a "slow march,"[16] but for the remainder of Tuesday and the day following he let the men stay in camp, busying themselves with getting the horses shod, with repairing and refitting and, probably, with a certain amount of just resting after nearly two weeks of unbroken marching and fighting.

Meanwhile, Forrest rode on into town, reported to General Johnston who was just about to follow the last of his troops on the road to Murfreesborough, and was by him instructed to report to General Floyd, who was to be left in command in Nashville, under orders to forward subsistence stores and other public property southward.

On that morning, Tuesday, there had been an effort made to distribute some of these stores in satisfaction of wages due "thousands of poor women who had labored faithfully for the Confederate government for months past" but when the warehouse doors were opened, the rush of the mob was such that not many of the "poor women" were able to get their hands on what was intended for them.[17] Another start at a distribution was made on Wednesday but was soon suspended, under the orders of Floyd to ship the stores south.

66

The people who had come with wagons, wheelbarrows, baskets, flour sacks, shawls or just bare hands to carry away what they hoped to get, jammed about the doors of the warehouses as they were closed. To disperse the crowds, according to the author of *The Great Panic*, cavalrymen charged into them with "reprehensible recklessness," and with such swearing as caused him to feel that the familiar simile "to swear like a trooper" was entirely too feeble. Expressing wonder that there was no serious injury done, the pamphlet adds that "little was accomplished" toward getting the supplies to the railroad stations.[18]

So passed Wednesday of the week of the Great Panic. That night the two bridges across the Cumberland were destroyed as a matter of "military necessity." Citizens protested the decision, both because of the inconvenience it would cause without any necessity which was plain to them, and also because of civic pride in the two structures, but military necessity prevailed.[19]

On the morning of Thursday the twentieth, as General Floyd was leaving for Murfreesborough, Forrest moved his command into the city, where he was to be left in charge for one more day—although, as it turned out, he was to stay four days. The bulk of the command, under Major Kelley, marched on southeastward, while Forrest and a small detachment turned to the business of getting the stores out of Nashville.[20]

Once more there arose the struggle with the people who felt that they had been promised these very supplies. As Forrest reported in his response to interrogatories of a Committee of the Confederate House of Representatives which afterward investigated the affair at Nashville, a "mob of straggling soldiers and citizens of all grades . . . had taken possession of the city to that extent that every species of property was unsafe. . . . I had to call out my cavalry, and after every other means failed, charged the mob before I could get it dispersed so as to get wagons to the doors. . . ."[21]

"After the mob was partially dispersed and quiet restored," he continued, "a number of citizens furnished wagons and assisted in loading them. I was busily engaged in this work on Friday, Saturday and Sunday." The last two days, it will be noted, were beyond the time set by Floyd for his departure but no bluecoats had arrived, and Forrest was not one to go off and leave stores if there was any way to get them moved.

On Friday morning there was more trouble with the clamorous mob, in another and even more persistent effort to break into the warehouses. This time, the steam fire engine was called upon to play a strong stream of ice-cold, muddy Cumberland River water over the crowd, with "magical effect." When leaders were knocked down and others were drenched, "those who escaped laughed most heartily. The passions of the people . . . were cooled down, everybody was soon in a good humor, the crowd was dispersed, and a disgraceful riot prevented. So much for cold water!"[22]

That was the end of the troubles with the mob but not the end of Forrest's transportation problems. The railroad trains which had gone south on the Chattanooga Road, and also on the new Tennessee & Alabama, not yet completed to the Tennessee River, were asked for by telegraph. While the trains were being brought back, drays, carts, vehicles of all sorts and men to drive them were impressed and set to work hauling supplies to the depots. And then, on Saturday the twenty-second, there came another torrential rain, which washed out two near-by bridges on the only railroad through to the south. Five hundred barrels of Confederate government liquor were destroyed, when it was found that they could not be moved, but other supplies still left at the depots were loaded again in wagons and hauled out beyond the breaks in the Chattanooga line, to be picked up there by trains.

Forrest paid special attention to the artillery and artillery ammunition in the city. He proposed by telegraph to Johnston, at Murfreesborough, that he remove the forty fieldpieces which were in the city, and also the dozen unmounted heavy guns which were to have been used at Fort Zollicoffer, five miles down the river. This proposition had the sanction of the General but the guns, meanwhile, had been burned and spiked by order of General Floyd.[23] Forrest did succeed, however, in taking out a large amount of fixed ammunition for light artillery which he had found in the arsenal, as late as Sunday morning, by the expedient of hauling it out beyond the city in wagons, to be picked up later by trains.

Meanwhile Buell had been having his troubles with high waters also, first in getting his troops and trains across Big Barren River at Bowling Green, and then on the way to Nashville. Despite all the panic at Nashville, it was not until Saturday morning that Buell got started south from Bowling Green with about 1,000 men on railroad cars which the Confederates had failed to carry off or destroy, and even then there were further delays along the line because of washouts.

It was not until about nine o'clock on the morning of Sunday the twenty-third—just a week after the panic began—that Federal pickets appeared in Edgefield, across the river. A squad of half a dozen blue-coated cavalrymen rode down to the bank, seized the steamboat which was being used as a ferry in the place of the destroyed bridge, and held it on the right bank. Once more Mayor Cheatham crossed the river, this time in a rowboat, to interview the military, which this time was in blue uniform. Returning, he once more addressed the people on the Public

Square, repeating the assurances which he had received from a captain of an Ohio cavalry regiment that property and persons would be scrupulously protected. After a week of fearsome expectations of the imminent arrival of panoplied columns in blue, commanded by high and glittering rank and accompanied by bristling gunboats, Nashville was being taken over by a mere Ohio captain and half a dozen men!

Those craving more of the pomp and circumstance of war may have been a little better satisfied when a colonel showed up in Edgefield that afternoon, sent for the Mayor to make another of his rowboat crossings, and told him that a general would be along in a day or two to take possession—which news the Mayor relayed to another assemblage on the Public Square.[24] It was not until Tuesday the twenty-fifth that the Federal occupation of the city itself took place, but on Sunday afternoon, being requested to do so by the civil authorities, and having removed all of value which he could get away, Forrest and his little detachment marched out toward Murfreesborough, where he reported in person that night to General Johnston.

The panic in Nashville, Forrest told the committee of the Confederate Congress, was "entirely useless and not at all justified." The loss of public stores, which he estimated at "millions of dollars," could have been saved but for the fact that every officer of the Quartermaster's and Commissary Departments, save one, left the city before his arrival, and that one left on Friday.

Hundreds of sick and wounded soldiers were sent to Chattanooga. They traveled in unheated boxcars in freezing February weather, but more could have thus escaped capture, Forrest said, had not the available trains been used to carry away civilians and their belongings, during the early days of the panic. "The city was in a much worse condition than I can convey an idea of on paper," Forrest reported.[25]

Nashville became and remained, for the rest of the war, an advanced base and headquarters for Union operations in the West, while Johnston's men wearily slogged their way southward through rain and mud.

Johnston, at Murfreesborough, found himself for the time being the most universally execrated of generals, the object of clamorous outcry of which he took no public notice whatever. Already, even as Nashville was being evacuated, he had formed his plans for a junction of all his forces somewhere south of the Tennessee River, the first line on which he could possibly make a stand.

On February twenty-third, the Sunday on which Forrest and his clean-up detachment reported at Murfreesborough, Johnston announced a reorganization of the "Central Army" in three divisions, a reserve brigade and two unattached cavalry units. Forrest's battalion and Whar-

69

ton's Eighth Texas. Floyd was sent on to Chattanooga with 2,500 men, and the rest of the army was ordered to "move on the 26th, by Decatur, for the valley of Mississippi."[26]

Already in the "valley of Mississippi" was Beauregard, who had proceeded there after the evacuation of Bowling Green to take command of the troops west of the Tennessee River, effectively separated from Johnston's army by the loss of the railroad. Ever fertile and even exuberant in invention, Beauregard already had sent, on February twenty-first, confidential circulars to the governors of Alabama, Louisiana, Mississippi and Tennessee, outlining the precarious plight of the forces in West Tennessee and Kentucky, and calling upon each for from 5,000 to 10,000 men with whom, added to his own forces and those which he expected to get from Earl Van Dorn, west of the Mississippi, Beauregard proposed to "march on Paducah, seize and close the mouths of the Tennessee and Cumberland Rivers; aided by gunboats I could also successfully assail Cairo, and threaten, if not indeed take, St. Louis itself." The gunboats, twelve of them, he expected to get from New Orleans, he wrote Van Dorn, asking, "What say you to this brilliant programme?"[27]

What Van Dorn thought is not on record but General Johnston was thinking of no such "brilliant programme." He was content to assemble forces—all the forces he could get—at the obvious point of concentration, Corinth, Mississippi, and only hoped that he would be able to accomplish the concentration which he described as a "hazardous experiment," without Federal interference.

Interference from the Federals would have been more likely had not they too suffered from divisions of command. Buell, from Nashville, was advancing slowly after the retreating Central Army of Johnston, rather expecting that at any moment it might turn on him and assume the offensive.[28] Halleck, at St. Louis, was obsessed with the idea that his forces were "terribly hard pressed,"[29] was calling for reinforcements and was, at the same time, applying what now would be called high-pressure selling methods to secure his own promotion and enlargement of his command. As early as the seventeenth he was importuning McClellan to "give me command in the West."[30] Grant, meanwhile, went on up the Cumberland to Nashville on February twenty-seventh to assist Buell, who had reported his force there insufficient.[31] Grant was back at Fort Donelson on the twenty-eighth, but Halleck, trying to control a situation of which he had little real information, burst forth in querulous inquiries as to why "no one down there can obey orders?"[32] To McClellan, commanding at Washington, he wired, "I can get no returns, no reports, no information of any kind" from Grant, and that he was "worn-out and tired with this neglect and inefficiency."[33] Later, on March fourth, acting on a "rumor . . . that since the taking of Fort Donelson General Grant has resumed his former bad habits," Halleck relieved him of command, and put the veteran C. F. Smith in charge to "restore order and discipline."[34]

During three weeks of division and fumbling uncertainty in the Federal command, Johnston continued his retreat to the line of the Memphis & Charleston Railroad, leaving Murfreesborough on the twenty-seventh. Forrest was sent on to Huntsville, Alabama, in the region which was home for several of his companies. There he was authorized to furlough his men for a fortnight, under orders to report again at that point on March tenth. Promptly on the day appointed, the furloughed companies reported back to a man, in many cases bringing recruits with them. There reported, also, a new company raised in Memphis and captained by another Forrest brother, Jesse.

Following the railroad toward the point of concentration, on March sixteenth the regiment met, at Iuka, Mississippi, still another new company, raised in Fayette and Hardeman Counties, Tennessee, by the adjutant, Captain C. A. Schuyler. Having now a full regiment of cavalry, there was a reorganization of the command. Forrest was elected colonel, Kelley was moved up from major to lieutenant colonel, and Private R. M. Balch, who in civil life had been associated with Forrest in business, was elected major. To replace Adjutant Schuyler, Sergeant Major J. P. Strange was named Adjutant. The result of the elections having been reported to the Confederate authorities for the issuance of the necessary commissions, the new colonel and his regiment marched out from Iuka on the road which was to lead to Shiloh.[35]

71

CHAPTER VI

BATTLE AT THE PLACE OF PEACE*

March 16, 1862-May 30, 1862

THROUGH the month of March 1862 fighting men were converging from every quarter upon an unknown little log church in the Tennessee woods, bearing the name of Shiloh, which being interpreted means the Place of Peace, there to meet in the early days of April in the bloodiest battle, by far, which up to that time had been fought on the American continent.

Shiloh Church itself was of no military importance. Pittsburg Landing, some three miles to the northeast, was of little more importance—a store and two or three houses on the riverbank where, in prerailroad days, a small area of Tennessee and Mississippi, including the town of Corinth, shipped and received freight by Tennessee River packet.

A few years before, Corinth had become a railroad junction of importance, at the crossing of the Mobile & Ohio Railroad, north and south, and the Memphis & Charleston, east and west. Through connections at Grand Junction, rail transportation reached southward to New Orleans, and at Chattanooga to all of the eastern South. For that reason, Corinth had been chosen by Albert Sidney Johnston as his place of concentration for making a stand below the Tennessee River.

To Corinth he ordered the troops retreating from Bowling Green and Nashville. The frowning fortress at Columbus was evacuated, part of the guns and the garrison sent to New Madrid and Island No. 10 to continue the blockade of the Mississippi, and the remainder, under Major General Leonidas Polk, drawn back along the railroad to Corinth. The zeal and activity of General Beauregard began to bear fruit with the arrival at Corinth of 5,000 men under Brigadier General Daniel Ruggles, "borrowed" from the defenses of New Orleans, and 10,000 more from Mobile and Pensacola, where for nearly a year they had been trained under a strict disciplinarian and drillmaster, Major General Braxton Bragg. Smaller detachments were gathered in from along the line of the Memphis & Charleston, under Brigadier General James R. Chalmers, an able young Mississippi lawyer, and Brigadier General L. P..Walker of Alabama, who had been the first Confederate Secretary of War.

So general was the feeling that the South was to be defended best by

---

* The field of operations covered in this chapter is shown on the map on pages 48 and 103.

concentrating an army at Corinth that commanders in other sectors and even the governors of states were willing to see their own local defenses weakened, or even stripped, to add to Johnston's strength. Governor John Gill Shorter of Alabama, indeed, went so far as actually to urge that troops be sent out of his state, on call from Beauregard.[1]

By the end of March there had been assembled in the vicinity of Corinth a force of some 40,000 Confederates. Still others had been sent for, notably the 15,000 troops from across the Mississippi under Major General Earl Van Dorn, but due to lack of quick transportation they had not arrived.

From the north, during the same period, two armies were moving on Pittsburg Landing, twenty-two miles northeast of Corinth and across the state line in Tennessee. First to arrive was Grant's victorious force, reinforced to a strength of six divisions instead of the three which had won Fort Donelson, steaming up the Tennessee in an "immense fleet" of transports, convoyed by gunboats. Grant himself being still under suspension as a result of Halleck's displeasure, C. F. Smith led the expedition to Savannah, on the east bank of the Tennessee River, where headquarters were established.

On March sixteenth, the same day on which Forrest reached Iuka, Mississippi, William T. Sherman, commanding the most advanced division, made camp at Pittsburg Landing, nine miles upstream from Savannah and on the opposite side of the river, toward the Confederate concentration at Corinth. Back from the landing the country rises into a plateau, averaging a hundred or more feet above the water, bounded on the south by the steep valley of Lick Creek and on the north by Owl Creek, flowing into Snake Creek, which in turn flows into the river some four miles below the mouth of Lick. Some five miles back from the river, the headwaters of the two creeks come close together, making a rough quadrilateral of the tableland enclosed between them and the river.

Finding the site high, dry and spacious, "admitting of easy defense by a small force and yet affording admirable camping ground for a hundred thousand men," Sherman urged that the army be concentrated there.[2] Grant, now restored to command, so ordered, except that headquarters were kept at Savannah, the principal town in that section of the river, toward which Buell was marching cross-country from Nashville, 125 miles to the northeast, with four divisions.

News of Buell's advance to a junction with Grant was brought back by a timely scout of a detachment of Forrest's newly organized regiment of cavalry into Middle Tennessee, and promptly reported to Johnston.[3] Forrest remained at Iuka and when next Sherman made a reconnaissance toward the railroad, landing troops at Eastport eight miles away, he found

73

Confederate cavalry vigilantly guarding the road. It being no part of Sherman's orders to bring on a fight, he withdrew and dropped back down the river to Pittsburg Landing.[4]

On that day—Tuesday, April 1—the troops at Iuka were the extreme right of Johnston's forces, which were stationed along the railroads from that point to Corinth, and thence northward to Bethel Station in Tennessee—the line roughly conforming to the "corner" made by the Tennessee River where it abruptly changes its westward course to flow north to the Ohio. In number, Johnston's command was about equal to that of Grant encamped on the Shiloh tableland, but it was far from ready to give battle. Some of the commands were described by Bragg as a "mob, miscalled soldiers," while none of the newly named Army of the Mississippi had been properly organized for successful handling in large-scale combat. But, ready or not, Johnston knew that another army, Buell's, almost as large as the one Grant already had, was on the march toward Pittsburg Landing.

Just before midnight of Wednesday, April 2, therefore, Johnston determined to seek out Grant and attack him where he lay, before Buell could come up. Warning orders were issued before 2:00 A.M., to get the troops in readiness for movement "as soon as practicable" on Thursday, with three days' cooked rations in haversacks and forty rounds of ammunition in cartridge boxes. The plan was to have the army in position in the woods below Shiloh, ready to strike at daylight of Saturday, April 5, while Buell was yet too far away to help Grant.[5]

There was delay in getting started on Thursday, however, with the leading corps not getting under way until well into the afternoon. There was crossing of corps in the march order prescribed by Beauregard, second-in-command to Johnston, with consequent blocking of the few narrow and bad roads available for the advance. There were all the things that could and did happen to so large a force making its first combined movement. There was fretting and fuming among the commanders, and a vast lot of standing still waiting for a chance to move on the part of the columns. Instead, therefore, of bivouacking Thursday night beyond the hamlet of Monterey, a dozen miles out of Corinth, as was planned, the various corps were strung out clear back to Corinth. And that night it rained, a torrential downpour which made the bad roads, already cut to pieces by the wheels of wagons and guns, all the worse.

Breckinridge's reserve division, to which Forrest's cavalry was temporarily attached, did not leave Burnsville, a village on the railroad east of Corinth, until the morning of Friday, April 4, but that day made a good march of twenty-three miles to the vicinity of Monterey.[6] Forrest, being

74

detached from Breckinridge, was sent on the next day to picket the country south of Lick Creek. That night, on the extreme right of the army, he bivouacked within three miles of the river, along the road leading to Hamburg, the next landing upstream from Pittsburg. And that night again the heavens opened and the rain descended upon the Confederates sleeping in the open.[7]

On the following day—Saturday the fifth, when Johnston had planned to fight his battle—the Confederates commands made short marches forward to and beyond "Michie's [or Mickey's] house," and deployed in line of battle. Hardee's corps, the first line, actually deployed before noon within a mile and a half of Shiloh Church, near which Sherman, commanding the most advanced of the Union camps scattered about the tableland, had his headquarters.[8]

Forrest's men, during this day, skirmished with Federal outposts along Lick Creek, driving back a cavalry company which seems to have been the escort to Colonel James B. McPherson, sent to examine the defensibility of the ground at Hamburg and, if advisable, to lay out camps for Buell's four divisions, whom Grant planned to station there, "when they all get here."[9]

Neither the driving in of McPherson's escort, nor the other brushes between advanced Confederate elements, nor the general disturbance created by the deployment of an army within less than two miles of his camps, served to warn Grant of an imminent attack, probably because he was so certain in his own mind that he would make his junction with Buell and then go to seek out again this Confederate force which, for two months, had been falling back before him.

As late as Saturday night, while Forrest's men guarding the fords across Lick Creek were so close to his camps that they enjoyed the music of the Union army's band,[10] Grant was writing Halleck, "I have scarcely the faintest idea of an attack (general one) being made upon us, but will be prepared should such a thing take place."[11]

Actually, though, no real precautions had been taken to observe the approach of the Confederates who, in spite of all orders, had come up in noisy, holiday-soldier fashion, cheering and shouting and blazing away at rabbits scared up out of the brush, or just firing off their guns to see if the nights in the rain had spoiled their charges. No fortified lines had been thrown across the narrow neck between the headwaters of the two creeks which covered the flanks of the Union position—a precaution which would have made it all but impregnable. The divisional camps were scattered about in the area between Shiloh and the Landing with an eye to convenience of camping, not defense against attack.

Beauregard was so convinced that Grant *must* know the whereabouts

75

and intentions of the 40,000 Confederates who had spent all day Saturday deploying almost in sight of Sherman's camps, that he urged a return to Corinth and abandonment of the attack. At a conference of corps commanders, held at a crossroads less than two miles from Shiloh Church, Johnston quietly announced, "Gentlemen, we shall attack at daylight tomorrow." Before dawn, at a final meeting of the generals at Johnston's campfire, Beauregard renewed his urging of a retreat to Corinth. Firing was heard from the front. "Gentlemen," said Johnston, "the battle has opened. It is too late to change."[12]

It was Sunday morning, April sixth. Just after five o'clock Johnston's army struck. The surprise, so far as attack by the main Confederate army is concerned, was complete. Sherman's men, in front of Johnston's left, were busy about their Sunday morning camp chores. Grant was a dozen miles away from the scene of the blow, at his headquarters in the Cherry House in Savannah. The roar of artillery, reduced to a dull mutter by the distance, was his news that a battle had begun. Brigadier General B. M. Prentiss, a "civilian" general whose division had been at Shiloh only three days, seems to have been the one Union commander who took the trouble to send troops to find out about all the disturbance down in the woods.

This regiment of Prentiss, sent out a mile and a half, was the first force struck by the advance of the Confederate line of battle. Prentiss' whole division was soon engaged, along with Sherman's, and both were driven back upon the divisions of McClernand and S. A. Hurlbut and that of C. F. Smith, under the command of W. H. L. Wallace, which were encamped farther to the rear. The Union army, broken into fragments but stubbornly fighting, fell back through the woods, and across the little farm clearings and deep ravines and gullies, toward the Landing.

The exultant Confederates pressed forward, but broken into fragments, too. Their order of battle, prescribed by Beauregard, would have been exceedingly difficult to hold in the best of circumstances—Hardee's corps plus one brigade of Bragg deployed clear across the front of battle as the first line; Bragg's corps deployed 500 yards to the rear as a second line, clear across the front; Polk's corps and Breckinridge's troops, 800 yards behind, as a third line. In the dense country this difficult order of battle, with its lack of channels of command and communication from rear to front, was soon lost.

But in spite of disorganization and confusion, in spite of the gallant futility with which generals rallied odd bits of companies and battalions about them to advance in desperate charges behind waving flags, while other and larger units waited in the woods for someone to direct them, in spite of all the things that could and did happen in their first great battle to new troops who could find no room in which to execute the parade-ground maneuvers which made up most of their training, in spite of everything, the tide of battle was pressed northward toward the Landing.

Sherman's division began to give way shortly after eight o'clock, and by ten he had given ground completely, to join forces with McClernand in his rear. Prentiss fell back at nine o'clock, to take position between Hurlbut and W. H. L. Wallace. Wallace was mortally wounded, his division began to retire, and Prentiss was left, all but surrounded, holding the Hornet's Nest—a position which became, for the most of the day, a focal point of battle, never to be forgotten by the men of either side.

Under orders received direct from Johnston the night before, Forrest held his men on the south side of Lick Creek during the morning hours, assigned to watch for any possible advance of an enemy force which might have come ashore at Hamburg. Assigned to like duty was Colonel George Maney's First Tennessee Infantry. About eleven in the morning, having satisfied himself that no enemy was approaching from this extreme right flank, Maney started to the main battle, leaving Forrest to guard the fords of the creek. Forrest, riding in from his outposts, assembled his regiment and addressed them.

"Boys, do you hear that musketry and that artillery?"

"It means that our friends are falling by the hundreds at the hands of the enemy, and we are here guarding a damned creek! Let's go and help them. What do you say?"

With a roar of approval, the regiment started at the gallop for the sound of the advancing battle, by that time seemingly four or five miles away.[13] Pushing to the scene of the heaviest fighting, Forrest formed his men behind the division of Brigadier General Frank Cheatham, which had just been repulsed in one of the several charges against the Hornet's Nest. Two Federal batteries opened on the newly arrived cavalry.

Forrest felt that he must move his men either forward or back—preferably forward. Cheatham's command, after hours of hard fighting ending in a savage repulse, was in no condition to renew the charge at the moment, nor did Cheatham feel like giving Forrest orders to do so.

"Then I'll charge under my own orders," the intrepid Colonel announced, and away he went against the enemy positions. The mounted men bogged down in a marsh forty yards short of the troublesome batteries, but the horsemen were closely followed by Cheatham's infantry, who pressed home the charge.[14]

By the middle of the afternoon, the Union army, except for Prentiss' force cut off but still fighting, was being pressed back against a convex ridge surrounding the Landing itself, under the protection of a huge

77

battery of more than fifty guns marshaled and emplaced there by a fore-thoughted staff officer. Under the bluffs and along the riverbank cowered thousands of fugitive soldiers who, according to the reports of men of Buell's command, had given up the fight. At this point of the fight, about 2:30 in the afternoon, General Johnston, bringing forward troops on the right, was struck by a chance ball. An artery in his leg was cut. He did not notice, or disregarded it. Within half an hour he was dead, and command passed to Beauregard.

The fight, however, went on. Forrest, after his charge with Cheatham, moved over to the right and became part of the grouping of troops which cut between Prentiss and his reserves, completely encircling him and, after more hard fighting, bringing that doughty commander to surrender himself and the remnants of his division, 2,200 men, at about 5:30 P.M.[15] Meanwhile, about five o'clock, the first of Buell's brigades had come on the field, ferried across the river after a forced march through the swampy lowlands on the east side from Savannah, where they had camped on Saturday night.

As late in the day as it was, efforts continued to organize a mass Confederate attack on the convex ridge, crowned with its fifty-gun battery, which seemed to be all that stood between the Union forces and final defeat. From taking part in the capture of Prentiss,[16] Forrest passed on to skirmish vigorously against this final Union position, with such results that he sent back word to Polk, commanding in that part of the field, urging a general and rapid advance. Troops under Chalmers and J. K. Jackson tried it but they were small and weary brigades trying to breast a steep and encumbered slope against concentrated fire.

With their repulse, just before dark, ended the fighting of the first day at Shiloh, just as the orders from Beauregard came around to break off the battle to allow a chance to reorganize the commands for another day's fighting.[17] Forrest found himself at the close of the day's fighting in a wooded ravine partially flooded with backwater, on the extreme Confederate right and near the river.

Having been for hours without news of Willie, his fifteen-year-old son who had followed his father into battle, he started a search of the field, fearing to find him among the dead or wounded. To Mary Montgomery Forrest, with a husband under fire scores of times, and with her one child beside him, the war years must have been one long anguish, but an anguish of which she made no complaint, or none that is recorded, as is the way of women in war. Military risks and dangers for her men she seems to have accepted with the philosophy that the situation enforced, but she did worry about the lack of suitable companionship of his own age for her boy. Not long before Shiloh Forrest rode two days to the

78

headquarters of General Polk to "borrow" two suitable companions for Willie, the young sons of Bishop Otey of the Episcopal Church and of General Daniel S. Donelson of Tennessee.[18]

On the first night of Shiloh Forrest failed to find trace of Willie and his young companions, but the youngsters turned up safe enough with a batch of a dozen or so Federal stragglers whom they had surprised in one of the deep ravines falling steeply down to the river, and audaciously had made prisoners.[19]

In the course of the evening Colonel Forrest and his scouts—most of them in captured blue overcoats—worked well down the riverbank, and in sight of the Landing. There they saw steamboats arriving, and heard the orders given for the unloading of fresh troops—actually, though Forrest did not know it at the time, T. L. Crittenden's command whom he had last seen in January, in his scouting along Green River. Crittenden, who arrived about nine o'clock, was having "great difficulty in landing" because of the "6,000 to 10,000 entirely demoralized soldiery" who packed the bank of the river.[20]

To Forrest's mind, everything was clear. Action was demanded. Back he went, hunting for forces with which to act. The nearest command was Chalmers' brigade, sleeping on the ground where Prentiss had been captured. To Chalmers, then, he went, to tell him of the landing of reinforcements by the thousands, and of the need to strike and strike now.

"About midnight," Chalmers said, "Forrest awoke me, inquiring for Generals Beauregard, Bragg and Hardee, and when I could not tell him the headquarters of either, he said, in profane but prophetic language, 'If the enemy come on us in the morning, we'll be whipped like hell.' With promptness he carried the information to headquarters—" although as appears from other accounts he was not able to find General Beauregard, such was the confusion of the Confederate bivouacs on the field of battle—"and, with military genius, suggested a renewal at once of our attack; but the unlettered Colonel was ordered back to his regiment 'to keep up a strong and vigilant picket line,' which he did. . . ."[21]

Forrest and his men must have slept little that night, for scouting down the river continued until two in the morning, at which time reinforcements were still pouring up the river, while Forrest himself is noted as having reported during the night to General Breckinridge and twice to General Hardee, as well as to Chalmers.[22]

Monday morning came—the second day of Shiloh, a day of lowering clouds and spiteful storms. During the night Lew Wallace's Union division arrived, and the rest of Buell's fresh army of 30,000 men. Worn and now hopelessly outnumbered, the Confederates stubbornly fought

79

from half past five in the morning until two in the afternoon, and then, quietly and determinedly, started back to Corinth.

The first movement of the morning, a swarm of skirmishers thrown out by Buell's fresh troops who had come in during the night, came against Forrest's picket line. For an hour and a half Forrest held them off, slowly falling back, to gain time for the lining up of the infantry a little to the rear. At seven o'clock, under orders from Hardee, Forrest's cavalry retired through the infantry to form in the rear what would now be known as a "straggler line." Through the morning hours the Confederates held their own with astonishing steadiness. About eleven o'clock Forrest and his improvised "military police" were sent by Breckinridge to the right flank, where, within the next two hours, they had three brisk brushes with Union forces attempting advances. Toward one o'clock, under orders from Beauregard, Forrest moved to the center, dismounted his men, and fought them as infantry in helping to turn back the last heavy Federal attack before the retreat began.[23]

In the retreat from the scene of Sunday's victories there was nothing of the rout. It was an orderly withdrawal, with face to the enemy. Breckinridge's division, covering the retreat, established a line in the vicinity of the little church of Shiloh, the Place of Peace around which, in two days, 20,000 men had suffered wounds or death in battle. Toward evening, the Confederate line was withdrawn some three-quarters of a mile, and there, still in advance of the jump-off line of Sunday morning, the Confederates bivouacked on Monday night.[24]

Tuesday morning, the eighth, Breckinridge withdrew his line another three miles, leaving behind to check pursuit a collection of fragments of cavalry commands—part of Forrest's regiment, Wirt Adams' Mississippians, Wharton's Texas Rangers, and Captain John Morgan's Kentuckians—numbering in all only about 350 men, under command of Colonel Forrest.[25]

That morning Brigadier General William T. Sherman led the pursuit, "advancing . . . cautiously" along two roads. Finding a camp of Confederate cavalry in his way, he sent forward an Ohio regiment of infantry which "he took for granted . . . would clean the camp," and held a regiment of Illinois cavalry in readiness to follow up with a charge.

But Forrest, true to his instinct, had no idea of awaiting a charge. As the advancing enemy crossed a small stream, they fell into momentary disorder. Forrest's quick eye saw his opportunity and he charged first. "The enemy's cavalry came down boldly to the charge," Sherman reported, "breaking through the line of skirmishers, when the regiment of infantry, without cause, broke, threw away their muskets, and fled."

That the infantry broke "without cause" is not strictly true, for it appears that Forrest's men "in superb order and spirit" were upon them almost before they realized it, let them have a volley from shotguns at twenty paces and kept coming right on into their ranks, with pistol and saber.

As the infantry broke, the Union cavalry "began to discharge their carbines and fell into disorder." In a moment, Forrest and his men were upon them, also, and for a few minutes drove them, in wild disorder, through a stretch of miry ground and across a belt of fallen timber, right back against the brigade which Sherman had drawn up as a rallying line.

In the thick of it all, cutting and slashing, and firing away with his pistol, charged Forrest. In his impetuous ardor he charged beyond his own men who, at sight of Sherman's steady brigade drawn up to receive them, turned back, gathered up the seventy prisoners whom they had taken, and retired. Forrest, keeping up the pursuit until he was within fifty yards of the battle line, found himself surrounded by the very men he had been chasing, and being fired upon from all directions. One ball struck him in the left side just at the point of the hipbone, and plowed through to the spine. Another struck and mortally wounded his horse, as Forrest turned to shoot and slash his way out of the predicament into which he had charged. Clearing a way with his pistol, he started back. To protect his rear from the shower of bullets aimed at him, he seized a hapless bluecoat as he dashed by, and swung him up behind—to be dropped when the horse and his two riders were out of range.

"The check sustained by us at the fallen timbers," Sherman wrote, "delayed our advance so that night came upon us before the wounded were provided for and dead buried, and our troops being fagged out by three days' hard fighting, exposure and privation, I ordered them back to camp, where all now are."[26]

This little affair on the Corinth Road was the closing act of the great Battle of Shiloh. Back toward Corinth that night, Confederate wagons were lurching and struggling through the quagmires of roads, pelted with rain and hail, burdened with untended wounded. Forrest, with a wound which the surgeons thought would be fatal, started back to Corinth on horseback. Intense pain forced him to give up his horse for a buggy. Excruciating agony drove him back to his horse, on which, after an all-night ride, he staggered into Corinth, where the poor horse sank and died of its wounds.

Corinth had become one vast hospital. Schools, churches, the Tishomingo Hotel by the railroad depot, the depot itself, all were filled with wounded awaiting treatment. Trains were sent off with the overflow to Memphis. On one of them went Colonel Forrest, with a sixty-day leave of absence.

But, wounded or not, Forrest did not rest easy in his leave at home.

81

Word came to him from Corinth of disaffection in his regiment due to dissatisfaction with camp conditions and subsistence—the sort of thing which to his practiced business eye was always of such importance. On April twenty-ninth, therefore, only three weeks after he was wounded, and while he still carried the Union Minié ball embedded near his spine, he was back in camp. As good a commissary and quartermaster as he was a fighter, he was soon able to remedy conditions and relieve the discontent.[27]

Such was the man's vitality and stoic endurance that he even took to the saddle and resumed active field duty, with a bullet resting against or near his spine. A week later, however, as Halleck's ponderous siege of Corinth was getting well under way, while out on reconnaisance Forrest jumped his horse over a log in the woods and "started" the bullet from its bed, with agonizing results. Dr. J. B. Cowan, his medical officer and kinsman,[28] had to operate without anesthetics to extract it, and Forrest was forced to take another leave of two weeks in Memphis—the last time but one he was to see his home town until the war was over.

While at home recuperating, he seems likewise to have been busy recruiting, to judge from the following advertisement which ran in the *Appeal*:

200 RECRUITS WANTED!
I will receive 200 able-bodied men if they will present themselves at my headquarters by the first of June with good horse and gun. I wish none but those who desire to be actively engaged. My headquarters for the present is at Corinth, Miss. Come on, boys, if you want a heap of fun and to kill some Yankees.
N. B. FORREST
Colonel, Commanding
Forrest's Regiment.

How many recruits presented themselves in response to this double-barreled appeal is not recorded but Forrest himself was back at Corinth not long before the end of May when Beauregard, unable longer to fend off Halleck's ponderous and glacierlike encircling of his position, gave him the slip and fell back down the railroad farther south in Mississippi to Tupelo.

CHAPTER VII

FROM MISSISSIPPI TO KENTUCKY

June 1, 1862-September 25, 1862

ON JUNE 11, 1862, almost exactly one year after his enlistment in the Confederate service, Bedford Forrest enacted for the first time a part with which he was to become familiar—taking leave of a body of troops which he had raised, equipped, trained and fought, and going forth to do the like for another command.

General Beauregard, struck with Forrest's performance at Shiloh, determined both to increase his sphere of usefulness and to solve a difficult organization problem, by sending him to Chattanooga, in the area under command of Major General Kirby Smith, with special instructions to take command of the several cavalry regiments in that vicinity and organize them into a brigade, for action as a unit. "Forrest hesitated at first," according to General Beauregard's biographer, "modestly alleging his inability to assume such a responsibility; but yielded, finally, when again urged by General Beauregard, and after receiving the promise that his old regiment should be sent to him as soon as it could be spared from the Army of the Mississippi."[1]

Forrest, consequently, turned over the "Old Regiment" to Lieutenant Colonel Kelley, and set out from Tupelo across country with an escort of ten men led by his redoubtable brother, Captain Bill Forrest.[2]

On the same day on which he started, as it happened, the Union advance upon Chattanooga, interrupted more than two months before when Buell was called to assist in Grant's movement against Corinth, was resumed in earnest. With Corinth at last disposed of, Halleck ordered Buell to start again for the point which, as both sides were beginning to realize, was the true gateway to both East Tennessee and Georgia.

Buell's original advance toward Chattanooga had been down the railroad from Nashville, through which he could maintain connection with his base on the Ohio River at Louisville. Instead of permitting him to continue along this line, however, Halleck ordered him to base on Memphis, which the Union gunboat fleet had captured on June sixth, and to advance eastward along the Memphis & Charleston Railroad,

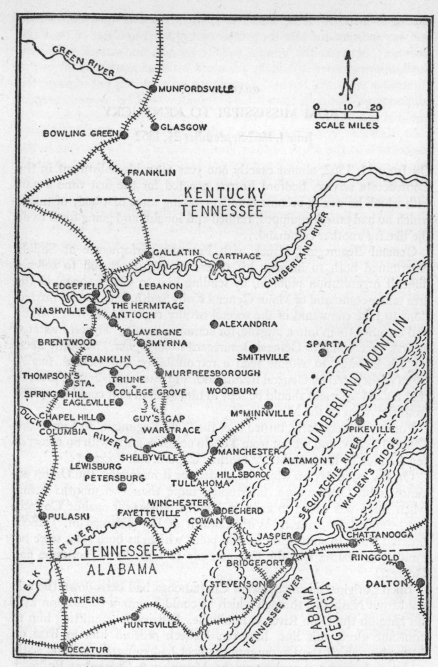

MIDDLE TENNESSEE AND NORTHERN ALABAMA

84

putting it in repair as he went—in spite of the fact that the railroad line was and remained for the greater part of the war a sort of unofficial "frontier" between the armies, subject to raid and attack by either. Buell, obeying orders, gradually advanced his headquarters as far east as Huntsville, Alabama, but at the same time he prudently put in repair the railroad from Nashville toward Chattanooga which, he correctly judged, would afford him a safer and more practicable line of advance.[3]

As Buell's army worked its way eastward, Forrest and his little party passed well to the south of their lines, to arrive at Chattanooga in the third week of June. The task of organizing the assortment of independent cavalry commands there into a unit was not easy. The Colonel of one regiment, from Louisiana, was his senior in rank. The members of another regiment, from Kentucky, which had been enlisted originally for twelve months' service by Ben Hardin Helm, brother-in-law of Mrs. Abraham Lincoln, were anxious for their discharges so that they might re-enlist in a distinctively Kentucky command. Of all the troops assigned to Forrest's new brigade only Terry's Rangers, the Eighth Texas, made no objection to fighting with him. Some of them, indeed, had already done so, handsomely, at the affair of the fallen timbers on the road from Shiloh to Monterey.

Finding the brigade assigned to his command not only somewhat disaffected toward its new commander, but also, in his opinion, in need of both training and supplies, Forrest characteristically "proposed active duty as a training scheme and the enemy as a source of supply for needed equipment."[4] Before engaging in this program, however, the internal situation was somewhat eased when General Kirby Smith ordered the Louisiana regiment northward to Kingston, west of Knoxville, planning to replace them in Forrest's brigade with Morrison's First Georgia Battalion of cavalry, then stationed at Kingston, while Lawton's Second Georgia Cavalry, just up from Atlanta, was added to the brigade which Forrest was ordered to take into Middle Tennessee, to find out what Buell was doing and to hold him in check until Chattanooga could be reinforced.[5]

On July ninth, the little column consisting of only the Texans and Lawton's Georgians, hardly more than 1,000 men, crossed the Tennessee River, climbed steep Walden's Ridge, dropped down into the long, narrow trough of Sequatchie Valley well to the north of the Federal forces in the same valley at Battle Creek, and climbed again to the plateau of Cumberland Mountain, where, on the night of the tenth, the troopers bivouacked around the little mountain courthouse at Altamont.

On the eleventh, they marched on past the long columned portico of the summer hotel at Beersheba Springs, where they turned down the mountain and, after a thirty-mile march, halted at the county-seat town of McMinnville. There they were joined by Morrison's Georgians, who had come directly from Kingston, by two companies of Tennessee cavalry under Major Baxter Smith, and by two Kentucky companies—bringing the total force up to about 1,400 men.

On the twelfth, the very day on which Buell's repair forces completed their work on the railroad from Nashville to the crossing of the Tennessee River at Bridgeport, Alabama, 120 miles away and only thirty miles short of Chattanooga,[6] Forrest completed the organization of his brigade, and assigned to each of the commands which composed it parts in the work ahead. The morning was spent in the work of organization and preparation. Horses were to be shod, rations prepared, ammunition distributed, everything checked—for at one o'clock in the afternoon the new brigade was to start on a march which, before dawn of the next day, was to carry them fifty miles and into their first fight.

The march was made "with no halt, except for a short time to feed and water the horses,"[7] at the village of Woodbury. There, at eleven o'clock on Saturday night, the people turned out to welcome Forrest's troopers with hospitable attention for man and beast—including the cakes and pies and other delicacies which the Woodbury housewives had prepared for their own Sunday dinners. That afternoon, Forrest was told, a Federal patrolling party had raided the village and carried off many of its men to the jail at Murfreesborough, under vague charges of giving aid and comfort to the Confederacy.[8]

Being himself headed for Murfreesborough, Colonel Forrest reassured the people of Woodbury, summoned his men from their pleasant midnight halt, and at one o'clock on Sunday morning, July thirteenth—the day being his own forty-first birthday—was on the road again.

The garrison at Murfreesborough, the largest and most important along the railroad, consisted of two regiments of infantry, a cavalry detachment and a four-gun battery—the whole force being about equal in number to that which Forrest was bringing against it. For some weeks previously the post had been under command of Colonel Henry C. Lester, of the Third Minnesota Infantry, which, with Hewett's Kentucky battery, was camped about a mile and a half northwest of the town. In the eastern edge of the place there were camped the Ninth Michigan Infantry, Colonel William Duffield, and a detachment of the Seventh Pennsylvania Cavalry. One company of the Michigan regiment, serving as a provost guard, held the center of the town, including the courthouse and the jail—the latter filled with Confederate sympathizers, including several under sentence of death.[9]

Command of the post had been taken over by Brigadier General T. T.

86

Crittenden on the morning of the twelfth—just about the time that Forrest's riders, nearly fifty miles away, were getting ready to make their start—but he had as yet made no changes in Lester's dispositions. He recognized that the camps of the several units should be concentrated, but there was no great rush about getting it done. He ordered the cavalry patrols which went out every day on the five turnpikes radiating from Murfreesborough to be doubled in number, but nobody told him that it was the practice of the patrols to come in each night, trusting to the fact that there had been no Confederate force nearer than Chattanooga during the five months' occupation of the place, and to the belief that this was still true.[10]

And so, on the night of the twelfth, General Crittenden, with his plans for the morrow, went peacefully to bed at his headquarters in the town, and Colonel Duffield, second in command, retired to his tent in the Michigan camp, while Forrest and his men marched, and marched fast.

At 4:30 in the morning, half an hour before reveille, with no one in the Federal camps awake except a few cooks chopping wood for the breakfast fires,[11] Forrest's men struck. Wharton and the Texans, in the lead, were told off to assail the camp of the Michigan infantry and the Pennsylvania cavalry east of the town. Morrison's Second Georgia was to sweep on into the town to take the jail, the courthouse and the private buildings occupied by the Federals. Lawton's First Georgia and the detached companies of Tennesseans and Kentuckians were to pass on through the town and attack the camp of the Minnesotans and the Kentucky Union artillery beyond.

Through a mishap, the greater part of Wharton's regiment followed the rush into the town, instead of turning off to attack the camp assigned to them, but this "did not abate their commander's courage or that of his men." The fragment of the regiment which made the attack charged "over the tent ropes right into the camp," where they were met by men who, in spite of being roused from their Sunday morning sleep, fought with courage and resolution. Almost at the outset of the fight, both the Michigan Colonel Duffield and the Texas Colonel Wharton were wounded. Lieutenant Colonel John G. Parkhurst of the Michigan regiment rallied his men for a countercharge which pushed the small body of Texans back far enough, and held them back long enough, to permit the creation of a strong defensive position, with a cedar-post fence in front and baggage wagons and baled forage blockading the flank approaches. And there, throughout the hours of the morning, Parkhurst and his men maintained themselves under punishing fire, giving as good as they got.

Meanwhile, the rest of the Confederate command swept on into and through the town, the hoofs of their horses beating out on the hard metaled road "a strange noise like the roar of an approaching storm," as the sound of deliverance drawing near seemed to one of the prisoners held in the jail under sentence of death.[12] One part of the Second Georgia surrounded and stormed the jail, though not until a vindictive guard had fired the building and made off with the keys, leaving the prisoners to be burned to death unless sooner rescued with axes and crowbars—as they were. Others of Morrison's men battered their way into the guarded courthouse, while still others rounded up the Federal officers who had their lodgings in near-by private dwellings—including General Crittenden and his provost marshal, Captain Rounds, whose unpopularity with citizens of the town is attested by the gleeful persistence of the tradition that he was captured under the bed in the house of a citizen.[13] The town was in a joyous uproar. "We sprang from our beds and rushed to the windows to see the streets full of gray-coated, dusty cavalrymen," a lady of Murfreesborough wrote, "while . . . bang! bang! bang! was heard in every direction. The glad cry of 'our boys have come' rang from one end of the town to the other, and staid, elderly citizens clapped their hands in delight . . . that day when the rebels burst so suddenly upon us was the happiest day experienced by the citizens of Murfreesborough during the war."[14]

The uproar in the town wakened and warned the outlying camp of Colonel Lester, who advanced his regiment to a little rise in the ground, about a mile west of Murfreesborough. There he drew them up in line, with a section of artillery on either flank. They were rather too much for Lawton's small regiment and the four detached companies to tackle by themselves, but there Lawton held them immobile through the early hours of the morning, while Forrest's men finished up the job in the town itself.

That done, Forrest hurried out to take a hand in the desultory fight west of the town, swept around Lester's flank, charged into his camp, drove off or captured his camp guards and destroyed tents and baggage. Leaving Lawton with seven companies to keep on holding Lester in play, he rushed back to the other side of town, where Parkhurst's men, behind their breastworks of fence rails, wagons and baled hay, kept up the fight. At the same time, he started the prisoners already taken toward McMinnville, under escort, and also sent off in captured wagons and with captured teams as much of the captured stores as he could transport.

It being now nearly noon, and there being a virtual certainty that news of the attack had stirred up the heavy garrisons along the railroad, some of Forrest's officers suggested that enough had been done, and that prudence dictated a prompt withdrawal from their exposed position. "I didn't come here to make half a job of it. I'm going to have them all," was his response.

With the troops which had been shifted from the other fights Forrest was able to bring to bear a heavy preponderance of force on the beleaguered encampment of Parkhurst. With his men in position, he sent in under flag of truce a demand for surrender, the first of a sort which he was to use more than once:

"COLONEL: I must demand an unconditional surrender of your force as prisoners of war or I will have every man put to the sword. You are aware of the overpowering force I have at my command, and this demand is made to prevent the effusion of blood.

"I am, Colonel, very respectfully, your obedient servant,
"N. B. FORREST,
"Brigadier-General of Cavalry, C. S. Army."[15]

This communication Parkhurst forwarded to his wounded commander, Colonel Duffield, who was in a near-by residence, asking for his "order or advice." Duffield left the matter to his subordinate's discretion. With half his force killed or wounded, with no sign or hope of help from Lester, and with a strong feeling that if Forrest did take his place by assault he "evidently intended . . . to execute the threat contained in his demand for a surrender," Parkhurst gave up the fight at twelve o'clock, and surrendered.

Free to concentrate on the forces west of the town, Forrest moved that way again, and again sent in one of his notes demanding immediate surrender to "save the effusion of blood." The Minnesota Colonel asked for an opportunity to confer with Duffield, who, by that time, was a prisoner in Forrest's hands. The interview was arranged, to assure Lester that the other parts of the garrison had surrendered. As he was taken through the town, to and from the house where Duffield lay, through the tree-shaded vistas of the Murfreesborough streets he caught fleeting glimpses of Confederate soldiery—although, had the Colonel but known it, quite frequently they were one and same column being maneuvered for him to see.

While this military mummery was going on, others of Forrest's men were busy sending off prisoners, loading up captured stores, destroying what could not be loaded, burning bridges and tearing up track on the railroad, doing all the damage they could, preparatory to pulling out for McMinnville as soon as Lester's inevitable surrender should be completed.

89

With that accomplished in midafternoon, the total bag of prisoners was brought to nearly 1,200 officers and men, and perhaps a quarter of a million dollars' worth of property, including more than fifty road wagons with teams and harness complete, a considerable quantity of much-needed cavalry equipment and small arms and, most prized of all by Forrest's men, their first artillery—the three 6-pounder brass smooth-bores and one 10-pounder Parrott of the Kentucky Union battery. Forrest's own loss was never definitely reported, although it was probably higher than the tentative and preliminary estimate of "about 25 killed and from 40 to 60 wounded" included in his report.[16]

By six o'clock the day's work was done and the last of Forrest's men was out of Murfreesborough. Major Baxter Smith's two companies were sent southeast along the railroad to destroy bridges over small tributaries of Stones River, while the remainder of the command followed the train of the prisoners and the captured property back toward McMinnville. Nine miles they marched that night, to camp at Readyville—making a total march of nearly sixty miles, besides twelve hours of fighting, in about thirty hours. Finding next morning that he did not have enough men both to maintain proper guards and to drive all the captured teams and artillery, Forrest promised the enlisted prisoners that if enough of them would volunteer to act as teamsters, all would be paroled and released at McMinnville—an arrangement which was entered into and faithfully kept on both sides.[17]

This first independent operation of Forrest as a brigade commander was afterward summarized by General Viscount Wolseley as a "rare mixture of military skill . . . and bluff,"[18] while at the time, General Braxton Bragg, who on June twentieth had succeeded Beauregard as Confederate commander in the West, described it as a "gallant, brilliant operation. . . . Such successful efforts deserve immediate reward, and I will cheerfully meet with you [the letter was addressed to Kirby Smith] in recommending Colonel Forrest. This affair, added to his gallantry at Shiloh, where he was severely wounded, mark him as a valuable soldier."[19]

The affair at Murfreesborough, however, was more than a brilliantly successful local raid. By the time Forrest was back in McMinnville, local garrisons in Middle Tennessee were being called in for the protection of Nashville against his force, estimated by Union commanders as high as 7,000 men, while larger bodies of troops were ordered back from Buell's army strung out along the Memphis & Charleston Railroad. Before Forrest left McMinnville for his next operation, on July eighteenth, Brigadier General William Nelson's division had been moved up from Alabama to Murfreesborough, and other brigades were marching into Middle Tennessee.[20] And even these movements were but incidents in the larger picture of protecting Chattanooga by delaying Buell's advance. "The safety of Chattanooga depends upon his [Forrest's] cooperation," Kirby Smith telegraphed General Samuel Cooper, the Adjutant and Inspector General of all the Confederate forces, on July nineteenth, adding that his operations might "delay General Buell's movement and give General Bragg time to move on Middle Tennessee."[21]

It was not until July twenty-first, however, that General Bragg definitely determined to move the main western army of the Confederacy from Tupelo to Chattanooga. Two independent forces were left in Mississippi—one under Major General Earl Van Dorn to defend Vicksburg against attack from the river, the other under Major General Sterling Price to guard the state against Grant's possible advance from the Memphis-Corinth line.

Bragg's cavalry and artillery horses were started across country, the guns sent part way by rail, the infantry sent by rail from Tupelo south to Mobile, there to be ferried twenty miles across the bay and up the Tensas River to the end of the new railroad and thence sent on by rail again through Montgomery and Atlanta to Chattanooga[22]—the first time an army had been so shifted from one theater of action to another, by rail. The movement was accomplished far more quickly than it could have been by marching but, even so, it was to take time, and time was what Forrest had been sent to Middle Tennessee to gain.

"Our cavalry is paving the way for me in Middle Tennessee," Bragg wrote to his friend and predecessor in command, Beauregard. ". . . Crittenden is quite a prize, and the whole affair [at Murfreesborough] in proportion to numbers more brilliant than the grand battles where strategy seems to have been the staple production on both sides. . . ."[23]

By the time this was written Forrest had gone on to other exploits. After paroling his prisoners, sorting out his captured property, and sending what was not immediately required back to safety in East Tennessee under command of the wounded Wharton, Forrest left McMinnville again at noon on July eighteenth.[24] In the week which followed, his small command was to ride almost into the suburbs of Nashville, to break again the newly repaired railroad, to cause the concentration of 10,000 men in pursuit of him, and to gain more time for Bragg's arrival at Chattanooga.

Learning that the Federal garrison had returned from Nashville to Lebanon, and hoping to repeat there the surprise attack he had made at Murfreesborough, Forrest made a fifty-mile forced march to reach Lebanon at sunrise on Sunday the twentieth, only to find that the new garrison had taken alarm and left, in a hurry, the night before.[25] The people of Lebanon did their best to solace the disappointment of Forrest's men by feeding them upon poultry, roast pig, choice hams and other "Sunday dinner" fixings, and by sending them away on Monday morning with three days' supply of such provisions.[26]

Forrest's appearance at Lebanon started the wires to buzzing again. From points as far away as Bowling Green, Kentucky, messages as to his whereabouts and intentions began to fly in. The commandant at Bowling Green, indeed, contributed a cryptic gem to the general uncertainty of the situation when he wired Nashville that "Forrest is at Lebanon, Tenn., with large rebel force. Without doubt he will move on Gallatin or Nashville, or probably make his way to Kentucky."[27]

From Lebanon, Forrest moved directly on Nashville. Midday of the twenty-first found him at Andrew Jackson's "Hermitage," twelve miles from Nashville, where the command was given an hour's rest, which some of them improved in converse with a party of ladies and gentlemen who had driven out to celebrate the first anniversary of the Confederate victory at Manassas.[28]

That afternoon Forrest pushed on down the Lebanon Pike to within five miles of Nashville, in sight of the tower of the state capitol, where he captured part of the Union picket and drove in the rest, before swinging around the city toward the Chattanooga railroad. There, before dark, he cut the telegraph, battered down the stockades with his captured artillery, and began the work of destroying the bridges at three crossings of Mill Creek. Before he reached the wires, however, they were buzzing with messages about him. Brigadier General William Nelson, who had been brought back from northern Alabama with his division as a result of the affair of the thirteenth, figured that Forrest would return by the way he had come, and started a heavy column out from Murfreesborough toward Lebanon to cut him off. Hardly had the column been got together before another wire came that Nashville itself was threatened by Forrest—who had no idea whatever of attacking the garrisoned city with his little band, even though he did report afterward his regret that he did not have enough men to attempt "a more solid demonstration."[29]

Upon receipt of news that Forrest was threatening Nashville, Nelson recalled his column and started them in that direction. Hard marching brought them, by ten o'clock on the night of the twenty-first, to within ten miles of Nashville, but no enemy could be found. Forrest, having accomplished what he had come to do in breaking the railroad line again—thereby delaying any possibility of a Union advance for another eight critical days[30]—and having killed and captured more than 100, without the loss of a man, simply disappeared from the Nashville-

Murfreesborough pike on which Nelson's men continued their march.

Turning aside on the Chicken Pike, Forrest's men camped for the night within easy hearing of the pound of the marching feet of Nelson's column. With the coming of morning they marched back into the main pike behind the Federal column, and coolly proceeded toward Murfreesborough, while their pursuers countermarched down the dusty pike on a July day.[31]

Six miles short of Murfreesborough Forrest swung away from the main pike again, circled around the town which was too heavily garrisoned for him to dare an attack with Nelson's column at his back, and pushed on to McMinnville. Nelson's weary men footed it back into Murfreesborough, whence, on July twenty-fourth, their General reported to Buell his scorn for the way he had been misled by the panicky messages from Nashville, together with his own plans for catching Forrest when other troops came up. "When they do come," he wrote, "I will have about 1,200 cavalry, and Mr. Forrest shall have no rest. I will hunt him myself."[32]

On the day of this dispatch the advance brigades of Bragg's army began to detrain at Chattanooga, while their commander and Kirby Smith were working out plans for their combined campaign into Kentucky— one of the most soundly conceived and, up to a fatal point, most brilliantly executed movements of the whole war. While the main armies moved, the gadfly Forrest stayed in Middle Tennessee, delaying "the completion of Buell's arrangements," as Kirby Smith wired Bragg, and "giving time for your advance."[33]

Buell himself testified afterward that "the consequence of this disaster [the capture of Crittenden and his command at Murfreesborough] was serious. The use of the railroad from Nashville, which had been completed the very day before and which I was depending on to throw supplies into Stevenson for a forward movement, was set back two weeks; the force of Forrest threatened Nashville itself and the whole line of railroad through Tennessee. . . . It became necessary to move northward some of the troops in North Alabama to drive out the rebel force and guard against further embarrassment. Nelson's division was ordered by rapid marches to Murfreesborough, one brigade going by railroad through Nashville; two brigades of Wood's division were ordered from Decatur to Shelbyville by forced marches . . ."[34]—all as the result of the work of one newly organized and imperfectly equipped cavalry brigade!

To Halleck, who had telegraphed from Washington that "there is great dissastisfaction here at the slow movement of your army towards Chattanooga," Buell explained that his lines of communication had been "constantly beset by a vastly superior cavalry force. They have been twice seriously broken in that way just as they were finished. The army could not be sustained in its present position, much less advanced, until they were made secure. We have therefore found it necessary to fortify every bridge over more than 300 miles of road."[35]

As the trains bringing Bragg's men up from the south continued to roll into Chattanooga, the cavalry force which chiefly had accomplished this result stayed on in Middle Tennessee, alert to do all the damage and cause all the delay possible. On the morning of July twenty-seventh, two weeks after the affair at Murfreesborough, Forrest struck again, this time at Manchester, on the branch railroad from Tullahoma to McMinnville. There, for the first but not for the last time, Forrest's forces met those of Brigadier General William Sooy Smith, of whom they killed three and captured fifteen. Once more they raised the alarm all along the railroad— and once more they vanished. Ordered out by Buell from Murfreesborough to reinforce the hunt, Nelson responded, somewhat wearily it would seem: "I leave tomorrow. I have been detained by all sorts of vexations."[36]

Nelson was still at Murfreesborough on the twenty-ninth, however, sending Buell another telegram complaining of the nonarrival of cavalry.[37] On the next day, still at Murfreesborough, he disgustedly answered his commander's query why he had not gone out after Forrest on the twenty-eighth as he promised, with the same reason that he had no cavalry and that "to chase Morgan and Forrest, they mounted on race horses, with infantry this hot weather is a hopeless task." In further explanation, he added that "neither troops nor officers have had a change of clothing or the shelter of a tent since we left Athens," that being more than two weeks before.[38] The chase of "Mr. Forrest" was turning out to be a wearing affair.

Finally, however, on the morning of August second, Nelson got in motion with nearly 4,000 infantry and cavalry combined. One column marched from Murfreesborough toward McMinnville by way of Woodbury; another, under Brigadier General Richard Johnson, toward Sparta by way of Liberty. Sooy Smith at Manchester and Thomas J. Wood, about Tullahoma, were ordered to hold brigades ready to support Nelson in case of need.

Nelson reported his arrival at McMinnville on August third, but Forrest was not there. He was, according to Nelson, thirteen miles away, toward Sparta. Expecting that Johnson's column would block Forrest's movement in that direction, Nelson reported: "I march tomorrow in pursuit and will not stop till I drive the enemy across the mountain."[39]

On the fifth, however, as Nelson was continuing his pursuit of the elusive brigade toward Sparta, he received an imperative dispatch from

Buell to turn back southward, to meet a reported advance of Bragg's whole army—which, as a matter of fact, was not to happen for nearly another month. Nelson countermarched as soon as he received his orders, "within five minutes," the more willing perhaps because the cavalry which he had ordered to be at Sparta on the third had not yet shown up.[40] That night he was back in McMinnville, under instructions from Buell to "make no permanent advance . . . control the country in your vicinity . . . and destroy Forrest if you can."[41]

As Nelson fell back to McMinnville, Forrest closed in again. On the seventh Nelson sent out a regiment to the Caney Fork River "to attract Forrest's attention," intending, as soon as Johnson was in position with the supporting Union cavalry and artillery, "to move myself and envelop him." The plan failed, and on the following day, according to Nelson's reports, Forrest was at large between McMinnville and Sparta "with 2,500 to 3,000 men."[42]

While he was sparring with Nelson's force between McMinnville and Sparta, Forrest received Kirby Smith's notification of August fourth that his commission as a Brigadier General, dated July 21, 1862, had been received from Richmond and would be forwarded to him as soon as a safe opportunity offered. Two new Tennessee regiments of cavalry—one commanded by the physician Colonel James W. Starnes, who had fought with Forrest at Sacramento—and a howitzer battery were being sent him, the dispatch said, and another Georgia regiment was promised. Finally, he was ordered to maintain himself in that section of the country where he was, at the request of General Bragg, most of whose infantry had by that time completed the rail journey from Tupelo to Chattanooga.[43]

Summoned to Chattanooga for conference with General Bragg, the new Brigadier General left his command in camp above McMinnville and set off across the mountains. Four days later, having ridden 200 miles, he was back with his troops, intent on carrying out Bragg's idea of "harassing Nelson out of all idea of advancing."[44] Meanwhile, John Hunt Morgan and his Kentuckians had whirled away on one of their daring raids against Buell's communications between Nashville and Louisville,[45] while Buell had ordered two more brigades, under Wood, to reinforce Nelson at McMinnville.[46] On the sixteenth Nelson himself was ordered away to take command north of the Cumberland River,[47] and George H. Thomas took command of the combined Union forces at McMinnville.

The opening moves in Bragg's Kentucky campaign came this same week, when Kirby Smith left Knoxville for Lexington, by-passing and containing the Union garrison under Brigadier General George W.

Morgan at Cumberland Gap. Bragg, at Chattanooga, began "crossing and massing" his troops from Tupelo preparatory to advancing on Kentucky, so threatening Buell's communications that he might give up Nashville and Middle Tennessee. "My infantry is all up," Bragg wrote Kirby Smith on the fifteenth, "the artillery coming in daily, and part of my train is arriving." To Forrest he wrote two days later, "My cavalry is slow in coming in, so that you have not been reinforced as I have desired, but as soon as it comes you shall have the whole." Bragg was uneasy about the situation of his advanced cavalry, for, as he wrote to Kirby Smith, Buell had "taken such position at McMinnville and Sparta as to render it impossible for Forrest to operate there at all.[48]

To Forrest he declared, "It is perfectly evident you cannot cope with the enemy in our front as he is now located." The commanding general's suggestion was that he leave a "mere corps of observation" on the west side of the Cumberland Mountain, and drop back across into Sequatchie Valley, to interfere with the Union communication lines in the lower end of that Valley.[49] There is no certainty that Forrest received this message sent on the seventeenth. Forrest himself made no reports of this phase of his operations, but from the Federal reports it appears that, by August eighteenth, he was already well beyond McMinnville, threatening Johnson's force at Smithville, which was reinforced by two regiments and a battery.

The scare, in fact, extended clear to Nashville whose garrison Buell ordered reinforced by troops brought up on a forced march, if necessary, and whose defensive works he ordered hastened to completion.[50] At the same time stockades and bridge guards for the Tullahoma-Manchester-McMinnville railroad were ordered. On the twenty-fourth Buell reported to Halleck in Washington that "our communications have now been effectually cut for twelve days"—the result of the combined activities of the Confederate cavalry commands operating in his rear.[51] As late as August twenty-sixth, being concerned about reports that "Forrest and Morgan are reported at Lebanon, to attack Murfreesborough or Nashville," Buell inquired of Thomas, "Do you know a colonel fit to command a light brigade of cavalry, artillery and infantry to operate against Forrest?"[52] On the twenty-seventh Federal reports had Forrest at Woodbury and, later in the day, as having captured the trains of a division near Murfreesborough.[53]

The affair which gave rise to this report, apparently, was one covered in a later report by the commander of the Union Tenth Brigade, that an attempt by Forrest against his wagon trains at Round Mountain near Woodbury, in the afternoon of the twenty-seventh, was met by two regiments and a battery which "handsomely repulsed" the Confederates,

96

MURFREESBOROUGH, 1862

The courthouse with Union troops encamped on the grounds. The building is
still in use.

WITH HIS GENERAL'S STARS

From an unpublished *carte de visite* photograph of Forrest probably
made in 1864. Comparison made with the civilian photograph
made about three years earlier shows something of the wear of
war on Forrest.

and "pursued and drove them over 2 miles, scattering them in every direction."[54]

On August twenty-second, with the first touch of asperity in their relations, Bragg had ordered Forrest, as soon as he had accomplished his object, "to return and act according to the instructions you have previously received."[55] There is no record of when Forrest got the order, but at the time of the brush at Woodbury he was on his way out of Middle Tennessee, heading for the top of Cumberland Mountain, where he was to await the coming of Bragg's army—and showing the same skill in dodging fights as he had earlier shown in seeking them, when it was to his advantage to do so.

By the second morning after the brush at Round Mountain, Forrest had crossed the guarded line of the McMinnville-Manchester railroad, and headed into one of the long, narrow coves leading back into the Cumberland plateau beyond, marching for Altamont. In the early morning of the twenty-ninth one of the cloud of scouts by whom his march was preceded and surrounded came in with the news that McCook's Union division, which for so long had been in the lower Sequatchie Valley, had fallen back to the top of the mountain and occupied Altamont. From this force, moreover, a column was even then marching down the mountain toward Forrest. Almost at the same time, other scouts came in with news that in the rear Federal columns were converging from three different directions—Winchester, Manchester and McMinnville. Forrest was never to be in a tighter spot.

Pushing his horse to a commanding spur of the mountain from which he could overlook the floor of the valley for miles, he spotted the approaching blue columns and, at the same time, made his plan for avoiding them. Turning back down the cove, he led his men into the dry bed of a creek, deep cut between overhanging banks, whence they emerged when the converging columns had passed on in pursuit of the rebel raiders.[56]

With McCook at Altamont, it was obvious to Forrest that he would have to make his junction with Bragg's advancing army farther north, at Sparta, so to Sparta he headed. The safest way to get there without fighting was to recross the line of the railroad, swing west and north, and pass behind the Federal garrison at McMinnville—which he proceeded to do.

That afternoon the force which was supposed to have been "scattered in every direction" two days before recrossed the railroad line eight miles southwest of McMinnville. There, according to Federal reports, Forrest attacked the bridge stockade and its garrison, and was repulsed. "The rout was complete, the rebels throwing away arms and fleeing, leaving on the field their dead and several of their wounded."[57] To Forrest and his

97

men, however, the attack was a mere bluff and a dare, from which they went on their way to their appointed place.[58]

On the very next day, as they passed northward across the McMinnville-Murfreesborough road at Little Pond, Forrest's men were "routed" again. This time, according to reports, "the rebels fled in the utmost consternation and confusion," losing by capture "General Forrest's light spring wagon, riding-horse, and body servant of Captain Forrest, brother to the general."[59]

All of which led up to Thomas' exultant dispatch of August thirty-first to Buell:

"Thursday Forrest was whipped . . . near Woodbury. Friday he attacked the stockade on the railroad 8 miles from McMinnville and was whipped again. . . . Started yesterday for Bragg's camp by Altamont; was met by McCook's advance and again whipped. He then returned toward Woodbury again, but was pursued by one of Wood's regiments, overtaken and attacked . . . and again badly whipped and dispersed."[60]

Not taking quite so seriously the reports of his "whippings," Forrest and his "dispersed" command marched on toward Sparta where, on September third, they met the advance of Bragg's army, and after two months on their own inside the enemy's lines entered upon the next phase of their work in the Kentucky campaign.

Bragg from Sparta and Buell from Murfreesborough and Nashville were in a foot race for Louisville. Forrest was ordered to operate far out to the left of Bragg's column, both to cover it and to hang on Buell's flank and rear, and impede his progress. Before leaving Sparta, Forrest was reinforced by a section of artillery and by the four Alabama companies of the "Old Regiment"—still referred to in the reports as "Forrest's Cavalry"—under Captain W. C. Bacot.[61]

Straight west from Sparta Forrest pushed to Lebanon, only thirty-two miles short of Nashville. From Murfreesborough, General McCook reported on September sixth that his "cavalry was just in from Lebanon" with advice that "a strong cavalry force of the enemy" was advancing on that point from Sparta.[62] Forrest's men pressed on from Lebanon to Murfreesborough, which he entered on the seventh as McCook's rear guard was leaving, being in time to save the courthouse and the center of the town from destruction by fires set by irresponsible Union stragglers.[63] To reports of his whereabouts and activities, Forrest added an urgent and characteristic recommendation of an "energetic movement forward."[64]

Something akin to panic was, by this time, spreading in the North. In central Kentucky, Kirby Smith had, on August thirtieth at Richmond, completely defeated the Union forces under Nelson, and advanced to Lexington, Frankfort and beyond. All business houses in Cincinnati were closed, while the citizens feverishly fortified the place to resist his expected assault. In Virginia, at the same time, John Pope's army had been astonishingly defeated at Second Manassass, and Lee had crossed the Potomac into Maryland. Washington was hearing rumors that Bragg, too, was heading for Virginia and a junction with Lee. President Lincoln asked the Union commanders in Cincinnati and Louisville, on the seventh, whether, indeed, even then Bragg "might not be in Virginia?"[65] On the evening of the eighth, he addressed a like question to Buell at Nashville, to which, on the ninth, Buell replied that "Bragg is certainly this side of the Cumberland Mountains with his whole force."[66]

By that time, in fact, Bragg was north of the Cumberland River and well on his way into Kentucky. Forrest, fulfilling his appointed task, moved north from Murfreesborough on the morning of the eighth—reporting, meanwhile, to Bragg, where there was a large amount of "good flour at $10 a barrel," and offering to send for it; crossed the Cumberland near the mouth of Stones River, near the Hermitage; and on September eleventh struck the Union pickets at Tyree Springs, Tennessee, eighteen miles south of Franklin, Kentucky. "I have halted their whole command," he reported, "and they still remain where we left them," shelling the woods. "I shall continue to annoy them as far as Franklin,"[67] he added.

Thomas, commanding Buell's rear guard, reported on the twelfth that he was "thinking of sending out an expedition" for Forrest's capture the following night,[68] but by that time Forrest was well away harassing and delaying Buell's march by bold and persistent attacks which forced the Union forces to waste precious time in deploying to beat him back.

By special orders issued at Bragg's headquarters at Glasgow, Kentucky, on September fourteenth the cavalry of the command was divided into two brigades—one, under Colonel Joseph Wheeler, assigned to Hardee's left wing of the army; the other, under Forrest, assigned to Leonidas Polk's right wing.[69] Forrest was ordered by General Polk on the next day to "dispose of his baggage trains and everything else that may be in the way of his rapid movements via the Louisville turnpike, and prepare his command to move at a moment's notice."[70]

On that day the Confederate army was closing in on Munfordville, where the Louisville & Nashville Railroad crosses Green River. Forrest's movement was part of the encircling of that place which resulted, on the seventeenth, in the surrender of the post and its garrison of more than 4,000 men. General Bragg had won his race. His army was squarely between Buell and his base. Louisville was added to the list of cities in panic.

In that third week of September 1862 the affairs of the Confederacy reached high tide, with Lee in Maryland outfacing the great army of McClellan across the Antietam, and with Bragg in Kentucky having Buell, as one of his officers put it afterward, "in the hollow of his hand." With the necessary withdrawals of Lee after the bloody stand at Sharpsburg, and with the never really explained decision of Bragg to "open his hand," the tide began its long ebb, to run out to the end.

During the few days before Bragg decided to stand aside from Munfordville and let Buell pass to safety, Forrest pushed forward along the railroad to Elizabethtown, whence he turned eastward to Bardstown, picketing out toward Louisville and toward Frankfort as well. On September nineteenth Polk ordered him to "leave a detachment to protect his baggage train" where it was, while he returned to Munfordville immediately. "The presence of your command is of importance to us,"[71] he added. Forrest sent the majority of his brigade back, retaining only the wagon train, the unfit men and horses and enough others to keep out his pickets. He himself, "being disabled," remained with the baggage train.

Receiving another order from Polk two days later "to make a demonstration on West Point, at the mouth of Salt River, and to break up the railroad," he protested the impossibility of complying with it for lack of men and horses.[72] By the twenty-third, however, following Bragg's order to march to central Kentucky, Polk himself had come up to Bardstown with infantry support and Forrest was ordered forward another twelve miles along the turnpike to Louisville, with picket guards out right and left toward Taylorsville and Shepherdsville.[73] At ten o'clock that night Forrest, from his camp two miles beyond Cox's Creek, replied that he had furnished so many guards and pickets that he had not a full company left in his command, but that he would make up a detail from different companies and send it out to report on the whereabouts of the enemy[74]—that being, incidentally, about as close as the Confederates came to Louisville.

On the next day but one, September twenty-fifth, army headquarters having moved to Bardstown, Forrest was summoned to meet General Bragg, by whom he was informed that he was to be relieved of duty in Kentucky and sent back to Middle Tennessee, authorized to raise there four regiments of infantry and two of cavalry, muster them into the Confederate service, and with them and such other troops as he might find, to operate against the enemy in all practicable ways. He was to be permitted to take with him as his escort, and to keep in his command, the four companies of the Old Regiment under Captain W. C. Bacot.[75]

100

And so at the end of September Forrest's part in the fateful and promising Kentucky campaign ended as it had begun in mid-June, by his taking leave of a command which had been stamped with his name and personality, and setting forth with a small escort to raise another.

CHAPTER VIII

THE FIRST WEST TENNESSEE CAMPAIGN

September 25, 1862-January 3, 1863

IT WAS part of the evil chance which beset the Confederacy in the West that, until very nearly the end of the war, President Jefferson Davis was to see Bedford Forrest through the eyes of General Bragg, and that Bragg could not see him except through the fine-print pages of the drill books. Despite his expressed confidence in Forrest's "energy, zeal and ability"[1] he did not realize, and apparently could not realize, that a man not professionally trained in the minutiae of the regulations might nevertheless be a first-class soldier and not a mere partisan raider.

When Forrest was sent back from Kentucky his mission was to operate against the Union forces remaining in Middle Tennessee by "cutting off supplies, capturing trains, and harassing them in all ways practicable."[2] He was sent, in other words, "on partisan service, for which and which alone [Forrest and Morgan] are peculiarly and especially suited," as Bragg afterward wrote to President Davis.[3]

The Union forces remaining in Middle Tennessee consisted chiefly of a garrison of something more than 12,000 men under Brigadier General James S. Negley,[4] concentrated in Nashville, where the troops had been left largely at the insistence of Andrew Johnson, Military Governor of Tennessee, that the capital of the state must be held at all hazards. To operate against this garrison, there were about 1,700 Tennessee state troops, or militia, and about 1,000 Confederate cavalry, all fresh-raised and entirely green. These half-organized and untrained bands were encamped at La Vergne, halfway between Nashville and Murfreesborough, when Forrest arrived at the latter point from Bardstown after a five-day march of 165 miles. Forrest brought with him Bacot's battalion of cavalry, veteran soldiers, and found at Murfreesborough one trained infantry regiment, the Thirty-second Alabama, and Captain S. L. Freeman's battery of two 6-pounder guns and two 12-pounder howitzers, bronze.[5]

The Alabama regiment was sent forward to the advanced position at La Vergne, where at dawn of October seventh a Federal force from Nashville struck in a surprise attack, front and flank. The Tennessee levies

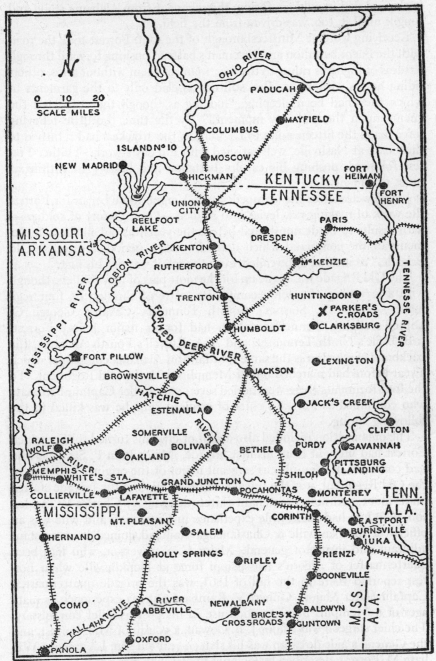

WEST TENNESSEE AND KENTUCKY AND NORTHERN MISSISSIPPI

The following place names appear on the map:

OHIO RIVER

PADUCAH

MAYFIELD

COLUMBUS

MOSCOW

ISLAND Nº 10

NEW MADRID

HICKMAN

FORT HEIMAN

KENTUCKY
TENNESSEE

FORT HENRY

UNION CITY

REELFOOT LAKE

MISSOURI
ARKANSAS

PARIS

DRESDEN

KENTON

OBION RIVER

RUTHERFORD

McKENZIE

TRENTON

HUNTINGDON

PARKER'S C. ROADS

MISSISSIPPI RIVER

FORKED DEER RIVER

HUMBOLDT

CLARKSBURG

TENNESSEE RIVER

FORT PILLOW

LEXINGTON

BROWNSVILLE

JACKSON

HATCHIE

JACK'S CREEK

ESTENAULA

RIVER

CLIFTON

SOMERVILLE

RALEIGH
WOLF

BOLIVAR

BETHEL

PURDY

SAVANNAH

OAKLAND

PITTSBURG LANDING

RIVER

SHILOH

MEMPHIS

WHITE'S STA.

GRAND JUNCTION

POCAHONTAS

MONTEREY

TENN.

COLLIERVILLE

LAFAYETTE

ALA.

MISSISSIPPI

MT. PLEASANT

CORINTH

EASTPORT

BURNSVILLE

HERNANDO

SALEM

IUKA

HOLLY SPRINGS

RIPLEY

RIENZI

BOONEVILLE

MISS.
ALA.

COMO

TALLAHATCHIE RIVER

NEWALBANY

BALDWYN

ABBEVILLE

BRICE'S CROSSROADS

GUNTOWN

OXFORD

PANOLA

N

0 10 20
SCALE MILES

broke and fled in wild confusion; the regiment from Alabama stood and fought until it, too, was driven from the field.

Receiving word at Murfreesborough of the rout, Forrest took the road with the Bacot battalion and Freeman's battery, pushing forward through streams of fugitives riding to the rear, many of them without arms, others riding horses without saddles, still others clad only in the garments in which they had been sleeping, "looking as though they expected the enemy upon them at any moment." By the time the little relieving force made the fifteen miles to La Vergne, the attackers had returned to their base at Nashville, well satisfied with the day's work. Thither Forrest followed, pushing his cavalry battalion and battery to within six miles of the city.[6]

In the weeks after the stampede at Le Vergne there began for Forrest the work of making raw levies into soldiers—Forrest's sort of soldiers—with results to be demonstrated before the year was out in the achievements of the command which dates from this period—Forrest's "Old Brigade," as it came to be called, even though it was not his first.

The Old Brigade was made up for the most part of new soldiers, though with a leavening of veteran companies scattered through its four regiments—James W. Starnes's Fourth Tennessee Cavalry; George G. Dibrell's Eighth Tennessee, which had for its major Jeffrey Forrest; J. B. Biffle's Ninth Tennessee; and A. A. Russell's Fourth Alabama, the backbone of which was the same four faithful Alabama companies which a year before had marched out of Memphis with the Old Regiment. To the four regiments there were added seven guns under Captain Freeman, who continued as Forrest's chief of artillery until he was killed in the following spring.

The organization included also a staff of civilians turned soldier which Forrest had brought from his first brigade. Major John P. Strange, who had come out of Memphis as sergeant major of the original battalion of the Old Regiment, was the brigade adjutant. Before the brigade started on its first expedition, Lieutenant (afterward Major) Charles W. Anderson, who had had mercantile experience in Cincinnati and who was an official of the Nashville & Chattanooga Railroad, joined it as assistant adjutant and inspector general. Major C. S. Severson, who had been quartermaster of Alcorn's Mississippi force at Hopkinsville when Forrest reported there in the fall of 1861, was the brigade quartermaster. Captain (later Major) Gilbert V. Rambaut put his experience as manager of a Memphis hotel to good use in his post as chief commissary. The chief surgeon was Major J. B. Cowan, a cousin of Mrs. Forrest, and the General's aide-de-camp was his sixteen-year-old son, Lieutenant William M. Forrest, described by Colonel Kelley, who was a sort of unofficial chaplain to the staff, as "the youngest and gentlest" of the staff group.[7]

Others joined later but, except for Major Severson, who retired in 1864, these staff members served Forrest through all his promotions and in all grades, to the surrender in 1865. One who joined the command, but not the staff, before its first expedition was Lieutenant John W. Morton, a nineteen-year-old veteran, who had already won attention at Fort Donelson by his handling of Porter's battery after the wounding of its captain, who had served a time as a prisoner in the North, and who, at the age of twenty-one, was to become Forrest's chief of artillery.[8]

While he was organizing his new command Forrest was appealing to everybody in authority in the Confederacy whom he could reach for arms and equipment—and getting very little of either. When Major General Sam Jones, commanding in East Tennessee, had none to spare for him, he went direct to Secretary of War Randolph with the plea that "if you can only send me 1,000 short arms and sabers for cavalry, they will be invaluable." From Colonel Josiah Gorgas, chief of Ordnance of the Confederacy, there came back, very promptly and definitely, the answer, "impossible."[9]

The arms actually issued to just one company of Starnes's regiment, as afterward recalled by one of its soldiers, "such as they were," included "Enfield rifles, Belgian muskets, shotguns and what were called 'Mississippi Rifles,' probably because these guns were made in Nashville, Lebanon and various other towns."[10] Dibrell's regiment drew 400 flintlock muskets, which with sabers drawn at the same time were the "only issue of arms ever made to this regiment by the Confederate government."[11]

It appeared then, as afterward, that Forrest's best source of supply was to be the enemy.

Toward the end of October his independent command terminated with the arrival of Major General John C. Breckinridge, who had been unable to get from the far South to Kentucky in time to help Bragg in his campaign, and had been diverted with 3,000 troops into Middle Tennessee.[12] Breckinridge set up headquarters at Murfreesborough, while Forrest took over the advanced post at La Vergne, with pickets and scouts beyond, right up to the hills which ring Nashville.

The main armies on both sides, meanwhile, were making their way back toward Middle Tennessee. Bragg, after the bloody and tactically indecisive battle of Perryville on October eighth, had decided that he could no longer stay in Kentucky, and was making his way through the breaks of the Cumberlands, in eastern Kentucky, heading for East Tennessee. Buell, not undertaking to follow the retreating Confederates through this difficult and ill-supplied country, broke off the direct pursuit and started his army back down the railroad toward Nashville.

While Bragg was yet in East Tennessee, and before Negley had been reinforced, Breckinridge sent Forrest against Nashville in a demonstration in force, backed up by two brigades of infantry. The cavalry moved forward on the night of November fourth, along seven of the macadamized or "metaled" turnpikes which radiated from the city to the east and south. At daylight of the fifth, they began to "drive in the Abolitionists' pickets"[13] on all seven roads, with the main column—the Fourth Alabama cavalry, followed by two brigades of infantry and four batteries—on the Murfreesborough Pike. When the advance reached Dogtown, three and a half miles out, the cavalry dismounted and drove in the pickets on the fortifications, one and a half miles beyond. The first line of fortifications was carried, and Confederate batteries, emplaced on outlying hills, began to bombard the heavy inner fortifications.

At the same time Edgefield, the suburb across the river, was attacked by a force under John H. Morgan, operating north of the Cumberland.[14] "The engagement now became general," Forrest reported. "The firing was kept up until 10 o'clock, when I withdrew my forces."

Forrest's version of the end of the first phase of the day's operations, contained in his report made from La Vergne on the following day, does not support the statement made in his biographies that the withdrawal was directed by Breckinridge, acting under orders from Bragg, still far away in East Tennessee,[15] nor do such orders appear elsewhere in the contemporary records. Whatever the original intention of the demonstration against Nashville, it was not carried out as a serious attack.

Covering the return of the infantry, Forrest moved the Starnes and Dibrell regiments and two batteries westward to the Franklin pike where they met Negley's men in a confused running engagement, back and forth, that can scarcely be recognized in the accounts of the two sides as the same affair. Negley, conceiving that he was dealing with a force which "positively exceeds 25,000, of which at least 5,000 are cavalry," felt that he had done well in not being gobbled up,[16] and a week later, "respectfully suggested extreme caution in operating against Forrest's cavalry."[17] Forrest's men, on the other hand, realizing that they were but a handful going up against a garrison four times their own number, felt that the victory was theirs when the last of Negley's regiment retired within the works surrounding the city.

A week after the demonstration against Nashville, the main Confederate army was back in Middle Tennessee, and General Bragg, with headquarters at Tullahoma, was again in direct command. On November thirteenth, under his orders, his newest and youngest cavalry general, Joseph Wheeler, was put in command of all the cavalry, and Forrest was ordered to report to headquarters for instruction.[18] "Little Joe" Wheeler, the new cavalry chief, was of Connecticut ancestry and Georgia birth, a graduate of West Point, twenty-six years of age, diminutive in size, gravely courteous in manner, immensely industrious, devoted to duty and as brave as any man could be. His command consisted of the three brigades which Bragg referred to as his "regular brigades," and two others, Forrest's and Morgan's, which were considered by Bragg to be suitable for no more than partisan service.[19]

While the Army of Tennessee was coming in from the east the main Union army was massing again in Nashville. It came back under a new commander, Major General William S. Rosecrans, who had been put in Buell's place because of the "slowness" of the latter's movements.[20] The new commander, who had been with Grant in northern Mississippi, was expected to pursue a more vigorous and aggressive policy, but he found right at the beginning some of the same difficulties that had beset Buell. His railroad line from Louisville had been cut behind him by Morgan, who had burned the wooden linings of the twin tunnels above Gallatin. The stage of the Cumberland was too low for his transports to pass the Harpeth Shoals below Nashville. Until he could get his railroad in running order, which took weeks, and until the winter rains raised the river, he could not accumulate at Nashville enough supplies to make him independent of temporary interruptions, and dared not attempt the forward movement upon which the War Department at Washington was so impatiently insisting.

During the same weeks Grant was working away at his problem of supplying an army advancing from West Tennessee through northern Mississippi, with Vicksburg as its objective. Vicksburg had already, in the summer of 1862, beaten off a combined attack by Farragut's Gulf Squadron from below and the river gunboat flotilla from above. The next campaign against Vicksburg, therefore, was not to be purely a naval affair. It was to include an overland advance, following the railroads southward, with an attack upon the hill fortress from the land side.

Grant's supplies were drawn entirely by rail from a base at Columbus, Kentucky, with a line of supply along the Mobile & Ohio railroad through Jackson, Tennessee, to Corinth, Mississippi, and another from Jackson along the Mississippi Central Railroad through Bolivar and Grand Junction. By December the army so supplied had advanced below the university town of Oxford, where Grant had established his own headquarters, with an advance base of supply at Holly Springs.

Lieutenant General John C. Pemberton, just put in command of the inadequate Confederate forces in Mississippi, appealed to Bragg for help. On November twenty-first Bragg wired that he would send "a large cavalry force under Forrest" to create a diversion in his favor by

107

operating in Grant's rear.[21] Such a plan, "if successful," Bragg wrote President Davis, "may force the enemy to retire from Mississippi."[22]

Bragg was justified in entertaining some doubt of the success of the plan. The operation which Forrest was to undertake was difficult in the highest degree—indeed, in ordinary hands, impossible. Merely to get at the enemy, he had to cross, in wintry December, the lower reaches of the Tennessee, one of America's major rivers. The banks of the river in the stretch where the crossing would have to be made were inhabited for the most part by a people of strong Union sympathies. The stream itself was patrolled by gunboats.

Once across and in enemy-held territory, Forrest's movements would have to be over "dirt roads" which were just passable for wheeled vehicles in summer and during the winter rains were considered bottomless and hopeless. At all times his men would be exposed to attack from garrisons and mobile columns stronger than their own force. And finally, and most difficult of all, when they were through with their job they would have to come out the way they went in, recrossing the wide Tennessee in the face of an aroused enemy of overwhelming strength. In comparison with this first independent operation of Forrest's into West Tennessee, most of the famed raids "around the armies," on both sides, or even the longer raids into enemy territory, appear as something in the nature of military picnics.

To General Bragg, Forrest protested that half of the force of 2,100 men with which he was to accomplish his mission were armed with ancient muskets of various designs—some of them, even, 1812 flintlocks and many of those without flints[23]—while many had no arms at all. Appeals to the commanding general, however, could get no others, even though only a month before, on November third, Bragg had written Adjutant General Cooper at Richmond that, "for the first time in the war we have to complain of a want of men to handle our arms. We have now a large surplus."[24]

Protests and objections notwithstanding, Forrest, being then at Columbia, forty-five miles south of Nashville, received on December tenth final orders to go with what he had. The job ahead was to be done with the means at hand—but Forrest was at work to enlarge his means and increase his chances of success.

A "citizen" not otherwise identified was sent on to Memphis, Federal headquarters in West Tennessee, to procure and bring back a supply of the percussion caps without which the more modern of Forrest's weapons could not be fired.[25] Other men he sent ahead on a job less risky but equally necessary—preparing means of crossing the wide and icy Tennessee.

His men and his horses and their equipment he subjected to the rigid inspection which was part of his method. And then, as ready as he could make them with the means at hand, he put the force in motion for the river at Clifton, seventy miles to the west of Columbia.

Arriving there on the fifteenth, they found that the advance party had built two small flatboats, hidden in a slough behind an island near the eastern bank of the river. As the brigade arrived, a chain of pickets was strung out up and down the stream to observe and signal the approach of any inquisitive Yankee gunboat patrol, while the work of crossing went on, in a driving winter rain, all that night, all the following day, and into the next night.

By morning of December seventeenth, with everything across, the precious flatboats were sunk in a creek, and the command marched out some eight miles, away from prying eyes on passing boats. There they built the first fires they had had in two cold days and nights, dried clothing, groomed horses, and once more stood inspection and a check on equipment and ammunition.

At this halt the unnamed "citizen" came in from Memphis with the percussion caps, 50,000 of them—enough to do until some more could be captured.[26] Two of Forrest's worries were past. He was across the river and his men could fire their pieces.

The crossing, however, had been neither unexpected nor unobserved. On the very day Forrest left Columbia, Rosecrans telegraphed from Nashville to Grant at Oxford, "tell the authorities along the railroad to look out for Forrest,"[27] while on the day the command reached Clifton, Brigadier General Jere C. Sullivan, Union Commander at Jackson, Tennessee, dispatched that "Forrest's cavalry, or rebel cavalry, are crossing the Tennessee River at Clifton today."[28]

With "timely notice of Forrest's advance," Grant ordered a concentration of troops at Jackson, the center of West Tennessee and the junction point of railroad lines from three directions, sending men back by rail from Oxford, Bolivar and Corinth, and calling for other troops from the garrisons at Columbus and at Forts Heiman, Henry and Donelson.[29] From the beginning of the expedition, then, Forrest was to face a concentration of troops which should have been overwhelming—but wasn't.

The first force he met was a cavalry column sent out from Jackson toward the Tennessee River on the night of the sixteenth—an Illinois regiment, another of West Tennessee Unionists, a battalion from Ohio and a section of an Indiana battery, all under the command of Colonel Robert G. Ingersoll. From the first light encounter at Beech Creek, five miles east of Lexington, Ingersoll fell back to the edge of the little town, where he took up a position covering two roads with his two guns placed to command the crossing of a creek. Forrest was not so obliging as to come that way but followed his favorite tactics of a demonstration in front while part of his force swung well to the flank. Before Ingersoll realized it, troops of the Fourth Alabama were driving in on his left. Attempting to fall back to a new position, he "found that the enemy were pouring in on all directions." In a few minutes his West Tennessee regiment "came back in confusion and on the full run, pursued by the enemy. It was impossible to stop them."[30]

"Ingersoll made a good fight," one of Forrest's soldiers wrote afterward, ". . . but if he really believed that there is no hell we convinced him that there was something mightily like it."[31] In a few minutes despite the good fight of the battery and the Illinois regiment, the rout was complete, with a loss of about 150 prisoners, including Colonel Ingersoll himself and both guns, fine rifled three-inch steel Rodmans which became the nucleus of Morton's famous battery.[32]

The captured commander, not yet become famous, was just a Yankee colonel to young Frank Gurley, the Alabama captain who led the flanking force which captured him. With a somewhat airy persiflage, perhaps to cover up chagrin at his discomfiture in his first battle, the Colonel asked Gurley, "Is this the army of your Southern Confederacy for which I have so diligently sought? Then I am your guest until the wheels of the great Cartel are put in motion."

Asked if the prisoners were all his men, the Colonel answered, "These are the Illinoisians. The Tennesseans have ingloriously fled." Asked where he was from, he continued on his note of grandiose persiflage, that he was "from everywhere but here, and I hope to be from here just as soon as I can obtain your genial approbation to that effect."[33]

The "genial approbation" came three days later, when the Colonel, having lost all his money in a friendly and social game of four-card draw with nothing wild with his captors, and having been staked by them so that he might keep on playing, was paroled and released along with his men and many other prisoners captured by that time.[34]

The remnants of Ingersoll's command were pursued twenty miles to within four miles of Jackson. There Forrest kept up the game of bluff which he had started as soon as he crossed the Tennessee River. Ingersoll's men went into the town with stories of "overpowering numbers." Ingersoll himself believed, even after his capture, that Forrest was "at least 5,000 strong, with eight pieces of artillery."[35]

Other Federal commanders set the figure as high as 10,000[36] and the numbers grew even greater as Forrest used every manner of artifice to foster the illusion. Troops were ostentatiously marched in sight and sound of the enemy, with kettledrums beating at widely separated points

110

to give the impression of marching infantry. Friendly inhabitants, many of whom "rushed to their front gates with whatever of good things to eat they happened to have," as Forrest's men marched past, were regaled with stories of the number of men in the command.

"How many soldiers have you got?" one woman asked Private Tom Jones of the Fourth Tennessee.

"Madam, I would tell you if I could. Do you know how many trees there are standing in West Tennessee? Well, we've got enough men to put one behind each tree, and two or three behind the biggest ones."[37]

Federal commanders weren't taken in by such palpable exaggerations, of course, but by the time Forrest reached the neighborhood of Jackson, they had come to accept the idea that he was accompanied, or at least closely followed, by as much as an infantry division, usually described as Cheatham's.[38]

It all had its effect. Though by the evening of the eighteenth he had in Jackson not less than four times as many soldiers as Forrest had in West Tennessee, Brigadier General Jere Sullivan, the Union commander at Jackson, was convinced that he was threatened by overwhelming numbers. One brigade which left Corinth that morning with "pleasing prospects" of a Christmas furlough at home in Iowa, and which had been plucked from the train as it passed through Jackson that afternoon, was set to defend the depot "to the last extremity and if overpowered . . . to retire to the courthouse."[39]

On the same evening other troops, brought up on the trains from Bolivar by Brigadier General Mason Brayman, were sent out to meet the fleeing remnants of Ingersoll's column, which they did some three and one-half miles out. There they spent a cheerless and fireless night, enviously watching the campfires of the Confederates[40]—though they did not know that one purpose of these fires was to cover up the fact that a good half of Forrest's force already had marched away to circle around Jackson and cut the railroads leading north, southeast and southwest.

At daybreak of the nineteenth, Forrest, with Starnes's and Biffle's regiment, two companies under Woodward and a portion of Freeman's guns, advanced against the Federal force posted on a ridge near old Salem Cemetery.[41] He had not the slightest intention of developing more than a demonstration to keep the Union forces in Jackson busy while the real work of the day was being done elsewhere, but even so it resulted in successive retirements of the enemy to positions behind the creek running between the cemetery and the town. The cavalry which had fought the day before at Lexington, indeed, "fell back about 1 mile toward Jackson without having first obtained any orders from me to that effect," as the commander of the force delicately put it.[42]

111

At the same time that Forrest was demonstrating east of Jackson, Dibrell's regiment struck the railroad eight miles to the north, at Webb's Station, captured the stockade and its garrison of about 100, tore up the track and switches and cut the telegraph wires.[43] A few minutes after General Sullivan received word of this attack, news came from the Corinth railroad that "the bridges 12 miles south were burned, and that a large force had crossed going toward the railroad leading to Bolivar." This force consisted of Russell's regiment and Cox's Second Tennessee Battalion, which, after a night march, put in the day on their appointed task of breaking the rail lines leading to Grant's army.[44] The break in the Bolivar line was not accomplished, however, until after Fuller's Union brigade, sent back from Oxford, Mississippi, had passed up on its way to Jackson.[45]

Upon the arrival of Fuller's force in midafternoon of the nineteenth, Sullivan sent six regiments under General Brayman against Forrest's two cavalry regiments, east of the town. Forrest, leaving a mere screen to keep up a show of fight, started north on his real business. On the next morning, the twentieth, Sullivan left a garrison of 2,000 in Jackson and with the rest of his force pushed eastward in search of Forrest—who wasn't there.[46]

That day—December 20, 1862—was one of double calamity for the Union forces. To the south, at Holly Springs, Earl Van Dorn's cavalry division burst in upon Grant's advanced supply depot, destroying in a day the stores which had been accumulated for the overland advance to Vicksburg. And on the same day, while Sullivan was pursuing a phantom force, Forrest started the destruction of the railroad north of Jackson, the effect of which, as Grant wrote Sherman, was to "cut me off from supplies, so that further advance by this route is perfectly impracticable."[47]

It was a common complaint of commanders on both sides of the war that cavalry could not be relied upon to get down and do the hard work necessary to wreck a railroad thoroughly. Sherman's cavalry, sent in 1864 to destroy the railroad from Atlanta to Macon, had hardly finished reporting its destruction when the whistle of Confederate engines running over it was heard. No such complaint could lie against Forrest's men or his methods of railroad destruction in West Tennessee, especially north of Trenton. When they finished their job it took new bridges, new rail and a deal of time to make that railroad serviceable once more.[48]

The first destruction attempted on the twentieth, however, failed when Dibrell's regiment could not get at the bridge over the Forked Deer River, between Jackson and Humboldt, before its stockaded garrison was

112

reinforced by a trainload of troops coming out from Jackson.[49] While Dibrell was banging away at the bridge, however, Starnes went on ahead to capture Humboldt, where the Memphis & Ohio railroad crossed the Mobile & Ohio. While Starnes was busy destroying track, trestles and depot there, with a fine accompanying display of daylight fireworks from the explosion of ammunition stored in some of the burning buildings, Biffle and Cox came up from below Jackson, where they had completed their mission of the nineteenth, and passed beyond Humboldt to Trenton.[50]

The Trenton garrison, largest between Jackson and Columbus, was posted in the railroad station, which was barricaded with cotton bales and hogsheads of tobacco, and in a stockade "secure against any force . . . unless accompanied by artillery." But Forrest had artillery, which put sixteen shell into the defenders' position in rapid succession. Seeing that he was surrounded and "completely in their power," Colonel Fry surrendered unconditionally,[51] bringing that day's bag of prisoners up to 700.

On that night, Saturday the twentieth, and for part of the next day, while Sullivan was making his way back to Jackson from the fruitless chase to Lexington, Forrest held his command together at Trenton, busily arming and outfitting them with captured arms and stores. One item in the capture, for which no official use appeared, was a quantity of counterfeit Confederate money, of no value as a circulating medium because it was so much better engraved and printed and on so much better paper than the genuine article that it could be detected on sight. But, as Private Dan Beard wrote, it was "just as good to play poker with as gold," and so the Confederates added it to the stock of military necessities and sutlers' luxuries with which they left Trenton Sunday evening.[52]

For himself Forrest took from the Trenton captures a saber of the United States Dragoon pattern, which, after he had had its regulation dull edge sharpened to razor keenness, he used throughout the rest of the war. Although he was naturally left-handed, he was ambidextrous by training, wore his sword in the usual position on the left side, and drew it with his right hand—although occasionally in combat he might shift it to the left.[53]

While the Confederates were refitting at Trenton, Forrest paroled the 1,200 prisoners already taken. In the very manner of doing so, he insured that they would help to magnify the force of their captors. As the paroles were being made out and signed, courier after courier would be sent forth from the presence of the prisoners bearing orders to this or that general to come up with their commands.

As night settled over Trenton, campfires were built here and there, while after dark detachment after detachment was passed between these fires and the guarded prisoners, with such marchings and commands as created the impression that they were, indeed, fresh forces arriving.[54] On Sunday morning the body of prisoners was started north, under flag of truce, to report to the Federal commander at Columbus, whence it was expected that they would be furnished transportation home.

Having completed the destruction of stores at Trenton, Forrest started northward along the railroad, with his whole command united again, and all of them busy. At Rutherford Station, twelve miles north, two companies were captured. Five miles beyond, at Kenton, some 250 men were taken, while all during the day the work of tearing up track went steadily on. Monday, the twenty-second, and the forenoon of Tuesday were spent in doing the major railroad damage of the expedition where for fifteen miles the line ran through the wide and swampy bottoms of the Obion River, with numerous short bridges and long trestles. At first, the working parties used axes pressed from the citizens. Finding the "trestles as hard as horn and the axes as dull as froes," half the men were put to work splitting dry kindling and the other half to building brisk fires on top the trestle and around each bend, with highly satisfactory results, despite the melting of the sleet and ice which encased the structures.[55]

While part of the force worked, the rest marched on to Union City, the junction of the Mobile & Ohio with railroads northeast to Paducah and southwest to McKenzie, Tennessee. There another garrison of 100 men was gobbled up on the afternoon of the twenty-third, and there Forrest stayed through Christmas Eve, while the working parties finished destroying the bridges across the north and south forks of the Obion and the four miles of trestle work between them. Other parties were at work on the railroads from Union City northward toward Columbus and Paducah, and eastward toward Dresden.

From Middleburg, near Union City, Forrest got off a preliminary report to Bragg on the twenty-sixth, asking to be excused from making out a report of strength because "we have been so busy and kept so constantly moving that we have not had time." Actually, Forrest's strength was growing, despite the inevitable losses from the breaking down of men and horses in so strenuous a campaign. His battle losses had been negligible—fewer than twenty-five men, he reported—while at Union City, Colonel T. A. Napier had joined with his battalion of some 400 men.[56]

While Forrest was at and about Union City, General Sullivan at Jackson was organizing an expedition to follow him, and at the same time trying to get General Davies, commanding the heavy garrison of more than 5,000 men at the great fortified base at Columbus, to move against him from above.[57] The latter, however, had been told by Halleck to take no chances on giving up Columbus, and was taking his instructions so seriously[58] that Forrest's working parties destroyed the railroad bridge at Moscow, Kentucky, only ten miles from his position, without interference. Indeed, Davies loaded much of the stores at Columbus on steamboats, and had heavy guns at Island No. 10 and New Madrid dismantled and spiked, and powder thrown in the river—all to keep it from falling into the hands of Forrest. In obvious relief he reported that "by the movement of trains and circulating reports," he had "kept Forrest for several days under the impression that I was going to give him battle outside."[59]

On Christmas Day Forrest started southeast along the Northwestern Railroad toward the Tennessee River. Davies, even though reinforcements from up the river had brought his force at Columbus up to 7,000 men, continued too apprehensive of some design on the part of Forrest to take the chance of leaving his fortified position. It was felt at Columbus, as shown by a letter from one of the subordinate commanders, Brigadier General Clinton B. Fisk, written on December twenty-seventh, that "Cairo, Paducah, Columbus and vicinity" were in danger of becoming "a prey to the marauding chieftains, Forrest and Cheatham," who had a "force of about 15,000 very near us."[60]

As Forrest started from Union City toward the river, Sullivan started from Jackson with a division to intercept him, despite a gloomy misgiving of a "design of the rebels to weaken this post by making me send off my men, and then, marching rapidly to the rear, capture and destroy the stores." But, since Grant was determined that he must go, he added that "what can be done shall be done."[61]

Drenching December rains began on the day after Christmas. By the morning of the twenty-eighth, when Forrest turned south from McKenzie's Station, the wide and swampy bottoms of the sluggish South Fork of the Obion were everywhere overflowed—and there were no bridges along the way which he must go save one rickety and decayed structure, reached by a long, narrow causeway on either end. Sullivan was entirely justified in telegraphing Grant, as he did on December twenty-ninth. "I have Forrest in a tight place. . . . The gunboats are up the river as far as Clifton and have destroyed all bridges and ferries. . . . My troops are moving on him from three directions, and I hope with success."[62]

On that morning Forrest emerged from the Obion bottoms at McLemoresville after an all-night passage over the all but abandoned causeway, in which he "made a hand" in bracing up the rickety bridges with forked timbers cut in the woods and, finally, himself guided the first

115

team across the treacherous surface. The General made it across but the next two teams slipped off the narrow track into the icy swamp. Man-handling was resorted to to get the vehicles across—twenty men to a wagon, fifty to a gun. The deeper mudholes were filled with logs and chunks and even, in some cases, sacks of flour or coffee, in lieu of sand-bags.[63]

On the same morning on which Sullivan sent his optimistic dispatch General Fisk at Columbus, not knowing within forty miles where Forrest was, sent an even more definite and optimistic message that "the brigand Forrest's . . . bands are now scattering. . . . I have been begging General Davies to let me take 4,000 men and go out there and whip him but the General will not allow it, is quite nervous about the post, but I am fully convinced we could defeat or skedaddle the entire rebel horde. I know I am a young general but I believe I am old enough to see through a mill-stone with so large a hole in it."[64] Even the "young generals" began to think that they had Forrest in a corner.

And indeed he was in a desperate position. He had nothing much to fear from the 7,000 men at Columbus, but all over West Tennessee columns were moving to cut him off. Between him and the Tennessee River that morning were Sullivan's two brigades, either one virtually equal to his own in strength. Farther east, and closer to the river, was a mixed force under Colonel Lowe, based on Fort Henry. Coming up from Corinth was the force of General Grenville M. Dodge, much closer to the crossing at Clifton than was Forrest. Coming out of Jackson was still another brigade, under Colonel Lawler, likewise closer to the critical point of crossing. The river was rising and the gunboats were up as far as Clifton.

As Forrest emerged from the Obion bottoms he had to wait to let the rear of Sullivan's Third Brigade, under Colonel John W. Fuller, pass on its way to Huntingdon. Sullivan's Second Brigade, under Colonel Cyrus L. Dunham, which was already at Huntingdon, was ordered out on the afternoon of the twenty-ninth to intercept Forrest, correctly reported to be moving from McLemoresville toward Lexington. The roads on which the two commands were marching converged at Parker's Cross Roads, also known as Red Mound. There, on the morning of the last day of the year, Forrest's advance found Dunham drawn up and waiting for him, and there, from nine o'clock in the morning to three in the afternoon, was fought a pitched battle as curiously mixed in its course and its results as any fight well could be.

There are three distinct stories of the battle of Parker's Cross Roads. There is the battle according to Dunham and his subordinates, the battle according to Fuller and his, the battle according to the Confederates.

116

The Dunham account[65] represents that with 1,554 men and three guns (although one of his subordinate commanders, Colonel Rinaker, says 1,800) he started "to try to coax or force a fight out of" Forrest, who had, he thought, 8,000 men with twelve pieces of artillery. Forrest accommodated him with a slow-moving and confused engagement in which Dunham retired from the west to the east of the Huntingdon-Lexington road. In his final position, suffering severely from Confederate artillery fire, he was suddenly attacked front, flank and rear, while Confederates cut in between his battle position and his trains and train guard. "This was the crisis of the day, and nobly did our gallant men meet it," he reported. "The main line was faced at once to the rear and drove the enemy back. . . . The repulse was complete. . . . This substantially closed the fighting for the day. . . ."

Colonel Dunham reports that he indignantly rejected a demand from Forrest for surrender, while Colonel Rinaker adds that "Forrest was unable to rally his men again, and was in full retreat when the Second Brigade came in sight, the appearance of which greatly added to the celerity of the rebels' flight and afforded our gallant Ohio friends no opportunity to participate in the rout of a force we could have destroyed had the Second Brigade arrived in time, which they would have done but for the genius for tardiness exhibited by General Sullivan."

The Second Brigade (Fuller's) tells quite a different story.[66] They marched from Huntingdon, according to their report, at 5:00 A.M. At Clarksburg, ten miles south, where Dunham had bivouacked the night before, they heard firing from the direction of Parker's Cross Roads. The sound came first from the right, or to the west of the road; then, in about a half-hour, directly in front; later, after another half-hour, to the left, or east of the road. Finally, during the last half-hour of the march—much of which was made at the double-quick—there was no more firing. The fight, apparently, had moved eastward, and then ceased.

When Fuller was two miles short of Parker's house an orderly galloped up from Sullivan with orders to wait for the rear guard, three miles behind, but Fuller, acting on reports from his scouts, drove ahead without waiting and burst upon Forrest's rear in a complete surprise attack.

Firing from Dunham's forces had ceased, "nor did the command of Colonel Dunham fire a shot at the enemy as he moved past their flank to their rear," Fuller reported. Colonel Zephaniah Spaulding, of Fuller's brigade, goes further to say that "firing had ceased on both sides, and flags of truce were passing between the parties engaged. The enemy had surrounded Dunham's brigade on three sides, so that we now came upon them [the enemy] in their rear." Colonel Edward F. Noyes is still more definite as to the situation when the Second Brigade arrived. "A part, if

117

not all, of Dunham's artillery, together with several hundred prisoners, had fallen into the hands of the enemy. The moment was a critical one and the day seemed inevitably lost . . . the three regiments composing the Ohio brigade came upon the enemy together, just in time to prevent disaster and to secure a brilliant victory."

Forrest was indeed surprised in battle, for the first and only time, though not for lack of precaution.[67] When he started his march along the road from McLemoresville to Parker's Cross Roads, he sent four companies across country to Clarksburg, to observe and report the approach of Union troops from Huntingdon. With the rest of his column, except Biffle's regiment which was coming in from a side operation in the direction of Trenton, he marched on toward Lexington. Meeting Dunham near the Cross Roads, he settled down to a leisurely, casualty-saving artillery attack, not knowing that his scouting companies had misunderstood and failed in their missions, and relying on them to give him timely notice of the approach of the rest of Sullivan's command. Had he known of Fuller's near approach, he said, he "could have terminated the fight by making it short and decisive, when without such advice I was whipping them badly with my artillery and unless absolutely necessary was not pressing them with my cavalry." The artillerymen, who carried the brunt of the fight, were all given high praise by the general, with special mention of Captain Freeman and Lieutenant Morton, commanding batteries, and of Sergeant Nat Baxter of Freeman's Battery.[68] Casualties among the Union soldiers who had taken shelter behind a snake fence of rails were especially heavy, when accurate shelling converted its rails into missiles.

After midday, with artillery placed to enfilade both flanks of Dunham's line, Forrest sent Russell's regiment around to the right to charge the Union rear, and Starnes to strike on the other flank. As a result, the Confederates soon captured Dunham's three guns, his wagon trains, about 300 of his. men, and, as white flags began to break out along the line, demanded unconditional surrender. And then it was, between fifteen and thirty minutes after firing had ceased, that Fuller's brigade struck, with complete surprise, upon Forrest's rear.

Forrest became, even while living, almost a legendary figure among the soldiers of the western armies. One of the legends originated at this double action of Parker's Cross Roads, where he was squarely caught between two lines of battle, either equal or superior to his own in fire power.

"General," asked a staff officer, "what shall we do? What shall we do?"

"Charge them both ways," was the instant reply, according to the story.

118

The story is apocryphal but as a matter of fact that was almost what was done. When Russell and Starnes, who were behind Dunham or on his flank, heard the lull in battle broken by an outburst of rifle and artillery firing *behind* the rest of the Confederate force, those alert commanders divined the situation instantly and ordered a charge at Dunham's rear which acted to keep him out of the action in his front. Quick action by the other half of the Forrest brigade, and especially the gallant conduct of the Dibrell regiment which joined the General's escort in a charge to cover the withdrawal of the rest of the command, checked Fuller's advance long enough for most of Forrest's men to draw off from between the two lines of battle.

Six of the nine pieces with which the Confederates entered the battle were carried off, but the other guns and the three which had been taken from Dunham had to be abandoned for lack of teams to pull them. Three hundred dismounted men were captured when their horses, picketed in the peach orchard at Parker's house, were stampeded by the outburst of fire from the rear. There was "much confusion, as our horse-holders were demoralized and many men were captured trying to get their horses," Dibrell reported, but the savage counterattacks from the improvised rear guard mustered under the General's personal leadership checked any serious attempt at pursuit.

In fact, General Sullivan hardly felt that there was any hurry about the pursuit, as at six o'clock on the evening of the last day of the year 1862, he dispatched Grant: "We have achieved a glorious victory. We met Forrest, 7,000 strong. After a contest of four hours, completely routed him with great slaughter."

Three days later, so serenely confident was he that he reported from Jackson: "Forrest's army completely broken up. They are scattered over the country without ammunition. We need a good cavalry regiment to go through the country and pick them up."

To which, on the same day, Grant replied: "You have done a fine job—retrieved all lost at Trenton and north of you. I sent a fine regiment of cavalry to you. They left here on the 31st. . . . Dodge is now out after Forrest's band."[69]

But even before these gratulatory messages passed over the wires, Forrest was back over the Tennessee River, by the way in which he had come.

From Parker's Cross Roads, Forrest marched away with Union prisoners about equal in number to the 300 of his own men lost by capture, the latter including Major John P. Strange, his adjutant, who single-handed had captured Dunham's ammunition train of eighteen wagons and was busily inventorying it when Fuller's men burst upon him.[70]

119

Lexington, twelve miles south of the battlefield, was reached the same night. After a halt for feeding men and animals, and attention to the wounded who had been brought off, the column marched out toward Clifton. On the morning of New Year's Day 1863, they met head-on Colonel William K. M. Breckinridge's Union cavalry regiment, sent up from below by Dodge, and brushed it aside in a sharp little fight.[71] From behind, Forrest was followed—though not closely—by part of Sullivan's brigade and by a fresh force, 3,000 strong, sent out from Jackson under Colonel Lawler.[72]

That day Forrest reached the river at noon, marching over roads which his pursuers, who did not reach the river until two days later, described as "horrible."[73] The flatboats which had been hidden by sinking them were raised and put to work ferrying the men, the wagons and the guns. Boats were poled upstream half a mile or so, and then shoved out into the current, to be swept downstream as they were being worked across. Returning, the process was reversed. Horses, this time, were made to swim. And so, for twelve busy hours, they worked their way across. By midnight, everything was over.

Fifteen days earlier they had gone into West Tennessee half-armed, ill-equipped, new and green in their organization. They came out, armed and equipped with the best the Federal stock afforded, and with surplus equipment, a keen, veteran organization. They had killed or captured more men than they had;[74] had taken or disabled ten guns; had carried off or destroyed stores and ammunition valued in the millions of dollars; had kept more than ten times their own number frantically busy for a fortnight and, by destroying Grant's line of supply, had helped to compel the abandonment of his promising campaign against Vicksburg, saving that fortress to the Confederacy for yet another six months.

Battle losses, even including the prisoners lost at Parker's Cross Roads, had been fewer than the recruits gained. What the campaign had cost in effort and physical weariness, however, cannot be calculated. It had been march, march, fight, bluff, watch, work, work all the way and every day, with little rest and less sleep for men or for animals. When Forrest's men crossed back over the river at Clifton, they must have been weary with a vast weariness, though it is not to be noted in reports and accounts of their two weeks' midwinter campaign. The Union soldiers who gained the supposed victory at the Cross Roads, however, "reached Corinth ragged, shoeless, dispirited and worn-out,"[75] after giving up the profitless pursuit on the west bank of the Tennessee two days after Forrest's men had crossed over to safety, to the plaudits of the people, the official congratulations of the Confederate Congress and even the praise of General Bragg.

"The expedition under Forrest has fully accomplished its object," Bragg wrote Samuel Cooper at Richmond.[76] And again, in his official report of the Battle of Murfreesborough, he wrote "the complete success which attended [Forrest's expedition in West Tennessee] commends him to the confidence of the Government and the gratitude of the country."[77]

CHAPTER IX

MIDDLE TENNESSEE: THRUST AND PARRY
January 3, 1863-April 10, 1863

FORREST returned from West Tennessee to find the Army of Tennessee in the new position to which it had retreated after the great battle of Stones River or Murfreesborough, fought on the last day of December and the first two days of the new year.[1] The close of the fighting on January second left both commanders, Rosecrans and Bragg, not quite certain who had won and who had lost. Another day they stood facing each other until, on the night of the twenty-third, Bragg settled the question by dropping back some thirty miles to take up a new line along the Duck River. Army headquarters were established at Tullahoma, with the two infantry corps posted about Wartrace and Shelbyville in Bedford County, and the cavalry wings curving away right and left on a total front of about eighty miles.

Marching in from the west, Forrest's force became the left horn of the long crescent of the Confederate line. To General Johnston, commanding west of the Appalachians, who was apparently giving further consideration to the idea of sending Forrest to Mississippi, Bragg wrote on January seventh, "I implore you not to remove Forrest and Roddey from my left, or the enemy will compel me to fall back." Forrest, Bragg reported, had done his work in West Tennessee "most successfully," having "fitted out his whole command, which was poorly equipped, in splendid style."[2]

Forrest's new post was at Columbia on the Duck River less than twenty-five miles west of his birthplace at Chapel Hill. This land of his birth and his boyhood to which he now returned for a season is a saucer of irregular shape hollowed out of the general level of the highlands of Middle Tennessee by the action of the Cumberland, the Duck and their tributaries. It is a rolling land, with rich valleys of limestone soil on which the bluegrass grows by the beneficence of nature, alternating with wooded ridges and knobs. The general elevation ranges from about 500 feet above sea level, in the valleys, to as much as 1,000 or even 1,200 feet on the tops of the hills. It was, in the sixties, a land of long-established and solid agricultural prosperity—not a cotton country but a country of corn and wheat and grass and the livestock which go with them. It was dotted with substantial farmsteads and, even then, threaded with turnpikes of macadam, lined in large degree by characteristic stone walls laid without mortar by the patient skill of a breed of builders now extinct. To the region geologists give the general name of the Nashville Basin. To the poet John Trotwood Moore, it was the "Dimple of the Universe."

Through the greater part of January Forrest remained at Columbia, recuperating, reconditioning and re-equipping his command after its extraordinary exertions of the previous weeks. His growing reputation, however, was causing his presence to be rumored, or even positively reported, simultaneously from points as far separated as northern Kentucky and central Mississippi. When the indefatigable Wheeler, Bragg's chief of cavalry, captured four transports and the lightly armored gunboat *Sidell* at the Harpeth Shoals of the Cumberland River on January thirteenth, Quartermaster General Meigs, feeling quite sure that Forrest was at the bottom of this break in Rosecrans' river communications, warned him that he must have gunboats to convoy his transports through safely against such forces as Forrest led.[3] "Are there any horses left in the country for Forrest to seize?" he concluded.

"There are some horses in the country for Forrest to steal," Rosecrans replied, "but if we can get a start, we mean to steal them ourselves. Our men have commenced to practice unofficially in this way. Unfortunately the quartermaster's department has been the chief sufferer so far."

At the very last of January, spurred on perhaps by the success of Wheeler's attack of the thirteenth on the boats at the Harpeth Shoals, it was decided to interrupt once more the navigation of the Cumberland by Rosecrans' supply steamers.

Just whose was the idea and whose the planning is not entirely clear. Wheeler, in his official report to General Bragg, says that "in obedience to instructions, I ordered General Wharton's and a portion of General Forrest's brigades to proceed, with a full complement of ammunition, to the most favorable position on the Cumberland River, to interrupt the navigation as far as practicable." He was not with the command when it started, apparently, but "overtook it after it had passed Franklin."[4] Neither Wharton nor Forrest made a report of the affair but in Jordan and Pryor's *Campaigns*, which Forrest saw and approved in the manuscript, it is stated that he was summoned to army headquarters on January twenty-sixth, and there told by General Bragg that a portion of his brigade was included in an expedition which already had started under Wheeler's command, and which Forrest should overtake and join. This he did, after two days' hard riding, in the vicinity of Palmyra, a

123

village on the Cumberland, some twenty miles upstream from Fort Donelson.

There he had an inspection of the 800 men of his brigade who had been brought along on the expedition—the sort of inspection, extending from the shoes of the horses to the ammunition of the artillery, which was part of the Forrest method. To his dismay, he found that his men had been ordered out with no more than twenty rounds of ammunition apiece. A similar inspection of Wharton's men, made at the same time, showed a like state of supply. The artillery was little better off, having less than fifty rounds per gun.[5]

General Wheeler, meanwhile, according to his official report, had learned that the enemy, "being apprised of our presence on the river, had determined not to send any more boats either up or down the river while we remained in position to interrupt their passage." So long as the Confederates held their position, that is, they were accomplishing a major part of the object of the raid—interrupting navigation.

"After maturely considering the matter," however, General Wheeler decided to attack the garrison and fortifications at Dover-Fort Donelson[6]—for no sound reason which now appears. The reward, if the post were captured, promised to be no more than a handful of prisoners and the temporary tenancy of the small new post adjacent to what John Morton called "memory-haunted" Fort Donelson. No one had any idea that the small Confederate force could maintain itself a hundred miles within the enemy's line for more than a few hours, or a day or two at most. And even during that period, they would be in no better position to blockade the river at Dover than they already were at Palmyra.

The expedition was not Forrest's sort of operation. The decision to attack the fortified post at Dover was even less so. The risks and difficulties were too great to justify possible results, and Forrest fought for results, being as diligent in dodging fights which did not promise commensurate rewards as he was eager in seeking those which did.

To Captain Anderson and Dr. Ben Wood of his staff, Forrest confided his objections and his misgivings as the command started for Dover, saying that he had protested against the move, that his protest had been disregarded, that he had spoken to no one else about it and would not do so, that he intended to do his duty, but that if he were killed he wanted the fact of his protest made known.[7]

At Cumberland Iron Works, nine miles from Dover, there was a brush with a Union scouting company from which men escaped to carry warning to the fort. Colonel A. C. Harding, commanding the post, recalled the steamer *Wild Cat*, which he had just started up the river to Palmyra, carrying two field guns and a company of infantry protected by baled hay. Before noon he had his whole command in readiness to receive the expected assault.[8]

Arriving in the vicinity of the post in the early afternoon, Wheeler ordered a simultaneous attack from two sides, Forrest from the southeast, Wharton from the west. One regiment of Wharton's brigade was sent out toward Fort Henry to guard against an attack from the rear by the garrison of that post.

Under flag of truce, a note was sent in, signed by Wheeler as "chief commander" and by the two brigadiers, each described as "commanding cavalry division," demanding an immediate and unconditional surrender—to which Colonel Harding returned an immediate and unconditional refusal.[9]

As Wheeler left him on the east side of the town, to ride around to Wharton's side, Forrest saw a movement in the fortifications which caused him to believe that the garrison were trying to escape to the river-bank. Quickly remounting his men, he charged down the slopes from the ridge on which he was deploying, across a hollow—the same one through which just a year before he had led his first regiment out of Dover to freedom and himself to fame—and up the opposite slope toward the line of fortifications.[10]

The Illinois troops, however, were not abandoning the works, and were ready to receive with concentrated rifle and artillery fire the few hundred men with whom Forrest tried desperately to drive on into their lines with the defenders who were shifting position. In the forefront of the charge Forrest's horse was killed.

Repulsed, Forrest drew back, dismounted, told off every fourth man to hold the horses, and with the others returned to the charge, this time with his men on foot. Again Forrest had a horse killed under him. This second attack was partially successful and gained a foothold in the houses on the east side of the village. Once more, however, Forrest and his men mistook a movement of the enemy, this time taking it to be a threat against their held horses. To protect them, they abandoned the foothold they had won and rushed back across the hollow to where the horse-holders were.

With virtually no more ammunition, Forrest's men were to all intents and purposes out of the fight before Wharton had well begun his attack from the west of the town. Wharton took some houses on that side, and held his position until nightfall, by which time he too was all but out of ammunition. During the afternoon he did capture and succeed in bringing off one brass 12-pounder, while after dark, a boat loaded with provisions lying at the landing was successfully fired and burned.[11]

What small success there was in the bungled affair of the day was

125

Wharton's but by the time active firing ceased, shortly after dark, it was apparent that the Confederates could not long remain where they were, without ammunition and with very limited supplies of food or forage. At eight o'clock they began marching away, leaving details behind to search the fields of battle for wounded.

That night, with the Union commanders at the two river forts sending off justly jubilant dispatches, the Confederates moved away to Yellow Creek Furnace, three miles from the river, where they bivouacked while the gunboats, which had come up after the fighting, noisily shelled the woods. The three generals, according to subsequent accounts, were together in the same room of a farmhouse, Wheeler sitting beside the fire dictating his report, Wharton sitting opposite him, and Forrest, who had been severely bruised and shaken when the second horse of the day was shot under him, stretched on the floor, feet on the hearth, head propped up on a turned-down split chair. He was sore in mind as well as body—angry over the result of the day's work, sick over the loss of about one-fourth of the men he had carried into the two charges.

As Wheeler dictated his report of this phase of the affair, Forrest heaved himself up from his chair to declare in tempestuous tones that his men had done their duty, that he had remonstrated against the attack to no avail, that nothing which could be said now would bring back the dead or the wounded then freezing on the slopes above Dover, and that, as for himself, never again would he fight under Wheeler's command.[12]

The young West Pointer kept his temper and, to his everlasting credit and the great advantage of the Confederacy, did not accept Forrest's offer to resign rather than serve under him. With dignity and good judgment he arranged things so that thereafter, so long as both served with the Army of Tennessee, Forrest should not be called upon to fight under his immediate command. Within less than six months, indeed, he was to prove his friendship by risking his command and his life to keep open a bridge over which Forrest's column was expected to retreat.

On the morning of February fourth, the shaken Confederates started away from the ill-fated area about Fort Donelson, to molest it no more. The Fort Henry garrison came over to join in the pursuit, while the column of the Union Brigadier General Jeff C. Davis marched westward from Franklin to intercept the retreat. Swinging to the west, the Confederate column crossed the Duck River at Centerville, whence they marched to Columbia. General Davis cut off and captured only about thirty men, who were scouting and foraging along the eastward flank of the march. Among them, however, was Captain Rambaut, Forrest's chief commissary, and Colonel Charles Carroll, an acting aide.[13]

Back in Columbia, Forrest went to work on the more complete organization and conditioning of his command, against the time when he should be called into the field again. Dress parade was ordered twice a week, drill went on daily, supply arrangements were tightened up, further efforts were made to supply deficiencies in arms. All in all, as Forrest reported to Wheeler on February eighteenth, he was getting his men "in very good condition."[14]

Actually, however, Forrest was having internal difficulties in his new organization. Russell's Fourth Alabama was transferred at this time from the Old Brigade to one of Wheeler's Alabama brigades, being replaced by the assignment of Holman's and Douglas' battalions of Partisan Rangers, both of which had been raised in Middle Tennessee. These battalions, together with two detached companies, were combined to form the Eleventh Tennessee Cavalry. Major D. C. Douglas being a prisoner of war in Federal hands at the time, and Major D. W. Holman having just been seriously, and, it was reported, mortally wounded in the affair at Dover, the command of the new regiment was given to Captain James H. Edmondson, of one of the detached companies, the Bluff City Grays of Memphis. Something on the order of a near mutiny followed, with both battalions of partisan rangers protesting that the consolidation was "against the wishes of every man" composing them. As a result, many of the officers were ordered by Forrest into arrest and close confinement at Columbia. The officers in arrest were soon released, upon appeal to General Van Dorn when he took command shortly afterward, while Major Holman took command of the regiment later in the year, when he reported for duty after recovering from his Dover wound. In the meanwhile, however, the Eleventh Regiment had gone on to do excellent work for Forrest under Edmondson's command.[15]

From General Bragg's headquarters at this time there issued general orders calling on cavalry commanders to use vigorous means to search out "the great numbers of men who have joined cavalry commands, and avail themselves of that peculiar service to roam over the country as marauders, avoiding all duty," and to transfer them to "infantry regiments, where they can be more easily watched and compelled to perform their duties."[16]

It was a situation which was to plague the Confederate commanders, particularly in the light of the requirement that cavalrymen were expected to provide their own mounts. Forrest, however, seems to have suffered less from chronic absenteeism and disability of men and horses than most of the mounted commanders. According to those field returns of that period in which the figures for the several cavalry commands can be compared, his brigade mustered 78 percent of its enrolled strength as present, and 90 percent of those present as effective, making 70 percent effectives out of the whole command. For the remainder of the cavalry of the army, the effective present strength was but 58 percent of the aggregate. Forrest, apparently, was not only good at marching and fighting but also at administration.[17]

While he was reconditioning his command, he was at the same time vigilantly scouting toward Franklin, the strongly held right flank of the Union line, where, he reported, the Federals had about 6,000 men. They had repaired the railroad and the telegraph south from Nashville, also, and were repairing the railroad bridge over the Harpeth, indicating preparations for an advance south of that stream. To General Wheeler, Forrest suggested the possibility of a combined operation, to cut in on the advancing Union force from three directions, in hope of capturing or cutting them to pieces.

Despite the stormy scene at Yellow Creek Furnace, personal relations between Forrest and Wheeler continued good. In Forrest's dispatch of February eighteenth, there is a note of thanks for a helmet which Wheeler had sent him, while on the next day he appealed to Wheeler for help in getting the arms he so badly needed for his command.[18]

Forrest was expecting the arrival of a new commanding officer, Major General Earl Van Dorn, whose transfer from Pemberton's army in Mississippi to Bragg's in Tennessee had been ordered in January by the supreme Confederate commander in the west, General Joseph E. Johnston. Van Dorn was looked upon by many as the ablest, as he was certainly the most experienced, of the Confederate cavalry commanders in the West. A graduate of West Point, he had served with distinction in the War with Mexico, had had wide experience in warfare on the plains, including service in Robert E. Lee's famous regiment of dragoons, and had commanded all the Confederate forces west of the Mississippi, from which territory he had brought his army east at the call of Albert Sidney Johnston. Arriving too late for Shiloh, he had served under Beauregard and Bragg, had enjoyed a season of independent command in Mississippi after Bragg's departure for Kentucky and, finally, as cavalry commander under Pemberton, had staged the great raid on Grant's base at Holly Springs at the same time that Forrest was raiding the Union rail communications in West Tennessee. Van Dorn was a brave and enterprising commander, touched with brilliance but dogged with fatal ill fortune.

The command he brought from Mississippi consisted of the cavalry divisions of Brigadier Generals William T. Martin and William H. Jackson. To these divisions Forrest's brigade was added to make Van Dorn's cavalry corps, which on February twenty-fifth was set up as a separate component of the army, had about 11,500 men enrolled and some 6,300 present and effective. The corresponding corps under

128

Wheeler had an aggregate strength of about 18,000, with about 8,800 effectives present.[19]

Van Dorn's new corps found its first active employment early in March when, in making a reconnaissance in force toward Franklin, it encountered a like movement toward Columbia by a Union column under Colonel John Coburn—four infantry regiments, a battery and some cavalry, 2,837 men of all arms.[20] Colonel Coburn started his march from Franklin on March fourth under a plan which called for a junction at Spring Hill, twelve miles north of Columbia, with another column sent out from Murfreesborough under command of Brigadier General Philip H. Sheridan.[21]

Less than four miles out, Coburn began to meet Confederate forces, which forced him to deploy and carry on a long-range, delaying engagement through the afternoon. That evening, from a camp only four miles from his starting point, he sent back to the general commanding at Franklin a slightly bewildered message, ending on the plaintive note of, "What shall we do?"[22]

Coburn, however, was a brave and determined commander and, without waiting for further instructions, he marched on south on the morning of the fifth. He was encumbered with a train of eighty wagons which he was to fill with forage collected from the countryside and send back to Franklin. About ten in the morning, as he breasted a ridge some ten miles south of Franklin and a short distance north of Thompson's Station, he discovered stronger Confederate forces ahead.

The forces consisted of three brigades of Jackson's cavalry division, drawn up dismounted across the pike just to the south of the station, and Forrest's brigade, posted well out to their right, a total of about 6,000 men all under command of Van Dorn. Coburn believed, however, that the small force opposed to him numbered not less than 15,000 men, and perhaps as many as 17,000.[23] He had another four miles to go to his rendezvous with Sheridan at Spring Hill, but his conviction of the overwhelming strength of the opposition, together with threatening movements on his left flank, caused him to decide to retire.

The cavalry and artillery, according to the reports of the infantry officers, anticipated his decision. The cavalry, Coburn reported, "went off. I saw them no more," while the "artillery followed hastily."[24] The artillery did not follow, however, until after Forrest had sent Freeman's battery forward to a high hill, half a mile in advance of the Confederate line, from which it was able to throw twenty rounds into the enemy battery. In this, the last fight in which Freeman fired, he demonstrated again that, as was said of him after his death, his "favorite distance" for his guns was "as close as his general would let him go."[25]

Left alone, Coburn's infantry fought stubbornly and well. Three times

Jackson's men charged to the crest of the ridge they held above Thompson's Station, each time to be driven back with heavy loss. On one charge, indeed, when the Third Arkansas Cavalry lost its commander, Colonel Samuel G. Earle, and its color guard from a withering volley, seventeen-year-old Alice Thompson rushed from the residence where she was sheltered, raised the fallen flag and rallied the wavering regiment.[26]

In prolongation of the Confederate battle line to the right, Forrest placed Starnes's Fourth Tennessee and Edmondson's Eleventh Tennessee, dismounted. As Jackson's division launched its frontal attack against the Union position, Forrest, mounted on his favorite war horse "Roderick," rode up to these regiments as they lay in line, taking fire, called on them to "move up," and led them in a charge through the cedars clothing a rocky ridge in their front, against the Union left flank. As the Union flank was rolled back westward across the railroad and the turnpike, Roderick was struck three times. Turning Roderick over to his son and aide, the seventeen-year-old Lieutenant Willie Forrest, to be led to the rear, the General mounted his son's horse and continued the charge. Arrived at the position of the horse-holders, Roderick was relieved of saddle and bridle, for his greater comfort, and was not haltered. The habit of the horse had been to follow his master about, much as a favorite dog would do. Relieved of restraint, the wounded animal turned, pricked up his ears at the sound of the battle still raging, and tore away headlong across fields, outstripping all pursuit, jumping three fences on the way, and receiving a fourth and fatal wound as he reached his master.[27]

The two other regiments which Forrest had on the field—Biffle's Ninth Tennessee and Cox's Tenth—he had sent on a wide swing to the right. Coming in from that flank, they cut across the turnpike in Coburn's rear, deployed, dismounted, sent the horse-holders and held horses to the rear and, just before four o'clock in the afternoon, with Forrest himself on foot at their head, drove home the charge which, according to the reports of both Coburn and Van Dorn, "decided the fate of the day."[28] When the charging line was within twenty feet of the Union troops, Forrest reported, they "threw down their arms and surrendered."[29]

Among the losses of the day was the death of Captain Montgomery Little, who had organized Forrest's personal escort company in Middle Tennessee when the Old Brigade was formed in October of the year before. A planter and Memphis businessman of middle age, Captain Little had been a Union man in sentiment before the outbreak of the war. A man of good general education, though without specific military training, he had shown pronounced aptitude in the exacting business of leading the daredevil company whose business it was to keep up with Old Bedford, to carry his messages and, as at Thompson's Station, to charge where he charged.[30]

The bag of Union prisoners at Thompson's Station numbered 1,221, including seventy-eight officers, among them Colonel Coburn himself and Major William R. Shafter, the same who thirty-five years later was to command the American forces before Santiago de Cuba.[31]

The capture of Coburn's column disrupted the plan for a combined movement on Columbia but did not bring it to an end. Having "heard heavy firing south of Franklin" all day of March fifth, Sheridan's advance under Colonel Robert H. G. Minty backtracked to Triune. Meanwhile, on the sixth, Confederate infantry and artillery forces under Brigadier General Patton Anderson, moved out from Shelbyville toward Triune, to intercept Sheridan's advance, and Van Dorn was ordered by Lieutenant General Polk to move eastward in co-operation. On the night of the seventh Van Dorn and Forrest encamped at College Grove, some twenty miles east of Spring Hill. There Forrest "sent out men on all roads," and learned that the Sheridan force from Murfreesborough, together with Steedman's command of four regiments of infantry and one of cavalry, were in camp about three miles north of the Harpeth, in the vicinity of Triune. Anderson, "not deeming it prudent to go beyond Eagleville," returned to Shelbyville, while the Union forces on the eighth went on westward to Franklin, to take part in a renewed expedition to Columbia. Van Dorn, released from his orders to co-operate with Anderson, returned to the country between Franklin and Columbia.[32]

This time the Union advance was made with columns both on the Columbia Pike and on the Carter's Creek Pike, roughly paralleling it to the west. The fresh memory of what had happened to Coburn, however, together with the brisk resistance of the rear guards left behind under Forrest, caused the Federal columns to advance with a very respectable degree of caution. On the afternoon of March ninth the two columns made a junction at Thompson's Station, camping that night at Spring Hill. The Union advance of all arms was in such force that Van Dorn decided to give ground before it. On the next day light forces of Forrest's held the line of Rutherford Creek, half a dozen miles south of Spring Hill, fending off attempts to cross. In a "terrible storm," with the creeks and rivers rising to flood, the principal Confederate forces were busy that day getting wagons and guns across the swollen Duck on a pontoon bridge, which broke that night and was swept away in the swift current. Confederate forces remaining north of the Duck had to march eastward to White's Bridge, more than twenty miles upstream, to find a crossing. By that time Major General Gordon Granger, the Union

131

commander at Franklin, had joined infantry forces to the cavalry under Sheridan and, on the morning of the eleventh, an advance across Rutherford Creek was ordered. Forrest's rear guard drew off to the eastward to cover the upstream movement of the retiring Confederates, somewhat to the mystification of the Federal cavalry commanders, who marched the remaining five miles to Duck River without opposition of consequence. There, Van Dorn's force being safely out of reach, they gazed across the bottoms and the booming current of the Duck to Columbia on its hills beyond, and decided to go back to Franklin, which they did by a forced march.[33]

Van Dorn's resilient force followed as soon as the pontoon bridge at Columbia could be opened again, and by March fifteenth were back at Spring Hill, with the advanced line stretching east and west through Thompson's Station. "Red" Jackson's division lay to the west of that point, while Forrest's newly formed division, consisting of his own brigade, now under direct command of Starnes, and that of Frank C. Armstrong, extended to the east as far as the turnpike between Franklin and Lewisburg, with advanced pickets out to the Harpeth River at College Grove.[34]

From this line came the next thrust in the fencing match which was to go on in the debatable land between Franklin and Columbia for yet another three months, the prize being the possession of the fruitful country upon which Bragg's army was depending for a great part of its food and forage.

This next thrust was not to be at Franklin but at Brentwood, nine miles to the north and halfway between Franklin and Nashville, where there was a substantial garrison with army stores, and a stockaded railroad bridge across the Little Harpeth. On the evening of March twenty-fourth Forrest started after these prizes. Starnes, with part of the Old Brigade, crossed the Big Harpeth at Half-Acre Mill, six miles east of Franklin, at midnight and marched for Brentwood. In crossing the Federal line, however, he failed to capture all the pickets. Those who escaped made their way into Franklin by three in the morning, to give the alarm—but not before Starnes's men had cut the telegraph wires above Franklin. Approaching Brentwood from the east by daylight of March twenty-fifth, Starnes held his men in hand behind a range of hills, awaiting the arrival of Forrest with Armstrong's brigade, from the west, as planned.[35]

Armstrong, however, had been delayed by difficulties in getting the section of guns which accompanied him across the Harpeth below Franklin. Starnes waited until after seven in the morning, then concluded that some unforeseen circumstance had prevented the co-operating column from coming up. Being himself without artillery, he decided to march west to the Hillsborough Pike, along which the Armstrong brigade was to have advanced. Arriving at that road, he found that the column had already passed to the north, toward Nashville, and was moving by a crossroad eastward to Brentwood.

Arrived at Brentwood, Forrest went ahead with his plans without the help of Starnes. At the hamlet itself there was an entrenched camp, surrounded by a quarter-mile belt of felled trees and garrisoned by more than 500 Wisconsin troops. A mile and a half to the southward, where the railroad crossed the Little Harpeth, was a strong stockade garrisoned by nearly 300 Michigan troops. Forrest determined to capture both garrisons, with all their equipment, stores and wagons, and to burn what he could not carry off.

To hasten the operation, he sent Captain Anderson forward to Brentwood, carrying what turned out to be the only white handkerchief in the staff aloft on his saber as a flag of truce, with a summons to Lieutenant Colonel Bloodgood to surrender or take the consequences. Bloodgood, who had been at Thompson's Station under Coburn but had made his escape with the same troops he was now commanding, first "sent back word to General Forrest to come and take us" but within a short while, finding himself surrounded, observing that two pieces of artillery were being brought to bear on his position, and feeling that there was "no hope of aid from any quarter," changed his mind and surrendered.

Prisoners were quickly rounded up, stores and equipment were loaded on captured wagons, and the whole were started away to the westward to the Hillsborough Pike, by way of which they were to be taken south. To prevent interference from the direction of Nashville, and to spread the scare, the First Tennessee was ordered to demonstrate in that direction, which it did with such success that it came within three miles of the city, at which distance it circled clear around the southern environs, in sight of the tower of the capitol.[36]

With the rest of the command—less the details sent out to watch for the approach of Union reinforcements—Forrest turned immediately to the business of capturing the bridge stockade garrison, to the south. After one opening shot from his artillery, Forrest again sent in a demand for immediate surrender. Anderson, having lost the handkerchief used a short while before, was ordered by his chief to use the only other passably white cloth he had—his shirt. It proved to be just as efficacious, however, as the more conventional handkerchief and in a few minutes the Michigan garrison, surrounded, outnumbered and outgunned, surrendered.[37]

Warned of the irruption of Confederates into his rear, Gordon

133

Granger, commanding the Union forces at Franklin, started a column of about 700 cavalry under Brigadier General Green Clay Smith back up the pike to see what the disturbance was about. By the time Smith reached Brentwood, Forrest had finished his work and departed for the Hillsborough Pike. When the rear of the Confederate column, the Fourth Mississippi Cavalry, was no more than a mile from the burning stockade, Smith closed upon it and charged. The rear company checked Smith's charge with a volley and fell back to the next hill, where two more companies were formed to receive him. "Three fires" altogether the rear guard gave them, the colonel of the regiment reported with chagrin, when Smith "charged me while my guns were empty, and I was forced to make a precipitate retreat," after which, he added, "I am mortified to confess, I was forced by overwhelming numbers to become a part and parcel of the disgraceful number who stampeded in front of me without ever firing a gun."[38]

The troops in front were the Tenth Tennessee, whose commander gives quite a different account of what happened. The panic, he wrote, was created by a "company of stragglers from other commands" who came dashing through his regiment with the cry that the enemy were upon them, "causing the greatest disorder and confusion."[39]

Regardless of cause, there is no doubt of the panic, in which teamsters lashed their horses into a lather as the wagons bumped and careened over the narrow lanes leading away from Brentwood, while soldiers of the rear guard sought to force their flying horses past, to escape to the head of the column. It was a sight which the Union General Smith described with the most joyful exultation, ascribing it to the fact that his men, armed with five-shooters and rapid-fire Burnside carbines, "shot with wonderful and fearful aim," and did powerful execution. His small force, he reported, "drove more than twice their number, with two pieces of artillery, over 6 miles, perfectly dismayed and whipped," and "but for overwhelming forces, numbering not less than 5,000, would have gained an unquestioned success."[40]

The real cause of the reversal of fortune which overtook General Smith, however, was not overwhelming numbers but was Forrest himself, with the unshaken head of the column, and Starnes, with Forrest's own brigade. Starnes, who had not been in the fights at Brentwood, was chasing a Federal wood-gathering train on the Hillsborough Pike when he learned that the Confederate forces "were falling back rapidly and the enemy following them with great vigor." Ever prompt in action, he turned back and struck Smith's Union force on the right flank, causing him in turn "to fall back . . . with great precipitation."[41] When Smith rallied on a hill and began to deploy as if for another go at the retreating column, Biffle's regiment and Starnes's own, under Major McLemore, moved on them again, while Forrest himself, riding back from the head of the column with such scraps of companies and squads as he could gather up, stormed into action.

One of Biffle's soldiers, Sergeant J. G. Witherspoon, tells the story of how he came. Witherspoon's squad was posted behind trees and rocks, facing the Union command, which had taken position behind a stone wall across a creek. "In a very short time," the Sergeant wrote, "General Forrest came charging up the pike, cursing a blue streak as he came. He had a considerable force, seven or eight hundred men. (I learned afterward that in coming up the pike he had gathered a conglomerated medley of men of different commands that had been stampeded.) He had a flag in his hand, which he waved over his head. As he came up I heard him say, 'Fall in! every damned one of you!' I presume that he thought we had stampeded too. We fell in, of course. We couldn't have stayed out if we had wanted to.

"I dropped in immediately in his rear, and we charged up the pike like the Old Scratch was after us. When we got within good long range of their muskets, which we could see glistening from behind the stone fences, two or three to one of us, and I began to think, 'Old man, I wonder if you are going to charge those fences in the shape we are in'—for we were going then in column of fours—he reined up his horse and commanded 'Halt!' Turning his horse he looked back down the line, then said coolly as if he were simply on his way to church, 'Boys, I'll be damned if it will do to charge like that.' Then I thought again: 'Old man, you have certainly said something.' In an instant he gave the command: 'March to the left flank!—double quick!' and when we had cleared their right he threw us into line on their right flank, dismounted us, and in less time than it takes to tell it we had them whipped, chased them back about two miles toward the railroad and were bothered with them no more that day."[42]

In his counterattack Forrest retook the wagons which Smith had recaptured, but was unable to bring them off. Everything else, however—the prisoners, some 800 of them, and the rest of the wagons, mules and horses—were marched to Columbia, while Forrest moved back to his headquarters at Spring Hill, watchfully guarding against any further attempt at recapture.

"Many of the men in the command who were unarmed got guns in the field," Forrest reported, "and many who had inferior guns, muskets, shot-guns, etc., exchanged them on the field, placing (or, at any rate, so ordered) their old guns in the wagons in lieu of them"—a practice which seemed to him no more than just to the men who had marched and

135

fought to capture the guns but which ere long was to get Forrest again in difficulties with his superiors.[43]

Despite the loss of twenty-nine prisoners in the stampede of the rear guard, the little affair at Brentwood, coming on top of the larger one at Thompson's Station, was sweet to Forrest's men. It took some of the sting out of the failure at Dover, and it even brought to them and their General special commendation in general orders issued by General Bragg on March thirty-first.[44]

It brought no letup, however, in the incessant activity in the territory between the fronts of the two armies—small affairs all, raids for information, for diversion or even for so prosaic and practical a purpose as cutting out and driving off herds of beef cattle gathered for the use of the Union army.

Activity rose on April tenth, with a movement by Van Dorn against Franklin itself, interpreted by Gordon Granger as an actual attempt to take the place but described by Van Dorn as a forced reconnaissance. At any rate, in the middle of that morning Jackson's division drove in the Federal pickets on the pike from Spring Hill, while Forrest advanced on the pike from Lewisburg. The attack along the pikes leading into Franklin from the south and southeast was pushed with such a lack of vigor through the noon hour that Granger began to believe that the whole thing was a feint to cover another move against Brentwood. Receiving a message from the commander there that his pickets were being driven in—a false alarm as the event proved—Granger started Green Clay Smith and his cavalry back to Brentwood, thereby losing their use for the rest of the day just as the Confederates, about two in the afternoon, began to push their attack into the outskirts of Franklin.[45]

Meanwhile, Major General David S. Stanley, commanding Rosecrans' cavalry corps, had approached to within four miles of Franklin, from the direction of Murfreesborough. Hearing heavy firing about 2:30 P.M. he crossed the Harpeth and started looking for the fight.[46]

Stanley's flank movement from the right caught Forrest at a peculiarly unfortunate time. Armstrong's brigade, with two guns of Freeman's six guns, was in front, battering away at Franklin. Starnes, with Forrest's own brigade, was coming up some two miles in the rear, Biffle's regiment leading. Behind Biffle, marching in route order and without flank protection, came Freeman and the other four guns of his battery. Suddenly, the Fourth U. S. (Regular) Cavalry burst out of a woodland to the right, not more than a hundred yards away, and charged the limbered and unprotected guns. Before the battery could fire a shot, the cavalry were among the men, capturing the guns and a large part of the men, including Captain Freeman.

136

The near-by Confederate cavalry regiments were prompt to the charge, "threatening to surround" the force which had just overwhelmed Freeman. To extricate themselves the Union cavalry abandoned the guns and caissons captured, after doing them minor damage, released all but about thirty of the prisoners they had taken in the first rush, and hastily made their way back across the Harpeth.[47]

In the haste to escape, the Confederate prisoners, dismounted, were forced to run at the point of the pistol. While so running, Captain Freeman was shot dead by a Federal trooper when he failed to keep up the pace set by his mounted captors. Freeman's body was recovered, along with his guns, before nightfall. The manner of his death, learned from Confederate prisoners after their exchange, became the inciting cause of a special feud between Forrest's men and the Fourth Regulars, who were to meet in battle more than once.[48]

It was from this surprise attack at Franklin that there originated one of the "Forrest stories" which illustrates both his cool readiness and resource and the grip he had on the imaginations and the confidence of his soldiers. The story as told to Viscount Wolseley by an unnamed Confederate general officer (who may well have been Frank Armstrong himself) is that as the Union cavalry struck his extended column in flank, messengers rushed forward to the General with the alarming word that "General Stanley has cut in behind you, has captured the rear guard battery and many prisoners, and has now got into General Armstrong's rear!"

"You say he's in Armstrong's rear?" Forrest roared. "That's where I've been trying to get him all day, damn him! I'll be in *his* rear in about five minutes! Face your line of battle about, Armstrong; push forward your skirmish line; crowd 'em both ways! I'll go to the rear brigade and you'll hear from me there directly!"

"The distinguished General who is my informant," Wolseley added, "tells me that there was not a private soldier who was then present who does not to this day believe that General Stanley fell into a trap that Forrest had deliberately laid for him. Forrest afterwards admitted that at the moment he thought his whole command was 'gone up.' "[49]

Van Dorn fell back to Spring Hill while Stanley's cavalry, after remaining a day at Franklin, marched back to Murfreesborough, "burning on our way ten dwellings and outhouses belonging to persons who had sons in the Confederate Army, as per order of Major General Stanley," according to the report of Colonel D. M. Ray of the Second Tennessee (Union) Cavalry, commanding a brigade.[50]

This method of making war moved Brigadier General James B. Steedman, commanding a Union division operating about Triune, between

Franklin and Murfreesborough, to protest to his corps commander, not against the burning of dwellings but against the incidental loss of forage for which Steedman had sent his wagons, to find only smoking ashes. "In the destruction of property under the order of Major General Stanley to his command to burn the houses of all citizens who have sons or near relatives in the Confederate service, a large amount of forage was burned. . . ." he reported. "I do not suppose that General Stanley knew anything about the destruction of the forage, or that he would have permitted it had he known that it was being done."[51]

On the same afternoon during which Van Dorn and Forrest were thrusting against Franklin, Rosecrans ordered out from Nashville an expedition intended to carry deep into the South systematic destruction of supplies for the army, of the manufactories which might produce them, and of the railroads which might transport them. Though Forrest knew nothing of it at the time, as he fell back to his headquarters at Spring Hill, Colonel Abel D. Streight was even then starting on the raid which was to do more than any one thing which had yet occurred to spread the fame of Forrest.[52]

CHAPTER X

THE PURSUIT AND CAPTURE OF STREIGHT

April 10, 1863-May 5, 1863

IN MID-APRIL of 1863 the Union armies in the West began to use against the Confederates the pattern of long-distance cavalry raid developed by Forrest and Morgan, driving deep into enemy-held territory to strike at remote bases and lines of communication and supply.

Two such raids were launched simultaneously. One, that of Colonel B. H. Grierson of Illinois, from the vicinity of Memphis through the length of the state of Mississippi, was a distinct success in disturbing and disrupting Confederate communications at the critical time when Grant was transferring his army across the Mississippi and establishing himself in the rear of Vicksburg.

The other, that of Colonel Abel D. Streight of Indiana, starting from Nashville with intent to travel a circuit of nearly 1,000 miles by steamboat and muleback to get into north Georgia and there "cut the railroads which supply the rebel army by Chattanooga," ended in failure and captivity.

Streight had the longer and more difficult road to follow. He had, too, the problem of finding and fighting his way back—or rather, would have had, could he have reached his objective—while Grierson had only to keep going south to come out at Baton Rouge, Louisiana, already held by Union forces coming up the river from below. Grierson, moreover, had the good fortune to strike a virtual vacuum in the Confederate defenses, while Streight was to meet the fierce resistance of Forrest—an experience which was to be reserved for Grierson until the following year at Okolona and Brice's Cross Roads.

Streight's "Independent Provisional Brigade designed for special secret service" was made up of four regiments of infantry from Indiana, Ohio and Illinois, who were to be mounted, and two companies raised in north Alabama but designated as Middle Tennessee Cavalry (Union). On the afternoon of April tenth, as Van Dorn and Forrest were falling back from their fruitless demonstration against Franklin, Streight's command filed down to the steamboat landing at Nashville, loaded their stores, and drove aboard the 800 quartermaster mules on which a portion

139

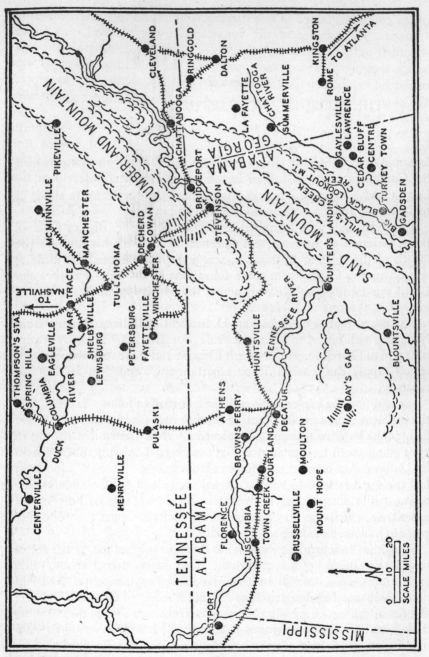

SOUTHERN TENNESSEE, NORTHERN ALABAMA, NORTHWESTERN GEORGIA

140

of the command hoped to ride diagonally across northern Alabama into Georgia. The balance of the command, it was planned, was to be mounted on horses and mules gathered up in the countryside through which they were to pass—one purpose of the expedition being, as was explained in a book published afterward by Colonel Streight, "to cripple the enemy" by "seizing the animals whose labor furnished subsistence for the rebel armies."[1]

On the morning of the eleventh, Streight's flotilla of eight transports backed out from the landing at Nashville, turned in the stream and "sped irresistibly along," as one member of the expedition described the scene, "before the mighty force of the river's current and power of the steam engine," with the "spiral columns of white steam ascending from the exhaust pipes . . . forming behind us, over vale and hill, a milky track of the circuitous course of the Cumberland."

That evening the boats landed at a "heap of black and charred ruins" which "in the palmy days of peace" had been the village of Palmyra. There men and mules disembarked, while the steamers proceeded down the Cumberland to the Ohio, where they were to pick up forage and rations, and come up the Tennessee to Fort Henry, to which point the command was to march overland, gathering up horses and mules on the way.

At Palmyra the idyllic humors of the morning's start from Nashville first began to fade. It was discovered that the mules brought down on the boat were not so good as they should have been, many of them being wild and unbroken. It was found, also, that the infantrymen who were to ride them "were at first very easily dismounted, frequently in a most undignified and unceremonious manner."[2] A day and a half were spent at Palymra in this manner of equestrian exercise, while parties were out scouring the country for additional mounts.

At noon on the fifteenth, the day appointed to meet the boats, Streight arrived at Fort Henry, having picked up some 500 mounts as he marched across from Palmyra, and having lost through distemper and exhaustion about 100 of those with which he had left Nashville. At Fort Henry Streight met his first delay when the fleet failed to put in its appearance until the evening of the sixteenth. That night was spent in loading the 2,000 men and 1,200 animals aboard and, on the morning of April seventeenth—the same day on which Grierson left La Grange, near Memphis, on his raid into Mississippi—Streight's expedition started southward, up the Tennessee River to Eastport, Mississippi, head of navigation at the then stage of water.

At Eastport Streight was to meet an expedition under Brigadier General Grenville M. Dodge, sent out from Corinth to advance beyond the

Muscle Shoals section of north Alabama as a screen and blind behind which he could disembark, complete his preparations and get started across the state of Alabama to his first objective at Rome, Georgia. The original plan called for the meeting on the sixteenth, but the delayed start and further delays to the fleet on account of low water prevented Streight from reaching the rendezvous until the afternoon of Sunday, April 19, late on his schedule by three full days.[3]

Dodge, meanwhile, had moved out to Bear Creek, twelve miles above Eastport, with some 7,500 men. Thither Streight repaired on Sunday evening, leaving the unloading and coralling of his precious mules to subordinates. Returning to the bivouac at Eastport at midnight, he found that there had been a stampede among the mules, and that 400 had escaped. Two days were spent trying to round up the scattered mules, of which only about half were recovered—another two days lost on the schedule.[4]

It was not until the morning of the twenty-second, therefore, that Streight moved up to the rear of Dodge's command, whose eastward advance up the Tennessee Valley was intended to cover Streight's movements until he was in position to cut loose on his independent dash for Georgia, to distract Confederate attention from that move and, if the move should be discovered, to keep the Confederates too busy to follow him.

During the nearly two weeks in which Streight was on the move from Nashville to Eastport, and getting started from there into Alabama, neither his movements nor those of Dodge were of concern to Forrest. A scout did report the passage of transports with troops up the Tennessee River on the seventeenth. Colonel P. D. Roddey, the Confederate commander at Tuscumbia, Alabama, engaged in stubborn resistance to the advance of Dodge in that direction, and relayed another scout's report that "transports were landing an army at Eastport" on the nineteenth. Both reports were duly passed on to General Joseph E. Johnston, supervising all Confederate Western operations, at his headquarters in Chattanooga.[5]

Thus it happened that while Union forces from Mississippi and Tennessee, numbering nearly 10,000 altogether, were moving into northwestern Alabama against Roddey's 1,200 Confederate cavalry, Van Dorn and Forrest were left at Spring Hill, watching the Federal forces at Franklin. Relations between them, which had been growing more and more strained during the two months of their service together, came near to an open flare-up of personal encounter on the very last day on which they were to be together. That there was no such open break and the reasons why there was not reflect the good sense and patriotism

142

of two high-strung, high-tempered soldiers of opposite and clashing temperaments.

Three accounts of this incident have come down, all from members of General Van Dorn's staff. From them it appears that Van Dorn reproached Forrest with having permitted some member of his staff to write articles for the Chattanooga *Rebel*, in which the honors at Thompson's Station were claimed for Forrest rather than Van Dorn, and with having improperly reported property captured at Brentwood which he now refused to turn over to the army authorities, as ordered. The story, as told by General Van Dorn to Captain H. F. Starke of his staff immediately after the incident, goes on:

". . . without mincing matters, I called his attention to the reports I had heard, and accused him of misrepresentation at headquarters. This he warmly denied and expressed his conviction of my too great willingness to listen to stories to his discredit. One thing led to another, until at length I threw off all restraint and directly expressing my belief in his treachery and falsehood, suggested that then and there was as good a time and place to settle our difficulties as any, and suiting the action to the word, I stepped to where my sword was hanging against the wall, snatched it down and turned to face him.

"Forrest (said Van Dorn with a smile) was really a sight to see. He had risen and advanced one step, his sword half drawn from its scabbard, and his face aflame with feeling. But even as I unsheathed my own sword and advanced to meet him, a wave of some kind seemed to pass over his countenance; he slowly returned his sword to its sheath, and steadily regarding me said, 'General Van Dorn, you know I'm not afraid of you—but I will not fight you—and leave you to reconcile with yourself the gross wrongs you have done me. It would never do for two officers of our rank to set such an example to the troops, and I remember, if you forget, what we both owe to the cause.'

" 'I never felt so ashamed of myself in my life,' General Van Dorn went on to say, 'and recalled by Forrest's manly attitude and words to our true position, I immediately replied that he was right, and apologized for having used such expressions to him. And so we parted to be somewhat better friends, I believe, than we have been before. Whatever else he may be, the man certainly is no coward.' "

While it may be doubted that General Van Dorn gave to the conversation quite the literary finish with which it was afterward reported by his staff officer to the Confederate Veterans' Association, there can be no doubt that from the incident Van Dorn gained, as he said, "a higher opinion of General Forrest than I have ever held before."[6]

143

About eleven o'clock on the night of April twenty-third—the day, probably, of the near-clash between the Confederate commanders— orders from General Bragg reached Forrest at Spring Hill to take his Old Brigade southward to the Tennessee River, there to join Roddey and to take command of the combined forces opposing the threatening advance of Dodge's Union force.[7] No one on the Confederate side, as yet, was concerned with what Streight was up to.

Before daylight of the twenty-fourth, the advance of the brigade was under way for the Tennessee River. Thirty-six hours later the brigade was ninety miles away, at Brown's Ferry, below Decatur, Alabama. There Dibrell's Eighth Tennessee, with a section of guns under John Morton, was detached to work down the north bank of the river to Florence, with orders to block any attempt on the part of Dodge to cross over or, if no such attempt developed, to make such a demonstration as might make Dodge apprehensive of a Confederate crossing to the south bank.

With the remainder of the brigade Forrest ferried the broad Tennessee on the twenty-sixth, and on the twenty-seventh marched westward through Courtland and on to the vicinity of Town Creek, between that point and Tuscumbia. There, on the twenty-eighth, Forrest joined Roddey in an all-day resistance to the crossing of that stream by Dodge's force.[8]

That day's fighting at long range, in truth, was but part of the Union plan to give Streight a good start on his way to Georgia. The twenty-fifth and twenty-sixth he had passed at Tuscumbia, where the medical officers gave his command a thorough going-over, checking every man for physical fitness for the grind ahead. Through this winnowing his strength was reduced, according to Streight's report, to 1,500 men, but they were picked men. At the same time he was furnished by Dodge with 200 more mules and six ammunition and ration wagons, according to Streight's account, or with 500 mules and twelve wagons, according to the account of Dodge. This left him still short mounts for 150 men.[9]

At eleven o'clock on the night of Sunday the twenty-sixth, the day on which Forrest crossed the Tennessee River, Streight's column slipped out of Tuscumbia, heading south to Russellville, where it was to turn eastward to Moulton. The march was made in a hard rain and through mud and darkness which, Streight reported, made progress slow, especially as the pace of the mounted men was held down, both to permit the men on foot to keep up and to afford an opportunity for parties to scour the country along both sides of the line of march to bring in additional mounts.

All day of the twenty-seventh Streight's men plodded along through

144

the hill country that lies to the south of the broad and level Tennessee Valley. That night, having made thirty-four miles from the starting point, the advance encamped at the village of Mount Hope in Lawrence County, where Streight received word from General Dodge that the Confederates had been driven off up the valley, and that he should push on. Not until ten o'clock in the morning of the twenty-eighth, however, did all Streight's command come up to Mount Hope. More delay.

During that day James Moon, an intrepid scout of Roddey's, headed northwest for the battle along Town Creek with the news that a column which he estimated at 2,000 had left Mount Hope that morning, marching toward Moulton, which would put them well into the rear of Forrest's left flank. The information reached Forrest at dusk, just about the time that Streight, by this time having all but fifty of his men mounted, was marching into Moulton.[10]

At midnight of the twenty-eighth Streight marched away from Moulton, headed southeastward toward Blountsville by way of Day's Gap. During the same night Forrest's camp, a day's march north of Moulton, was a scene of most intense activity. From the fragmentary information which came in through scouts, and from his own observation of the course of the day's fighting along Town Creek, he had arrived at the sound conclusion that Dodge's force was but a blind, and that the real threat was from Streight. Still, with the limited knowledge which he had, it was not safe to hazard everything on such a conclusion. Roddey, therefore, was ordered to place his own command, plus Edmondson's Eleventh Tennessee and Julian's battalion, between Dodge and the assumed position of Streight's column, to prevent either from sending reinforcements to the other. Biffle's Eighth Tennessee and Starnes's Fourth Tennessee, temporarily under Major McLemore, with two of Morton's pieces and Ferrell's six-gun Georgia battery, which had been with Roddey, were told off for the pursuit of Streight. Orders were sent across the river to Dibrell to intensify his demonstration toward Dodge's rear, with the idea of causing him to retreat westward, while the remainder of the command was left in front of Dodge, to fight him if he came forward or to follow him if he fell back.

All night long these soldiers who for five days had marched and fought almost continuously worked to get ready for the test ahead. The portable forges of the farriers were fired up, and anvils rang as horses were shod. Ammunition was checked and inspected, the best animals were selected for the artillery and guns and caissons were double-teamed. Rations were cooked, two days' feed of shelled corn to be carried on the saddle was issued, supplies and gear of every sort were gone over, with

145

Forrest himself planning, directing, overseeing the whole of the preparations. He did not know just who Streight was nor what he was up to but he did know that a formidable column was loose and headed into the South, where there were no Confederate forces, and that it had a long head start.

At dawn of the twenty-ninth Forrest marched for Moulton, some six hours after Streight had marched away from that little courthouse town of Lawrence County. Thirty-five miles Streight made that day, to rest in camp that night at the foot of Day's Gap, where the rough road climbed through a narrow and winding defile to the top of the plateau of Sand Mountain—the local name for the final southwestern extension of the great Appalachian chain.

"On the morning of April 30th, 1863," Colonel Streight's aide afterward wrote, the rains which had plagued their march were over and "the sun shone out bright and beautiful, as spring day's sun ever beamed; and from the smouldering camp fires of the previous night the mild blue smoke ascended in graceful curves, and mingled with the gray mist slumbering on the mountain tops above. The scene was well calculated to inspire and refresh the minds of our weary soldiers."[11]

Colonel Streight, marching at the head of his column as it wound up the mountain, may well have felt some sense of elation, after all the vexatious delays of the three weeks since his men had marched aboard steamboats at Nashville. He had had good hunting the day before, with sufficient haul of horses and mules to mount his whole force at last, including the replacement of many of the failing and broken-down mules brought from Nashville. He was in a country of pronounced Union sympathies from which, indeed, most of the men of the two "Middle Tennessee" cavalry companies under Captain D. D. Smith had been recruited. "Many were the happy greetings between them and their friends and relations," he reported. He did not know that Dodge had begun his retirement to Corinth, Mississippi, the day before.[12]

Ahead of Colonel Streight at sunrise on that last day of April 1863 the way seemed open to great results and much glory. Behind him, he thought, was the protection of Dodge's force to engage and hold off any possible Confederate pursuit—when, as he reached the top of the mountain two miles from his starting place, his ears were assailed by the boom of cannon.

Forrest, having marched a day and half the night to cover the fifty miles from the battle line along Town Creek, had bivouacked at midnight only four miles behind Streight, and at sunrise was driving in his rear.

The force immediately behind Streight was that which had been sent under Roddey to keep between him and Dodge, while the regiments of Biffle and Starnes were to climb the mountain by another gap to the northward and get upon Streight's flank or rear. Getting word of this movement, Streight put up a strong delaying fight with his rear guard at the head of the Gap, while the main column pushed ahead through a "country which was open, sand ridges, very thinly wooded, and afforded very fine defensive positions."[13]

Selecting one such position, some three miles back from the brow of the mountain, Streight formed line of battle on a ridge, with his right resting on a precipitous ravine and his left on a marshy run. The mules and horses were sent to a place of safety in a ravine to the rear, skirmishers were sent out to front, flanks and rear, both to prevent surprise and "to prevent any straggling of either stray animals or cowardly men." The plan was for the rear guard, when everything was set, to retreat rapidly toward the center of the position, leading their pursuers into ambush.

The plan worked. As the Alabama Union cavalry fell back on the run, closely followed by Captain Bill Forrest's company of scouts, the Union lines rose from the underbrush where they lay and, with the addition of two 12-pounder mountain howitzers, poured into the charging Confederates a destructive fire. One of the wounded was Captain Forrest, who suffered a shattered thigh bone.

Reinforcements coming up, the Confederates advanced again, this time running the two guns of Morton's battery under Lieutenant Wills Gould to within 300 yards of the Union line. An effective countercharge by Streight's men drove the Confederates back in confusion, and ended in the capture of Gould's guns with their caissons—a fact which put Forrest in a towering, thunderous rage and which, indirectly, was nearly to cost him his life within the month.

As more and more Confederates came up after their terrific ride from the Tennessee River—barely 1,000 men had been in hand during the early stages of the battle at Day's Gap—Forrest formed a new line of battle for another charge to avenge the check his men had suffered and to recapture his guns. Raging up and down the line, he ordered the men to tie their horses to the saplings in the thin piny woods. No horseholders this time, he told them, and no use for horses if they did not bring back those guns.

At eleven o'clock in the morning, after a fight of some five hours, Streight decided that he had done enough fighting for the time and, fearing the approach of one of Forrest's flanking parties, skillfully withdrew from his position and "resumed the march," just in time to avoid Forrest's attack from the rear. The first blood and the first honors were Streight's, for, after all, his mission was not to fight barren battles on top of remote Sand Mountain but to make his way to Georgia and cut railroads.

Six miles beyond the battleground of the morning, with Forrest closing in on his rear again at Crooked Creek, Streight was compelled to lose time again by deploying in line of battle on a ridge called Hog Mountain, where, from about an hour before dark until about ten o'clock, Forrest attacked under a full moon, with the general order to his men to "shoot at everything blue and keep up the scare."

Forrest's force at Hog Mountain consisted of the Starnes and Biffle regiments, which had come up after their unsuccessful detour to get in Streight's rear, the General's escort company, Captain Bill Forrest's scouts and the artillery. Edmondson's regiment had been sent away that afternoon to move parallel with Streight to the northward so as to head off any attempt to break back toward the Tennessee River in that direction, while Roddey and his men had been sent back to make sure that Dodge did not pounce upon Forrest's back as the latter had upon Streight's.

The Hog Mountain fight was one of bold and venturesome determination on both sides, carried on in the darkness by the light of the flashes of artillery and small arms. Forrest, leading in the very front of the fight, had horses shot under him three times. Finally, when a detachment of Biffle's regiment passed around Streight's flank and threatened his mule-holders, Streight once more "resumed the march," leaving behind the Confederate guns whose loss had so roused Forrest.

About midnight Streight set another ambush, leaving Lieutenant Colonel Gilbert Hathaway's Indiana regiment behind in a dense thicket alongside the road to check the pursuit by firing into it at short range. The ambush, Streight reported, caused "a complete stampede of the enemy," although Confederate accounts have it that the advanced point of the pursuing column sensed the ambush, which was located by scouts, and shelled out of the woods by two pieces of Ferrell's battery pushed forward by hand, without noise, along the road of soft sand shimmering in the moonlight.[14]

Colonel Streight, as he explained, hoped that by "pushing ahead" he could get down from the top of Sand Mountain to a region where he "could feed before the enemy could come up with us, and, by holding him back where there was no feed, compel him to lay over at least a day to recuperate." Consequently, he marched on through the night. By two in the morning, however, Forrest was again crowding his rear to the point where it was necessary to halt, deploy and lay another ambush.[15]

After another brisk affair in the moonlight Forrest halted until daylight to water and feed, and to give an opportunity for those with the weaker horses to close up.[16] Meanwhile, Streight pushed on wearily to the village of Blountsville, forty-three miles from Day's Gap, where he arrived about ten in the morning of Friday, May first.

When Forrest's men took up the march again shortly after daylight of the same day, they had been on forced march or fighting ever since leaving Spring Hill a full week earlier. In the three days since they had arrived in front of Dodge at Town Creek, they had fought one day, worked one night, marched all the next day and night, and marched and fought still another day and most of the night.

The weariness with which men and horses picked up the march that morning can hardly be imagined. And yet pick it up they did, for Old Bedford led, and they picked it up with such spirit that well before noon, and before Streight's men finished feeding their animals in Blountsville, Forrest was driving in his rear pickets. The two commands went through the little village in a running fight and a whirl of dust. During his halt, Streight had sought to lighten his column by transferring ammunition from his wagons to pack mules and burning the wagons. So closely did Forrest press him, however, that the hungry Confederates managed to put out the fires before the store of provisions which the wagons had carried was entirely spoiled.

Beyond Blountsville, Streight took up the same tactics which he had developed the day before—marching ahead with his main body, setting ambushes with small parties of his rear guard and so forcing upon the pursuit a certain caution, at the same time continually scouring the country for mounts, both to supply himself and to insure that no fit animal should be left behind for the mounting of Forrest's men as their horses failed, using and then destroying bridges, obstructing the road. All these advantages of the pursued, Colonel Streight, an able man as well as brave, with a command of real soldiers, exploited with skill and persistence.

Beyond Blountsville the running fight went on all day until, late in the afternoon, Streight made another general stand to give the command a chance to get across the deep and difficult ford of the East Branch of the Black Warrior River, under cover of the two howitzers emplaced upon the farther bank. From there he pushed wearily on toward Gadsden, plodding through the night "though the command was in no condition to do so," because of a report from scouts that another Confederate column was moving on a parallel road with evident intent to get ahead and cut him off. Forrest, on the other hand, sent no more than an advance guard forward to keep up the attack, while the main body was given three hours' rest at the crossing of the Warrior, refreshed

149

somewhat by rations which Streight had lost when two of his pack mules drowned at the ford.[17]

Marching again before midnight, Forrest was hard upon Streight's rear at the crossing of Big Will's Creek, in the valley below the southern point of Lookout Mountain. There Biffle's regiment, which had been in the advance, was allowed a short rest while the remainder of the command pushed on.

Four miles on in the direction of Gadsden, and about nine o'clock in the morning of May second—the ninth day of almost continuous fighting and marching for Forrest's men—Streight got across Black Creek on "a fine wooden bridge, which was afterwards burned by our rear guard. This, it was thought, would delay Forrest's forces long enough to enable us to reach Rome, Georgia, before he could again overtake us, as the stream was very deep and seemed to be unfordable."[18]

While the bridge was yet burning, Forrest and his escort company, riding hell-for-leather at the head of the pursuing column, tore up to the stream, to be met with sharp fire from the opposite bank. It did look, for a moment, as if Forrest were balked. But only for a moment, for from a neighboring farmhouse, home of the Widow Sanson and her two daughters, came unexpected help.

"Can you tell me where I can get across that creek?" Forrest asked of Emma, sixteen-year-old daughter of the house.

Miss Emma knew, she said, of a trail about 200 yards above the bridge, and on the Sanson farm, where the cows sometimes crossed at low water, and offered to show it to the General if he would have a horse saddled for her.

"There is no time to saddle a horse; get up here behind me," he said, as he backed his mount up close to the bank on which she stood.

Over the momentary objection of her mother, who feared that "people would talk about" Emma if she went off with the soldiers, she swung up behind the General and guided him to the neighborhood of the lost ford, where, coming in sight of the Union sharpshooters, she suggested that they dismount to be less conspicuous. As they came close to the ford, creeping through the bushes, she happened to be in front. Forrest stepped ahead, saying, "I'm glad to have you for a pilot but I'm not going to make breastworks of you."[19]

Amid a burst of fire—bullets passed through the billowing skirts of the young girl—she pointed out the marks and bearings of the ford. Returning to the house, Forrest ordered the widow and her daughters to seek safety from the Federal fire, while he went about the business of getting the command across the creek. When the Union forces marched on, fondly believing that they had placed an impassable stream

150

between themselves and pursuit, the Sanson ladies returned to their house.

On the way they met Forrest, who told Emma that he had left a note for her in the house, asked for a lock of her hair, asked that they see that Robert Turner, a Confederate soldier killed in the skirmishing across the creek and "laid out" in their home, be buried in some near-by graveyard, got on his horse and with his men rode away in the implacable pursuit. "My sister and I sat up all night watching over the dead soldier who had lost his life fighting for our rights," Emma Sanson wrote in the brave and simple recital of her deed which she gave Doctor Wyeth thirty years afterward.

The note which Forrest left for her, written in a clear hand and published in facsimile in Wyeth's *Forrest*, reads:

"Hed Quaters in Sadle
"May 2, 1863
"My highest regardes to Miss Ema Sanson
for hir gallant conduct while my forse was
skirmishing with the Federals across Black
Creek near Gadisden Allabama
"N. B. Forrest
"Brig. Genl   Comding N. Ala—"[20]

Disappointed in their hope of some respite at Gadsden, east of Black Creek, Streight's men seem to have believed that Forrest was shown the ford by "a young man by the name of Sanson" who had been "among a lot of prisoners captured by us in the morning and paroled, who, as soon as set at liberty, made his way direct to the pursuing force of General Forrest," in violation of his parole. "From this incident," Streight's aide wrote, "the rebels manufactured the bit of romance" about Emma Sanson.[21]

With Forrest at his heels Streight paused in Gadsden only long enough to destroy army and commissary stores of the Confederacy found there, and forced himself and his weary column on. "It now became evident to me," Streight reported, "that our only hope was in crossing the river at Rome and destroying the bridge, which would delay Forrest a day or two and give us time to collect horses and mules and allow the command a little time to sleep, without which it was impossible to proceed."

From Turkeytown, eight miles east of Gadsden, therefore, he dispatched "200 of the best mounted men selected from the whole command," under Captain Milton Russell, to push ahead to Rome, seize the bridge across the Oostenaula River there, and hold it until the main command could come up.[22]

151

Rome and rest looked a long way off but on Streight's men plodded, in a continuous rear-guard skirmish all through the day until four in the afternoon, by which time they had reached Blount's plantation, twelve miles east of Gadsden. "Here I decided to halt," wrote Streight, "as it was impossible to continue the march through the night without feeding and resting." While details fed and watered the animals, the rest of the command formed line of battle on a ridge. After a skirmish in which Streight's second-in-command, Colonel Hathaway, was killed, Forrest drew back to a parallel ridge and began massing his men, Streight thought, for "a more determined attack."

The little battle at Blount's having revealed that much of the ammunition was worthless by reason of a wetting in fording some creek, and that much more was worthless because the paper cartridges had worn out and the powder had sifted away in the men's cartridge boxes or pockets, and darkness coming on, Streight decided to slip away "unobserved, if possible" and lay another ambush in a thicket half a mile to the rear.[23]

The ambush failed when Forrest discovered it and started a flank movement around it. Streight and his men, many of them now without mounts and others with stock "jaded, tender-footed, and worn down," withdrew as silently as possible and started for another dreadful night of marching. After some delay for a skirmish at the village of Centre, they reached the ferry across the Chattooga River, a short distance above where it falls into the Coosa. Captain Russell had passed that way but had neglected to leave behind a guard for the means of crossing the considerable stream, and by the time the main body arrived citizens had spirited away the ferryboat.

The indomitable Streight turned wearily northward, with intent to cross on a bridge reported to be standing near Gaylesville, some seven or eight miles upstream. On the way it was necessary to cross extensive "coal choppings." Here the timber had been cut and burned for charcoal to supply the near-by Round Mountain Iron Furnace, where nearly 1,000 hands were engaged in making charcoal pig iron to be used by the foundry and machine shops at Rome in casting cannon and building engines for the Confederacy. One of Streight's scouting parties partially destroyed the furnace—the one tangible result achieved by the raiders—but the passage of the "choppings" that Saturday night was an ordeal which contributed to the disastrous end of the expedition as a whole.[24]

The old choppings were a maze of wagon tracks running in all directions through the scrub second-growth timber. It was night, the guides were none too sure of their way at best, men and animals were staggering along, scattered, lost and wandering in a nightmare of utter confusion and weariness approaching exhaustion. Not until daylight did the command get across the Chattooga on Dyke's Bridge, which they burned, turned back southward toward the Rome road and pushed on beyond Cedar Bluff, with exhausted men and worn-out animals dropping by the wayside.

Toward nine o'clock on the morning of Sunday, May third, Streight decided that there was nothing for it but to halt for rest and feed, which he did at the plantation of Mrs. Lawrence in the Straightneck Precinct of Cherokee County, Alabama, and a little more than twenty miles short of his first objective at Rome, Georgia.[25]

Through the Saturday night on which Streight's men toiled across the coal choppings, Forrest sent one squadron directly on their trail with orders to "devil them all night," while the remainder of the command took their rest.[26]

While Forrest's men rested and Streight's toiled on, and Captain Russell's troop of 200 selected Federal soldiers pushed ahead to seize the bridges at Rome, messengers sent forward from Gadsden by Forrest were swinging well north of their line of march to reach Rome with warnings of their coming. Meanwhile, however, on the south side of the Coosa, a quick-witted volunteer was pushing forward on his own account to reach Rome first with the warning.

John H. Wisdom, forty-three-year-old rural mail carrier, returning from his rounds, drove up to the east bank of the Coosa River at 3:30 in the afternoon Saturday, to find the ferryboat (his own property, incidentally) sunk, and Gadsden, on the far side of the stream, in possession of Streight's raiders.

Hallooing across the river to a neighbor to tell his family that he was riding on to warn Rome of the approach of the Yankees, he turned his mail-driver's buggy and started on a ride of sixty-seven miles. Two hours later the approach of darkness found Wisdom and his rig twenty-two miles away at Gnatville. There the Widow Hanks undertook to care for his worn-out horse and to lend him a lame pony, the only mount she had, on condition that he ride it no farther than Goshen, five miles away, where he hoped to be able to get another horse.

At Goshen, twenty-seven miles from the start and forty miles from the finish, Farmer Simpson Johnson let Wisdom have a horse for himself and sent his son along on another, to bring both back. Into the night Wisdom and young Johnson went at a swift gallop another eleven miles to the home of Preacher Joel Weems, at Spring Garden, where after some delay a new horse was had. Eleven miles farther the Weems horse carried Wisdom, on into Georgia, where, near Cave Spring, he left that horse with John Baker, from whom another was borrowed. Twelve miles the Baker horse made, when he too gave out, and, six miles from Rome, was replaced by another for the last lap. Just before midnight Wisdom galloped into Rome with his warning.[27]

At the request of the local authorities he galloped through the streets to sound the alarm and waken the people. "Everybody jumped out of bed and the excitement was great," was the way Wisdom recalled the scene afterward. "A Citizen of Rome," writing in the Rome *Tribune* less than a week later, was stronger in his language. "Tremendous excitement, and be it said to the discredit of some, much liquor was wasted, doubtless to screw up their courage to the fighting point."[28]

When the children heard "The Yankees are coming!" as one mother recalled the events of the night, they "jumped up and got under the bed. . . . There was one little girl who was terribly frightened. She had no idea whether the Yankees were men or horses, or what kind of animals they were. She just knew they were something dreadful."[29]

"Bill Arp" (Major Charles H. Smith), in a nearly contemporary account of the Rome "battle" in the Atlanta *Southern Confederacy*, written in the style of dialect and unorthodox orthography so popular with humorists of the time, says that with the sounding of the alarm, "there were no panik, no skedadlin, no shakin of nees—but one universal determination to *do sumthin*. The burial squad organized fust and foremost and began to inter their money, and spoons and 4-pronged forks, and sich like about the premises."[30]

Having buried valuables in one place, as one Roman lady related, "we would begin to imagine that because *we* knew where these things were, the first Yankee that appeared would know too, and often we would go and take them all up from there and dig another hole and put them in that, so that our yards came to look like graveyards."[31]

Throughout the night and early morning hours, according to Bill Arp's humorously exaggerated account, "reports were brought into these Head Quarters, and all other quarters, to the effeck that 10,000 Yankees were kummin, and 5,000 and 2,000 and any other number; that they were ten miles from town, and 6 miles, and 2 miles, and any other number of miles; that they were on the Alabama Road, and the Cave Spring Road, and the River road, and any other road . . . that they had tuck the Steembote Laura Moore, and Cherokee, and Alfaretta, and any other steembote; that they had shot at a scout and hit him in the coat tail, or his hosses tail, or any other tale. . . . In fak, a man could hear anything by gwine about, and more too."[32]

But despite the intense excitement and real terror in the little city which had never seen a Yankee soldier and, until Wisdom came galloping in at midnight, had no idea there was one nearer than the army lines 'way up in Tennessee, there did begin to emerge a state of defense. There was no organized Home Guard in Rome, but convalescent soldiers turned out from the military hospitals, and citizens, including those from the neighboring country, were mustered with shotguns and squirrel rifles.[33] The main dependence for local defense, however, was upon cotton-bale barricades thrown up across the bridges spanning the Etowah and Oostanaula Rivers, which flow together at Rome to form the Coosa. Two ancient and cranky cannon were resurrected and emplaced so as to sweep the approaches to the bridges, it was hoped, while the roadway planking was covered with straw soaked in turpentine, to be fired if other means of defense failed.[34]

As the critical "Citizen of Rome" remarked, there was enough preparation "to make a pretty formidable fight if they had been under any sort of organization but the organization amounted to as near none as possible." At that, while it would not have withstood an attack pressed home by even a small body of troops, the show of resistance resulting from Wisdom's warning did in fact play a considerable part in the final result of the Streight raid.

Shortly after sunrise on Sunday morning, May third, while Streight was still more than twenty miles to the westward, and just about the time Forrest's men were getting under way to close in for the kill, the advance party of the Union raiders, under Captain Russell, came over the crest of Shorter's Hill, within sight of Rome. Through their field glasses they saw the "fortifications" at the bridges and glimpsed the bustling activity in the town behind them. An old Negro woman, asked if there were any Confederate soldiers around, assured the invaders that the town was "full of sojers!" On the way Captain Russell had captured a garrulous mail carrier who, either believing or seeming to believe that the captain was a Confederate, had freely given him "much valuable information concerning the numbers and disposition of the troops and defenses of the city"—most of which were nonexistent. Captain Russell, therefore, "reconnoitered the defenses and military strength" of Rome, found them "indeed quite formidable," so reported by courier to his commander, and early on Sunday afternoon started back to join the main body.[35]

Meanwhile, at sunrise of Sunday, Forrest and his men, now numbering fewer than 600 after their driving, punishing march all the way from Tennessee, rose from their rest, refreshed, and pushed on to Dykes Bridge. Finding the bridge burned, they forded the Chattooga, holding the ammunition high above their heads as they splashed across, and dragging the two guns of Ferrell's battery across on the bottom of the stream, with long ropes carried across to double teams on the far side—a

155

method of crossing at which they had become adept in their pursuit of Streight across bridgeless streams.[36]

By nine o'clock, but a short time after Streight had ended his all-night march with the halt at Mrs. Lawrence's, Forrest closed on his quarry. Even before Forrest struck, Streight had found it "almost impossible to keep the men awake long enough to feed." When his pickets were driven in, Streight abandoned breakfast for man and beast, and formed line of battle on a ridge a half-mile from the plantation house. "The command was immediately ordered into line," he reported, "and every effort made to rally the men for action, but nature was exhausted, and a large portion of my best troops actually went to sleep while lying in line of battle under a severe skirmish fire."[37]

Sending McLemore to the right with the Fourth Tennessee, or what part of it had managed to stand the pace of the pursuit, and Biffle to the left with the Ninth Tennessee, Forrest and his escort, with a few troops besides, began a demonstration in the center against Streight's line.

His real reliance, though, was not on force with a two-to-one superiority of numbers against him, but on craft. Captain Henry Pointer of his staff was sent forward with a flag of truce to demand immediate surrender "to stop the further and useless effusion of blood."[38]

"Most of my regimental commanders," Streight reported, "had already expressed the opinion that, unless we could reach Rome and cross the river before the enemy came up with us again, we should be compelled to surrender." A council of war was called to canvass the situation.

Streight knew that his men and mounts were "in a desperate condition," with not more than twenty of the animals drawn in Nashville still going, and the men "overcome with fatigue and loss of sleep." He believed, too, that he was "confronted by fully three times our number," a belief which Forrest was doing nothing to dispel.[39] Sergeant William Haynes of the Fourth Tennessee, a young man of mien so solemn and inspiring of confidence that he was known by the nickname of "Parson," captured in the fighting of Saturday and closely questioned by Streight, had assured him that Forrest had with him his own brigade, Armstrong's, Roddey's and one or two other commands which Haynes could not recall.[40] To add to all his other distress, word came to Streight that Captain Russell had been unable to take the bridge at Rome.

"Yielding to the unanimous voice of the regimental commanders," Streight asked for parley with Forrest, and they met in a patch of woods. Even then Streight refused Forrest's demand for surrender unless it could be demonstrated to him that he was indeed faced by a force superior to his own. At this juncture a section of Ferrell's battery, the only artillery Forrest had in reach, galloped up in full sight. When

156

Streight protested against movement of troops nearer than a certain ridge while negotiations were going on under flag of truce, Forrest sent Captain Pointer to order the artillery back. The alert young captain, responding to a covert nod from his commander, enlarged upon the order to such an extent that the same two guns appeared, disappeared and reappeared at so many points as to seem almost a column of artillery.

As Forrest described the scene afterward, he was standing with his back to the guns, while Streight faced them. "I seen him all the time we was talking," Forrest is quoted as having said, "looking over my shoulder and counting the guns. Presently he said, 'Name of God! How many guns have you got? There's fifteen I've counted already!' Turning my head that way, I said, 'I reckon that's all that has kept up.' ..."[41]

As the conference continued, Forrest interspersed his talk with Streight with an occasional order to Captain Pointer for the disposition of some entirely imaginary command. Catching the spirit of the game, McLemore and Biffle, off the flanks, marched portions of their commands around and around the conical hills of that section until the weary and worried Streight, after returning for further consultation with his officers, finally came to the conclusion that the hills and hollows must be filled with armed Confederates.

Toward noon Streight yielded to the desire of his officers to give up the hopeless fight, and agreed to surrender upon condition that all his men be treated as prisoners of war, officers to retain side arms and personal baggage—terms which Forrest was perfectly willing to grant.[42]

Forrest's men, indeed, were in but little better state than those whom Streight was so reluctantly surrendering. Streight's men were asleep in line of battle, it is true, but many of Forrest's were nodding as they stood with bridles in hand at the drooping heads of their horses. Forrest's men had come farther under forced draft, but they had been better handled, with the three opportunities for short rests which had been given them—and they were led by Forrest. But not until the arms were stacked, and Streight's officers and men were separated, with the Confederates interposed between them, could Forrest really breathe easy after his game of bluff.

The prisoners surrendered at Lawrence numbered 1,466. The enlisted prisoners were put in charge of Biffle, whose regiment by that time was reduced to little more than 200 men, and were marched that afternoon to a bivouac halfway to Rome. With the officers in custody, Forrest pushed on to the town, on the way gathering in Captain Russell's force which he met as it marched back from its fruitless dash for the bridge. The addition of Russell's men brought the total bag of prisoners to nearly 1,700, or roughly three times the force Forrest had at hand.

157

Forrest, having sent couriers ahead to Rome with news of the surrender, reached there with the first batch of prisoners about six o'clock on Sunday evening, to be met with an exuberance of gratitude which insisted upon expressing itself, among other ways, in firing a salute from the guns which had been shotted and emplaced to rake the road from Alabama, along which Forrest himself was now coming—without remembering to remove the shot. Only bad aim prevented fatal results.[43]

"I am told that when Forrest entered Rome with his prisoners," Kate Cumming wrote in her journal when she visited the hospitals there three months later, "he was met by the ladies and presented with a wreath of flowers, and the pathway of his gallant army was strewn with them."[44]

"The excitement was worse than any camp meeting you ever saw," one Roman lady said of that evening. "Everybody was flying from one end of the town to the other. Suppers that were just ready to be cooked were never cooked or eaten; there was a general jollification. . . . Every lady insisted on going up and speaking to the General and shaking hands with him and his forces."[45] Another account has it that several young women snipped off locks of his hair, and that had he yielded to the requests of all the ladies who asked for them, he would have been bald-headed.[46]

When Mrs. George Ward went up to speak to the General, carrying her baby daughter, "he took her and kissed her. He told us that his prisoners were coming into town, and he wanted them to have rations. He said, also, that his own men had been riding hard . . . and he wanted something for them to eat at once."[47]

Forrest was ever the quartermaster and commissary, and not even the the exultance of conquest, the vast weariness of the flesh which must have been his on that evening, nor the adulation of the ladies, diverted his mind from the business in hand. Officer prisoners he lodged in the county courthouse, enlisted men in bivouac at the Choice House, site of the present-day principal hotel of the city which, appropriately enough, bears the name "General Forrest."[48]

Heeding Forrest's request for rations for his prisoners and his own men, "everybody went home," Mrs. Ward continued, "and there was just a regular wholesale cooking of hams and shoulders and all sorts of provisions that we had, and everything was sent down to the respective camps. We were quite willing to feed the Yankees when they had no guns"[49]—treatment which Colonel Streight's aide thus acknowledged in his subsequent book: "We remained in Rome until Tuesday morning, May 5, under orders of General Forrest, who, to his credit be it said, furnished us with sufficient rations for our subsistence, and also with comfortable quarters."[50]

Since Streight had cleaned the country of riding stock as he came through, and Forrest had been unable to obtain remounts for such of his animals as were broken down, he reached Rome with fewer than 600 horses. Streight had three times as many horses as Forrest at the time of the surrender. His animals, moreover, had for the most part marched but one, two or three days, and had not accomplished the whole exhausting march from Tennessee, as had Forrest's. Using the best of the captured animals, therefore, to remount those of his own men whose horses were done for, Forrest sent the remainder direct to Chattanooga under escort, with the request to General Bragg that they be returned to north Alabama for distribution among the people from whom they had been taken by the raiders.[51]

Having turned over his prisoners to the troops sent up from Atlanta by the provost marshal, and seen them started for prison on the little Rome railroad on the morning of the fifth, Forrest and his men turned to the business of rest and refitment, and to the enjoyment of Roman hospitality.

A popular subscription to buy a fine horse to be given to the General himself, the Rome newspapers announced, was oversubscribed in an hour or two, when it was found that A. M. Sloan, a local citizen, had anticipated the popular movement by personally presenting the General "his splendid saddle horse, for which he would not on any other account have taken the best negro fellow in the State." The money which had been raised was turned over to the General, therefore, for the benefit of the sick and wounded of the command.[52]

Plans were announced, also, for a great picnic for "Gen. Forrest and His Brave Men," with appeals to all to come, bringing "sufficient supplies, ready cooked and prepared; bring for 20 men if you can, or for 10 men, or for 5, besides a sufficient supply for your own family which will attend."[53]

But Forrest and his men were not to be there, for on the night of Tuesday, May fifth, only a little more than forty-eight hours after their arrival in Rome, word came that another raiding column had left Tuscumbia, headed toward Jasper and Elyton, site of the present Birmingham. In the early morning of the sixth, therefore, Forrest and his men were in the saddle again, backtracking through Gadsden to meet the new threat.[54] The Romans were left to consume the bountiful basket dinners which had been provided, to observe an official day of thanksgiving and prayer for their deliverance, to start organizing a Home Guard company for future emergencies, and to tell over and over again the stirring story of the Sunday when Streight and his men came to Rome as prisoners, not as conquerors.

CHAPTER XI

RETREAT WITH THE ARMY OF TENNESSEE*

May 5, 1863-July 6, 1863

AT GADSDEN, which he reached on the afternoon of the second day of his hurried march back from Rome, Forrest was met by some of his own scouts whom he had left behind to keep an eye on the movements of Dodge, with the news that he had returned to Mississippi.[1] There being no new raids into Alabama to be repelled, Forrest headed his column back to station in Tennessee by the most direct route, through Decatur.

On the way he was met by orders to send the command on to Spring Hill but to report himself to General Bragg at Shelbyville,[2] a summons due, no doubt, to the fact that Major General Van Dorn had been killed by a local citizen of Spring Hill on May seventh, leaving vacant the command of the cavalry of the Confederate left wing.[3]

Turning the command of the brigade over to Colonel Biffle, Forrest took train on May eleventh at Huntsville, where he was greeted by a turnout of the citizenry and presented with another splendid charger,[4] and whence he journeyed to Tennessee by way of Stevenson and the same Nashville and Chattanooga Railroad which he had so effectively harassed the summer before when it was in Union hands.[5]

Forrest's exploit, small in scale as it was, was resounding through the western South by this time, and was being heard of even in Richmond, as absorbed as the capital was in the great news from Chancellorsville.[6] When Forrest reached Shelbyville on May thirteenth he was received by General Bragg with "unwonted warmth and cordiality," and told that his promotion to Major General would be recommended. "To this, however, Forrest replied," according to the account most nearly contemporary with the facts, "that he preferred the promotion of another officer, whom he suggested, as having more capacity for the functions which properly belonged to the rank of major-general."[7] It is not stated in this account, which was seen and approved by Forrest, but from a letter to Governor Harris of Tennessee from General Gideon J. Pillow it appears that Pillow may have been the officer so suggested.[8]

---

* The field of operations covered in this chapter is shown on the map on page 84.

Although Forrest declined the promotion proffered him—and, as events turned out, never did receive it at the hands of General Bragg—he was sent back to Spring Hill to take over Van Dorn's vacant command. Included in the command were two brilliant young brigadier generals out of the old United States regular army, William H. Jackson and Frank C. Armstrong. Jackson commanded the small division with which he had come up from Mississippi in February. To "balance" this division Forrest organized his own brigade and Armstrong's into another such division, with Armstrong in command. Dibrell and his regiment were transferred to the Armstrong brigade, of which Dibrell became commander, while Starnes was placed in command of Forrest's own Old Brigade.[9] Organization was completed by the assignment of Major John H. Rawle as chief of the artillery, which included Freeman's old battery, now under Captain A. L. Huggins, and the newer battery of John Morton.[10]

Almost as soon as the organization was formed, however, it began to be dissolved—an experience which Forrest was to know time after time. Events in Mississippi called for the return of "Red" Jackson's division to that army, reducing Forrest's force by about one-half.[11]

With the force which remained Forrest ranged wide through the debatable land of the rich Harpeth Valley through the pleasant month of May and into June, with vigilant scouting all along the front and occasional sharp skirmishing. Upon one such occasion, a reconnaissance in force against the Union stronghold at Franklin rather than a mere skirmish, Forrest experienced one of those occasional acts of quixotic generosity between enemies which distinguished the war between the American states, when he mistook a signal flag on the Union fortifications for a flag of truce. He sent in his own flag of truce and, to meet it as promptly as possible upon its return, followed it closely to within pistol-shot range of a hedge behind which a strong Federal force was posted. As he did so, there rose up from behind the hedge a Federal officer who waved him back with the warning exclamation:

"General Forrest! That isn't a flag of truce. It's a signal flag. Go back, sir, go back!"

Raising his hat in polite response to this generous warning, Forrest turned and as quickly as possible removed himself from the immediate vicinity of the Federal guns in Franklin, no doubt with the momentary expectation of feeling between his shoulder blades the bullet of some soldier with a conception of warfare less knightly than that of the officer who extended the warning.[12]

Ten days later, not in battle but in the hall of his own headquarters building, and not from some Yankee gun but from the pistol of one

161

of his own officers, Forrest was to receive his second wound of the war, and the cavalry of the left wing was to miss narrowly the loss of another commander by private assassination.

The transfer to another command of Lieutenant A. Wills Gould, commanding a section of Morton's battery, together with Forrest's blunt refusal to discuss with the young officer the reasons for his transfer, constituted the immediate cause of the attack. Back of that was some dissatisfaction with the Lieutenant on the part of Forrest, as to which there is conflict of testimony. The widely circulated story that Forrest told Gould he was being transferred because he had been repeatedly reported by his battery commander for cowardice, is indignantly rejected by Morton himself, who says that to the contrary he had commended Gould to the General for his courage and competence.[13] Forrest's dissatisfaction sprang, more likely, from either the loss at Day's Gap of the two guns commanded by Gould or from his handling of the guns in the subsequent reconnaissance in force at Franklin.[14]

Whatever the detailed cause may have been, the high-spirited young Lieutenant, brooding over what he deemed an unjust reflection upon himself, sought out the General for an interview and explanation. They met by arrangement early in the afternoon of June fourteenth in the hall of the Masonic Building at Columbia, used by Forrest as his headquarters. The only close witnesses—although their presence was unnoticed at the time—were four little boys of Columbia, tremendously thrilled at the return of the man who had captured Streight, and tagging along as close to him as ever they could, as is the way of boys.[15]

As the two officers stood in the hall Forrest idly twirled a small pocket knife. Lieutenant Gould, standing with his hand thrust in the pocket of a linen duster he wore over his uniform, talked with angry heat until the General curtly closed the interview and started to turn away. As he did so, Gould thrust the pistol he was holding in the pocket of the duster almost against Forrest's left side and fired.

With his powerful left hand Forrest seized and held Gould's pistol hand, while with his teeth he opened the penknife in his right hand and, still holding Gould, stabbed him in the abdomen. At the blow of the knife, Gould jerked away from Forrest and ran.

When a hasty examination of Forrest's wound by the nearest doctor indicated that it might prove fatal, he swore, "No damned man shall kill me and live!" Without waiting for treatment, he broke away from the doctor's office, snatched a pistol from the saddle holster on a horse standing before the door and raged forth, looking for his assailant.

Gould, meanwhile, had run across the Public Square and into a tailor shop, where he fell upon a low bench near the rear door. Two doctors, hastily summoned, had begun to examine his stab wound when Forrest stormed into the front door. As he did so, Gould rolled from his bench and out through the door into an alley behind, where he started running again. There Forrest fired at him and missed, the ball ricocheting and striking one of Armstrong's troopers, mentioned by description only as "a Dutchman belonging to Armstrong's escort," in the fleshy part of the leg. As Forrest started after Gould once more, the Lieutenant fell in a patch of tall weeds behind the stores facing the square. Bystanders believed, and persuaded Forrest, that he was dying.

His rage fading as rapidly as it had flamed, Forrest submitted to treatment of his own wound. When the probe showed that the ball lodged in his side above the hip had touched no vital spot, and the doctors proposed to cut it out, Forrest interrupted them with the impatient exclamation, "It's nothing but a damned little pistol ball! Let it alone, and go get Lieutenant Gould. Take him to the Nelson House and make him as comfortable as you can. Spare nothing to save him. And, by God, when I give an order like that I mean it!"

But Lieutenant Gould was not to be saved, either by the efforts of the doctors or the loving care of the young lady of Columbia to whom he had become engaged to be married when the battery was first stationed there in February. Before his death a few days later, and while Forrest too was still abed with his own wound, the young Lieutenant asked to see the General. Forrest was carried to the hotel, where the hot-blooded and high-tempered officers were reconciled in an affecting scene of farewell.

The affair was a cause of deepest regret to Forrest, as well as to the command. In the biography by Jordan and Pryor, the only account of his career which the General saw and approved, there is no reference whatever to the incident—a significant omission. Even when Doctor Wyeth wrote, thirty-five years later, the story is given without the name of the Lieutenant—not that it was unknown to the author, of course, but as part of the general reticence and hesitation to reflect upon a young man who had paid so fully for his mad rashness.

In Captain Morton's account of the affair there is no such reticence, but rather an attempt to set forth what was in the minds of his lieutenant, whom he considered a courageous and competent officer, and of his general, whom he idolized. Returning from detached service to duty with his battery on the morning of June fourteenth—the day of the tragedy— Morton learned from Major Rawle that the General had ordered Gould's transfer. From Gould, he found that Forrest's action had grown and festered in his mind into a conviction of monstrous and intolerable injustice. Knowing both men, and seeing both points of view, Morton rode from camp into Columbia that morning to see the General, if pos-

163

sible, and attempt to explain the difficulty to the satisfaction of both. Had he succeeded in seeing the General before Gould did, it is altogether likely that he could have averted the needless tragedy.

On June twenty-fourth General Rosecrans started the Union army forward from the lines about Murfreesborough which it had held ever since the great battle at that place nearly six months before. The Union right wing at Franklin and Triune closed in toward the center, while a strong body of infantry, under Gordon Granger, feinted toward the Confederate left center—between Forrest's wing and the main body of the army—to distract attention from the main Union advance around the other flank.

On the morning of June twenty-fifth, therefore, that being the twelfth day after his wound, Forrest left his bed at Columbia and took to the saddle, to march hard eastward through the valley of Duck River toward Leonidas Polk's Confederate infantry corps at Shelbyville.

To the Union commanders then, as so often afterward, it became a matter of moment to know where Forrest was and what he was doing. "No news from Forrest's force yet" was the dispatch from his old antagonist, D. S. Stanley, commanding the Union cavalry, on the night of June twenty-fifth. Twenty-four hours later, Gordon Granger, commanding the Union corps with which the movement on Shelbyville was being undertaken, telegraphed Rosecrans that he "was keeping a portion of the cavalry . . . watching the movements of Forrest, whose whereabouts I am unable to ascertain. He will turn up yet in some unexpected place."[16]

While the Union forces were watching for him, Forrest moved eastward by way of Riggs' Cross Roads, not far from Eagleville,[17] through torrential rains which, as Granger put it, "made the whole country a perfect quagmire." Flooded creeks delayed him half a day on the twenty-sixth, and before he could make contact with the infantry the whole Confederate Army of Tennessee was in retreat, turned out of its long-held lines about Bell Buckle, Wartrace and Shelbyville by Rosecrans' skillfully planned and boldly executed maneuver.

The retreat of the Confederate army began late on the twenty-sixth, when Rosecrans forced Liberty Gap and Hoover's Gap, on the Confederate right beyond the positions of Hardee's infantry corps.[18] That night orders went forward to Polk, commanding the Confederate left, to evacuate Shelbyville, lest his corps should be outflanked and cut off.[19]

Polk's withdrawal started early on the morning of the twenty-seventh, but before the last of his infantry and his long wagon trains were out of the town and across Duck River on the way to Tullahoma, Gordon Granger burst through the Confederate outer line at Guy's Gap, on

164

the turnpike from Murfreesborough, and, meeting "no resistance to speak of," pushed on down the pike for Shelbyville with Stanley's cavalry in the lead.[20]

That morning, also, Forrest came floundering along through the rain and mud, not heading directly for Shelbyville but, as ordered, marching for the turnpike north of that point, to join forces there with the other Confederate cavalry. By midafternoon, as he neared the turnpike, he was met by the sound of firing which by the direction of its drift to the south showed unmistakably which way the fight was going. Armstrong, in the lead of Forrest's column, was pushed ahead to join in, but so rapidly did Stanley's cavalry force the Confederates back toward the environs of Shelbyville, and so difficult was the cross-country movement to intercept it, that Armstrong was never able to come up with the fight.[21]

The Confederate rear guard in Shelbyville consisted of a small cavalry force under Wheeler. Its main job was to hold back the overwhelming strength of Stanley's cavalry and the infantry corps of Granger right behind it, while the Confederate wagon train, miles and miles of it, was dragging through mud almost without bottom and up the long slopes of the single road leading to the plateau on which Tullahoma stands.

Wheeler was expecting Forrest to come by Shelbyville, either to join in the fight there or to retreat by the Skull Camp Bridge across the Duck at that point. After his afternoon of fight in front of the town and in its streets, with repeated charge and countercharge, Wheeler finally decided that Forrest was not coming that way, withdrew his rear guard of some 600 men across the river and was about to burn the bridge, when Major Rambaut, of Forrest's staff, rode up to report that the Forrest command was in sight of the town and hastening on, expecting to cross there.[22]

Back across the river came Wheeler and his second-in-command, Will T. Martin, with a volunteer force of some 400, determined to hold for a while longer the town and the streets leading down to the bridge. A good portion of the men who came back across were out of Russell's Fourth Alabama, which had served under Forrest. One of them was a young private of that regiment, John Allan Wyeth, who never served under Forrest but who that day fought for him and who, long years afterward and after he had become one of the nation's great surgeons, wrote the biography of Forrest to which all students of the man are so deeply indebted.[23]

The fight was not long in coming, a close, hard, hand-to-hand affray, with sabers swinging and the butt-ends of carbines and pistols used as clubs when there was no time to reload. It was a short fight, though, with

165

weight of numbers telling. The blue cavalry rode through and over Wheeler's thin line, and on and over the two light guns which he had brought back across the river. A caisson overturned on the bridge and there were Wheeler and his men, with the bridge blocked and the Union force between them and the river. Some of Wheeler's men scattered up and down the stream to make their escape in the gathering dusk. More were captured. Others, some sixty in number, turned and with Wheeler and Martin in the lead, charged through the cordon of blue-clad troopers between them and the bank, hacked their way through to the precipitous bluffs above the river, spurred their horses over the bluffs at top speed and shot out into the air to fall into the river fifteen or twenty feet below, and there struck out swimming for the other side through a driving shower of lead from the guns of the startled Yankees on the bank above them. Many never made it, although the two generals and more than a score of others did.[24]

Forrest, meanwhile, not knowing of Wheeler's gallant and generous attempt to hold the bridge, and rightly judging from the shift in the sounds of battle that this way of retreat was closed to him, deflected his course to the west of the town, crossed the Duck four miles below in the early evening, and before bivouacking that night—in the rain, again—pushed on five miles beyond.[25]

That night, had they but known it, was one of golden opportunity for the Federal commanders at Shelbyville. At eight o'clock Granger reported that the Confederate wagon train could not be more than nine miles away, moving on "very heavy roads," and that he expected to move within an hour in pursuit.

Men and horses had been "too exhausted to move" that night, however, Granger reported the next morning, while "Forrest pressed around our rear last night, moving eastward. Had I known he was so doing," he added, "I could have thrown my force between the retreating rebel army and his forces, but even then our men and horses were too badly used up to insure any prospect of success."[26]

By the time this dispatch was sent, on the morning of June twenty-eighth, Granger's opportunity was past. Forrest had interposed his force between the wagon train and any chance of effective pursuit. By four o'clock in the afternoon, both wagon train and cavalry rear guard had reached the lines of the main Confederate army at Tullahoma.[27]

By that time, however, Tullahoma itself was rapidly becoming untenable. Manchester, twelve miles to the northeast, had already been occupied by the Union forces the day before—the same day on which Shelbyville was evacuated—and the main Union army was steadily closing up to and beyond that point, while aggressive cavalry columns under Brigadier General Philip H. Sheridan and Colonel John T. Wilder were pushing still farther on, beyond the Confederate right flank, threatening the safety of the bridges on the railroad back to Chattanooga upon which Bragg was absolutely dependent.

Upon the arrival of the Forrest troops at Tullahoma, therefore, they were passed through the town and on out the Manchester road, all in the same drenching rains in which the whole campaign was fought. During thirteen days there was never a day without its downpours, never a time when the soldiers were dry. Through the days men and horses slogged along in the mud. Through the nights, sitting against trees or stretched out on brush or fence rails piled up to keep them out of the water, they napped and shivered in their wet clothes—for in the Tennessee highland country into which the campaign moved the nights even in June have a nip in them. More than one soldier on either side of the campaign has recorded his recollections of its discomforts—not the least of them for mounted men being the saddle galls that came from the long continued chafing of wet leather and wet breeches against wet skin.[28]

On the afternoon of June thirtieth, the second day after their arrival upon the Tullahoma plateau, the Forrest command suffered its greatest single loss of the campaign when, in a small affair of skirmishers on the Tullahoma-Manchester Road, a bullet ended the promising military career of Colonel James W. Starnes, whom Forrest, when raised to divisional command, had selected for the command of the Old Brigade.[29]

That afternoon and night of the last day of June, Bragg gave up Tullahoma and started falling back again, uncertain whether to fight at the crossings of the Elk River, or to fall back twenty miles or so to the foot of the Cumberland Mountain and there make his stand.[30]

Rosecrans' aggressive forces, continuing their pushing around the Confederate right, crossed the Elk well to the north of the Confederate positions on July first. Before the close of that day the commander of the Army of Tennessee decided that neither the line of the Elk nor the Cumberland Mountain could be held and, at 1:30 in the morning of July second, issued orders to fall back across the mountain and even cross the Tennessee River. By six in the morning the columns were on the march again, Hardee's corps heading for the crossing of the mountain at Brakefield Point, Polk's for that at University Place, the location of the infant University of the South.[31]

The work of the cavalry on the retreat was to cover the flanks and hold the rear, first at the crossings of the Elk which had not already been forced, and then to follow on to and over the mountain. By the afternoon of July third, as the long columns of the infantry and wagons wound their way up the roads leading over the crest of the Cumberland

Mountain, the cavalry was being crowded back against its foot, fighting little delaying actions, breaking away to fall back, fighting again, falling back once more.

In the last of these little affairs Forrest, at the rear point of the rear guard, came through the village of Cowan, at the foot of the mountain, on the run. As he and his men fell back, one of the local ladies singled him out for special denunciation. "You great big cowardly rascal," she screamed at him as he retreated past her home, "you big cowardly rascal, why don't you turn and fight like a man, instead of running like a cur? I wish old Forrest was here. He'd make you fight!"[32]

From Cowan, Forrest's men brought up the Confederate rear, rather ineffectually trying to obstruct the road up the mountain by felling trees with the half-dozen axes available. On that day, however, Rosecrans, having outrun his supply arrangements, dropped close and immediate pursuit. He had not brought Bragg to bay for a general battle but in a nine days' campaign he had accomplished the feat of turning him out of the rich territory of Middle Tennessee and causing him to fall back more than 100 miles across the mountain and river.

On the Fourth of July—the same Fourth of July on which Pemberton surrendered Vicksburg to Grant, and on which the armies of Meade and Lee, after three days of battle, lay watching each other from the heights on either side of the little town of Gettysburg—Forrest's men remained on the mountaintop above Cowan, while the main Confederate Army of Tennessee continued its march down the other side of the plateau and through Sweeden's Cove into the Sequatchie Valley. As the army continued its retreat the rear guard followed along, no longer molested by immediate pursuit.

During the next two days the army, and then the cavalry, crossed the broad Tennessee, partly by ferry and partly by marching across the planked-over surface of the railroad bridge at Bridgeport, Alabama, just below the state line.[33] On the night of July sixth, with the last of the command across, the bridge was again burned, as it had been in the first great retreat after the fall of Nashville.

General Bragg was back to the position from which, a year before almost to the day, he had sent Forrest forward across the Tennessee as a prelude to the campaign into Kentucky.

CHAPTER XII

VICTORY WITHOUT FRUITS

July 6, 1863-September 20, 1863

THROUGH six weeks of summer the main armies lay quiet, with the broad current of the Tennessee and the sparsely settled Cumberland Mountain region between them. To General Bragg, still standing on the defensive, the mountains were not a protecting barrier, however, but rather a screen behind which Rosecrans might be shifting his forces to mass for a crossing of the river either above Chattanooga or below—anywhere, indeed, on a front of 150 miles.

On the Confederate left Wheeler's cavalry was detailed to stand watch and ward over the long southwestward reach of the Tennessee from Chattanooga into northern Alabama. At Chattanooga itself, and upstream as far as the mouth of the Hiwassee River, was massed almost all of the Confederate infantry. Farther out to the right came Forrest's cavalry, with its headquarters at the ancient village of Kingston, one-time capital of Tennessee, pleasantly situated where the Clinch River falls into the Tennessee, seventy miles north of Chattanooga and forty-five miles west of Knoxville.

Kingston was the "hinge" between the lines of the two chief Confederate forces in East Tennessee—Bragg's army, with headquarters at Chattanooga, facing west toward Rosecrans, and the corps of Simon Bolivar Buckner, with headquarters at Knoxville, facing north against the anticipated advance of Major General Ambrose E. Burnside's force from eastern Kentucky.

While Forrest's soldiers enjoyed the sport of splashing and swimming in the clear, cool mountain rivers on either side of the camp at Kingston,[1] their General's ever-active brain was turning back to the great river on whose banks so much of his life had been spent. The Father of Waters, in Lincoln's phrase, was flowing unvexed to the sea—a state of affairs which Forrest believed he could change to the advantage of the Confederacy.

On August ninth, in a letter addressed to the Adjutant General of the army at Richmond, and forwarded through military channels, he submitted his plan—that he take about 400 men and one four-gun battery

169

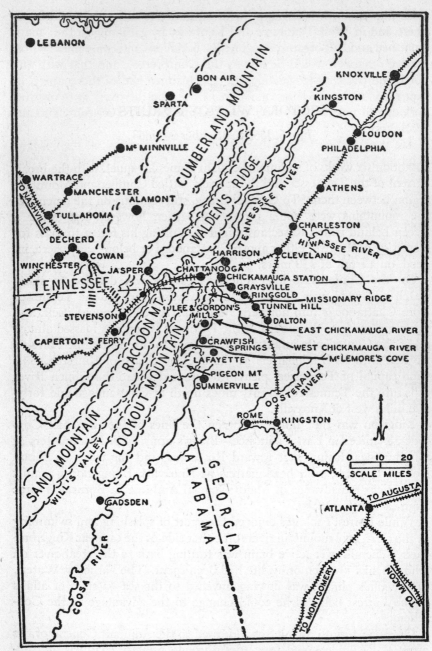

THE CHICKAMAUGA CAMPAIGN

with him to north Mississippi, with authority to raise additional forces there and in West Tennessee and Kentucky by gathering in the "many unarmed and half-organized regiments, battalions and companies" whose service otherwise would be lost to the Confederacy, and that with this force and the knowledge which he and his men had of the country, he would so "move and harass and destroy boats on the river" as to obstruct seriously, if not entirely, the Federal use of the river between Cairo and Vicksburg.[2]

He proposed to take with him his escort company, 60 men, Major Charles McDonald's battalion, 150 men, and Colonel Thomas G. Woodward's Second Kentucky Cavalry, 250 men. The McDonald battalion was a remnant of the original Forrest regiment raised in 1861, and a natural choice for the work. Behind the selection of the Second Kentucky, however, is a story illustrative of the effect upon soldiers of service under Forrest.

Forrest's first contact with soldiers of this organization was at Chattanooga in July 1862, when most of the men whose one-year enlistments were then expiring declined service in Forrest's first brigade, to which the regiment was assigned, and either re-enlisted in other outfits or went home to Kentucky. Colonel Woodward, a West Point graduate, thereupon went back to Kentucky, gathered in old and new men and reformed the command. In the autumn of 1862, having been driven out of Kentucky, the regiment was ordered by the Confederate War Department to be mustered for three years and to become a part of Forrest's second brigade.

"All declined," according to the report of the inspector and mustering officer, "except those whose names are here enrolled"[3]—an action afterward explained by a member of the command as due to the fact that "at that time Forrest was as much feared and despised as he was afterward appreciated and beloved. So the men refused to submit to the terms proposed and the regiment went to pieces."[4]

Colonel Woodward and the remnants remained with Forrest, however, and served through the first West Tennessee campaign in December 1862 to become the nucleus of the regiment now specially selected by Forrest himself for the proposed service along the Mississippi.

As to arms and equipment, Forrest asked for long-range Enfield rifles for the men and four 3-inch rifled Parrott or Dahlgren guns for a battery. For transportation he wanted eight No. 1 horses to each piece and caisson and two wagons for the battery, and one pack mule for every ten soldiers, with 200 rounds of ammunition for each of his 400 men and his four guns.

Through Forrest's letter there runs the pride of a successful com-

171

mander. "I shall leave this department with many regrets," he concluded, "as I am well pleased with the officers in command, and with the division serving under me. I shall especially regret parting with my old brigade; it was organized by me, and a record of its past services and present condition will compare favorably with any cavalry command in the service; and nothing but a desire to destroy the enemy's transports and property, and increase the strength of our army, could for a moment induce me voluntarily to part with them."[5]

Ten days after starting his proposal through regular channels, Forrest sent a copy direct to President Jefferson Davis—another Mississippi River plantation owner—because he had "understood that it was likely" that the original "would not be forwarded by General Bragg, and he believed the matter of sufficient importance to warrant the President's consideration."

General Bragg, however, had forwarded the original communication promptly upon its receipt, and with a most complimentary indorsement:

"I know no officer to whom I would sooner assign the duty proposed, than which none is more important, but it would deprive this army of one of its greatest elements of strength to remove General Forrest."

Before the end of the month, the two copies of Forrest's letter, together with General Bragg's indorsement, were passed upon by the President in Richmond, in the following fifth indorsement:

"The indorsement of General Bragg indicated the propriety of a postponement. Subsequent events have served to render the proposition more objectionable. Whenever a change of circumstances will permit, the measure may be adopted.

"J. DAVIS."

What other "subsequent events" the President may have had in mind do not appear but one such event, no doubt, was the fact that even before Forrest forwarded the second copy of his letter, General Rosecrans had begun the forward movement of the Union Army of the Cumberland.

The general advance, after the pause of six weeks, began on August sixteenth. The first encounter took place on the next day, when Minty's Union cavalry, advancing from McMinnville, engaged near Sparta the outposts of Dibrell's Eighth Tennessee, a regiment which Forrest had sent back across the Cumberland Mountain to its home country for the double purpose of recruiting and remounting and keeping watch on Rosecrans' movements.

172

In running fights along Wild Cat Creek and the little Calfkiller River, Dibrell held his own and inflicted upon Minty losses which were the major part of the total of only about 100 casualties suffered by the whole of Rosecrans' army in the masterly maneuver by which they crossed the Cumberland plateau and the Tennessee River and turned Bragg out of his headquarters city of Chattanooga. Dibrell fell back from the Calfkiller to the western brow of Cumberland Mountain, near Bon Air, to meet reinforcements Forrest was sending him. From this position he reported on the eighteenth, and correctly as the event demonstrated, that Minty's movement was but part of a general advance by Rosecrans upon Chattanooga.[6]

Three days later, on August twenty-first, Rosecrans' advance reached the north bank of the Tennessee opposite Chattanooga. The day, as it happened, was one appointed throughout the Confederacy for fasting and prayer for the success of Southern arms. Observance of the day in Chattanooga, however, was punctuated and interrupted by Northern shell screaming across the river and bursting in the little city.

The shelling of Chattanooga—a token shelling rather than an attack—was part of the general demonstration by which Rosecrans designed to impress upon Bragg the idea that the Union crossing of the Tennessee was to be above Chattanooga. His real advance, however—though this was not to appear for yet another week—was to be along the railroad line from Nashville, which dips well down into Alabama, in seeking the most practicable passage through the Cumberland range. At Stevenson, Alabama, forty miles southwest of Chattanooga, the line comes within two miles of the Tennessee River, turns northeastward and follows upstream to a crossing at Bridgeport, thirty miles below Chattanooga and still in Alabama.

While two of Rosecrans' three infantry corps—Thomas' Fourteenth and McCook's Twentieth—advanced to the vicinity of Stevenson, the third corps, Crittenden's Twenty-first, kept up an ostentatiously active demonstration all along the forty-mile stretch of the river above Chattanooga, as far as the mouth of the Hiwassee. Fires were lighted at wide intervals along Walden's Ridge, the spur range of the Cumberland plateau which closely parallels the course of the river. Bodies of troops, including artillery, were moved about in view of the Confederate pickets. Down along the riverbank there was sawing and hammering of planks and pounding of barrels to sound as if boat-builders were busily at work, preparing for a crossing.

Concerned at what he construed to be preparations for an advance north of Chattanooga, which would have cut between his own force and that of Buckner at Knoxville, Bragg called Buckner to move down closer to him. On August twenty-second Forrest called in the Dibrell regiment and others on advanced outpost duty. Two days later he was ordered to fall back from Kingston to join the concentration of Buckner's force at Loudon, where the railroad crossed the Tennessee thirty miles below Knoxville.[7]

Meanwhile, 125 miles away to the southwest in Alabama, Rosecrans made his first crossing of the Tennessee River at Caperton's Ferry near Stevenson, on August twenty-ninth, unopposed and almost unnoticed. Not until two days later, indeed, and only after a pontoon bridge had been put across the river at Caperton's, the railroad bridge at Bridgeport had been repaired, and the two corps of Thomas and McCook were on the south bank of the river, was the fact of the crossing reported to army headquarters at Chattanooga.[8]

On August thirtieth, the day after Rosecrans began to cross the Tennessee but before Bragg yet knew of it, Buckner's force, including the cavalry of Forrest, was ordered on south, to cross the Hiwassee River and take position about Charleston, Tennessee, forty miles northeast of Chattanooga.[9]

At that point, orders were received from Bragg on September third, adding to Forrest's cavalry corps the small division of Brigadier General John Pegram, which had been operating in upper East Tennessee under Buckner, and placing Forrest in command of all the cavalry north of Chattanooga.[10]

Among the troops who thus came under his command was a remnant of Morgan's men who had escaped back across the Ohio from his ill-starred raid into the North in July. They had been gathered up, reorganized, remounted and rearmed under the lead of Colonel Adam R. Johnson and Lieutenant Colonel Robert M. Martin—the same two daredevils who had served as Forrest's scouts on the night of the surrender of Fort Donelson. This remnant of "Morgan's men" was to serve with Forrest but a short while—during the Chickamauga campaign—but in that time was to do such service as would lead Forrest to exclaim, "Any man who says that Morgan's men are not good soldiers and fine fighters tells a damn lie."[11]

During the first days of September, while the manipulations of Crittenden's corps north of Chattanooga held Bragg bemused as to Federal intentions, Rosecrans passed without opposition the next natural obstacle in his way—Sand Mountain which, at its northern end, is known locally as Raccoon Mountain. By September fourth, Rosecrans had the two maneuvering corps of Thomas and McCook down from Sand Mountain into Will's Valley, the long narrow trough lying between it and Lookout Mountain.

On that day, being no longer in doubt as to Rosecrans' whereabouts, but still uncertain as to his intentions, Bragg wrote to Lieutenant General Daniel Harvey Hill, who had come out from the East to take over the command of Hardee's old corps, that "we must do something and that soon." The "something" suggested was that Hill, commanding the Confederate infantry north of Chattanooga, should cross the Tennessee and fall upon and crush Crittenden's corps. "By selecting fords," he added, "Forrest promises to cross infantry on his horses."[12]

In the light of the explosive end to personal relations between Forrest and the commander of the Army of Tennessee, to come within the month, it is of interest to note this little additional item indicative of Bragg's rising estimate of Forrest as a soldier. By the end of the Chickamauga campaign, however, Forrest was to grow so outdone with the fatal fumblings of his commanding general that the restraining power of military subordination, never too strong with him in any case, was to give way entirely. It was not that Forrest was inherently insubordinate or intractable—his life-long friendly personal and official relations with his subsequent commanders such as Stephen Lee, Dabney Maury and Richard Taylor show the contrary—but that he was intolerant and impatient at what seemed to him to be official incompetence and stupidity, regardless of rank.

When Bragg wrote Hill on September fourth, he thought that the Union troops already across the Tennessee would move southwest down Will's Valley, heading for Gadsden, or perhaps for Rome. Rosecrans did neither, however, but marched east up and across Lookout Mountain— the long, narrow ridge of steep, forested slopes crowned with vertical, palisaded cliffs, which rises abruptly 1,500 or more feet from the bank of the Tennessee River just below Chattanooga, and extends southwestward nearly 100 miles across a corner of Georgia and into Alabama. Thomas' corps breasted the height of Lookout up the zigzag road leading to Stevens' Gap, twenty-five miles below Chattanooga, and McCook's at Winston's Gap, another twenty miles to the south—still without meeting serious opposition.

General Bragg had been neatly outmaneuvered, and once more was exposed to fatal interruption of the communications upon which his army depended—in this case, the State of Georgia's railroad, known as the Western & Atlantic, from Chattanooga back to Atlanta. As it had been when he was faced with a like threat at Tullahoma in July, he had little choice but to give up his headquarters city and again fall back to cover his communications.

This time, however, there was a tremendous difference in the nature and possibilities of the withdrawal—for General Rosecrans, who had come so far so well, had made the mistake of underestimating his enemy, and of scattering his three corps so widely that no one of them was in position to support any other—although Bragg had yet to learn that fact.

Bragg's decision to abandon Chattanooga and move the Army of Tennessee south was announced to his commanders in an order of Sunday, September sixth, to march on Rome, which Bragg still believed was Rosecrans' objective. The march was to be made in four "columns" moving on two roads—Leonidas Polk's and D. H. Hill's commands to march on the more westerly road through La Fayette and Summerville; Buckner's corps and a demi-corps under Major General W. H. T. Walker, made up of reinforcements recently arrived by rail from Mississippi and Virginia, to follow another road some five to ten miles to the east.

The march toward Rome was, in effect, a march by the left flank and in the direction in which Wheeler's cavalry were operating. In the circular ordering the march Forrest was ordered to "move rapidly to the front" of the marching columns, with part of his cavalry, leaving behind a sufficient force to picket the Tennessee River crossings north of Chattanooga, and to bring up the rear of the march, "with all other cavalry marching on different roads to cover all"—an order as difficult to understand exactly as it must have been to excute to the full.[13]

"Promptness," wrote D. H. Hill in the march order to his corps, "is the greatest of all military virtues"[14]—a precept more preached than practiced in the Chickamauga campaign.

Bragg's order, however, found Forrest already in motion. From Ringgold, on the railroad twenty miles southeast of Chattanooga, he sent word ahead to Wheeler, who was farther south, that one brigade had marched for Rome at eight o'clock in the morning of September sixth, while another would be under way at two the same afternoon.[15] The main army, however, did not get started that day. The orders of the morning were countermanded in the afternoon, and new orders were issued on the morning of the seventh for an advance to start "at dark tonight,"[16] but it was not until well into the day of Tuesday, the eighth, that the troops finally cleared Chattanooga, marching for Rome through heat and dust described as "terrible."[17]

During the uncertainties, vacillations and delays in getting the Army of Tennessee started toward Rome, Forrest kept pushing south. As he dispatched Wheeler, a day's march beyond him, on September eighth, he was under "instructions by General Bragg to impede their advance on Rome as much as possible." But, never being a purely defensive fighter, Forrest enlarged upon his instructions with the closing remark that "if the enemy does not advance, we must move on them."[18]

To resolve the uncertainty as to the two columns of blue-clad soldiers which by now were snaking their way down the steep eastern slope of Lookout, Forrest, with the aid of a detail of 300 men from Wharton's command, made a reconnaissance of the enemy's position in the vicinity of Alpine, south of Pigeon Mountain, on the ninth.[19] This, with a like reconnaissance made in McLemore's Cove, north of Pigeon Mountain, revealed to Bragg that Rosecrans, in his haste to get at the rear of his enemy, had dangerously divided and separated his own troops.

To understand the situation which the events of the ninth unfolded to General Bragg, it is necessary to consider the geography of the country just to the east of Lookout Mountain. Closely paralleling the northern end of the mountain, and separated from it by the narrow valley of Chattanooga Creek, is the miniature mountain of Missionary Ridge. South of the Ridge and thirty-five miles below Chattanooga the spur of Pigeon Mountain juts out from Lookout itself, curving east and north before falling away into a low range of hills south of Crawfish Spring— the present town of Chickamauga, Georgia. In the space enclosed between Lookout and Pigeon Mountains, known as McLemore's Cove, there rises the West Fork of the Chickamauga, the little river whose name, in the Indian tongue, was the "River of Death."

On the ninth, Thomas' corps, the center column of the Union army, coming over Lookout by way of Stevens' Gap, was debouching into McLemore's Cove. McCook's corps, the right column, was coming off the mountain away to the south into the Broomtown Valley about Alpine, leaving between the two corps more than twenty miles of distance and the difficult range of Pigeon Mountain. And on this same ninth of September Rosecrans' third corps, under Crittenden, was just coming into evacuated Chattanooga, more than thirty miles away to the north of the Cove.

From wing to wing of Rosecrans' army lay sixty difficult miles—with Bragg's army directly between them and on the one direct road by which the scattered corps might be reunited. Bragg's whole army, indeed, was closer to two of Rosecrans' three corps than any one of them was to any other. The Confederate commander, with his force in hand in the Chickamauga Valley, had but to fall upon the scattered Union corps singly and in detail, and to crush them one by one—such an opportunity as came to no other commander during the whole four years of the war.

General Bragg's failing was not in lack of recognition of his opportunity. Before midnight of the ninth he issued orders for the closing up of the rear columns of the army, preparatory to a concerted attack from north and east upon the advanced elements of Thomas' corps, then moving into McLemore's Cove.[20]

On the same night Forrest's cavalry was pulled out of the concentration of infantry at and north of La Fayette, and assigned to cover the rear against any advance and attack from Crittenden's corps which that day had occupied Chattanooga and moved out to the south. In addition to Crittenden's advance it was reported—though erroneously—that Burnside was coming down from Knoxville. Forrest, therefore, sent Hodge's brigade back toward Cleveland, Tennessee, to watch out for Burnside. Scott's brigade, another one of those recently assigned to Forrest, was sent to Ringgold, to watch for movements of Crittenden down the railroad. John Pegram was left at Pea Vine Church, where he might observe and obstruct Crittenden's advance, whether it came by way of the road through Lee and Gordon's Mills, or by way of Ringgold. Frank Armstrong's brigade, at the request of General Polk, was left with the infantry in the vicinity of La Fayette. Forrest, keeping with him only his escort and the 240 "Morgan men," set up headquarters at Dalton, twenty miles east of La Fayette and on the railroad.[21]

Fighting began on the tenth, when Pegram, out on reconnaissance in the vicinity of the Georgia-Tennessee state line, found himself confronted with Crittenden's infantry coming down the railroad, a day's march to the east of the direct road south from Chattanooga, and by so much the more separated from the rest of Rosecrans' army, and exposed to attack in detail.

Forrest, who came up late in the afternoon to join in Pegram's fight, sent word of what he had found to Polk, commander of the nearest corps of infantry, and also to General Bragg, both of whom had their headquarters in the vicinity of Lee and Gordon's Mills. So assured was Forrest that his message would bring infantry bent on Crittenden's destruction, that he went ahead that night with all advance preparations for an attack early the next morning, including arrangements for passing behind Crittenden and seizing the Red House bridge by which he had come out from Chattanooga.[22]

Getting no word of such an attack, at midnight he rode to headquarters where he found that General Bragg had gone forward to La Fayette, near which point he was concentrating his infantry. Bragg, through that whole day of the tenth, had been trying by his orders to push forward troops from Polk's corps, lying just north of the mouth of the Cove, and from Hill's corps, at La Fayette, for a converging attack upon Thomas' advanced divisions in the Cove.

The reasons for the failure to deliver the attack became matters of controversy between the General and his lieutenants—such controversy as seemed to be an inevitable aftermath of General Bragg's major operations—but whatever the reasons, the attack was not made on the tenth, nor, indeed, was it to be made on the eleventh, despite the General's personal presence on the ground.

Forrest, not being able to get the infantry force needed for an attack on Crittenden's separated troops on the eleventh, went back before daylight and with such of his own force as was available undertook to hamper and delay the Union advance down the railroad in the direction of Ringgold and Dalton.

The indefatigable Wilder, commanding Crittenden's mounted advance, struck Colonel Scott's brigade of Forrest's command at daylight of the eleventh, two miles north of Ringgold. After a sharp skirmish Scott fell back to the little town where, with Forrest himself on the field and in command, the Confederates made a stubborn stand of two hours. A division of Union infantry coming up on the Confederate left, Forrest fell back, fighting, along the railroad, to make another and final stand dismounted and fighting as infantry, at Tunnel Hill, where the welcome reinforcement of Dibrell's brigade came up.[23]

In the fight at Tunnel Hill, in which the Union advance down the railroad was brought to a halt, Forrest received another wound. It was not serious enough to cause him to leave the field or give up his command, or even to be mentioned in the Confederate official reports. By army grapevine, however, news of the wound did get across to the Union side, where it received official, and slightly exultant, mention.[24] The effect of the wound upon Forrest himself, so far as it is recorded, was faintness from pain and loss of blood which caused him, upon the orders of his surgeon, to do what he never did except when sick or wounded— take a drink of whisky.[25]

On this same eleventh of September, the mishandling of the concerted Confederate attack upon his advanced divisions in McLemore's Cove gave warning to Thomas that this enemy whom the Union army had been pressing back for almost a year was turning to fight—and was in position to do the scattered and disjointed Federal forces immense mischief. Thomas pulled his advance back out of the Cove and began to mass his force up Lookout Mountain, through Stevens' Gap.

On the twelfth, while McCook remained where he was away to the south at Alpine, Crittenden was called to move from Ringgold over toward Thomas, involving a march across the valley of the Chickamauga to a point of concentration near Lee and Gordon's Mills—where the Confederates had been two days before. Part of Pegram's division gallantly opposed Crittenden's march in a "fight almost literally hand to hand" at Leet's Tan Yard, whence Pegram sent timely word of his movement to General Bragg.[26]

Bragg had missed his opportunity to crush Thomas in detail in

179

McLemore's Cove but here was another opportunity, to crush Critten-den farther down the valley of the Chickamauga. Twice during the evening of the twelfth, Bragg sent dispatches to Polk, whose troops were nearest Crittenden, to attack him "at day dawn tomorrow." The response was a message from Polk, at 11:00 P.M., that he had taken a strong position for defense and a request for reinforcement. At midnight Bragg renewed his orders for attack, explaining the situation as it was developing, and urging the necessity for "forcing the enemy to fight at the earliest moment before his combinations can be carried out." Buckner was on the way with reinforcements but, he added, Polk "must not delay attack for his arrival, or another golden opportunity may be lost by the withdrawal of our game."27

Orders were issued at midnight for the attack but none came, at "day dawn" or any other time on the thirteenth. The information as to Crittenden's whereabouts given in Bragg's order to Polk was vague and erroneous, the reinforcements under Buckner were recalled before their arrival for no particular reason now appearing, and the paralysis of uncertainty settled on the whole movement, for reasons which were to become part of another of those controversies with his lieutenants which were so customary a part of General Bragg's after-battle routine. Crittenden, unmolested, brushed on past Pegram's little force, picked up one of his own divisions which had come out from Chattanooga on the direct road south, and moved on toward his junction with Thomas in the Cove.28

On the same day, the thirteenth, Rosecrans ordered McCook back from his separated position about Alpine, and started him to join Thomas. Because of the lay of the land and the position of the Confederates on the flank of the direct route, however, McCook did not come straight across Pigeon Mountain but marched back over Lookout, turned north in Wills Valley, and then recrossed the mountain to come down in Thomas' rear—nearly sixty miles over atrocious roads, requiring two crossings of the mountain and three full days of the hardest sort of marching.

Three more days, then, were to be vouchsafed to General Bragg to strike the Union army before it was again fully concentrated—days which he used not for that purpose at all but in confused and pointless marches and countermarches in the area between La Fayette and the railroad, twenty miles to the east.

Up this railroad there had been coming supplies and a trickle of reinforcements from Mississippi and Virginia. Greater things were expected, for on September ninth Lieutenant General James Longstreet had started to Georgia with the famed First Corps of the Army of

Northern Virginia, traveling south through the Carolinas to Augusta, Georgia, and thence to Atlanta and up to the railhead at Ringgold. The total distance was 835 miles—the movement could have been made by the short line of 540 miles through Lynchburg and Knoxville had it been undertaken a few weeks earlier—and the railroads were rickety, but the troops from Virginia were on their way and, all things considered, were making very fair time.

Even without considering them, the anxious Rosecrans had enough ground for anxiety during those mid-September days—the fourteenth, fifteenth and sixteenth—while in desperate haste he was reconcentrating the army he had so lavishly scattered over the Georgia countryside.

The campaign was made not in rain and mud, as had been the case in Middle Tennessee in July, but in a season of dry streams and choking dust. The feet of marching men and of the animals, the wheels of the guns and the creaking wagons, all raised powdery clouds to settle in eyes, nose and mouth, to coat the skin of face and hands, to sift into knapsack and clothing, to make of the long day's march a choking, itching torment.

By the sixteenth, what with his own hard marching and the fumbling indecision of the Confederates, Rosecrans was able to telegraph to his colleague Burnside, supposed to be approaching from the direction of Knoxville, that he had his army massed in the Chickamauga Valley, from fifteen to twenty miles south of Chattanooga, while Bragg's main force was between La Fayette and Ringgold. "It is of the utmost importance," he added, "that you close down this way to cover our left flank. . . . We have not the force to cover our flank against Forrest now."[29]

On the seventeenth the armies were aligned along the Chickamauga— the Union force on the west bank, the Confederates on the east. The Confederate force was the farther north, or downstream, and thus closer to Chattanooga than the Army of the Cumberland. In this position Bragg determined to attack with his whole force, waiting no longer for Longstreet and the rest of the reinforcements from Virginia. The battle order issued on the night of September seventeenth called upon designated troops to cross at the various little timber bridges and shallow fords on the morning of the eighteenth, and, turning to the left, to sweep up the Chickamauga seeking the enemy.[30]

The right element of the Confederate infantry was to be an improvised division under command of Bushrod Johnson, the same with whom Forrest had gone into his first heavy fighting on the Confederate left at Fort Donelson.

Acting under orders previously received, Johnson had started from

181

Ringgold toward La Fayette early that morning and marched for two hours before he received his orders for the day. Countermarching, he went back to Ringgold and there turned west on the direct road to Reed's Bridge, where he was ordered to cross and make a lodgment on the west bank of the Chickamauga.[31]

Four miles west of Ringgold, and at eleven o'clock in the morning of September eighteenth, as Johnson was forming line of battle to meet the enemy reported in front, Forrest came up with the detachment of Morgan's men under command of Bob Martin, "proceeded to the front to develop the position of the enemy, and was soon skirmishing with them"[32]—the opening guns of the great battle.

Through the early afternoon of the eighteenth of September the Confederate right drove Minty's cavalry across Pea Vine Creek, and toward Reed's Bridge. About three in the afternoon Forrest was strengthened by the arrival of John Pegram's division, and the Confederates forced the crossing of the Chickamauga, crowding the defenders of the bridge so closely as to prevent its destruction.

At this juncture Major General John B. Hood, just arrived from Virginia, came up from the railroad to take over the command of the Confederate right. The line pushed on to Jay's Steam Saw Mill, a mile west of the bridge. There, about four o'clock, the infantry began its shift leftward and upstream as ordered, leaving Forrest's men to continue the advance through the gently rolling, forested country between the Chickamauga and the eastern foot of Missionary Ridge.[33] That night the Confederate right, infantry and cavalry, bivouacked on the field of what was to be the greatest of all battles in the West, and the bloodiest of the whole war—a soldier's battle, in which they were to pay with blood for the blunders of their commanders.

Early on the morning of Saturday, September nineteenth, Forrest was ordered to move out toward the right to develop the situation on that flank. What he found was serious. While Bragg had been moving his army southward up the Chickamauga and away from Chattanooga, Rosecrans had been sliding his long line in the opposite direction, northward and toward Chattanooga. All through the night Thomas' and McCook's corps had been on the march. Thomas had moved from the center to pass behind Crittenden and take place as the left corps of the new line. McCook had closed in to take over the positions vacated by Thomas. So now, early in the morning of the nineteenth, when Forrest's men went skirmishing out beyond Jay's Saw Mill, they found the woods, which had contained no more than light cavalry forces the day before, filled with long lines of steady blue infantry. Instead of overlapping the left flank of the Union army as he had planned, General

182

Bragg found it squarely in his front and, indeed, on Forrest's flank, overlapping his own right.

Fighting began near Jay's Saw Mill about 7:30 in the morning, between Forrest's cavalry and John Croxton's brigade of Brannan's division. Half an hour later Van Derveer's brigade of the same division came into the fight, on Croxton's left and well beyond Forrest's right flank. The great battle had been joined, not where or how General Bragg had planned it, but at a point in the Chickamauga woods a good two and one-half miles to the north and east.

Forrest started fighting and sent for help. Polk was asked for the return of Frank Armstrong's division but could send only Dibrell's brigade. Meanwhile Pegram's division were down off their horses and fighting infantry the infantry way, "with such regular lines that those opposed to them supposed they were engaged with infantry."[34]

Dibrell's brigade, which "arrived shortly after we engaged the enemy," Forrest reports, was likewise "speedily dismounted and formed" to fight the infantry way.[35]

Later in the battle D. H. Hill, the same who had made himself unpopular with the mounted services of the army in Virginia by his remark that he had yet to see a dead soldier with spurs on, rode by where Forrest's men were fighting.

"What infantry is that?" he asked.

"Forrest's cavalry, sir," was the reply.[36]

General Hill was seeing a new sort of cavalry. By tradition the cavalry had been the dashing and romantic element of the army. Its task was of the greatest importance—to provide information of the enemy, to screen movements of his own troops, perhaps to pursue a beaten and broken enemy—but the hard, slogging, toe-to-toe fighting and dying was the infantry's trade. When serious fighting began, orthodox cavalry was usually withdrawn to a flank, or perhaps held in reserve to be used in supreme emergency as mounted shock troops thrown against the enemy with weight of horse and man—a use which the breech-loading rifle made dubious and the machine gun was to make impossible. But as they were to prove once more on the field of Chickamauga, there was little of the orthodox about cavalry whom Forrest led.

Finding that messages did not get him the help—infantry help—he must have if the Confederate right flank was to be saved, Forrest left Pegram in charge with orders to hold on no matter what happened. Pegram held on, though it cost the loss of one-fourth of the command that day,[37] until infantry from W. H. T. Walker's division began to arrive—and then he held on still, with the infantry, for there was no letup in the fight.[38]

The swelling fight in an unexpected quarter was drawing to itself units from both armies. On the Union side Connell's brigade of Brannan's division had come into action to Croxton's right, while Baird's division was in still farther to the south. The first infantry reinforcement to come up on the Confederate side, under the guidance of Forrest himself, was Colonel Claudius Wilson's Georgia brigade of Walker's division, which was thrown in on the left of Forrest's dismounted cavalry to meet the lines of blue as they extended to the south.

Forrest, conspicuous in the long linen duster he wore that day, with his sword and pistol belted over it,[39] led the combined force in a forward surge which took them for a quarter of a mile through tangled scrub oak thickets and briery underbrush, "driving the enemy back and capturing a battery of artillery."

Brought up short against a strong Federal infantry line which far overlapped his left, Forrest's mixed command was driven back by a gallant charge of John Croxton's brigade, supported by two of Baird's brigades on his right. Needing more help to sustain his position, again Forrest went back after it, picked up Ector's brigade of infantry on his own responsibility, brought it forward and formed it on the right of Wilson, pushing Pegram and Dibrell still farther out to the right, and kept on with the fighting. "The superior force of the enemy compelled us to give back until reinforced by General Ector's brigade," Forrest reported, "when the enemy was again driven back."[40]

It was an anxious time on the right. Forrest, who that day suffered the loss of the fine horse given him at Rome, stood beside a 6-pounder gun with one wheel gone but still firing, watching narrowly the battle in front while looking back and to the left for the additional reinforcements for which he had sent.[41]

Shortly before midday, they came—Major General W. H. T. Walker, bringing with him St. John Liddell's two brigades, Walthall's Mississippians and Govan's Arkansas troops. The reinforcements went into line on the left of the troops with which Forrest had sustained the morning's fight, and, at 12:15 P.M.,[42] moved forward against an enemy who, for the moment, could nowhere be seen because of the thick underbrush. The impetuous advance of the men under Walthall and Govan struck and overran the first and the second Union lines before them, capturing seven guns.

Coming up against the main positions, however, the Confederates found themselves overlapped by a long line of blue, spitting fire from field gun and musket. From around this line and squarely upon Govan's left flank, came Croxton's brigade which had been withdrawn after the early fighting for rest and replenishment of ammunition. Under the vigor

184

of their charge the Confederates fell back, losing all but one of the guns they had captured but which they had not been able to remove because of the loss of the battery horses. An hour the advance and retreat took, or maybe two—the reports differing, as reports of time in battle so frequently do.[43]

With Major General Walker in general command of the Confederate right flank by noon, Forrest took over the direct command of his own dismounted cavalry and of the two infantry brigades which he had earlier brought forward, and whose "fighting and gallant charges," he reported, "excited his admiration." During the hour or more in which the infantry battle on his left rolled forward and back, Forrest was working his two brigades of dismounted cavalry and Ector's infantry well out to the right of the battle, intent on his favorite tactics of a flank attack. He was, indeed, coming more upon the rear of the Union left than the flank. The charges and countercharges of the morning battle in thick woods in much of which no man could see fifty yards ahead, had brought about a quarter-turn change of direction, so that Colonel Ferdinand Van Derveer's brigade, still forming the left of Rosecrans' line, now faced south instead of east.

About one o'clock, or it may have been half an hour after that, such being the uncertainties of time in battle, Van Derveer discovered his danger, and whirled about to meet it—a most difficult movement, executed with admirable promptness and steadiness—with a well-placed line forming an obtuse angle opening toward the Confederate advance. Into the angle, despite the enfilading fire from its sides, Forrest's men drove their attack.

The advance was made up the slope on whose crest Van Derveer's line was posted, against the direct fire at first of infantry and of six guns. As the Confederates moved on against Van Derveer's left, their own left flank came under the "murderous and enfilading" fire of two regiments forming the right angle of the Union line, and of another section of artillery posted there. And still, as Van Derveer reported, they "steadily moved up" while he sent "messenger after messenger" for reinforcements, which arrived as the Federal guns, double-shotted with canister, and the blue infantry were pouring fire into Forrest's lines from front and flank.

"On came these men in gray in magnificent lines, which showed clearly through the open forest," wrote H. V. Boynton, who commanded the regiment on the extreme left of the Union line, "bending their faces before the sleet of the storm, and firing hotly as they advanced" to within forty yards of the goal, where the artillery "poured a nearly enfilading fire of canister down these long lines, standing bravely there

185

and fighting almost under the mouths of the guns." After the smoke lifted from the third round of this fire, however, "the front was clear of everything but the heaps of dead and wounded, and the work of the day at that point on the Union left was done."[44]

The Union left had had a close call—so close, indeed, that George H. Thomas, in general command on that flank, withdrew the divisions of Brannan and Baird, which had been engaged since early morning, to a defensive position on the rise of ground less than half a mile east of McDonald's, while the battle was taken over by other divisions which had arrived in that quarter—Palmer's, Johnson's and Reynolds'.

Forrest, too, fell back to the neighborhood of Jay's Saw Mill, where the fighting of the morning had started, leaving Van Derveer believing that the force which had come against him and which he had by so narrow a margin turned back was "two divisions of Longstreet's corps, one commanded by General Hood"—no mean impression to have been created by two brigades of cavalry, dismounted, and one of infantry.

As Forrest was making his flank attack against the Union left, and while Walker's brigades were falling back in the early afternoon, Frank Cheatham's strong Tennessee division came into action about one o'clock. Three of his brigades—John K. Jackson's, Preston Smith's and Marcus Wright's—first took over the battle, sweeping forward for nearly three-quarters of a mile and then, assailed on both unprotected flanks, falling back, after a fight of some two hours. Two more of Cheatham's brigades, George Maney's and Otho Strahl's, came forward to take over the positions vacated by Jackson and Smith, but they too were caught in flank and forced back.

"Seeing General Maney's brigade hard pressed and retiring before the enemy," says Forrest, "I hastened to his relief with Freeman's battery of six pieces, dismounting Colonel Dibrell's brigade to support it." When Maney "heard a battery open in rear of the right of my line," he reported, "I hastened to it and found that Forrest had been forced in on my right. General Forrest in person was with the battery, which was firing obliquely to the front and right, and, as I thought, too much in range with two companies of my right regiment. . . . General Forrest was apprised of this fact and requested to oblique his guns more to the right, which he did and continued firing, as he informed me the enemy was certainly approaching in force from that direction. . . . Forrest's battery was some protection to my right flank. . . ."

Under pressure from the left, however, Maney had to fall back. Forrest's guns, under the direction of Major Rawle, "kept up a constant and destructive fire upon the enemy until they were within 50 yards of the guns, getting off the field with all their pieces, notwithstanding the loss of horses. They were gallantly protected by Colonel Dibrell in retiring, who fell back with the line of infantry."[45]

It may have been in this affair—the last active engagement of Forrest on that day—that the General displayed his ever-ready resourcefulness by causing four troopers of his escort to throw the harness of a gun which had lost all its horses over their own saddled mounts, attach the traces and ride off through the woods dragging the guns behind them.[46]

As Cheatham's men were withdrawing in midafternoon, the two brigades under Liddell—Govan's and Walthall's—came again into action on Cheatham's right, but were borne back along with Cheatham's line. They, too, had their difficulties with Forrest's artillery "firing so closely over us as barely to miss the line," until ordered to cease firing.

After Maney's retirement in midafternoon, Forrest reports, "We had no further engagement with the enemy during the evening"—using "evening" in the old Southern sense of "afternoon and evening"—while the battle rolled away to the southward, a disjointed, piecemeal affair with divisions and even single brigades being fed in, virtually without plan or concert, in a succession of isolated and unsupported attacks against the Union positions.[47]

After dark, being still on the extreme right of the Confederate line, holding the road back to Reed's Bridge and the railhead at Ringgold where troops still arriving from Virginia were being unloaded from the cars, Forrest was reinforced by the arrival of Frank Armstrong's brigade, which had been released from service with Polk's infantry.[48]

In the middle of this same night, between the two bloody days of Chickamauga, Bragg took the extraordinary step of reorganizing his army in the midst of battle—dividing the army into two wings, the right under Leonidas Polk, the left under James Longstreet, who had that afternoon arrived from Virginia and who came on the field toward midnight.

Unhappily, brigade and division commanders, and even corps commanders, were not all told of the new arrangement until after the time set for the renewal of the Confederate attack on Sunday, the twentieth—a time set not by the watch but by the sun for "earliest day dawn." The attack was not to be made simultaneously all along the line but was to start on the right, and be taken up successively from right to left at the sound of the guns. The reorganization of the Confederate army in the middle of the night was so radically defective that D. H. Hill, whose corps was on the right and was to initiate the battle at "day dawn" received no notice of the fact until, after long delay, Bragg himself came to that flank and ordered the battle started.

In the golden early hours of the day when, from right to left, the

187

masses of Confederate infantry were supposed to be advancing against the breastworks of logs and dirt which the Union troops had thrown up during the night, nothing worth while was done. The commanders who had received their orders direct from army headquarters were alerted but other commanders rode through the Chickamauga woods looking for orders, couriers were out looking for commanders, and no one knew just what the plan of operations was nor his own part in it.

Forrest, whose cavalry still was the extreme right wing, received no orders or instructions of any sort until after the second day's battle was supposed to have been well under way.[49] There was, indeed, little general direction of the Confederate conduct of the second day's battle, either at the time of starting or during the day, when once more divisions and even brigades were fed into the battle in detail, without concert of action. Battle was not joined until after nine-thirty in the morning, and did not become general along the line until noon—a morning of daylight lost.

Forrest's advance that morning was to the Chattanooga-Rossville-Lee and Gordon's Mills road which was, in general, the front of battle between the two armies, and across the road to the vicinity of the Cloud house and spring. About eleven o'clock Pegram reported from the extreme right that the Union reserve corps was approaching. This corps, which had been left behind under Gordon Granger to guard the railroad from Nashville and the river crossings, had come forward to Chattanooga, and on to the gap in Missionary Ridge at Rossville. Now, with sound and soldierly sense, Granger was marching to the sound of the guns.

For two hours in the middle of the day Forrest's full force, fighting again as infantry, and using the eight field guns of Huggins' and Morton's batteries and eight more borrowed from Breckinridge, fended off Granger's advance, forced him to take out precious time to go into line of battle, and to deflect his course westward toward the foot of Missionary Ridge, before finally he was able, at the double-quick, to join Thomas' firm battle line on the horseshoe-shaped heights jutting out eastward from the Ridge, bringing not only a critical reinforcement of 4,000 men but also 100,000 rounds of sorely needed ammunition.[50]

A Federal counterattack drove Forrest's force back, across and away from the road whose use they had successfully denied to Granger earlier in the day, winding up with a destructive artillery duel at short range— the final firing on the Confederate right flank on the bloody closing day of Chickamauga.[51]

More decisive events, however, had taken place farther to the left. The continuing pressure of the Confederate right on Thomas, throughout the battle, had brought from him continued calls for assistance.

Before midafternoon, Rosecrans withdrew Woods' Division from its place in the right wing, and by some strange lapse failed to replace it at once. Into the gap thus left in his line came thrusting the Tennessee division of A. P. Stewart, followed by a column of brigades under Longstreet, prepared to exploit the break in the line in either direction. On his own initiative Longstreet turned to the right, pressed toward the Union left, and started the Union rout of Chickamauga.

The Union right and center melted and broke in flight for Chattanooga, carrying with them in the rush not only the division commanders—including so renowned a fighter as Phil Sheridan—and the two corps commanders, but even the commander of the army, General Rosecrans, and the Assistant Secretary of War, Charles A. Dana, who was there as a special observer for Secretary Stanton. A few brigades maintained their fighting organization and made their way northward to join Thomas, who doubled back part of his troops to face southward to meet the onslaught. The bulk of the Union army outside Thomas' horseshoe lines, however, left the field of Chickamauga, broken and disorganized, in headlong flight back across Missionary Ridge through McFarland's Gap, and so down the valley into Chattanooga.

Long before dark the Union commanders had reached that point, and even Thomas, standing stoutly on the Horseshoe Hill, had begun the withdrawal of his corps through the gap in Missionary Ridge behind him—an orderly withdrawal, however, made with face to the enemy. That night, from Chattanooga, Assistant Secretary Dana opened his dispatch to his chief in Washington with the words, "Chickamauga is as fatal a name in our history as Bull Run."[52]

Dana described the army which came into Chattanooga as a "panic-stricken rabble." Making allowance for the rhetorical flourish of the great editor and the natural impression which the scene he had just witnessed would make on the civilian mind, it still is apparent that fate and the hard fighting of its soldiers had given the Army of Tennessee another opportunity.

CHAPTER XIII

TO NEW FIELDS*

September 21, 1863-November 14, 1863

THE Battle of Chickamauga ended in the triumphant and never-to-be-forgotten shout raised when the soldiers of the right and the left wings of the Confederate army realized in the late afternoon of Sunday, September twentieth, that they had come together as the jaws of a giant nutcracker against the three-sided position held by Thomas—and that, at last and for the first time in major combat, definite and unmistakable victory had come to the far-marching and hard-fighting Army of Tennessee.

To the soldiers bivouacked that night on the field of Chickamauga, there was no doubt of victory and no question that tomorrow would be a day of pursuit. Not even the elation of victory, however, could erase the evidence all around them of the fearful price at which it had been won—a loss in killed and wounded which averaged, for the whole army, more than one man in three. The battle moon shining through the trees cast interlaced shadows upon ground silvered by the first frost of the year and dotted with bodies in all the grotesque poses in which death can strike.

The field was waterless, except for the scant dry-season supply in the wells and springs of the infrequent farm clearings in the forest, and the wounded suffered from thirst as well as chill. At the hospitals, under flickering lamps hung above kitchen tables, the surgeons were at their bloody work. On the sloping ground beneath the windows of a hospital near which Forrest's men bivouacked that night, the arms and legs amputated during the two days of battle lay in a pile twenty feet wide at the base and a dozen feet high—a sight which shocked at least one of Forrest's young soldiers more than all else he had seen on the field of Chickamauga.[1]

Despite the weariness of three days of fighting and three nights of camping on the battlefield—the last two without fires, and with scant food and horse feed—Forrest's men were in the saddle at four o'clock in the morning of Monday, September twenty-first, riding northward toward the gap in Missionary Ridge at Rossville,[2] in pursuit of the retreating enemy.

---

* The field of operations covered in this chapter is shown on the map on page 170.

Riding in the advance with Armstrong, Forrest spied a body of Federal cavalry, to whom he immediately gave chase at the head of some 400 of his own troopers. The Union troops fired one volley and departed in haste for the gap in the ridge. A ball from the volley struck Forrest's horse in the neck, cutting a large artery. Forrest leaned forward, thrust his finger into the hole made by the bullet to stop the spurting blood, and kept up the pursuit without slackening speed. As the pursuit ended, coming out on the point of a spur of Missionary Ridge overlooking the valley in which Chattanooga lies, Forrest withdrew his finger from the wound and dismounted, and the horse fell dead.[3]

The pursuit had been so rapid—it was not yet seven in the morning—that Federal lookouts perched on an observation platform in the tall trees on the spur of the ridge had not had a chance to climb down and escape. Forrest ordered them down, took over a pair of their fieldglasses, climbed up to the lofty perch just vacated and swept his eyes over the whole scene below him.

Across on the west side of the valley towered the wall of Lookout Mountain, ending in the Point at the bank of the Tennessee. On the east side Missionary Ridge stretched away, nearly to the river. To the north, across the river, the long, sharp line of Walden's Ridge closed the vista. And in all the valley thus spread out before him as if in an amphitheater, Forrest saw the feverish workings of what he took to be an army in retreat—certainly an army demoralized, which might be thrown into retreat.

Coming down from his perch, he dictated to Major Anderson of his staff a message which Anderson, using for a desk the flat shield of a stirrup leather stretched taut, wrote out on a sheet of pale-blue notepaper torn from a pocket memorandum book:

"ON THE ROAD, September 21, 1863.

"Lieut. Gen. L. Polk:

"General: We are within a mile of Rossville. Have been on the point of Missionary Ridge. Can see Chattanooga and everything around. The enemy's trains are leaving, going around the point of Lookout Mountain.

"The prisoners captured report two pontoons thrown across for the purpose of retreating. I think they are evacuating as hard as they can go. They are cutting timber down to obstruct our passing. I think we ought to press forward as rapidly as possible.

"Respectfully, &c,

"N. B. FORREST,
"Brigadier-General.

"Please forward to General Bragg."[4]

Subsequent writers, both Federal and Confederate, have said that Forrest was in error in his interpretation of the activities he saw spread out below him in the valley, and that Rosecrans was not preparing to evacuate Chattanooga and retreat. Some of the Federal writers, indeed, go so far as to claim that possession of Chattanooga was the "objective of the campaign," for the possession of which the great battle had been fought—even though Rosecrans had had Chattanooga in his possession ten days before the battle began, and had marched out of it to meet Bragg's army—and that he had no intention of abandoning the town voluntarily. As to the latter point, they are doubtless correct. Rosecrans was busy that morning of September twenty-first, desperately busy, fortifying Chattanooga and its environs with intent to hold the position.

On the Confederate side, when Doctor Wyeth sent General Longstreet a copy of Forrest's dispatch in 1896, the General melodramatically insisted that "it was this dispatch which fixed the fate of the Confederacy." He himself, Longstreet explained, had persuaded Bragg to a movement across the Tennessee above Chattanooga, to march around Rosecrans and cut his communications, when Forrest's dispatch misled Bragg into the idea that Rosecrans would retreat and that Chattanooga would drop into his lap.[5]

The real point of Forrest's dispatch, however, did not lie in the statement that he thought Rosecrans was getting ready to retreat from Chattanooga, but in that characteristic final sentence: "I think we ought to press forward as rapidly as possible."

There was the Forrest method. It was instinctive with him but it might have been taken from the well-nigh perfect prescription for the exploitation of a victory written by General Bragg himself at the conclusion of his official report on the operations of his corps at the battle of Shiloh. That battle, Bragg wrote, taught the lesson

". . . never on a battle-field to lose a moment's time, but, leaving the killed, wounded and spoils to those whose special business it is to care for them, to press on with every available man, giving a panic-stricken and retreating foe no time to rally, and reaping all the benefits of a success never complete until every enemy is killed, wounded or captured."[6]

"I think we ought to press forward as rapidly as possible," wrote Forrest, but no one else seemed to feel that way. Four hours later, at 11:30 A.M., he sent another dispatch to Polk, who was commanding the nearest infantry wing, reporting that the enemy "are evidently fortifying,

192

STREIGHT'S STARTING POINT

Nashville in 1863, from across the Cumberland River in Edgefield. The principal steamboat wharf is at the left.

From *Harper's Weekly*

WHERE STREIGHT LEFT THE RIVER

Transports and gunboats at Eastport, Mississippi, on the Tennessee River below the Muscle Shoals.

as I can distinctly hear the sound of axes in great numbers. The appearance is still as in the last dispatch, that he is hurrying on toward Chattanooga."[7]

Forrest, however, did not merely report the situation. The Dibrell regiment, commanded by Captain Hamilton McGinnis, he sent against the fortifications of the gap at Rossville, with Armstrong and Pegram deployed for advance on both sides of the Rossville road. Resistance at the gap was too strong to be dislodged, but Major McLemore, with the Fourth Tennessee Cavalry, bypassed the defenses and, before being recalled by Forrest, penetrated within three miles of Chattanooga and brought back a full bag of prisoners. Forrest's artillery, also, advanced along the Ridge to a point where they were able to engage the Union batteries in the town.[8]

It was a small-scale operation, however, against the whole Union army, and the precious day, the great opportunity for "pressing forward," was lost. The advance of the army was not ordered until 2:00 P.M., and then not on the direct road toward Chattanooga which Forrest had followed but down the valley to the east of the Missionary Ridge, with Polk's wing to rest that night at Chickamauga Station on the railroad, Longstreet's to the south of that point, and army headquarters at Red House Ford on the Chickamauga.[9]

Word of these dispositions reached Forrest at four in the afternoon, by which time he was "almost beside himself at the delay."[10] Before bedtime he rode back to headquarters at the Red House, interviewed the General and rode back to his post on the Ridge, muttering in his beard, "What does he fight battles for?"[11] It was, in another form, the same query "which all day Monday, 21st, you could hear among the soldiers (the privates), 'Why *don't* we follow our victory?"[12]

The truth is that it was the Army of Tennessee which had won a victory, not its commander. It was not a happy army under Bragg. Its corps and division commanders, or most of them, were in a state of half-suppressed hostility, which flared up in mutual criminations and recriminations after Perryville, and again after Murfreesborough, and was to flare up again more than ever after Chickamauga. Its junior officers reflected the feelings of their immediate commanders, while, as one of them wrote, "none of General Bragg's soldiers ever loved him." By most of them he seems to have been looked on as a savage and irascible tyrant, for whose strictness and severity there was no compensating habit of victory. "Dying on the field of battle and glory," one of them wrote, "is about the easiest duty a soldier has to undergo. It is the living, marching, fighting, shooting soldier that has the hardships of war to carry." Even so, the same soldier added, "more depends on a good

193

general than the lives of many privates. The private loses his life, the general his country."[13]

And on these days after Chickamauga, though few of them knew it at the time, General Bragg's soldiers were seeing the last great opportunity of the Confederacy, purchased with the lives of so many of their comrades, thrown away by the supineness, the fumbling indecision of their general.

Forrest's men were early astir on the morning of Tuesday the twenty-second, and by eight o'clock were lined up along the Ridge, ready for the general advance. After waiting for the army to move and detecting no signs that it was about to do so, Forrest went ahead with what he had, moved down from the heights and drove the Federals northward through the valley to within half a mile of the rapidly growing fortifications. Dibrell's brigade was detached and sent to the left to seize and hold the northern end of Lookout Mountain, where it abuts on the Tennessee River west of Chattanooga—a position which dominated both the river and the railroad by which Rosecrans normally would supply his army. Davidson's and Scott's brigades on the right moved down from the Ridge to close in on the Federal fortifications east of Chattanooga. Forrest himself, with Armstrong's troops, lay athwart the valley south of the town.

About one in the afternoon the first Confederate infantry came into the Chattanooga valley—Kershaw's brigade of McLaws' division, Longstreet's corps. To McLaws, Forrest proposed a joint undertaking against the Union forces but McLaws did not feel that his limited orders for picket duty permitted him to engage in such a venture. Forrest's small cavalry force, therefore, stood in line of battle that night, spread thin on a front extending from the river below Chattanooga at Lookout Mountain to the river above at Silvey's Ford.

Wednesday the twenty-third, and still no relief for the cavalrymen. That morning McDonald's battalion fought for and gained the Point of Lookout, the lofty perch beneath which the whole panorama of the campaign is spread out as on a living map. At last, toward noon of that day—the third after the great victory of Chickamauga—the higher command of the Army of Tennessee began to show a realization of the importance of the positions which Forrest's handful of men were fighting to hold, and started to replace him with infantry. As replaced, the cavalry were ordered into camp at Bird's Mill, near Tyner's Station, east of Chattanooga.[14]

There, on Thursday, Forrest put his men to work to shoe horses, check equipment and cook rations, making ready for the next service. Twenty-four hours later, on the morning of Friday the twenty-fifth, orders came

194

to move out a few miles to Harrison, there to meet a supposed advance of Burnside's corps from the direction of Knoxville.[15]

In less than forty minutes after the order reached Forrest's headquarters the command was on the march, although supplied only for the short move to Harrison and carrying only the ammunition which it had left over after Chickamauga—forty rounds to the man.[16] At Chickamauga Station, a second courier overtook Forrest with new orders to shift his course eastward to Charleston, on the Hiwassee River—a movement which, as things turned out, was to carry him on to within thirty miles of Knoxville.[17]

Following his usual tactics, at Charleston on the morning of the twenty-sixth Forrest sent flanking forces to cross the Hiwassee above and below, while he was to make the direct attack on Federal forces fortifying across the river. While waiting for the flanking parties to make their marches, Forrest himself went ahead and selected positions for his artillery. When the attack came, the artillery was led across the fields at a gallop to the positions selected, and at once opened fire to cover the advance of the horsemen as they splashed their way across the broad but shallow stream, dismounted on the far side and went into action as infantry.[18]

Before the Confederate flankers were able to gain their rear, the Union forces began a retreat—not soon enough, however, to avoid slashing attacks on the flank before they reached the town of Athens fifteen miles beyond. After the fight there, Forrest himself helped to hold one of his wounded soldiers through the agonizing ordeal of amputation, without anesthetic, of a leg.[18a] The retreat continued, with occasional stands, to Loudon. There the enemy crossed the Tennessee and the pursuit ended, with Forrest back where he had been just a month before.

While he was off on this fast-moving side operation against detached Union cavalry forces—Burnside, it developed, was not even thinking of moving his corps down toward Chattanooga—General Bragg was advancing in leisurely fashion to the formal siege of Rosecrans, who had been allowed ample time to fortify himself in Chattanooga. More prompt and vigorous action was not possible, Bragg explained, because of the great weariness of his men. His men were weary no doubt, as were Forrest's. But weariness did not halt men whom Forrest led—even such weariness as that of young Lieutenant Nat Baxter, Jr., of Huggins' Battery, who, riding along sound asleep at the tail of the column on one of the hard marches in East Tennessee, was raked from the saddle by a low branch, and fell to the road without waking while his horse, doubtless asleep also, plodded on behind the battery.[19]

Bragg's lackadaisical following up of the tremendous advantages which his army had won at Chickamauga was not so much due to weariness of men or lack of supplies—of which there were enough in Chattanooga—as to Bragg's own indecision and his excessive preoccupation with quarrels with his subordinates which, as usual, broke out after the battle. With his consuming passion for unloading blame on other shoulders Bragg soon found himself in active and open disagreement with the three lieutenant generals under his command, Polk, Longstreet and D. H. Hill, and with such senior major generals as Buckner, Hindman and Cheatham. After consulting with the other lieutenant generals, Longstreet wrote to the Secretary of War on September twenty-sixth a letter most bitterly critical of Bragg and all his works. ". . . Our chief has done but one thing that he ought to have done since I have joined his army," he said. "That was to order the attack upon the 20th. All other things that he has done he ought not to have done. I am convinced that nothing but the hand of God can save us or help us as long as we have our present commander. . . . It seems that he cannot adopt and adhere to any plan or course, whether of his own or of someone else."[20]

The reference to Bragg's inability to stick to a plan was due, doubtless, to the fact that he had not followed the plan which Longstreet had recommended on the morning after Chickamauga, and which he had understood was to be adopted—although Bragg himself closes his official report of the battle with the statement that "it is hardly necessary to say the proposition [Longstreet's] was not even entertained, whatever may have been the inferences drawn from subsequent movements."[21]

The "subsequent movements" referred to by Bragg were the long raid by Wheeler across the river and the mountains into Middle Tennessee by which it was vaguely hoped to break up Rosecrans' communications. This undertaking was apparently decided on before September twenty-eighth, for on that date, from army headquarters on Missionary Ridge, there went forth to Forrest, "near Athens," a curt and peremptory order, without reason or explanation: "The general commanding desires that you will without delay turn over the troops of your command previously ordered to Major-General Wheeler."[22]

The order, or some communication to the same general effect, must have reached Forrest that day, for from his headquarters "Five Miles from Charleston," he wrote to Wheeler that he was sending to him Davidson's and Armstrong's brigades and retaining Dibrell's and Pegram's.

Explaining that his command had started out under orders to march only as far as Harrison, Forrest added that all his brigades were "without rations, as we did not expect to be absent from our trains but a day or two, and unless they can be supplied they will be in no condition to cross the mountains . . . am satisfied that neither men nor horses are in condition for the expedition. We have had no opportunity of shoeing the horses since the battle of Chickamauga commenced."[23] In that period of ten days Forrest's men and horses had fought their way again to within thirty miles of Knoxville, and were now halfway back to Chattanooga.

On the following day, the twenty-ninth, in a special order from army headquarters Wheeler was "assigned to the command of all the cavalry in the Army of Tennessee, and will proceed without delay to execute the orders previously given."[24]

At one o'clock in the morning of the thirtieth and again at six in the morning Frank Armstrong wrote to his new commander, Wheeler, that "my command is totally unfit to start on any expedition; horses are very much in need of shoeing and my men have had no rations for thirty-six hours, and I can see no prospect of getting any. I am too unwell to start on any expedition across the mountain. I request that you will relieve me from duty with the brigade and allow me to report to General Forrest."[25] On the same day Forrest's aide, Captain Charles W. Anderson, wrote to Major E. S. Burford, Wheeler's adjutant, that the troops were on the way to Cottonport, on the Tennessee River, as ordered, but that they were short of supplies and had no way of getting more, as Forrest's trains were far away at Graysville, Georgia.[26]

When the three brigades—Armstrong's and Davidson's two, under Scott and Hodge—reported on the thirtieth, Wheeler found that they were "mere skeletons, scarcely averaging 500 effective men each. These were badly armed, had but a small supply of ammunition, and their horses were in horrible condition, having marched continuously for three days and nights without removing saddles. The men were worn out, and without rations. The brigade commanders made most urgent protests against their commands being called upon to move in this condition. With this state of things, I allowed the worst horses to be returned to the rear, and, with the remainder, crossed [the Tennessee, on October 1]."[27]

The raid then started lasted but eight days. It opened with a great success on October third, when a wagon train ten miles long was captured in the Sequatchie Valley and nearly 1,000 six-mule wagons were burned and the mules shot or sabered. It carried Wheeler and his men back through the familiar fighting grounds about McMinnville, Murfreesborough, Shelbyville and the Duck River country, but it ended with the near-destruction and substantial loss of Wheeler's command before he was able to recross the Tennessee at the Muscle Shoals. The operation, altogether, resulted in more of loss than gain for the Confederacy and was of no substantial effect on the plans or operations of

Rosecrans' main army in Chattanooga. It was, in truth, not Forrest's sort of operation—for Forrest would never have started on so long and difficult an expedition with a command in such condition.

To Forrest, indeed, the start of the expedition must have been reminiscent of the loose planning of the expedition to Dover and Fort Donelson back in February, as a result of which he had made his vow never to serve again under Wheeler's command. Nor was Forrest the only one who objected. Among his troops there were "prayers and entreaties" against the transfer,[28] and such "fearful discontent" that, according to one young officer, only the imminence of the movement into Middle Tennessee, which made men and officers unwilling to seem to be shirking active operations, was all that "prevented open mutiny of the corps."[29]

In Forrest himself the blow swept away almost, but not quite, all the restraints of subordination to a commander whom he had come to distrust and despise. Accounts of what happened and the exact sequence of events vary and cannot be entirely reconciled, but Forrest wrote a letter of fiery protest, of which no copy seems to have survived but the nature of which can be guessed from Forrest's remark to Anderson, as he finished dictating it, "Bragg never got such a letter as that before from a brigadier."[30]

The letter was followed up with a personal call on the commanding general, a day or two later. This call, as described in Jordan and Pryor's work, which was published in 1868 and approved by Forrest as to accuracy, resulted in assurance "that his old command should be recomposed at the conclusion of Wheeler's expedition." Whereupon Forrest, being virtually without a command or with pressing duties, applied for and received a ten-day leave of absence to go to LaGrange, Georgia, to see his wife for the first time since he had been in Memphis recovering from his Shiloh wound, eighteen months before.[31]

On October fifth, while at LaGrange, he received an order issued almost as soon as he had left the army, taking away the rest of his troops and placing him and them under the direct command of Wheeler. In view of the assurances which he had received and his well-known attitude as to military service under his friend Wheeler, Forrest with good reason took the new order as a direct and personal affront, and simply exploded. The last restraint of military subordination to Bragg was gone.

The detail of just what happened is not entirely clear. The substantial fact of fiery denunciation and blunt defiance of the commanding general by his great subordinate stands out in all accounts—except in the *Official Records*. Jordan and Pryor, in the most nearly contemporaneous account, say that Forrest resigned; that his resignation

198

reached army headquarters while President Jefferson Davis was there trying to iron out the friction between Bragg and his senior generals; and that the President, refusing to consider the loss of Forrest's services, wrote him a gracious autograph letter, declining to accept the resignation and making an appointment to meet him in Montgomery, Alabama, a few days later to discuss future plans.[32]

There is still another story, resting upon the good authority of Forrest's kinsman and chief surgeon, Dr. J. B. Cowan, who wrote it to both Doctor Wyeth and Captain Mathes, whose biographies of Forrest were published at the turn of the century. Cowan, summoned to ride with Forrest to Bragg's headquarters, found his chief grimly silent. Arrived at the commanding general's tent, Forrest strode past the sentry without acknowledging his salute—a circumstance which was so contrary to his usual courtesy in such matters as to attract Cowan's attention. As Forrest entered Bragg rose and offered his hand. Forrest refused the hand and, standing stiff and erect before the general, with the bony index finger of his left hand punctuating his every point with a quick, stabbing motion, unbosomed himself of the bitterness with which he had suffered under Bragg:

". . . You robbed me of my command in Kentucky . . . men whom I armed and equipped from the enemies of our country. . . . You drove me into West Tennessee in the winter of 1862, with a second brigade I had organized, with improper arms and without sufficient ammunition . . . in spite of all this I returned well equipped by captures . . . and now this second brigade, organized and equipped without thanks to you or the government . . . you have taken from me. I have stood your meanness as long as I intend to. You have played the part of a damned scoundrel, and if you were any part of a man I would slap your jaws and force you to resent it. You may as well not issue any orders to me, for I will not obey them, and I will hold you personally responsible for any further indignities you endeavor to inflict upon me . . . if you ever again try to interfere with me or cross my path it will be at the peril of your life."

As the torrent of denunciation poured forth, Dr. Cowan says, Bragg retreated to the rear of the tent behind a small field desk and seated himself in a camp chair. Forrest, when he had said his say, stopped as suddenly as he had begun, turned and stalked out the tent with Cowan behind him, still with never a word from the commanding general.

"Now you are in for it!" Cowan remarked, as the pair rode away.

"No," answered Forrest, "he'll never say a word about it; he'll be the last man to mention it; and, mark my word, he'll take no action in the matter. I will ask to be relieved and transferred to a different field, and he will not oppose it."[33]

Forrest, according to this account, had no thought of resigning, since that would have seemed an attempt to escape responsibility for his outburst.

Doctor Cowan does not date the affair between Forrest and Bragg, but it occurred, no doubt, before the visit of President Davis to the Army of Tennessee in an effort to compose the quarrels between Bragg and his senior officers. His quarrel with Brigadier General Forrest, indeed, while it may have been more direct, personal and violent, must have been in Bragg's mind but a minor affair, when he had already relieved from command his ranking lieutenant general, Polk, and one of his senior major generals, Hindman, and was within a few days to relieve Lieutenant General D. H. Hill as well;[34] when Longstreet and Polk had written Richmond urging his removal from command;[35] and when many of his senior generals had actually joined in a "round robin" to the President urging a new commander for the Army of Tennessee.[36]

To deal with this seething situation on the ground, President Davis arrived by special train from Richmond on the night of October ninth for a visit of five days during which he interviewed various generals.[37] Upon leaving for Mississippi, on October 14, he issued an address to the troops in which, in guarded phrase, he touched upon the troubles of their commander, urging that they "crown" the zeal, gallantry, energy and fortitude which they had shown "with harmony, due subordination and cheerful support of lawful authority."[38]

While with the Army of Tennessee, the President asked General Bragg about Forrest's August proposal that he be assigned to north Mississippi and West Tennessee. In response to his inquiry Bragg advised on October thirteenth that while he had previously declined to approve the transfer, "because I deemed the services of that distinguished soldier necessary with this army," he felt that the request could "now be granted without injury to the public interests in this quarter" and asked "that the transfer be made."[39]

Two weeks later, at the President's invitation, Forrest met him at Montgomery as he was returning from his inspection in Mississippi. He traveled with him to Atlanta, discussing his plans and his hopes. From Atlanta on October twenty-ninth, the President wrote General Bragg, approving Forrest's transfer to Mississippi, and passing on Forrest's suggestion that as a nucleus for his new organization he be allowed to take with him Lieutenant Colonel Woodward's battalion of the Second Kentucky, Major McDonald's battalion of Forrest's own old regiment, and a battery of four steel rifled guns, with Freeman's (now Huggins') or Morton's company to serve the pieces. The President commended the application to General Bragg's favorable consideration, at the same time furnishing a copy of the letter to Forrest.[40]

Forrest's request for troops, modest as it was, was not fully met. In reporting to the Adjutant General in Richmond his change of station, Forrest advised that the Woodward battalion for which he had asked had not been given him. He had been assigned, besides his escort company and Morton's battery, the battalion of Major McDonald, who had since been killed in the disastrous fight under Wheeler at Farmington, Tennessee, and the regiment of Colonel Jeffrey E. Forrest, who, his brother continued, "was, so I have just learned, killed last week near Tuscumbia, Alabama." There is no hint in the terse official dispatch that this Colonel Forrest was his own posthumously born youngest brother, whom he had raised as a son and made into a soldier. The dispatch simply went on to add that "as the regiment lately commanded by Colonel Forrest was composed of Alabama troops, he being killed, it is my impression that they will be unwilling to go and if so I will allow them to remain in General Bragg's department."[41]

Jeffrey, as it turned out, had not been killed but was only wounded and captured, although this was not known at the time of the assignment of troops and his regiment was withheld. Forrest, therefore, had as his entire command McDonald's battalion, with 139 effectives, young John Morton's battery of 67 men, his own redoubtable escort company of 65 men, and his staff of eight—an "army" of 279 effectives and 310 total.[42]

The regiments of the Old Brigade which he had raised in Middle Tennessee just a year before had to be left behind despite protests and petitions of officers and men. The brigade no longer constituted a unit, being scattered among the brigades of Wheeler's cavalry corps, according to special orders of the army issued October thirty-first.[43] Starnes's Fourth Tennessee, now under McLemore, and Holman's Eleventh were together in one of John Wharton's brigades. Woodward's Second Kentucky was in a brigade under John H. Kelly, while the three other regiments—the Eighth Tennessee, now under Daugherty, and Biffle's Ninth and Cox's Tenth Tennessee, together with McKenzie's Fifth Tennessee and the *other* Fourth Tennessee, known as Baxter Smith's or Paul Anderson's to distinguish it from Starnes's—were brigaded under George Dibrell in Frank Armstrong's division. Under Dibrell's command this largest fragment of the Old Brigade, which was again out on picket near Knoxville when Forrest took his leave, continued its service in East Tennessee, in Virginia and the Carolinas until at the very end of all things, along with a remnant of Morgan's men under Basil Duke, it formed the escort for President Davis and his cabinet up to the day of dispersal at Washington, Georgia, on May 5, 1865.

With his new "army" of 300 men, Forrest left the Army of Tennessee and marched to Rome, Georgia. In that beautiful little hill town, where he had last come as the conqueror of Streight, Forrest spent two days fitting his command for the march across the state of Alabama, by way of Talladega and Tuscaloosa, to its new field of operations in Mississippi.[44]

Forrest himself went ahead of his troops by rail through Atlanta and Montgomery to Selma, where he visited the Confederate arsenals in the hope of improving his equipment, and on to Meridian, where he called at the headquarters of General Joseph E. Johnston, commanding the department. There, on November 14, 1863, the General announced in orders Forrest's assignment "to the command of West Tennessee," an area then wholly and to all outward appearances completely within the Union lines.[45]

With something of prophetic vision, however, on November third the Federal commander of the area, Major General Stephen A. Hurlbut, from his headquarters in Memphis had already reported to Grant, by that time in full command of everything in the West, that "it is currently believed that Forrest has superseded Chalmers. If so, there will be more dash in their attacks."[46]

CHAPTER XIV

A GENERAL FINDS—AND MAKES—HIS ARMY*

November 15, 1863-February 12, 1864

THE twelvemonth beginning with his arrival at his new headquarters at Okolona, in mid-November 1863, was to be the great year of Forrest's military life, but its prospects at the beginning were anything but encouraging. He had his own band from the Army of Tennessee, which arrived on November seventeenth with horses—especially those of the artillery—much worn and jaded from the long overland march. He had about 150 men of his brother Jeffrey's regiment, ordered to him from northern Alabama, but indifferently armed and lacking the presence of their commander, who was still suffering from his wounds. He had the brigade of West Tennessee troops under Colonel R. V. Richardson, supposed to be about 1,000 strong and expected to become the nucleus of his new force—which proved to be almost imaginary. Of the nearly 1,000 men on its rolls hardly more than 250 could be mustered, while an inspection showed only 262 rifles, of seven different patterns. Most of his men, the brigade commander explained, having come out of West Tennessee without winter clothing or bedding, had gone home to get these articles, had taken their rifles with them, and had not come back.[1]

Forrest was starting on his new enterprise with little in the way of troops and even less of equipment, but he did have for once a commander willing to give him encouragement and opportunity—Major General Stephen D. Lee, South Carolina-born, West Point-educated, an artillery officer in the old army and now, at the age of thirty, just appointed to the command of the mounted forces in Mississippi. Lee had never met Forrest but as soon as he heard rumors that he might leave the Army of Tennessee he wrote General Bragg to ask for his assignment to Mississippi,[2] and when he learned that the stormy Tennessean was being sent there had hastened to welcome him.

"Whether you are under my command or not," Lee wrote, "we shall not disagree, and you shall have all the assistance and support I can render you. I would feel proud either in commanding or co-operating

---

* The field of operations covered in this chapter is shown on the map on page 103.

with so gallant an officer as yourself and one with such an established reputation in the cavalry service to which I have been recently assigned"—to which expression of esteem the obliging young Lee added a very practical "general order to my staff officers to fill your requisitions as far as practicable and afford you every facility in your new assignment."[3]

Forrest's first assignment was to go find himself an army in West Tennessee and "the Purchase" section of Kentucky—an area bounded on the west by the Mississippi, on the north by the Ohio, on the east by the Tennessee and on the south by the fortified and garrisoned line of the Memphis & Charleston Railroad, along which Sherman had just advanced on his way to reinforce Grant and Thomas at Chattanooga. Besides Union garrisons along the railroad from Memphis to Corinth, and Union gunboats patrolling the rivers, there were heavy fixed garrisons at Memphis and at Columbus, Kentucky, and smaller ones at Fort Pillow, Fort Heiman and Paducah.

The area within this cordon of Federal garrisons "at this time was full of little [Confederate] companies of from ten to thirty men willing to fight, but unwilling to go far from home or into the infantry service."[4] Many of them, indeed, were carried on the rolls of various Confederate regiments as deserters. Forrest's task was to get across the fortified railroad "frontier" into West Tennessee, round up the scattered small commands, enlarge their numbers by recruiting or conscription and bring them out to the Confederate army, to which they otherwise were quite lost.

"To go into West Tennessee with only a few hundred men and they poorly armed," Forrest wrote on November twenty-fifth to his new department commander, General Joseph E. Johnston, "would be rash." Nevertheless, having exhausted all the possibilities of getting more men, more guns and more horses, within a week he was on his way to West Tennessee with but 450 men and two pieces of artillery—the others had been left behind for lack of horses—and entirely without a supply of arms for the men whom he hoped to recruit within the enemy's lines.[5]

The time was to come when Joe Johnston would rate Forrest as the greatest soldier of the war, second not even to Lee or Jackson,[6] but at this time he was so far from recognizing the potentialities in him that he suggested to President Davis the transfer of Major General Wade Hampton from Virginia for the command in northern Mississippi.[7]

With none of this, however, was Forrest concerned as he started for West Tennessee, accompanied by the other cavalry in north Mississippi whom Stephen Lee led against the Yankee-held line of the Memphis & Charleston. As Lee's active demonstrations all along the section from Moscow to Pocahontas drew forces away from Saulsbury, fifty-eight miles east of Memphis, Forrest crossed the "frontier" there on December second and was on his way northward to Jackson, while Lee kept up active operations against the railroad for two days longer both to prevent the garrisons from pursuing Forrest's handful of men and to do such damage as he might to track, bridges and stations.[8]

Forrest's crossing was not unnoticed, for on the fourth Major General Stephen Hurlbut, commanding the Union Sixteenth Corps at Memphis, dispatched Brigadier General A. J. Smith, commanding the garrison at Columbus, that Forrest was across at Saulsbury with from 300 to 500 men.[9] Earlier Hurlbut had relayed to Sherman and Halleck reports that Forrest was going to West Tennessee, with promises that if he did so, he would be followed and pressed.[10] To this report Sherman—who had just joined Grant and Thomas in Chattanooga, preparatory to the great victory over Bragg at Missionary Ridge—contemptuously replied that "Forrest may cavort about the country as much as he pleases. Every conscript they now catch will cost a good man to watch."[11]

By the middle of December, however, this attitude of slightly amused tolerance had begun to change, for Forrest's venture, as its commander wrote to both Lee and General Bragg, was "succeeding beyond my most sanguine expectations." Success was due partly to the advance planning which had sent such men as Colonels Tyree H. Bell and J. J. Newsom into the territory ahead of the expedition, partly to the rallying in of such commands as Colonel W. W. Faulkner's Twelfth Kentucky, which had already been raised on the border of the two states of Tennessee and Kentucky,[12] and partly to Forrest's own vigorous management.

Ever the quartermaster and commissary as well as the field commander, he had hardly set up his headquarters at Jackson before he began rounding up the supplies which were fairly plentiful in West Tennessee—especially beef cattle—and starting them out to the south. To "succeed in raising troops, getting out absentees and deserters from the army, and army supplies and provisions," he reported to Johnston, "two articles are indispensably necessary—they are arms and money; and I hope, general, that you will be able to supply me with both. I have had to advance to my quartermaster and commissary $20,000 of my private funds to subsist the command thus far." For the purchase of horses, wagons and forage he asked that he be sent $100,000 of quartermaster funds, and for the pay of the troops, "many of whom have received nothing for a long time," $150,000 of pay funds.[13]

In dense woods and "bottoms" Forrest set up recruiting camps consisting of the type of shelter which came to be known among the troops as a "shebang," described by Sergeant William Witherspoon as "an oil cloth, seven feet by four, which Uncle Sam furnished all of Forrest's cavalry," stretched over a pole supported on two forked sticks about two feet above the ground. Insofar as his description covers the case, the "shebang" seems to have been the ancestor of the modern pup tent, but many of them were not made of Federal oilcloth but of blankets, or of boughs, planks or anything else handy.[14]

On December thirteenth, ten days after his arrival, Forrest sent out his first new regiment—without arms—under command of Colonel R. M. Russell. While these men safely made their way south, Forrest continued to recruit at the rate of from 50 to 100 men a day, including more than 100 Kentuckians who, having been conscripted by the Union forces in that state, made their escape and joined Forrest.[15]

While Forrest was gathering in his forces Hurlbut, Union commander at Memphis, was preparing to start after him as soon as the rivers in the interior of West Tennessee should fall and the roads should become practicable. "I do not think he will get away," he wrote.[16]

The movement which Hurlbut contemplated called for a column to come down from the north—A. J. Smith's garrison at Columbus had been strengthened for that purpose—at the same time that other columns moved in from the railroad line across the southern border of Tennessee. In addition to the columns which Hurlbut planned to send against Forrest, General Grant, now in command of the whole military area west of the Appalachians, ordered his own chief of cavalry, William Sooy Smith, to gather up a force in Middle Tennessee, Kentucky and northern Alabama and cross the Tennessee River to fall upon him from the east.[17] Sherman, too, had by this time come around to the opinion that a heavy cavalry force should be sent against Forrest to "get on his heels and chase him to the wall," but he doubted that Sooy Smith was the man for the job, deeming him "too mistrustful of himself for a leader against Forrest."[18]

On December eighteenth the concerted movement was ordered—one column under Brigadier General Joseph A. Mower to advance from the southeast at Corinth; another, under Brigadier General B. H. Grierson, from the southwest at La Grange; a third, under Brigadier General A. J. Smith, from the north at Columbus; while from Middle Tennessee Brigadier General William Sooy Smith was to start with still a fourth column, and Brigadier General George Crook from Huntsville, Alabama, with a fifth—altogether nearly 15,000 men to go after Forrest's 3,500, of whom not more than 1,000 had arms. Hurlbut had every reason, apparently, for saying as he did, "I think we shall cure Forrest of his ambition to command West Tennessee."[19]

Forrest, warned by his scouts of what was being planned against him, watched warily and wrote both to Stephen Lee and to Johnston to see what might be the prospects for enough help to enable him to stay where he was. He was "gathering up as rapidly as possible all the absentees and deserters" from the several West Tennessee regiments of infantry in the Army of Tennessee, he said, with intent to "use them until they can be returned to their proper commands." He believed that he could protect himself against any one move but that if there were too many he would "have more than I can manage with the raw and unarmed troops I have."[20] If Lee could move up into West Tennessee, however, he believed that "we can whip anything they may send against us." If not, he knew that "with my force of raw, undrilled and undisciplined troops it will not do for me to risk a general engagement with superior force."[21]

Before Forrest could hear from Lee as to the proposal for a supporting expedition Hurlbut settled the question by advancing so that Forrest knew that with his large numbers of untrained and unarmed men there was nothing for it but to get out of West Tennessee.

Behind him was the force of A. J. Smith, coming down from the north. Ahead of him were Mower's column closing in from Corinth via Purdy, and Grierson's, from La Grange via Bolivar—any one of the three forces far exceeding Forrest's own in the number of armed effective soldiers. Between Forrest and the railroad line, moreover, there were two rivers, the Hatchie and the Wolf, small streams both but swollen with the December rains and bordered by wide, low, swampy bottoms. Once across the rivers Forrest had still to cross the railroad line, along which troops were posted, with trains ready to run either way to intercept him. And to add to all his other difficulties he was encumbered with a wagon train carrying bacon and other supplies, and with a drove of some 200 beef cattle and 300 head of hogs, which he had no slightest intent of abandoning.

Warned by scouts of the close approach of the movements against him, on the morning of December twenty-third Forrest started south, sending word to Chalmers, commanding the Confederate cavalry in northern Mississippi, to ask for a demonstration against the railroad.[22] On the same morning, as it happened, Grierson, commanding the Union forces to the southwest of Jackson, sent a force up from La Grange to Bolivar with orders to scout all crossings of the Hatchie and destroy all means of crossing.[23] Forrest, however, pushed forward an advance detachment under Richardson to reach the crossing of the Hatchie at Estenaula in time to seize the last remaining ferryboat on the river, and in the early morning of the twenty-fourth to cross to the south side.

In the early afternoon of the day before Christmas the two advance detachments met in their first clash, about four and a half miles south of

207

the Hatchie. Richardson's men, being raw and indifferently armed, gave way under attack and were driven back some three miles to the Slough Bridge, where Colonel J. J. Neely had set up a covering line which successfully held off the Federal attack until after the rise of a bright, clear Christmas moon, about 8:00 P.M., when the Federal forces withdrew to Westville, twelve miles west of Bolivar.[24]

On the same day on which the advance detachment was sent forward to hold a crossing of the Hatchie, a second detachment under Lieutenant Colonel D. M. Wisdom was sent to the southeast of Jackson to meet and fend off the Federal column approaching from Corinth. High water had forced this column to swing east and north around the headwaters of the Forked Deer to the vicinity of Jack's Creek, where before daylight of the morning of the twenty-fourth Wisdom's detachment struck them, to start a noisy all-day fight which ended in the withdrawal of the Federal column toward Corinth. After an all-night march of thirty miles Wisdom's men came up with the rest of the command at the crossing of the Hatchie on Christmas morning.[25]

Meanwhile, Forrest had started his main body—some 2,500 men, mostly unarmed, with forty wagonloads of bacon and other supplies and with four-footed rations on the hoof, under command of Colonel Tyree Bell—to follow on to the crossing of the Hatchie. Forrest himself, having seen to all arrangements for getting out everything which could be carried south, left Jackson at six o'clock on Christmas Eve.[26]

By ten o'clock he had come up with Bell's column toiling away at the task of getting men, horses, wagons, cattle and hogs across the swollen, freezing Hatchie with its wide flooded bottoms. Forrest and his men passed on to the advance, where the aggressive Neely reported that the Union forces with whom he had fought earlier in the evening were bivouacked only five miles south of the river. The General and his escort—that amazing company which was so often expected to do, and did, the fighting of a regiment—pushed ahead to attack and drive Colonel Prince's 600 men. The attack was not made in any ordinary formation but in a single line of troopers spread ten paces or so apart, so that the sixty men of the company formed a line more than a quarter of a mile long. With his line so formed and with every junior officer and sergeant instructed to pick up and repeat orders as if he were commanding at least a company in a brigade drill, Lieutenant Nathan Boone, commanding the escort, roared out the order, "Brigade—Charge!" As the orders for the smaller units of the "brigade" rang out, the little command crashed its way through the still-standing dried stalks of a cornfield, keeping up a tremendous racket in the clear, frosty night.[27] So successful was the attack in convincing the Union commander that he was threatened, if not surrounded, by superior forces that he hastily moved again during the night, ten miles farther west to Somerville, which he reached at five o'clock on Christmas morning.[28]

While this Union force sent out to block him was marching away to the west through the night, Forrest went back to the critical crossing at Estenaula, where Bell's men were working back and forth across the dark waters by the ruddy light of fires built along the banks and the gleam of a cold moon shining through the bare branches of the giant hardwoods of the Hatchie Bottoms—an eerie sight for the night before Christmas.

As the new Major General—he had just had word of his promotion to that rank to date from December fourth—watched, the one frail ferry-boat capsized and pitched a wagon and team into the current. Ever ready to "make a hand" in emergency, he was down immediately into the icy stream, armpit deep, trying to cut the mules out of harness and save them. Up on the bank stood a hulking conscript—"big mouthed he was," as a soldier of Forrest's escort remembered the incident, "big-mouthed, stompin' up and down, tellin' everybody that he wasn't goin' to get down in that water, no sir, not for nobody he wasn't." Having completed his emergency job with the mules, the General clambered up the muddy bank, quickly stepped up to the grumbler, grabbed him by the neck and the slack of his pants, heaved him high and flung him into the stream. "And after that," the escort soldier remembers, "that fellow made a pretty good hand."[29]

With everything across the Hatchie by the afternoon of a bright, sunny Christmas day, Forrest's motley column moved on. His way out of West Tennessee, Grierson and Hurlbut confidently expected, would be along the relatively high and dry ground to the east of the headwaters of the Wolf—roughly the same route by which he had gone in.[30] To insure that he would have no choice but to go that way, all bridges across the flooded Wolf were ordered destroyed,[31] while bodies of troops were stationed along the railroad from La Grange, at the headwaters of the Wolf, eastward to Pocahontas on the upper reaches of the Hatchie, with the idea of closing the gap between the two streams. It did seem in the light of all these careful preparations that Brigadier General Tuttle, of the La Grange garrison, was justified in gleefully wiring to Hurlbut, "it looks to me like we will get them sure this time."[32]

Forrest, though, had other ideas. He knew that he was expected to pass out along the line of the Mississippi Central Railroad, or to the east of it, and he knew where the troops were stationed. His scouts reported also the location of three considerable detachments which had been sent north from the line of railroad to intercept him. Two of these detach-

209

ments—the one he had driven on the twenty-fourth and another coming up from the south—he met about nine in the morning of the day after Christmas at New Castle, between Bolivar and Somerville. There, after a morning of maneuvering and fighting during which Forrest ostentatiously displayed unarmed men to build up the impression of strength in his battle lines, the Union forces were routed—or, as it was put by their commander, "were compelled to retire, and, owing to the broken character of the ground, in considerable disorder."[33]

On this day Tuttle at La Grange was wiring the commanders still farther east, at Corinth, that "later information makes it sure that Forrest and Richardson are coming like hell."[34] Actually, however, after the skirmish at New Castle, instead of moving southeast as expected, Forrest turned due west through Somerville, where his precious wagon train and the droves of cattle and hogs were picked up again, and on six miles beyond to Whitehall where camp was made at eight o'clock that night.

From this camp Forrest sent a detachment of 700 men, of whom only fifty were armed, under command of Colonel W. W. Faulkner, to march down the north side of the Wolf River to the very vicinity of Memphis, where they were to seek a crossing of the river and railroad and make their way southward into Mississippi—a seemingly hazardous march which, by creating excitement and dividing attention, was to help Forrest with his main problem.[35]

During the morning of the twenty-seventh—a day during which the bright, sunny weather of the Christmas season turned to torrential, driving rain—Forrest's main column turned left at Oakland to march south in response to news from Lieutenant Colonel Thomas H. Logwood that there was at La Fayette (now Rossville, Tennessee) a bridge across the Wolf. Scouting that way the night before, Logwood and Lieutenant John A. Williamson had learned that the Union forces had not destroyed the bridge as ordered, but had only removed the flooring. The Confederate scouts had, in fact, seen the flooring relaid to permit Union reinforcements to pass north and had seen it again taken up and piled on the south bank of the river under the guns of a small earthwork guarding the bridge and the station on the railroad, which here runs closely parallel to the course of the Wolf.

Tyree Bell, with some 200 armed men—nearly half of all Forrest had—was ordered to push ahead through the rain over the dozen miles to La Fayette, while the rest of the armed men were thrown out as flank and rear guards. Forrest himself brought on the unarmed men, the trains and the herds in the center.

Before noon Bell's advance was on the north side of the Wolf at

La Fayette Station. As Bell's armed men fired their first and only volley, the garrison turned out, saw the swarm of men in sight, failed to see that only those in front had guns and promptly abandoned the work covering the bridge. Confederate troopers catwalked or "cooned" across on the stringers, relaid the floor in a jiffy with the boards so conveniently piled on the south bank, and took up the pursuit of the garrison.[36]

West of La Fayette Station, five miles away at Collierville, there was one Federal force and to the east there were others at Moscow, eight miles away; at La Grange, eighteen miles away, where Grierson had his headquarters; at Grand Junction, where a brigade was stationed with a railroad train held ready for movement; and still more at Pocahontas and Corinth. As Bell approached the station at La Fayette, the operator there got through a message to Grierson before the wires were cut, so that interception of Forrest's crossing was promptly ordered, and Federal troops advanced from both directions by road and by rail toward the point where Forrest was pouring his unarmed men across the Wolf and the adjacent railroad line.

In a rain so hard that, as one of the enemy commanders reported, "it was barely possible to see distinctly anything at a distance beyond 200 or 300 yards," Forrest followed his usual tactics of attack first. He sent most of his armed men against the detachment advancing from the west and drove them back toward Collierville, while the remainder of the men with guns, aided by the slowness and irresolution of the advance from Grand Junction on the east, held the Federal forces back until after dark, which at that season and in that weather came early.[37]

In the meanwhile unarmed men, livestock and trains marched hard for the neighborhood of Holly Springs in north Mississippi. As they marched, Forrest himself and his armed men pushed the simulated attack right up to the fortifications of Collierville to give the impression that they were advancing westward toward Memphis.

About ten o'clock on the night of the twenty-seventh, having thoroughly mystified and misled his enemies, Forrest abandoned his noisy demonstration against Collierville and drew off in the darkness and the rain to follow his precious charges southward. At midnight, two hours after Forrest had marched away, Collierville appealed by telegraph for help in resisting an attack by Forrest and 4,500 men, expected at daylight.[38] The brigade from Grand Junction, under Colonel William Morgan, was turned out again at 3:00 A.M. and plodded on west. The idea was to attack at dawn Forrest's rear as he went against Collierville but Morgan's column did not reach the vicinity of Collierville until eight in the morning, after a wearying, dispiriting march through a night of rapidly dropping temperature.[39]

211

Grierson had estimated the situation correctly at 11:40 p.m. of the twenty-seventh when he wired from La Grange that "Forrest has gone south like hell,"[40] and began to organize troops to take up the pursuit south of the railroad, in the hope—which proved to be vain—of catching up with him before he could cross the Coldwater, the next considerable stream south of the Wolf. Meanwhile, during the same night in which Morgan's men were making their way *to* Collierville, Forrest marched *from* Collierville to Mount Pleasant, across the state line in Mississippi, which he reached at daylight of December twenty-eighth,[41] and from which he marched that day to a camp south of the Coldwater and seven miles west of Holly Springs.

Behind him Forrest left the Federal columns, foot and horse, inconclusively marching and countermarching in the area between the Wolf and Coldwater—even though Colonel Morgan, commanding the infantry brigade from Grand Junction, as early as the twenty-ninth, had mournfully dispatched his superiors that "Forrest is certainly far away"[42]—and quarreling among themselves with charge and countercharge as to who it was that let him get away.[43]

From his camp below the Coldwater Forrest reported briefly on the twenty-ninth to Lieutenant General Leonidas Polk, who had succeeded as department commander early in the month when Joe Johnston left to take Bragg's place in command of the Army of Tennessee. He regretted that he had had to leave behind in West Tennessee about 3,000 men whom he "could not get together in time" to bring out with him. "If arrangements can be made to go back again," he added, "can bring out at least 3,000 men."[44]

To Stephen Lee, his immediate commander, he wrote on the same day that he had brought out about 2,500 men, and that Faulkner had with him 800 more, of whose safe crossing he hoped to hear by the next day—which, in fact, he did, Faulkner having crossed the railroad line that very night at White's Station, halfway between Memphis and Germantown and within less than five miles of the Federal headquarters.[45]

To Lee, Forrest wrote further that "if I could have stayed ten days longer, could have almost doubled the number" brought out. He reported the safe movement of his wagon train and artillery also, despite "such weather and roads" as he had never experienced, but added that his stock was "much jaded and requires rest." For that purpose and for the urgently necessary job of organizing the miscellaneous force with which he had come out of West Tennessee, he suggested his preference for withdrawing south of the Tallahatchie River.[46] To Chalmers, who had moved northward to the vicinity of Germantown to create a diversion in aid of Faulkner's coming out, Forrest sent a request to see him at Holly

Springs, "as I am unwell and much fatigued"[47]—as well he may have been, though it is a note not often found in Forrest's war correspondence.

The projected encampment south of the Tallahatchie was not approved apparently, nor was much account taken of Forrest's fatigue and indisposition, for three days later, on January first, Forrest's headquarters were established at Como Station on the Mississippi & Tennessee Railroad, forty-three miles south of Memphis. There, on the morning of January 1, 1864, Chalmers' troops came in from Tennessee with Faulkner's men, having marched in "the coldest weather ever known in the country the entire command, including artillery, having crossed creeks on ice," many of the men being frozen so stiff that they could not dismount upon reaching Como.[48]

At Como, Forrest set to work vigorously to make a cohesive fighting force of the heterogeneous units who had come with him from West Tennessee. Among the 3,500 men with him were fragments of at least "sixteen different commands, with companies composed of 13 to 35 men each," as Forrest wrote Samuel Cooper, the Adjutant and Inspector General at Richmond, on January 2, 1864. Muster rolls of many of the regiments which had been forwarded to Richmond were "not legal," he added, and "there are no regiments except upon paper. . . . I can see no way of making these troops effective or organizing them, except by an order from the War Department annulling all authorities previously given to raise troops, accompanied with an order to consolidate into full companies and full regiments. . . .

"There are hundreds of officers in West Tennessee," he continued, "with an authority from various colonels, pretending to be raising companies for various regiments; they have collected together or mustered into the service squads of 15 or 20 men; they have no desire to complete a company and never expect to do so, but are using the authority to recruit as a means of keeping out of the service." To correct this situation Forrest recommended revocation of the authorities, which was partially granted by the War Department on January twenty-fourth, and consolidation of the troops into a limited number of organizations, which was authorized by Secretary of War Seddon.[49]

Having gathered up fifty or more Federal prisoners on his way out of West Tennessee, one of Forrest's first acts upon reaching camp in Mississippi was to propose to Hurlbut at Memphis an exchange, rank for rank and man for man, to spare the "fatigue and exposure necessary to send your men to Richmond," and thence to the regular places of exchange. After a correspondence marked with mutual courtesy this practical proposal resulted on January thirteenth in such an exchange being

213

set up for Hernando, although Hurlbut wrote that his orders were such that "with this exchange, I am compelled to close the system."[50]

On January thirteenth Forrest was called to department headquarters at Meridian, Mississippi, for a meeting with Lee and the department commander[51] at which some of his supply, organization and administrative difficulties were dealt with. A new command area was created, "Forrest's Cavalry Department," including all cavalry commands in West Tennessee and in northern Mississippi as far down as a line drawn across the state just to the north of Columbus, Grenada and Cleveland, and arrangements were made to supply Forrest with arms, accouterments and ammunition. From the conference at headquarters Forrest returned to Como where, on January 25, 1864, he issued his General Orders No. 1, assuming and announcing the limits of the new command;[52] No. 2, announcing his staff—principally the same which had served him so well ever since the organization of the Old Brigade in Middle Tennessee in the fall of 1862; and No. 3, announcing the reorganization of the command into four small brigades.[53]

Brigades were to be commanded by Brigadier General R. V. Richardson, who had five regiments and two separate battalions of West Tennessee troops; Colonel Tyree H. Bell, with five regiments of Tennessee troops including the Second Tennessee Cavalry, a veteran regiment commanded by Clark R. Barteau, former teacher and editor, native of Ohio and graduate of a college in that state, who had come South only five years before the war, and whose regiment was transferred to the new command on its own earnest petition;[54] Colonel Robert (Black Bob) McCulloch, with his own Second Missouri, now commanded by his cousin, Lieutenant Colonel R. A. (Red Bob) McCulloch, Faulkner's Kentucky regiment, a battalion of Mississippi cavalry, another of Texans, two Tennessee battalions and a fragment of the Second Arkansas; and Colonel Jeffrey E. Forrest, whose brigade included the troops which his brother had brought with him from General Bragg's army, the Seventh Tennessee, a veteran outfit which now included the company in which both the Forrests had been privates in June 1861, and three regiments and a battalion of Mississippi troops. The McCulloch and Jeffrey Forrest brigades were combined to form a division under Brigadier General James R. Chalmers.

With a command recruited as most of his had been, Forrest was plagued from the start with the problem of surplus officers. Many of those who came out of West Tennessee with him had seen service in the infantry during the first year of the war but had been out of touch with the service since. Now, with the consolidation of fragments of regiments into the comparatively compact organization Forrest was setting up, there simply were not enough places for all the would-be lieutenants and

214

captains and field officers—many of whom had already served in such capacities in other outfits.

To the problem of the officers rendered surplus by reorganization, there was added the problem of the unwilling, or half-willing, soldier. Many of the enlisted men gathered up in West Tennessee were described as "of that class of soldiers who went home on the expiration of the first twelve months of their service, the time of their enlistment, not feeling themselves bound to remain longer."[55] Others had never been in the service, and quite a number did not want to be.

With all the sources of dissatisfaction and with the bitter winter weather and the shortage of warm clothing, arms and munitions,[56] there is little wonder that not a few of the soldiers did undertake to go back to their homes, with or without authority. Absence without leave might almost be called a custom of the Confederate service, and its close kinship to desertion was not apparent to many a soldier.

This disposition to decamp without permission culminated finally early in February, when nineteen of the West Tennessee recruits started home in a body. They were pursued, caught, brought back, tried, and seventeen were condemned to death, with the idea that so flagrant and wholesale a case of desertion should receive nothing less than the most extreme punishment. On Friday, February twelfth, the date set for the execution, Bell's brigade, from which the desertion had taken place, was marched out to a field near Oxford and formed on three sides of a square—the fourth being a line of the condemned, each with his coffin and his grave before him. The petitions for clemency which poured in to Forrest from the citizens—and especially the ladies of Oxford—apparently had left him unmoved. The firing squads marched out, took their places and were just about to receive the order "Fire!" when one of Forrest's staff rode up with a pardon from the General. The brigade, realizing what had happened, broke into a cheer,[57] while men and women ran from house to house in Oxford with the news, lifting the terrible gloom which had hung over the little town at the thought of the mass execution.

"There were no more desertions," one of Forrest's new officers wrote afterward, "and the men learned that General Forrest was not cruel, nor unnecessarily severe, but they also learned that he would not be trifled with. The effect was marvelous. The old soldiers who had served under him laughed and said 'We knew he would do it,' and the recruits said, 'me too.'"[58]

From material which in ordinary hands would have been almost impossibly difficult, Forrest was forging an army—and an army which, within little more than a fortnight after his order of reorganization and

215

less than six weeks after the most of it had come out of West Tennessee, unarmed, unorganized, untrained and not more than half-willing, was to be called upon to meet the test of invasion by a trained, disciplined, well-equipped and confident force of more than double its numbers.

CHAPTER XV

OKOLONA: DEBUT IN VICTORY

January 8, 1864-February 26, 1864

WHILE Forrest still had before him the seemingly impossible task of making an effective fighting force of discordant material and scant resources, Major General William T. Sherman came back to Memphis to resume command of the Union forces along the Mississippi, full of plans for active winter campaigning.

The campaign planned by the ever-active Sherman inaugurated a sort of warfare new to the struggle of the sixties which was to be made famous before the end of that year by the same commander in his march through Georgia—the heavily destructive infantry raid, directed not so much against armies in the field as against the resources and transportation without which armies are helpless.

Sherman's plan for the first operation of the sort, as outlined to Halleck, called for the advance of a column of infantry from Vicksburg eastward along the railroad "to strike Meridian and it may be Selma," with a co-operating cavalry column to move from Memphis southeastward to strike the Mobile & Ohio Railroad and follow that line down to a junction with the infantry at or near Meridian.[1]

Sherman himself was to command the infantry column, made up of troops from McPherson's Seventeenth and Hurlbut's Sixteenth Army Corps. The cavalry column was to be commanded by Brigadier General William Sooy Smith, Grant's chief of cavalry, who had crossed the Tennessee River with five regiments on January 8, 1864,[2] too late to head off Forrest and his unarmed recruits but soon enough, Smith felt, to pursue him. "I have been anxious to attack him [Forrest] at once," he wrote to Grant, "but General Sherman thinks I had better await his movement, and in the meantime collect, organize and supply my command."[3]

The command was to consist of the five regiments which Sooy Smith had brought from Middle Tennessee, a brigade from A. J. Smith's Columbus, Kentucky, garrison, commanded by Colonel George E. Waring, and the cavalry of Hurlbut's corps, commanded by Brigadier General B. H. Grierson—in all, 7,500 men, well mounted, well equipped and well

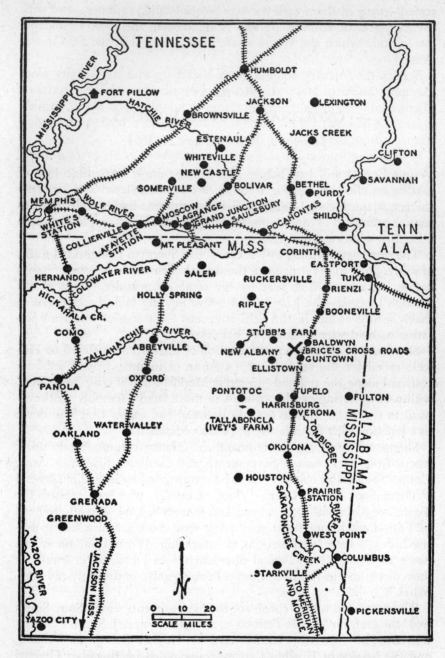

WESTERN TENNESSEE AND NORTHERN MISSISSIPPI

218

armed—many of them with the new breech-loading carbines—and with twenty pieces of artillery. It was to be, indeed, the most formidable cavalry force which the Union armies had yet put into the field in the West.

Besides the infantry column from Vicksburg and the cavalry from Memphis, Sherman planned still a third expedition into the interior of Mississippi, to go by gunboat and transport up the Yazoo River, possibly as far as Greenwood, for the purpose of dividing the defense and drawing attention from the main movements.

In gathering up the force needed for operations of such magnitude, Sherman ordered the recall of the garrisons along the Memphis & Charleston Railroad from Corinth back to Collierville, twenty-four miles east of Memphis, which became the new railhead, where Sooy Smith's cavalry force was to be concentrated.[4]

In final instructions issued as he was leaving Memphis for Vicksburg on January twenty-seventh Sherman turned over to Smith the command of all the cavalry, "the best and most experienced troops in the service," and believed "to be superior and better in all respects than the combined cavalry which the enemy has in all the State of Mississippi." With this force Smith was instructed "to move from Collierville on Pontotoc and Okolona; thence sweeping down near the Mobile & Ohio Railroad, disable that road as much as possible, consume or destroy the resources of the enemy along that road . . . and finally reach me at or near Meridian. . . ." The object in view was to destroy communications "to Meridian and thence eastward to Selma." Smith was instructed also to "take liberally" of forage and standing corn, as well as horses, mules and cattle, and to use mills, barns and the like but "as a rule" to "respect dwellings and families." The idea of the expedition, he was warned, was "celerity."[5]

From the time of his arrival in West Tennessee Smith had been busy in preparation for the move. He had found, as he wrote Grant, that "nearly all the cavalry in the district needed a great deal of shoeing after racing about after Forrest," which was being done "with all diligence."[6] Each man was to carry also an extra set of horseshoes, fitted, and with the necessary nails. Baggage was to be limited to blacksmith's tools, five days' light rations on the person of the soldier, and an additional five days', to be carried along with the ammunition on pack mules,[7] since no wheeled transport other than ambulances was to go with the expedition. Artillery was to be doubled-teamed.[8] All in all, General Smith was well warranted, so far as numbers, equipment and preparations went, in telling Sherman that he felt able "to pitch into Forrest wherever I find him."[9]

Perhaps because of General Smith's somewhat odd middle name there has been some disposition to write of the man himself and his expedition with a disparagingly humorous twist, but he was, in fact, No. 6 in the West Point class of 1853 which included among its high-ranking graduates James B. McPherson, John M. Schofield and Joshua W. Sill, together with Philip H. Sheridan, who was No. 34, and John B. Hood, who was No. 44. That he was a man of capacity and courageous imagination is indicated by his career as an engineer and constructor after the war, which included the building of the world's first all-steel railroad bridge.[10]

His second-in-command, Brigadier General B. H. Grierson, was of an entirely different background and training—a teacher of piano, cornet, clarinet, guitar and voice in the college town of Jacksonville, Illinois, at the outbreak of the war, as well as a band leader, piano tuner, composer and arranger, amateur painter, rhymester and song writer—but he had early shown the dash, boldness and organizing ability which caused Sherman to rate him, by the end of 1862, as "the best cavalry officer I have yet had." To this reputation he added greatly by his successful cavalry raid from Tennessee through the length of Mississippi and into Louisiana in the spring of 1863.[11]

Forrest was neither ignorant nor unmindful of all the organizing and preparing going on in Memphis. As early as January eleventh word came out to him from Captain Thomas Henderson of his scouts that a movement into Mississippi was impending.[12] Word of the threatened raid was at once sent on to Lieutenant General Leonidas Polk, the Confederate department commander, at his headquarters in Meridian.[13] More positive information from Henderson, received on January sixteenth,[14] was likewise passed on to Polk who on the nineteenth informed Governor Charles Clark of Mississippi, for the benefit of the Mississippi state troops.[15]

Before the end of January, and in fact almost as soon as Sherman's plans were reduced to final operations orders, Forrest and Polk were informed that Mississippi was to be invaded from Vicksburg, from the vicinity of Memphis and up the Yazoo,[16] although they did not yet know the exact composition of the columns or the exact direction and object of their movements.[17]

While Forrest was thus warily watching the enemy and busily building an army with which to oppose him, there arrived at General Polk's headquarters an officer from General Joseph E. Johnston with seven long lists of "absentees without leave and deserters from the Tennessee regiments" of Johnston's army "supposed to be in General Forrest's command," to the number of 2,869, seeking Polk's "aid in recovering them" for their proper commands.

220

Polk indorsed the letter on to the harassed Forrest but at the same time told Johnston's agent, Colonel Pressly, that he "did not think this a proper time to attempt to recover these men," partly because of the impending invasion, partly because they had "been so short a time with General Forrest that any attempt to detach them now would result in a general stampede. They would almost all desert and return to West Tennessee." The Colonel might, however, attempt it, Polk added, if he thought best, and so reported to General Johnston on February third. Two days later, on the fifth, Forrest sent to Polk, from Tupelo, this laconic dispatch: "Have telegraphed General Lee to come up. Desire greatly that you meet him here. If matters are not arranged to my satisfaction I shall quit the service."[18]

What "matters" are there referred to does not appear, but whatever they were they seem to have been arranged, for Forrest did not resign and no more was heard at that time of Colonel Pressly's mission to recover absentees from the infantry regiments of the Army of Tennessee.

While Forrest was still vexed with the affair of the absentees Sherman's invasion of Mississippi began on February third, with the simultaneous advance of a column of 20,000 infantry and artillery from Vicksburg to the east, and a gunboat and transport expedition up the Yazoo. So far, however, there had been no advance from the vicinity of Memphis, despite the reports of scouts. At the summons of Leonidas Polk, the department commander, Forrest therefore fell back below the Tallahatchie, so as to put himself in closer supporting distance of the troops in central Mississippi threatened by Sherman's advance from Vicksburg.[19]

With the advance of Union troops southward from Memphis toward Holly Springs, reported on the sixth, and more complete information about the concentration of all the cavalry in West Tennessee and Kentucky about Collierville, which came in on the seventh, Forrest halted the southward movement of his troops—except for one regiment which was sent on to take part in resisting the boats coming up the Yazoo—and waited to see what was coming from Collierville.[20]

At that point General Smith had gathered all his forces, awaiting the arrival of Waring's brigade of 2,000 men, which was making its way slowly and heavily southward from Kentucky across the flooded bottoms of the several small rivers which flow westward into the Mississippi across West Tennessee. Just before leaving for Vicksburg Sherman heard rumors of the delay to Waring's force and sent to the commanding officer at Columbus a blistering blast at the "disgrace to the cavalry arm of the service that they cannot cross a creek," concluding that "of course the use of that cavalry is lost to us in this movement."[21]

As to that, however, Sherman was in error, for General William Sooy

221

Smith, after much consideration and with considerable misgiving, had decided to wait for its arrival before starting into Mississippi. In explaining why he was thus deviating from the plan set for him, Smith again expressed his eagerness to "pitch into" Forrest but added that he knew that it was not Sherman's "desire to 'send a boy to the mill' " and thought it "wisest, best and most promising" to wait for the brigade which was needed to make up his full strength of 7,000 even though he was "deeply chagrined" at the delay.[22]

While Smith delayed his start, Sherman's infantry advance rolled relentlessly on and Polk evacuated Meridian to retire to Demopolis, across the Tombigbee River in Alabama. Sherman reached the appointed rendezvous at Meridian on the fourteenth and at once, while waiting for Smith and his cavalry to come up, began vigorous and systematic destruction. "For five days," he reported, "10,000 men worked hard and with a will in that work of destruction, with axes, crowbars, sledges, clawbars, and with fire, and I have no hesitation in pronouncing the work as well done. Meridian, with its depots, storehouses, arsenals, hospitals, offices, hotels and cantonments, no longer exists."[23]

While the work of destruction was going on, Sherman was wondering, too, what had become of the cavalry upon which he was counting for help in carrying the war on to the Confederate foundries and arsenals at Selma, and perhaps, even, to the seaport of Mobile. "It will be a novel thing in war," the impatient commander noted, "if infantry has to wait the motions of cavalry"[24]—but so it was to be, and moreover to wait in vain.

General Smith—though Sherman did not know this as yet—did not get away from Collierville until February eleventh. His road to Meridian was about 250 miles—say 100 miles farther than Sherman's route. His command, however, was mounted, was "in splendid condition" and "provided with everything and eager for the work." The weather was "beautiful, the roads getting good."[25] In front of him was nothing but Forrest—and Forrest, Sherman had positively assured Smith, "could not have more than four thousand cavalry, and my own movement would give employment to every other man of the rebel army not immediately present with him." Sherman had warned Smith also of "the nature of Forrest as a man, and of his peculiar force," and "told him that in his route he was sure to encounter Forrest, who always attacked with a vehemence for which he must be prepared. . . ."[26] In fact, it is possible, as things turned out, that Sherman may have overdone the business of warning Smith of what he was to meet.

Forrest, in fact, had even less force than Sherman had estimated. With all the territory he had to watch he could muster but 2,500

222

soldiers—mostly new soldiers and not all of them even armed—with which to meet Smith's invading column. From the very beginning of Smith's movement, however, he correctly divined that the movement from Memphis toward Panola was "only a feint," the "real move" being that from Collierville southeastward to Pontotoc and so on to strike the railroad in the rich corn-growing prairie region about Okolona, and thence to a junction with Sherman.[27] To meet such a movement Forrest left no more than a skirmishing and delaying force along the Tallahatchie, and started to shift to the east, both to keep ahead of Smith's anticipated march and to put himself in closer touch with Stephen Lee's forces in central Mississippi.[28]

Smith, starting off as if "resolutely bent on the destruction of the last vestige of Forrest's troublesome little army," crossed from Tennessee into the "rough, hopeless, God-forsaken" country of Tippah County, Mississippi, as one of his brigade commanders described it. "Its hills were steep," he wrote, "its mud was deep, its houses and farms were poor, its streams, torrents of bottomless muddy water, fast swelling from the thaw."[29] The crossing of the Tallahatchie was completed on the seventeenth "without firing a shot," and the column headed for Pontotoc, still without real opposition.

On that day the Confederate Secretary of War, Seddon, took the extraordinary step of sending orders direct from Richmond to Forrest to "leave General Chalmers with his cavalry to check the enemy in North Mississippi and proceed with dispatch to aid General Lee in operations against the enemy in East Mississippi." Lee, however, having been placed in command of all cavalry west of Alabama, dispatched Forrest "to use your discretion as to all movements against the enemy"[30]—in sharp contrast to the attempt to handle by remote control from Richmond the details of a campaign in Mississippi. Forrest, using his discretion, was keeping out of Smith's way, falling back toward the main force as he concentrated his scattered troops.

But notwithstanding the absence of opposition General Smith was not easy in his mind, and grew less so the farther he got from Memphis. Through the nineteenth the only armed opposition he had met was what he called "Gholson's rabble of State troops,"[31] sent out to observe his progress, which he easily brushed aside, but as he got beyond Pontotoc and neared the Mobile & Ohio railroad he kept hearing reports, "quite conflicting," of concentration by Forrest farther down the road of a force which somehow had grown from 4,000 to 8,000 or 9,000—more than equal to his own, at least in numbers. From the outset of the expedition Smith had been apprehensive that Forrest would not fight him close to Memphis but would do so "as low down as Pontotoc, where he could concentrate a larger force and where we would be to some extent jaded and farther from home." And here he was beyond Pontotoc, and still Forrest did not stand to fight! By the night of the nineteenth Smith was worrying no little about the "most disastrous" effects of a defeat so far from home.[32]

And as he entered what Colonel Waring described as the "marvellous prairie region of Northeastern Mississippi, an interminable, fertile, rolling prairie before us in every direction," he had other worries as well. His orders were to devastate as he went along, to the extent of capturing stock, destroying cotton, hides and the immense quantities of corn and meat which had been collected by the Confederate commissaries in that well-favored region, and doing as much damage as possible to the railroad. As the expedition moved along, however, it began to attract and collect "contrabands," until it was plagued by a train of 3,000 of them, with the mules, horses and wagons on and in which they had left the plantations to join the blue-clad column of liberation.[33]

And to add to all of General Smith's other troubles, his orders as to devastation were receiving a too-liberal application at the hands of soldiers or contrabands, or both. "During two days," wrote Colonel Waring, "the sky was red with the flame of burning corn and cotton," all the way down to West Point. The Negroes, "driven wild with the infection, set the torch to mansion houses, stables, cotton gin and quarters," and "came en masse to join our column, leaving only fire and absolute destruction behind them."[34] General Smith, "deeply pained" at the disgrace of "incendiarism of the most shocking kind," ordered the arrest of "any one caught setting fire to property of any kind without orders," and even posted a reward of $500 for the first person detected in such an act.[35] Even so, there was enough authorized and required burning to mark his line of march with fire by night and smoke by day.

On the twentieth, for the first time, Smith began to feel opposition. On that day he called in his wing from Aberdeen, concentrated his column at Prairie Station, fifteen miles north of West Point, and advanced toward that place where, according to the reports he had, Forrest was concentrating.

Forrest, however, was still under the necessity of spreading wide to meet advances on any one of several possible routes.[36] His own headquarters were at Starkville, Mississippi, by the night of the eighteenth with forces spread fanwise in front and on both flanks of Smith's march, all being under orders to avoid anything like a general engagement. Tyree Bell's brigade—commanded by Colonel C. R. Barteau because of the sickness of Bell—was sent clear across the Tombigbee to Columbus to guard against the possibility that Smith might advance down the

THE "FORT PILLOW MASSACRE"

This highly imaginative drawing from *Harper's Weekly* is typical of the pictorial treatment of the fight at Fort Pillow, both at the time and subsequently in even more vivid lithographs, which did much to fix the "massacre" in the public mind as the "atrocity" of the war.

FOUR OF FORREST'S OPPONENTS—1864

Above: Left—Brig. Gen. William Sooy Smith; *Right*—Maj. Gen. Samuel D. Sturgis.

Below: Left—Maj. Gen. Cadwallader C. Washburn; *Right*—Brig. Gen. Benjamin H. Grierson.

eastern side of that stream toward Alabama, rather than follow the railroad on the west side.

As Smith advanced upon West Point on the morning of the twentieth, he was met by Jeffrey Forrest's brigade, which had marched in from Aberdeen at two o'clock that morning,[37] and which fell back skirmishing and avoiding a fight, leading Smith on into a pocket formed by the swampy bottoms of the Sakatonchee and Oktibbeha Creeks on the west and south, and on the east the Tombigbee River, into which they flow. The rest of Forrest's forces, except Bell's brigade already sent across the Tombigbee and the dismounted men held at Starkville, were drawn back across the Sakatonchee, with its steep and high banks and miry bottom, but Forrest left standing Ellis' Bridge and the causeway, three miles southwest of West Point, by which he expected, if opportunity should offer, to recross the stream and take the offensive.

On the morning of February twenty-first General Sherman got tired of waiting for Smith at Meridian, gave up any idea he had of "going on to Mobile or over to Selma" as unwise "without other concurrent operations," and started back to Vicksburg, making what he himself described as "a swath of desolation 50 miles broad across the State of Mississippi, which the present generation will not forget."[38]

On the same morning of February twenty-first, though knowing nothing of Sherman's move back toward his base on the Mississippi, Smith decided that orders or no orders he had gone far enough. He had made nearly two-thirds of his allotted journey without a real fight as yet, but he kept on hearing rumors, most disturbing rumors, of Forrest's growing strength. He found to his right, to his left and to his front, swamps which could be crossed only by narrow defiles and against strong opposition. He heard reports of movements threatening his rear. He was ten days late anyhow and could get no communication through to Sherman, and so he decided to make a feint of a push to the front while his main body and his incumbrances, "contrabands," pack train and captured stock, would start back by the way he had come. He was not going to move his "encumbered command into the trap set for me by the rebels."[39]

That morning Chalmers' division held the crossing of the Sakatonchee, with Jeffrey Forrest's brigade north of the stream and McCulloch's on the south bank, covering and holding Ellis' Bridge. Against them Smith sent his rear guard to deliver a smart two-hour attack while the balance of the force started back to Okolona on the way to Memphis.

Forrest himself, who had been away with the eastern column, came up as the fight was going on to find Chalmers standing on the causeway leading to the bridge. "His manner was nervous, impatient and imperious," said Chalmers, who tells the story of this first fight in which he saw Forrest engaged. "He asked me what the enemy were doing, and when I gave him the report just received from Colonel Duff, in command of the pickets, he said sharply, 'I will go and see myself.'"

Chalmers followed his new commander across "the bridge, about thirty yards long and then being raked by the enemy's fire." As they reached the other bank they met a panic-stricken Confederate soldier, hat, gun, everything thrown away, running to the rear. Forrest jumped from his horse, dragged the fleeing soldier to the roadside, thrashed him with a piece of brush, straightened him up on his feet, faced him to the front and started him back to the battle. "Now, God damn you, go back there and fight; you might as well be killed there as here, for if you ever run away again you'll not get off so easy," he said.[40]

The affair of Forrest and the runaway soldier at Ellis' Bridge became the subject of an illustration in *Harper's Weekly* of "Forrest breaking in a conscript" but it was not his usual method of making soldiers and binding them to himself. His favorite command, "Come on, boys!" was, according to one of his soldiers, the main secret of his success in leading men.[41] "The safest place is over yonder," he would say, pointing toward the enemy. "Come on!"[42] To one group, rejoining just as the fight was coming on, unarmed and asking for weapons, Forrest's command was "Just follow along here, and pretty soon there will be a fight over yonder, and you can get you some guns"[43]—illustrating his original and individual methods of both command and supply.

By the middle of the morning of February twenty-first Forrest had satisfied himself that the attack at Ellis' Bridge was a mere feint to cover a retreat and had begun to make his dispositions accordingly, as the Federal advance guard, now the rear guard, started its withdrawal "in compliance with orders," as its commander reported, although he himself was "thoroughly convinced of two facts, viz., first, that the enemy had no artillery at that place, and, second, that the Federal force was at least 4 to the enemy's 1."[44]

Forrest had commands, small but vigorous, on three sides of Smith's retreating column that afternoon. Bell's brigade, which had been across the Tombigbee at Columbus the day before, was crossing back over that stream and moving northward parallel to Smith's line of march on the east. Chalmers was disposing other forces to prevent Smith's breaking out to the west across Sakatonchee Creek. Only the force which had fought in the morning, however, was close enough for actual contact with the retreating Federal forces.

Forrest realized the overwhelming disparity in force against him, which enforced a certain caution in the advance, but he dispatched Chalmers that afternoon, "I think they are badly scared," adding that he would "follow on as long as I think I can do any good."[45] It had not been his intention, as he afterward reported to Polk, to bring on a general engagement at the crossing of the Sakatonchee, but when he "found the enemy had begun a systematic retreat, being unwilling they should leave the country without a fight," he had ordered the advance, despite the plan to fall back to a junction with Stephen Lee's forces.[46]

"No sooner had we turned tail," wrote Colonel George E. Waring, commanding one of Smith's brigades, "than Forrest saw that his time had come, and he pressed us sorely all day and until nightfall."[47] The retreating Union forces made their strongest stand and hardest fight about four miles north of West Point, taking advantage of a position in a skirt of post-oak timber which could be reached only by a narrow causeway and bridge. To attack such a position Forrest dismounted his men, sent one regiment around to strike the enemy in the rear and threw the rest of the force against their front.

"This was their first fighting under their new commander, Forrest," wrote the historian of the Seventh Tennessee Cavalry (the regiment which then included the company in which Forrest had once been a private), "and his immediate presence seemed to inspire every one with his terrible energy, more like that of a piece of powerful steam machinery than of a human being."[48]

The combined attack caused a hurried withdrawal of the enemy. Forrest's men remounted and took up the pursuit, driving the enemy from several short stands and keeping so close to them that with the coming of night Forrest's men mistook their own General and his escort for a party of the enemy and fired a volley into them, killing one man and putting a bullet through Forrest's clothes.[49] With this near-repetition of the tragedy of Jackson and his men at Chancellorsville, pursuit was called off for the night,[50] with the pursuing troops occupying a Federal campground fourteen miles south of Okolona in which they found much forage and subsistence left by its retreating owners, and even burning campfires and the wood to keep them going, especially grateful on a sharp February night.[51]

The retreating Federal column continued the weary march through the night until 2:00 A.M.,[52] to put ten miles of distance between themselves and their troublesome pursuers before camp was finally made about four miles south of Okolona. Forrest had his men up at four in the morning of February twenty-second and before dawn was on his way after the enemy. Having outdistanced his main body, Forrest and his seemingly tireless escort overtook the Union pickets four miles south of Okolona, and followed them as they fell back through the town to a line of resistance formed a mile or so beyond.

To deliver the attack which the Union line was ready to receive Forrest had with him at the moment no more than his staff and escort company, but looking to the east he spied across the open prairie country which surrounds Okolona another Confederate force—Bell's brigade which its temporary commander, Barteau, had put in motion at three o'clock that morning, despite the fact that they had crossed and re-crossed the Tombigbee on successive nights and had marched all of the two preceding days. Barteau, indeed, had been on the field for an anxious hour, facing an overwhelming force of the enemy and wondering when Forrest and the pursuing troops would get up from the south.

Leaving his escort to keep up some sort of demonstration in front of the Union forces, Forrest himself rode across the prairie to the point where the Bell brigade was keeping up a lively skirmishing to gain time.[53] But even with this brigade Forrest was in the uncomfortable position of being on an open plain with one small brigade and one company in the face of an enemy which, rightly handled, could easily have turned upon him and ruined him.

But Forrest had an instinctive realization of the value of the offensive in defense. It may have dated to an incident of his boyhood at Chapel Hill, when he was thrown into the midst of a snarling savage pack of dogs by a colt which he was breaking. He hit the ground expecting to be torn. Instead the dogs, frightened by having an object as large as a boy thrown at them, turned tail and fled. Forrest never forgot it. Even in his first important fight, at Fort Donelson, according to the story related by Gideon Pillow at a memorial meeting in Memphis just after Forrest's death, he applied the lesson. Threatened with a charge by heavy forces, he turned to Pillow, under whose command he was, and asked for orders to charge first, saying, "We can't hold them but we can run over them."[54]

On the prairie at Okolona, Forrest applied the same principle. As he galloped across the short front of Bell's brigade with hat upraised in polite acknowledgment of the cheers of recognition which greeted him, he asked Barteau, but one question: "Where is the enemy's whole position?"

"You see it, General, and they are preparing to charge."

"Then we will charge them," was the instant reply, followed, as he reached the right of the line, with the order to mount and charge. When the charge ran into difficulties from the heavy fire of breech-loading carbines of the Federals, delivered from behind a fence, Forrest put himself at the head of the Second Tennessee Cavalry, Barteau's own regiment, rose to the standing position in the stirrups which added to his height and that of his horse to make him a truly gigantic and fearsome figure in a charge, called "Come on, boys!" and swept round to attack the flank of the Federal line.[55]

As he did so, the brigades pursuing from the south happily came into sight and the Federal stampede began—by coincidence when the Second Tennessee Cavalry (Union) gave way under the charge of the Second Tennessee Cavalry (Confederate). The Union regiment, along with the Fourth Regulars, first was "forced to retire in haste," according to their brigade commander, and then, getting mixed up with the Third Tennessee (Union), all three regiments "became entirely disorganized."[56]

With this break in the Federal lines just above Okolona the pursuit "became general and eager" in a five-mile running fight, with Forrest himself in the lead. Six of Smith's guns—"little pop guns" he called them in his report—were lost almost immediately when, as their commander reported, the road on both sides of them was filled with "flying cavalry . . . in perfect confusion . . . some hallooing 'Go ahead or we will be killed!' "[57]

The first real organized resistance by the Union forces was undertaken some five miles beyond the beginning of the stampede, when Waring's brigade was formed in line to check pursuit while McCrillis' broken brigade streamed through it, "in such confusion," Waring reported, "as to endanger the morale of my own command." Waring thereupon fell back a mile to another stronger position, which they held for a time until Hepburn's brigade—which had formed the rear guard on the day before—could form a new line on a carefully selected position, some seven miles northwest of Okolona, on the road to Pontotoc.[58]

The position was well selected, in a hilly wooded section where the road to Pontotoc, running along a narrow "hogback" ridge, makes an abrupt bend just in front of the houses, stables, ginhouse and other buildings of a large plantation known as Ivey's Hill. Artillery was emplaced, skirmishers and flankers were thrown out, and protected positions were chosen from which to stop the relentless pursuit. Bell's brigade, which had taken the lead during the morning and early afternoon of that day—most of its men had advanced, fighting, on foot for nine miles since the morning's fight began—was replaced in the Confederate advance by Jeffrey Forrest's and McCulloch's men. These two brigades, too, had suffered from the breakdown of horses in the running fight of the past two days but on they came, exultant in pursuit, to charge the new Union position.

As the charge swept forward the Union line crackled with fire—artillery and small arms. At the first volley McCulloch was wounded in the right hand, and Jeffrey Forrest killed by a ball through his neck. The

229

two brigades were shaken and stopped by the volley and the loss of their commanders. Bedford Forrest, seeing his best-beloved brother fall, rushed to his side, dismounted, lifted his body in his arms and held him tenderly, calling him repeatedly by name until he realized that Jeffrey was indeed dead. During the few minutes of this scene—less than ten minutes altogether—there was something of a lull in the fight, until the General, once more in command of himself and the situation, laid down the body of his brother, covered his face, quickly surveyed the field before him, started Colonel W. L. Duckworth, who took over the command of Jeffrey's brigade, around to the left to fall on the Federal flank and rear, lined up the escort company and ordered Jacob Gaus, his bugler, to sound the charge.[59]

As Gaus brought from his battered bugle—it had the marks of two bullets on it—the notes of the charge, Forrest and the escort drove hard, directly at the Federal line which "broke to the rear and retreated at great speed," although it was speedily rallied.[60] Into the re-formed line Forrest plunged with the little band of men who had been able to keep up with him, for a hand-to-hand fight with saber and pistol in which, it is said, Forrest himself disposed of three enemy soldiers. So desperate seemed his plight and that of the handful of men with him, however, that "Black Bob" McCulloch, whose wound had by that time been dressed, came charging to the rescue of his general, waving the blood-soaked bandages of his wounded hand above his head as a flag.[61]

A mile beyond, where another fence with plantation buildings furnished a rallying place, another Union line awaited the headlong dash of Forrest's men. As they charged, the General's horse was killed and his saddle shattered under him. Private J. B. Long of his escort turned over his own horse to the General but soon this animal also was shot dead—just as the orderly brought up from the rear the General's own favorite charger, King Philip, who too was wounded, though not fatally, before the day was over.[62]

In all the rush of the fight and even on this day of great personal loss and bereavement, Forrest had eyes for detail and willingness to relieve unnecessary suffering. As the Federal line broke back once more, to the fifth position of the day, and Forrest dashed through the position just vacated, he heard from a hut used as a hospital such a cry of agony that he dismounted, entered, and found a Federal soldier who, in the midst of having his leg cut off, had been left by the fleeing surgeons with an amputating saw stuck fast in the marrow of the bone of his leg. Forrest administered with his handkerchief some of the precious little supply of chloroform which the Confederates had left, and sent for Doctor Cowan to take charge of the case and complete the amputation.[63]

Doctor Cowan was at the time engaged in another errand of mercy upon which the General had sent him, just after the first horse to be killed under him that day was struck. While changing horses Forrest had noted a terror-stricken mother and her brood of children huddled behind their log cabin in a corner of the stick-and-daub chimney, as the retreating and pursuing tides of battle swept over their little place. To Cowan Forrest had entrusted the duty of placing the woman and the children for safety's sake in a pit in the corner of the yard from which the mud used in chinking the cabin and daubing the chimney had been dug.[64]

"Ten miles from Pontotoc," Forrest reported, "they made a last and final effort to check pursuit. . . . They had formed in three lines . . . directly in our front . . . at intervals of several hundred paces. . . . As the advance of my column moved up they opened on us with artillery. My ammunition was nearly exhausted, and I knew that if we faltered they would in turn become the attacking party, and that disaster might follow. Many of my men were broken down and exhausted with clambering the hills on foot and fighting almost constantly for the last 9 miles."

In most characteristic fashion Forrest "determined, therefore, relying upon the bravery and courage of the few men I had up, to advance to the attack. As we moved up, the whole force [of the enemy] charged down at a gallop, and I am proud to say that my men . . . standing firm, repulsed the grandest cavalry charge I have ever witnessed. . . ." They drove back each successive wave of the charge as it came forward, with rifle and revolver fire, and in turn captured another piece of artillery as the Union troops fell back from their position.[65]

How the Confederate line withstood and broke the charge which so excited Forrest's admiration was thus explained, after the war, by Lieutenant William Witherspoon of the Seventh Tennessee, to one who was in the Federal charge:

". . . We opened ranks to extend across the field. As the line was formed, Forrest rode into the field, in our rear, saying to us, 'I think they are going to charge you, boys, hold this line for me.' He passed on down the line, repeating it. . . . Now, when you charged that line, it was not one Forrest you were contending with, but every man in that line was a Forrest."

However, as Lieutenant Witherspoon went on to explain, there were reasons of tactics as well as of morale for the result.

"You made a formidable appearance, mounted, with your chargers well reined and sabres drawn. . . . At the sound of the bugle you dashed for-

231

ward, holding your horse with the left hand and the sabre grasped by the right. We were meeting each other, you in a mad gallop, with us at a halt. Forrest's style was always to meet a charge with a counter-attack. . . . When you were near enough for our rifles to do good work we commenced pumping lead. Some of you were firing occasionally, but the greater part of you were intent on holding that rein and sabre. As you got within seventy-five yards we dropped our carbines (which were strung by a strap across the shoulder), drew the navy sixes, one in each hand—we had discharged sabres as a fighting weapon—then we fed you on lead so fast and furious you whirled with your backs to us. Then it was again with the carbine until you got back into the woods and we saw you were forming again. 'Well, boys, we whipped the first charge, and we can whip the next,' was the universal remark with us. . . ."

And so it was with the second and third charges, Lieutenant Wither-spoon explained, aided in the latter case by a flank fire from the Second Missouri.[66]

The charges, after all, were made only to cover the continuing retreat of the main Federal column. Night was at hand, half of Forrest's men were entirely out of ammunition, all of them, men and horses, were worn out with two days of fighting and marching which had carried them from the crossing of the Sakatonchee, below West Point, to within ten miles of Pontotoc—a total distance of nearly fifty miles.

At this time, after dark, Gholson came up with his small brigade of Mississippi state troops, to whom Forrest turned over the pursuit of Smith's column through the night. That night, for a brief period, Smith rested some three miles south of Pontotoc, to resume the weary march at 3:30 on the morning of the twenty-third, and not to halt again that day until he had safely recrossed the Tallahatchie at New Albany, and put another dozen miles between himself and pursuit. On the twenty-fourth and twenty-fifth Smith's column marched back toward Memphis unmolested by Forrest, but nevertheless at a round pace of retreat. The march, Colonel Waring wrote, was "almost incessant, day and night," with men and horses "allowed" only the fewest possible hours in the very dead of night for hasty cooking and scant repose. "We were a worn and weary lot . . . worn and weary, and sadly demoralized, and almost dismounted . . . broken in spirit and sadly weakened in discipline."[67]

On the twenty-sixth the expedition arrived in its camps about Memphis to find that stragglers, who had preceded them, had filled the city with reports that the expedition had been "totally defeated and scattered."[68]

Such a report, of course, was not true. Neither, for that matter, was the view expressed in General Sooy Smith's report that "we retired, fighting for over 60 miles, day and night, and had the fighting all our own way except at Okolona."[69] Each of Smith's subordinate commanders, it is true, gives a picture of an orderly and controlled retreat without confusion or disorder, but only so far as his own command is concerned. When it came to units other than their own, descriptions of the action of February twenty-second abound in such phrases as "wildest disorder and confusion," "panic-stricken and flying," in a "terrible rush from the rear," a "motley crew seeking to get out of harm's way," "breaking up and stampeding," a "human tornado." About the mildest reference in these reports is that other commands were "retiring in haste, entirely disorganized," or were in a "rather disturbed condition."[70]

As good a summing up as any is that of Colonel Waring, who described the rapid retreat to Memphis—it took only half as long to go back as it did to come out—as a "weary, dis-heartening and almost panic-stricken flight, in the greatest disorder and confusion."[71] Major General Hurlbut, Union commander in the Memphis area, observed that such a retreat before an inferior force, at the rate at which Smith retreated, "demoralized the cavalry very seriously."[72]

Sherman, the hardheaded realist who had sent Smith on the expedition, and whose plan for passing beyond Meridian into Alabama was wrecked by his failure, was vigorous in his censure, both for the delay in starting and for "allowing General Forrest to head him off and to defeat him with an inferior force."[73]

General Grant's estimate of the meeting between Forrest and Smith was that "it was decidedly in Forrest's favor," but in extenuation he explained—quite erroneously—that while in numbers Smith's command was nearly double that of Forrest it was "not equal, man to man, for the lack of a successful experience such as Forrest's men have had."[74] Actually Forrest men were not only considerably less than half Smith's in number but for most of them the affair about Okolona was their first fight, and for nearly all of them the first under Forrest.

The affair became the subject of a handsome general order issued by Lieutenant General Polk, congratulating Stephen Lee and Forrest and the men of their commands "upon the brilliant and successful campaign just closed."[75]

But not even "brilliant and successful campaigns" were enough to appease the high gods who presided over army paper work at Richmond. Forrest had written a letter direct to President Davis on February fifth, dating it from "Hdqrs. Cavalry Dept. of W. Tenn and N. Miss," and telling the President of his plans and hopes for making an army of the fragments of material he had brought from West Tennessee and especially his plan to go back there for more. The letter lay unnoticed, apparently, until March ninth, two weeks after the rout and pursuit of Sooy Smith—which, it would seem, might have made Forrest's command tolerably well known at Richmond—when the Adjutant and Inspector General's office added a first indorsement referring the letter to General Bragg, the President's new "Chief of Staff," with no mention of its contents but with the curt notation that the "Cavalry Department of West Tennessee and North Mississippi is not known at this office." To which, in the course of a week, General Bragg's office added a second indorsement that "an inspection of this command has been ordered."[76]

CHAPTER XVI

THE "OCCUPATION" OF WEST TENNESSEE AND KENTUCKY*

February 26, 1864-April 10, 1864

WHILE the authorities at Richmond were concerning themselves with the legality and the state of organization of his command, and while the members of the command itself were recuperating and enjoying the warm hospitality of the citizens of Columbus and Starkville, the pleasant Mississippi towns in which Forrest's headquarters and those of Chalmers were established after the rapid repulse of William Sooy Smith, Forrest himself was driving ahead on his plan to go back to West Tennessee after those 3,000 men whom he had had to come away without at Christmastime.

At the summons of Leonidas Polk, the department commander, Forrest and Stephen Lee went together to headquarters at Demopolis, Alabama, in the last days of February, traveling most of the way by railroad handcar.[1] There Forrest was informed that three small regiments of Kentuckians were to be assigned to his command, and to be mounted for cavalry service. The best place to find horses for them, he believed, was in their home state—wherefore his plans were extended beyond Tennessee into Kentucky.

At the same time Polk sent Forrest a Kentucky brigadier general, Abraham Buford, graduate of West Point in the class of 1841, veteran of service in the Mexican War and on the western plains and at the Cavalry School at Carlisle, Pennsylvania, who had resigned from the army and was in 1861 engaged in raising racing stock in his native state of Kentucky.[2]

Orders to Forrest were to take on the "short campaign" which was planned such part of his command as might be necessary, in addition to the orphan Kentuckians, and to leave the rest in northern Mississippi to hold the enemy in check while he was gone. Artillery and wagon trains were to be left behind in the vicinity of Columbus, where they were to be repaired and refitted.[3]

When the Kentucky regiments reported at Columbus, Forrest effected

---

* The field of operations covered in this chapter is shown on the map on page 103.

a reorganization of his entire command in orders issued on March 7, 1864, dividing them into two divisions to be commanded by Chalmers and Buford. Chalmers' division included Richardson's brigade of Tennessee troops, to which was added the Seventh Tennessee out of Jeffrey Forrest's brigade, and McCulloch's brigade of Missourians, Texans, Mississippians and Tennesseans. Buford's division consisted of Tyree Bell's brigade of Tennesseans and Colonel A. P. Thompson's brigade, which included the three new Kentucky regiments—the Third, Seventh and Eighth—together with Faulkner's Twelfth Kentucky, and the Alabama regiment which had been Jeffrey Forrest's and which still bore his name.[4]

Two days after the reorganization, however, Forrest relieved Chalmers from duty with his division and directed him to report to Polk for orders,[5] while only a day or two later Richardson, commanding one of Chalmers' brigades, was "relieved on account of charges preferred against him by Colonel Green," one of his regimental commanders. McCulloch was put in command of the division and Colonel J. J. Neely in command of the Richardson brigade.[6]

Richardson's separation from the Forrest command was permanent; that of Chalmers, temporary. There were no charges against Chalmers, the difficulty apparently being entirely in a clash of temperament which, fortunately, was resolved and accommodated by being brought into the open. Chalmers, a graduate of South Carolina College, had organized the first military company in Forrest's old home town of Hernando, had become colonel of a Mississippi regiment even before Sumter and a brigadier general before Shiloh, and had been in command of the cavalry in North Mississippi when Forrest arrived in that theater. It is not to be wondered at that when Chalmers was put under the command of Forrest there were incidents and annoyances.

This culminated when, according to letters from Chalmers to Polk and to the Adjutant and Inspector General of the Army at Richmond, "General Forrest took my only tent from me and gave it to his brother," and Chalmers wrote Forrest "a letter which he considered disrespectful." This letter, which Forrest said "speaks for itself," was not preserved but on the following day, March ninth, Forrest relieved Chalmers of command. "He has never been satisfied since I came here," Forrest wrote Polk, "and being satisfied that I have not had and will not receive his support and cooperation, deemed it necessary that we should separate. I must have the cordial support of my subordinate officers in order to succeed and make my command effective. . . . I hope you may be able to place him where he will be better satisfied than with me."[7]

Chalmers obeyed under protest and demanded a court on inquiry.

Polk promptly ruled that Forrest had exceeded his authority and referred the subject to the War Department at Richmond, which on March sixteenth sustained the ruling that Forrest had not the power which he had assumed to exercise, but could only have Chalmers "tried if amendable to charges"—which obviously he was not. Chalmers was restored to command, therefore, and ordered to report to Forrest for duty, which he did on March twenty-fifth, in good time to play a major part in the West Tennessee campaign in which by that time Forrest was deeply engaged.[8]

No other temperamental clash of the sort is preserved in the records, but at this period, before the antagonisms engendered while Forrest was forging discordant elements into a fighting force were lost and forgotten in the power of his leadership and the glow of his victories, there must have been more than one officer or soldier who resented his command. One young Mississippian, who prided himself on belonging to the "aristocracy," thus recorded his resentment in a diary entry:

"The dog's dead: finally we are under N. Bedford Forrest . . . and I must express my distaste to being commanded by a man having no pretension to gentility—a negro trader, gambler—an ambitious man, careless of the lives of his men so long as preferment be *en prospectu*."

But even this young gentleman completed his entry with the significant remark that "Forrest may be & no doubt is, the best Cav officer in the West, but I object to a tyrranical hotheaded vulgarian's commanding me."[9]

But despite all difficulties, external and internal, Forrest drove ahead with his preparations for the West Tennessee-Kentucky expedition, and on March sixteenth started north again, taking with him Buford's division, without wagons, with sixty rounds of ammunition and five days' cooked rations,[10] and leaving behind that of Chalmers, temporarily under McCulloch, whom he had recommended for promotion to brigadier general. Subordinate commands of the division left behind were ordered to "breast the country" in several sections of Mississippi to gather up and arrest all men absent without leave or subject to conscription, and to collect all squads and unattached companies of calvalry. "Impress upon the officers commanding the regiments sent out to scour and breast the country," Forrest's order ran, "to do the work thoroughly and catch, if possible, the men who are going through the country and impressing and stealing horses without authority." In certain sections the troops were ordered also to "destroy all distilleries"—altogether a commentary on the state into which the much-fought-over country of northern Mississippi had fallen.[11]

On his 150-mile northward march to Jackson, Tennessee—which he reached before noon of March twentieth—Forrest found plenty of additional evidence of the distress of the people. From Tupelo on to Purdy, Tennessee, the country had been laid waste until there was no longer subsistence for its inhabitants, he reported, let alone anything to support contemplated troop movements. Some small import of supplies was being made with handcars on the railroad tracks as far north as Corinth, he wrote, and recommended that the railroad be put in order for the running of trains that far, for the double purpose of helping to relieve the inhabitants and making it possible to establish at Corinth a depot to which he might send back recruits, there to be supplied and forwarded on south by rail. "The whole of West Tennessee," he added, "is overrun by bands and squads of robbers, horse thieves and deserters, whose depredations . . . are rapidly and effectually depleting the country."[12]

Forrest was accompanied by Isham G. Harris, the valiant Governor of Tennessee, the same who back in 1861 had issued Forrest's first commission to raise a cavalry command, and who since the fall of Fort Donelson had been an itinerant executive, with his "capital" wherever Tennessee soldiers served.[13]

At Jackson the people were found in distress over the operations of Colonel Fielding Hurst and his Union regiment, described by Forrest as "renegade Tennesseans." Hurst, Forrest reported, had levied cash tribute upon Jackson and had arrested, carried off and confined citizens, while his men were responsible for the murder and, in some cases, mutilation of five named members of Forrest's command who had fallen into their hands. Demand was made upon the Federal authorities at Memphis for restitution of the money extorted, for the release of citizens held in confinement at Fort Pillow and elsewhere, and for the surrender of Hurst and the officers and men of his command to be tried and dealt with for their offenses. When the demand was refused, as was to be expected, Forrest issued from Jackson a proclamation of outlawry against them.[14]

From Jackson Forrest sent back orders for the division left behind in Mississippi to move up toward Memphis, while with Buford's division he pressed on to Kentucky. From Jackson, also, he detached Colonel W. L. Duckworth, of the Seventh Tennessee Cavalry, with a small force to gobble up a garrison at Union City, in the northwest corner of Tennessee just below the Kentucky state line.

The Confederates arrived in front of Union City before daylight of March twenty-fourth, intending to attack at dawn. When the light from a burning house showed that the position of the defenders was stronger than they had been led to expect, with earthworks and an abatis against which it would have been folly to throw men without artillery, Colonel

Duckworth called to his aid the spell of the name of Forrest and his own considerable histrionic and diplomatic ability, developed by his dual career in private life of physician and preacher of the gospel.

By ingenious play acting, with horse-holders in the rear raising loud cheers at intervals, as if in welcome to arriving reinforcements, with much sounding of bugles from various points about the town, and with a judicious half-display of log "cannon" mounted on wagon wheels and maneuvered about in the bushes in the half-light of dawn, Duckworth managed to create the impression that he had artillery and that reinforcements were continually feeding in. Toward midmorning he sent in his flag of truce with a demand for immediate and unconditional surrender, bearing the signature of "N. B. Forrest, Major-General commanding."[15]

By one of the odd coincidences of the war the demand of Duckworth, commanding the Seventh Tennessee Cavalry, C. S. A., was received by Colonel I. R. Hawkins, commanding the Seventh Tennessee Cavalry, U. S. A., the same whom Forrest had captured in West Tennessee in December 1862. Hawkins knew Forrest, of course, as a result of that experience, and demanded an interview. Duckworth, however, was equal to the emergency. "I am not in the habit of meeting officers inferior to myself in rank under a flag of truce," the pseudo Forrest wrote, "but I will send Col. Duckworth, who is your equal in rank, and who is authorized to arrange terms and conditions with you under instructions."

Colonel Hawkins was the more disposed to surrender because he believed, and the day before had telegraphed Brigadier General Mason Brayman, Union commander at Cairo, that Forrest was expected to attack his post within twenty-four hours "with five times our numbers," a figure which grew in Brayman's dispatches to 7,000 men.[16] On the other hand Hawkins had been assured by Brayman's adjutant that reinforcements were on the way to him from Columbus, and even from Cairo by steamer to Columbus and thence by train, and he had been ordered to hold on.[17] The powers of persuasion and intimidation displayed by Colonel Duckworth were such, however, that his opponent was convinced that "it would save a great many lives if we would surrender," and over the objections of most of his officers decided to do so. About 11:00 A.M. on the twenty-fourth, while the train bearing relieving troops from Columbus, Kentucky, was only six miles away—although on the far side of a bridge which Duckworth prudently had had burned—the surrender was accomplished. Duckworth's ruse had netted some 500 prisoners, which was more men than he had with him, some 300 horses and a quantity of arms and stores, all "almost without the loss of blood or the smell of powder."[18]

On the same day on which Duckworth captured Union City and its

239

garrison, Forrest, with the Kentucky troops, was marching for Paducah, where the Tennessee River falls into the Ohio. From Nashville, where he was busy hastening the concentration of the force with which he planned to attack Joe Johnston's Army of Tennessee in northern Georgia, General Sherman wrote on this day that "Forrest's cavalry has gone up toward Columbus, where he can do us little harm, and it would be folly for me to push him"[19]—an opinion which he was to amend before the expedition ended.[20]

Having covered the 100 miles from Jackson in fifty hours, despite the spring mud of the roads, Forrest was at Paducah by two in the afternoon of March twenty-fifth. The garrison, commanded by Colonel Stephen G. Hicks, was ordered into the works of Fort Anderson in the western edge of the town at the double-quick, with Forrest's advance hard on their retreating heels. It was no part of Forrest's plan to attack the fort itself, especially since it was reinforced by the gunboats *Peosta* and *Paw-Paw* standing off in the Ohio River, but merely to hold the town and keep garrison and gunboats occupied with part of his troops, while others gathered up and removed the army stores, and especially the government horses, which were the chief reason for coming to Paducah.

But Paducah or its vicinity was home to many of the men of Colonel Thompson's brigade, including the Colonel himself, this was their first fight as a unit, and they had marched nearly 300 miles for it. It was foreign to the nature of those Kentuckians not to make trial of strength of the fort and garrison, and so when Colonel Hicks staunchly refused Forrest's customary demand for surrender to "avoid the unnecessary effusion of blood," Thompson on his own responsibility and without orders led his little brigade forward to storm the works.

In the quick and bloody repulse which resulted, Colonel Thompson himself was among the killed. As soon as Forrest, busy on the other side of town, heard of the assault, he sent peremptory orders that there should be no further attack and kept on with the business of rounding up horses and supplies, and destroying what could not be carried away, including the marine ways and the steamer *Dacotah* on them for repair.[21] Forrest held the town until nearly midnight and "could have held it longer," he reported, "but found the small-pox raging and evacuated the place."[22]

During the hours that Forrest held the town, and longer, the guns of the fort shelled it above the heads of the Confederates, while the gunboats, ranging up and down the river, shelled the upper part of the town, especially houses along the water front and facing the fort, which, it was believed, were occupied by Confederate sharpshooters. Firing from the fort ceased about 8:30 P.M., but the "rebels having commenced to

240

destroy property," at 10:30 the naval commander was requested by Colonel Hicks, to "protect the fort and let the town go to hell." Bombardment was renewed until it was found that one party being shelled on Jersey Street were Federals and not Forrest's men. In other sections the bombardment continued until midnight, when the *Peosta* stopped firing because its ammunition was nearly exhausted.[23]

The town was much damaged, which, thought Lieutenant Commander James W. Shirk, in command of the flotilla, would be a good lesson to Southern sympathizers.[24] General Brayman, the Union commander at Cairo, in his congratulations to Colonel Hicks upon his determined and successful defense of Paducah, expressed gratification that the town was "made a ruin," because the "rebel instincts" of the people "rendered it quite certain that the town would not have been occupied [by Forrest] without their consent."[25]

Amid a flurry of reports from Union commanders that he had or would cross the Tennessee and the Cumberland Rivers to the east of Paducah, Forrest marched southwest to Mayfield.[26] There the regiments raised in that vicinity were furloughed to go to their homes, secure clothing and mounts, gather up recruits and report back at the end of the month—which, without exception, they are reported to have done. Buford brought his Kentuckians on south to arrive on April third at Trenton, Tennessee, where Bell's brigade, meanwhile, had rendezvoused after a like program of going home for remounting, refitting and recruiting.[27]

The gravity of Forrest's repulse from Fort Anderson at Paducah and the extent of his losses were greatly exaggerated in the minds of the Union commanders. Such glowing reports of the thrashing administered to Forrest were forwarded to Grant, then commanding all the Union armies, that from his headquarters at Culpeper, Virginia, he telegraphed to Sherman, his successor in the western command, that "Forrest should not be allowed to get out of the trap he has placed himself in at Paducah. Send . . . all your cavalry with orders to find and destroy him wherever found."[28]

"The whole object of Forrest's movement," Sherman wrote later from Nashville, "is to prevent the concentration going on here as against Georgia. . . ."[29] Forrest's original object, however, had been much more limited and local. He went to West Tennessee and Kentucky for more men, mounts and supplies but, being there, holding possession of all the interior of the country save for a few posts on the rivers,[30] and in position to observe through his scouts what passed up and down the rivers which surrounded him, he soon sensed the nature and purpose of what he saw.

From Jackson, therefore, he reported to General Joseph E. Johnston, commanding the Army of Tennessee in north Georgia, what had been observed, and added this significant statement:

"I am of the opinion that everything available is being concentrated against General Lee and yourself. Am also of opinion that if all the cavalry of this and your own department could be moved against Nashville that the enemy's communication could be utterly broken up."[31]

Thus early, on April sixth—a month before the great co-ordinated advance of the Union armies in the East and the West and at a time when the Confederate high command was without policy or plan to defeat Sherman's advance—did Forrest, carrying on a local campaign in a far corner of the war, penetrate the grand Union design and suggest the one plan which, as the event was to demonstrate, would have had any real chance to bring it to defeat.

Forrest's possession of the country between the rivers was not entirely peaceable, of course, in view of the orders of Grant and Sherman that he be hunted out at any cost. Grierson was ordered out of Memphis with his cavalry, to "follow and attack Forrest, no matter what the odds," while Brigadier General James C. Veatch, with an infantry division destined for the great concentration against Johnston at Chattanooga, was ordered "to hurry up the Tennessee [River, by steamer] and strike inland to intercept Forrest" about the headwaters of the Hatchie, in the vicinity of Purdy, Tennessee.[32]

Grierson had ordered Colonel Fielding Hurst out "to hang upon and harass" Forrest, on March twenty-fourth—the same day as the Paducah fight—with special caution against allowing his men to "straggle and pillage,"[33] while Veatch, spurred on by a second order from Sherman, was at Purdy by noon of the thirtieth. On the day before, however, Colonel Neely, on his way up from Mississippi in response to Forrest's call, had struck Hurst's Tennessee Unionist regiment between Bolivar and Somerville and there had "whipped" them according to Union accounts, or, according to the Confederates, had routed and scattered them and driven them, including Hurst himself, "hatless into Memphis."[34]

Veatch, finding no evidence that Forrest was coming by Purdy, and hearing a sufficiency of rumors and reports that instead he was going to cross the river into Middle Tennessee, marched back on the day after his arrival, re-embarked on his transports, and dropped back down the river to Clifton, whence he marched away toward the concentration at Chattanooga—much to the chagrin and displeasure of Sherman.[35]

Veatch's withdrawal from the headwaters of the Hatchie, however, did not have nearly the direct effect upon the course of the campaign which Sherman felt that it would—for Forrest was not coming that way, at least not any time soon. He had, rather, on March twenty-ninth sent for Chalmers, who had resumed the command of his division in that week, to move up into Tennessee and establish himself between Jackson and Memphis, so as to keep Forrest "fully posted of all movements of the enemy from the direction of Memphis and Fort Pillow."[36]

Besides his instructions to Veatch to strike in from the Tennessee River on the east and to Hurlbut to "come out from Memphis" on the west with infantry and cavalry, "to catch Forrest in flank," Sherman had also instructed Brayman, commanding at Cairo, "to feel for Forrest out from Columbus."[37]

Sherman's instructions to Brayman to scout against Forrest came to nothing, Brayman being concerned, indeed, with destroying the ferry-boats and skiffs all along the lower Ohio River lest Forrest be about to cross over to join forces with supposed Copperhead plotters in southern Illinois—a fear which the exasperated Sherman called "ridiculous nonsense."[38]

The Federal troops in Memphis did not attempt their first real advance against Forrest until April third, and even then it was conducted with a prudence which afterward was described by the caustic Sherman as "timidity."[39] The advance was fanwise on several roads to the east of the town. Colonel Waring, whose brigade was on the Somerville Road, met a Confederate force some thirty miles out from Memphis. The Confederates after a skirmish retired in such fashion as to induce Waring to fear that they were decoying him into a trap. Actually the only Confederate force at hand was the remnant of the original Forrest regiment, just a little more than 150 men commanded by Lieutenant Colonel J. M. Crews, but Crews so disposed his men as to create the illusion of strength and the appearance of flank attacks in force—and got away with it. Being under orders not to bring on a general engagement, Waring fell back to the village of Morning Sun, where General Grierson came up, took over the command and ordered a further retreat to Raleigh, only fifteen miles out from Memphis—for lack of forage, Grierson reported, because they had been "repulsed and driven back," according to Crews.[40]

On the same night on which Grierson's cavalry fell back before the handful of the Old Regiment, General Sherman determined to take steps which would put an end to this troublesome Forrest business. A trusted officer, Brigadier General John M. Corse, clothed with power to use Sherman's own name, was put on board the fleet dispatch steamer *Silver Wave* at Nashville and sent down the rivers, with orders to stop at

Paducah, Cairo, Columbus and Memphis, delivering to the commander at each place special instructions for his part in the grand roundup of Forrest's force. That done, Corse was to continue on down the Mississippi and up the Red River in Louisiana until he should meet Major General A. J. Smith, who with his excellent division had been lent by Sherman to N. P. Banks for his grand Red River expedition.

Instructions were that the posts at Paducah, Cairo and Columbus should be held in force, sending out no more than mere excursions designed to attract Forrest's attention; that Veatch, whom Sherman then supposed to be about Purdy, should remain there to strike Forrest in flank as he tried to get out of West Tennessee; that Hurlbut, operating from Memphis, should strike the opposite flank; and that A. J. Smith should immediately return from the Red River, pausing at Vicksburg only long enough to replenish his supplies, to push on up the Yazoo to Greenwood, where he was to disembark and march rapidly across country to Grenada, Mississippi, whence he was to operate on Forrest's rear.[41] Smith's appearance at Grenada with 10,000 men, Sherman gleefully calculated, "will be a big bomb-shell in Forrest's camp," which would "in a measure compensate for the ill effects of William Sooy Smith's repulse and Forrest's recent raid." With some satisfaction Sherman reported to his chief that "dispositions are complete to make Forrest pay dear for his foolish dash at Paducah."[42]

Before many days, however, General Sherman was to learn that where Forrest was concerned, making dispositions was one thing and carrying them out was frequently quite another.

After Veatch left his assigned position on the headwaters of the Hatchie to proceed on to the rendezvous at Chattanooga, Hurlbut's troops in and about Memphis were the only mobile force in position to operate against Forrest. The Confederate leader estimated this force at 6,000 men, although the actual number was nearer twice that many,[43] but with his usual audacity he determined to bluff and blockade this force with one of Chalmers' brigades, while with the other brigade of Chalmers and all of Buford's division, he went ahead with his own plans.

On April fifth, therefore, he directed Chalmers to send Neely's brigade toward Memphis on a demonstration designed to impress Hurlbut with the idea that he was threatened with attack.[44] When Hurlbut ordered his cavalry out again after Forrest on the seventh, he was assailed with so many and such circumstantial rumors of Forrest's own advance that the troops were recalled, and all troops in Memphis were ordered to stand to arms at daylight the next day to repel the anticipated attack. Instructions were that if they could not hold their ground against it, they should

244

"retire concentrically," burning behind them any public buildings containing stores which it might be necessary to abandon.[45]

At the same time Sherman, "after consultation with General Grant," decided that to attempt to use A. J. Smith's 10,000 men against Forrest would render it impossible to get them to Chattanooga in time for the grand concentration against Joe Johnston, which was the prime point of Federal strategy in the West. "The object of Forrest's move is to prevent our concentration as against Johnston," Sherman wrote, "but we must not permit it."[46] On April nineteenth, therefore, orders to Smith were changed, although as it turned out, the difficulties and delays in getting the Banks expedition out of the Red River were such that Smith's troops played no part in the operations of the early summer against either Forrest or Johnston. On the same day on which Corse was advised of the changed orders for Smith, Sherman himself gave up hope of destroying Forrest in West Tennessee, and telegraphed Grant that "Forrest will escape us."[47]

During these days, when Brayman was reporting Forrest as still near Cairo with 9,000 men and the commander at Columbus was hearing reports that he was approaching that post with 20,000 men; when Hurlbut at Memphis was sure that the bulk of Stephen Lee's cavalry had joined Forrest, and belligerent old Colonel Hicks at Paducah was "looking and waiting for Messrs. Forrest & Co.," strong in the feeling that "there is an awful shaking among the timid, but the righteous are bold as a lion,"[48] Forrest himself met with Buford, Chalmers and some of his brigade commanders in a conference at Jackson, where he laid out to them plans for his further operations in West Tennessee and Kentucky.

Buford was sent with the Kentucky brigade to pay a return visit to Paducah, chiefly for the purpose of capturing 140 head of government horses which Northern newspapers were gleefully reporting had escaped capture during the attack of March twenty-fourth because they had been skillfully hidden in an old rolling mill or foundry.

On his way from Trenton to Paducah, Buford detached 160 picked men under Captain H. A. Tyler, accompanied by Captain David E. Myers of his own staff, to try a game of bluff on the fortified position at Columbus. At daylight on April thirteenth the detachment drove in the pickets on the various roads out from Columbus and followed them to the edge of the woods about the fortifications. There in full view of the garrison the attacking force went through evolutions, half-seen through openings in the trees, designed to create the impression of great force. At six o'clock, Buford's staff officer, Captain Myers, went in under flag of truce with the usual demand for surrender "to avoid the shedding of blood," closing with the threat of no quarter to the Negro troops if the

245

place had to be taken by storm. The note was signed "A. Buford, Brigadier-General," although Buford himself, with the main body, was a day's march on the way to Paducah.

Colonel William Hudson Lawrence, the Union commander at Columbus, hospitably provided the Confederate envoys with breakfast and other refreshments while he consulted with his officers. Lawrence, as his contemporary report shows, was convinced that his position was surrounded by Buford with a division, mostly mounted infantry. However, one armed steamer happened to be at the post, which he detained, and another with 1,500 troops aboard was only a few hours behind. The Columbus commander, therefore, played for time, which exactly suited the Confederates as they had no desire to receive the actual surrender of the garrison and would, indeed, have had a problem in doing so without revealing their own weakness. Finally, however, fearing that their seeming indifference to so long a delay would of itself excite suspicion, the Confederate messengers called for an answer, whereupon Lawrence declared "surrender out of the question." The Confederate forces hovered about Columbus all afternoon, accomplishing the double purpose of causing the news to go out that Buford was at Columbus, and of preventing reinforcements from that garrison being sent to Paducah.[49]

Buford himself, meanwhile, marched on for Paducah, which he reached at noon of the fourteenth.

Having come only for horses, and such other supplies as he might be able to gather, Buford had no intention of attacking the fort, into which the Federal garrison promptly retired. Wishing to create the opposite impression, however, he notified Colonel Hicks that he would allow women, children and noncombatants an hour to get out of the town, in order that they might not be endangered. Colonel Hicks accepted the proposal for an hour's time "to let the women and children out" of the town. "After that time come ahead," he wrote. "I am ready for you."[50] Buford, however, had come to Paducah for horses and supplies, and as soon as those were garnered—as they were—he was ready to depart. Leaving a rear guard under Faulkner to keep up the show until after dark, Buford and the main body marched out during the afternoon with their spoils, headed for Dresden in West Tennessee.[51]

At the same time that Buford and his Kentuckians were making what turned out to be their last ride into Kentucky, Forrest sent orders through Chalmers for Neely's brigade to move as if preparing to attack Memphis from the east, for Duckworth to threaten Memphis from the north and for Colonel John McGuirk's Mississippi state troops to advance from the direction of Holly Springs. Engineer working parties were to prepare ostentatiously for the crossing of Wolf River by boats or pontoon bridges—one of them actually demonstrated within five miles of Memphis—while the whole force was to keep up an active demonstration on April tenth and for two or three days thereafter, before falling back toward Jackson.[52]

The purpose, as was explained under strict seal of secrecy to those in command, was to bluff the garrison at Memphis and hold them fixed to their fortifications while Forrest and Chalmers captured Fort Pillow.[53]

CHAPTER XVII

"FORREST OF FORT PILLOW"

April 10, 1864-April 13, 1864

"ATROCITIES" were not an invention of the First World War propaganda organizations. American newspapers of the Civil War period, North and South, abounded in them. Southern newspapers described the savagery of the invading armies, charging that Northern soldiers, authorized and even ordered by their officers, made theft, assault and murder a part of their regular duties. Northern papers were no less lurid in their descriptions of the dishonor, infamy and ferocity of the Southern soldiers— coming to a climax in a Boston paper's description of Robert E. Lee flogging a slave girl with his own hands and then rubbing brine on her bleeding wounds.[1]

But Fort Pillow was *the* "atrocity" of the war. Forrest's men stormed the fort. Incompetent and blundering command of the defense brought extraordinary losses to the defenders. Bitter local animosities and racial antipathies added to the slaughter. A Congressional committee of inquiry made the "atrocity" official. Its report, of which 40,000 extra copies were printed, became a prime campaign document in the bitter election of 1864.

During the weeks and months in which Fort Pillow was being thus established in popular belief as a "massacre," neither Forrest himself nor the Confederate government made any corresponding effort to present the other side of the story to the people in either North or South. Forrest's reason for public silence, as expressed in a letter to Stephen Lee ten weeks after the affair, was that "as my official reports are in the hands of the Department at Richmond I did not, nor do I, consider that I have any defense to make, or attempt any refutation of the charges. . . . I have taken pains in my official report made to Lieutenant-General Polk, to place all the facts in the possession of the Government in order that they might meet any demands made by Federal authority."[2]

The Confederate government was silent during these critical weeks because it had not received the report. After the death of General Polk during the Atlanta campaign the report was found among his papers by his aide, Lieutenant W. D. Gale, and forwarded to Richmond. On

August tenth the President suggested to Secretary of War Seddon that "It would be well to have the report and accompanying papers published in refutation of the slanders promulgated by the Government of the enemy. . . ."[3] By that time, however, four months after the event, the "Fort Pillow Massacre" had become established, and so remains in most minds. In course of time the story was added to and embroidered by spurious "dispatches" supposed to have been sent by Forrest, and published as evidence of both his illiteracy and his ferocity.[4]

Fort Pillow was erected originally by the Confederates in 1861, at the First Chickasaw Bluff of the Mississippi, forty miles north of Memphis in a direct line and twice that far by the meanders of the river. The original trace of the fort was a line two miles long at a distance of 600 or more yards from the river, enclosing the angle between the Mississippi on the west and Coal Creek on the north. Finding this work entirely too large for any available garrison to hold, Brigadier General Villepigue, subsequently commanding for the Confederates, built a second and much shorter line inside the original work. In the great Confederate retreat after the siege of Corinth in the early summer of 1862 the position was evacuated, and passed into Union possession. The new occupants built a third and still smaller work, only about 125 yards in length and enclosing no more than the high clay bluff in the apex of the angle between creek and river. The Villepigue trenches were retained as an outer line of rifle pits.

When Sherman was gathering up troops from small and isolated posts to make up the columns for the Meridian and the Red River expeditions, he removed the garrison from Fort Pillow. In a short while, however, the post was reoccupied by the Thirteenth Tennessee Cavalry (Union), then being organized under Major William F. Bradford—an officer described by Major General Stephen A. Hurlbut, his commander, "as a very young officer, entirely inexperienced in these matters."[5] To reinforce the garrison and to provide an experienced commander, General Hurlbut subsequently on March twenty-eighth sent up from Memphis four companies of heavy artillery and a section of light artillery, colored troops, under command of Major L. F. Booth, "an old soldier who had served in the regular army." Booth, in whom his general "had great confidence," reported that "he could hold the post against any force for forty-eight hours."[6] With the arrival of Booth and his men the garrison consisted of 557 officers and men, of whom 295 were white and 262 colored, with an armament of six guns.[7] In addition to the garrison of the fort itself, the gunboat *New Era*, Captain James Marshall, was stationed offshore, to take part in the defense of the place.

To add to the tensions to be expected between Confederate soldiers

249

and a garrison made up of Negro troops and white soldiers of the sort whom the Confederates called "renegades," "Tennessee Tories" or "homemade Yankees," the recruiting, scouting and foraging activities of the white Union regiment had been carried on with a rigor which, to the Confederate neighbors of Fort Pillow, appeared more as pillage and persecution. From the time that Forrest entered West Tennessee in March, therefore, there had come to him a series of reports from local citizens of outrages on property or persons ascribed to the Fort Pillow garrison. As early as April fourth Forrest had written to Polk that "there is a Federal force of five or six hundred at Fort Pillow, which I shall attend to in a day or so . . ."[8] but it was not until a week later that the movement against the fort was actually started.

Orders for the movement went out on Sunday, April tenth, from Forrest's headquarters at Jackson to Bell's brigade, encamped at Eaton in Gibson County, and to McCulloch's brigade at Sharon's Ferry on the Forked Deer River, the whole force of about 1,500 men to be under the direct command of Chalmers. Bell, having seventy miles to go, marched at midnight Sunday, almost as soon as orders were received. McCulloch, with a shorter march of fifty miles to make, started Monday morning. Both brigades marched hard Monday and Monday night through drizzly rain over roads of deep mud and across weak bridges, with no more than brief halts for rest and feed, to arrive before Fort Pillow about 5:30 on the morning of Tuesday, April twelfth. Pickets were driven in with a rush and by sunup the Confederates were inside the original works built in 1861.[9]

The early-morning fight was carried forward with skill and vigor under the command of Chalmers. Lieutenant Mack J. Leaming, adjutant of the regiment of Tennessee Unionists and during most of the day post adjutant of Fort Pillow, reports that by 8:00 A.M. two companies of skirmishers which had been thrown forward to hold the advanced rifle pits were "compelled to retire to the fort after considerable loss." With the defenders driven into the shrunken space of the fort proper, Lieutenant Leaming adds, "the firing continued without cessation, principally from behind logs, stumps, and under cover of thick underbrush and from high knolls, until about 9 A.M., when the rebels made a general assault on our works, which was successfully repulsed. . . ."[10]

There is no mention of this general assault and repulse in the Confederate reports but it is plain that already, by midmorning, they dominated the situation. The "high knolls" mentioned by Lieutenant Leaming enabled them to fire into the fort at ranges of not more than 400 yards, while the logs and stumps left in the felling of the timber inside the original 1861 works gave shelter to the Confederate sharpshooters. "We suffered pretty severely in the loss of commissioned officers by the unerring aim of the rebel sharpshooters," Leaming reported, including the loss of the commanding officer, Major Booth, who was killed about nine o'clock, and his adjutant, killed shortly after. From that time on, indeed, the defense of the place was hopeless, for already the Confederate marksmen were in such position that they could take both faces of the fort proper in reverse and pick off the defenders even as they stood behind the heavy parapets upon which they relied.

These parapets, four feet thick at the top, rising eight feet high above a ditch which was itself six feet deep and twelve feet wide, were but one of the elements of the defense which had caused Major Booth to report that he regarded the place as "perfectly safe,"[11] and which were to lead his inexperienced successor in command, Major Bradford, to attempt to hold the place even after it was untenable. The other illusory element of strength upon which Bradford relied was the gunboat New Era, which throughout the morning engagement was noisily and ineffectively shelling the woods and the ravines as glimpses were caught of the gray-clad Confederates, first to one side and then the other of the fort.

Forrest himself came upon the field about ten in the morning, having ridden the sixty-five miles from Jackson in a day and night. Not long after his arrival McCulloch's men advanced with a rush to take possession of the rifle pits abandoned earlier in the morning by the advanced companies of the garrison—the time being fixed as about 11:00 A.M. in the reports of both Chalmers, for the Confederates, and Adjutant Leaming, who made the only comprehensive Union report on the operations of the morning.

Most significantly in the light of later allegations that the Confederates attained their positions close to the fort by improper use of a flag of truce during the afternoon, Adjutant Leaming says:[12]

"At about 11 A.M. the rebels made a second determined assault on our works. In this attempt they were again successfully repulsed with severe loss. The enemy succeeded, however, in obtaining possession of two rows of barracks running parallel to the south side of the fort [italics supplied] and distant about 150 yards. The barracks had previously been ordered to be destroyed, but after severe loss on our part in the attempt to execute the order our men were compelled to retire without accomplishing the desired end, save only to the row nearest the fort. From these barracks the enemy kept up a murderous fire on our men, despite all our efforts to dislodge him.

"Owing to the close proximity of these buildings to the fort, and to the fact that they were on considerably lower ground, our artillery could not be sufficiently depressed to destroy them, or even render them untenable for the enemy."

The buildings referred to in Lieutenant Leaming's report were situated in a ravine, thus described in the report of the Congressional committee which investigated the "massacre":[13]

"Extending back from the river on either side of the fort was a ravine or hollow, the one below the fort containing several stores and some dwellings, constituting what was called the town. At the mouth of that ravine and on the river-bank were some government buildings containing commissary and quartermaster's stores. The ravine above the fort was known as Cold [sic] Creek ravine. . . .

"The gunboat *New Era*, Captain Marshall, took part in the conflict, shelling the enemy as opportunity offered . . . as they were shelled out of one ravine they would make their appearance in the other. They would thus appear and retire as the gunboat moved from one point to another. About one o'clock the fire on both sides slackened somewhat, and the gunboat moved out in the river to cool and clean its guns, having fired 282 rounds of shell, shrapnel and canister, which nearly exhausted its supply of ammunition."

At this hour of one o'clock when, as appears from Captain Marshall's testimony,[14] the gunboat fired its last shot the Confederates had for some two hours been in possession of the ravines which, it was afterward alleged, they secured only by violation of a flag of truce sent in about 3:30 P.M.

Upon his arrival at the fort Forrest began one of his usual close-up, naked-eye reconnaissances of the position. Almost immediately a rifle ball fired from the fort struck and mortally wounded his horse. Frantic with pain, the animal reared and fell over backward, carrying his rider with him and inflicting upon the General bruises and injuries which were painful and even serious. Undaunted, Forrest mounted another horse which, in turn, was shot and killed. Over the remonstrance of his adjutant, Captain Anderson, he mounted still a third time, declaring that he was just as liable to be shot on foot as on horseback and that he could see better from his horse. Before the painstaking reconnaissance was completed, Forrest's third mount of the day was struck, though not killed.[15]

Fighter that he was, Forrest was not accustomed to sacrifice men needlessly. He got results but he wanted them as cheaply as possible. Throughout the time of his reconnaissance and afterward, he kept his men working forward through the underbrush and stumps toward the fort in short rushes, each advance being covered by the fire of sharp-shooters converging from both sides upon the defenders behind the parapet.

252

By 1:00 P.M.—the time at which the gunboat ceased trying to shell the Confederates out of the ravines—the Confederate lines were already formed "on the declining ground from the fort to a ravine, which nearly encircles the fort" at a distance varying "from 50 to 150 yards of the works," according to Anderson's report. Anderson adds:[16]

"The width or thickness of the works across the top prevented the garrison from firing down on us, as it could only be done by mounting and exposing themselves to the unerring aim of our sharpshooters, posted behind stumps and logs on all the neighboring hills. They were also unable to depress their artillery so as to rake these slopes with grape and canister, and so far as safety was concerned, we were as well fortified as they were; the only difference was that they were on one side and we on the other of the same fortification. They had no sharpshooters with which to annoy our main force, while ours sent a score of bullets at every head that appeared above the walls."

In this state of affairs when, as Anderson wrote, "it was perfectly apparent to any man endowed with the smallest amount of common sense that to all intents and purposes the fort was ours," the fight died down because Forrest was approaching the end of the ammunition which his men had brought with them, and was waiting for the arrival of his ordnance wagons, dragging their way through the April mud of the roads from Brownsville.

Upon the arrival of the wagons about 3:30 P.M. the Confederates sent in a flag of truce with a note to Major Booth. "My men have received a fresh supply of ammunition, and from their present position can easily assault and capture the fort," the note said, demanding "the unconditional surrender of the garrison, promising you that you shall be treated as prisoners of war" but declining, if the demand were refused, "to be responsible for the fate of the command," that being another form of the same threat which Forrest had so often and so successfully used ever since his first capture of Murfreesborough by stratagem and bluff.[17]

And then began a correspondence carried on from the Union side entirely in the name of Major Booth, dead for more than six hours. First Major Bradford asked, in the name of Booth, for "one hour for consultation and consideration with my officers and the officers of the gunboat." Forrest, observing a steamer "apparently crowded with troops" approaching the fort, seeing "the smoke of three other boats ascending the river," and "believing the request for an hour was to gain time for re-inforcements to arrive, and that the desire to consult the officers of the gunboat was a pretext," replied with a note allowing twenty minutes.[18]

Meanwhile the troop-laden steamers—the *Liberty* from above and the

253

Olive Branch from below, as appears from subsequent Union testimony —continued to approach in apparent violation of the truce, with no signal of any sort being made to them from either fort or gunboat to turn back or stand away toward the Arkansas shore.[19]

In this state of affairs, believing that the defenders were playing for time for the arrival of reinforcements and seeing the approach of what might well have been reinforcements, with no effort being made to warn them of the existing truce, Forrest ordered his adjutant, Anderson, to move 200 men of McCulloch's command down the ravine in which they already were safely ensconced, to the steamboat landing below the bluff on which the ford stood, and sent Barteau with another 200 down the Coal Creek ravine to prevent landing of reinforcements at either point.

It was this movement, plainly observed by those in the fort and on the gunboat, which became the basis for the later charge that Forrest violated the truce to put his men in position to storm the fort—"the very position," Lieutenant Leaming reported, "which he had been fighting to obtain throughout the entire engagement."[20] Actually, so far as the storming of the fort was concerned, the move down the ravines put 400 men—one-fourth of the entire force—out of the assaulting columns. The move was purely one of precaution against what seemed to be an attempt to land reinforcements, although, as will appear, the detachments in these positions did play a part in the final act of the impending tragedy in preventing the escape of those who sought to flee along the riverbank beneath the bluffs.

While this was transpiring, Bradford sent out another note signed "Booth," to the effect that "negotiations will not attain the desired object." General Forrest, who had ridden forward to the point where the flags-of-truce transactions were taking place in order to convince the Union negotiators that he was indeed there in person, received the evasive answer and sent back a peremptory demand for "an answer in plain, unmistakable English. Will he fight or surrender?"[21]

Having no real hope of holding the fort, apparently, but relying on an insane scheme of defense concocted with Captain Marshall of the gunboat, Bradford sent back the defiant message, "I will not surrender."[22]

Forrest, without a word, rode rapidly back to his position a quarter of a mile from the line and ordered Gaus to sound the charge. As Jacob Gaus brought from his battered bugle the notes of the charge, the assaulting line sprang forward, not pell-mell or helter-skelter but as if they had been rehearsed in detail in crossing ditches and scaling parapets. While the sharpshooters redoubled their already effective efforts to keep down the heads of the defenders, the assaulting troops crossed the few intervening yards to the twelve-foot-wide ditch, jumped down into the

254

mud and water in the bottom, clambered and helped one another up its six-foot sides to the little ledge below the parapet, paused there for an instant—all without firing a shot—and then, with guns loaded, climbed and pushed one another over the eight-foot wall.

As the first assaulting wave, boosted from below by their fellows, came over the wall they emptied their guns at point-black range into the bodies of the garrison crowded on the fire step of the parapet. Before the garrison, which had fired at the first apparition of the charging line, could reload, the second wave was over, to empty another 600 guns into the mass below them. The "rebel charge," reported Lieutenant Leaming, was "as if rising from out the very earth."[23]

"In the meantime," Leaming told the Congressional committee, "nearly all the officers had been killed, especially of the colored troops, and there was no one hardly to guide the men. They fought bravely, indeed, until that time," when with the assaulting Confederates pouring over the supposedly impregnable parapet, a company of colored troops, according to Leaming's report and that of other white troops, broke and fled. "I do not think the men who broke had a commissioned officer over them," Leaming added.[24]

The testimony of the colored soldiers, on the contrary, was to the effect that "the Tennessee cavalry broke, and was followed down the hill by the colored soldiers."[25] Regardless of which element of the garrison first broke, it is agreed that almost instantly the whole garrison, or such of them as had not been already killed or wounded, ran from their positions back through the little enclosure of the fort to the brow of the bluff above the river side, and plunged over.

"Major Bradford signaled to me that we were whipped," Captain Marshall, commanding the gunboat New Era, told the Congressional committee. "We had agreed on a signal that if he had to leave the fort, they would drop down under the bank, and I was to give the rebels canister."[26]

And so, with the flag of the fort still flying and with arms still in their hands, the garrison dropped below the bluff, with apparent intent to continue resistance there, while the gunboat was "to give the rebels canister." But not a shot was fired from the gunboat. Instead, the prudent Captain Marshall, having found that he was nearly out of ammunition and fearing that the victorious rebels would turn the guns of the fort on him—as they actually did—closed his portholes and steamed away out of range.

When the fleeing garrison found that there was to be no blast of canister at their pursuers, panic seized them. Some continued their resistance; others thought only of safety in flight. As they rushed southward along the riverbank, they were met with a volley from the detachment under Anderson, which had come down to the steamboat landing to prevent reinforcements from coming ashore from the approaching transports, and which now fired their first shots in the assault. Turning the other way, the demoralized troops of the garrison met the fire of Barteau's men, beneath the bank on the other side of the fort. Others rushed into the river where they were shot or drowned—and all the while the flag of the fort still flew from its staff, until Private Doak Carr of the Second Tennessee (Confederate) cut it down.

"For the survivors it was a fortunate occurrence that some of our men cut the halyards and pulled down their flag, floating from a high mast in the center of the fort," reports Anderson, who was under the bluff. "Until this was done our forces under the bluff had no means of knowing or reason for believing that the fort was in our possession, as they could from their position see the flag but could not see the fort."[27]

What happened under the bluffs was described by Lieutenant Leaming as a "horrid work of butchery," which continued from the fall of the fort "until dark and at intervals throughout the night."[28] Others who testified, including both those who were there and those who were not, were more profuse and harrowing in their detailed accounts of rebel savagery in the 128 pages of the report of the Congressional committee. And there can be no doubt, nor has it ever been denied, that some men —perhaps a considerable number—were shot after they, as individuals, were seeking to surrender. However, as Second Lieutenant Daniel Van Horn of the colored artillery regiment put it in his report, "there never was a surrender of the fort."[29] Instead, as Colonel Barteau described the situation in an interview published in 1884, "they made a wild, crazy, scattering fight. They acted like a crowd of drunken men. They would at one moment yield and throw down their guns, and then would rush again to arms, seize their guns and renew the fire. If one squad was left as prisoners . . . it was soon discovered that they could not be trusted as having surrendered, for taking the first opportunity they would break loose again and engage in the contest. Some of our men were killed by negroes who had once surrendered."[30]

As the Federal flag fell Forrest spurred his horse from the knoll a quarter of a mile away, from which he had watched the fight, into the fort, promptly ordered all firing to cease and, with the help of Chalmers and other officers, began to restore order.

"The unwounded of the garrison were detailed, under the supervision of their own officers, to bury the dead and remove the wounded to the hospitals, tents and buildings," Anderson reports, while he and Captain John T. Young, of the Fort Pillow garrison, went up along the riverbank with a white flag, in an endeavor to open communication with the master of the gunboat *New Era*, and try to get him to send ashore for the wounded.[31] The *New Era*, however, steamed away, being "fearful that they might hail in a steamboat from below, capture her, put on 400 or 500 men, and come after me,"[32] and so the wounded were left unattended for the night and most of the dead unburied.

With the coming of night Forrest started back to Jackson but, by reason of the severe shaking-up he had received in the fall of his horse that day, he stopped for the night about three miles from the fort. Chalmers likewise left the fort with the coming of dark, and marched his command well back and away from the works before making camp about two miles from the river. If, as Lieutenant Leaming and others testified, shooting, bayoneting and butchering of men went on all night at Fort Pillow, it was the work of stragglers or prowlers and not of organized Confederate forces, none of whom were in or about the place until the next morning, the thirteenth.[33]

At daylight of the thirteenth, acting on orders from Forrest, Chalmers sent back to the fort details to bring away the captured artillery and other arms and to "burn all houses at the fort, except the one used as a hospital . . . [and] leave with the wounded . . . slightly wounded men sufficient to wait on them . . . [and] five or six days' supply of provisions and any medicine they may need."[34]

While Chalmers' men were engaged in this work, including "applying torches to barracks, huts and stables," there appeared before the fort from below the gunboat *Silver Cloud* (No. 28), accompanied by the transport *Platte Valley*, sent up from Memphis in response to news that the fort had been attacked. The gunboat shelled the fort and woods for about an hour until 8:00 a.m., when Captain Anderson, sent back by Forrest for the purpose, succeeded in making a truce for the day, under the terms of which the Federals would be put in full possession of the fort until 5:00 p.m. "for the purpose of burying our dead and removing our wounded," as Acting Master William Ferguson of the gunboat reported. Wounded were "brought down from the fort and battlefield and placed on board the *Platte Valley*. Details of rebel soldiers assisted us in this duty."[35] Another Union observer reported that "the rebels rendered us efficient aid, facilitating as much as possible getting the wounded on board transport"[36]—quite at variance with the report of Lieutenant Leaming that "while the U. S. gunboat No. 28 from Memphis was shelling the enemy, who at the same time was engaged in murdering our wounded, Forrest sent a flag of truce to the commander granting him time . . . to bury our dead and remove the few surviving wounded, he having no means to attend to them."[37] In the anxiety to

257

make out a case of cold-blooded butchery against Forrest and his men, the inconsistency in the two attitudes ascribed to them in the same sentence seems to have escaped attention.

In one of the hearsay statements included in the Union reports it is said that the Confederates "took out from Fort Pillow about one hundred and some odd prisoners (white) and 40 negroes. They hung and shot the negroes as they passed along toward Brownsville until they were rid of them all."[38] In fact, the prisoners captured, other than the wounded who were turned over to the boats on the day after the fall of the fort, were promptly removed to Mississippi and arrived in Okolona on the evening of April twentieth.[39]

During the truce of the thirteenth, while the parties from the Federal steamers were removing the wounded with some Confederate assistance and burying the dead, Chalmers' men were removing the captured arms, ammunition and other supplies for which they had transportation. Ox teams were impressed to haul away the six pieces of artillery captured, while the muskets—269 of which were picked up below the bluff, where they had been carried as part of the scheme to continue resistance with the help of the gunboat—were loaded into the ordnance wagons along with captured ammunition.[40]

By 4:00 P.M. the work of the day was completed, the landing parties returned to the steamers in the river, Chalmers and his men marched inland, the gunboat lowered her flag of truce, ran up the United States flag and steamed off, and Fort Pillow was left alone with its dead.[41]

General Forrest, in a dispatch to Polk from Jackson, said that "the loss of the enemy will never be known from the fact that large numbers ran into the river and were shot and drowned. . . . The river was dyed with the blood of the slaughtered for 200 yards."[42] With the Federal reports of the number in the garrison, however, and the fuller information which became available later, it is possible to arrive at the loss with reasonable accuracy. Of the 557 members of the garrison the names of 226—168 whites and 58 Negroes—appear upon the lists of prisoners carried away from the fort by the Confederates. Captain Ferguson took on board the *Silver Cloud* and the *Platte Valley* "some 20 of our troops" before the truce of April thirteenth began, and "found about 70 wounded men in the fort and around it," during the truce.[43] Elsewhere, in the official reports of the navy there is a receipt from Ferguson to Anderson for 3 officers, 43 white privates and 14 Negroes, and also a nominal list of 58 wounded taken aboard during the truce.[44] In addition to those taken off by Ferguson's boats "some 20 more" were placed on the *Red Rover*,[45] making a total of from 100 to 110 wounded taken off on that day. Two days later Captain LeRoy Fitch took off ten more wounded soldiers,[46] bringing the total number of wounded in Federal hands to from 110 to 120.

It appears then that of the garrison of 557 there were at least 336 survivors, of whom 226 were unwounded or only slightly wounded and approximately 100 seriously wounded. The dead of the garrison may be calculated as not more than 231, which accords with the burial reports. Captain Ferguson says that his men "buried, I should think, 150 bodies."[47] Captain Marshall, who returned to Fort Pillow during the truce of the thirteenth, buried 64.[48] Others were buried by Lieutenant Commander Fitch whose gunboat, the *Moose*, was at Fort Pillow on the fourteenth. Some of the last, however, appear to have been reburied— bodies hastily and imperfectly buried before.[49] In addition to the dead of the garrison there were doubtless some deaths among the enlisted civilians, sutlers, traders and the like, who elected to take part in the defense of the place. The loss of life approximated forty percent of the garrison—by no means an extraordinarily high rate for a place carried by assault as Fort Pillow was.

During the investigation made by Senator Benjamin F. Wade and Representative Daniel W. Gooch, a subcommittee of the Joint Select Committee of Congress on the Conduct of the War, special efforts were made to show that, with the exception of about a score, all the loss of life occurred after organized resistance ceased. Lieutenant Leaming, for example, having previously testified that the commanding officer of the post and his adjutant and indeed "nearly all the officers" had been killed during the fight, and having testified to the "murderous fire" and the "unerring aim of the rebel sharpshooters," was led by questioning to testify that of the eight officers of his regiment in the battle only two remained alive, all but one of the others having been killed after "we were driven from the fort."[50] Sergeant Weaver of the colored troops, in response to a question from Senator Wade, "supposed" that before the fort was captured not "over a dozen" of the whites and "probably not more than fifteen or twenty of the negroes" were killed. He somewhat spoiled the answer, however, by adding that "there were a great many of the negroes wounded, because they would keep getting up to shoot, and were where they could be hit."[51]

The Congressional committee arrived at Cairo, Illinois, on April twenty-second, took testimony there for two days, went down the river to visit Columbus, Memphis, Fort Pillow and the gunboat *New Era*, taking testimony at each place, and returned to Cairo on the twenty-eighth. During their investigation the committee interrogated sixty-seven persons about Fort Pillow, of whom forty-two were in the fort on the day of the fight—seventeen colored soldiers, twenty-one white soldiers,

259

one colored civilian and one white, one white officer and one surgeon. The remainder included four officers of the gunboat *New Era*, ten persons who came to the fort the next day, six surgeons of the Mound City, Illinois, hospital, and five army and navy officers of rank who gave general testimony. In addition to those interrogated, the committee was furnished by General Brayman, commanding at Cairo, with affidavits from five white soldiers and four civilians who were in the fort and four others who came there the next day.

From this mass of testimony the Congressional committee reported, in summary, that the rebels took advantage of a flag of truce to place themselves in "position from which the more readily to charge upon the fort"; that after the fall of the fort "the rebels commenced an indiscriminate slaughter sparing neither age nor sex, white or black, soldier or civilian"; that this was "not the result of passions excited by the heat of conflict, but of a policy deliberately decided upon and unhesitatingly announced"; that several of the wounded were intentionally burned to death in huts and tents about the fort; and that "the rebels buried some of the living with the dead."[52]

Long afterward Dr. Wyeth collected sworn testimony from half a hundred Confederate survivors and eyewitnesses of the fight, indignantly denying these and like charges. Disregarding this and other Confederate evidence on the subject, however, and relying only on statements from Union sources, it is apparent that no one of the five principal points of the committee's report can be sustained upon critical examination of the record.

As to the first, that of advancing under flag of truce to a better position for assault, it is clear from the Federal statements that Forrest's men were in the ravines below reach of the guns of the fort, and as close as fifty yards, before noon and some four hours before the truce began. Marshall of the gunboat testified that he was signaled from the fort to shell them out and tried to do so, but failed. Leaming testifies to like effect, although at another point he does say that the Confederates advanced under flag of truce. The movement he referred to, obviously, was that to the riverbank, made for the purpose of preventing the possible landing of reinforcements from the approaching troop-laden transports. That these transports were approaching and that they were not signaled from fort or gunboat to keep away is confirmed by the testimony of Brigadier General George F. Shepley, of the Union Army, who was on the *Olive Branch* going up the river, and who mentions the *Liberty*, bound downstream.[53]

The Confederate detachments which went to the riverbank, moreover, did not put themselves in better position for the assault. They put themselves entirely out of that part of the action.

The description of the slaughter in the second principal point of the committee's report is rhetoric. The aged, the women and children, and the civilians in the fort who did not wish to join in the fight, were placed in a coal barge early in the morning and towed by the *New Era* "to a big island up the river," as testified to by Captain Marshall and referred to by other witnesses.[54]

Of those engaged in the fight, the slaughter was by no means so great as it would have been had there been an order or a determination to exterminate the garrison, as is implied in the committee's report. About two-fifths of the garrison were killed, and another one-fifth wounded. It is impossible to know now how many had been killed before the mad rush away from the stormed parapet in an attempt to take up the fight from a new position, but from the testimony and reports it is apparent that there must have been heavy loss during the hours of fighting from the "unerring aim of the rebel sharpshooters," and probably still heavier loss as the assaulting waves came over the parapet, emptying 1,200 rifles into the crowded defenders at hand-to-hand range. It must be remembered too that there never was a surrender of the fort, nor an entire cessation of resistance until perhaps twenty minutes after the storming of the parapet. Had there been, the loss of life would have been less.

The third main charge, that the "atrocities committed at Fort Pillow" were the result of deliberate policy, does not stand up under examination of the Union record. Without doubt men were killed and wounded who should not have been, and the loss of life was greater than it would have been but for the attempt to prolong resistance beneath the bluff while the gunboat was supposed to be shelling the Confederates in the fort.

Undoubtedly, too, this was intensified by the bitter animosities, many of them personal, existing between the Tennessee white Unionist defenders of the fort and the assailants, and by the feeling of many Confederate soldiers toward those whom they looked upon as slaves in blue uniforms. In all the circumstances it would have been a strange and wonderful thing had there been no cases of individual assault in the closing portions of a fight which came to a ragged, scattering and indefinite end.

The finding of the committee as to a deliberate policy of destruction of the garrison rests partly upon Forrest's note demanding surrender and partly upon testimony of wounded survivors that "officers," or "Chalmers" or "Forrest" had ordered a slaughter of the defenders. As to the note demanding surrender, Forrest was probably correct in saying that he could not be responsible for the consequences if the demand was refused, but this was by no means the same as saying that he was ordering a slaughter. As a matter of fact, it was no more than a repetition of the device which he had used before and was to use again with success in securing surrender of places with minimum loss of life to his own command and, for that matter, to the defenders.

The testimony of survivors on the point of the attitude of officers is mixed. The very first survivor examined—Elias, a colored soldier—said that the rebels "killed all the men after they surrendered, until orders were given to stop. . . ."

"Till who gave orders?"

"They told me his name was Forrest."

The same witness told of seeing a soldier shoot one of the wounded men in the hand, when "an officer told the secesh soldier if he did that again he would arrest him."[55] Lieutenant Leaming testified that when there were shots outside the hut to which he had been carried after being wounded he heard an officer ride up and say: "Stop that firing; arrest that man," and that another officer-prisoner told him "that they had been shooting them, but the general had had it stopped."[56]

One witness, Frank Hogan, colored, testified that a "secesh first lieutenant" shot a captain of the Negro regiment,[57] while others testified that they were told that the shootings were ordered by General Forrest. One imaginative witness, however, declared that "towards evening, General Forrest issued an order not to kill any more negroes, because they wanted them to help haul the artillery out."

"Were colored men used for that purpose?"

"Yes sir. I saw them pulling the artillery, and I saw the secesh whip them as they were going out, just like they were horses."[58]

The only witness in the whole record who professed to have seen Forrest ordering, or otherwise participating, in the shootings was Jacob Thompson, colored civilian, who told the committee that he fought with the garrison.

"When were you shot?" he was asked.[59]

"After I surrendered."

"Who shot you?"

"A private."

"What did he say?"

"He said, 'God damn you, I will shoot you, old friend.'"

"Did you see anybody else shot?"

"Yes, sir; they just called them out like dogs, and shot them down. I reckon they shot about fifty, white and black, right there. They nailed some black sergeants to the logs, and set the logs on fire."

"When did you see that?"

"When I went there in the morning I saw them; they were burning all together."

262

"Did they kill them before they burned them?"

"No sir, they nailed them to the logs; drove the nails right through their hands."

"How many did you see in that condition?"

"Some four or five; I saw two white men burned. . . ."

"Did you notice how they were nailed?"

"I saw one nailed to the side of a house; he looked like he was nailed right through his wrist. I was trying then to get to the boat when I saw it." [This, it is to be noted, was after the arrival of Ferguson and his two boats, with their numerous landing parties—none of whom reports having seen such sights.]

"Did you see them kill any white men?"

"They killed some eight or nine there. I reckon they killed more than twenty after it was all over; called them out from under the hill, and shot them down. They would call out a white man and shoot him down, and call out a colored man and shoot him down; do it just as fast as they could make their guns go off."

"Did you see any rebel officers about there when this was going on?"

"Yes, sir; old Forrest was one."

"Did you know Forrest?"

"Yes, sir; he was a little bit of a man. I had seen him before at Jackson."

"Are you sure he was there when this was going on?"

"Yes, sir."

Beside this one bit of positive evidence to connect Forrest with whatever shootings went on after resistance ceased, from a witness who knew him as "a little bit of a man," there is the statement of Sergeant Benjamin Robinson, colored, that "General Forrest rode his horse over me three or four times. I did not know him until I heard his men call his name. He said to some negro men there that he knew them; that they had been in his nigger yard in Memphis. He said he was not worth five dollars when he started, and had got rich trading in negroes."[60]

Other references to Forrest in the testimony are to the effect that soldiers hallooed "Forrest says, no quarter! no quarter!" and the next one hallooed, "Black flag! black flag!"[61] or that the "general cry from the time they charged the fort until an hour afterwards was, 'Kill 'em, kill 'em; God damn 'em; that's Forrest's orders, not to leave one alive."[62]

That some of Forrest's men believed that he had made some such order is indicated in the letter of Sergeant Achilles V. Clark, of the Twentieth Tennessee, written from Brownsville to his sisters on the nineteenth:[63]

"The slaughter was awful. Words cannot describe the scene. The poor, deluded negroes would run up to our men, fall upon their knees and with uplifted hands scream for mercy but they were ordered to their feet and then shot down. The white men fared but little better. . . . I with several others tried to stop the butchery and at one time had partially succeeded but Gen. Forrest ordered them shot down like dogs and the carnage continued."

That Sergeant Clark was mistaken in his belief as to Forrest's orders is shown by the mass of sworn testimony subsequently assembled by Dr. Wyeth from staff officers of Forrest and Chalmers, from brigade and regimental commanders, and from surviving Confederate officers and soldiers of all ranks.

None of them denies that there was firing after the garrison broke from the fort to the prepared positions under the bluff where, in addition to the arrangements with the gunboats, "six cases of rifle ammunition were found . . . with tops removed and ready for immediate distribution and use," and where "about 275 serviceable rifles and carbines were gathered up between the water's edge and the brow of the bluff, where they had been thrown down by the garrison when they found the gunboat New Era had deserted them and escape impossible."[64] Several Confederate survivors testify to the effect that Forrest, as soon as he reached the scene, "rode down the line and commanded and caused the firing to cease."[65] After this order was given, according to the testimony of Dr. W. J. Robinson, there was but one shooting and the guilty soldier was at once arrested and placed under guard by General Chalmers.[66]

That Chalmers protected another of the garrison is attested, also, in a letter from Dr. C. Fitch of Chariton, Iowa, written to the General in 1879, after he had become a member of Congress and had been assailed on the floor for his participation in the "Fort Pillow Massacre." Dr. Fitch, who was the surgeon of the post, said that when his captors were about to strip him of his boots he appealed to the General, "who cursed them, and put a guard over me, giving orders to the guard to shoot down the first one that molested me.

"I am not aware that there was any formal surrender of Fort Pillow to Forrest's command," he added. "I looked upon many things that were done as the result of whiskey and a bitter personal hate, especially as regards the Thirteenth regiment. There was considerable alcohol outside the fort, which Forrest's men must have got hold of long before the charge was made. I have always thought that neither you nor Forrest knew anything that was going on at the time under the bluffs. What was done was done very quickly."[67]

There is abundant testimony from Confederate sources that wide-

264

spread and almost general intoxication among the garrison contributed to the frenzy of the scattered resistance offered between the time the parapet was stormed and the time Forrest could restore order below the bluffs. Most of the fifty men who furnished affidavits to Dr. Wyeth mention the presence of whisky in the fort, and the evidences of its too-liberal use by the garrison. Barrels of whisky found along the parapet, with tin dippers attached, were kicked over and spilled by prudent officers of the attacking forces. Among the officers who mention this circumstance are Colonels Tyree Bell and Robert McCulloch, commanding the two assaulting brigades, Colonel Barteau and Captain Anderson, Forrest's aide and only staff officer during the Fort Pillow operation.[68]

That men were killed who had ceased to resist is clear, and is not denied. That this was due to a policy, and not to the circumstances of the fight, is not established. That Forrest himself did exert effective efforts toward stopping any indiscriminate slaughter is clear.

The fourth principal point in the indictment of Forrest's men at the hands of the Congressional committee is that wounded men were burned to death in the huts and tents about the fort. That burned bodies were found by the burial parties from the *Silver Cloud*, the *Platte Valley* and the *New Era* on the thirteenth is not disputed. The explanation offered by Captain W. A. Goodman, Chalmers' adjutant, is that when the *Silver Cloud* began to shell the position that morning, the officer in charge "ordered the tents which were still standing . . . to be burned, intending to abandon the place. In doing this, the bodies of some negroes who had been killed in the tents, on the day before, were somewhat burned; and this probably gave rise to the horrible stories about burning wounded prisoners which were afterward invented and circulated."[69]

The greater part of the testimony before the Congressional committee is not inconsistent with this explanation, being simply statements to the effect that charred bodies were seen in the tents, or that the witness had been told that someone else had seen them. One witness, Ransom Anderson, colored soldier, says that "they put some in the houses and shut them up, and then burned the houses," and that he knew they were there because he "went and looked in" and "heard them hallooing when the houses were burning."[70] He places this on the night of the twelfth, however, while all other evidence is that the tents and huts were burned on the following day. Lieutenant Leaming, who was wounded, was in one of the buildings on the morning of the thirteenth. He testified that after the *Silver Cloud*, or *No. 28*, began to shell the place the Confederate officer in charge decided to burn the tents and buildings, but that he was "gotten out, and thinks that others got the rest out."[71]

Except for Ransom Anderson's inherently improbable story, which

265

fits in with none of the other evidence, there is but one other piece of testimony of intentional burning. Eli A. Bangs, mate of the *New Era*, who accompanied the burial party sent ashore on the thirteenth, says that in one burned tent he found the body of a man through whose clothing and cartridge box nails had been driven into the floor. Three corroborating witnesses support his statement, agreeing that there were other bodies found in the same tent but that "this man in particular was nailed down."[72] In the absence of any direct evidence to the contrary, it may be taken as possible that some vicious person, whether a Confederate soldier or some skulker or prowler, may have perpetrated such an outrage. Beyond this, however, there is no real evidence of value to sustain the committee's conclusion.

The fifth and last of the principal points made by the committee was that the "rebels buried some of the living with the dead." If living men were buried with the dead it was not by the rebels, for the entire work of burying the dead was carried out by Union soldiers, first by prisoners of the garrison and on subsequent days by burial parties sent ashore from the gunboats and transports in the river.

The weight of the evidence—even the Union evidence, when sifted and analyzed—is that any excessive loss of life among the garrison was due to the character of the command and the plan of defense which permitted no definite, clean-cut and readily understood surrender or end to the fighting. This uncertainty gave full play to the tensions between defenders and assailants and the passions aroused in the day of battle. It is plain that there was no planned and ordered "massacre," and that there was no considerable loss of life after the fact of general surrender was well established. The loss was from the sharpshooting throughout the day, in the storming of the parapet and in the period of uncertainty between that time and the arrival of Forrest in the fort after the flag came down—a period which Anderson estimates as "not to exceed twenty minutes."[73] Marshall of the *New Era* says that "the rebels kept firing on our men for at least twenty minutes after our flag was down"[74]—so that there is a fair degree of agreement as to the period of time involved.

The development of the "massacre" theory of the capture of Fort Pillow may be traced in the columns of the Memphis *Bulletin*, a newspaper of strong Union complexion. Its first story, in the issue of Wednesday, April thirteenth, reports the arrival the night before of the steamer *Liberty No. 2*, bringing down families and refugees from Fort Pillow, along with the report that the place was under attack but that "no apprehensions were felt for its safety." On the next day, the fourteenth, the *Bulletin* reported the capture of the place by Forrest's force of 4,000, with an estimate that 300 of the garrison had been killed or wounded in the early fighting and storming of the works which, it was said, "were carried with the national flag waving over them." On the fifteenth the *Bulletin* stated that the gallant defenders had been massacred but again declared that the "greater portion of the garrison had been killed or wounded during the earlier part of the fight."

Two days later, on the seventeenth, an editorial in the *Bulletin* included some of the atrocity stories. On the twenty-first, in a dispatch from Cairo, new atrocities such as burying wounded men alive were added, and the dead Major Booth was praised for his order of the day, "Soldiers Never Surrender!" Finally, on the twenty-seventh, after the visit of the Committee of Congress, portions of its report making the "atrocity" official were published, along with an editorial denunciation of the "infamous General Forrest."

Two years later, on May 30, 1865, and after the end of the war, the same paper considered Fort Pillow once more, concluding that "there was much misrepresentation about the Fort Pillow affair. It is not true that the rebels took no prisoners. On the contrary, about 200 were taken prisoners and carried South."

Even before the Congressional committee was named to make the investigation which was to make of Fort Pillow *the* "atrocity" of the war, a military investigation had been started. Secretary of War Stanton on April sixteenth ordered Sherman to "direct a competent officer to investigate and report minutely, and as early as possible, the facts in relation to the alleged butchery of our troops at Fort Pillow."[75] To this order, Sherman responded a week later that the investigation was under way. He added:

"I know well the animus of the Southern soldiery, and the truth is they cannot be restrained. The effect will be, of course, to make the negroes desperate, and when in turn they commit horrid acts of retaliation we will be relieved of the responsibility. . . . The Southern army, which is the Southern people, cares no more for our clamor than for the idle wind, but they will heed the slaughter that will follow as the natural consequence of their inhuman acts."[76]

The military investigation thus ordered was carried out by General Brayman, Union commander at Cairo, who on April twenty-eighth sent a copy direct to Secretary Stanton, as ordered, and gave another to the Congressional committee when it visited Cairo.[77]

Sherman's judgment of the "massacre at Fort Pillow" as expressed in his *Memoirs* is that:

267

"No doubt Forrest's men acted like a set of barbarians, shooting down the helpless negro garrison after the fort was in their possession; but I am told that Forrest personally disclaims any active participation in the assault, and that he stopped the firing as soon as he could. I also take it for granted that Forrest did not lead the assault in person, and consequently that he was to the rear, out of sight if not of hearing at the time, and I was told by hundreds of our men, who were at various times prisoners in Forrest's possession, that he was usually very kind to them."[78]

To this expression may be added his contemporary judgment expressed in action. "If our men have been murdered after capture," Grant telegraphed Sherman from Virginia, "retaliation must be resorted to promptly."[79] Sherman made his own investigation, and had an opportunity to study that made by the Committee of Congress—but there was no retaliation, and General Sherman was not a man to shrink from ordering retaliation had he felt that it was justified.

CHAPTER XVIII

A SWORD AGAINST SHERMAN'S LIFE LINE*

April 14, 1864-June 9, 1864

THE DIRECT military consequences of the storming of Fort Pillow were small, outside a great flurry among the gunboats all along the Mississippi and its tributaries. Three boats were sent down from above and six ordered up from below, from points as far away as Fort De Russy up the Red River in Louisiana,[1] to be followed in a few days by two more ordered from the mouth of White River on the rumor that Forrest was about to attack Memphis.[2] While Forrest's men were marching back inland to Jackson the wooded hills about Fort Pillow felt the crash of heavy shell thrown from the patrolling gunboats at small bodies of men or sometimes, apparently, just on rumor or general suspicion of rebels about.

On the way back from Fort Pillow, Major Bradford, the unfortunate commander of the ill-fated post, was killed by his Confederate captors. The circumstances are obscure and the testimony contradictory, but it appears that Bradford, whether by violation of parole or otherwise, escaped and was making his way to Memphis in civilian clothing, when he was gathered up in the conscription dragnet which Forrest was spreading through that part of West Tennessee,[3] was recognized and was sent on toward Jackson, to be sent south with other prisoners. In the vicinity of Brownsville he either attempted to escape and was shot, according to one story, or, according to another, was taken into the woods by a small party of his captors and shot. "I knew nothing of the matter until eight or ten days afterward," Forrest wrote the Federal commander at Memphis, adding that "if he was improperly killed nothing would afford me more pleasure than to punish the perpetrators to the full of the law."[4] There is no record of any such action, however, any more than there is record of action by the Federal authorities against Colonel Fielding Hurst on like complaints and charges made by Forrest.

Back in Jackson, Forrest received an order from General Polk to move promptly back to Okolona to meet, in conjunction with Stephen Lee,

---

* The field of operations covered in this chapter is shown on the map on page 218.

an anticipated raid from Middle Tennessee into Alabama. "It is my opinion that no such raid will be made from Decatur or any point west of there," Forrest wrote—an opinion which the event confirmed as correct. His own suggestion, offered in a letter of April fifteenth to President Davis, was that his force be combined with that of Stephen Lee for a "move into Middle Tennessee and Kentucky which would create a diversion of the enemy's forces and enable us to break up his plans, and such an expedition, managed with prudence and executed with rapidity, can be safely made."

Thus again, three weeks before Sherman was to start on his great campaign toward Atlanta, Forrest proposed the one movement which Sherman really feared the Confederates would make—a raid in sufficient force against his railroad line from Louisville through Nashville to Chattanooga to stop the forward movement of his supplies. The letter, which President Davis referred to his military adviser, General Bragg, for comment, came back with an acid endorsement chiefly devoted to captious criticism of the fact that Forrest had sent his letter to Richmond by the hand of William McGee of a Louisiana artillery command, who had expressed a desire to shoot the guns under Forrest. Men, said General Bragg, were being "enticed from their commands and employed in violation of orders." Moreover, he wrote, Mr. McGee "should be arrested and sent to his proper command, and General Forrest made accountable for his unauthorized absence." And where, the General wanted to know after doing a little arithmetic, were all those men whom Forrest was supposed to have raised in West Tennessee? The only reference to the point of the letter, the proposed joint movement into Middle Tennessee, was the remark that it was of the "utmost importance."[5]

Meanwhile, under orders, Forrest was starting his command south. Chalmers, to whom Forrest made handsome acknowledgment in his report for "prompt and energetic action" and "faithful execution of all movements necessary to the successful accomplishment of the object of the expedition,"[6] was sent on to Okolona.[7] Other than Buford's brigade, which was still in Kentucky, only small units were to be left north of the Mississippi line, and these were to be brought out as soon as Buford returned.

It appearing, however, that the rumored raid into Alabama was in fact a false alarm, Forrest somewhat delayed his departure, meanwhile using the small commands of Colonels Duckworth, Crews and Wilson to keep the Union forces in Memphis "practically in a state of siege," as General Hurlbut described it, or "penned up in Memphis," in Sherman's more forthright language.[8]

270

Forrest reported himself upon arrival at Jackson as "suffering from exhaustion caused by hard riding and bruises received in the late engagement," in which a wounded horse fell on him.[9] He did not mention it in his report, but while he had been away on the Fort Pillow expedition, his brother, Lieutenant Colonel Aaron Forrest, who had last been reported in February "on the Yazoo River with one regiment fighting gunboats and transports," died of pneumonia—the second of the brothers to meet death in the service of the Confederate States in two months.[10]

As Chalmers marched south into Mississippi he met the order revoking the command for Forrest to leave West Tennessee forthwith, and not only sent along the countermanding order but also sent back Bell's and Neely's brigades, both of which were put to work in the vicinity of Memphis to "drive the country, gathering all conscripts and absentees."[11] Forrest knew that he did not have long to stay in West Tennessee and he planned to take out with him, when he went, as many men and as much of everything as he could.

To that end, he urgently requested that the railroad be put in operation as far above Tupelo as possible to haul out the supplies which were being sent to Corinth by wagon and thence on south by handcars to which mules were hitched—the beginning, perhaps, of what came to be known as the "system of mule trains" on the railroads in northern Mississippi.[12] Rambaut, still in Mississippi, was ordered to get up rations to Okolona, and the wagons were called up as far as Tupelo. Plans were put on foot to get the horses shod as soon as they got back to Mississippi, and put in shape for further service.[13] Disciplinary problems received attention as well, to judge from an order to Chalmers to send Captain W. H. Forrest, the General's brother and a famous scout, to the general commanding at Tupelo, and to "have the men with him arrested and taken to Tupelo"—for what reason does not now appear.[14]

Just as busy as Forrest on logistic problems, and on a vastly larger scale, was General Sherman, 150 miles northeast of Jackson, at Nashville. General Sherman was getting ready to carry out the grand design of a co-ordinated advance— Grant upon Lee's army and Richmond, himself upon Joe Johnston's army and Atlanta—and the time was growing short. This Forrest, moreover, was a troublesome and unpredictable factor in the problem, given to breaking out at unexpected times and places. He must be kept busy and penned up, even if not run down, but it must be done without "interrupting my plans of preparation for the great object of the spring campaign."[15] Hurlbut, Sherman had come to believe, could not be expected to do the job. He was therefore relieved of his command at Memphis on April eighteenth and replaced by Major General Cadwallader C. Washburn.[16] The new commander at

Memphis was the youngest of three distinguished brothers, the others being Israel, war Governor of Maine, and Elihu, Congressman from Illinois and chairman of the Military Affairs Committee of the House of Representatives and early patron and backer of an unknown ex-officer of the United States Army, U. S. Grant. Cadwallader had served three terms as a Congressman from Wisconsin before the war—all three brothers had been in Congress together at one time—and had resigned to enter the army. After the war he too was to become a governor, of Wisconsin, and the organizer of one of the world's greatest milling companies.[17]

On the same day on which Washburn was ordered to take command at Memphis a new cavalry commander was sent there by Sherman. The new commander, Brigadier General Samuel D. Sturgis, was a graduate of West Point in the famous class of 1846, which numbered among its members George B. McClellan and Thomas Jonathan Jackson, better known to fame as "Stonewall," besides corps and division commanders in both armies such as John G. Foster, Jesse Reno, Darius Couch, George Stoneman, Dabney Maury, Cadmus Wilcox and George Pickett. He had served in the War with Mexico and in numerous affairs on the Western plains; had been brevetted and promoted to brigadier general of Volunteers for "gallant and meritorious conduct" at Wilson's Creek in 1861, with a second brevet at the battle of Fredericksburg, and had commanded cavalry operations in Virginia, Kentucky and East Tennessee. He was not only a gallant soldier but one whose self-confidence was such that Sherman could not say of him, as he had of William Sooy Smith, that he was "too mistrustful of himself" to make a good commander against Forrest.[18]

"I have sent Sturgis down to take command of that cavalry," Sherman wrote to Grant's chief of staff, "and whip Forrest, and, if necessary to mount enough men, to seize any and all the horses of Memphis, or wherever he may go." Hurlbut was advised that Sturgis was on his way to Memphis "to assume command of all the cavalry, and to move out and attack Forrest wherever he can be found." Grierson was directed to seize as many horses and mules as might be necessary to get the cavalry ready for Sturgis' coming, and Brigadier General R. P. Buckland, commanding the infantry garrison, was told to get ready to move out with the cavalry. Like orders were sent to the new commander, Washburn. "The great object is to defeat him, if possible, and prevent him from getting off with his plunder." To which Sherman added a final admonition: "I know there are troops enough at Memphis to whale Forrest if you can reach him."[19]

Under all these admonitions Washburn arrived in Memphis on April

272

twenty-third and Sturgis a day later. To Grant's chief of staff Washburn reported that Forrest was at Jackson with seven brigades, about 8,000 men altogether, all well mounted. "I regret that my force here is not sufficient to enable me to move out and assail him," he added—which reads not at all differently from what Hurlbut had been saying to his superiors. Hurlbut had been removed from command for "marked timidity in the management of affairs" as against Forrest and here was the new commander reporting already: "While with the force I have here I feel perfectly secure against any mounted force they may bring, I do not feel that I could venture to go in pursuit of Forrest without hazarding the city unless I have more force."[20]

Forrest had, in fact, but a fraction of the force attributed to him, but there was about him and his operations an aura of uncertainty and invincibility which most certainly affected the resolution of commanders sent against him. "The very name of Forrest is a host in itself," an infantry soldier who did not serve under him wrote in his diary in an entry describing how, in this same month of April 1864, a small body of foot soldiers operating near Florence in north Alabama captured a cavalry detachment in the night by charging them under the battle cry, "Forrest! Forrest!" After their surrender, he noted, the Yankees "were much surprised that 'Gen. Forrest' had only 150 men, and they afoot, but we would not undeceive them. . . ."[21]

Sherman at Nashville, struggling with the immense task of getting his great expedition under way, evidently sensed something of the effect of Forrest upon the minds of his new commanders at Memphis, for he wrote Washburn a confidential note rechecking the reports as to strength there, and admonishing him to "try and not exaggerate the forces of the enemy or your own weakness, but use your force to the best advantage. Don't let Forrest insult you by passing in sight almost of your command."[22]

Washburn not only seized all the horses in Memphis but called on the commander at Vicksburg for cavalry reinforcements, whose arrival he was awaiting. "The moment they arrive I shall send out a force that I am certain will whip Forrest and drive him from the State," he added. Hurlbut, hearing of these efforts to increase the force, offered the sardonic comment that General Washburn "sent to Memphis expressly to punish Forrest . . . which 'marked timidity' on my part prevented from being done, should use only the material which I left there."[23]

Before leaving his headquarters at Nashville for his advanced position at Chattanooga, on April twenty-eighth Sherman telegraphed Grant, "I must imitate Forrest's example and help myself [to horses]. I began here yesterday, and at once have got 1,000 good horses." More im-

273

portant, he renewed his instructions to Washburn to do likewise. "We are now all in motion for Georgia," he said. "We want you to hold Forrest . . . until we strike Johnston. *This is quite as important as to whip him.*"[24]

At the same time Rear Admiral D. D. Porter, commanding the vast naval fleet on Western waters, was asked by Sherman to "keep a bright lookout up the Tennessee that Forrest don't cross and cut my roads when I am in Georgia."[25]

To his trusted lieutenant, McPherson, Sherman wrote: "The only danger I apprehend is from resident guerrillas, and from Forrest coming from the direction of Florence. I did want A. J. Smith on the Tennessee, about Florence, to guard against that danger, but Banks cannot spare him, and Grant orders me to calculate without him."[26] This admonition McPherson passed on to Washburn:

"You may not be able with the troops at your disposal to assume the offensive with as much boldness as is desirable against an enemy like Forrest, and force him to fight or be driven out of West Tennessee. It is of the utmost importance, however, to keep his forces occupied, and prevent him from forming plans and combinations to cross the Tennessee River and break up the railroad communications in our rear."[27]

With all this activity directed against him, Forrest spent the last days of April in West Tennessee with his "entire command engaged conscripting and arresting deserters . . . scattered in all directions, but moving toward" Jackson, where he expected to have "all concentrated by the 30th," and to reach Tupelo by May fifth or sixth. When he got there, Forrest wrote, he hoped that time and opportunity would be allowed "to render to the department proper field returns and inspection reports." Before he started out of West Tennessee, however, he was advised by Polk from department headquarters at Demopolis, Alabama, that "an officer from Richmond is here on his way to Tupelo to inspect your command; you will leave such of it as you may desire in Tennessee and Kentucky and proceed yourself immediately to Tupelo to meet him." Forrest did not start immediately—he could not, with the responsibility for withdrawing his command from West Tennessee upon him—but wrote Polk that he wanted his command "thoroughly inspected," and asked that the officer from Richmond remain at Tupelo until he could get there.[28]

Buford's whole division, Bell's Tennessee brigade and the Kentucky brigade were assembled in Jackson before the end of April, as was Neely's brigade. On May first the three brigades left Jackson under Buford's command, convoying a long ox train heavy-laden with supplies and subsistence and some 300 prisoners, to march around the head-waters of the Hatchie by way of Purdy to Corinth and thence down the railroad to Rienzi, where supplies and prisoners were to be transferred to the railroad while the command moved on to Tupelo.[29]

Early on the morning of April thirtieth Sturgis' column of 3,000 cavalry and 3,400 infantry, with twenty guns, marched out of Memphis "in pursuit of Forrest." Two and one-half days were spent making the first forty-five miles to Somerville. From there, at 1:00 P.M. of May second, Sturgis sent forward 700 select men under Colonel Joseph Kargé, with a section of artillery to locate the enemy. Forrest had closed his head-quarters at Jackson that morning and started south by way of Bolivar.[30] As he reached that point in midafternoon he learned that 200 troopers of McDonald's battalion—his own Old Regiment—under Lieutenant Colonel Crews, were fighting what was reported as a Federal cavalry force 2,000 strong west of the town.

Such a fight was too close for Forrest and his escort to miss. The arrival of the General and his hundred daredevil companions brought Crews's force up to about 300, without artillery. After driving the Federal troops with his first impetuous charge Forrest drew back into the old entrenchments just west of the town, thrown up there during the Federal occupation in 1862, and kept up a "severe fight" for two hours—the while his wagons and the unarmed men whom Crews was convoying moved on south. Finally, at dark, the Confederate force fell back through the town, destroyed the bridge over the swollen Hatchie and followed on south without close pursuit.[31] Among Forrest's losses in the fight was his adjutant, Major Strange, wounded.

Washburn reported to Grant that Sturgis was "in hot pursuit" of Forrest, although Sturgis himself was more concerned to point out the delays he was suffering from rain, high water, bad bridges and slow infantry than he was to claim any very close contact with Forrest's re-treating forces.[32] Indeed, he did not follow the main body, which had passed down through Purdy on the east of the Hatchie, but followed Forrest himself and his little detachment through Ripley on the west of that stream—which may have been why the wily Forrest marched that way instead of with his main body and his subsistence trains.

Finally, at Ripley, which Sturgis reached on May sixth, he found "that the rear of Forrest's command had passed . . . nearly two days before." Hoping against hope, he said, he still would "have continued the pur-suit had it not been for the utter and entire destitution of the country from Bolivar to Ripley, a distance of forty miles. My horses had scarcely anything to eat, and my artillery horses absolutely nothing. . . . I need hardly assure you that it was with the greatest reluctance . . . that I decided to abandon the chase as hopeless. . . . Though we could not catch the scoundrel we are at least rid of him and that is something."[33]

But it was not the "something" that was of greatest importance to Sherman, as Sturgis may have realized, judging from this explanatory letter which he wrote to Sherman after his return to Memphis:[34]

"My little campaign is over and I regret to say, Forrest is still at large. He did not come to West Tennessee for the purpose of fighting, unless it might so happen that he could fall upon some little party or defenseless place. . . . It is idle to follow him except with an equal force of cavalry, which we have not in this part of the country. I say except with an equal force of cavalry, but even then he has so many advantages and is so disposed to run that I feel that all that could be done in any case would be to drive him out unless, indeed, he might be trapped. . . . I regret very much that I could not have the pleasure of bringing you his hair but he is too great a plunderer to fight anything like an equal force, and we have to be satisfied with driving him from the state. He may turn on your communications and I rather think he will, but see no way to prevent it from this point and with this force."

On May fifth, as Sturgis was marching toward Ripley, three days behind Forrest, Grant was across the Rapidan and into the Wilderness, and in Georgia Sherman moved along Rocky Face Ridge to open the campaign for Atlanta. At last, after three years of war, from the logic of the chain of events started two years earlier at Fort Henry and Fort Donelson, a great strategic design had emerged.

On the same day Forrest, the threat above all other threats to Sherman's striking force which was to cut through the heart of the South while Grant hammered Lee's army on the anvil of Richmond, reported at Tupelo, leading in his troops and his trains, loose and free of entanglements, and ready, with a "little rest, ammunition, etc.,"[35] for the next service which the Confederacy or his superior officers might require.

Through the month of May, Sherman was driving ahead in north Georgia, skillfully using his superior numbers and resources to outflank the Army of Tennessee which Joe Johnston as skillfully withdrew from its successive positions, from Dalton to Resaca at the crossing of the Oostenaula, to Cassville and on across the Etowah into the broken hills north of Kennesaw Mountain.

Johnston's was a losing game, however, and must continue to be, so long as Sherman could keep open his life line to the rear—the railroad back through Chattanooga and Nashville to the Ohio River.

"That single line of railroad, four hundred seventy three miles long," Sherman wrote, "supplied an army of 100,000 men and 35,000 ani-

mals. . . . The Atlanta campaign was an impossibility without these railroads; and possible only then because we had the means and the men to
maintain and defend them in addition to what were necessary to overcome the enemy."[36]

There were not wanting men on the Confederate side who saw this
situation and who believed that the way to defeat Sherman was to cut
his life line of rails. As early as April twenty-second, while Forrest was
still in West Tennessee and before Sherman had begun his advance,
General Bragg proposed to President Davis that while Johnston took the
offensive into East Tennessee, "Forrest might move into or threaten
Middle Tennessee."[37] Johnston himself, as soon as Sherman's advance
started and even before the retreat from Dalton began, suggested "the
immediate movement of Forrest into Middle Tennessee."[38] In the early
days of the advance, in fact, there were so many and such various reports
from subordinate Federal officers as to the whereabouts of Forrest in
Tennessee, in Alabama and even in north Georgia, that they provoked
from Sherman the remark, on May fifteenth, that "Forrest on the 6th
was retreating before Sam Sturgis in Mississippi, toward Tupelo. In
person he may be at Rome, but if his horses are there they can out-
march ours."[39]

Sherman's deduction was correct. Forrest was still in Mississippi, busy
with the recruitment of his horses, the refitting of his men and the inspection and reorganization of his command. The reorganization included
the creation of an artillery battalion of four batteries—Morton's Tennessee battery of three-inch rifled guns under command of Lieutenant
T. Saunders Sale, the Arkansas battery of Captain J. C. Thrall and the
Tennessee battery of Captain T. W. Rice, both equipped with 6-pounder
brass pieces, and Captain E. S. Walton's Mississippi battery of two brass
10-pounders and two 12-pounder howitzers. Commanding the battalion
was Captain Morton, the "pasty-faced boy" whom Forrest had indignantly rejected when he reported at Columbia eighteen months before
and who now, being still in his twenty-first year, had become his chief of
artillery.[40]

Forrest's usual close attention to horses was extended at this time to
their ownership as well. "Not a day passes," ran his order announcing
$500 reward for the detection, delivery and conviction of any member of
the command guilty of horse stealing, "without many complaints being
made from both officers and soldiers and citizens. It must be stopped,
and the major-general commanding is determined if severe punishment
inflicted on those convicted of it will stop it, that it shall be done. No
mercy will be shown in these cases."[41]

Another side of the life of the command is shown in an order suspending military duties on Sunday, May fifteenth, as far as possible so as to permit "all soldiers who are disposed to do so" to attend special divine services of thanksgiving and intercession to be held at headquarters at Tupelo by the chaplains of the command.[42]

The general state of the command at this time appears from the reports of the two inspecting officers sent out from Richmond, Brigadier General George B. Hodge and Colonel George William Brent. Colonel Brent noted that horseshoes and nails, forage sacks and proper horse equipment were lacking. The Confederate saddles furnished, he added, were indifferent in quality and destructive of the horses' backs—which may have been another reason why Forrest seemed to prefer to equip his men with what he could capture from the enemy. There was a great lack of funds for the purchase of supplies while, as appears elsewhere, few of the troops in the department had received pay in six months or more.[43]

As to the troops themselves, Colonel Brent reported that McCulloch's brigade of Chalmers' division was made up of old organizations, while the other brigade of the division, Neely's, had but one old regiment, Duckworth's Seventh Tennessee, and three others "composed of the debris of Richardson's brigade, and many other partisan and irregular organizations raised in West Tennessee." Crossland's brigade of Buford's division, he reported, consisted of the three newly mounted Kentucky infantry regiments, augmented by recruits recently obtained in Kentucky, plus Faulkner's regiment which "claims to be an old organization, but by what authority, or when raised and first organized, investigation has not yet disclosed. It was a fragmentary command when it reported to General Forrest." Bell's brigade, also of Buford's division, was made up of one old regiment, the Second Tennessee, and three newly organized commands. Of Forrest's other brigade, commanded by Brigadier General S. J. Gholson, he simply reported that it had just been transferred from the Mississippi state forces to the Confederate service.

"The present organization of Forrest's command is irregular and without authority," Colonel Brent reported, but in explanation he recited the facts as to Forrest's arrival with a handful of men in his new field of operation, to find there only one organized command—the brigade of Chalmers, now commanded by McCulloch. Colonel Brent added:

"All the other commands were either in a chaotic, disorganized condition or incomplete, and claiming to be followers of different leaders. Their commanders found it impossible to keep their commands together. . . . The necessity for reconstruction and reorganization of all these scattered, disorganized, and fragmentary bodies became necessary. General Forrest accordingly informed the commanders that unless by the 5th of

278

February, 1864, they could reassemble their commands he would assume the power of reconstructing them. The commanders having failed to reassemble their commands, General Forrest . . . proceeded . . . to reconstruct and reorganize all these bands into battalions and regiments . . . assuming and exercising the power of appointing both field and staff for many of these commands. . . . It is impossible to trace out the origin and subsequent history of all these organizations. It is equally so to reinstate them in their original condition. To do so would produce endless confusion and controversy. To avoid such calamity, the good of the service would be best promoted by accepting the existing organization."[44]

Colonel Brent did find, however, comparing the muster rolls with a list of deserters from the Army of Tennessee, that 654 men so listed were included in Forrest's command, and ordered their arrest and return to Johnston's army. Forrest took the matter up with the Major General Stephen D. Lee, who had succeeded to the command of the department on May ninth, when Lieutenant General Polk and most of the infantry were sent to Georgia to help fend off Sherman's advance.

"There are about 1,000 men in my command who left the army at its reorganization in spring of 1862," he telegraphed Lee, representing that to return these men at this time would result in wholesale desertion and loss to the service. "Some officers are here from infantry to identify and get their men," he wrote, asking for a temporary suspension of the order. "I have given them free access to the muster rolls in order to get a list of men claimed, but I am firmly of opinion that until such times as all the regiments who have absentees here can . . . have officers present to identify their men, that any attempt on the part of the few officers now here to recover their men will result in the loss of 800 or 900 men; for as soon as you commence arresting, the balance, anticipating a similar fate, will take to the woods with arms, equipment and horses."[45]

Failing to get the order suspended, Forrest proceeded vigorously to its execution, giving "every facility in his power to accomplish the object of my mission," Colonel Brent reported. On Sunday, May twenty-second, under Forrest's orders both divisions of his command held dress parades *on foot*, at which time designated men to the number of 653, taken from ten regiments, were arrested and forwarded under guard. The men so arrested turned in their arms and equipments and turned over their horses to the division quartermasters, who had them appraised and receipted for them—the Confederate cavalryman's horse being his own property, not his government's.[46]

Despite his care, however, Forrest's fear of heavy desertions as a result of the action taken proved to be well founded. From the three newly organized regiments of Neely's brigade, desertions during the day and night of May twenty-second numbered 126 out of an aggregate present of 1,629.[47]

Despite all these difficulties in administration and organization—difficulties from which Forrest was never to be free—Assistant Inspector General Hodge found that though "the force is principally of new recruits, and consequently undisciplined and undrilled, the material is good." The horses he found "in tolerable condition, but the arms and equipments very deficient. It needs quite 3,000 guns and accouterments."[48]

The latter lack the department commander undertook to supply by stopping in transit at Selma arms and accouterments being shipped to General Kirby Smith in the Trans-Mississippi department, and sending them to Forrest at Tupelo.[49]

Lee was trying to help Forrest get ready for the movement into Middle Tennessee, which he had suggested to Adjutant General Samuel Cooper at Richmond. On May seventeenth Cooper authorized the movement, suggesting that "it should be prompt and vigorous." On the very day on which the order was received, however, Lee wired back to Richmond that he did not "deem it prudent to make movement suggested now," because an enemy raid in force was expected from Memphis, and at the same time he advised Joseph E. Johnston, who by this time already had been forced back from Dalton to Resaca, Georgia, that the order for Forrest's movement into Middle Tennessee had been suspended.[50]

The change in plans stemmed from reports received by Forrest from his redoubtable chief of scouts, Captain Thomas Henderson, whose lameness from an old wound kept him on crutches but in nowise slowed up his activity on horseback or the thoroughness and pervasiveness with which his men hovered round the Union camps.[51] "I don't understand why Henderson's scouts are constantly about us," Colonel Waring wrote his new commander at Memphis, General Washburn, adding, "They usually have some communication with Forrest."[52] At this particuliar time, indeed, despite Washburn's official closing of the lines about Memphis to all trade and passage without express military permit, they were getting out to Forrest news of the preparations being made for a movement against the territory he was assigned to defend.[53]

Forrest himself acquiesced in the suspension of the movement to Middle Tennessee. He had an effective total of 9,220 men, he wrote Lee, but 3,804 of them were still without arms. The Tennessee expedition was to have taken 3,500 of the best armed and equipped men while 1,400 were stationed about Panola and Grenada, in the central part of Mississippi, leaving only 700 muskets with Chalmers for the defense of the prairie country, "the only abundant and available" source of supply for "breadstuffs and provisions" in the whole region. It would be "impolitic," Forrest thought, "to leave the prairie country almost unprotected" in this fashion, while he felt, also, that 3,000 men was "too small a force to send into Middle Tennessee."[54]

Lee disagreed with Forrest on the last point, deeming 3,500 men a sufficient force for the Tennessee expedition, but countermanded the order for the movement[55]—which was exactly the reaction calculated upon by Sherman who was using, and for the remainder of the critical summer of 1864 would continue to use, the threat from Memphis against Mississippi as the most effective way to keep Forrest off his railroads in Middle Tennessee.

By that time the receding tide of battle in Georgia had rolled on back from the Oostenaula to the Etowah—the Army of Tennessee crossed that considerable stream on May twentieth—and the idea of using Forrest to cut in behind Sherman was being discussed by Confederate civilians of such diverse stations as the Rebel War Clerk J. B. Jones and Confederate States Senator Gustavus A. Henry of Tennessee, who addressed to Jones's Chief, Secretary of War Seddon, this pertinent inquiry:[56]

"Now that the enemy are drawn far into Georgia would it not be a great move to order Forrest with his whole force to fall in behind the enemy and cut off his trains of supplies and make such a demonstration in his rear as will destroy his army."

By the time Senator Henry addressed the query, however, Forrest's forces had begun to be dispersed, despite the fact that the Federal "raid still threatened from Memphis." On May twenty-third Chalmers was sent to central Alabama with Gholson's brigade and his own division, less three regiments left to make up a new brigade commanded by Colonel Edmund W. Rucker, apparently for defense against possible Federal raids from Georgia.[57] The movement which was to take nearly half of Forrest's effective force out of action for critical weeks was apparently another, and extreme, expression of the policy of the dispersed defensive which was to keep small and almost impotent bodies of Confederate soldiers scattered about covering territories all over the South while the great concentrated forces of Sherman and Grant struck for their objectives.

On the same day on which Chalmers left on this fruitless expedition, Sherman was wiring from Georgia directions for "a threatening movement from Memphis on Columbus, Miss., to prevent Forrest and Lee from swinging over against my communications."[58] Sherman knew

281

where his danger was and he knew the weakness in Southern policy on which to play.

Although Forrest was left after Chalmers' departure with only some 5,000 men, spread all across north Mississippi from Panola to Corinth, Federal scouts continued to bring into Memphis rumors and reports of heavy concentrations under Forrest, which Washburn reported as "from 10,000 to 12,000 men, at Corinth and Tupelo," while other Federal commanders raised the sights to 15,000 and even to 30,000 men, poised ready for "some big enterprise."[59]

Forrest himself on May twenty-sixth outlined to Lee several lines of action, in the alternative—to go into Middle Tennessee, starting from Tupelo rather than Corinth; to strike the Mississippi River at Commerce below Memphis, or at Randolph above, and obstruct navigation; or to go against Memphis itself—all moves which might "create diversions which will be of advantage."[60]

Before hearing from Lee, Forrest sent from Tupelo on May twenty-ninth the brief and decisive dispatch:

"The time has arrived, and if I can be spared and allowed 2,000 picked men from Buford's division and a battery of artillery, will attempt to cut enemy's communication in Middle Tennessee."[61]

Forrest's decision was based, in part at least, upon a report received from Brigadier General P. D. Roddey, commanding the light Confederate forces in north Alabama, that the Tennessee River was low and "fordable for large horses" while Sherman's railroads were "all guarded by negro troops."[62]

On May thirty-first Lee authorized Forrest to carry out his plans with his "disposable force," to which Forrest replied on the same day that on the following morning, June first, he would leave Tupelo with about 2,200 men, six pieces of artillery and ten days' rations, marching by way of Russellville, Alabama, for the Tennessee River, leaving behind in Mississippi 1,400 men at Tupelo and Corinth under Colonel Russell, and 1,500 at Oxford under Colonel Rucker.[63]

On the day on which Forrest started his march for Tennessee, however, the Federal expedition ordered by Sherman left Memphis under instructions from his lieutenant, McPherson, to "smash things" in north Mississippi.[64] The new expedition made up and fitted out by the indefatigable Washburn was the largest and best equipped which had yet gone against Forrest—3,300 cavalry under Grierson, 5,000 infantry under McMillen, 250 wagons, 22 guns, the whole under command of the ardent Sturgis, whose disappointment that Forrest had not accommodated him with a fight a month earlier had been so vigorous and vocal. "The force sent out was in complete order and consisted of some of our best troops," Washburn reported. "They had a supply of twenty days. I saw to it personally that they lacked nothing to insure a successful campaign. The number of troops deemed necessary by General Sherman, as he telegraphed me, was 6,000 but I sent 8,000."[65]

Of the three infantry brigades in the expedition, one of 1,200 men commanded by Colonel Edward Bouton was made up of colored troops who, as Washburn afterward admitted in correspondence with Forrest, had taken an oath to avenge Fort Pillow and to show Forrest's troops no quarter.[66] General Hurlbut had stated, indeed, that "in case of an action in which they [colored troops] are successful, it will be nearly impracticable to restrain them from retaliation" for Fort Pillow.[67]

Despite the vigor of his assertions and the ardor of his troops, however, General Sturgis moved out from Memphis slowly, even in the absence of any substantial opposition. On Sunday, June fifth, from Forrest's boyhood home of Salem, Mississippi, a flying column of 400 men under Colonel Kargé was sent ahead to strike the railroad at Rienzi, destroy bridges and trestlework there, and rejoin the main column.[68] Before Kargé got back, Sturgis was already thinking of turning back to Memphis. At Ripley on June eighth he called a council of his senior officers to whom he put his difficulties and exposed the state of his mind. It was raining, the roads were bad, the streams flooded. There was, he felt, "great probability that the enemy would . . . concentrate an overwhelming force against us in the vicinity of Tupelo," and he was particularly impressed with the "utter hopelessness of saving our train or artillery in case of defeat."

"All agreed with me in the probable consequences of defeat," he reported. "Some thought our only safety lay in retracing our steps and abandoning the expedition. It was urged, however, (and with some propriety, too) that inasmuch as I had abandoned a similiar expedition only a few weeks before . . . it would be ruinous on all sides to return without first meeting the enemy. . . . Under these circumstances, and with a sad foreboding of the consequences, I determined to move forward. . . ."[69]

During the week in which Sturgis was marching the seventy-five miles between Memphis and Ripley, Forrest had marched from Tupelo into north Alabama, where he was to add 1,000 of Roddey's men to his own 2,200 and had sent Captain Anderson and Captain John G. Mann, his chief engineer, on ahead to arrange for crossing the Tennessee. At Russellville, Alabama, however, on June third orders were received from Lee to return immediately to repel the Sturgis expedition. Prompt movement and marching brought Forrest back to Tupelo on the fifth—the day on which Sturgis was at Salem, fifty miles to the northwest.[70]

Sturgis, as he plaintively reported, was moving blind with "information exceedingly meager and unsatisfactory." Forrest, on the other hand, knew where Sturgis was, but his timid and hesitant moves taken with the divergent movement of Kargé's column made it difficult to determine where he was going—whether toward Corinth or Tupelo. Buford, therefore, was sent up the railroad to Baldwyn, eighteen miles north of Tupelo, whence on the eighth he moved another dozen miles north to Booneville.

It was at Booneville that Forrest's troops witnessed their first military execution for desertion in the face of the enemy. Three men, or rather two men and a boy, were confined for the night of the eighth in a boxcar on the railroad tracks. "A preacher was with them," wrote Sergeant Frank T. Reid of Morton's Battery, years later, "and I can still hear their loud voices in prayer and singing hymns." The next morning, June ninth, the troops were drawn up in the old sedge field, in the center of which there were three newly dug graves. At the last minute the boy was pardoned, while a firing squad of twelve men took position at ten paces distance for the execution of the two men. "A sharp command, a crack of musketry, and two lives were snuffed out like worthless tallow candles," wrote Sergeant Reid, but Lieutenant Hanson, who likewise remembered and recorded the scene, was impressed with the fact that one of the deserters was not killed instantly by the fire.[71]

On this same ninth day of June, after two days' skirmishing across the front of Sturgis' advancing column, Rucker reported to Forrest at Booneville with his new brigade which had been left behind about Oxford when Forrest started for Tennessee, while Bell's brigade was ordered on to Rienzi, seven miles north of Booneville, where it would be in better position to cover Corinth should that turn out to be necessary. On this day also Colonel William A. Johnson, one of Roddey's brigade commanders, marched into Baldwyn with the 500 men of his brigade who had been able to hold the pace in a week's forced march from Alabama. The Kentucky brigade of Buford's division, commanded by Colonel Hylan B. Lyon, remained this day at Booneville.[72]

"I cannot hear of Forrest," Sherman dispatched on this same day from Acworth, Georgia, below the Etowah, "though I believe the expedition which left Memphis June 1 . . . will give him good employment."[73]

The expedition referred to on this ninth of June moved through Ripley and on southeast some twelve miles toward Guntown, a station on the Mobile & Ohio Railroad. That evening Sturgis' force, compactly concentrated, made camp at Stubbs's Farm. This news, promptly borne to Forrest, was the first clear and unmistakable indication that the "upper route" by which Sturgis might have moved to strike the railroad at Rienzi or Booneville was abandoned, and that he definitely was headed for Tupelo by way of Guntown.

On the same evening General Lee, who had been with Forrest at Booneville, went south by rail to attempt to gather in about Tupelo, or even below toward Okolona, reinforcements upon which Forrest might fall back before giving battle to Sturgis' advancing force. Lee left to Forrest's discretion what was to be done, and how[74]—discretion under which that most audacious man made one of the most audacious decisions of his fighting career.

The result, on the next day, was the battle variously known as Guntown or Tishomingo Creek or Brice's Cross Roads but, by whatever name known, one which, in the words of Viscount Wolseley, was "a most remarkable achievement, well worth attention by the military student"[75] —an opinion shared by Lieutenant Colonel William A. Mitchell of the United States Military Academy, who years later wrote, "for use of cavalry in battle, no better example can be found than Forrest's employment of cavalry at Brice's Cross Roads."[76]

CHAPTER XIX

BRICE'S CROSS ROADS: HIGH-WATER MARK OF VICTORY*
June 10, 1864-June 13, 1864

AUDACIOUS as was Forrest's decision to head off and fight Sturgis' overwhelming force where he found him, it was a calculated audacity. True, Sturgis could have put two men on the firing line to Forrest's one, what with the necessity for every fourth man of the cavalry acting as a horseholder, and the disparity in artillery strength was nearer three to one. True, too, Sturgis had his whole force concentrated within less than ten miles of the place where Forrest planned to meet him and give battle, while Forrest's forces were widely scattered. Johnson's fragment of a brigade, 500 men, was at Baldwyn, six miles from the field. Lyon and Rucker, with no more than 1,500 men between them, and the two batteries of artillery under Morton were at Booneville, eighteen miles away. Bell, with nearly 2,800 men, more than half the available force—Chalmers and Roddey being clear away in Alabama—was still farther off at Rienzi, twenty-five miles north of the scene of the coming fight.

But June 10, 1864, the day that was not yet dawning as Forrest got his command under way, was going to be a "scorcher" in Mississippi. "Their cavalry will move out ahead of their infantry," Forrest explained to one of his brigade commanders, Rucker, "and should reach the cross roads three hours in advance. We can whip their cavalry in that time. As soon as the fight opens they will send back to have the infantry hurried up. It is going to be hot as hell, and coming on a run for five or six miles, their infantry will be so tired out we will ride right over them. I want everything to move up as soon as possible. I will go ahead with Lyon and the escort and open the fight."[1]

It was characteristic of Forrest that while he counted upon the exhaustion and distress of the enemy's infantry as a factor in his battle, he assumed as a matter of course that his own men, even though they had more than twice as far to come on that hot and steamy morning, would be fit to fight when they arrived. And it is equally characteristic of men who followed Forrest that they were!

---

* The field of operations covered in this chapter is shown on the map on page 218.

Having sent his wagon trains south by another road east of the railroad, Forrest started his march from Booneville at four o'clock in the morning, moving "as rapidly as the jaded condition" of horses which had just made the march to Alabama and back "would justify, intending if possible, to reach Brice's Cross-Roads in advance of the enemy."[2] The march was along the road then known in the country roundabout as the Wire Road, because it had been the route of the early telegraph line to New Orleans before railroads were built. Eighteen muddy miles south of Booneville and six miles west of the station of Baldwyn on the Mobile & Ohio, this road crossed at right angles another running southeast from Ripley to the railroad at Guntown—the road on which Sturgis was marching.

The crossing of the roads was on a low ridge, or rather plateau, rising between wide bottoms through which small streams cut deep, winding, steep-banked channels in soil of the sort which, when wet, "balls up" on the wheels of wagons or of guns, and weights down the plodding feet of men and horses. The plateau on which the roads cross was covered with a thick growth of scrub oak or blackjack, broken with occasional small open "prairies" and sedge fields.

At the crossing of the two roads there were in 1864 only the two-story house of William Brice, another dwelling, a vacant storehouse and the little chapel and burying ground of Bethany Church—in and of itself a place of no importance except as the almost accidental meeting place of converging forces.[3]

At Old Carrollville, where the roads from Booneville and from Baldwyn to Brice's come together, Forrest, moving in advance of the command, received word that the Union cavalry were within four miles of the crossroads where he intended to intercept them. Lieutenant Robert J. Black, temporarily attached to his staff, was sent ahead "with a few men from the Seventh Tennessee" to meet the enemy's advance, while the General hurried forward troops for the battle.[4]

Sturgis' cavalry, under Grierson, had marched out from its bivouac at Stubbs's Farm, nine miles northwest of the crossroads, at 5:30 A.M., an hour and a half after Forrest was on his way. Brice's—still a point of no particular importance in the calculation of General Sturgis—was reached by the advance of the cavalry after some inconsiderable skirmishing across the bottoms of Tishomingo Creek, at 9:45 A.M.[5]

Ahead of the advance brigade of Union cavalry, roads led away from Brice's in three directions, southwest toward Pontotoc, southeast toward Guntown, north of east toward Baldwyn. Learning that "Forrest and Lee with their whole commands" had passed up toward Baldwyn two

287

or three days before, Colonel Waring, commanding the advance, sent a strong patrol in that direction. About a mile out, the patrol "came upon a heavy force of the enemy" and sent back for help.[6] The situation being reported to Sturgis, he sent forward orders that a small body of cavalry should remain at the crossroads to precede the infantry on its march toward Guntown, while the remainder was to "drive the enemy toward Baldwyn . . . as I didn't propose to allow the enemy to draw me from my main line of march."[7] Forrest's annoying force, in short, was to be brushed off to the left of the Union advance.

As the whole of Waring's brigade—1,400 men and six guns—pushed out the Baldwyn road they met at first no more than a couple of companies of Faulkner's Kentuckians under the dashing Captain H. A. Tyler. Tyler's companies, however, were so disposed and handled in the thickety woods as to give an exaggerated impression of strength—a fact on which Forrest had counted in laying his plans. "The country is densely wooded," he said that morning to Rucker, "and the undergrowth is so heavy that when we strike them they will not know how few men we have."[8]

For the first hour or so of the fight Forrest had up only Lyon's Kentucky brigade of Buford's division, about 800 men, and his escort company of Tennesseans, under Captain John C. Jackson, reinforced for the occasion by a company of Georgians under Captain Henry Gartrell.[9]

By the time these reached the scene of the fight and long before the other troops, strung out along the muddy roads from starting points as much as twenty-five miles away, could get there, Waring's leading Union brigade was in position and ready to advance, while the other Union cavalry brigade under Winslow—1,500 men and four guns—was coming up to the crossroads and pushing out along the Guntown road to go into position on Waring's right.

Forrest, however, had no intention of surrendering the initiative that day by merely standing to receive an attack. Lyon's men, dismounted, came into action charging. It was not meant as a serious charge—Forrest did not want to bring on a "general engagement until the balance of my troops and the artillery came up"[10]—but was to be just enough of a charge to puzzle the Federal commander and make him think that there must be a lot more troops back there in the dense woods from which these few so boldly emerged.

The charge, described by the opposing commander as "exceedingly fierce" and the first of "three desperate attempts to take our position,"[11] succeeded in its purpose. The advance Union brigade dismounted and remained in position while Lyon's little band busied itself making

CAPTAIN BILL FORREST RIDES IN

Entrance into the Cayoso Hotel without troubling to dismount, during the Memphis Raid, August 21, 1864.

From *Harper's Weekly*

THE RAID ON MEMPHIS

Attack and defense of the Irving Block Prison. This building still standing became in Reconstruction times the reputed head "hasty fortifications of rails, logs and such other facilities as presented themselves."[12]

The feint worked for an hour. By that time Rucker with his 700 Tennesseans and Mississippians came up on the run after a march of eighteen muddy miles from Booneville that morning, to be dismounted and put immediately into action on Lyon's left, extending the line toward the Guntown road, to match the Union battle line stretching in that direction.[13]

Once more there was a feint at a Confederate charge made by Lyon, Rucker and Johnson, who had come up with his 500 Alabamians and gone into action on Lyon's right, while Duff's Mississippi regiment (of Rucker's brigade), mounted, was pushed well out to the left of the whole Confederate line to guard against flank attacks from that direction. With the arrival of Johnson, Forrest had on the field two-thirds as many men as Grierson, the Union cavalry commander, but as yet no artillery. Morton's guns were coming as fast as horseflesh could drag them with the help of straining cannoneers through the worst mudholes. Bell's Tennessee brigade, too, was being urged forward by Buford, the division commander. "Tell Bell to move up fast and fetch all he's got,"[14] was the order sent by Forrest to his largest brigade—but Bell had a long, hard way to come. Forrest's problem through the morning and midday hours, without Bell and without Morton's guns, was to whip the superior cavalry force of the enemy and do it before the even more overwhelming infantry force reached the scene.

"We had a severe skirmish with the enemy . . . until 1 o'clock" is the way Forrest himself described the midday fight.[15] To Grierson, commanding the Union cavalry, however, the Confederate advance appeared to be "in large numbers, with double lines of skirmishers and line of battle, with heavy supports." Grierson, indeed, was convinced during, and even after, the battle that the troops facing him included infantry forces and not merely dismounted horsemen. "We succeeded, however, in holding our own and in repulsing with great slaughter three distinct and desperate charges," he reported, while to General Sturgis he sent back word that he "had an advantageous position and could hold it if the infantry was brought up promptly."[16] The battle was working out according to Forrest's plan.

The Union infantry did not start its march on this morning of June tenth until 7:00 A.M. and after. Encumbered as it was with long and heavy wagon trains, the column spread along nearly five miles of road space. Marching at the head of the infantry column, General Sturgis received word about five miles from Brice's of the expanding fight in his front.

He immediately pushed forward to the scene of battle, arriving at noon to "find considerable confusion about the cross roads with the artillery and ambulances and led horses jammed in the road," and to learn that Waring "would have to fall back unless he received some support," while Winslow, according to Sturgis' report, was "almost demanding to be relieved"—a statement, however, most indignantly denied by Winslow's men, who said that they were withdrawn by Sturgis' order for "use on the flanks, mounted," in aid of the Union infantry.[17] At any rate, Forrest was making progress in his plan to have the cavalry whipped before the infantry came up.

As he left the head of the infantry column Sturgis left orders with McMillen, commanding the division of infantry, to "move up . . . as rapidly as possible without distressing the troops."[18] It may not have been quite so hot in Mississippi that morning as Forrest had profanely predicted, but on both sides all agreed that it was a sultry and oppressive day. Forrest himself fought most of his battle in his shirt sleeves, sleeves rolled up and with his uniform coat of a Major General laid across the pommel of his saddle.[19]

In this heat the Union infantry started forward at a round pace, which was increased by the repeated messages coming back from the fight to "make all haste" and "lose no time in coming up."[20] Even without such urging, in a mixed column of men and wagons marching closed up on a narrow road there was the inevitable "accordion" effect of slack running in and out as the tail of the column alternately lost distance and had to double-quick to regain it.

General Sturgis declared afterward that he had "specially ordered" that the infantry should not be brought up on the double, despite his repeated urgings of haste, but brigade and regimental commanders who were back in that hastening, panting column agree that for the greater part of their frantically hurried march to the crossroads, they did move at the double-quick, with the result that many men were "sun struck," and all were "blown" and in great distress.[21] Colonel Hoge, commanding the leading brigade, justified the haste which caused him to bring up his men in such condition by the "peremptory order" to hurry up "as the only thing that would save us was the infantry."[22] The second phase of Forrest's battle was opening, likewise according to his plan.

As the first of the Federal infantry brigades came up to the crossroads Bell's brigade came up on Forrest's side of the fight, and with it Morton's guns. The hour was about one o'clock in the afternoon, by which time "everything at the cross roads," according to the observations of the arriving Federal infantry commander, McMillen, "was going to

290

the devil as fast as it possibly could."[23] Winslow's cavalry on the Union right was giving way, and Waring's on the left was likewise falling back, thus shortening the semicircular line in front of the crossroads.[24] As Hoge's infantry brigade came up and went into position, with the second Union infantry brigade under Wilkins coming in close behind, Grierson asked for authority to have the cavalry relieved and taken out of line, "as it was exhausted and well-nigh out of ammunition."[25]

The first stage of Forrest's battle was over. The cavalry had been "whipped" according to plan, but it had been no easy fight. Charges had been pressed home to the point where men fought with clubbed carbines across "doubled-down" rail fences and brush barriers but always the initiative had been kept by the intrepid Confederates until their opponents were convinced that they were on the point of being "overwhelmed by numbers."[26]

Shortly after one o'clock, with all his troops up after their long and punishing marches, Forrest started his first real attack of the day against the rapidly growing line of Union infantry drawn in a close semicircle about the crossroads. Morton's guns went into action with such precision that the enemy reported that "from the commencement of their firing they had our range exactly," with "every shell bursting over and in the immediate vicinity of our guns."[27] Forrest put Bell's newly arrived brigade into position on Rucker's left, reaching across the Guntown road, pushing Duff's regiment (of Rucker's) still farther out to the left toward the Pontotoc Road, and placing even beyond Duff as the extreme left of the Confederate line his own daredevil escort and the little battalion commanded by Captain Tyler.

Forrest had no idea, however, of depending entirely upon a straight frontal advance against the inner, and therefore shorter and much more strongly held Federal lines. He had left word at Old Carrollville at the very beginning of the fight for Buford to detach one of Bell's regiments when they arrived at that point and send it across on a wide sweep to the enemy's left rear—an order with which Buford complied by sending Barteau's experienced Second Tennessee Cavalry.[28]

And so, with all things in readiness, Forrest began the next phase of his battle—whipping the infantry. It was to be a stubborn, even a desperate, fight, without signs of definite result for more than two hours. Bell's brigade on the Confederate left had to advance through dense undergrowth to within thirty yards of the enemy's position before he could launch his assault. As the Confederate left became heavily engaged, fighting with "great fury," Forrest sent a staff officer over to Buford, whom he had put in charge of the right of the line, to move

Lyon's and Johnson's men forward and press the enemy. Meanwhile, the counterpressure of a determined Union attack forced back Newsom's regiment in Bell's part of the line, and threatened to engulf units on either side, until charges from the flank by Duff's regiment and Forrest's escort, with Wilson's Tennessee regiment which had just come into line, checked the Union advance and relieved the pressure.[29]

Fearing that his order to Buford to throw forward the right had miscarried, Forrest himself rode along the line until he found him. At the same time, through Captain Anderson of his staff, he had all the guns brought forward and put into action, before riding back to the center and left for the final concerted advance all along the line.

While these preparations were in the making there was a distinct lull along the front, as the two battle lines drew back just far enough apart for the dense trees and undergrowth to obscure sight of each other. Men on both sides fell to the ground for rest and lay panting in the heat under the dense shade of trees whose leaves hung motionless in the breathless air. During this pause the soldiers "had a bountiful supply of water from the rills fed by the recent rains," one of them remembered. "I never tasted better," he added, "and the cessation of battle was as grateful as the water."

The pause, though, did not last long until Forrest came riding back along the line on a big sorrel horse, "looking the very God of War," as the same soldier remembered him—but a very practical "god of war" in his shirt sleeves.

"Get up, men," was his order. "I have ordered Bell to charge on the left. When you hear his guns, and the bugle sounds, every man must charge, and we will give them hell."[30]

"I noticed some writers on Forrest say he seldom cursed," another soldier who was in this part of the field afterward wrote. "Well, the fellow who writes that way was not where the Seventh Tennessee was that day. . . . Our movement was too slow to suit Forrest, he would curse, then praise and then threaten to shoot us himself, if we were so afraid the Yanks might hit us. . . . He would praise in one breath, then in the next would curse us and finally said, 'I will lead you.' . . . We hustled, and across that narrow field was a race—double quick nowhere in it."[31]

It was a desperate charge through fields and entanglements of blackjack and brushwood, with fierce fighting hand-to-hand as "guns once fired were used as clubs, and pistols were brought into play, while the two lines struggled with the ferocity of wild beasts."[32]

"The battle was fierce and the enemy obstinate," Forrest reported

292

laconically, but the Confederates pushed home their attack. Morton, under orders of his General, had his guns double-shotted with canister in the front rank, pushing them forward by hand, firing as they went at musket range or closer. To the extreme left of the line Forrest sent a message through Lieutenant George Cowan of his escort that the time had come to "hit 'em on the e-e-eend!"[33]—and the escort, with Gartrell's company and Captain Tyler's little command, knew that the General meant a flank attack. The attack, smartly delivered, carried them beyond and behind the Federal right and on into the bottoms of Tishomingo Creek. And far away to the other side of the battle, the Second Tennessee attacked the Federal lines from the left and rear, so far behind their flank indeed that shell from the Confederate artillery fell among Barteau's advancing men.[34]

There were only about 250 of them, but they attacked widely deployed to exaggerate their apparent strength, with Bugler Jimmy Bradford galloping along the line, sounding the charge at long intervals for imaginary regiment after regiment.[35] So many bugle calls, blown so loudly and so far apart, made the skeleton regiment scattered through the woods seem a veritable host.

About the time that the advance of the third Federal infantry brigade—the Negro troops commanded by Colonel Edward Bouton—came into action, the Confederate center burst from the woods into the cleared ground about Brice's house, the flank attacks closed in on both sides and the last Federal line, drawn close about the crossroads, gave way under what Forrest described as "the steady advance of my men and the concentrated, well-directed and rapid fire from my batteries." Then it was, about five o'clock in the afternoon of the long hot day of battle, that as Forrest put it, "the retreat or rout began,"[36] or as Sturgis reported, "Everywhere the army now drifted toward the rear and was soon altogether beyond control. . . . Order gave way to confusion and confusion to panic. . . ."[37]

Most of Bouton's colored brigade, which had brought up the wagon train, had not yet been seriously engaged, however. The wagon train had reached a field in the Tishomingo Creek bottoms in the early afternoon, and had there been ordered off the road and into park. Before the train was completely parked it was decided to turn it around, no small task for 200 or more four and six-mule wagons crowded together, and one which was not to be finished. With the wagon train and its guards in this state of confusion the backward drift of defeated cavalry and dispirited infantry struck them and, not far behind the debris of their own breaking army, the shells of Morton's relentless batteries. General

Sturgis "now attempted to get hold of the colored brigade . . . but before I could do so the troops from all directions came crowding in like an avalanche from the battlefield, and I lost all possible control over them."[38] About the bridge over Tishomingo Creek there was by this time, as Colonel Winslow describes it, "one indiscriminate mass of wagons, artillery, caissons, ambulances, and broken, disordered troops,"[39] into which the Confederate artillerymen were dropping shells not only from their own guns but from the Federal guns captured, with ammunition, about the crossroads and now turned upon their former owners.[40]

The third phase of the battle, pursuit, had begun. Attempts were made by the Union commanders to form new lines, but every such attempt was fruitless and, indeed, hopeless. Colonel Bouton reports that his soldiers of the colored brigade fought with "terrible desperation," forming lines of defense and falling back five successive times between the beginning of the rout and sundown, to no avail.[41]

Wagons of the train, such of them as had got turned around and out of the park, onto the road and across Tishomingo Creek before the rout began, were all this time breaking for the rear. The artillery, such of it as had not already been captured, "came up and went ahead of us, and forced everybody to give the road to them," reported an officer in charge of trains. To this officer Sturgis issued orders to halt the trains beyond the point where he hoped to make a stand until dark, and "in the meantime issue rations and ammunition to the troops, after which he would burn the God-damned train with the remaining supplies."[42] Before the order could be executed, however, the position on the ridge north of Tishomingo was abandoned and the flight of the train resumed. Teamsters, unable to get ahead with their wagons, abandoned them where they stood in the road, in some cases setting them afire, cut the teams out of harness, mounted the horses and joined the rush to the rear. The artillery and the train, Sturgis announced early in the evening, "had already gone to hell" and could not possibly be saved.

Colonel Winslow of the cavalry, "finding no order, no attempted efforts to reorganize the retreating troops, took up a line of march . . . moving through the woods parallel to the road, now full of the debris of a retreating army." He thought of trying to form a new line for defense, he added, but decided that "it could not be done without losing my horses," presumably to dismounted men who wanted to join the cavalry in getting away from Brice's Cross Roads.

Marching on without halt, Winslow soon "overtook the general commanding expedition," who seems to have been well to the front of the retreat. From Sturgis he received orders to form his cavalry, "the only organized force in the army," at Stubbs's, to put no obstacle in the way of retreat and, after the routed troops had passed, to bring up the rear.[43]

And all the while, acting under Forrest's orders to "keep the skeer on 'em,"[44] the Confederates crowded the rear of the retreat and the Confederate guns, reinforced by captures, kept up their fire upon what had become, in the words of Federal officers, a "regular stampede." Many of the retreating soldiers had thrown away their arms, and of those who had arms many more were without ammunition, which had been shot up or just thrown away in what Sturgis called an "uncontrollable panic."[45]

Sturgis "attempted the destruction of his wagons, loaded with ammunition and bacon," Forrest reported, "but so closely was he pursued that many of them were saved without injury, though the road was lighted for some distance."[46] William Witherspoon of the Seventh Tennessee tells how some of the wagons were saved. As one batch was burning, Forrest himself dashed up to find a group of soldiers succumbing to the fascination of watching the fire. "Don't you see the damned Yanks are burning *my* wagons?" he demanded. "Get off your horses and throw the burning beds off!" And, Witherspoon adds, "in a jiffy every wagon was surrounded by men as close as they could stand and off the burning beds went."[47]

"It being dark," Forrest reported, "and my men and horses requiring rest"—they had marched from eighteen to twenty-five miles that day, fought hard for from five to seven hours and pursued hard for four or five more—"I threw out an advance to follow slowly and cautiously after the enemy, and ordered the command to halt, feed, and rest."[48] It was the tactics of the Streight raid repeated on a larger scale—Forrest's main body resting while small advance forces harassed and pursued the enemy. This time there was the difference that Forrest's men were not dependent upon their own meager supplies for rations. Well-filled wagons were scattered all along the line of the rout and every soldier could become "his own commissary sergeant,"[49] as one of them put it. General Forrest declared, and the man who reported the observation thought with justice, that the army "foundered to a man on the fresh, crisp hardtack and nice, thin side bacon"[50] which was such a contrast to the stringy, blue beef on the hoof and the soldier-mixed and soldier-cooked doughy bread which was apt to be the Confederates' mainstay for rations.

Between Dr. Agnew's house, three miles from the battlefield, where the last attempt at a stand was made, and Stubbs's Farm the road to Ripley crossed the muddy "bottoms" of one of the headwater streams of the Hatchie. Federal guns and wagons which had thus far escaped the perils of shell, fire and abandonment, were there mired down with the way completely blocked by "abandoned ambulances, drowned and dying horses and mules, and the depth of the mud."[51] Picking his way past this blockade, Colonel Bouton of the colored brigade went on to find General Sturgis at Stubbs's about 11:00 P.M. There, as he told the story to the Board of Investigation, he said:

"General, for God's sake don't let us give up so."

"What can we do?" was the reply.

"I told him," Bouton says, "to give me the ammunition that the white troops were throwing away in the mud and I would hold the enemy in check until we could get those ambulances, wagons and artillery all over that bottom and save them. I told him that if he would give me one of those white regiments to help me lift the wagons and artillery over, that I would stake my life that I would save the whole of them."

The General, perhaps reflecting upon the fact that the ammunition which was made a condition precedent to the rescue of the train and artillery was no longer his to give but was scattered in the mud all through the nine miles back to Brice's, replied:

"For God's sake, if Mr. Forrest will let me alone, I will let him alone. You have done all you could and more than was expected of you, and now all you can do is to save yourselves."[52]

"Mr. Forrest," however, had no intention of letting Sturgis alone. "At 1 A.M. on the 11th," he reported, "the pursuit was resumed. About 3 o'clock we came again upon the enemy's rear guard of cavalry." This was, apparently, in the vicinity of the bottom on the south prong of the Hatchie, where, Forrest reports, "they had abandoned the balance of their wagon train, all their wounded, and 14 pieces of artillery."[53]

Young William Witherspoon tells a little more about the rich haul at the Hatchie crossing. "Somewhere between midnight and day," he wrote, "we came to a wide slough or creek bottom; it was miry and truly the slough of despair and despond to the Yanks. Their artillery and wagons which had heretofore escaped capture were now bogged down and had to be abandoned. This slough was near kneedeep in mud and water, with logs lying here and there. On top of every log were Yanks perched as close as they could be, for there were more Yanks than logs—reminded me of chickens at roost. . . . We who were in front were ordered to pay no attention to prisoners, those in the rear would look after that."[54]

And so through the warm and showery night the weary retreat went on, with the fresher pursuers continually crowding the rear and occasionally pushing up among the fugitives. To one such trooper a dejected Union horseman made remark:

"Old Forrest gave us hell today."

To the noncommittal grunt which he received in reply the plodding but talkative fugitive went on, "Yes, and we were fooled about Old Forrest's strength. He certainly had 50,000 men in that fight. The woods were full of them, they were everywhere"—whereupon he was informed that he too was a prisoner of one of "Old Forrest's" men.[55]

The soldier whose gloomy imagination filled the woods with 50,000 Confederates differed only in degree from his officers, who reported that the Federal troops gave way to "overwhelming numbers," "odds of four to one" and the like, and who estimated Forrest's force all the way from twice to six times its actual strength.[56]

In these overestimates of Forrest's force the Union commanders were aided to no small degree by the inhabitants of the country through which they passed. "At Ripley, going out," the Federal Colonel DeWitt C. Thomas testified, "a lady whom I took to be a very intelligent person, Mrs. Faulkner, wife of Colonel Faulkner of the rebel service, informed me, in a laughing manner, in answer to my question as to where Forrest was, that Forrest had gone away from there with two divisions to reinforce Johnston, but had returned again and that we would have plenty to do in a few days. I asked her if she knew of the number of men Forrest had, and she said he had some 28,000. On my return she had breakfast prepared, and she called me in and I took breakfast with her. She wanted to know if I did not find her words very nearly correct."[57]

Mrs. Faulkner's kindness in feeding the Union invader both breakfast and misinformation was in keeping with the observations of Colonel Waring about the ladies of Ripley. Going out, he said, the rebel women of Ripley were "spiteful," but as the Federal column came back, after "marching all that long night [of the tenth] without food and without rest," the same women were to the fore in succoring and comforting the pitiable wounded.[58]

Sturgis and McMillen were in Ripley at dawn, "sitting under a tree in the center of the town," but the Federals were not to stay long. "We came upon them again about four miles east of Ripley," Forrest reported, but "they made only a feeble and ineffectual resistance, the Seventh Tennessee and my escort driving them from position."[59] At the town itself, some small effort was made to organize a real resistance, but upon Forrest's arrival before the town about eight in the morning, the usual slashing attack, this time with Colonel Andrew Wilson's Sixteenth Ten,

297

nessee with Lieutenant Colonel Jesse Forrest in the advance, striking in front, and the ubiquitous escort on the flank, started the retreat all over again.[60]

"From this place . . . the enemy offered no organized resistance," Forrest reported, "but retreated in the most complete disorder, throwing away guns, clothing, and everything calculated to impede his flight," while Faulkner's Kentucky regiment, that day commanded by Major Thomas Tate, and Duckworth's Seventh Tennessee, mounted, slashed away at the rear.[61]

The retreat was described at the time by General Sturgis himself, according to one of the infantry officers, as " a hell of a stampede" in which "every man would have to take care of himself,"[62] while the commander of the rear guard complained:

"The day was very hot. The soldiers had eaten nothing since the morning of the 10th. . . . They were without rations; many had thrown away or destroyed their arms, and all the infantry near the rear had reduced their clothing as much as possible, hoping to keep in advance of the rear guard; but the general in command was leading the retreat so rapidly that I was obliged to leave hundreds every mile . . . who could keep up with ordinary marching, but were unable to keep up while marching as fast as we were."[63]

The complaint of the officer of the rear guard against the pace set by General Sturgis in the retreat was mild compared to some of those made by the infantry officers about the cavalry. Colonel Eaton, commanding an Ohio regiment in Wilkin's First Brigade, declared that the cavalry "began to march at such a rapid pace that it became utterly impossible to keep up with them." While he was trying to keep as close as possible to the cavalry ahead of him, he added, a cavalry regiment acting as "rear guard to the whole command suddenly made a rush to the front, riding through the ranks of my regiment, causing the men to scatter in all directions to avoid being ridden over," just as the enemy made an attack on his rear.

This device of "seeking safety in the woods,"[64] or as another of the infantry colonels put it, "breaking to the brush,"[65] was about all that was left to the infantry as Buford came up and took over the direct pursuit, while Forrest with his escort and Bell's brigade swung out on another road, seeking to reach Salem ahead of the retreating column. Buford, however, pressed them so hard that the attempt to intercept the column failed—particularly since so large a part of it had "scattered on all by-roads leading towards the Memphis and Charleston Railroad, re-treating through the woods in squads and avoiding capture that way."[66] Behind them, Forrest's men ranged the ridgy, broken and wooded coun-try between Ripley and Salem in small bodies, rounding up fugitives.

"On we went," wrote Colonel Waring, "and ever on, marching all that day . . . and all that interminable night and until half past ten the next morning, when we reached Collierville and the railroad, reinforce-ments and supplies, we marched, marched, marched, without rest, with-out sleep, and without food."[67] But pitiable as was the condition of the cavalry, that of the infantry was even worse. It had taken a week to march out from Collierville to Brice's Cross Roads but the return march, ninety miles without rest and virtually without food, was made by men on foot, after a day of battle, in two nights and a day.

Railroad trains bringing 2,000 infantry reinforcements, with food, forage and ammunition, met the retreating expedition at Collierville on the afternoon of the twelfth, but not yet were the fugitives to be allowed to rest.[68] There was no pursuit, it is true, but there were rumors of pur-suit, and that night at dark the march toward Memphis started all over again—seventeen miles more through the night to White's Station, where the command dragged itself in on the morning of the thirteenth with horses dead-beat and men "so stiffened as to require assistance to enable them to walk" and "some of them, too foot-sore to stand upon their feet, crawling upon their hands and knees to the cars."[69]

Perhaps it was only the tonic of victory which kept Forrest's men from being almost equally weary. Tyree Bell's brigade, between four o'clock in the morning of the tenth of June and eight on the night of the eleventh, marched twenty-five miles over miserable mud roads, fought hard for five hours and pursued the enemy for fifty-five more miles, while the other cavalry regiments marched almost as far and some of them fought even more hours. Morton's artillery marched eighteen miles, fought from one o'clock until dark and pursued the enemy for forty-three miles, all in thirty-eight hours, and all over deep, muddy and rutted roads and through blazing heat.

Forrest marched as far as any man, fought as long as any and carried the anxiety and responsibility for the whole. Not even his giant, steel-tempered frame could stand that sort of pace forever. Mack Watson, private in the escort company, used to tell that as he rode close behind the General on the afternoon of the day of pursuit, on nearing his boy-hood home of Salem, Forrest fell asleep on his horse. Watson reported the fact to Captain Jackson, commanding the escort.

"Go wake him up, Mack," was the order.

"No, sir, you wake him!" answered Watson.

"Tell Colonel Bell," was the amended order.

"Ride ahead and wake him up, Mack," said Bell.

"No, sir, *you* do it," Mack replied.

The horse, probably asleep also, settled the question of who should wake the General by doing so himself when he left the road and ran into a tree.[70]

On this same day, with pursuers exhausted almost as much as the pursued, Private Watson was sent back by Forrest with an order to General Buford to "gallop up."

"Tell General Forrest, by God, that my men can't gallop up," was the worn-out Buford's reply.

"Very well, sir, I'll tell the General what you say," answered the orderly—"but," he added, "before I could get good started back to General Forrest, I heard Buford's bugle sound and they 'galloped up.' "[71] From privates to division commanders no one trifled with that hair-trigger temper of Forrest's.

From White's Station the Sturgis expedition limped back to Memphis to report losses of 2,240 men, of whom 223 were killed, 394 wounded and 1,623 missing. His artillery was all gone, and more than 200 fine six-horse wagons—and he brought back not one single strand of that "hair" of Forrest's which he had so bumptiously promised General Sherman. "Yet there is some consolation," he reported, "in knowing that the army fought nobly while it did fight, and only yielded to overwhelming numbers."[72]

Forrest's report of losses indicates that Sturgis' men did fight and fight well, while they fought. In his small force, there were 96 killed and 396 wounded—a loss proportionately almost as heavy in killed as that of Sturgis, and in wounded almost three times as heavy. The great difference was in captures. Forrest lost nothing, neither man nor gun nor wagon, while he captured 60 officers and 1,558 enlisted men, 16 guns, 1,500 stand of small arms, nearly 1,000 rounds of artillery ammunition and 300,000 rounds for small arms, 176 wagons, mostly six-horse, with vast supply of harness, quartermaster, medical and other equipment and supplies.[73]

A disproportionate part of the Federal loss in killed and wounded fell upon Bouton's brigade of Negro troops, who had almost as many wounded as any other of the five brigades in Sturgis' command, and nearly as many killed as all the others combined.[74] Washburn, commanding at Memphis, protested at what he said seemed to be a repetition of "the massacre at Fort Pillow," to which Forrest made reply that he had had reports of oaths taken by the Negro troops in Memphis, "on their knees, in the presence of Major-General Hurlbut . . . to avenge Fort Pillow, and that they would show my troops no quarter," with the result that "the recent battle . . . was far more bloody than it would otherwise have been but for the fact that your men evidently expected to be slaughtered when captured, and both sides acted as though neither felt safe in surrendering, even when further resistance was useless." In accepting Forrest's offer to exchange the wounded, man for man, Washburn agreed that he believed "that it is true that the colored soldiers did take such an oath but not in the presence of General Hurlbut," and inquired as to the status of colored prisoners. "My prisoners, both black and white, are turned over to my government to be dealt with as it may direct," Forrest replied, referring Washburn to the authorities at Richmond for information as to how they were "regarded by my government, and the disposition which has been and will hereafter be made of them."[75]

"If there was, during the war, another engagement like this, it is not known to the writer," in the opinion of a Federal officer who fought under Waring, writing more than twenty years later. "It is the fate of war that one or the other side should suffer defeat, but here there was more. The men were cowed, and there pressed upon them a sense of bitter humiliation, which rankles after nearly a quarter of a century has passed."[76]

Colonel Waring's own explanation of the result was that the Sturgis expedition was "sent out by Sherman as a tub to the Forrest whale," while at the scene of the battle itself, the Union infantry came on the scene "a regiment at a time, or only so fast as the Forrest mill could grind them up in detail."[77]

It was close work, though, depending for its success upon the incredible marching and fighting of men whom Forrest led. From the beginning to the end of the fight there was never a time when Forrest had on the field and in line of battle much more than half as many men as Grierson and Sturgis could have thrown against him, while always, at each crisis of the long day of battle, it was the command which had just come up that saved the day for Forrest.

The Memphis *Bulletin*, the newspaper of Union sympathy published in Memphis during the Federal occupation, offered another explanation in reporting Sturgis' return. He had, the paper said, met "superior numbers" under General Kirby Smith, with Lieutenant General Stephen D. Lee as second in command, who "pressed our troops on all sides."

Still another explanation, current at the time and much inquired into

301

by the Board of Investigation which conducted an examination of the disaster, was that Sturgis was intoxicated. This his officers, some of whom displayed no very high regard for Sturgis otherwise, positively denied,[78] although there was testimony that he was seen to take a drink of liquor several times during the advance and retreat—once before breakfast, once at the head of the infantry column when the first word of the fight at the crossroads came back, once when the first attempt was made to form a line upon the retreat, and once as the last line was formed, about sundown.[79]

"I will have the matter of Sturgis critically examined," Sherman wrote from Big Shanty in Georgia, "and, if he is at fault, he shall have no mercy at my hands."[80] A Board of Investigation headed by Brigadier General R. P. Buckland of the Memphis garrison completed its work on July 30, 1865, and submitted testimony and exhibits "as the result of their labors," without recommendations.[81] General Sturgis, however, was not again assigned to active duty during the Confederate war or until late summer of 1865, when he was sent on frontier duty at Austin, Texas.[82]

Sherman was disappointed, of course, and chagrined at the result of the Sturgis expedition. Sturgis had been his own choice for the command.[83] He had been sent out to keep Forrest from "breaking into Tennessee from some quarter," as Sherman wrote home on June twelfth. "Jno. Morgan is in Kentucky," he said then, "but I attach little importance to him or his raid, as we don't draw anything from Kentucky, and there are plenty of troops there to capture and destroy him. Forrest is a more dangerous man. I am in hopes that an expedition sent out from Memphis on Tupelo about the 1st of June will give him full employment."[84]

On the day on which this letter was written, as it happened, General Morgan suffered defeat at Cynthiana, Kentucky, but the expedition which was to give Forrest "full employment" was streaming back toward Memphis in utter rout.

The expedition did, however, achieve Sherman's "chief object to hold Forrest there [in Mississippi] and keep him off our [rail]road," as Sherman wrote Secretary of War Stanton from Big Shanty on June fourteenth, when he had news of Sturgis' defeat. "Forrest has only his own cavalry . . . and the militia under Gholson," he added. "I cannot understand how he could defeat Sturgis with 8,000 men. . . ."[85]

"I cannot but believe Sturgis had troops enough," he wrote the Secretary of War a day later after further reflection. "I know I would have been willing to attempt the same task with that force; but Forrest is the very devil, and I think he has got some of our troops under cower. I have

302

two officers at Memphis that will fight all the time, A. J. Smith and Mower. . . . I will order them to make up a force and *go out and follow Forrest to the death if it costs 10,000 lives and breaks the Treasury. There never will be peace in Tennessee until Forrest is dead.* . . ."[86] (Italics supplied.)

Besides the new and larger expedition which he ordered out to keep Forrest in Mississippi, Sherman sent word to William Sooy Smith, then in Nashville, that he might "send notice to Florence [Alabama] that if Forrest invades Tennessee from that direction, the town will be burned, and if it occurs you will remove the inhabitants north of the Ohio River, and burn the town and Tuscumbia also."[87] There can be no doubt that Sherman was in earnest about keeping Forrest away from his supply lines in Tennessee, and that despite the losses suffered by Sturgis' expedition he had carried his point, for the time at least.

Forrest's victory, however, was by no means barren of strategic results above and beyond his captures of men and matériel. The Union division of Brigadier General John E. Smith, at Huntsville, Alabama, and the brigade of Colonel J. H. Howe at Decatur, both on the way to reinforce Sherman in Georgia, were held where they were, "in consequence of the repulse of Sturgis by Forrest."[88] More important still, Major General A. J. Smith, back from the Red River with excellent troops intended for an expedition against Mobile, was sent to Memphis and given, instead, the task of keeping Forrest away from Tennessee[89]—a task which was to occupy his summer so completely that he neither reached Mobile nor joined Sherman in Georgia.

But the people of the central South, when they heard of the victory at Brice's Cross Roads, were not thinking of Sherman away over in Georgia. They did not see that Sherman had so played upon Confederate susceptibilities as to win a major point in the high strategy of the whole war by keeping Forrest away from his railroad. They saw only that once more Forrest and his men had turned back from the Confederacy's greatest remaining granary overwhelming invasion, by overwhelming defeat.

Nor was high strategy Forrest's responsibility. His task was to defeat Sturgis, and the performance of that task was truly a military masterpiece—a masterpiece of marching, of timing, of tactics and of morale. It was for Forrest and his men their high mark of victory. Never again after that would they know another so complete, so overwhelming, so smashing. They were to rejoice in the impudence of a successful raid into the very Union headquarters at Memphis. They were to capture gunboats, to destroy supply bases, to wreck communication lines. They were to enjoy three times more the thrill of marching north into the

303

Tennessee country which was home to so many of them. They were to fight for almost a year longer, but never again, after those June days in Mississippi, were they to meet in open, pitched battle and to send back in complete, reeling defeat an army of the enemy, which had come forth against them in the pride of what should have been overpowering equipment, armament and numbers.[90]

CHAPTER XX

HARRISBURG: AN INVASION REPELLED BY VICTORY*

June 14, 1864-July 23, 1864

THE Confederacy's last chance was being fought out in those midsummer weeks of 1864 in the north Georgia hills above Atlanta. Grant in Virginia was "fighting it out" with appalling loss and, so far as appearances went, disappointingly small results. Farragut's squadron in the Gulf had not yet pushed past the forts and the torpedoes into Mobile Bay. It was an election year in the North, and the Northern people were showing disconcerting signs of wearying of the war.

In Georgia, through the month of May and into June, Sherman had relentlessly forced Joe Johnston back seventy miles from Dalton to Big Shanty, on the slopes leading up to Kennesaw Mountain. His losses had been great and in the unsuccessful assault upon Kennesaw itself were to be greater, but great as they were Sherman had, and knew that he had, the strength to outfight or outflank Johnston—*if*.

Sherman's *if* was his line of supply. From the Ohio River to Nashville his chief reliance was the railroad from Louisville, but in addition he had the Cumberland River during the season when it was open to navigation and the Tennessee River to Johnsonville, whence the unfinished Northwestern Railroad had been hastily completed to Nashville by the Union military forces. From Nashville south to Stevenson, Alabama, he had two lines—the direct railroad southeast from Nashville to Chattanooga and an alternative route south from Nashville to Decatur, Alabama, and thence east to Stevenson. From Stevenson there was but a single line of railroad for forty miles across the Tennessee River and the mountains to Chattanooga, and thence forward to Sherman's battle front a hundred miles beyond.

"I wish we could make an accumulation of stores somewhere near," Sherman wrote home in mid-June, "but the railroad is taxed to its utmost to supply our daily wants."[1] With 100,000 men and 35,000 animals to be fed and supplied it was hard, indeed impossible, to do much accumulating, certainly while the army was also to be kept fighting—for fighting eats up and burns up supplies and Sherman's margin was thin. He was

---

* The field of operations covered in this chapter is shown on the maps on pages 218 and 306.

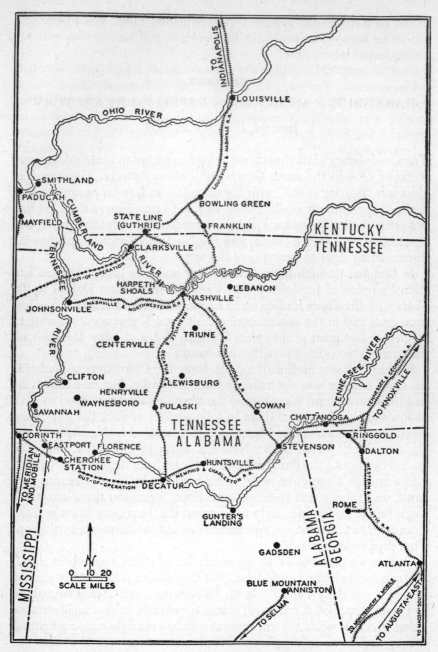

SHERMAN'S SYSTEM OF COMMUNICATIONS—
ATLANTA CAMPAIGNS, 1864

all but on a day-to-day, almost a hand-to-mouth, basis. His supply line had to be kept open, his trains had to run—and had to run without consequential interruption.

Over in north Mississippi was the one threat which gave Sherman serious concern—Forrest. "He whipped Sturgis fair and square," Sherman wrote to Major General Lovell Rousseau, whom he had left in command in Middle Tennessee, at the same time warning him to be prepared for Forrest's appearance at the crossings of the Tennessee River.[2] But after all, as Sherman wrote Grant, "even Sturgis produced the effect which formed the chief purpose of his attempt,"[3] for "he kept Forrest away from us."[4] And so, as soon as he heard of the Sturgis disaster and in the same message in which he ordered its investigation, Sherman ordered out a new and stronger expedition against Forrest, even though it meant taking the troops which had been made ready for a long-planned movement against Mobile, and abandoning that expedition entirely.[5]

The new orders contemplated not only the destruction of Forrest's forces and the death of the General himself—"there never will be peace in Tennessee until Forrest is dead," Sherman had written[6]—but also "devastating the land over which he has passed or may pass, and [making] him and the people of Tennessee and Mississippi realize that, although a bold, daring and successful leader, he will bring ruin and misery on any country where he may pause or tarry. If we do not punish Forrest and the people now, the whole effect of our past conquests will be lost."[7]

There was in this something new in the war, at least as an avowed policy, "to punish Forrest and the people," not as a military measure aimed against armies but a punitive measure applied to peoples.

To carry out the new plan Sherman designated Major General Andrew J. Smith and Brigadier General Joseph A. Mower, both regular army officers of capacity, and directed Washburn to furnish them with a force of infantry, cavalry and artillery "large enough to deal with him [Forrest] handsomely," to be "got ready and started with all dispatch"[8]—a force, indeed, which Washburn was to describe as "ample to whip anything this side of Georgia."[9] To Mower, "one of the gamest men in our service," Sherman promised promotion to a major-generalcy if he were to be successful in complying with the order "to pursue and kill Forrest," and registered the promise with President Lincoln, asking that "should accident befall" Sherman, the President would "favor Mower, if he succeeds in disposing of Forrest."[10]

While Forrest was receiving all this flattering attention from the enemy, there were not lacking those on the Confederate side who saw as clearly as Sherman himself where the critical spot in the whole strategy of the war was, and the possibilities that lay in the use of Forrest to affect the decision there. As early as May tenth, immediately after Leonidas Polk had come to Georgia, General Johnston had suggested to Stephen Lee that Forrest's "advance [into Middle Tennessee] will be of great importance"[11]—an idea which he was to renew with increasing insistence not only to Lee but also to General Bragg, the President's military adviser, and to President Davis himself. Johnston wrote in his memoirs:[12]

"Early in the campaign, the accounts of the cavalry in Mississippi . . . gave me reason to believe that an adequate force to destroy the railroad communications of the Federal army could be furnished . . . under an officer fully competent to head such an enterprise—General Forrest. I therefore suggested the measure to the President, directly on the 13th of June and 10th of July, and through General Bragg on the 3d, 12th, 13th, 16th and 26th of June. . . . I made these suggestions in the strong belief that this cavalry would serve the Confederacy far better by contributing to the defeat of a formidable invasion, than by waiting for and repelling raids."

In this suggestion the Commander of the Army of Tennessee was strongly backed by two of his corps commanders. On June thirteenth Lieutenant General Polk, in the last official dispatch he was to send before meeting his death on Pine Mountain, urged his old West Point friend Jefferson Davis to send Forrest against Sherman's communications, to which recommendation Lieutenant General Hardee added, "I concur."[13]

To these military urgings for the use of the man whom Johnston described as "the most competent officer in America for such service,"[14] there were added the strong urgings of the Georgia civil authorities. "Could not Forrest . . . do more now for our cause in Sherman's rear than anywhere else?" Governor Joseph E. Brown asked the President on June twenty-eighth,[15] while on the next day a delegation sent by Brown called upon Benjamin H. Hill, Confederate States Senator from Georgia, to enlist his powerful aid in having Forrest ordered against Sherman's line of communications. Before taking the matter up with the Confederate authorities Senator Hill called on General Johnston at Marietta, where he was told that the only way to get Sherman's army out of the country was by such an attack on his rear.[16] With these views in hand he proceeded to Richmond and laid the subject before Secretary of War Seddon.

To Secretary Seddon, also, appealed General Howell Cobb. Unless something of the sort were done, he wrote, "I see no end to the slow process of Sherman's advance through Georgia. If his communication was cut for ten days his army would be destroyed, and Georgia, as well as Alabama and Mississippi, saved, and Tennessee recovered. To effect such a result could we not afford to uncover for a short time the country protected by Forrest?"[17]

To all of which from General Bragg and President Davis the answer was the same. The President's military adviser, commenting upon Governor Brown's suggestion after making arithmetical comparisons, declared that the Confederate forces in Mississippi were "in proportion to the enemy confronting them, much weaker than General Johnston," and that Stephen Lee needed "his troops now with Johnston more than the latter can need Forrest"[18]—disregarding entirely the relative strategic values of the fields entrusted to the two forces.

Accepting this estimate of the situation, the President curtly answered the Governor of Georgia that "the disparity of force between the opposing armies in northern Georgia is less as reported than at any other point. . . . Forrest's command is now operating on one of Sherman's lines of communication, and is necessary for other purposes in his present field of service."[19]

The doughty Governor lost no time in repeating by wire his suggestion that "ten thousand good cavalry under Forrest be thrown in Sherman's rear," going on to say:[20]

"The whole country expects this though points of less importance should be for a time overrun. . . . We do not see how Forrest's operations in Mississippi . . . interfere with Sherman's plans in this State as his supplies continue to reach him. Destroy these and Atlanta is not only safe, but the destruction of the army under Sherman opens up Tennessee and Ky. to us. Your information as to the relative strength of the two armies in North Georgia cannot be from reliable sources. If your mistake should result in loss of Atlanta . . . the blow may be fatal to our cause and remote posterity may have reason to mourn over the error."

All on the same day, July fifth, the President snapped back, with studied sarcasm:[21]

"I am surprised to learn from you that the basis of the comparison I made on official reports and estimates is unreliable. Until your better knowledge is communicated, I shall have no means of correcting such errors, and your dicta cannot control the disposition of troops in different parts of the Confederate States. Most men in your position would not assume to decide on the value of the service to be rendered by troops in distant positions. When you give me your reliable statement of the

309

comparative strength of the armies, I will be glad also to know the source of your information as to what the whole country expects, and posterity will judge."

"I regret the exhibition of temper with which I am met in your dispatch," Governor Brown wrote back from his capital at Milledgeville to the President in Richmond,[22] adding:

". . . if you continue to keep our forces divided and our cavalry raiding and meeting raids while enemy's line of communication, nearly 300 miles from his base, is uninterrupted, I fear the result will be similar to those which followed a like policy of dividing our forces at Murfreesborough and Chattanooga. If Atlanta is sacrificed and Georgia overrun while our cavalry are engaged in distant raids, you will have no difficulty in ascertaining from correct sources of information what was expected of you by the whole people, and what verdict posterity will record. . . ."

And so, regardless of military or civilian suggestion or remonstrance—or it may have been in part, even, *because* of the sources and tone of them—the Confederate war authorities elected to cling to the end to the policy of the dispersed defensive. The greatest soldier in the West—indeed, in the opinion of at least one of the officers under whom he served "the greatest soldier of his time"[23]—was to be used not to "insure the defeat of a great invasion," if that might have been done, but to "repel a mere raid."[24]

Unconcerned about all the correspondence and controversy over what use should be made of him and his force, Forrest was busy making his command ready to meet the "formidable expedition" from Memphis which he well knew was coming soon. Scouting went on without intermission, with McCulloch's regiment pushed forward on outpost duty to Abbeville, another under Lieutenant Colonel Jesse Forrest at Ripley, and with scouting parties all around Memphis under orders to Captain Thomas Henderson, chief of scouts, "not only [to] learn all they can but to see for themselves."[25] While Forrest complained at one time of the "meagre and unreliable information received" about affairs in and about Memphis, a check of his dispatches against developments there indicates a most considerable knowledge of Federal plans and preparations, and an astonishingly accurate prevision of what was to come.[26]

In anticipation of the coming expedition Forrest likewise was gathering troops, such as he could. Chalmers, who on the day that Brice's Cross Roads was fought received his orders to return from Alabama, marched 120 miles in three days to reach Columbus, Mississippi, and there meet the news of the victory.

310

A brigade of Arkansas and Mississippi troops, commanded by Colonel Hinchie P. Mabry of Texas, was ordered up from the Yazoo country to reinforce Forrest and was stationed at Okolona.

Buford's division was quartered in the vicinity of Guntown, near the scene of the recent victory, while Roddey, leaving but a few hundred men in Alabama, was moved into the northeastern corner of Mississippi about Corinth. Gholson's brigade was transferred to Wirt Adams' command in central Mississippi.

While all this shifting and preparing was going on, there came to Forrest through department headquarters a letter from Brigadier General Gideon Pillow claiming that under authorities to raise troops previously issued to him by Generals Johnston and Bragg and "now confirmed . . . in an order dictated by the President himself in the presence of the Tennessee Senators," he was "entitled to the four regiments of West Tennessee troops recently organized into a brigade by General Forrest, and now commanded by Colonel Bell."

"When General Forrest went into West Tennessee," General Pillow wrote, "he ordered these troops out with him . . . and subsequently blended the regiments together in disregard of my rights and of the authority of the officers, I had authorized to raise them, and formed them into a command for himself. . . ." Expressing the opinion that Forrest would "promptly repair the injustice done me" if the facts and the order of the Government were brought to his attention, Pillow added that if he were mistaken in this feeling, he looked to Stephen Lee "to do me justice."

Called upon by Lee for a statement, Forrest referred the communication to Tyree Bell, who recited the story of the raising of the command in question, "with which I am well satisfied, and so are the men," and expressed "the highest regard for General Pillow both as a man and an officer" under whom he would have no objection to serving as division commander, but "preferred" remaining where he was.

To this Forrest added his own surprisingly temperate and diplomatic statement:

"The troops now under Colonel Bell I do not claim as my troops, but are Confederate troops, and subject to the orders of the major-general commanding department. I do claim, however, to have perfected and completed their organization, and to have been the means of gathering them up and placing them effectively and promptly in the service, by consolidating and placing together the various parts of which the brigade was to be composed. . . . The troops and their officers are desirous of remaining in my command. I am much attached to them and desire them to remain with me, and am of the opinion that it would not be

311

for the good of the service to take them from the command against their wish. At the same time they, with all other troops in my command, are subject to orders from department headquarters."[27]

The rank and rights of officers and the organization of commands were not the only personnel problems with which Forrest had to deal. There was the usual run of absentees and deserters, complicated in the case of Forrest's command by what he called "the scare consequent upon the action of the Government in taking out and sending back absentees from the infantry."[28]

Forrest set up a special camp near Tupelo for men who had lost their horses, or whose mounts did not pass a rigid inspection designed to weed out "all horses unable to stand the fatigues of service." The purpose was to avoid "loss of the services of both man and horse," to cut down "straggling and scattering men along the line of march," to "recruit horses that a few days' service at this time would render worthless" and, while accomplishing all these desirable ends, to get from the temporarily dismounted men the equivalent of a "good brigade of infantry." At first, however, some of the men "ran away rather than come to the dismounted camp," although most of them—between 500 and 600—"once in camp and assured of the design to recruit their stock and render it serviceable, appear very well satisfied."

To these dismounted men Forrest purposed to add, by rigid examinations, a large number of "attaches, employes and detailed men," provost guards, purchasing agents, presumed officers of state reserves, and others who, he felt, would bring up his dismounted force to at least 2,000 men. Many of these "exempts" of various sorts were beyond Forrest's reach but his own detailed men were to be armed with "gun and necessary accouterments to go into the fight," and subordinate commanders were held accountable to see that they did so.[29]

And all the while there was the unending work of improving the physical condition of the command—sick men and those wounded in the recent fight to be sent promptly to the rear; arms and ammunition to be checked; serviceable horses to be shod and horse equipments to be repaired; transportation to be strengthened by the issue of the well-equipped wagons and fine harness just captured (wagons being one thing of which Forrest now had enough) with stringent orders to teamsters, wagon masters and commanding officers as to their care.[30] Supplies of forage and subsistence were set up on prospective routes of operation. Forrest was doing all that he could do with the resources at hand but, like some of his soldiers, he must have "noticed the smallness of the companies, and when on the march the regiment did not string out as it formerly did."[31]

On June twenty-fifth Forrest outlined to Lee the situation as he had figured it out from the reports of his scouts. The new expedition in the making, he felt, was not going to join Sherman but did "meditate the destruction of the Mobile and Ohio Railroad as far down as possible and then turn across to the Central Railroad, destroy it and return to Memphis"—quite an accurate statement of Smith's instructions and intentions, even to the detail of moving well out east of Memphis on the railroad before turning south, except that it omitted the emphasis in Sherman's orders to Smith "to pursue and kill Forrest"[32] and Washburn's instruction that it was "of the utmost importance to him [Sherman] to hold Forrest."[33]

On June twenty-sixth Major General A. J. Smith moved out of Memphis with what Washburn, the district commander there, described as a "fine force" of 14,000 men of all arms—infantry, cavalry, artillery—following the railroad east.[34] On the twenty-eighth, with Smith at La Grange, Washburn reported "he will probably not leave the line of railroad for a week." On the same day Forrest reported that Smith would "probably start . . . in six days."[35]

At the same time Forrest offered his congratulations to Lee, his department commander and friend, upon his promotion to the rank of Lieutenant General, which had just come through from Richmond, and asked him to take command of the forces since he was "suffering with boils."[36] Captain Morton reported that Forrest's keen suffering "depleted even his iron constitution"[37] but, boils or no boils, there was to be no rest and no relief for him. The pressure on the department, with other smaller expeditions threatening from Vicksburg and Baton Rouge, was such that the new Lieutenant General could not spare the service of Forrest.

In anticipation of Smith's starting south from the railroad early in July, the outpost about Ripley was strengthened by the addition of Hyams' Mississippi regiment of McCulloch's brigade. The rest of the forces under Chalmers were moved from Columbus up to Verona closer to Buford, and all troops were ordered to have prepared and ready to issue six days' rations of hard bread and bacon. Forrest was making ready to meet whatever might come.[38]

On July 5, 1864, A. J. Smith started south from La Grange with his cavalry under Grierson, moving from Saulsbury parallel and to the east —the side of the marching column on which Forrest's men were. The march orders were strict in the extreme. Every canteen was to be filled so that there might be no excuse for falling out of line to get water. Frequent halts were made for the same purpose of removing any excuse for falling out, and rolls were to be called three times daily to check up on stragglers.[39]

And so, in a movement described by Stephen Lee as "exceedingly cautious and careful,"[40] Smith moved into Mississippi, without opposition except for a skirmish above Ripley on the seventh, in which the little force of Jesse Forrest and Hyams was promptly pushed back out of the way.[41] On the eighth, pursuant to instructions for punishment of Forrest and the people, much of the village of Ripley—the courthouse, the Methodist and the Cumberland Presbyterian churches, the Masonic and the Odd Fellows' Halls, and a number of residences—were given to the flames,[42] and the column marched on, leaving a swath of desolation ten miles wide.[43]

On the ninth the column crossed the Tallahatchie at New Albany and marched on toward Pontotoc,[44] on the route followed in February by William Sooy Smith in the first of the series of expeditions against Forrest, of which A. J. Smith's in July was the fourth—though not the last.

Forrest, the chief object of the expedition, had no idea of giving battle until General Lee should come up with reinforcements but he did send Buford, with Bell's brigade and Mabry's assigned to him for the occasion, from Tupelo to Ellistown to observe Smith's approach. When Smith did not come that way but moved through New Albany and Pontotoc, Buford was ordered to hang on his flanks and develop his strength but to avoid a general engagement. By an all-night march of the ninth Buford put himself in position to carry out the order.[45]

Meanwhile, Forrest ordered Chalmers to put one brigade of his division into Pontotoc ahead of the enemy, holding the remainder of his troops in the area between Pontotoc and Okolona.[46] At Pontotoc, Chalmers took command of both his own and Buford's troops and began to offer to Smith his first real resistance, under orders from Forrest to "hold the enemy in check two days longer, if possible," while preparation was being made to receive him near Okolona.[47]

Having in mind what had happened to his predecessors in this risky business of hunting Forrest, Smith came on toward Pontotoc very slowly, moving "usually with a line of battle and skirmishers about one mile in length," but steadily pushing on. During the morning of the eleventh, he forced McCulloch's brigade back through the town and occupied it.

On the morning of the twelfth about nine o'clock there came a message from Forrest to Chalmers "to let the enemy come on if he would, as everything was ready to receive him."[48] The prudent A. J. Smith, however, declined to "come on" that day, other than to send out from Pontotoc on various roads reconnaissance parties, all of which were checked and driven in. The principal advance party, sent down the road to Okolona on which Sooy Smith had made his advance and retreat, found that the Confederates had obstructed the marshy passage of two small creeks in a bottom by felling trees, and held a prepared position on the ridge beyond.[49] They were indeed ready, but so ready that Smith decided not to ram his head against the position.

At 6:00 P.M. of July twelfth the retrograde movement of the Confederates from Pontotoc toward Okolona, for which orders had been issued earlier in the day, was canceled with word that Generals Lee and Forrest would be up that night to the position below Pontotoc and that other troops were on the way—a sudden change of orders after the original movements were under way and just as night fell, which produced some confusion.[50]

The background of the decision of the department commander to hasten the fight is to be found in his correspondence with General Bragg and Major General Dabney H. Maury, in command of the defenses at Mobile, a port which in July 1864 still was open to the blockade-runners making their way in and out under the watchful guns of Farragut's squadron out in the Gulf. Maury, expecting an attack, wanted reinforcements. "As soon as I fight I can send him 2,000, possibly 3,000," Lee wrote Bragg, but the understanding between the two commanders in the field was that if A. J. Smith did not "succeed in delaying the battle," Lee would have "time to wind up his fight" before doing so.[51]

At four o'clock in the morning of July thirteenth A. J. Smith abruptly changed his line of march. Instead of continuing southeast from Pontotoc to Okolona he turned squarely to the left and headed directly east for the railroad at Tupelo[52] on a road which, as a result of the confusion from the change in orders by the Confederate command the night before, was that day left open and unguarded.[53] Upon this road, then, marched Smith "with his column well closed up, his wagon train well protected, and his flanks covered in an admirable manner."[54]

Although there was no Confederate force in Smith's front as he marched for Tupelo, eighteen miles away, Forrest fell upon his rear while both Buford and Chalmers, marching hard along parallel roads, attacked his flank. All attacks, however, were beaten off without serious loss,[55] while the marching column, with a good start in the morning, pressed on. Grierson and the cavalry were in Tupelo by noon and fell to work destroying the railroad in both directions from the town. The infantry, halting occasionally and turning to beat off rear or flank attacks, marched until nine o'clock at night, when the rear of the column made camp at Harrisburg, an ancient village now become a suburb of its younger neighbor, Tupelo, on the railroad.[56]

That night the Union troops encamped in line of battle with a line

315

nearly two miles in length, facing west with its left or southerly flank drawn back to face south, and with the wagon trains parked behind the left, further protected by Grierson's cavalry on the flanks. During the night General Smith's veterans strengthened their line with fence rails, logs, timbers from houses in the village torn down for the purpose, cotton bales in one part of the line and anything else which came to hand which might stop a bullet. At 3:00 A.M. of Thursday, July fourteenth, they were under arms, awaiting attack—and ready for it.[57]

Coming upon the field about nine o'clock on the evening of the thirteenth, as the Confederates were going into camp opposite and about two miles from the Union position, Forrest dismounted, took off his coat, stretched himself full length upon the ground and seemed lost in thought, or perhaps weariness from the intense heat and heavy work of the day. In a little while he sprang up, called Lieutenant Samuel Donelson, one of his aides, and started off on a reconnoitering ride clear around and through the camps of the enemy—a ride on which they were once suspected and challenged by Federal pickets but from which, by the boldness of their bluff and the darkness of the night, they were enabled to return safely, even though they did ride away in a shower of bullets.[58] A bullet might have done him good, Forrest remarked jokingly, if it had hit and opened one of his boils.[59] In his official report Forrest merely mentioned that "at a late hour in the night, accompanied by one of my staff officers, I approached Harrisburg and discovered the enemy strongly posted and prepared to give battle the next day."[60]

Whether Forrest himself wanted to give battle on the next morning, the fourteenth, or whether he did so only in obedience to the orders of his superior officer, Lieutenant General Lee, is a point of uncertainty and even of controversy. At the time it was widely believed among Forrest's men that he had merely acquiesced in the fighting of the battle of Harrisburg because Lee had ordered it, and it was generally accepted that Lee had done so because of the pressures upon his department from other directions which required the imminent breakup of the forces drawn together to resist Smith.

Forrest himself never said this, however, in any writing which has been preserved and published. He did say in his official report, written seventeen days after the battle, that "on the morning of the 14th Lieutenant-General Lee ordered the attack to be made, and the troops were disposed for that purpose." Lee being the ranking officer, however, these expressions do not necessarily imply any disapproval of the attack on the part of Forrest. Many of Forrest's associates stoutly maintained, however, that while Forrest was no doubt in agreement with the general idea of fighting A. J. Smith, he did object earnestly to fighting him as he was

316

found in a situation to which Forrest referred in his official report as "overwhelming numbers in an impregnable position."[61]

Major Anderson, Forrest's assistant adjutant and as close to him as any member of the staff, relates that on the morning of July fourteenth, and before the decision was made to attack, his General said to Lee in Anderson's presence:

"The enemy have a strong position—have thrown up defensive works and are vastly our superior in numbers and it will not do for us to attack them under such conditions. One thing is sure, the enemy cannot remain long where he is. He must come out, and when he does, all I ask or wish is to be turned loose with my command. I will throw Chalmers' Division on the Ellistown Road, and if Smith undertakes to cross the country to Sherman, turn south to devastate the prairies, or return to Memphis, I will be on all sides of him, attacking day and night. He shall not cook a meal or have a night's sleep and I will wear his army to a frazzle before he gets out of the country."[62]

While he did not cite it as a statement of Forrest himself, Colonel Edmund Rucker expressed the like opinion that "had Forrest, and no one else, been in command at Harrisburg, he never would have permitted the enemy to get a roasting ear. He would have harassed him so by remaining in his front, flank and rear, that sooner or later he would have had to make a disastrous retreat. As it was, his retirement was without honor."[63]

On the other hand, in an address before the Southern Historical Society in 1879, two years after Forrest's death, General Chalmers denied that General Lee "made the fight from supposed necessity, and without the concurrence of General Forrest." Chalmers said:

"Lee, Forrest, Buford and I were riding to the front, when the battle was about to begin. Buford said to Lee and Forrest, who had spent the night and morning together in consultation: 'Gentlemen, you have not asked my opinion about this fight, but I tell you, we are going to be badly whipped.' Forrest replied sharply: 'You don't know what you are talking about; we'll whip 'em in five minutes.' Buford replied: 'I hope you may be right, but I don't believe it.' "[64]

Even Chalmers' story, however, does not clear up the matter. The battle had been decided upon and Forrest, regardless of what he might have said earlier to Lee, might very well have been turning to Buford and the whole army, for that matter, a front of confidence in the result. The battle having been decided upon, in loyal support of his commanding officer, he could scarcely have done less.

In that state the question was left until thirty-seven years after the battle when General Lee, who made no official report at the time, published his account.[65] "Whatever others may say," he wrote, "Gen. Lee and Gen. Forrest were in perfect accord as to delivering battle, and Gen. Forrest personally never shrank from his responsibility before or after the bloody battle." In the same account, however, General Lee says that:

". . . the troops were all of Forrest's command, and he should have had supreme command, but he insisted on Gen. Lee's, the department commander, assuming the responsibility and being present. Forrest had just won his splendid victory at Brice's Cross Roads, over Gen. Sturgis, and his troops had confidence in him. Gen. Lee used this argument to insist on his commanding the field, but he said no; that the responsibility was too great, and that his superior in rank should assume and exercise the command; that he considered the Confederate troops inadequate to defeat Smith."

The last clause of the sentence quoted hardly sounds as if Forrest was "in perfect accord" as to delivering battle, but whatever the facts of the day may have been, General Lee's publication brought on a storm of protest from the surviving associates of Forrest, who objected not only to Lee's statements as to their chief's military judgment but even more to other statements to be noticed hereafter, that Forrest had failed to carry out the plan of battle agreed upon. Through correspondence and letters published in the newspapers, all carried on with the most complete courtesy of expression, but with the fiercest of spirit, the aging warriors once more fought the Battle of Harrisburg from records and recollections.

With such a conflict of evidence and with the reasons which prevented the two principals from showing other than perfect accord at the time of the battle, it is impossible to say positively whether Forrest did or did not agree with the idea of attacking A. J. Smith at Harrisburg on the morning of July 14, 1864, but the preponderance of evidence seems to be that he merely acquiesced in what he could not help.

Nothing of this, however, appeared that morning to the eager young Confederates looking across the low ground in front of their position and up the long, bare slope to the crest of the low ridge on which the Federal line had been thrown up during the night. Inside the line were Smith's two divisions of veteran infantry, the First and the Third of the Sixteenth Army Corps, and Bouton's brigade of Negro infantry—about 11,000 in all. Along the line there were six batteries of artillery while to the rear and on the left flank, extending to Tupelo and the railroad, was Grierson's cavalry, some 3,200 men. The whole position was ad-

318

mirably chosen, with a clear field of fire across a rising slope over which an attack must advance for something like half a mile.

On the Confederate side there were Buford's cavalry division with Mabry's brigade attached on the left, facing east, and the small division of Roddey on the right, facing north. Coming into position between them, and still somewhat to the rear, was Chalmers' division, while still farther back, in reserve, was a provisional division of foot soldiers, made up of Lieutenant Colonel Beltzhoover's battalion of heavy artillerists from Mobile, Gholson's Mississippi troops, dismounted, and Neely's brigade, which had come in from Alabama, likewise dismounted—about 2,100 men in all, under the temporary command of Brigadier General Hylan B. Lyon, whose Kentucky brigade was commanded for the day by Colonel Ed Crossland. To Morton's artillery battalion of four batteries was added a fifth, Ferrell's, which had come up with Roddey. The total Confederate force was approximately 9,000 men, of whom, after deducting necessary horse-holders, not much more than 5,500 rifles could be put in the assaulting line.

Fighting with the Kentucky brigade that day was a remnant of John Morgan's men. The anabasis of this band, who made probably the longest ride of the war through enemy-held territory, had started a month before at Cynthiana, Kentucky, 65 miles from Cincinnati where 106 of Morgan's horse-holders, caught in a stampede of 3,000 horses when Morgan was disastrously defeated, made their escape, held together, elected Captain William Campbell to lead them and started west and south to join Forrest. In their wanderings they saw the Ohio River, somewhere above Louisville. Unarmed—only fifteen had saved their rifles—they bluffed the Federal garrison at Bardstown into surrender, to get rifles. Wandering on, dodging the swarming enemy, they neared the Ohio River again at Owensboro, crossed the Green at Calhoun, passed through Cadiz, forded the Cumberland near by, the season being dry, and, after much trouble and the loss of several horses and one or two men, managed to get across the wider Tennessee by swimming, having to keep a sharp eye out for patrolling gunboats. Passing on through West Kentucky and clear across Tennessee, they kept themselves mounted as their stock gave out by the irregular practice of "exchanging" horses with citizens on the line of march. Finally they met near Corinth, Mississippi, a small band of Forrest's scouts, "hard looking and very dirty," the diarist of the anabasis notes, but nevertheless a delight to see. By them Morgan's men were escorted on south in time to take their gallant part in the tragedy of Harrisburg, with a loss of one-third their number.[66]

Even with soldiers of such mettle, an attack against a position such as

319

Smith's by forces no more numerous than those commanded by Lee and Forrest, could have had no more than an outside chance of success— and what chance there was, was lost by failure to bring about a simultaneous, co-ordinated attack all along the line.

The Confederates had to make an approach march averaging two miles to get into position for the assault. To this was added a certain amount of misdirection and countermarching to correct the alignment,[67] with some distress to troops not accustomed to foot maneuvers. Morton, who for the first time had twenty guns at hand, proposed to General Lee that they be massed to breach the Federal line at a critical spot near the main axis of the coming battle, along the Pontotoc-Tupelo road. The general, instead, divided the guns among the infantry commands, putting some in reserve and, as events turned out, clear out of the battle —much to Morton's disappointment.[68] Lee's plan of battle, according to his subsequent account, was that he offered command of either wing to Forrest who chose the right wing (Roddey's division), while he, Lee, took the left. The front line of the left wing was Mabry's Mississippi and Arkansas brigade on the extreme left, then Crossland's Kentuckians, with Bell's Tennessee brigade behind as a support. Chalmers' division and the provisional division of Lyon were still farther in the rear as a reserve.

About 7:30 in the morning "Lieutenant-General Lee gave the order to advance," Forrest reported, "and directed me to swing the right around upon the enemy's left. I immediately repaired to General Roddey's right with all possible speed, which was nearly a mile distant, and after giving him the necessary orders in person I dashed across the field in a gallop for the purpose of selecting a position in which to place his troops . . ."[69] —all things which should have been done, it would seem, before the order to advance was given.

While Forrest was away on the right the left began to move forward, with a fatal lack of timing and co-ordination. Mabry's brigade obliqued too much to the left, Crossland's too much to the right, opening between them a gap into which Buford, the division commander, hurried forward Bell's brigade. Before he could get his lines right, however, the Kentuckians "raised a shout and charged."

"Though ordered to move surely and steadily, it was impossible to restrain the ardor of my men,"[70] Colonel Crossland reported—and so the very intrepid daring which gave the Confederate plan of battle what little chance of success it had, ruined even that chance. The Kentucky brigade charged forward ahead of its fellows, a handful against an army, seemingly confident that the long, steady line in front would break and give back before them as they had seen so many others do. But here was something new—a line which held its fire and then, rising up, blasted

320

The United States of America.
District of West Tennessee

In the Circuit Court of the United
States of America, within and for the Sixth Circuit and District of West Tennessee, September
Term in the year of our Lord Eighteen Hundred
and Sixty four—

The Grand Jurors of the United States of
America, within and for the Sixth Circuit and
District of West Tennessee, elected, empanneled,
sworn and charged to enquire in and for the body
of the District aforesaid upon their oaths present
that on the first day of January in the year of our
Lord one thousand eight Hundred and sixty two
and long before, and continually from thence hitherto an open and public Rebellion insurrection and
war with force and arms was existing and is yet existing and prosecuted and carried on against the
Government and Laws of the United States of America by divers persons claiming to exercise the powers
of Government within the said The United States of
America, styling themselves "the Confederate States
of America" and that Nathan B Forrest
late of said District aforesaid being an inhab-
itant of and resident within the said The United
States of America and owing allegiance and
fidelity to the said The United States of America
well knowing the premises but not weighing and

INDICTED FOR TREASON

Opening of the four-page indictment against Forrest by the Federal grand
jury, growing out of his raid into his home town of Memphis.

this Court in pursuance of such their traitorous intentions and purposes aforesaid he the said Nathan B Forrest with the persons so as aforesaid traitorously assembled armed and arrayed in manner aforesaid most wickedly and maliciously and traitorously did ordain prepare and levy war against the said The United States of America, contrary to the duty of the Allegiance and fidelity of the said Nathan B. Forrest, and contrary to the form of the statute in such case made and provided and against the peace and dignity of the United States of America

A true Bill
J. E. Merriman
Foreman
W A Jones
W Bayly
Sanford Hill M.D.
J. Ogden
F. Erickson
E. F. Comers
W M Gans
James Tipping
D C Trader
Joseph Dobrecka
Peter Miller

"A TRUE BILL"

Last page of Forrest's indictment for treason as a result of the Memphis raid signed by the grand jurors, some of whom were his former neighbors and associates.

the very ground over which the Kentuckians advanced, while from far to the right and the left, enfilading and oblique fire from field guns and rifles poured into them. Gallantly they pushed forward again and again —a few of them almost to the line of breastworks itself—and as gallantly first Mabry's men and then Bell's, who had farther to come, rushed up the slopes to their aid, but always they were disjointed attacks by single brigades, not the steady determined push all along the line which might possibly have succeeded.

"On reaching the front [to put Roddey in position for the assault]," Forrest reported, "I found the Kentucky brigade had been rashly precipitated forward, and were retiring under the murderous fire concentrated upon them. I seized their colors"—Forrest was ever one to go wherever the boldest of his men might go—"and after a short appeal ordered them to form a new line, when they held their position."[71]

Meanwhile Buford's other brigades had made their charges forward, with the artillery assigned to each of them being pushed forward by hand, firing as it went, and they too had been driven back by the concentrated, converging fire from all along the line. Chalmers' division, called up from reserve, was coming into action, but "while moving received three different orders"—from Forrest to bear right to support Roddey, from Lee to go to the left to support Mabry, from Buford to go to the center. Chalmers, in a quandary, started to follow Forrest's order, but before he got there received a fourth order, this time from Lee, dividing the command, leaving McCulloch's brigade in reserve and sending Rucker's to the left "to charge at the double-quick and with a shout." Rucker and his men "behaved with as much gallantry as men could . . . yet they were unable to accomplish anything."[72]

To Forrest, rallying the Kentucky brigade for another try, it was apparent that the enemy were in "overwhelming numbers in an impregnable position, and wishing to save my troops from the unprofitable slaughter I knew would follow any attempt to charge his works, I did not push forward General Roddey's command when it arrived, knowing it would receive the same concentrated fire which had repulsed the Kentucky brigade."[73]

The Confederate right, therefore, was never seriously engaged, and the reserve under Lyon was not even brought up to the field, while the shattered brigades of the left, with from a fourth to a third of their men lying dead or wounded on the slopes leading up to Harrisburg, with hundreds of others prostrated by the heat of the charge of as much as a mile across plowed ground in some cases, with their ammunition exhausted and the hopelessness of their disjointed charges apparent, were withdrawn under cover of McCulloch's brigade.

As seen by the Union General Smith, the Confederate charges "seemed to be a footrace to see who could reach us first . . . yelling and howling like Comanches . . . gallantly made, but without order, organization, or skill. They would come forward and fall back, rally and forward again, with the like result. Their determination may be seen by the fact that their dead were found within thirty yards of our batteries."[74]

There is the usual conflict of testimony as to just how the Confederate attack was met and terminated. Some of the Union subordinate commanders describe how their units rose up and fired into the faces of the charging Confederates with such effect that they turned and fled in "the utmost disorder," exclaiming as they went, according to one account, "My God! My God!"[75] but the accounts given by Generals Smith and Mower are much more matter of fact. "After about two hours fighting in this manner," says Smith, "General Mower, losing all hope of their attempting any closer quarters, advanced his lines about a quarter of a mile, driving the enemy before him from the field and covering their dead and wounded."[76]

"This ended the hard fighting of the day," General Smith reported, while General Mower explained that there was no attempt at further pursuit because of the exhaustion from the march of nineteen miles and the fighting of the day before.[77] At 1:00 P.M. the Federal troops who had advanced from one-quarter to one-half a mile after the repulse of the Confederate attacks were recalled to the lines of the morning whence, at sundown, they fell back some 600 yards farther for the night.

The fighting activity of the rest of the day and evening of the fourteenth, curiously, was on the part of the Confederates who had been so bloodily repulsed before 10:30 in the morning. Harrisburg was burned by the Union forces that night, while Chalmers with McCulloch's brigade and Forrest with Rucker's drove in their outer lines upon the main body, which opened upon them what Chalmers described as "the heaviest small arms fire heard during the engagement,"[78] but one which did little execution. The chief effect of the audacious night attack was to keep a considerable proportion of the Union troops under arms for a second night.[79]

Of the seven mounted brigades of Confederates on the field three were not closely engaged. Deducting horse-holders, the four brigades which charged the Union position in succession were able to put on the line approximately 3,000 men. Their reported losses in killed and wounded were 1,259, missing 49, or more than 40 percent of those actually in the attack—such a loss as befell hardly another cavalry command during the war.[80] Only one of the four brigade commanders escaped unwounded. In seven regiments of Buford's division every field officer was a casualty. One regiment, the Second Tennessee, came out of the fight under the command of Lieutenant George Seay.[81]

The three batteries which charged with the infantry suffered like losses, though not included in the totals above. One of the guns in Lieutenant Tully Brown's section of Morton's battery lost seven of the eight men of its crew, and every horse. A sergeant in the battery recalls Lieutenant Saunders Sale, its commander, sitting his horse in a storm of lead, laughing at the efforts of a very small pony harnessed to a limber in the stead of a big wheel horse. "Brown," he called, "damned if he don't believe he's a wheel horse!"[82] The gun had to be brought off by hand with the aid of Captain Titus' company of sharpshooters, a body of about fifty military prisoners under confinement for serious offenses, released just before the battle and allowed to fight on probation, as it were—and doing it right gallantly.[83]

"The command engaged went in by piecemeal and were slaughtered by wholesale. . . . It was all gallantry and useless sacrifice of life."[84]

Why? Forrest himself in the report of the battle made on August first offered no word of apology or explanation, other than the remark that while he was away lining up the troops on the right wing the Kentucky brigade was "rashly precipitated forward." In the work of Jordan and Pryor, which he saw and approved, it is said:

"General Lee's orders really were that his centre should stand still, while the right (Roddey) should have time to swing around into a position as near to the enemy as that held by Buford, but from a misunderstanding, the Kentucky brigade prematurely began the attack. . . ."[85]

General Stephen Lee made no report at the time but thirty-seven years later, after his distinguished career as college president, he wrote in his published account of the battle that Forrest changed the plan of battle by not ordering Roddey forward "at the signal agreed on."[86]

"Gen. Lee moved to the right [he said, using the third person throughout]. . . . He soon met Gen. Forrest, and said to him: 'Why did you not carry out the plan of attack?' Forrest replied: 'Buford's right had been rashly thrown forward and repulsed. In the exercise of my discretion I did not move Roddey forward but I have moved him to the left, and formed a new line.' Gen. Lee said, 'In doing as you did, you failed to carry out the plan of battle agreed on.' Gen. Lee replied that it was then too late to remedy the matter. . . ."

Replies to this paper were immediately forthcoming from three of the brigade commanders at Harrisburg—Bell, Rucker and Lyon, the last having been at West Point with Lee—and also from D. C. Kelley, who had commanded Forrest's Old Regiment that day, H. A. Tyler, who had commanded a special detachment of Kentuckians, Anderson, Forrest's assistant adjutant general, Morton, his chief of artillery, and Samuel Donelson, one of his aides. Colonel Kelley, in a statement submitted to and approved by the others named, made the point that there was no signal gun fired for the beginning of the battle as General Lee had related, and supported the point with Captain Morton's statement that he had received no orders to have such a gun fired and that none had been. With expressions of distinguished esteem the veteran soldier-minister called attention to the fact that General Lee, having made no contemporary official report of the battle, was now after thirty-seven years of silence on the subject trusting to memory which "after a long lapse of time is not always reliable."

General Lee in reply reaffirmed his statement that a signal gun had been fired for the opening of the battle, that being a point on which his memory was most positive, and explained the lack of a contemporary report by the circumstance that almost immediately after the battle he had been transferred to the command of a corps in the Army of Tennessee and had not received or seen Forrest's report. The report, as Colonel Kelley promptly pointed out, had been made in due course to Major Powhatan Ellis, Lee's department adjutant general, as was then the custom of the army. After another round of letters between them Lee closed the correspondence with a courteous final letter, leaving Kelley to "occupy the field alone."[87]

And there the controversy may well be left, with mention of the fact, conceded by all that the friendship between Forrest and Lee remained unbroken until the day of Forrest's death for, as Lee said of the sadly mixed management of Confederate affairs on the field of Harrisburg, "I am sure he [Forrest] did the best as he saw it. I am sure I did my best as I saw it."

Regardless of causes or responsibility for the handling of the troops at Harrisburg, there is no doubt that it was a defeat for the Confederates which, with more dash and boldness on the part of A. J. Smith, might have been turned into a disaster. Despite the defeat of the fourteenth, however, and the great losses suffered, it was the Confederates who held the initiative after the fight and who on the morning of the fifteenth resumed the fighting. Buford attacked the Federal left flank, not seriously but enough to drive in the skirmishers on the main line, while Chalmers moved around their right flank toward the Ellistown road—the movement which, according to his assistant adjutant general, Forrest had wanted to make the day before.

By noon Chalmers reported that the enemy was in retreat in that direction, and "the pursuit began"—truly a strange pursuit in which an overwhelmingly superior force which had just won a pitched battle with

324

losses little more than half those of its weaker antagonist, drew away, leaving the field to the losing side—and actually congratulating itself that it was getting safely away!

General Smith was retreating, he reported, because he had found that much of the twenty-days' supply of bread with which he had started only ten days before was spoiled, leaving him with but one day's rations[88]— and that right at the edge of the greatest granary of breadstuffs in the Confederacy!

Leaving his more seriously wounded men behind in Tupelo, Smith started back on the long, devastated road to Memphis, with his mission uncompleted except that for a season he had kept Forrest from Sherman's lines.

As the Confederates occupied Smith's position at Harrisburg, General Lee ordered Forrest to resume the command of the troops and to take up the pursuit, which Forrest's men did with eagerness. Late that afternoon at Old Town Creek, five miles northwest from Tupelo, Buford, with Bell's brigade in the advance, drove in the Union cavalry with a rush—almost a stampede—but was himself repulsed as he struck the solid infantry forces under Mower.[89] McCulloch's brigade coming up on the gallop with Forrest himself leading was almost surrounded and was driven back, while Chalmers, with Forrest's Old Regiment newly reconstituted under its old Lieutenant Colonel D. C. Kelley, struck in on the flank with no success. Horses and guns were withdrawn safely, however, and the Confederate line held, half a mile away,[90] while once more there was not the strong counterattack to be expected from the Federal forces. General Smith was too intent on getting back to Memphis intact.

There might have been such a real counterattack perhaps if the Union commanders had known then the news which soon was to run through all the western South, that in the swirling fight back and forth across the creek bottom, just before sunset of July fifteenth, Bedford Forrest had suffered a crippling, disabling wound. The ball struck him in the foot— the big toe, according to one account—but it inflicted a wound so painful, taken with the boils from which he still was suffering, that Forrest had to turn over the command to Chalmers.[91]

Despite repulse Chalmers' men resumed the pursuit on the morning of the sixteenth, and harried the rear and flanks of Smith's overwhelming force as it marched still cautiously and "acting always on the defensive"[92] back through New Albany and on to Salem, where on July nineteenth, after four days' march, it met supplies sent out from Memphis. On the twenty-first the command was back on the railroad at La Grange, whence it had started seventeen days before.

325

From New Albany on the seventeenth A. J. Smith sent to Washburn his message of victory closing "I bring back everything in good order; nothing lost"[93]—a message so different from those which had come back from other Generals sent out after Forrest that Washburn was almost exultant in passing on the word to Sherman.

But that redheaded realist of war was not so much impressed with the victory as Washburn and Smith thought he ought to have been. This business of marching back to Memphis, even if it was "in good order; nothing lost" and for the purpose of replenishing supplies, was not what he had sent Smith out to do.

"Order Smith to pursue and keep after Forrest all the time,"[94] his message to Washburn began, while to Halleck and Grant he explained that he had ordered Smith out again "to hang on to Forrest to prevent his coming to Tennessee."[95]

"General Smith . . . thinks you have a wrong impression in regard to his fight," Washburn replied to Sherman. "He returned for lack of supplies. That he whipped the enemy very badly there is no doubt." To which, in response to Sherman's instructions, he added, "I have ordered General Smith to put his command in order to again move against Forrest. He will so move as soon as he can get ready, unless you should think he had better go to Mobile."[96]

Harrisburg, then, was a battle satisfactory to no one in its results. From the Federal standpoint it was better than what had gone before but inconclusive—except that it had kept Forrest from Tennessee for a season. From a Confederate standpoint it was badly planned and worse executed. The only justification for fighting it on that day was the anxiety of the department commander to get it over with so that he might break up the scanty force assembled to meet Smith's invasion, and send its parts back to meet threats to other portions of his department—as was, in fact, done a few days after the battle, when Mabry and Gholson were returned to central Mississippi and Beltzhoover and his artillerists to Mobile, and Roddey's force was sent to repel a threatened move into Alabama, leaving Forrest again with only his two divisions—Chalmers' and Buford's.

The real reason for fighting at Harrisburg that day, however, and the real cause of the headlong precipitate way the battle was fought, in all probability, was the half-conscious Confederate attitude toward these repeated expeditions sent out from Memphis after them—Sooy Smith who had turned back from Okolona, Sturgis who had turned back from Ripley and on his second trial had been chased back from Brice's Cross Roads, and now this fourth expedition after Forrest. But this time was to be different. There was no chance to "run" the Yankees

326

home again—but, curiously, Forrest's men did turn them back and did it short of the prairie country, the defense of which was their special charge. This time the invasion had been turned back by giving battle, even though the battle resulted in defeat. The next time, soon to come, it would have to be turned back by stratagem.

CHAPTER XXI

MEMPHIS:
THE RAID THAT RECALLED AN INVADING ARMY*

July 24, 1864-August 25, 1864

THE NEXT invasion of Mississippi was not long in coming. General Smith got back to Memphis on July 23, 1864, and on the same day began getting ready for his return. His preparations, no doubt, were spurred by a message of the twenty-fifth from Sherman, who had just fought the Battle of Atlanta and was drawing his lines close for the prolonged siege of that doomed city. To Washburn, commanding in West Tennessee and north Mississippi, he wired:

"It was by General Grant's special order that General Smith was required . . . to pursue and continue to follow Forrest. He must keep after him till recalled by me or General Grant, and if Forrest goes toward Tennessee, General Smith must follow him. . . . It is of vital importance that Forrest does not go to Tennessee."[1]

By the morning of July twenty-eighth Smith had the first of his brigades ready to move out along the Memphis and Charleston Railroad, which was being put in repair eastward to Grand Junction, fifty miles. From that point the construction and repair crews of the United States Military Railroads were to work south along the Mississippi Central beyond Holly Springs to the Tallahatchie River "for the purpose of moving troops and supplies for an expedition against Forrest."[2] There was to be no going back for supplies this time. They were to be brought out to the column.

This column—18,000 men of all arms—was enough to "whip the combined force of the enemy this side of Georgia and east of the Mississippi," Washburn told Sherman on August second. "I shall push across the Tallahatchie as soon as possible," he added—evidently using "I" in a military sense rather than as the first personal pronoun. "Will not stop short of Columbus, Mississippi. Forrest's forces were near Okolona a week since, Chalmers in command. Forrest not been able to resume command by reason of wound in fight with Smith. I have a report today that he died of lockjaw some days ago. . . ."[3]

---

* The field of operations covered in this chapter is shown on the map on page 218.

"After General Smith reaches Columbus he should march for Decatur, Ala., and thence report to me," Sherman replied. ". . . Let General Smith impress on the people the fact that as long as Forrest lives their country is doomed to be harassed. . . . Is Forrest surely dead? If so, tell General Mower I am pledged to him for his promotion, and if Old Abe don't make good my promise then General Mower may have my place."[4]

"Old Abe" made good, however, even though Mower had not succeeded in his assignment of killing Forrest, and, as it happened, issued Sherman's commission to the permanent rank of Major General of Regulars on the same day as Mower's to the temporary rank of Major General of Volunteers. In expressing his thanks to the President for both commissions, Sherman observed that while Mower's "task was to kill Forrest" and he had "only crippled him," he was "a young and game officer" deserving of the promotion.[5]

Except for the report of Forrest's death, Washburn's dispatch was substantially accurate. Chalmers was still in command of the Confederate forces in northern Mississippi—his own and Buford's divisions—reduced to barely more than 5,000 men all told after the losses at Harrisburg.[6]

Though Forrest was not in active command he did manage to get about among the camps in the Tupelo-Okolona area, riding in a farm buggy with a rack projecting over the dashboard to carry his painfully wounded foot, "sick-looking, thin as a rail, cheekbones that stuck out like they were trying to come through the skin, skin so yellow it looked greenish, eyes blazing."[7]

General Lee had left the department to take command of John B. Hood's corps, the latter having been put in command of the Army of Tennessee defending Atlanta when the President removed Joseph E. Johnston. Suceeding Lee as department commander was Major General Dabney H. Maury of Virginia, West Point graduate of the class of 1846 along with Stonewall Jackson and George B. McClellan, kinsman of General Johnston and Commodore Matthew Fontaine Maury, and a scholarly and experienced soldier. While in command of the defense of Mobile, Maury had learned somewhat of the manner of man Forrest was, and had pondered well the lesson of the Battle of Harrisburg. To Forrest, therefore, he wrote upon taking over the command:

". . . I intrust to you the operations against the enemy threatening an invasion of North Mississippi. I would not, if I could, interfere with your plan for conducting these operations, but must confine myself to the duty of sending you the means, as far as I can, of accomplishing the successful results it has been your good fortune so constantly to achieve. . . . You know as well as I the insufficiency of my means. . . . But we must do the best we can with what little we have, and it is with no small satisfaction I reflect that of all the commanders of the Confederacy you are accustomed to accomplish the very greatest results with small means when left to your own untrammeled judgment. Upon that judgment I now rely."[8]

In acknowledgment of Maury's courteous letter Forrest reported to him the situation—his command reduced by losses in battle, especially "deficient in field officers and brigade commanders," with Bell the only experienced brigade commander on duty, and the "greater number of field officers in Bell's brigade wounded or killed.

"Nevertheless," Forrest wrote, "all that can be done shall be done ... I have not the force to risk a general engagement, and will resort to other means. ..."[9]

As Smith moved cautiously forward from Grand Junction toward Holly Springs, Forrest, now able to "take the saddle with one foot in the stirrup," resumed active command in the early days of August. On the fifth he advised Maury that he thought Smith's move down the Central Railroad was a feint to "draw my forces west and give him the start toward the prairies"—in which estimate the events of the next few days proved Forrest to be in error—but he was disposing his limited forces to meet, as best he could, any move which Smith might make. Buford's division he was holding about Okolona to await developments. Neely's brigade was moved forward to Pontotoc. Mabry, whose brigade had just been returned to Forrest's command, was started back from southern Mississippi to Grenada. Chalmers himself with McCulloch's brigade and a battery went to Abbeville, on the Central Railroad just south of the Tallahatchie River, with instructions to fortify the crossings of that stream and its tributary the Tippah, as he might think necessary, and to blockade the fords which he did not fortify. The directions to Chalmers were to "take every negro you can get your hands on to do the work" and to impress not only hands but the tools for them to use. Orders were issued also to destroy the railroad bridge across the Tallahatchie above Abbeville and the trestlework from the river south to Oxford, although as late as August eighth Forrest still did not think the enemy would come that way, expecting that they would strike farther east on the old route by way of Pontotoc.[10]

Smith's menacing advance into Mississippi was not the only problem which Forrest had to face upon his return to command early in August. On the seventh, while Smith was approaching the Tallahatchie below Holly Springs and while Forrest was still at Okolona, he received orders from Richmond requiring an election of field officers in the West Tennessee regiments which he had organized in February, because of "irregularities and illegalities."

Forrest immediately wrote President Jefferson Davis, recalling once more the circumstances in which the fragmentary companies composing these commands were brought out of West Tennessee and the impossibility then of holding elections. He continued:

"With great labor, and under many difficulties and disadvantages, I succeeded in bringing order out of confusion, and organized and placed in the service a majority of the troops now constituting my command. The enemy in heavy force is in my front, and any attempt, by elections, to fill the field positions in the West Tennessee regiments I am satisfied will disorganize the command and be injurious to the service. . . . Election will surely result in the loss of the best field officers I have, who by strict discipline have kept the men together and are not popular with the men. . . . At this particular time it would be disastrous to change the field officers of the West Tennessee regiments, and it is my firm conviction that to do so at any time will be highly injurious."

To this eminently sound and practical proposition he added the hope that nothing would be done to "destroy the effectiveness or weaken my influence and control" over a command which "since its organization has performed more and better duty than perhaps any other new cavalry command ever did in the same length of time."[11]

Neither the argument that appointment of field officers was the proper and legal way of choosing them in commands organized as these had been, nor Forrest's closing appeal, was effective with the President and the Adjutant and Inspector General at Richmond. The law, it was held, was that these West Tennessee troops were raised as regiments under authority granted by General Pillow, and not as "independent companies," and that therefore field officers must be elected and not appointed. The President approved the Adjutant General's finding and instructed the Secretary of War to inform General Forrest—though not, fortunately, until after his immediate operation was over and done with.

Meanwhile, however, and before Forrest had to start on the next of his major operations, the papers fell into the hands of the Assistant Secretary of War, John A. Campbell, who in the days before the war had been an Associate Justice of the Supreme Court of the United States. Judge Campbell examined the law more closely and with a more liberal and practical eye, and found to his own satisfaction—and apparently to that of the Department since no further action was taken—that under an act of October 11, 1862, the President could determine the condition under which commands raised as these had been should be accepted into

331

the regular service, and could, if he desired to do so, appoint field officers for them.[12]

While Forrest was watching the several possible lines of advance and at the same time having to deal with Richmond about the status of his field officers, Smith completed the movement of his infantry to Holly Springs by rail. With his whole command in hand, on August eighth he moved in strength to the Tallahatchie River, crossed the stream on driftwood lodged against the piers of the destroyed railroad bridge, as well as by flatboat, and drove the little defending force back "to the first big hill" to the South. During the night and the next day a bridge was thrown across the river.[13]

The crossing of the Tallahatchie having made plain the direction of Smith's advance, Forrest sent word to Chalmers at Oxford to "contest every inch of ground" and started toward him with everything he had in the way of reinforcements.[14]

Fortunately for Forrest, Smith's movements, even after he was across the Tallahatchie, continued to be supercautious. On August tenth his advance pushed the Confederates back across Hurricane Creek, and six miles beyond to the little university town of Oxford. Chalmers evacuated the town and fell back across the Yoconah River to the south, with the idea that the Federal cavalry would follow. Instead, learning that a Confederate column was approaching from the east, they evacuated Oxford during the night of the tenth, and fell back northward to the vicinity of the Tallahatchie crossings.

Forrest, with Bell's and Neely's brigades and Morton's battery, marched in from Pontotoc at eleven o'clock that night, so that the citizens of Oxford, having gone to bed with their town occupied by Federal soldiers, awoke to find the public square and the streets leading into it filled with soldiers in Confederate gray, stretched out or curled up on the ground, each man holding the reins dangling from the drooping head of his horse, man and mount both sleeping with the weariness of the forced march of the night before.[15]

There followed a week of watchful sparring in the rain, with feint and thrust on both sides, but no major movement on either. In that season—the "wet August" as it came to be known in those parts where August ordinarily is a dry month—the Confederates found that not even the best constructed "shebang," made of a captured oilcloth stretched over a pole resting in two forked sticks stuck in the ground, or over a sapling bent and tied down to the ground to form a ridgepole, could keep them even moderately dry, the ground beneath them being saturated. "Rations were in plenty," one Confederate private wrote, "but we could scarcely get dry wood enough to cook them."[16]

"Owing to very heavy rains for the last few days, washing the railroad badly, there has been some delay in getting supplies forwarded," Washburn reported to Sherman on August eleventh. Two more days, however, he thought would place "everything on the south side of the Tallahatchie"—13,000 infantry plus three Minnesota regiments, strength not given, 3,000 colored troops and 4,000 cavalry. The report concluded with an ominous statement—for Washburn and Smith—"General Forrest is not dead."[17]

Smith's failure to advance was due to the wait for supplies; Forrest's to a total lack of the strength which he needed to resist so formidable a force as he faced. During the period of relative inactivity he did send the Seventh Tennessee and his own Old Regiment out to strike in behind Smith from the east and cut the railroad between Holly Springs and Grand Junction, but the expedition proved abortive.[18]

On August seventeenth, the weather being still rainy and the roads deep in mud, Smith started forward again from his camps about the Tallahatchie, heading south for Oxford and beyond. The movement was not simultaneous, however, as some units moved on the eighteenth and nineteenth and others not until as late as August twenty-first.[19]

Forrest was well advised of the situation and of Smith's movements. So were the soldiers under him. Four times, now, they had seen invasions turned back from the country they were assigned to protect—two by smashing defeats of the invading forces, another by reason of the lack of resolution of its commander, and the fourth by a fight so desperate and so resolute as to make the invading general anxious in his mind to the point of returning to Memphis. Each invasion had been on a scale larger than the last, while the forces available to meet them were dwindling. It had become apparent that all had been done that could be done in the way of fighting the columns sent out from Memphis. This one must be turned back some other way.

"We knew we couldn't fight General Smith's big fine army," said Lieutenant Tully Brown, "and we knew that we couldn't get any reinforcements anywhere, and we boys speculated about what Old Bedford was going to do."[20]

The situation was desperate; the remedy was to be characteristic—and successful.

At five o'clock in the afternoon on August eighteenth Forrest gathered about him on the public square of Oxford detachments of Bell's and Neely's brigades and Morton's battery—nearly 2,000 men in all, after a "weeding out of sick men, sore back and lame horses."[21] In a pelting rainstorm—when it was already nearly dark because of the lowering clouds—he led them out of town to the west. Chalmers, left behind with something more than 2,000 men, was under orders to demonstrate so vigorously and with such a show of force as to hold Smith where he was for at least two days, and to prevent him from learning that nearly one-half of the Confederate force had left his front.

All night the raiding force under Forrest plodded along westward, through rain, through mud knee-deep at times, across swollen creeks, up and down long slippery hills. Two hours before daylight there was a halt to rest the horses. At daylight they pushed on. At seven in the morning of August nineteenth the column reached Panola, where the Mississippi and Tennessee Railroad crossed the Tallahatchie. Finding the streams so high and the road so wet and bottomless, Forrest there turned back to Grenada the ambulances with which he had started, two guns of the Morton battery and about 100 men whose horses had begun to show signs of failing. With the balance of the men and with two guns under Lieutenant Sale, ten horses to the gun, he crossed the Tallahatchie at Panola, and stretched away northwestward for Memphis.[22]

All that day, the nineteenth, the sun shone on Forrest's men as they marched, while back in front of Oxford Chalmers was boldly bluffing the overwhelming force against him. Forrest bivouacked that night at Senatobia, fifty miles from his starting point and a little more than half-way to Memphis.

A mile north of Senatobia on the morning of the twentieth he struck the flooded Hickahala Creek—bankfull, sixty feet wide in the current. "I had no idea of giving up my visit to Memphis," Forrest said afterward, "nor did I intend to lay around the creek waiting for it to fall." Whereupon, with characteristic versatility, he turned his cavalrymen into bridge-building engineer troops. The raw materials of his bridge were trees of the forest used for the supports of his suspension span; the wild grapevines festooning the trees, cut down and woven together to form the suspension cables; a small flatboat found at the crossing, used for a float or pontoon to support the center of the span where it hung lowest, and two bundles of poles, tied together with grapevines, placed as pontoons on either side of the flatboat; and, finally, the plank floors taken up from the ginhouses for miles about and brought in on the shoulders of the cavalrymen to form the floor of this remarkable span— homemade, using the materials of nature which came to hand, and completed by willing workers in an hour.[23]

Six miles beyond the Hickahala lay the Coldwater River, twice as wide, with banks brimful, a booming current coursing through the flood, and one small ferryboat which could carry only four horses at a time. There was nothing for it but another and bigger bridge, which was built of the same sort of materials and finished in three hours. Across these swinging, swaying bridges the men led their horses. The guns, unlimbered, were drawn by hand and the wagons—what few there were of them—were unloaded and pulled across empty, while the soldiers carried their contents in small packs. Forrest himself, limping on his wounded foot, was "the first man to carry across an armful" of corn in the shuck unloaded from one heavy wagon, an example that was hardly needed. "I never saw a command look more like it was out for a holiday," one soldier wrote,[24] while Forrest said, "I had to continually caution the men to keep quiet. They were making a regular corn shucking out of it. Wet and muddy, but full of life and ready for anything. . . . Those were great soldiers."[25]

The last troops were across the bridge at the Coldwater a little before sunset. Ten miles beyond, at Hernando, the home of Forrest's young manhood, the whole command rested for a while that Saturday night, before marching the last twenty-five miles to Memphis. At three o'clock the next morning, Sunday, August twenty-first, the 1,500 men whose horses had been able to keep up under the strain of the march were in the outskirts of that city.

Memphis at that time had been held securely by Union forces for more than two years—ever since the June day in 1862 when the Union gunboats demolished the Confederate fleet of converted river steamers.

The presence of large numbers of officers and soldiers, and of sutlers, army contractors, speculators in cotton or government vouchers and pay claims, and other commercial followers of the army, had given to the town something of the air of a Northern center of business. New York houses, and those of St. Louis, Chicago, Indianapolis, Columbus, Pittsburgh or Wheeling, filled columns of the *Bulletin* with announcements of their Memphis branches or offices, or with advertisements of sutlers' goods, insurance, "Sherman" tobacco, or Chesapeake oysters from Baltimore. More tantalizing than any of these, probably, to the Confederate soldiers into whose hands the amazingly free circulation of newspapers back and forth between the belligerents would put the *Bulletin* or the *Review*, were the numerous and alluring advertisements of Madeira, or sherry, of Moselle or Rhenish wines, of French brandy or cognac, of "segars" from Havana, and of coffee—especially coffee. Memphis was the land of plenty.

Theaters were booming. There were the New Memphis, the Olympic, the National. *East Lynne* was shown, and *The Daughter of the Regiment, The Lady of Lyons, Susan Hopley, or the Trials and Vicissitudes of a Servant Girl, The Innkeeper's Daughter, or the Graveyard Murder*. To these and others forgotten thrillers of the day admission to the dress circle or parquette was seventy-five cents. "Improper characters"—of whom there is persuasive evidence that the town was entertaining more than its usual quota—were not admitted.

Not infrequently the columns of the papers would note the marriage of some young lady of Memphis to an Illinois lieutenant, or one from Iowa or Indiana. Captain James H. Burk, of the Indiana Military Agency, was busy collecting contributions for a volume of *Poetry, by Indiana Soldiers.*

So far as attack by Confederate forces went, no city could have seemed more secure than Memphis. There had been some little trouble with guerrillas sniping at trains running out on the Charleston Railroad, but the commanding general had met that with his Special Order No. 74, published in the newspapers late in July, directing that "forty prominent secessionists be arrested and put on the trains," with one seated beside the engineer, one beside the fireman and others in exposed places, and that "no train be allowed to leave Memphis without a Secesh Guard until this murderous business is desisted from." It was further directed that the "Secesh Guard" be quartered at Memphis and Grand Junction and "tenderly cared for when not on duty on the trains." Some officer of the staff of the Military Division of West Tennessee must have fancied himself as a humorist.

The Memphis *Review*, published weekly during the Federal occupation, had a correspondent, "More Anon," with the expedition of Smith. On August fifteenth, from Abbeville, Mississippi, under the headline, "The Rout Complete—Our Cavalry Pursuing," More Anon described the crossing of the Tallahatchie, the defeat of the "rebels 10,000 strong," and their retirement upon Oxford. More and better news was promised for the next week's paper.

The *Review* containing this dispatch was published on Saturday evening, August twentieth. In the same issue was published General Washburn's Special Order No. 107 prohibiting the "crying or selling of newspapers on Sunday between the hours of 9 A.M. and 5 P.M.," the better to preserve the peace and quiet of the day unbroken.

That Saturday night, according to the next issue of the *Review*, was a peculiarly peaceful one, with soft clouds, a rare sunset and a moonrise of surpassing serenity. "Sunday, with its sacred duties, was about dawning on us, and unhaunted by the calls of a business day all were resting in the folds of Morpheus," continued the reporter, "when, stealing through the deep fog, about one thousand rebels fell upon our soldiers and the roar of musketry startled our citizens from oblivion. . . ."

There were in Memphis at the time three general officers of the Union Army—Major General Cadwallader C. Washburn, commanding the District of West Tennessee, Major General Stephen A. Hurlbut, his predecessor in command, and Brigadier General R. P. Buckland, commanding the Memphis garrison. Forrest had quite complete information as to the location and disposition of Union troops, brought out to him by some of Captain Henderson's scouts. As the command neared the city special parties were told off to the different jobs to be done, with definite and explicit instructions. One general instruction, to all officers and men of all the detachments, was that the work was to be done quietly with no unnecessary gunfire or cheers.

The advance of the movement into the town was under the General's brother, Captain Bill Forrest. His task after getting past the sentry lines was to ride straight to the Gayoso House to round up the Federal officers quartered there—one of whom, it was understood, was General Hurlbut. Lieutenant Colonel T. H. Logwood, with detachments from Lieutenant Colonel J. U. Green's Twelfth Tennessee and Colonel F. M. Stewart's Fifteenth Tennessee cavalry, was to support Bill Forrest's move and also to establish detachments at the steamboat landing and at the corners of Main and Beale and Shelby and Beale Streets.

To another brother of the General, Lieutenant Colonel Jesse Forrest, was entrusted the task of capturing General Washburn, who occupied the Williams residence on Union Street.

The troop encampments in the southern outskirts of the city were to be attacked by Colonel Neely with a command made up of detachments from Lieutenant Colonel "Red Rob" McCulloch's Second Missouri, Lieutenant Colonel Raleigh White's Fourteenth Tennessee and Lieutenant Colonel Alex Chalmers' Eighteenth Mississippi regiments of cavalry. In reserve—although as events turned out in very active fighting, too—was to be Tyree Bell's command, made up of parts of Newsom's and Russell's Tennessee regiments, and the Second Tennessee commanded, because of the wounding of all its field officers at Harrisburg, by Captain W. A. DeBow. Lieutenant Sale and his section of artillery were left in the outskirts to cover the withdrawal.

At a quarter past three in the morning, with officers and men well instructed in their parts and strictly enjoined to silence, the column crossed the bridge at Cane Creek, four miles from town, moving quietly at a slow walk, with Captain Bill Forrest in the lead, riding alone through the blackness sixty yards ahead of the next man.

The first picket post was captured with the firing of but one rifle, but at a second post, a quarter of a mile beyond, there was a flurry of gunfire, followed in a moment by the rebel yell. The discipline of Forrest's men, never very rigid, gave way under the excitement of the early morning charge into the city that for so many of them was home. Orders or no orders, they broke into cheers and yells as they swept on toward the center of the city.

In the lead was Captain Bill Forrest and his band of scouts. At the

337

Gayoso, Captain Bill and the men nearest him did not take time to light and hitch but rode through the broad, high doors of the hotel and into the lobby, demanding of the startled and half-awake night clerk the whereabouts of the General after whom they had come. Hurlbut, however, had that night slept away from the hotel at the quarters of Colonel Eddy, and thus by social accident escaped capture, although not a few officers were taken in the quick roundup made of the Gayoso.[26]

General Washburn had slept at his own quarters that night, but as Jesse Forrest's men were riding at top speed toward him, the shouts and shots in the suburbs alerted the sentries, who woke the General just in time for him to make his escape in what the reporter of the *Review*, had he mentioned the incident at all, would doubtless have called his "nocturnal habiliments." In the more official language of the Assistant Inspector General of the Sixteenth Army Corps, "Major-General Washburn ... left his residence as early as possible, and made his way to Fort Pickering, without having given any command as to what should be done by our troops. He could much more easily have retired to headquarters of provost guard than have gone to the fort, as the fort is full one-half mile from the house, and but three squares to the provost-marshal's office."[27] In Washburn's own language he had "barely a moment to escape,"[28] no reference being made to the fact that in his haste it was necessary to leave behind his uniform and all his accouterments—a circumstance which brought from Hurlbut the unforgotten quip:

"They removed me from command because I couldn't keep Forrest out of West Tennessee, and now Washburn can't keep him out of his own bedroom!"

While the district commander raced away for the safety of Fort Pickering with its ninety-seven guns, which not even Forrest had the remotest idea of attacking, the Confederate parties attacked, unsuccessfully, the Irving Block building on Second Street, used as an armory and military prison. The provost guard in the inner part of the city rallied, under the command of Buckland, who also had made his escape from pursuing Confederates. The alarm gun for the calling out of the Enrolled Militia—2,000 civilian employees of the army and Memphis citizens of Union sympathies—began to sound, and the streets to fill with hurrying soldiers and the armed militia. At the wharf the *Red Rover* got up steam and went alongside the gunboat *Erie*, whose engines were down for repair, to tow her into the stream beyond the reach of marauding Confederates.[29]

Meanwhile in the southern outskirts of the city, where the General himself had remained, what serious fighting there was that day was going on. Neely's brigade was checked by a strong infantry line which

338

had time after the alarm was given to get into position. Forrest himself, seeing the check, rode to strike the enemy in flank. On the way he in turn was fired upon from a cavalry encampment on his own left. Quick as thought, he turned toward the fire—he was riding King Philip that day—and riding down the yard and garden fences intervening "like a scythe over a wheat field,"[30] led his escort and the men of Bell's brigade in a rush which rounded up nearly 100 horses and half as many men.

Neely, having overcome his temporary check, drove the Federal infantry into the stout brick building of the State Female College a few hundred yards away, where he was joined in the fight by Bell's brigade and by Lieutenant Sale, who put a few shell into the building. No serious assault was made or intended, however, for the time had come to draw off from the Union headquarters city.

Recall was sounded for Forrest's men in the city proper at about the time that the Federal troops began to get themselves well organized. The withdrawal began about 9:00 A.M. The Confederates, in small parties and even singly, made their way back through streets familiar to many of them to the rendezvous south of town. There was some fighting on the way out, though none of serious proportions, and some soldiers who lingered too long were cut off and picked up by the Union parties, who reported a total of twenty-five prisoners captured.

It was hard, indeed, to get all of Forrest's men out of Memphis. As the Confederates moved about the streets they were greeted with delirious manifestations of joyous welcome, especially by the ladies of the city who, despite the early morning hour and the state of their dress, waved from windows or even rushed out to the front gates to greet the Southern soldiers. One young soldier recalled years afterward the delighted thrill with which he hailed his mother and sister as he rode past his own front gate, and nearly escaped their recognition because in the faded, tattered and bespattered figure before them they could not at first see the neat young soldier in gray whom they had sent away to the wars more than two years before.[31]

The greatest difficulty encountered in the withdrawal was the Seventh Wisconsin battery, which had been charged and dispersed first by Bill Forrest as he went in and then by Logwood's party, but which had returned to its unharmed guns and was ready to turn them on the Confederates as they passed on their way out.

The first pursuit was organized hastily by the alert Colonel Matthew H. Starr of the Sixth Illinois Cavalry, the same who had rushed the first word of his danger to General Washburn. Overtaking the rear of the Confederate column south of town, Colonel Starr led a charge which, in the fashion of single combat of old, brought him face to face with General Forrest himself in a saber duel which ended in the desperate wounding of the aggressive Colonel and the repulse of his pursuing column.[32]

At 11:30 A.M., under orders of Colonel Winslow, all the cavalry about Memphis, some 650 in number, were gathered up and sent down the Hernando road after Forrest. Near Nonconnah Creek about 2:00 P.M. they met a flag of truce from General Forrest, advising that he had some 600 prisoners, most of them captured without shoes or clothing other than that in which they had slept, whom he was prepared to release on parole if their word not to fight until regularly exchanged would be honored by Washburn. If not, Forrest proposed that he would wait at the Nonconnah Creek crossing until clothing and shoes might be sent out to them.

Major Anderson, bearer of the flag of truce, returned with the message that General Washburn was not authorized to accept the parole of the prisoners but that he would send out clothing, which later came forward.[33]

While straightening out the clothing question, Forrest also sent in to General Washburn his own uniform captured that morning—a personal courtesy which was recognized soon after by General Washburn sending to Forrest under flag of truce a fine Confederate uniform made in Memphis by Forrest's own tailor to his well-known measurements—such being the occasional amenities of warfare as practiced between Americans in the sixties.[34]

The pursuing column, having been sent out without rations or forage, waited through the time of the truce and afterward, understanding that they soon would be supplied.[35] Through some mix-up, however, the supplies were not forthcoming until morning of the twenty-second, when the pursuing cavalry moved on to Hernando, which was reached about two in the afternoon, at least five hours after the last Confederate troops had left.[36]

This little effort at direct pursuit, however, was not the real reliance of General Washburn. At noon of the twenty-first he started messages to General Smith by telegraph to La Grange—Forrest had not cut the wires, part of his plan being that word should get through to Smith—with orders to the commander of the post there to forward them immediately to Smith with a mounted escort of 100 men. The burden of his messages—there were three—was that Forres⁺ had attacked Memphis in force after a two-day march from in front of Smith, that he was on his way back via either Panola or Holly Springs, and that Smith, if he would but "move rapidly and spare not horse flesh," could certainly catch him.[37]

Washburn was quite critical of Smith in his comments to Sherman and

Canby and in his official report, both for letting Forrest leave his front and march away to Memphis without Smith, who had 5,000 cavalry, learning of it, and for not following the directions to intercept him as he returned from Memphis.[38]

As to the first point, while Forrest was away Chalmers succeeded perfectly in his work of bluffing and blinding the enemy in his front. The news that Forrest was in Memphis came to Smith and his cavalry commanders, Grierson and Edward Hatch, as so complete a surprise that even when they heard it they "could not believe it."[39]

Chalmers, in an exceedingly ticklish position with an overwhelming force in front of him and a rising stream behind, had hung on and kept up the bluff with considerable misgiving, under orders from Forrest and, after he was away and out of touch with the telegraph wire, from Maury at Meridian.[40]

On August nineteenth, the first day that Forrest was away, Chalmers concealed his weakness by the bold front of an advance against the enemy at Hurricane Creek north of Oxford, which led Grierson to report that the Confederates were "found in force" but were driven away.[41] The twentieth was another day lost to General Smith as he brought his brigades forward, while on the twenty-first, the Sunday on which Forrest was in Memphis, the Union forces moved slowly on toward Oxford.

During the morning of Monday the twenty-second, the day on which Forrest was riding to and crossing the Tallahatchie at Panola, General Smith occupied Oxford, Chalmers having finally fallen back. But, strange to say, on the same afternoon General Smith's "big fine army" about-faced and started back toward Holly Springs, though not until after public buildings, including the courthouse, unoccupied houses, and at least one that was occupied, that of Jacob Thompson, former Secretary of the Interior, were burned.[42] "Where once stood a handsome little country town," the correspondent of the Chicago *Times* wrote, "now only remained the blackened skeletons of the houses, and smouldering ruins. . . ."[43]

The immediate cause of the prompt countermarch from Oxford—some commands did not so much as halt before turning back—is not stated, but in time it coincided with the arrival of the armed escort with the incredible news that Forrest was in Memphis itself. These messages were delivered in Oxford about eleven o'clock on the twenty-second.[44]

Washburn's directions to Smith to cut off Forrest as he attempted to recross the Tallahatchie at Panola formed the basis of his subsequent complaint that Forrest would have been caught had Smith followed instructions. The message, however, reached Smith at Oxford only half a day before Forrest was across the river. In fact, Forrest was sending in-

341

structions to Chalmers at the same time that if the Union forces did fall back, as he figured they would when they got the news from Memphis, he should "pursue them hard."[45]

In his report and messages Washburn treated the "whole affair" as an "utter failure" on Forrest's part, while other Federal officers reported that he had accomplished nothing "of any considerable account" and had "failed entirely in the object of his expedition."[46] Accepting these reports at face value, Sherman promptly sent word to Forrest through Washburn that he "admired his dash but not his judgment" in "running his head against Memphis."[47]

Forrest's own brief report, sent from Hernando on the night of the raid, said no more than that "we killed and captured 400 . . . with about 300 horses and mules. Washburn and staff escaped by darkness of morning, leaving his clothes behind. My loss, 20 killed and wounded," the latter being an understatement of the actual Confederate loss of about 35.[48]

The major capture which Forrest had sought, that of a brace of major generals, did not come off, much to his chagrin. But the expedition did not fail in its principal object—its effect upon the imaginations and apprehensions of the Federal command.

The scare which Forrest's raid started was not over even when he headed south. On Tuesday, August twenty-third, when Forrest and his troops were two full days' march away, a report ran through the city that he was coming into Memphis again. General Washburn requested the naval commander to send a gunboat below Fort Pickering and shell the southern approaches of the town, which was done without discovering any rebels.[49] Alarm bells rang in the city and the regiments of the enrolled militia and citizens "eager for the fray"—among them the editor of the *Review*—stood to arms all day, "while hundreds of negroes presented themselves and were armed." Special Order No. 204, calling for the return to the arsenals of these same arms, under threat of severe punishment, was published in the *Review* of the twenty-fifth and for several days thereafter.

As late as September third a recruiting advertisement for the Eleventh Tennessee Infantry (Union) was headed:

> "TENNESSEE INVADED!
> MEMPHIS THREATENED!
> FORREST COMING!"

The Nashville *Union*, publishing a dispatch from Memphis, put Forrest's force at 3,000, but announced that General Washburn "expects to capture a large portion of the attacking party."

342

General Washburn did so expect and wrote as much to his influential brother Elihu B. Washburne, chairman of the Committee on Appropriations of the House of Representatives, friend of Lincoln, and "discoverer" of Grant:[50]

"We had a big thing here on Sunday morning, and ran a very narrow escape, indeed it was almost a miracle that I was not either killed or captured. One main drive of the Expedition was to catch me. Forrest fooled A. J. Smith very badly, leaving his immediate front at Oxford and making a dash at Memphis without Smith knowing it, tho he had 4500 Cavalry with him. Had not Smith disregarded my orders he would have caught Forrest on his retreat. The whole Expedition was barren of fruits. They were in so great a hurry to get away that they carried off hardly anything. I lost two fine horses, which is about the biggest loss of anybody. . . ."

On the afternoon of August twenty-fifth the last of the Federal forces recrossed the Tallahatchie above Abbeville in such haste as to leave the railroad bridge intact. Indeed the whole retreat was conducted in such haste and with Chalmers' forces pressing so closely that the Federals left behind and lost ninety-seven miles of telegraph wire from Abbeville back to White's Station, the line having been "operated until the last moment, and Forrest's forces advancing as fast as General Washburn's fell back."[51]

There was no doubt in the minds of the Southern people as to the effect of Forrest's raid on Memphis. "You have again saved Mississippi. Come and help Mobile," General Maury wired Forrest on August twenty-fourth.[52] "Our people think that old Forrest is the greatest man of the age," a young Mississippian, who was at home recovering from wounds received in the fighting in Virginia, wrote to one of his comrades. "He is a trump and heavy one at that."[53]

But perhaps the most sincere tribute to the effectiveness of his operations came from the other side, when the grand jury of the Circuit Court of the United States for the District of West Tennessee, meeting in Memphis for the September 1864 term, returned an indictment against Nathan B. Forrest for treason. Reciting the existence of "an open and public rebellion, insurrection and war with force and arms . . . against the government and laws of the United States of America by divers persons . . . styling themselves 'the Confederates States of America,'" one of the persons being Nathan B. Forrest, "late of said District aforesaid," the grand jurors declared that he, on the twenty-first day of August 1864, "and on divers other days and times as well before as after that day . . . not weighing the duty of his said allegiance but wickedly

343

devising and intending the peace and tranquillity of the said the United States of America to disturb, and to stir, move, excite, aid and assist in said Rebellion, insurrection and war . . . with force and arms unlawfully, falsely, maliciously and traitorously did raise and levy war . . . with a great multitude of persons whose names to the grand jurors aforesaid are unknown . . . armed and arrayed in a warlike manner . . . with guns, swords, pistols and other warlike weapons as well offensive as defensive . . . did . . . in a hostile and warlike manner array and dispose themselves against the said the United States of America . . . most wickedly and maliciously and traitorously did ordain, prepare and levy war against the said the United States of America, contrary to the duty of the allegiance and fidelity of the said Nathan B. Forrest . . ." and so on and on.[54]

To all of which the Marshal of the United States Court, in whose hands there was placed the capias for the arrest of "the said Nathan B. Forrest," made return with unintentional humor—"Defendant not to be found in my district."[55]

CHAPTER XXII

TO TENNESSEE—TOO LATE

August 25, 1864-October 10, 1864

WHATEVER plans Forrest may have had for the rest and recruitment of his men, his horses and himself after the tremendous exertions of their dash into Memphis lasted no longer than August thirtieth. On that day Major General Dabney Maury, temporarily in command of the department, sent another and more urgent message: "Enemy reported moving troops . . . probably to Mobile. You are my only hope of succor."[1]

And so one week after he had settled down at Grenada Forrest was once more on the move, this time south to the relief of Mobile. Even the week at Grenada had been far from one of rest, what with getting the several brigades posted where they might best find forage and subsistence, and at the same time keep a watchful eye on the enemy; getting the question of the dividing line between his territory and that assigned to Brigadier General Wirt Adams settled; making arrangements for the issue of 1,000 new short Enfield rifles which were expected, and for the disposition of the inferior arms and surplus ammunition he was turning in; and the whole round of discipline, drill, scouting, shoeing horses and the never-ending detail of care and administration.[2]

And there was, too, the continuing question of organization. On August thirtieth, the day on which Maury called for succor at Mobile, Forrest issued and forwarded to Richmond his General Orders No. 73, announcing as "permanent" a new organization of his command and in some cases new assignments of commanders.[3]

The new organization consisted of two divisions, those of Chalmers and Buford, of two brigades each. Chalmers had the brigade commanded by Colonel "Black Bob" McCulloch, consisting of Missouri, Texas and Mississippi regiments, and another brigade of Tennessee troops, to which Colonel Edmund W. Rucker was assigned as permanent commander. Buford had the Kentucky brigade, to the command of which Brigadier General Hylan B. Lyon was assigned, and the Tennessee brigade of Colonel Tyree Bell.

The reorganization had the merit of bringing together troops of the same state in accordance with Confederate policy. The permanent appointment of Rucker to command one of Chalmers' brigades, however,

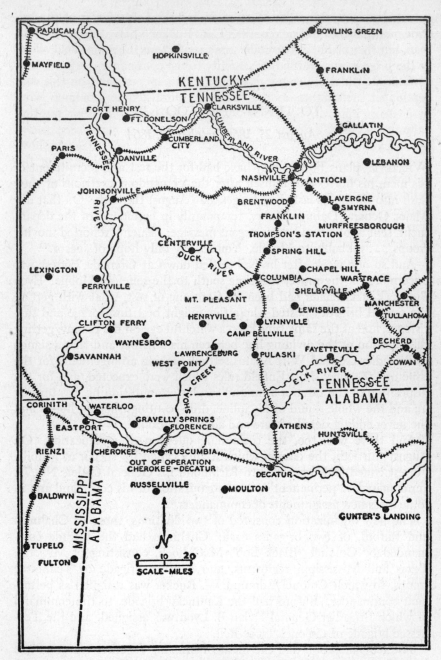

THE TENNESSEE CAMPAIGNS—1864

346

"created considerable dissatisfaction among the field officers of the brigade, not that they did not consider Gen. Rucker a brave and competent man, but they claimed that under army regulations the senior field officer of the brigade was entitled by seniority to the command. . . ."[4]

So firmly did most of the regimental commanders stand on this conception of their rights, indeed, that they protested to Chalmers who, in a sharp note on September twelfth, declared that their position "afforded scarcely a decent pretext for hesitating to obey orders issued by or coming through Colonel Rucker."[5] Still refusing to obey, however, five regimental commanders—Colonels W. L. Duckworth of the Seventh Tennessee, J. J. Neely of the Fourteenth, F. M. Stewart of the Fifteenth and J. U. Green of the Twelfth Tennessee regiments, and Major Philip T. Allin of McDonald's battalion, now bearing the designation of Twenty-sixth Tennessee—were suspended from their commands, not to return during the war to active command under Forrest.[6]

As soon as he received Maury's call for help Forrest started moving. Chalmers was called back from his advanced position about Water Valley to Grenada, whence he was to move across to the Mobile and Ohio Railroad. From there he was to send 2,000 of his best men and horses ahead by rail, and to march with the rest for Meridian.[7] The troops sent ahead to Mobile—McCulloch's brigade less the Fifth Mississippi—as things turned out, went on to west Florida, where although "much dissatisfied," and despite Forrest's efforts to get them back, they were kept for half a year doing picket duty around the Union base at Pensacola.[8]

On September 2, 1864, the day on which Chalmers' movement south was ordered, Atlanta fell to Sherman's long siege. And then at last, after the real opportunity had passed, the Confederate military authorities decided to do that which Robert E. Lee had recommended to President Davis as far back as July twelfth—"to concentrate all the Cav^y in Miss^{pi} & Tenn: on Sherman's communications."[9]

Just before Atlanta fell, accordingly, Wheeler's cavalry had been detached from the Army of Tennessee and sent off on a raid swinging wide to the eastward, which, between September first and eighth, was to carry him north into East Tennessee, west across the Cumberland Mountains into Middle Tennessee and on to the Nashville-Chattanooga Railroad which was Sherman's main supply artery—but which in the end was to result in less damage to Sherman's communications than to Wheeler's own command.

On September fifth, three days after the fall of Atlanta—though there is no certainty that Forrest had heard of the catastrophe by that time Forrest telegraphed direct to President Jefferson Davis:

"If permitted to do so with 4,000 picked men and six pieces of artillery of my present command, I believe I can proceed to Middle and West Tennessee, destroy enemy's communications or cripple it, and add 2,000 men to my command."[10]

By that time Maury had learned that the fears for the safety of Mobile were exaggerated—actually Mobile was to be the last of major Southern cities captured—and two days earlier had telegraphed the President, "Shall send Forrest to Tennessee. I meet him at Meridian tomorrow."[11]

These dispatches to the President were sent from Meridian, Mississippi, but from Maury's memoirs it would seem—although no date is given—that at some time between August thirtieth and September third Forrest had been at Mobile also. "My wife wished to entertain him," Maury wrote, "and gave him a dinner, inviting some lady friends who were desirous of meeting this great hero. His natural deference to the sex gave them all much pleasure. He was always very courteous to women, and in their presence was very bright and entertaining. He had for women that manly courtesy and respect that marks the truly brave man. Under all circumstances he was their defender and protector from every sort of wrong. His wife was a gentle lady, to whom he was careful in his deference."[12]

This moment of social relaxation at Mobile must have been of the briefest, however, for on September fifth Forrest met Lieutenant General Richard Taylor, the new commander of the department of Alabama, Mississippi and east Louisiana, at Meridian, where Taylor had just arrived from the Trans-Mississippi.

When Taylor received a telegram from his brother-in-law, the Confederate President, quoting the substance of what Forrest had wired Mr. Davis and suggesting that it might be well to employ him in such an operation on the enemy's lines of communication and supply, Taylor promptly replied that "five minutes after my arrival at Meridian, I issued the orders contemplated in your dispatch; the movement is now in process of execution."[13] To General Bragg, the President's military adviser, he telegraphed the same information, with more of the reasoning back of the step he had taken:

"Regarding the campaign in Georgia of paramount importance, I have ordered . . . the operation of Gen. Forrest's entire cavalry force on the line of Sherman's communications. This will be productive of more benefit than the detachment of a portion of it for the defense of Mobile. The former is of general, the latter of local, interest. . . ."[14]

The closing sentence of the dispatch indicates the exceptional breadth of Taylor's conceptions as a commander able to see beyond local defense to the general strategy of the war. Like Forrest, Taylor had come into the Confederate army from civil life but from a very different background and experience. Son of General Zachary Taylor, President of the United States, and brother of the first wife of Jefferson Davis, he was a man of education and affairs, both in the United States and Europe, who had entered the army as colonel of a Louisiana regiment, had served with distinction in both the Army of Northern Virginia and with the armies across the Mississippi and now, with the rank of Lieutenant General, had been put in charge of the difficult department between the great river and the state of Georgia. There were few men in the war on either side who saw men and things with the breadth and clarity which Taylor demonstrated both in his contemporary dispatches and his subsequent memoirs, *Destruction and Reconstruction*. His own story of his first meeting with Forrest, and the giving of the orders to go to Tennessee, constitutes, therefore, one of the best of all pictures of the great cavalryman. He wrote:

". . . A train from the north, bringing Forrest in advance of his troops, reached Meridian, and was stopped; and the General, whom I had never seen, came to report. He was a tall, stalwart man, with grayish hair, mild countenance, and slow and homely of speech. In a few words he was informed that I considered Mobile safe for the present, and that all of our energies must be directed to the relief of Hood's army, then west of Atlanta. The only way to accomplish this was to worry Sherman's communications north of the Tennessee River, and he must move his cavalry in that direction at the earliest moment.

"To my surprise, Forrest suggested many difficulties and asked numerous questions: how he was to get over the Tennessee; how he was to get back if pressed by the enemy; how he was to be supplied; what should be his line of retreat in certain contingencies; what he was to do with prisoners if any were taken, etc. I began to think he had no stomach for the work; but at last, having isolated the chances of success from causes of failure with the care of a chemist experimenting in his laboratory, he rose and asked for Fleming, the superintendent of the railway, who was on the train by which he had come. Fleming appeared—a little man on crutches (he had recently broken a leg), but with the energy of a giant—and at once stated what he could do in the way of moving supplies on his line, which had been repaired up to the Tennessee boundary. Forrest's whole manner now changed. In a dozen sharp sentences he told his wants, said he would leave a staff officer to bring up his supplies, asked for an engine to take him back north twenty miles to meet his troops, informed me that he would march with the dawn, and hoped to give an account of himself in Tennessee."[15]

Taylor's memoirs were written more than a dozen years after the event, and the phrase "march with the dawn" may have been due to faulty memory, or perhaps was intended only to convey an impression of promptness and dispatch. Actually Forrest displayed both those in a degree unusual even for him—for was he not going, at last, to have an opportunity to do the thing that he had been preaching through all that disastrous summer? But an expedition of the sort ahead of him was not one on which Forrest, at any rate, would "march with the dawn," or at any other time until he had had a chance to make every last preparation for success which was within his power.

Before Forrest could get started, indeed, there came to Taylor from General Hood on September eleventh an impatient message to "hasten Forrest and get him to operating upon Sherman's communications. It is all-important."[16] By that time the ill-starred effort under Wheeler to cut Sherman's railroad from the east had failed of any real effect, with the dispersal and loss of much of Wheeler's command, and with the trains running through again between Nashville and Atlanta on September tenth, almost immediately afterward.[17] "Cavalry usually do so little damage to a road," Sherman wrote, with some scorn, "that it can be repaired faster than they damage it."[18] As Hood ruefully commented in a message urging upon Wheeler still another effort to "move against the road . . . and keep it continually broken," Sherman's men did indeed "repair very rapidly,"[19] but they were soon to experience another sort of cavalry destruction which would wreck a road so that it would stay wrecked.

Ten days of close planning and intense preparation followed the order for Forrest to go to Middle Tennessee. For all his dash in action Forrest left few things to improvisation in emergency. His method was to think out in advance every facet and angle of every conceivable situation—thinking it all out in fierce concentration, furiously impatient at interruption. Usually, as one of his soldiers afterward recalled, while planning he sat immobile, chin sunk on his chest, or walked head down with his hands clasped behind him beneath the tails of his coat. During the period of his planning for the move to Middle Tennessee he was observed walking round and round the little railroad station at West Point, Mississippi, lost in deep study. An importunate applicant for consideration of some sort continued to interrupt him on his rounds, demanding that the General listen to his grievance. Finally, hardly looking up as he walked, Forrest let fly with his fist, knocked the man out and kept right on his rounds, calmly and unconsciously stepping over the prostrate body as he came round again.[20]

To command in Mississippi while he was gone, Forrest left Chalmers with only Mabry's brigade, the one regiment which McCulloch had left behind, and a motley assortment of state reserves,[21] or short-term militia for strictly defensive purposes within the state, whom the soldiers in the regular Confederate service derisively dubbed "tax in kind" soldiers.[22]

To go with himself Forrest took both brigades of Buford's division and Rucker's brigade of Chalmers', temporarily commanded by Colonel D. C. Kelley, in all 3,543 effectives, according to the report of Forrest's adjutant, Major Strange, who had just returned to duty after his Harris-burg wound.[23]

On September sixteenth the command moved from the vicinity of Verona, Mississippi, carrying five days' cooked rations, forty rounds of ammunition, one blanket and one change of clothing per man. The mounted men marched but the guns and caissons, the extra ammunition, the subsistence and quartermaster stores, and 450 men without horses moved by rail up the Mobile and Ohio road to Corinth and thence east-ward on the long disused Memphis and Charleston line to Cherokee Station sixteen miles west of Tuscumbia, Alabama.

The rail movement, something of a novelty for men of Forrest's com-mand, was made in five freight trains loaded inside and out. Stops were frequent, where bridges and trestles had to be repaired or cuts to be cleared of their accumulation of earth, logs and rubbish, or while the soldiers cut wood by the wayside for the locomotives, or brought water in buckets from near-by streams for their thirsty boilers. Despite all diffi-culties and delays, however, the whole command was at Cherokee by the evening of September nineteenth.[24]

The next day, while the command was being readied for the work ahead by cooking rations, shoeing horses and the like, Forrest went on to Tuscumbia to meet Major General Joe Wheeler, who was there with as much of his command as he had brought out of Middle Tennessee after the unsuccessful raid early in the month. Wheeler was disheartened, Forrest reported after his talk with him, and his men were "demoralized." Wheeler generously ordered to join Forrest's expedition the Fourth Tennessee Cavalry, Starnes's old regiment now under Lieutenant Colonel McLemore, and Biffle's Ninth Tennessee[25]—what he had of Forrest's famous Old Brigade. They were, however, but sixty men. "When I left the brigade with him last November," Forrest wrote Taylor, "it then numbered over 2,300 for duty. I hope to be instrumental in gathering them up."[26]

Taylor, from department headquarters just moved to Selma, replied that he was "pained to hear" this report of the condition of Wheeler's command but, evidently recalling that Wheeler ranked Forrest as a major general, and not knowing that Hood was recalling Wheeler to the Army of Tennessee, Taylor hastened to tell Forrest that he relied greatly upon his "skill and energy in accomplishing the object of the present movement, and to this end desire and authorize you to be guided in your operations by your own good judgment, reporting directly to me and acting independently of any officer, regardless of rank, with whom you may come in contact."[27]

Forrest's crossing of the Tennessee began with the march from Cherokee to the river at daylight of September twenty-first. "An officer who knew Forrest well," Viscount Wolseley wrote in 1892, told him of breakfasting with the General that morning on corn meal and treacle, on the bank of the river, as the column passed—blankets, shoes, equipment, legibly stamped with "U.S.," artillery with eight horses to the piece, wagons with six mules each, four-horse ambulances and "every gun, rifle, wagon and ambulance, and all the clothing, equipment, ammunition and other supplies . . . he had taken from the Northern armies opposed to him."[28] The artillery, ordnance and wagon trains were sent on up the river with Major Anderson in charge to be ferried across at Newport, where General Roddey's men had prepared flatboats for that purpose, while the mounted men crossed the ford at the head of Colbert's Shoals, picking their way in column of twos along a narrow, tortuous, jagged and rocky underwater path, some two miles from bank to bank as it wound and twisted its way across the broad Tennessee.[29]

On the night of the twenty-first the command camped north of the Tennessee five miles west of Florence, Alabama, having accomplished a march that day of twenty-five miles besides crossing the river. "In the early forenoon of a perfect day," September twenty-second, Forrest, mounted on King Philip and riding at the head of his escort, came into Florence from the west and marched out to the east through streets "lined with men, women and children, whose shouts were ably supplemented by the yells of the visiting soldiers," as one of them described the scene. "To have stood on Mitchell's corner that day, as I did, would mark an event in a life otherwise filled with adventures," he added.[30]

On the same day at Shoal Creek six miles east of Florence, Forrest picked up the troops of Brigadier General P. D. Roddey, who had crossed the river farther upstream. Roddey himself was not with his troops, on account of illness, and Colonel William A. Johnson, the same who had fought with Forrest at Brice's Cross Roads, commanded them. Even with this accession Forrest had only about 4,500 men, of whom 400 were without horses, trudging along hopefully waiting for animals to be captured from the enemy.

The night of the twenty-second was passed by the main body of the

THE PRESIDENT OF THE UNITED STATES,

To the Marshal of the District of West Tennessee--Greeting:

You are Hereby Commanded to take the body of *Nathan B. Forrest* if to be found in your District, and him safely keep, so that you have him before the Judge of the Circuit Court of the United States, at a term of said Court, to be held for the District aforesaid, at the Court House in the City of Memphis, on the first Monday in *March* next, then and there to answer the *United States* ~~State of Tennessee~~ on a Bill of Presentment against him, for *Treason* Herein fail not, and have you then and there this writ.

Witness The Hon. ~~Roger B. Taney~~, *Salmon P. Chase* Chief Justice of the Supreme Court of the United States, and the seal of said Circuit Court, this *First* Monday in *September* 1865 and *90th* year of American Independence.

A. S. Mitchell Clerk.

Isaac Morrison D. Clerk.

A WARRANT FOR FORREST'S ARREST

The United States Marshal, being directed "to take the body of Nathan B. Forrest" for treason, made laconic return on the reverse of the capias, "Deft. not to be found in my District."

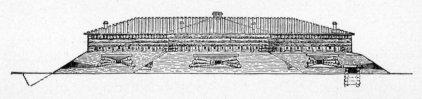

RAILROAD FORTIFICATIONS

Types of defense erected at bridges, trestles and other critical points along the railroads from Johnsonville on the Tennessee River, through Nashville and Chattanooga, to Atlanta—Sherman's line of communication and supply. First and last, Forrest captured and destroyed more than a score of them.

command at Masonville on the road from Florence to Athens, Alabama. About ten o'clock that night, however, Lieutenant Colonels Jesse Forrest and Raleigh White of the Twentieth and the Fourteenth Tennessee Cavalry regiments were sent on ahead in a night march to break the railroad and telegraph line between Athens and Decatur, twelve miles south, where the main Union garrison along the Tennessee River was stationed.[31]

Forrest's irruption into the territory north of the Tennessee was a complete surprise to Brigadier General Robert S. Granger, commanding the Union District of Northern Alabama. "Some time previously," he reported, he had intimated to General Sherman his apprehension that Forrest might invade Middle Tennessee but "was assured by him that I had nothing to fear from General Forrest." And here on the afternoon of the twenty-third of September Forrest "made his appearance unannounced," five miles from Decatur.[32]

Both Granger at Decatur and Colonel Wallace Campbell, commanding at Athens, sent out columns to drive the troublesome detachment under Jesse Forrest away from the railroad. Both Union columns reported success in their missions and between them they did clear the tracks, but during the early evening the Confederate circle—the main body was coming up at sunset—closed around Athens and the fort south of the town.

This fort, a considerable work a quarter of a mile in circumference, with a ditch fifteen feet wide and an elevation of seventeen feet from the bottom of the ditch to the top of the parapet, encircled by both a palisade and an abatis of felled trees, with an ample water supply inside the walls and with rations and ammunition enough to stand a siege of ten days, was looked upon as the strongest post between Nashville and Decatur.[33]

In the fighting which attended the encircling of the position during the early part of the night of the twenty-third the government storehouses in the town itself, more than half a mile to the north, were fired. Still more unfortunately for Colonel Campbell, commanding the defense, he captured in the little brush two of Forrest's men who solemnly assured their captor that he was surrounded by Forrest with 10,000 to 12,000 men. To add further to the disquietude of Campbell's mind, Colonel Prosser of the Second Tennessee (Union) Cavalry, who had brought out the relieving column from Decatur that afternoon, refused to remain, saying he did not believe the fort could be held with their combined forces.[34] Colonel Campbell, though he had never heard of the not-yet-invented term, was about to become the victim of "psychological warfare."

During the night, in a downpour of rain, Forrest completed his encirclement of the place with Barteau's Second Tennessee and the escort company cutting the railroad to the north,[35] Bell's brigade on the east, Kelley on the southeast, the regiments under Jesse Forrest and White to the south and Buford, with Lyon's brigade, closing the circle to the west, with Johnson in reserve. And so Forrest and his men rested, as much as the pelting rain would let them rest in the open, on that night of September twenty-third, with the place completely invested and with the eight guns of Morton's and Hudson's batteries moving into position to bear upon the fort.[36]

By seven in the morning of the twenty-fourth, everything being in readiness, Forrest started his attack on the fort. Morton's eight guns opened fire "from three different sides, casting almost every shell inside the works," according to the Union report. With his guns having the range and his troops in assaulting position Forrest sent in his accustomed demand for "immediate and unconditional surrender." Campbell, having first refused the demand, yielded to a second demand so far as to consent to a personal interview with Forrest—and so doing, was lost.[37]

Forrest opened the interview with earnest expressions of a desire to avoid unnecessary bloodshed, although the reports he had received from Kelley that another relieving column was approaching from Decatur doubtless had no little to do with his haste to get the Athens fight over and done with as soon as might be. So confident was he of his ability to take the fort, Forrest said, that he would be willing to have the commander of the defense inspect the Confederate forces and see for himself that there were not less than 8,000 men, with ample artillery. Colonel Campbell consented to take a look at the forces surrounding him and, as so many other commanders opposed to Forrest had done, he "saw double" at least. Having reviewed Forrest's force, and seen most of it two and three times as it was mounted, dismounted, remounted and moved about to simulate bodies of infantry and cavalry,[38] Colonel Campbell returned to the fort, saying, " 'The jig is up; pull down the flag'—thus surrendering the best fortification on the line of the Nashville and Decatur Railroad," as his disgusted officers put it in a bitter statement sent back from their place of captivity at Enterprise, Mississippi.[39] Forrest's first captures at the fort consisted of 450 colored infantry and 125 of the Third Tennessee (Union) Cavalry.[40]

The real fight of the twenty-fourth, however, was not at the fort but along the railroad from Decatur, where Kelley with Rucker's brigade fended off the advance of a relief column of some 700 Michigan and Ohio troops who, as Forrest testified in his report, fought their way forward "with great gallantry and desperation." The commander of the

354

relief column, Lieutenant Colonel Jonas Elliott, was mortally wounded, while Forrest's brother Jesse on the other side of the fight was so seriously wounded that not until almost the end of the war was he able to resume field duty. Finally, after three hours of fighting and heavy loss, the relief column was overpowered and brought to surrender when within sight of the walls of the fort, "just in time to see the garrison march out and stack arms."[41]

Forrest cleaned up the situation around Athens by the capture of two near-by blockhouses, No. 5 with a garrison of 40 men who surrendered on demand, and No. 6 with a garrison of like size commanded by Captain A. Poe, who at first boldly refused to surrender but promptly changed his mind when Morton began to put shell through the crevices between the logs forming the walls of his work. "Your shell, sir, bore through my blockhouse like an auger!" he cried as he rushed out with a white flag.[42]

The blockhouses and combustible parts of the fort were burned, along with two locomotives and trains of cars captured at Athens. Other captures included 2 twelve-pound howitzers, 38 wagons with much more than enough of supplies and stores to load them, and 300 horses. The first day's bag of 1,300 prisoners and the captured property, except the horses turned over to Forrest's dismounted men, were started for Cherokee that afternoon, under a guard commanded by Colonel Nixon.[43]

In the early afternoon of September twenty-fourth Forrest started north from Athens toward the next considerable town, Pulaski, Tennessee. Four miles north of Athens another blockhouse guarding a railroad trestle was surrounded and captured, the whole place being "in blazing ruins twenty minutes after we reached there,"[44] Forrest reported. In the capture of this and other blockhouses—he was to take and destroy eleven altogether on this expedition—Forrest made good use of the whilom defiant captain of No. 6, "ostentatiously parading the captured commander . . . and on this convincing proof that blockhouses could be taken, quite a number of them surrendered without a fight," as Forrest afterward told Lieutenant Colonel William E. Merrill, chief engineer of the Union Army of the Cumberland and designer of many of the works defending Sherman's rail line.[45]

Two miles farther on, at Sulphur Branch, stood the highest and longest trestle on that part of the railroad, 72 feet high by 300 feet long,[46] defended by two double-cased blockhouses, with walls forty inches thick, and an earthen fort, the whole garrisoned by 400 colored infantry, 200 Indiana cavalry and 400 Tennessee (Union) cavalry. The place was promptly invested early in the morning of the twenty-fifth, with Morton's eight guns so emplaced as to be able to throw shell into the works from all four sides while the assaulting troops moved into position. Surrender having been sternly, even haughtily, refused, the bombardment began. Colonel William H. Lathrop, the commanding officer, was killed early and Colonel J. B. Minnis of the Tennessee Unionist regiment was struck senseless by a bit of shell. After a two-hour bombardment, in which 800 rounds were fired, with the blockhouses "perforated with shell, and the dead lying thick along the works of the fort," as Forrest described the scene, the Confederate fire was suspended and another chance to surrender was offered the garrison, this time to be promptly accepted.

The captures at Sulphur Trestle other than 300 horses to finish mounting Forrest's men—1,000 prisoners, two guns, and arms, ammunition, stores and wagons in which to haul them away—were started back across the Tennessee in charge of Colonel Logwood that afternoon, as the blockhouses, the buildings in the fort and the great trestle they were built to protect went up in flames.[47] The wounded were cared for and the dead buried, a useless sacrifice, Forrest's men felt, to a stubborn stand which had in it none of the elements of real defense, decision or leadership.

Forrest, indeed, was beginning to face something of a problem in disposing of his captures. He wrote General Taylor asking that troops be sent up from Mississippi to the railhead at Cherokee to receive and guard his prisoners, but Taylor, for lack of troops, was unable to comply.[48]

Having used up so much of his artillery ammunition in the bombardment and reduction of the works at the Sulphur Trestle, Forrest also sent back from there both the four guns which he had captured and four of his own, retaining only the Morton battery.[49]

From Sulphur Branch, Forrest moved on north toward Pulaski. On the twenty-sixth at Elk River, a considerable stream, the blockhouses were found to be evacuated and the bridge undefended, for reasons which appear in the report of Colonel George Spalding, of the Twelfth Tennessee (Union) Cavalry. Colonel Spalding, having reached Elk River with about 800 Indiana and Tennessee cavalry on the night of the twenty-fifth, became convinced by 3:00 A.M. of the twenty-sixth that if he did not withdraw, Forrest would have him "surrounded by daylight." Accordingly, he sent for the officers commanding the colored infantry who composed the garrison of the two bridge blockhouses, explained to them the situation, exhibited to them dispatches that reinforcements were on the way from Pulaski and even from Nashville, and received their promise "to hold the blockhouses until they were knocked to pieces."

"Accordingly," Colonel Spalding reported, "I moved off gently in the direction of Pulaski until daybreak, when I halted to learn the location of the country. To my great surprise I found that the negro soldiers and their officers that I had left to hold the bridge had abandoned the stockade and been in advance of my cavalry all the morning, having evacuated the stockades without firing a shot."[50]

Continuing his "gentle" movement toward Pulaski, Colonel Spalding found the officer in command of the blockhouses guarding the 200-foot-long truss bridge of the railroad over Richland Creek packing up and getting ready to go to Pulaski also. To this prudent officer Colonel Spalding "immediately sent directions ... to make a stubborn resistance, and also stated that I would support him and shoot every officer and soldier that I found deserting his post." Regardless of mingled exhortation, encouragement and intimidation, the blockhouse and its garrison of fifty were promptly surrendered, Colonel Spalding and the cavalry having gone toward Elkton to meet Buford, advancing from that direction. They returned, however, in time to offer resistance to the Confederate crossing of Richland Creek in a fight which can scarcely be recognized in the Union and Confederate accounts as the same affair.[51]

Before leaving the Richland Creek area Forrest issued to the entire command from the captured stores several days' rations, including "as much sugar and coffee as they needed," and fitted them up with "boots, shoes, hats, blankets, overcoats, oil-cloths and almost everything necessary for their comfort."[52] Early on the next morning, September twenty-seventh, the advance was resumed toward Pulaski, six miles away, against increasing resistance. The Pulaski garrison had been strengthened, both by the cavalry from below who had fallen back to that point, and by Major General Lovell H. Rousseau's troops—infantry, cavalry and artillery brought down by train from Nashville in response to the call of the post commander for aid "at once, and then it would be too late, as it was."[53]

With the reinforcements at hand the Pulaski garrison far outnumbered Forrest's attackers. The Federal cavalry nevertheless made a "retrograde movement" of some six miles during the morning, retiring within the fortified lines of the town by 1:00 P.M. Against these lines Forrest advanced from south and east, with a bold and noisy show but with no slightest notion of a serious attack.[54] Having, as the Union Major General George H. Thomas put it, "thoroughly destroyed" a section of the Nashville and Decatur railroad,[55] enough to put it out of commission for more than six weeks,[56] Forrest felt that it was time to be about the more important and more difficult business of doing likewise to the direct Nashville and Chattanooga railroad, two hard days' march to the eastward.

Night coming on, Forrest ordered campfires built up along his entire

357

line "for the purpose of deceiving the enemy," threw out pickets to prevent discovery of the deception and marched away in the darkness. That night camp was made eight miles east of Pulaski; the next night, the twenty-eighth, five miles northeast of Fayetteville. "It was pleasant to see school boys and girls climbing upon the fences to see the soldiers," one man of the column remembered. "It was more like peace than war."[57]

The march was made through steep and hilly country, away from the macadamized turnpikes which even in that day radiated spokewise from Nashville through Middle Tennessee, and on narrow roads muddy from recent rains and much cut up by the passage of the column. In these circumstances Forrest came across a captured caisson stuck in the mud, beyond the efforts of the crew to move it.

"Who has charge here?" he demanded.

"I have, sir," spoke up Captain Andrew McGregor.

"Then why in hell don't you do something?" Forrest began, following with profane and uncomplimentary expletives.

"I'll not be cursed out by anyone, even a superior officer," was the angry and spunky response, as McGregor seized a lighted torch and rammed it into the ammunition chest—an apparently suicidal act which sent Forrest away as fast as he could clap spurs to his horse.

"What infernal lunatic is that just out of the asylum down there?" he demanded of his staff. "He came near blowing himself and me up with a whole caisson full of powder."

Those who knew that the caisson was empty, having been unloaded in the effort to get it out of the mudhole, laughed uproariously at McGregor's joke on the General and the General joined heartily in the laughter but, as Morton observed, after that he never cursed McGregor.[58]

From his camp twenty-five miles from Sherman's principal rail line, on the night of the twenty-eighth, Forrest threw forward Captain Nathan Boone with twenty of the escort company and Captain J. J. Kelleher with thirty men of the Twelfth Kentucky, to strike the railroad above and below Tullahoma and tear up track and wires. The breaks accomplished by these small parties, one three miles north of Tullahoma and the other near Decherd, were the only damage which Forrest was to do to the Chattanooga road. They were promptly repaired within a day, and the road was again open on September thirtieth.[59]

From Pulaski, Forrest had written Taylor on the night of the twenty-seventh that the enemy was "concentrating heavily" against him. By the time he reached Mulberry on the morning of the twenty-ninth he had more idea of just how heavy the concentration was, with a "strong

358

force at Tullahoma, and at all other vulnerable points on the railroad," and with reinforcements to the number of not less than 15,000 being "hurried forward from Atlanta, Chattanooga and other points." Considering the reduction of his own forces by losses and detachments of men and the breakdown of horses, and the depleted state of his ammunition supply, especially for artillery, Forrest decided that further movement against the overwhelming numbers being concentrated on the Chattanooga railroad was "hazardous and unwise," and determined, therefore, to "go where there was prospect of accomplishing more good."[60]

As Forrest marched across country from Pulaski toward Tullahoma, Rousseau had been moving his troops by rail around through Nashville to reinforce the 3,150 men whom Major General R. H. Milroy had to guard the line between Murfreesborough and the Cumberland Mountain tunnel at Cowan. At the same time Major General J. B. Steedman was sending troops from Chattanooga, while two divisions of infantry, Wagner's (or Newton's) and J. D. Morgan's, had been started back from Georgia to meet Forrest. Sherman meanwhile had called forward from Kentucky all available troops there, while Grant, the commander-in-chief of the armies, had ordered "all recruits and new troops from Western States to Nashville" with dispatch. Burbridge, the Union commander in Kentucky, was recalled from an expedition against the Confederate saltworks in southwest Virginia to meet the threat of Forrest. From the west came Washburn, sending 3,000 cavalry under Edward Hatch overland from Memphis, and loading 1,300 infantry and a battery on steamboats to come up the river to Johnsonville on the lower Tennessee.

The "whole resources of Tennessee and Kentucky," in Sherman's phrase, plus the divisions sent back from the main army in Georgia, and all the reinforcements to be gathered in the Western states, were to be "turned against Forrest . . . until he is disposed of." To take direct charge of the job of disposing of him Sherman's great second-in-command, Major General George H. Thomas, was sent from Atlanta back to Tennessee.[61]

In explanation of such a stir and disturbance Sherman wrote to Halleck that Forrest's "cavalry will travel a hundred miles in less time than ours will ten. . . . I can whip the enemy's infantry but his cavalry is to be feared."[62]

Meanwhile, the commander of the cavalry responsible for the commotion did the unorthodox thing of dividing his command in the vicinity of the enemy. Buford, with part of his division and with Kelley's and Johnson's brigades and Morton's artillery, was sent south toward the

359

Tennessee River, with orders to capture Huntsville, Alabama, if possible and to damage the railroad from that place to Decatur, before crossing to the safety of the south bank of the river. Forrest himself, with parts of the brigades of Bell and Lyon, and with the Seventh Tennessee and the Old Regiment but with no artillery, turned west to draw off pursuit from Buford, and to see, as well, what further damage might be done to the railroad from Nashville to Decatur.[63]

Appearing before Huntsville on the afternoon of the last day of September, Buford sent in a demand for surrender, by the hand of Colonel Kelley who as a young minister had organized and led forth his first cavalry company from that town more than three years before. Brigadier General R. S. Granger, in command, politely refused to surrender the little city and invited Buford "to come and take it as soon as you get ready." Granger, indeed, would have welcomed the fight even though he did believe that Buford was 4,000 to 5,000 strong and that Forrest himself was near by—a belief encouraged by the fact that a subsequent communication threatening an attack "tomorrow morning from every rock, house, tree and shrub in the vicinity" was signed "N. B. Forrest, Major General."[64]

But Granger, as one of his officers wrote home, was "feeling very badly. He was surprised. The railroad under his charge is seriously injured and he has lost 3,000 to 4,000 of his command. These are hard blows for an officer to stand up under."[65] And so Granger and his men worked all night, making ready for the fight of the morrow, barricading the streets of the town and building cotton-bale traverses in the fort against enfilading fire. Buford, however, had no intention of accommodating Granger with a real fight, and when threats failed to accomplish their result, marched away westward on the morning of October first. Four miles away he tore up railroad track which the pursuing division of Brigadier General J. D. Morgan, coming up from Georgia on the cars, had to work all that night in the rain to repair.[66]

That afternoon Buford appeared before Athens which had a new garrison of 200 Indiana and Tennessee Union soldiers and a Tennessee Unionist battery. On the morning of October second, following a night spent in the open in drenching rain, after a short bombardment Buford demanded the surrender of the place, was refused and drew off westward on the road to Florence, where he crossed the Tennessee without molestation while Morgan's division of infantry struggled on in futile pursuit more than a day behind.[67]

Forrest himself, meanwhile, marched down the Duck River Valley once more, by "obscure, circuitous roads." The night of the twenty-ninth he camped at Petersburg, Tennessee, within eight miles, according to the reports of his scouts, of a strong Federal force moving from Pulaski to Tullahoma in pursuit of him. On the thirtieth, the day on which Buford was using his name before Huntsville, he marched through Lewisburg, crossed Duck River at Hardison's Ford—not far from his birthplace of Chapel Hill—and pushed on northward. Toward noon of October first he struck the railroad at the familiar village of Spring Hill.[68]

There he turned south, destroying track as he went, and gobbling up blockhouses and their garrisons. The cordwood stacked for the railroad engines was used to build fires on the rails, firmly spiked down at both ends so that heat expansion would do the work of bending and kinking the iron.[69] During the same afternoon three blockhouses were summoned to surrender and did so, and the bridges they guarded were burned. Late in the afternoon, however, Forrest's men struck a blockhouse whose commanding officer took literally the instructions posted in all of them headed, in big type, NO SURRENDER.[70] This officer, described by Forrest's men as "a Dutchman" who "swore profusely"—he was Lieutenant J. F. Long of the Seventh Pennsylvania Cavalry—refused to yield. Without artillery Forrest had no means of making good an assault without too great loss but, as dark came on, a party of "ten gallant men" who volunteered for the duty managed to fire the 150-foot truss bridge over which he stood guard. By the light of its burning timber Forrest's men marched on south, to camp that night near Columbia.[71]

On the next day, October second, Forrest threatened Columbia from the north and west while detachments burned small railroad trestles south of the town and other detachments gathered up fat beeves and supplies in the rich country roundabout. On the same day Lovell Rousseau was about ready to start from Nashville with a mobile force, with the expressed hope that he would "give Mr. Forrest very little time to assail any place."[72] Forrest, however, was no longer figuring on assaults. His business in Tennessee was not fighting, certainly no more than he had to do, but destroying railroads and disrupting the enemy's supply arrangements and troop dispositions. The time had come for him to pull out of the hornet's nest he had stirred up and, as one of his soldiers said of him, Forrest was "pretty good on a *git*."[73]

Forrest, with fewer than 2,000 men and no guns, was being followed from Nashville by Rousseau with 3,500 cavalry and a like number of infantry, the latter "mounted" on seats of plank laid across the beds of army wagons. To the southeast there was J. D. Morgan's infantry division, moving from Athens toward the crossings of the Tennessee. Directly across country, coming west from Wartrace, was Croxton's cavalry brigade. To the west, moving up the Tennessee River, was Washburn with 3,000 cavalry, ordered to strike inland and join in the pursuit. Two gunboats were up the lower river which, after the season of hard and general rains, was no longer fordable and was rapidly rising, while from above, Lieutenant Moreau Forrest, United States Navy, was sending gunboats of the upper river flotilla down toward Florence.[74]

Thomas was entirely justified in saying, "I do not think we shall ever have a better chance at Forrest than this," while Sherman had good reason for his feeling that "we will never have a better chance at him than now."[75] To the commanders of his several columns Thomas issued orders to get together and "press Forrest to the death."[76]

On the night of the second Forrest camped at Mt. Pleasant, twelve miles southwest of Columbia. His march of the third was short, less than a dozen miles, with camp for the night eleven miles north of Lawrenceburg, Tennessee. The next day, however, possibly as a result of having received information from the cloud of scouts by whom his movements were surrounded, he stretched away for the river, down the old Military Road which Andrew Jackson's men had cut out in the marches between Tennessee and Natchez and New Orleans in the War of 1812. The night of the fourth he camped in Alabama, eighteen miles north of Florence where, on the morning of October fifth, he reached the river, much swollen by rains.[77]

Buford, who had reached there in advance of his chief, was already busy with such means of ferriage as were at hand, putting the train and artillery across the stream, here a mile wide and, on those days, broken by high winds into short choppy waves which threatened to swamp the skiffs and flats, forcing the men who were not at the oars to keep bailing them out.[78]

Upon the approach of Morgan's column from the east Forrest sent Colonel Windes of the Fourth Alabama back to Shoal Creek to hold him off, while the boats were dropped downstream to the mouth of Cypress Creek, where the work of ferrying was resumed. All that day of the fifth, all that night and during the next day the arduous and hazardous work went on. On the afternoon of the sixth, with more than 1,000 men still on the north bank, the enemy approached, "pressing the rear, which was greatly endangered."

Forrest was equal to the emergency, however. All troops, save one regiment, were ordered "to mount their horses and swim them across a slough about seventy yards wide, to a large island which would afford them ample protection and from which they could ferry over at leisure"[79]—though leisure is hardly the word most would apply to the work on the south side of the island where, hidden from the enemy by

362

the woods, the work of ferrying across the broad and stormy channel with three small boats was kept up for two days more.

Forrest himself, then as always, took an active hand in the work. As the last boat was leaving he made a round of his picket posts, and found four soldiers who had been overlooked. "I thought I would catch some of you damned fools loafing back here in the cane as if nothing was going on," he said. "If you don't want to get left all winter on this island you had better come along with me; the last boat is going over right away."

"When we reached the boat," says one of the four, "we were all made to take our turn at the oars and poles, and do our share of the work in ferrying across the river. The general, evidently worried and tired out, was on the rampage and was showing considerable disregard of the third commandment. There happened to be standing in the bow of the boat a lieutenant who took no part whatever in the labor of propelling the craft, noticing which, Forrest said to him: 'Why don't you take hold of an oar or pole and help get this boat across?' The lieutenant responded that he was an officer, and did not think he was called on to do that kind of work as long as there were private soldiers sufficient to perform that duty. As the general was tugging away with a pole when the reply was made, he flew into a rage, and holding the pole in one hand, with the other he gave the unfortunate lieutenant a slap on the side of the face which sent him sprawling over the gunwale and into the river. He was rescued by catching hold of the pole held out to him, and was safely landed in the boat, when the irate general said to him: 'Now, damn you, get hold of the oars and go to work! If I knock you out of the boat again I'll let you drown.' Forrest's rough and ready discipline was effectual; the young officer made an excellent hand for the balance of the trip."[80] And the command knew that the "Old Man" was working, in the emergency, harder than any of them.

Detachments of the Second, Seventh and Sixteenth Tennessee Cavalry and the Fourth Alabama were left behind on the north bank to skirmish with the enemy, divert his attention and keep him busy while their comrades crossed the river. "The strategy was successful," Forrest reported, giving high praise to these officers and men who "made no effort to escape from their perilous position," but hung upon the enemy's flanks, retired to the hills when pushed, subsisted on captured supplies, and came across the Tennessee only after the enemy commenced to withdraw.[81]

"Forrest has escaped us," Morgan reported on October seventh— "much to General Thomas' chagrin . . . as our force . . . ought to have crowded that rebel into the river," another report ran. The report excited some incredulity, although when it was finally accepted that he was indeed across the river except for 400 or 500 scattered men who were expected to be gathered in—but were not—Sherman issued directions to Thomas to "give such orders as will dispose of Forrest and break his railroad from Tuscumbia back toward Corinth. . . ."[82]

Sherman had in mind the approach of the gunboats with Washburn's force coming up the Tennessee River and the 3,000 cavalry coming across country from Memphis. The infantry, 1,300 men and a four-gun rifled battery under command of Colonel George B. Hoge, were aboard the transports *City of Pekin, Aurora* and *Kenton*, convoyed by the gunboats *Key West* and *Undine*, the naval commander being Lieutenant E. M. King. Orders from Washburn were to "land at Eastport, move rapidly out on the line of railroad near Iuka, and break up the road and destroy bridges. . . . After doing this hold Eastport . . . approach Eastport with care so as not to be ambuscaded."

The expedition, with the *Key West* in the lead, did approach Eastport with care at 1:30 P.M. of October tenth, and discerned no enemy. The gunboats dropped anchor in midstream to cover the landing, the transports tied up to the bank and ran out their stage planks, the troops and artillery started to go ashore while the Confederates—Kelley, with Rucker's brigade and a section of Walton's battery—watched the busy scene. When more than two-thirds of the troops were ashore Kelley opened a fire so vigorous and so accurate that both the army and navy Federal commanders reported that it was delivered by superior numbers of men and by nine rifled guns instead of the two actually engaged.

What followed, Colonel Hoge described as a "scene of confusion" with Confederate shell plunging through the gunboats, and setting fire to two of the transports besides exploding a caisson on one, with men ashore trying to scramble back on board, and the boats trying to get away from the Confederate fire. The naval commander, according to the report of his army associate, declared that "we must get the transports away at once, he going with them," and that "in spite of all I could do, the boats backed out, parting their lines, leaving about two-thirds of the command on the shore." The naval commander, on the other hand, tells how the troops on the bank "broke and fled pell-mell down the river. The battery of four guns was abandoned. The transports cut their lines and drifted downstream," while the gunboats remained firing "rapidly and well" for thirty minutes. "The gunboats were ready to assist in any movement that the colonel commanding might have suggested for the recovery" of the battery, he added. Two of the transports, the *Aurora* and the *Kenton*, drifted downstream disabled, but the *City of Pekin* put in to the bank twice after it got out of range of the Confederate guns, to pick up the

Federal soldiers scrambling along through the briery underbrush of the riverbank. Most of the men were picked up in this way and carried back down the Tennessee—but the expedition against Forrest's railroad and the immediate attempt to "dispose of" him were over.[83]

During its two weeks north of the Tennessee, Forrest's command captured 2,360 officers and men—not including the 75 captured by Kelley at Eastport—besides killing and wounding an estimated 1,000. The Confederate loss was 47 killed and 293 wounded. Captures included 800 horses, seven guns—one of Hoge's at Eastport slid off a stage plank into the river and was not recovered—2,000 stand of small arms, 50 wagons and ambulances, and great quantities of saddles and other ordnance, medical and commissary supplies. The railroad between Nashville and Chattanooga was scarcely damaged but that between Nashville and Decatur was so broken as not to be fully restored to service until well into November—all in all, a very respectable result for a force of 4,500 men hemmed in and pressed by many times their own number.

Nevertheless, the expedition failed of any major result. It came too late. Atlanta had fallen and the heavy fighting in Georgia was over. Sherman, moreover, had had a chance at last to make his accumulation at Atlanta of "ample supply of provisions and ammunition . . . so that he was not materially affected by the state of the railroad."[84] And with crops ripe, Sherman's men, as he wrote Grant, could "subsist luxuriously on the bountiful fields and potato patches" of Georgia.[85] "Even now," he wrote, "our poor mules laugh at the fine corn-fields, and our soldiers riot on chestnuts, sweet potatoes, pigs, chickens, etc."[86] Sherman was coming to the conclusion that it would be "a physical impossibility to protect the roads, now that Hood, Forrest and Wheeler, and the whole batch of devils, are turned loose without home or habitation," but he was about ready to abandon his line of communications anyhow and to strike out on his march to "make Georgia howl."[87]

Forrest had gone to Tennessee at last, but too late. "How fortunate" it was for the Union armies, as one of their officers wrote home, that Forrest's raid "did not happen before the capture of Atlanta, when no troops could have been spared. . . ."[88]

CHAPTER XXIII

AMPHIBIOUS OPERATIONS, 1864 STYLE*

October 10, 1864-November 13, 1864

WORN as he was by the tremendous exertions of the fast-moving raid into Middle Tennessee, Forrest had another task awaiting him—to go again into West Tennessee to seek supplies and recruits, and to interfere with Federal movements and supply arrangements.

To his department commander, Richard Taylor, Forrest wrote as soon as he was back across the river that he would "make the trip to West Tennessee" but hoped that "as soon thereafter as you can do so you will relieve me from duty for twenty or thirty days, to rest and recruit. "I have been constantly in the field since 1861, and have spent half the entire time in the saddle," he explained. "I have never asked for a furlough for over ten days in which to rest and recruit, and except when wounded and unable to leave my bed have had no respite from duty."[1]

Forrest might have added that even his wounds had scarcely taken him off duty—two weeks for the ball lodged against his spine in the fight at the fallen timbers at Monterey on the retreat from Shiloh; eleven days after the abdominal wound inflicted by Lieutenant Gould at Columbia; no time at all for the wound received at Ringgold; and no real respite from duty for the wounded foot at Harrisburg. Forrest had full justification for writing as he did, "My strength is failing and it is absolutely necessary that I should have some rest."

And there were, too, his private affairs to which, as he wrote, he had "never given a day's attention at any one time since the war began." His Mississippi plantations were still within the Confederate lines, but Memphis, where his other interests lay, had been in Federal hands for more than two years. Forrest's mother continued to live on her Shelby County farm northeast of Memphis, however, while his brother John, paralyzed below the waist by a spinal wound received in the Mexican War, lived in the city itself.[2]

The rest of Forrest's family were in the field—his brothers and the young Luxton half brothers and his son William in the army; his wife

---

* The field of operations covered in this chapter is shown on the map on page 346.

366

as near the army as conditions would permit. For more than eighteen months, from before the Fort Donelson campaign until after Chickamauga, she had not seen her husband and son. After Forrest's break with Bragg, however, she joined him at La Grange, Georgia, for his one ten-day leave, and after that she left her husband and son and "her" soldiers no more than was necessary. She could not follow them on the wild rides and raids they made nor into battle, but when they came back to the camps they found her waiting to minister to them. She was remembered as being "about headquarters during the war, an amiable, lady-like, religious woman,"[3] accompanied by the wife of Captain M. C. Gallaway, a man of about Forrest's own age who before the war founded the Memphis *Avalanche*, during the war served as the city's Confederate post-master while it still was in Confederate hands, and then as aide to Forrest, and after the war was famed as the co-editor of the Memphis *Appeal*. The light army ambulance in which Mrs. Forrest and Mrs. Gallaway usually traveled in the wake of the army became well known among the soldiers, many of whom would crowd around for a word with them. "She was always as near" to her husband and his soldiers "as prudence and the sudden exigencies of war would permit. . . ."[4]

In the same letter to Taylor in which he asked for the leave of absence—which, incidentally, he was never to get until the surrender terminated all Confederate military duty—Forrest discussed military arrangements. He wanted to get Chalmers back with him as a senior officer with whom he felt "that it would be safe to leave the command for a short time," and to reconstitute his force in two divisions under Chalmers and Buford. He wanted to get back McCulloch's brigade from Mobile or west Florida, and suggested that Mabry's brigade might be sent south in exchange. He wanted also to reassemble his "scattered" four-battery, sixteen-gun battalion of artillery, equipped from the nearly forty guns which he had captured since the beginning of 1864.[5]

Before he had time to hear from Taylor at Selma, Forrest wrote Chalmers to "telegraph General Taylor for permission to join me and with what troops. If he grants it, inform me and I will give you instructions what direction to move." Not knowing exactly where Chalmers was, except that he was in the vicinity of Memphis and consequently might be near the farm of his mother in that county, Forrest added to his note a message for her, "Say to my mother we are all well."[6]

Chalmers had moved up to Memphis with Mabry's brigade, now reduced in strength to fewer than 1,000 men, and with a small force of Mississippi State Reserves, upon whom he had had to use all his persuasive powers to get them to go north of the Tennessee boundary.[7] He had, nevertheless, managed to stir up enough of a scare to cause the barricading of Memphis streets, the calling out of the Enrolled Militia of the city, and more important, the retention in Memphis of troops who were being called for as reinforcements against Forrest. To such a call Brigadier General Morgan L. Smith, in command at Memphis, replied that "if you were in my place you would not allow an armed man to leave."[8]

Permission to recall Chalmers having been promptly granted by Taylor, Forrest as promptly laid out plans for the new West Tennessee expedition.[9] From the standpoint of getting out supplies, he saw in it small possibilities. "The amount of supplies in that region has been greatly exaggerated," he wrote Taylor, and Confederate currency could not be used to get what there was. "The people instead of collecting their surplus supply of hogs will scatter them in the woods to prevent their falling into our hands," he wrote, "and the same difficulty exists in purchasing wheat and any other supplies needed by our Government. . . . If you can furnish salt, or anything the people could use at home, I am satisfied they would interest themselves in hunting up and furnishing the Government with every article of supply they could possibly spare." Thus spoke Forrest the practical commissary and quartermaster and, so speaking, spoke a volume on the failing fortunes of the Confederacy.

As recruiting officer, also, he planned to "exercise the utmost diligence in getting up the large number of deserters and absentees. . . . As fast as these are gathered up, I would suggest that they be sent you and placed at once in the infantry service. The facilities of these men for running away is much greater in the cavalry service, and they should be placed in positions remote from home."

The line of the Tennessee River was picketed, Forrest said, from "Eastport to Jacksonville"—probably meaning Johnsonville—and he was endeavoring to intercept Washburn's force, a portion of which had been so handsomely repulsed two days before at Eastport, and would "fight him wherever he can be found, without regard to numbers."

But Forrest's "great predominating desire," as he told Taylor in his summary report of his situation and plans, was "to cut Sherman's line of communication." He had done "something toward accomplishing that result," he added, and was "anxious to renew the effort," but felt that nothing worth-while could be done unless the railroads were put in condition on to Tuscumbia, and a pontoon bridge were thrown across the Tennessee at Florence, using the piers of the destroyed railroad bridge there to support its ropes. Iron for the eastward extension of the road from Cherokee could be secured, he said, by tearing up the Memphis and Charleston line west of Corinth toward Grand Junction. If this were done, he added, "I could strike the Tennessee and Alabama road or the Nashville and Chattanooga road at pleasure, and return when hard pressed in safety."

Meanwhile, however, Forrest said, "the enemy derives much of his supplies from the Northwestern railroad, which are shipped up the Tennessee River to Johnsonville and thence to Nashville." Although men and horses were "greatly jaded by the labors of the recent raid . . . and need more rest than I am able to give them at present," Forrest stated that it was his "present design to take possession of Fort Heiman, on the west bank of the Tennessee River below Johnsonville, and thus prevent all communication with Johnsonville by transports." And so without rest for his men, his horses or himself Forrest started on another expedition.[10]

Word was sent to Chalmers to report at Jackson "with all the available men you have except enough to picket your front, fetching the two batteries with you." This was to be an artillery campaign to an extent greater even than the one in Middle Tennessee. And, added Forrest, "fetch your wagons," for it was to be a supply expedition, too. Chalmers was told also to "sweep the country Bolivar to Memphis and get up every absentee and straggler and bring them with you." For it was to be, also, a recruiting expedition.[11]

Chiefly, however, it was to be an expedition against Sherman's line of communication by way of the Tennessee River, Johnsonville and the Nashville & Northwestern Railroad. This railroad, which extended but twenty-one miles west of Nashville when war broke out, had been hurriedly built another fifty seven miles from Kingston Springs to the river by the United States Army, between October 22, 1863, and May 10, 1864, to provide for Sherman's Atlanta campaign an alternate route of supply as far as Nashville. At Johnsonville, named for Andrew Johnson, then Military Governor of Tennessee, there were extensive arrangements for the transfer of freight from steamboats to railroad cars, powerful hoisting machinery and ample buildings, platforms and storage space.[12]

The importance of Johnsonville as a transfer and storage point had made it the object of some solicitude as far back as July, when the timber on the west bank of the river opposite the depot was cut down so that it would not conceal or shelter approaching rebels.[13] This solicitude, increased by Forrest's irruption into Middle Tennessee, not only caused an increase in the garrison and strengthening of the defenses, but also made of Johnsonville a point of concentration for the flotilla of "tin-clad" gunboats in the lower Tennessee.[14]

Forrest started moving his forces into West Tennessee on October sixteenth. By the twenty-first he had his own headquarters at Jackson once more, with Chalmers' troops up from Memphis and with Buford around Lexington, between Jackson and the river. At Jackson, also, Rucker reported for duty, having recovered from his Harrisburg wound, to resume command of the brigade which Colonel Kelley had led so ably as to call for special commendation and a recommendation for promotion from Forrest.[15]

Forrest set about his several tasks in West Tennessee with accustomed energy and sagacity. To Taylor he wrote on the twenty-fourth recommending that some of the dismounted men in Mississippi be moved up to Corinth to protect that critical spot from possible Federal operations from the vicinity of Clifton, Tennessee. At the same time he recommended again that the railroad from Okolona north to Corinth and thence eastward to Tuscumbia be put in repair, "as its occupation and preservation may be of vital importance to General Hood and the Army of Tennessee."[16]

In this recommendation Forrest was anticipating a movement then being planned—the shift of the base of supply of the Army of Tennessee from Blue Mountain (the present Anniston), Alabama, to Tuscumbia, preliminary to Hood's contemplated march into Tennessee. Through the month of October 1864 Hood's army had campaigned against Sherman's railroad in north Georgia. The campaign was successful in breaking the railroad but did not have the hoped-for result of causing Sherman to loosen his grip on Atlanta. Like Forrest's slightly earlier operation against Sherman's railroads in Tennessee, Hood's effort came too late, for Sherman was in large degree independent of his railroad by this time, and had indeed, as early as September twentieth, proposed to Grant that he be allowed to break up the railroad, destroy Atlanta as a military base, cut loose and march to the sea, to meet new supplies to be sent him there.[17]

In such a state of affairs operations against his communications served rather to strengthen Sherman in his determination to "make the march and make Georgia howl"[18] but he was concerned in the meanwhile to "command the Tennessee River up to Muscle Shoals," as he dispatched Thomas, whom he had put in charge of affairs in Tennessee. He ordered, therefore, a renewal of the attempt upon Eastport which Kelley had so handsomely foiled a few days earlier.[19] On the very day, however, on which this new movement against Eastport was ordered Forrest started north to take into his own hands for a season the initiative in operations on the Tennessee.

The condition of Forrest's horses after the exertions they had made was such that he was compelled to let many of his men recruited in West Tennessee go home for remounts, reducing his strength to no more than 3,000 men, even after the arrival of Chalmers. Forrest reported,

370

likewise, that the enemy was still threatening to cross the river from Clifton, and that with such a threat in his rear he would not move farther down the river (north) but would remain where he was, collect absentees and, if the enemy did cross over from Clifton, would fight him.[20]

But while Forrest remained inland at Jackson, in the center of the area bounded by the Tennessee, Ohio and Mississippi rivers, with the West Tennessee troops scattered to their homes to get fresh horses and wardrobes, alarm ran all through the Federal posts along the rivers. Brigadier General Morgan Smith, commanding at Memphis, was so sure that he was about to be attacked by Forrest "in heavy force"—estimated at 20,000 men—that he loopholed the houses along the Bayou Gayoso, made an inner line of cotton-bale and hay-bale breastworks, and called for reinforcements from St. Louis above to the mouth of White River below. "The amount of Government property here is so vast," he wrote, "that the most strenuous efforts should be made to save it."[21] In his successful appeals for more men he was joined by Washburn, when the latter returned to active command at Memphis. "I have barely force here to defend this place [against Forrest and his 10,000 men]," Washburn wrote, "[and] should not be surprised if he should plant batteries above here, at Randolph and Fort Pillow."[22]

With the major post of Memphis in this state of mind, it was not to be expected that the minor posts of Columbus and Paducah, Kentucky, would escape the contagion. Everything in west Kentucky was withdrawn into these fortified posts, while Brigadier General Solomon Meredith, commanding, went into what seems to have been a state of chronic alarm, calling upon any and all commanders whom he could reach, loudly and almost daily during the last half of October and into November, for reinforcements to resist Forrest's imminent attack.[23]

Forrest meanwhile, being satisfied by October twenty-fourth that the enemy was not coming against him either from Memphis on the west or Clifton to the east, headed north toward the Tennessee River at the Kentucky-Tennessee state line—the once active but by this time neglected neighborhood of Fort Heiman on the left bank of the river, and Fort Henry on the right. Buford, in the lead, carried with him besides his field artillery two 20-pounder rifled Parrott guns sent up from the fortifications at Mobile by rail to Corinth, whence they had been dragged forward over wretched roads. A day's march behind Buford, within supporting distance, came Chalmers.[24]

Buford emplaced his troops and batteries on the west bank of the Tennessee on October twenty-eighth, with Lyon's Kentuckians and the two new guns from Mobile, worked by the men of Walton's battery, in

371

the old Confederate works at Fort Heiman, and a section of Morton's battery a few hundred yards downstream. Bell's Tennesseans with the other section of the Morton battery were placed five miles upstream at Paris Landing. Both groups were ordered to hold their fire until steamers were safely in the reach of the river between them—a "judicious disposition" which "effectually blockaded the river" and was approved by Forrest upon his arrival.[25]

Buford's men, with their guns all in place, were eager to try them out upon four steamboats which came down a little after nightfall. "Keep quiet, men, keep quiet, don't fire a gun," Buford warned them. "These are empty boats going down after more supplies for Sherman's army. I want a loaded boat, a richer prize. Just wait until one comes up the river, and then you may take her if you can."[26]

Buford's foresight and the patience of his gunners was rewarded the next morning, October twenty-ninth, when the new steamer *Mazeppa*, from Cincinnati, with a barge in tow, came round the bend below Fort Heiman, and unsuspectingly steamed past the Confederate guns and into the trap. After three rounds from the lower batteries she became unmanageable, drifted ashore on the opposite bank and was abandoned by her crew. A naked Confederate, with his pistol strapped around his neck, braving the possibility of further resistance from the boat, paddled across the river on a plank to take possession of the first prize of the expedition. With the steamer's yawl a line was got across the river, and willing hands soon warped the *Mazeppa* to the west bank.[27]

Her 700 tons of cargo consisted chiefly of shoes, of which there were about 9,000 pairs, blankets and warm winter clothing in anticipation of the approaching season. They included also subsistence supplies and at least one demijohn of French brandy—which last, according to the recollections of the diarists, fell into the hands of General Buford himself. "Plenty of meat, boys," he called out to the waiting soldiers as the boat was being warped into the bank, "plenty of hard-tack, plenty of shoes and clothes for the boys, but just enough brandy for the General!"[28]

Despite the air of holiday about the taking of the *Mazeppa*, Buford and his men unloaded it promptly and hauled its tons of supplies back from the riverbank, taking no chances of their recapture by three gunboats which, about this time, appeared below. The shore batteries, however, proved to be sufficent to turn the gunboats back downstream and as night fell quiet descended again on the broad current of the Tennessee.[29]

On the next day, October thirtieth, business on the river was brisk. The steamer *Anna*, bound downstream, was the first to arrive. She passed into the trap but managed to escape, partly because Buford, wishing to capture the boat uninjured, undertook to hail her into the bank under an understanding that his fire would be withheld. Promising to "round to" at the lower landing, the *Anna's* pilot took the chance of steaming full speed ahead past the lower batteries. When his course of action— the Confederate regarded it as "perfidy"—became plain, the lower battery opened on the *Anna* too late to stop or sink her, though she arrived at Paducah "badly damaged."[30]

The *Anna* had come down the river from Johnsonville as far as Sandy Island, only a few miles above the ambuscade, under the convoy of the gunboat *Undine (No. 55)*, which had started back to her base at Johnsonville forty miles up the river, when the Confederate fire on the *Anna* was heard. The *Undine* cleared for action, turned and steamed down the river to the sound of the firing.

The *Undine*, mounting four 24-pounder brass howitzers on each side, came first under the fire of the two guns at Bell's position of Paris Landing. After a fight of fifty-five minutes, according to the report of her captain, the escape pipe was shot off, the fire was knocked out of the furnace by a shell, four shots had gone through the gun casemates, four men were dead and three wounded and the boat was becoming unmanageable. He was able to make his way, however, to a point too far down the river to be reached by the Confederate guns at Paris Landing, and too far up to be reached by those at Fort Heiman.

There, while he was engaged in making repairs on his boat, and at the same time using his broadside guns with shrapnel against Confederate musketry fire from the bank, the transport *Venus* came down the river. The *Undine* signaled her to keep out of danger but the *Venus*, failing to heed the signals, came on into the range of the upper battery. She ran by the battery with small physical damage but with the loss of her captain and, shortly before two o'clock in the afternoon, came to anchor under cover of the *Undine's* guns.

"About twenty minutes after the *Venus* came down," Acting Master Bryant further reported, "another transport came down the river with a barge, and like the *Venus*, heeded not my signals, and ran under the batteries, where she had her steam pipe shot off. She then headed for the west bank and surrendered to the enemy. That steamer I afterward learned was the [J. W.] *Cheeseman*."[31]

During the day Chalmers arrived at the river, bringing with him Hudson's (or Walton's) and Rice's batteries of artillery, both of which were put into position on the bank above the section of Morton's guns at Paris Landing. While this was being done, Colonel Rucker reconnoitered the riverbank below and found a way by which guns could be moved through the thick and tangled underbrush to be brought to bear on the

Undine and the *Venus.* Two of Walton's guns were so moved and at 3:10 P.M. opened on the *Undine.* By four o'clock the gunboat, disabled by artillery fire, was run to the east bank of the river and abandoned. Kelley, to whose rifle fire the *Venus* surrendered, boarded her, crossed the river and took possession of the *Undine*—the same gunboat, as it happened, which had been under the fire of his guns three weeks before at Eastport.[32]

Meanwhile, another gunboat, the *Tawah* (No. 29) steamed down to the sound of the firing, dropped anchor a mile and a half away and began to shell the upper Confederate battery. Finding light field guns unable to reach the gunboat from that distance, Chalmers ordered the battery to move closer, supported by his own escort and the cadet company of the Seventh Alabama, to act as sharpshooters. Under the combined fire the *Tawah* soon weighed anchor and stood upstream out of range.[33]

Forrest, who came upon the scene on October thirty-first, decided to organize a temporary Tennessee River navy. The *Cheeseman,* too badly damaged in the fight to be of use, was unloaded of her stores and burned.[34] The *Undine,* mounting eight 24-pounder guns, and the *Venus,* upon which the two 20-pounder Parrotts brought from Mobile were mounted, were manned by volunteer crews. Lieutenant Colonel William A. Dawson on the *Venus* was named "Commodore," with Captain Frank M. Gracey of the Third Kentucky, who in civil life had been a Cumberland River steamboat man, in command of the gunboat. The thirty-first was spent in repair of the boats and "training" of the crews, to the extent of a few hours of practice maneuvers in the stretch of the river between the Confederate batteries.[35]

The new crews of the captured boats were willing to take them wherever Forrest might order but, as Colonel Dawson said to the General, he wanted a promise that "if we lose your fleet and come in on foot, you won't curse us out about it."[36] With that understanding and with strict orders to keep the boats between the upper and lower shore batteries, the amphibious command started up the Tennessee on the morning of November first. Chalmers moved in front to protect the "navy" of one regular gunboat and one homemade one from the three gunboats up the river at Johnsonville. Buford moved in the rear to perform a like service against the seven gunboats downstream toward Paducah.[37]

The day was rainy, the mud of the steep riverbanks deep, slick and slimy, the briers sharp and the brush thick. The river soldiers, finding life on the water easy, called elaborate commiserations across to their brethren, scrambling along the bank and pushing the artillery forward from position to position. The land soldiers had to be satisfied with calling back terrifying warnings of what would happen to their nautical comrades when the Yankee gunboats caught them.

On November first the expedition tied up and camped for the night in the neighborhood of the railroad bridge across the Tennessee at Danville. At 3:30 P.M. on the second, in the vicinity of Green Bottom Bar, only about six miles below Johnsonville, the predictions of the land soldiers began to come true. The *Venus*, become bold and overconfident perhaps, or perhaps tempted by the ease of steaming ahead while the land soldiers toiled on, got ahead of the land batteries and of the *Undine*, when she met, in a bend of the river, the Federal gunboats *Key West* (No. 32) and *Tawah* (No. 29), which immediately and vigorously attacked. With its light armament and lubber crew the *Venus* was soon overmatched and driven ashore. The crew ended their short naval careers by taking to the woods, while the Federal boats rejoiced in the recovery of the *Venus* and the capture of the two Confederate guns she carried. The *Undine*, which had attempted to come to the rescue of her sister ship in the Confederate navy, was driven back and made her escape downstream, where she was not followed.[38]

On November third, about noon, the now Confederate *Undine* made her appearance at the head of Reynoldsburg Island two miles below Johnsonville, offering a "dare" to the three Union gunboats above. Lieutenant E. M. King, in command of the Federal flotilla, rightly suspecting that the *Undine* was trying to decoy his boats within reach of land batteries below, declined to meet her thrice-repeated challenge.[39]

During that day, the night which followed and the morning of November fourth Forrest, without attracting attention, was putting his troops in position for the attack on Johnsonville which he had come there to make. The work, consisting chiefly of getting the batteries in position, was carried on with the utmost difficulty in the rain and through the woods and across the bottomless mud of the big "bottom" across the river from Johnsonville. Not only did guns have to be brought to bear on Johnsonville itself, but others had to be placed above and especially below, to cut off reinforcing gunboats.

The batteries below were the first to be engaged on November fourth, when at 8:00 A.M. Lieutenant Commander Le Roy Fitch stood up the river with six gunboats—his flagship the *Moose*, the *Brilliant*, *Victory*, *Paw Paw*, *Fairy* and *Curlew*, mounting a total of seventy-nine guns. At the same time, there came down the river Lieutenant King and his three gunboats, the *Key West*, *Tawah* and *Elfin* (No. 54), the three carrying twenty-five guns, or a total of more than one hundred guns afloat. Opposed to them were the captured *Undine* with eight guns and, on the land, two guns of Rice's battery, above the head of Reynoldsburg Island,

and, a little below, two of Walton's, bearing upon the narrow chute through which the channel of the river passed between the island and the west bank.

While weight of metal was overwhelmingly on the Federal side the advantages of position were with the Confederate land batteries. These advantages availed little, however, to the *Undine* caught between the gunboat fleets above and below, and there was nothing for Gracey to do but destroy and abandon her. This he proceeded to do by tearing open the mattresses of her crew, piling the shavings with which they were filled in the magazine and the cabins, soaking them in oil, and then, with everyone ashore but himself, applying the torch, wading ashore and taking to the woods as the last of Forrest's "navy" first burned and then exploded.[40]

But while the *Undine* was lost, the land batteries maintained their positions. The battery above the head of the island, Lieutenant King reported, was "too much for us," putting ten shell through upper works, seven through the berth deck and two through the hull of the *Key West*, out of a total of some thirty shots fired in twenty minutes. The upper flotilla, badly battered, drew off and steamed back to Johnsonville. The heavier fleet from below kept up the firing until eleven o'clock, but made no effort to come up through the Reynoldsburg Island chute. As Commander Fitch explained, the vessels would have had to come up single file against the current in a narrow and tortuous channel, which would have taken them at places within fifty yards of where they conceived several Confederate batteries to be placed, while if one boat should become lodged on the bar at the head of the chute there was no room for another to pass up to her assistance. And so it was that six gunboats less than four miles away were completely blocked off from the afternoon's fight at Johnsonville.[41]

While the lower land guns were holding off the gunboats from below, the rest of Forrest's artillery was being made ready for the bombardment of Johnsonville itself. Emplacements were prepared, above, opposite and just below the post, by digging gun pits in a natural levee lying between the river itself and the "bottoms" of the west bank. These positions were lower than the level of Johnsonville, the east bank of the river being here some twenty feet higher than the west, and much lower than the guns in the earthwork on the hill above the Federal post. One gun position immediately opposite and only half a mile from the place—that being the width of the river at this point—was so much lower than the Federal land guns that the latter could not be depressed enough to reach it, and at the same time was above the level of the river itself just enough to prevent the naval guns being elevated to reach it. This emplacement, selected by Morton personally, was occupied by a section of the Morton battery. Thrall's battery was placed half a mile above the town, with Walton's battery, two guns from Rice's and Morton's other two guns below the town. With much infantry help the guns were dragged through the bottoms, frequently having to be lifted by hand across the trunks of fallen trees, during the night of the third. The work not having been completed, it was continued during the morning of the fourth behind skillfully contrived camouflage of green boughs, blending with the thick underbrush along the bank.[42]

At 2:00 P.M., with all in readiness for the firing of the first guns, the concealed Confederates looked across the river to a busy scene—at the wharves, three gunboats, eleven transport steamers, eighteen barges, loaded and empty; on the ground, warehouses bulging with supplies, acres of open storage piled ten feet high with stores covered with tarpaulins; workmen busy unloading stores, two freight trains being made up, soldiers at their tasks, and nowhere any apparent awareness of the approach of destruction.[43]

Promptly at two o'clock the ten guns which Forrest was able to bring to bear upon Johnsonville opened fire. For forty minutes of consternation the Confederate batteries concentrated their attention upon the gunboats and the transports under their protection. Shell through boilers released scalding steam. Vessels afire and out of control drifted against others and spread the flames. And then, though the Confederates were not to know it until the publication of the reports long afterward, the Union naval commander, Lieutenant King, decided that the gunboats were fought out and whipped, and that they and the transports must be burned to keep them from falling into rebel hands. Convinced that Forrest had four times as many men and guns as he actually had,[44] Colonel Charles R. Thompson, commanding ashore, agreed and the work of destruction which Forrest's guns started was completed by setting fire to gunboats, transports and barges. The whole fleet burned to the water's edge and sank into the Tennessee where, as lately as the exceptional low water of 1925, their frames were still to be seen in the river, and where, doubtless, they are today.[45]

With the boats blazing away the Confederate artillery turned its attention more to the stores on the banks. Flames set by bursting shell and flames spreading from the burning boats soon made of the sheds and warehouses and the acres of piled-up stores a mass of roaring flames. One warehouse, on the hill above the town, contained a store of several hundred barrels of liquors. It caught fire, the barrels burst and blazing alcohol ran down the hills in a river of blue flame. Within two hours the whole place was ablaze, ashore and afloat, for a mile up and down the

377

stream. To one Federal officer it was a scene which, with the roar of artillery and the shriek of shell, with flame and smoke, terror and flee-ing panic, "beggared description; it was awfully sublime."[46]

On the west bank of the river the Confederates, their noses tantalized by the pungent odors of burning bacon, coffee and alcohol, were exultant. The infantry soldiers lined the bank as sharpshooters when opportunity offered but, as much as anything else, as cheering observers of what their artillery was doing. Forrest himself took a hand as gunner with the section of Morton's battery just opposite the town, with General Buford as number one at the gun and Colonel Bell as number four, "handling, loading and firing the piece with the enthusiasm of boy cannoneers on a Fourth of July." When a shot was reported too high the General's command would be to "elevate the breech of that gun a little lower!" but his volunteer gun crew knew what he meant.[47]

On the opposite bank there was much apprehension that Forrest might be about to cross the river, although the burning of the boats had made any such move impossible. Nevertheless, as was afterward reported, the railroad agent at Johnsonville "ran off with a train of cars" loaded with refugees. Upon reaching Waverly, twelve miles out and just short of the point where the railroad line begins to climb from the river bot-tom into the highlands, he was alleged to have cut off the engine and tender and run "light" to Nashville, leaving his refugees to shift for themselves.[48]

That night, having done what he had come to do as nearly as it was possible, Forrest started south, moving six miles by the glare upon the sky of the flames he was leaving behind him. To Taylor at Selma he reported briefly that he had "destroyed the town, burning three gun-boats, eleven steamers and 15 barges, a portion of the latter laden with quartermaster and commissary stores, also burnt most of the stores on the landing and in warehouses. The expedition thus far has resulted," he added, "in a loss to the enemy of four gunboats, of eight guns each, fourteen steamboats and seventeen barges, and quartermaster's stores estimated at from 75,000 to 120,000 tons."[49]

In his subsequent more complete report Forrest estimated the value of these stores and vessels, and the twenty-six guns of the enemy which he destroyed—there actually were not less than thirty-three so destroyed, including the eight on the *Undine*—at $6,700,000. The officers in charge who, it may safely be assumed, did not overstate their losses, set the value of the stores lost, including the steamboats and barges, at $2,200,-000 in one report, and at $1,500,000 in another, neither of them, appar-ently, including the value of the four gunboats and artillery lost. Forrest reported capture of 150 prisoners (there is no report of Federal casual-

378

ties otherwise) with a loss in his own command of two killed and nine wounded, and of the two Parrott guns lost with the *Venus*.[50]

Forrest marched away from Johnsonville under orders from General Beauregard, commanding the newly organized Military Division of the West, to join the Army of Tennessee. The first such order, issued on October twenty-sixth, the day on which Forrest moved out of Jackson toward Johnsonville, was that as soon as Forrest had "accomplished the objects of his present movement" he should move "toward Middle Tennessee" and put himself under orders of General John B. Hood at Bainbridge Crossing on the Tennessee below Decatur, Alabama.[51]

This first conditional order to Forrest to report to Hood did not reach him until October thirtieth when he was in the midst of the Johnsonville operation which he was directed to complete.[52] The order was repeated on November second. Again on November fourth orders went forward by special courier from Corinth, calling for Forrest to "report as ordered," as the Army of Tennessee would be ready to cross the Tennessee at Florence, Alabama, on November fifth and the crossing would be held up awaiting Forrest's arrival.[53]

By the time these orders reached Forrest—probably not before November seventh—he had completed his work at Johnsonville and was on his way south, as promptly as the rising streams, the state of the roads and the condition of his horses would permit. He had, indeed, undertaken on the sixth to comply with the earlier order to go into Middle Tennessee, attempting to make a crossing at Perryville thirty miles above Johnsonville. Two of the small boats saved from his short-lived "navy" had been hauled that far on wagons, while ferryboats were to be built of local materials, including the planking of vacant storehouses torn down for that purpose. Forrest "had his staff officers and escort company carrying plank and scantling on their shoulders down to the river," one of Chalmers' officers wrote and, while "ripping off weatherboarding with his own hands, was 'guying' the members of his staff because they did not carry better loads."[54] In black night, with rain falling in torrents, "the General was as busy as anybody."[55]

But the means of ferriage was too slight, and with the river going into a rise, carrying logs and driftwood on a booming current, it was impossible to swim the horses. For all these reasons and also, probably, because he had by that time received the positive and unconditional order to meet Hood at Florence, Alabama, Forrest discontinued the effort to put the command across the Tennessee, and on November seventh started his toilsome way south on the west side of the river. Rucker and the 400 men who were already across were ordered to make their way south on the east side, which they did, rejoining sixteen days later.

Forrest's was a slow, toilsome march. Even with sixteen to the gun, the artillery horses gave out. Oxen—four, six, even eight yoke to the gun—were impressed to drag the artillery through the almost bottomless mud of the country roads and across the rising streams. At the end of each day's march the owners of the oxen impressed for the work were allowed to take their slow-moving beasts back home, while others were secured for the next day's march.[56]

While Forrest was marching away from Johnsonville Federal reinforcements were pouring into the place. Major General John M. Schofield and the Twenty-third Army Corps, on the way back from Georgia by rail to be posted at Pulaski, Tennessee, as the front line against Hood's threatened advance, were diverted at Nashville and started to Johnsonville. The arrival of Colonel George W. Gallup with the first of these troops on the afternoon of November fifth was occasion of a heartfelt message from the commander at Johnsonville: "Colonel Gallup has arrived with 1,000 men, thank God. Is General Schofield on his way here, as reported?"[57]

The General arrived the following day, when "his presence had the effect of quieting excitement among the troops, who are now busily engaged constructing works for better defense of the position"—although, as events turned out, the position would never again during the war be of importance to either side. On November seventh, the same day on which Forrest turned south from Perryville, Schofield decided to leave two brigades as a garrison at Johnsonville, to halt the movement of the trainloads of troops headed that way, and turn them south from Nashville toward their original destination of Pulaski.[58]

Forrest, toiling southward through the mud in these early November days, had created more apprehension and excitement than he realized. On this same November seventh, that being the day before the Presidential election of 1864, Captain W. Fithian, Provost Marshal at Danville, Illinois, telegraphed to Major General Joseph Hooker, commanding the Northern Department at Cincinnati, a frantic report that "Forrest has been in disguise alternately in Chicago, Michigan City and Canada for two months; has 14,000 men, mostly from draft, near Michigan City. On 7th of November, midnight, will seize telegraph and rail at Chicago, release prisoners there, arm them, sack the city, shoot down all Federal soldiers, and urge concert of action with Southern sympathizers."

General Hooker, while expressing the belief that the report was "all stuff," nevertheless ordered troops sent from Springfield to Colonel Sweet at Camp Douglas, Chicago, to remain there through election day and night. Governor Yates of Illinois called out the militia also, while upon further reflection General Hooker ordered 500 soldiers from

Indianapolis and a regiment from St. Louis sent to Chicago, and finally went there himself.[59]

But Sherman took no stock in fantastic stories of Forrest being in Chicago or Canada. "That devil Forrest," he wrote Grant, "was down about Johnsonville making havoc among the gunboats and transports."[60]

Indianapolis and a regiment from St. Louis sent to Chicago, and finally
went there himself.

But Sherman took no stock in fantastic stories of Forrest being in
Chicago or Canada. "That devil Forrest," he wrote Grant, "was down
about Johnsonville making havoc among the gunboats and transports."

CHAPTER XXIV

ADVANCE: SPRING HILL AND FRANKLIN*

November 14, 1864-November 30, 1864

ON NOVEMBER 14, 1864, almost precisely a year after his separation from
the main Confederate command in the West, Forrest reported for service
once more with the Army of Tennessee.

In that year Forrest had created a command which in half a hundred
skirmishes and battles had put out of action nearly three times its own
number of the enemy, had taken forty-eight guns and destroyed nearly
as many more, had captured 10,000 stand of small arms, had taken or
destroyed four gunboats and fourteen transports, and land transportation which included 2,000 animals, 350 vehicles, five locomotives and
75 cars, together with many miles of railroad track. It was small wonder
that when Forrest rejoined the main army at Florence, Alabama, he was
"serenaded by the Tennesseans in the evening, to which he responded
in a very encouraging speech."[1]

In the twelvemonth in which Forrest had been elsewhere, the Army
of Tennessee under Bragg had fought and lost the battles about Chattanooga, ending with the disaster of Missionary Ridge. Under a new
commander, Joseph E. Johnston, with confidence and morale restored,[2]
the army had sustained the attacks of Sherman's mighty force from
Dalton back to Peachtree Creek. With still a third commander, the
thirty-two-year-old John B. Hood whose brilliant fighting in Virginia
had won the admiration and confidence of President Davis, the army
had taken the aggressive without success, had undergone the long siege
and final loss of Atlanta and had, in its turn, gone against Sherman's
communications with the North. And now, still under Hood, it had
marched away from Sherman nearly 300 miles, with intent to move
against his base in Tennessee, or perhaps even on to the Ohio—a
desperate march, as it proved to be, to disaster.

But in the beginning Hood's Tennessee campaign had one slender
chance of success in speed of execution, before Thomas, whom Sherman
had put in charge in Tennessee, could mobilize the strength available to
him. And yet, for reasons probably quite as much psychological as material, the ordinarily impetuous Hood was slow in starting.

---

* The field of operations covered in this chapter is shown on the map on page 346.

As early as October thirteenth he began his withdrawal from Sherman's railroad line in the vicinity of Dalton, Georgia, and on the eighteenth marched southwest to Gadsden, Alabama, which he reached on the twentieth. There, on the following day, he was joined by General Beauregard who, as commander of the newly created Military Division of the West, had a vague and ill-defined authority over both Hood and Richard Taylor.

Having become convinced that Sherman was not going to divide his forces so that he might be struck in detail, Hood "determined to cross the Tennessee River at or near Gunter's Landing," the point on the river closest to Gadsden, so as to "strike the enemy's communications again near Bridgeport, force him to cross the river also to obtain supplies, and thus we should at least recover our lost territory"[3]—an arrangement which Beauregard approved.

Starting toward Gunter's Landing, Hood deflected his course westward first to Decatur, Alabama, and thence on to Tuscumbia, for the double purpose of putting himself in touch with a railhead through which he could be supplied from the south by way of Corinth and the Mobile and Ohio Railroad, and of meeting Forrest, to whom Beauregard sent orders to join him.

Hood arrived at Tuscumbia on October thirtieth, bringing with him about 27,000 infantry and artillery, and Brigadier General William H. Jackson's 2,000 cavalry. North of the Tennessee River Thomas had at the same time, besides the considerable garrisons at such points as Nashville, Murfreesborough, Tullahoma, Chattanooga and Johnsonville in Tennessee, and Decatur and Huntsville in Alabama, some 4,500 cavalry under Edward Hatch and Croxton and the 13,000 men of Major General D. S. Stanley's Fourth Corps, sent back by Sherman from Georgia and stationed at Pulaski, Tennessee, seventy-five miles south of Nashville.

The opposing forces were more nearly equal in strength at the beginning of November than they ever were to be again. For Hood there were to be no reinforcements other than the 3,500 men whom Forrest was bringing out of West Tennessee. On the way to Thomas, however, were Schofield's Twenty-third Army Corps of 10,000 men coming back from Georgia; A. J. Smith's two divisions of the Sixteenth Army Corps, another 10,000 men, on the way from Missouri by steamboat; Wilson's dismounted cavalry force of 4,500 men awaiting only horses to take the field, and a variety of recruits and reinforcements from the northwestern states.[4]

For three weeks, however, while Thomas's strength grew, Hood waited on the Tennessee River. The delay, as he explained to Beauregard, who was insistent upon a prompt forward movement but who did not have, or at least did not exercise, any authority to order it, was for the double purpose of adding to his command the strength of Forrest's cavalry, and of accumulating at his starting point a twenty-days' supply of necessaries. These supplies, brought to the railhead of Cherokee over railroads of limited capacity, had to be brought on to Tuscumbia by a wagon haul of appalling difficulty.[5]

To these physical difficulties there was added a deep inner uncertainty on the part of the General commanding the Army of Tennessee. What was Sherman going to do? If Hood went to Tennessee, would Sherman turn back and follow? If he did not, should Hood abandon his proposed Tennessee campaign and follow Sherman wherever he might go in Georgia? Sherman, too, had like moments of uncertainty, though all the while believing that "popular clamor" would force Hood "to turn and follow me."[6] Sherman's uncertainties were the earlier resolved, however, in his final decision, made just about the time Hood took up his position on the Tennessee River, to go ahead with his march, "ruin Georgia," and bring up at the sea.

In this state of affairs, then, Forrest arrived at army headquarters, which had just been moved from Tuscumbia to Florence on the north bank of the river, and on the morning of November fifteenth was assigned to the command of all the cavalry operating with the Army of Tennessee. His new command included, besides his own troops under Chalmers and Buford, the division of "Red" Jackson and a demi-brigade under Colonel Jacob Biffle, neither of whom were strangers to Forrest. Buford's and Chalmers' command were much reduced in strength by detachments of men with unserviceable horses who had been sent south to Verona, Mississippi, and by the numbers of men furloughed in West Tennessee to secure remounts who could not be gathered up in time when the order came to hasten to Hood. So shrunken in number had all Confederate cavalry formations become by this period of the war, indeed, that the imposing-sounding three divisions under Chalmers, Buford and Jackson, into which Forrest's force was organized numbered in fact fewer than 6,000 men.[7]

On the morning of November sixteenth, as the new cavalry commander began passing his arriving troops over the pontoon bridge leading to Florence and the north bank of the Tennessee, General Sherman sat his horse at the top of a rise east of Atlanta, looking back at "the black smoke rising high in the air and hanging like a pall over a ruined city," and looking ahead along the gleaming gun barrels of his marching columns, as the bands played and the men sang, "John Brown's soul goes marching on."[8] The period of uncertainty, whether for Sherman or for Hood, was over. Sherman had started for the Atlantic; Hood was to start, after a few more days of gathering supplies, on a march to the

THE LAST MILITARY PHOTOGRAPH

The time and place of the making of this photograph—the finest of all Forrest portraits—and the location of the original are unknown to the author, but from the uniform it is apparent that it was made toward the close of his military career. The photograph was published in Captain Dinkins' *Personal Recollections* in 1897. Two years later it served as the model for the striking engraving which is the frontispiece of Doctor Wyeth's *Forrest*.

From the original by courtesy of Garnett Andrews

"RUIN TO OUR PEOPLE"

A personal and business letter of Forrest's after passage of the Military
Reconstruction Act of 1867.

north which, he hoped, might lead him to the Ohio River and, perchance, even on across the mountains to the aid of General Lee in Virginia.

Sherman was to meet on his march no opposition of consequence.[9] Hood was to meet opposition growing in power and steadiness until, at Nashville, he was to be overwhelmed by Thomas' final counterstroke. There may have been misgivings of some such result among the high commanders—at any rate, none but poor Hood was ever found willing to accept a full share of responsibility for the expedition, after it was all over—but the spirit of the army as it started for Tennessee was high and eager. To many of the troops it was a march back to their own country which they had not seen since they left it with Bragg, nearly eighteen months before. To all of them—the tried and tested veterans who had stuck through the battles and marches of that year and a half—it meant that the long retreat was over, that once more they were marching forward to seek the enemy.

The first fighting of the cavalry advance, on a small scale, was some ten miles out of Florence along Shoal Creek on November nineteenth, when Colonel Datus Coon's Union brigade cut its way out of what its commander called a "well devised trap," much to the "mortification and chagrin of the rebels," which, he said, was "made known by those hideous yells such as only rebels can make."[10]

The real movement forward of the whole army began on the morning of November twenty-first, a day which opened with an unseasonably early snowstorm and closed with a hard freeze—the beginning of a season of alternate thaw and freeze which made of the country roads deep-rutted quagmires.

The first objective was to cut off and destroy or capture the 23,000 men of the Union Fourth and Twenty-third Corps under Major General John M. Schofield in their advanced position at Pulaski, seventy-five miles south of Nashville and thirty miles south of Columbia, where both the railroad and turnpike crossed Duck River. For Columbia, then, seventy-five miles northeast of Florence, the Confederates headed, marching in three columns with Forrest's three divisions of cavalry leading.

To resist Forrest's advance the Union cavalry commander, Brigadier General Edward Hatch, had four brigades totaling about 4,300 men. From the twenty-first for three days there was "almost constant skirmishing," Forrest reported, in which the advancing Confederates "drove the enemy in every encounter."[11]

The left column of the Confederate cavalry, under Chalmers, was headed for Columbia by way of Henryville and Mt. Pleasant. Moving up toward Henryville in the afternoon of the twenty-third with Rucker

385

in the lead, it struck Capron's Federal brigade drawn up in line of battle. Sending Rucker forward "to keep up a slight skirmish," Forrest started Kelley, the same who had been sent on a like mission in Forrest's first fight at Sacramento three years before, around one flank to gain the rear, while he himself, with the escort company, took the other flank. The result was a "perfect stampede," which lasted until dark, and was repeated during the early evening when Rucker drove the enemy back upon a second ambuscade which Forrest and the escort laid in their rear.[12]

On the same day Jackson and Buford, marching east from Lawrenceburg for Pulaski, found that Schofield had that day evacuated his exposed advance position—and none too soon, as things turned out—and was halfway back to Columbia. The two Confederate columns turned northward, moving on country roads roughly parallel to the turnpike on which Schofield was marching, and from noon to night of the twenty-fourth had a series of sharp brushes with Hatch's cavalry, which was covering the flank of the infantry in its rapid withdrawal.[13]

On the same day, November twenty-fourth, at two o'clock in the morning Chalmers' column started by way of Mt. Pleasant for Columbia, driving the Federal cavalry before them. An hour later the Federal infantry division of Brigadier General Jacob D. Cox, which on the night of the twenty-third had camped eight miles south of Columbia, started for that point. From a point three miles out of the town Cox took a crossroad to the west, marching toward the sound of the fighting, to arrive just in time to keep Forrest's advance from going right on into Columbia with the Federal cavalry which Cox found "in hasty retreat," and so to seize the vital crossings of Duck River. Lining up his veteran infantry across the pike from Mt. Pleasant, Cox checked the pursuit in a fight in which Lieutenant Colonel William A. Dawson of the Fifteenth Tennessee Cavalry, who had been "Commodore" of Forrest's river navy, was mortally wounded as he was in the act of wrenching a Federal standard from the hands of its bearer.[14]

Cox's prompt action and firm stand gave opportunity for the rest of Schofield's infantry to march into Columbia. There, during the next two days, while Hood's infantry was toiling along on the difficult roads below Mt. Pleasant, Schofield entrenched, with a semicircular line of works running from the river above to the river below the town. Forrest's cavalry had the place invested by the night of the twenty-fourth, and kept up an annoying fire upon it during the three following days.[15]

With the coming up of Hood's infantry Forrest's force was relieved on the morning of the twenty-seventh, and sent farther out to picket the river and scout for crossings. During that night Schofield evacuated

Columbia itself and crossed to the north side of the Duck. With his crossing complete by 5:00 A.M. of the twenty-eighth, he burned his bridges and took up a position to carry out Thomas' instructions to delay Hood's northward march until the concentration of Union troops at Nashville should be complete.[16]

On the same night, the twenty-seventh, Forrest was called to a conference with General Hood at army headquarters at Mrs. Warfield's, three miles south of Columbia on the Pulaski pike, at which there was laid out a plan, both bold and sound, for the outflanking and entrapment of Schofield's two corps—a blow which, had it been delivered according to plan, would have given to the Army of Tennessee every chance of a successful campaign.[17]

Forrest's first task in the plan was to force the crossings of Duck River above and to the east of Columbia, so as to cover the laying down of a pontoon bridge for the infantry crossing. Before night of the twenty-eighth three of Forrest's columns—those of Jackson, Chalmers and Biffle, with whom Forrest himself marched—were across the river at fords from three to seven miles above Columbia. Buford, who was to have crossed still farther upstream at the Lewisburg-Franklin turnpike, ran into stronger opposition and did not succeed in forcing his way across until daylight of November twenty-ninth.[18]

In this operation of crossing Duck River, Forrest met in combat for the first time Major General James H. Wilson, the new Union cavalry commander in the West. Wilson, who had graduated from West Point only in 1860, had been a Second Lieutenant of the Topographic Engineers at the outbreak of the war. He had served as an engineer officer on the South Atlantic coastal operations and in the Vicksburg and Chattanooga campaigns, had served as Chief of the Cavalry Bureau at Washington, and had commanded a cavalry division with Grant's army in Virginia and under Sheridan in the Shenandoah Valley campaign. Finally, at the end of October 1864 he had been sent by Grant to Sherman to undertake the reorganization of the cavalry of the Western armies. Being one of the youngest of Union brigadiers, both in date of commission and in years—he was barely twenty-seven years old—he had been brevetted Major General to give him sufficient rank for the command to which he was assigned.[19]

Great things were expected of Wilson in carrying out the admonition of Grant to "not let Forrest get off without punishment."[20] The new Chief of Cavalry's doctrine was that "the only power of cavalry is in a vigorous offensive; therefore I urge . . . hurling it into the bowels of the South in masses that the enemy cannot drive back as it did Sooy Smith and Sturgis."[21] It was a conception which finally, in the failing days of the Confederacy, he was able to carry out. In November 1864, however, he did not consider that his new corps was yet ready to meet "Forrest, hitherto the most successful of the rebel cavalry leaders,"[22] although he did feel able to write on November twenty-eighth that "our force is now getting to be very respectable, and if Forrest will only wait for us, we shall soon be able to cope with him."[23]

Forrest, however, did not "wait for him," at least not that time, for at dusk of that very day the Confederate columns already across the Duck began to crowd the Union cavalry north and east, away from the river and away from Columbia. At 1:00 A.M. on November twenty-ninth, in a message sent from Hurt's Cross Roads on the turnpike leading from Lewisburg to Franklin, addressed on the outside "Major General Schofield by courier from Spring Hill. Important, Trot!!!" Wilson sent the news that not only was Forrest across the Duck in full force but that pontoon bridges were being laid for the infantry to follow him—information quite accurate except for Wilson's final deduction that the rebels would move toward Franklin on the pike from Lewisburg. To Schofield he proffered the advice to "get back to Franklin without delay."[24]

The message reached Schofield, still on the north bank of Duck River facing Columbia, at 7:30 A.M. of the twenty-ninth. Already, by that time, as Schofield reported, Forrest had "forced a column of cavalry between General Wilson and me, and cut off all communication between us."[25] Having had several warnings that the Confederate cavalry was across the river and to his left and that the infantry was expected to be there, Schofield tardily decided to start two divisions of infantry, his trains and most of his artillery back along the macadamized turnpike leading to Spring Hill, twelve miles north, and thence to Franklin.[26] For the rest of that day of November 29, 1864, destined to be the critical period in Hood's campaign into Tennessee, the village of Spring Hill, so familiar to Forrest and many of his men, became the focus of operations for both armies.

That morning, before dawn, Hood's infantry began its movement. Two divisions of Stephen Lee's corps were left behind in Columbia with nearly all the Confederate artillery, under orders to keep up such a demonstration as would conceal from Schofield across the river the fact that the bulk of the army had left his front. The other two infantry corps, those of Major General Frank Cheatham and Lieutenant General Alexander P. Stewart, with the division of Major General Edward Johnson out of Lee's corps, marched to the pontoon bridge at Davis' Ford, where Forrest had crossed the day before, and thence followed the country dirt roads lying between the Lewisburg-Franklin and the Columbia-Spring Hill-Franklin turnpikes.

388

Forrest's first duty of the morning, after Buford succeeded in getting his division across the river at daybreak, was to dispose of Wilson. By attacks front and flank the Federal cavalry, in number approximately equal to Forrest's command, was driven back from Hurt's Cross Roads, where it had concentrated the night before, northward along the Lewisburg pike five miles to Mount Carmel Church. There, as Wilson noted with some seeming relief, "the enemy ceased to press upon the rear of the column." Convinced that Forrest was "aiming for Nashville via Franklin," Wilson marched the rest of the day to get across Big Harpeth, in the meanwhile sending a warning to Thomas, "You had better look out for Forrest at Nashville tomorrow noon. I'll be there before or very soon after he makes his appearance."[27] The road junction of Spring Hill did not enter into Wilson's calculations that day, so that on the critical twenty-ninth of November, Schofield was "blind," with his cavalry "pushed off toward the East, and not connecting with our infantry nor covering the pike" on which Schofield was withdrawing by way of Spring Hill, with his "left and rear," as he reported, "entirely open to the enemy's cavalry."[28]

Forrest, having accomplished his first task of taking Wilson out of the play for the day, left Ross's Texas brigade of Jackson's division to follow Wilson's column as it retired to the north. "After waiting a short time for [his] troops to close up," Forrest himself, with the rest of the command, turned to the west and marched for Spring Hill.[29]

As the head of Forrest's column neared Spring Hill from the east it met, some two miles out, enemy skirmishers behind whom Wagner's division of Stanley's Fourth Corps was coming into the town on the double-quick, "just in time to meet the enemy's advance" by taking up a position extending from the pike above the town to the pike below, in a rough semicircle about one mile out from the village itself.[30]

And so just after noon of the twenty-ninth there began that affair of lost Confederate opportunities and eyelash escapes for the Union forces which, with different fortune or better management, might have been the decisive Battle of Spring Hill.

Forrest opened the fighting of that short late November afternoon, when from a hill near the tollgate on the Rally Hill pike, about a mile and a half southeast of the town, he ordered Chalmers to send a regiment against a near-by wood thought to be occupied only by cavalry patrols. The burst of fire by which the charge was met and repulsed showed the presence of substantial infantry strength. "They was in there sure enough, wasn't they, Chalmers?" commented Forrest.[31]

In reaching Spring Hill in time to stop the march of Schofield's column, even though he could not get across the pike and actually intercept it, Forrest had performed the second part of his task for the day. To hold Schofield's advance where it was while his own force was coming in from Mount Carmel and Rally Hill, and then until the Confederate infantry should arrive for the serious work of the day, Forrest made more than one attack.

It was not until about two in the afternoon that the last of Stanley's leading division—Wagner's—quick-stepped into Spring Hill as the guns rumbled into position on a rise of ground to the southwest of the town, while the long line of wagons—800 of them altogether—still were going into park west of the town as late as four in the afternoon.[32]

The first of Forrest's troops to arrive—Frank Armstrong's brigade of Jackson's division and the Kentucky brigade and one Tennessee regiment of Buford's—charged, mounted, and were repulsed. Receiving word from General Hood to hold his position at all hazards as the head of the Confederate infantry column was but two miles away and "rapidly advancing," Forrest sent Tyree Bell's brigade, dismounted, to make an attack on the left, where the enemy was "hurriedly moving his wagon train up the Franklin pike."[33]

As Forrest's men continued the fight to keep Schofield from passing Spring Hill, the Confederate infantry came marching north from Duck River on country roads roughly parallel to the Columbia-Spring Hill pike on which Schofield was moving, and angling over toward Spring Hill from the southeast on the Rally Hill turnpike. In the lead came Cheatham's corps and in the lead of that corps the division of Major General Patrick R. Cleburne, reputed to be the best infantry division in the whole of the Western armies. Close behind Cleburne in order came the divisions of Major Generals William B. Bate and John C. Brown, good commanders both and good divisions, though not touched, perhaps, with the same martial fire that was Cleburne's. Behind Cheatham's corps came the three divisions of Stewart's corps, with Edward Johnson's division of Lee's corps closing the column. And far away, from the south, came the muffled mutter of the cannonade which Lee was keeping up successfully, to cause Schofield to remain where he was with a major part of his infantry in front of Columbia.

Rarely in the whole war was a commander to have such an opportunity as was Hood's that November afternoon, with his troops in position to close and bar the way to Schofield and to crush or capture his divisions as they came marching northward strung out along the pike. The opportunity was lost. How it was lost, and whose was the responsibility, became the subject of long and bitter controversy and of an extended literature, controversial and critical, but in its details it is no part of the story of General Forrest save as he is fitfully glimpsed through that night of contradictory orders, varying recollections and fatal misunderstandings.

A little before four o'clock in the afternoon, as Cleburne came into action with the first of the Confederate infantry and Bell's brigade was driving ahead in its attack on the Federal line, things were going well for the Confederates. Wagner's was the only Federal division on the ground, and while it had the help of most of Schofield's artillery and the Confederates were virtually without guns, it was encumbered with the care and defense of Schofield's whole wagon train. The next Union division, Kimball's, was still south of Rutherford Creek, deployed to the east in anticipation of a possible attack by Hood from that direction, while the remainder of the two corps were still at Columbia, twelve miles away.

Cleburne, directed by Hood, went into action promptly on the left of Bell's brigade, and the two commands, infantry and cavalry, pressed forward with Cleburne and Forrest, riding together with swords drawn, personally directing the movement. Bell was charging with but four rounds of ammunition to the man, after the fighting of the past two days in which Forrest's troops had far outrun their ordnance wagons. Nevertheless, Forrest reported, the advance was made "with a promptness and energy and gallantry which I have never seen excelled."[34] A Union participant in the fight says that when Cleburne took them in flank and Forrest in front the brigade gave back on the run, with the Confederates so close after them that they could be distinctly heard "calling on them with loud oaths, charging Yankee canine descent, to halt and surrender." The right of the Union line, at all events, gave back until it uncovered the Confederate attackers to a battery of not less than eight guns which opened on them with shrapnel. The pursuit halted, and a new Union line was formed.[35] The time was about 4:30, half an hour before sunset.

And then, as Cleburne was re-forming his division to press home the attack and seize the pike, began the series of contradictory orders and misunderstandings which permitted Schofield to escape through the night from a position which, despite the calm assurance with which he was to view it in after years, he regarded that night as "extremely perilous."[36] An officer of General Cheatham's staff arrived with directions to make no attack until further orders. No "further orders" came, and soon after the fall of night Cleburne went into bivouac, still in line of battle facing the pike which he had first been ordered to take.[37]

Cheatham himself, meanwhile, was back at the Rutherford Creek crossing, two and one-half miles away, hurrying his troops forward. Bate's division, second of Cheatham's divisions to come on the ground, was directed by Hood to press westward to the vital Columbia-Spring Hill pike, get on it and swing southward toward Columbia, keeping in

391

touch with Cleburne's left. As Bate's skirmish line—he was advancing in line of battle—came within 100 yards of the pike at the Nat Cheairs residence, a mile and a half south of Spring Hill, he too received an order from Cheatham to halt, and form line on Cleburne's left. Bate hesitated to obey, since the enemy was before him passing on the pike and the order would pull his line away from his goal, but the order being repeated, he fell back from his position of advantage and after some delay went into bivouac between nine and ten o'clock that night.[38]

Brown, Cheatham's third division commander, was ordered to come up and form on Cleburne's right and to join him in the attack. Arriving about sunset (five o'clock), Brown discovered that the Federal line thrown out from Spring Hill, which he was to attack, overlapped his own right by several hundred yards and that "Forrest's cavalry, which I had been assured would protect my right, had been ordered to another part of the field. . . ." Feeling that it would mean "inevitable disaster" to advance, he stood fast and reported the situation to Cheatham, who soon came upon that part of the field. Cheatham approved what he had done, as also did General Hood a little later, said Brown, adding that he was directed to hold his division ready to advance at a moment's notice on orders to that effect after the arrival of Stewart's corps, which would come up on his exposed right. But, he added, the orders to advance never came.[39]

Cheatham undoubtedly thought that he gave such orders, for he rode off to the left of his corps to insure that Bate and Cleburne should be in readiness to take up the attack from right to left when Brown started. Cleburne and Bate so understood the arrangement and both waited, according to their orders, for the attack to open on the right. Brown, having no orders to do so, did not open the attack. Nor did Stewart come into position on Brown's right, as the arrangement was, for the reason that Hood had caused him to go into line of battle below Rutherford Creek, had held him there until after sunset, had let him come on only when it was already dark and had given him no orders to attack.[40]

But none of this did Bate, Cleburne or Cheatham know as they impatiently waited for the sound of Brown's rifles going into action. Finally, after dark, Cheatham rode back toward the right of his line to see why the battle did not start. On his way he met a courier from General Hood, calling him to conference at army headquarters. There Cheatham found Stewart also, and both were informed by the army commander that "he had concluded to wait till morning" and to be "in readiness to attack at daylight."[41]

Stewart, having finally been brought across Rutherford Creek, moved up under orders, according to Hood's report, to pass beyond Cheatham's

392

corps, advance on a road angling into the pike north of Spring Hill and block Schofield's line of retreat. Once more there was contradiction of orders as to where Stewart should align himself, and it was not until eleven at night that his weary men were in position. And even then, contrary to Stewart's judgment but according to the orders he had received, his line was formed away from the all-important pike and not toward it.[42]

As Stewart was being moved around by guides in the darkness he came across Forrest, whose men had been withdrawn, after the arrival of the infantry, to feed the horses and were in bivouac. From him Stewart learned something of the lines and positions of the Confederate forces and the movements of the enemy. Not being satisfied with the confused and contradictory orders under which he was being moved about, the competent and clear-minded Stewart and Forrest rode together back to Hood's headquarters to get the situation straightened out. When Hood was told that in view of the uncertainties and contradictions in the orders which had reached him, Stewart had put his men in bivouac, "he remarked, in substance, [as Stewart reported the conversation] that it was not material; to let the men rest."

Turning to Forrest, Hood asked if he could not take over the assignment of blocking the road with his cavalry. Buford and Chalmers, Forrest answered, having already expended sixty rounds of ammunition during the day, were "without a cartridge," and the ammunition wagons were far in the rear, with the army trains at Columbia. Hood ordered the infantry corps commanders to supply ammunition for Forrest's troops but neither Cheatham nor Stewart were able to do so, their ammunition wagons being back with the trains also. W. H. Jackson's division, however, had captured some ammunition during the day and with it, Forrest said, "he would do the best he could in the emergency."[43]

While Forrest was interviewing Hood, Bate arrived at army headquarters at the Thompson house to report to the commanding general that about dark he had reached the turnpike south of Spring Hill and had "caused a cessation in the movements of wagons, horsemen, etc., which were passing," but that in consequence of Cheatham's repeated order to halt and align himself with Cleburne's left, he had not passed on to the turnpike and swept toward Columbia as previously ordered. Now—the time being, as Bate placed it, between ten and twelve at night—he was uneasy about the continued passage of Federal troops along the pike which he had been sent to block.

"It makes no difference now," General Hood replied in substance, according to Bate's recollection, "or it is all right anyhow, for General Forrest, as you see, has just left and informs me that he holds the turnpike with a position of his forces north of Spring Hill, and will stop the enemy if he tries to pass toward Franklin, and so in the morning we will have a surrender without a fight. We can sleep quiet tonight."⁴⁴

Hood's remark certainly did not accord with what Forrest had just told him, that he would "do the best he could in the emergency" by sending Jackson's men to try to get on the pike, but it is of a piece with the foggy understanding and muddled management of Confederate movements that afternoon and night.

Ross's brigade of Texans, only about 600 strong, as it returned from its assignment of following Wilson's retirement had been upon the pike earlier in the evening, near Thompson's Station, where it had burned a few wagons and captured a train on the railroad, which here runs close and roughly parallel to the pike. With his new orders, received about midnight, Jackson called up Ross's brigade again, and also the stronger brigade of Frank Armstrong, and marched four miles north to strike the passing wagon trains and troops.⁴⁵

Schofield, the Union commander, reached Spring Hill at 6:30 P.M., after "considerable skirmishing along the right of the road as he approached town." At nine o'clock, having received reports of Ross's activity on the pike to the north, Schofield moved on to Thompson's Station, cleared the passage there with Ruger's division, and returned to Spring Hill to meet Cox, bringing up the three divisions which had not left Columbia until after dark. At midnight Cox took the advance and marched on for Franklin, twelve miles farther north. The wagon trains followed on immediately, with the men marching by the side of the wagons on the broad macadamized pike. And so it was that when a "small body of rebel cavalry," as Schofield described it, "made a dash upon the train a short distance north of Thompson's Station, they succeeded in destroying a few wagons and stampeding a few cattle," and no more.⁴⁶ Ross, the only Confederate commander who made a report of this affair, told of the capture or destruction of thirty-nine wagons and a stampede of teamsters and wagon guards, with the pike held and blocked for thirty minutes, after which his men withdrew to the "hills overlooking the pike ... and saw the Yankee army in full retreat" until daylight.⁴⁷ At that hour Cox, with the head of the column, was just going into Franklin, while the rear guard under Wagner was following the last of the wagons out of Spring Hill.

This little interruption of Schofield's hurrying retreat was the sole fruit of the great Confederate opportunity of the day and the night at Spring Hill except, perhaps, for what was garnered by the enterprise of individual Confederate soldiers who, as was reported by the Union General Stanley, caught Yankee stragglers for the contents of their

knapsacks. Union soldiers who took part in that hurried, straining retreat never forgot the march in silence and darkness, knowing that the
man in front had moved only when he was discovered to be not where he
was, knowing that he had stopped only when he was bumped into, the
start, stop, wait, start again, all through the night.[48]

Hood, both in his official reports and in his memoir, *Advance and
Retreat*, blamed various of his subordinates for the failure at Spring Hill.
They in turn vigorously defended themselves either in official reports or
in subsequent papers. On the Federal side there has been an almost
equally vigorous controversy not so much about the one affair at Spring
Hill as the conception and execution of the whole campaign, with Schofield critical of his superior, Thomas, and Stanley even more critical of
Schofield, and various subordinate officers lining up in one or another of
the camps.[49]

Out of it all the thing that stands out about Spring Hill is the opportunity that was Hood's. There were three things he might have done
during the few hours after sunset of November twenty-ninth, any one
of which probably would have wrecked Schofield's command, at the time
the largest and most experienced body of Federal troops west of the
Appalachians. He might have attacked Spring Hill directly; he might
have cut the pike below Spring Hill with Cheatham's corps; he might
have cut it above with Stewart's, in any case using part of his troops to
strike Schofield's extended marching columns in flank. He made a start
toward trying each one of the three possibilities, pressed none of them
home, did nothing effective, although he was on the field throughout the
evening and in personal charge of operations. As A. P. Stewart, who
was not one of those blamed by Hood, wrote, "The failure at Spring
Hill was General Hood's fault. . . . The remedy was entirely in his own
hands."[50]

Poor brave, devoted Hood was cast in a part beyond his capacity. He
was suffering from the disabling of an arm and the loss of a leg by battle
wounds, and no doubt was mentally worn and impaired by his physical
state. Neither his contemporary reports nor his subsequent memoir show
that he had a grasp of the situation with which he was dealing, while
the memoir shows frequent lapses of memory or recollection of things
which could not have happened as described. The book is less a history
of the campaign in Tennessee than a pathetic attempt at self-justification
by laying the blame for failures upon others, and even upon the army
as a whole. The Army of Tennessee, in his opinion, had developed such
a defensive psychology during the long retreat in Georgia under Joseph
E. Johnston that even "after a forward march of 180 miles, [it] was still
seemingly unwilling to accept battle unless under the protection of

breastworks,"[51] though how, after the events of the day following the failure at Spring Hill, he could ever again have believed that his army could not be brought to an aggressive fight is beyond imagination.

On that day, November 30, 1864, the Confederate infantry, which had lain still through the night and listened to the escaping enemy hurrying by on the pike, was hurled against an enemy ready and entrenched at Franklin, in charges as desperate, as devoted in their valor and as fruitless in their results as ever have been made by men. Franklin has been called "the Balaklava of America,"[52] but the name is inadequate in its suggestion of similarity to the charge of the Six Hundred, and appropriate only in its suggestion that in Tennessee, as in the Crimea, "someone had blundered."

All through the morning of the thirtieth Schofield's forces were streaming up the pike toward Franklin and, as they arrived, turning in to strengthen and improve the old entrenchments there, stretching across the neck of the loop of the Big Harpeth River in which the little town lay. All through the morning, too, the Confederates came marching north, with the main column on the direct pike from Spring Hill, Stewart's corps in the lead, followed by Cheatham's and in turn by Stephen Lee's, which had to march all the way from Columbia. The artillery, all but two batteries, was coming up from Columbia with Lee.

Having supplied Buford and Chalmers with ammunition borrowed from Walthall's division of infantry, Forrest moved at daylight into his usual place in the front and on the flanks of the march, covering the three pikes which converged from the south into Franklin—Chalmers to the west on the Carter's Creek Pike, Buford's Kentucky brigade to the east on the Lewisburg pike, Forrest himself with Jackson's division and Bell's brigade of Buford's on the pike directly north from Spring Hill, upon which Schofield had retreated.[53]

"Forrest's reputation as a 'raider' was so great that it was apt to be assumed on the national side that he never confined himself to the strictly auxiliary work of a cavalry column accompanying an army," the Federal Major General Jacob D. Cox wrote afterward.[54] In this instance Wilson made this very miscalculation, assuming that Forrest was starting on an independent "raid" to Nashville and placing the Union cavalry on the night of the twenty-ninth and morning of the thirtieth with reference to meeting such a raid.[55] But, as General Cox noted, "in this campaign, both on the advance and the retreat, Forrest proved that he could cover the movements of the infantry as brilliantly as he performed his independent raids. He had admirably assisted Hood as a flanking force all day on Tuesday, and now on Wednesday the thirtieth . . . he opened the way for the infantry, harassing our rear

396

guard, and making dashes at the trains, sticking closely to his work of helping Hood forward, and with no thought of distant expeditions."

Halfway from Spring Hill to Franklin, Forrest's troops overtook the rear of Schofield's retreating forces and pressed them on to Winstead's Hill three miles beyond, where the Federals were found to be strongly posted. As soon as Stewart's infantry column came up, about two in the afternoon, the Federal rear guard left its positions at Winstead's Hill and fell back across the open plain to the line of entrenchments about Franklin, two miles beyond. By that hour Schofield already had passed most of his wagon train across the Harpeth, using the railroad bridge planked over and an improvised footbridge, and had arranged that all the troops should be brought across after sundown, if in the meantime Hood did not attack—which no one on the Union side really expected him to do.[56] Schofield's real points of anxiety were his bridges across the Harpeth, and the fear that Forrest would cross the river above the town (east) and cut in between him and Nashville. "I have no doubt Forrest will be in my rear tomorrow, or doing some greater mischief," Schofield telegraphed Thomas at 3:00 P.M.[57]

And that, indeed, is what Forrest would have attempted had he had his way. Upon Hood's arrival at Winstead's Hill about 1:00 P.M., Forrest pointed out to him the strength of the Federal position at Franklin—entrenchments from river above to river below the town, well furnished with artillery, and the whole commanded by Fort Granger on an eminence across the river north of the town. Worse still, these entrenchments could be come at only by an advance for nearly two miles across an open, unsheltered, slightly rolling plain. Curving into the lovely pastoral scene from the east was the thread of the Harpeth which, as Forrest knew, could be forded at places above the town.

"Give me one strong division of infantry with my cavalry," he said to General Hood, "and within two hours' time I can flank the Federals from their works."[58]

But Hood, in his chagrin and disappointment at the miscarriage of his well-laid plans at Spring Hill, could not see the realities of the situation. Schofield, he believed, was in full retreat and, as Hood said to Cheatham who likewise advised against a frontal attack, he preferred to bring him to a fight at Franklin, where the Union troops had had but a few hours to fortify rather "than to strike them at Nashville where they have been strengthening themselves for three years."[59]

At Spring Hill, where there should have been attack in full force and vigor, there was none. At Franklin, where there should have been a flanking movement, the commanding General was fixed in his determination to make a direct frontal assault which, after the most desperate, the bloodiest fighting of the whole war, for the numbers engaged and the time it lasted, was to secure no more than could have been accomplished in the same time by the flanking attack which Forrest was not permitted to make.

As the infantry came up and began to deploy on the plain at the northern foot of Winstead's Hill, Forrest moved Buford and Jackson out to the right to make room for the infantry and to close the gap between its line and the river. Chalmers and Biffle, who had come up on the Carter's Creek Pike, were assigned to like duty on the left—so that Forrest's cavalry force, none too large at best, was divided. Wilson, on the other hand, had almost his entire force, which with the reinforcements he had received by this time considerably outnumbered Forrest's total, held together on the north side of the Harpeth in position to cover Schofield's left flank.

As the Confederate infantry moved up into assaulting position Buford's cavalry, dismounted, went forward with them "in line of battle on the right of Stewart's corps, covering the ground from the Lewisburg Pike to the Harpeth River." Jackson's division, still mounted, crossed the river at Hughes' Ford, three miles above Franklin, and sought out the enemy. It was a gallant fight on both sides, but a hopeless fight for the Confederates, outnumbered at least two to one and short of ammunition besides. Nevertheless, even though he could not do what Forrest would have attempted with his whole force, Jackson held on north of the river until dark.[60]

Schofield's anxiety as to events on his left flank is reflected in his report of the battle:

"A short time before the infantry attack commenced the enemy's cavalry forced a crossing about three miles above Franklin, and drove back our cavalry, for a time seriously threatening our trains, which were accumulating on the north bank, and moving toward Nashville. I sent General Wilson orders, which he had, however, anticipated, to drive the enemy back at all hazards, and moved a brigade of General Wood's division to support him, if necessary. At the moment of the first decisive repulse of the enemy's infantry I received the most gratifying intelligence that General Wilson had driven the rebel cavalry back across the river. This rendered my immediate left and rear secure for the time being."[61]

All this, the result of the work of but one of Forrest's three cavalry divisions, indicates what might have been accomplished had he been allowed to attempt his full plan for a flanking movement. The rest of Forrest's cavalry, however, formed the two ends of the infantry line which, in the failing light of the late afternoon of a short November day, was sent to slaughter at Franklin.

The main battle at Franklin was fought by Stewart's corps and that of Cheatham, with a subsequent attack by Johnson's division of Lee's corps. The rest of Lee's troops, with all but two batteries of the artillery, came up after their long march from Columbia too late to be engaged. Forrest's dismounted cavalry, Chalmers on the left and Buford on the right, did their work, and did it well, but the configuration of the ground and the trace of the Federal defenses was such that they were not called upon to go forward into hand-to-hand fighting at the cannon's mouth.

The story of the two hours' fight at Franklin, just before and just after dark, is not part of the story of Forrest, except as it affected the Army of Tennessee of which he and his men were a part. That story may be summed up as one of sickening losses, both among the men and the leaders. So many of the division and brigade commanders were killed or wounded that the Confederate reports of Franklin are incomplete, but it is known that out of fewer than 16,000 men in the two corps which carried the brunt of the attack, the loss in killed and wounded—most of it suffered within two hours time and a few hundred yards either way from the center of the Union line at the Carter House—was approximately 6,000.

The charge at Franklin had in it all the elements of mass grandeur and high individual heroism. There was no artillery preparation, for the guns had not come up from Columbia. The advance, in line of battle with the flags of corps, divisions, brigades and regiments bravely fluttering, was made over two miles of open country, exposed for almost every foot of the way to artillery, and later to rifle fire from the protection of prepared positions. And still they came on, steadily and without wavering, to make, just before sunset, the final rush at the Union entrenchments. And into the trenches they went, to be met by valiant countercharge, but there they stayed—the dead, the wounded, a few of the living fighting on—while the ground outside the works was covered with the dead and wounded, and with the living, holding on in the darkness and firing at the flashes of the enemy's guns on the parapets.[62]

Among the dead was Patrick Cleburne, idol of his division, and Brigadier General Hiram B. Granbury, commanding one of his brigades. Four regimental commanders in the division were killed, three were wounded, six were missing. John C. Brown, another of Cheatham's division commanders, was wounded. In his division Brigadier Generals Otho F. Strahl and States Rights Gist were dead; a third, John C. Carter, was mortally wounded; the fourth, George W. Gordon, was captured; while losses among the regimental commanders of the division were one killed and four wounded. In Walthall's division Brigadier General William A. Quarles was wounded, one regimental commander killed, eight wounded and one missing. In French's division the losses included Brigadier General F. M. Cockrell, wounded, three regimental commanders killed and four wounded. Loring's losses included Brigadier General John Adams, killed, Brigadier General T. M. Scott, wounded, one regimental commander killed and six wounded. Edward Johnson's division lost Brigadier General A. M. Manigault, wounded, and two regimental commanders killed, seven wounded, and one missing. Bate's division, which was less heavily engaged, nevertheless lost one regimental commander, killed, and two wounded. Clayton's and Stevenson's divisions were not engaged.

Total losses in the leadership of the Army of Tennessee in the Battle of Franklin in killed, wounded, missing and captured included two major generals commanding divisions, ten brigadier generals and fifty-four regimental commanders.[63]

To such a loss of leaders there was added the loss in men killed—1,750 out of the small force, killed in that short time. That was more men than Grant had killed in the two days' fighting at Shiloh, more than Burnside lost in the great Federal slaughter at Fredericksburg, more than McClellan lost in the Seven Days' Battle or Hooker at Chancellorsville, more than Rosecrans at Stones River, more even than his dead at Chickamauga, almost as many as Grant had killed at Cold Harbor—all of them "full dress" battles in which large Union armies fought from one to three days, or in one case even longer.[64]

Toward midnight the fitful fighting which had been going on in the dark all evening died down, as Schofield resumed his retreat with another night march, this time for the Union base of Nashville, eighteen miles away. The line of trenches, with the dead and wounded, were left to Confederate possession, though General Hood did not know it until next morning, when he was preparing to resume his battle.[65] If possession of the field be the test of victory, General Hood had won his battle—but he had wrecked his army through its losses in men, its losses in leadership and its loss of confidence in its commander.

CHAPTER XXV

THE REAR GUARD OF RETREAT FROM TENNESSEE*

December 1, 1864-December 28, 1864

FROM the failure at Spring Hill and the slaughter at Franklin the Army of Tennessee marched to predestined disaster at Nashville.

"Today," runs the entry in the war diary of Cheatham's corps for the day after the Battle of Franklin, "spent in burying the dead, caring for the wounded and reorganizing the remains of our corps."[1] Forrest's cavalry, however, having suffered no such crushing and disorganizing losses, was up and away at daylight. Buford and Jackson crossed the Harpeth east of Franklin, Chalmers to the west, and both columns pressed forward to converge at Brentwood, a spot familiar to Forrest, where it was hoped that Schofield's march might be interfered with, if not interrupted. Wilson's cavalry covered the retreat, however, without real difficulty, although at one or two places there was what General Hatch described as "severe fighting," involving the use of Morton's guns which had been brought to the front. By noon of December first, however, Schofield's infantry was marching into the safety of the works about Nashville.[2]

The Confederate cavalry, following close behind, encamped that night within sight of the tower of the State Capitol in Nashville, in a line extending from the Nolensville Pike on the right to the Granny White Pike on the left, while Lee's corps, the advance of Hood's infantry, which had marched from Franklin during the afternoon, was camped farther south.[3]

There probably was no city in America, with the exception of the capital cities of Washington and Richmond, more strongly fortified than was Nashville in 1864. The line of Union works, carefully laid out and heavily constructed, followed commanding hills looking down on the southern face to the valley of Brown's Creek, which flows into the Cumberland above the city, and on the west into the valley of Richland Creek and its tributaries, flowing into the river below the city. The whole bend of the Cumberland within which the city of 1864 lay was thus completely enclosed.[4]

To hold these works there were the lesser garrisons, which had been

---

* The field of operations covered in this chapter is shown on the map on page 346.

concentrated at Nashville by rail from points as far away as Decatur, Alabama, while Hood was marching up from Florence; the quartermaster and commissary troops and employees, drilled, armed and organized into a division, and another division of convalescents, suitable for holding positions in the strong inner line of entrenchments; new recruit regiments coming in by rail from the north; the 10,000 veterans of the Sixteenth Army Corps whom Andrew Jackson Smith had unloaded from the long rank of steamboats at the wharf on November thirtieth, and Steedman's 5,000 troops who came in by rail from Chattanooga on the following day—the same day on which Schofield and Wilson marched in from Franklin with two corps of infantry and the cavalry corps. Major General George H. Thomas, commanding for the Union at Nashville, thus had available for its defense not less than 60,000 men and more coming.[5]

Hood, pursuing some vague shred of illusory hope, undertook to besiege a fortified city so garrisoned with a force which, after Franklin, numbered fewer than 30,000 men of all arms. And then, to make his situation still more impossible, he detached Bate's division of infantry and Forrest and most of his cavalry to go against Murfreesborough, reported to be held by 8,000 Union troops under Major General Lovell Rousseau.[6] With not more than 23,000 men remaining, Hood sat down along the hills south of Brown's Creek within three miles of Nashville with a line which, as was well said, looked "more like the skirmish line of an investing army than of that army itself."[7] The main infantry line, extending only from the Murfreesborough Pike on the east to the Hillsboro Pike on the west, was lightly fortified, taking advantage of the stone walls so common in that section, with the addition of small detached and enclosed earthworks at critical points. The long stretch between the western end of the infantry line at the Hillsboro Pike and the Cumberland River below the town was covered by Chalmers' division of the cavalry.[8]

While Forrest, with Buford's and Jackson's divisions and Bate's infantry, was away at Murfreesborough on what proved to be a pointless and fruitless division of forces, Colonel Kelley with the Old Regiment and four guns set up a blockade of the Cumberland at Bell's Mills, six miles below Nashville by land and eighteen miles by river. On the afternoon of December third the transports *Prairie State* and *Prima Donna* were captured, with 56 prisoners and 197 horses and mules. Before the boats were completely unloaded of their cargo of forage and other supplies, the ironclad gunboat *Carondelet* and the tinclads *Fairplay*, *Moose*, *Reindeer* and *Silver Lake* came down from Nashville and retook the transports in a midnight battle but failed to drive off Kelley and his guns or to raise the blockade of the river. The blockade was made complete, in fact, by Federal orders forbidding steamers going down the river from Nashville or coming up above Clarksville. Two days later, on December sixth, another attempt was made to raise Kelley's blockade, with the ironclad *Neosho* leading the attack, but without success. On the seventh Rear Admiral Samuel P. Lee, commanding the Union naval operations in the Mississippi Valley, came as far up as Clarksville with the ironclad *Cincinnati*, but could come no farther in that heavy-draft vessel because of the stage of water on the Harpeth Shoals. And there the situation on the river rested with Kelley, who had taken part in Forrest's first fight with gunboats on the Cumberland back in 1861, and had shown such aptitude for fighting them on the Tennessee, maintaining his blockade until the very day of the opening of the Battle of Nashville.[9]

While one of Forrest's divisions was blockading the river approach to Nashville from the north, Buford's and Jackson's divisions were started southeast along the Chattanooga Railroad toward Murfreesborough on the afternoon of December second, destroying blockhouses and bridges as they went. Previously Bate's division of infantry had been sent by General Hood to undertake a like work of destruction closer to Murfreesborough. On December fifth the two commands joined four miles south of La Vergne, between them having taken and destroyed seven blockhouses—in all cases but one making the garrison prisoners—burned bridges and torn up track. With Forrest in command the combined forces advanced southward against Rousseau at Murfreesborough, whose defeat, they were informed, was regarded by Hood as "of the first importance."[10]

Since the great battle there earlier in the war, Murfreesborough had been continually and heavily garrisoned by Union forces, who during a period of two years had constructed to the north and west of the town, covering the Nashville railroad and both banks of Stones River, an extensive and most formidable group of earthworks, Fortress Rosecrans, enclosing 200 acres and mounting 57 guns.[11] On December sixth Forrest made a strong reconnaissance of this position, from which he was forced to the conclusion that so formidable a work with a garrison which largely outnumbered his own forces could not be attacked directly with any hope of success. Two small infantry brigades, Sears's and Palmer's, totaling about 1,600 men, arrived that evening to bring Forrest's total force up to about 6,500 men.

While Forrest had no intention of assaulting Rousseau in his works, he was not averse to fighting him outside. When, therefore, on the morning of December seventh, he discovered a column of the enemy—it was two brigades and six guns, 3,325 men in all, under command of Major

General R. H. Milroy—moving out of Fortress Rosecrans with intent "to make battle," Forrest lined up his troops to accommodate him.[12] The infantry, about equal in number to the Union troops, were to receive the attack while the Confederate cavalry, as planned, was to strike in on Milroy's flanks with intent to cut him off from retreat to the fortress.[13] In the meanwhile a detachment under Buford, with Morton's battery, had been sent around the town to come into Murfreesborough from the east—on the same Woodbury road, incidentally, by which Forrest had entered the town on his first raid there in 1862.

In the fighting of December 7, 1864, Forrest's command occupied some of the same ground held by the Union forces in the great Battle of Stones River while the Union forces were on ground then held by the Confederates. The fight, therefore, was over the same fields and rocky cedar glades where 100,000 men had battled for three days, over ground still littered with the wreckage of that struggle and with, here and there, the gleam of white bones protruding from some imperfect grave washed by the rains of two years.[14]

"The enemy moved boldly forward," Forrest reported, "driving in my pickets, when the infantry, with the exception of [Tom Benton] Smith's brigade, from some cause which I cannot explain, made a shameful retreat, losing two pieces of artillery." Bate, in charge of the infantry, offers the explanation that the attacking column which had passed from view in a wood and was supposed to have been retiring to the fortress, came upon the infantry suddenly and at close range; that the cavalry had given no information of the advance, which struck the left of the infantry line as it was being shifted leftward under Forrest's orders, with gaps between some of the brigades during the movement; and that the cavalry on that flank fell back "with but slight resistance." In fact, Bate added, "if the cavalry on either flank was seriously engaged, I was not aware of it."[15]

But whatever the reason, there is no doubt that the left of the Confederate infantry line broke and fled. "I seized the colors of the retreating troops and endeavored to rally them," Forrest wrote, "but they could not be moved by any entreaty or appeal to their patriotism. Major General Bate did the same thing but was equally as unsuccessful as myself."[16]

Forrest, as he is remembered that day by one of his soldiers, rode among the panicky men, calling on them to halt and form, mixing appeals and curses, laying about him with the flat of his sword. Even King Philip, whom he rode that day, seemed fired with the spirit of his master who, with his six feet and two inches of height raised in the stirrups of his great war horse, seemed little less than gigantic. Men flying to the rear

404

dodged and scurried to get by out of reach of the General and his sword—"right comical, if it hadn't been so serious," was the comment here—until finally one flying color-bearer passed near enough for Old Bedford to seize the flag, the staff of which he used as a bludgeon to strike at soldiers beyond the reach of his sword. Finally, in his exasperated fury, he hurled the flag, staff and all, at a man running by just beyond his reach.[17]

But Forrest was doing more than appealing to or bludgeoning panic-stricken soldiers. Through Major Strange, his adjutant, he sent word to the two brigades of Jackson's cavalry division—Armstrong's and Ross's—that everything depended upon the promptness and vigor with which they acted. "They proved themselves equal to the emergency by charging on the enemy, thereby checking his farther advance," Forrest reported.[18]

There was another reason also for the return of Milroy's forces to Fortress Rosecrans without further pursuit—a raid by Buford at this juncture into the town of Murfreesborough, pressed quite to the center of the town, with Morton's guns firing on the Union garrison in the courthouse itself. Vigorous countermeasures ordered by Rousseau, however, resulted in killing Morton's battery horses, but the Confederate guns and caissons, with the harness stripped from the horses killed, were successfully brought off by hand.[19]

On December ninth Bate's division was recalled to Nashville to take position in Cheatham's line, and was replaced in Forrest's detachment by A. J. Smith's brigade under the command of Colonel Charles H. Olmstead. During another week Rousseau remained in his fortified position, while Forrest's command foraged the country, completed the destruction of the railroad between La Vergne and Murfreesborough, and captured and burned a train of seventeen cars bringing 60,000 rations into Murfreesborough from the south, taking 200 prisoners.[20] Buford, meanwhile, on December eleventh was sent to the Hermitage neighborhood to picket the Cumberland River to prevent any flank movement from that direction.[21]

And all this while, for two weeks, Hood stayed on in front of Thomas' growing force hoping, as he wrote afterward, for reinforcements from the Trans-Mississippi and anticipating that Thomas would be forced to take the offensive against him. "Should he attack me in position I felt that I could defeat him, and thus gain possession of Nashville with abundant supplies for the army," Hood reported. "This would give me possession of Tennessee."[22] Such reasoning sounds like rationalization of the unhappy fact that there was nothing else for Hood to do. He had talked of a campaign north of the Cumberland into Kentucky, and even, in more expansive mood, on clear across the Alleghenies to reinforce Lee in Virginia. But at Nashville, with the winter on him, with his tenuous line of supply back to the Tennessee River, with the Cumberland patrolled as far up as Carthage by a fleet of a dozen gunboats to prevent his crossing the river, Hood seems to have given up the idea of going forward, while he felt that he could not, and would not, go backward, certainly not without a battle.

At Washington, however, and at City Point in Virginia where Grant had his headquarters, and in the Northern newspapers, none of these things was known or appreciated. The mere presence of Hood's army before Nashville and his apparent intent to stay there, if not to cross the Cumberland and break for the Ohio, excited the gravest apprehension. Stout Thomas, capable and imperturbable, was going about his business of organizing, arming and equipping the considerable number of poorly trained men transferred to him in emergency from the subsistence and other noncombat departments. Of greater importance, by far, he and Wilson were creating such a body of cavalry as had not been seen before on the Union side in the West—"a cavalry force," as Thomas reported to Grant, "sufficient to contend with Forrest."[23]

Thomas knew what the authorities at Washington and the Northern public did not seem to realize, that as the strength of his well-fed forces in their comfortable quarters in Nashville grew, the ragged, half-shod, half-equipped force of Hood, shivering and freezing on the hills beyond Brown's Creek, was losing strength daily. He was not going to be hurried into a fight until he had done all that he could do to insure its success—despite faultfinding, scolding, nagging telegrams from President Lincoln, Secretary Stanton, Major General Halleck and, most of all, Grant.

By December ninth he was almost ready, although Wilson had not yet completed the mounting and strengthening of the cavalry corps assembled at Edgefield, north of the Cumberland. His plan then was to advance against Hood on the eleventh, when he received warning that dissatisfaction with his delay in attacking Hood was such that unless there were an immediate attack he might be relieved of his command.

On that morning, December ninth, there began in the country about Nashville a "terrible storm of freezing rain," which by evening had covered the whole countryside with a sheet of ice. Thomas patiently explained to the impatient Grant that until the storm should end—it was to last four days—and there should be a thaw, military movements were simply impossible. The attack, said he, would be made after the storm, but if in the meanwhile the commander-in-chief wished to remove him from command he would "submit without a murmur." Thomas, in fine, had that moral courage which put the lives of his soldiers and the success of his cause above his personal glory or career. He had done all that he could, as quickly as he could, and he would not be stampeded into fighting until he could do so under the best possible conditions.

Grant relented rather ungraciously, while Thomas, and especially Wilson with the cavalry corps, completed their preparations. Before the thaw had set in, however, Grant's impatience again got the better of his military judgment. Orders were issued, though fortunately for the Union army not delivered, to put Schofield in command over Thomas, other orders were issued to put John A. Logan in command and Logan was sent to Nashville, and finally Grant himself started.[24] Amid all this fury of anxiety and impatience, Thomas went ahead with his preparations, the weather changed and, on the morning of December 15, 1864, the Union army, ready for its work, moved out against Hood.

The Army of Tennessee was aligned facing north, with Cheatham's corps on the right, beginning at Rains' Cut on the railroad to Chattanooga, Lee's corps in the center astride the Franklin Pike, Stewart's corps on the left, crossing the Granny White and extending to the Hillsboro Pike where its position ended in a line of detached redoubts facing west. From this point to the river, a distance of five miles in a direct line, there were no entrenchments and no troops other than Ector's infantry brigade posted along the Harding Pike and Chalmers' cavalry farther to the left along the Charlotte Pike and the river.

Thomas' plan called for a direct advance south against the infantry line but the main maneuver was to be a great wheel to the left through the wide gap between the end of the Confederate prepared positions and the Cumberland River. The outer wing of this wheel, with the longest distance to go, was Wilson's cavalry—now numbering 9,000 men mounted and 3,000 for whom no mounts had yet been secured.

The attack on the Confederate left, held by the cavalry, was begun in a dense early morning fog by the gunboats, shelling Kelley's battery on the riverbank. It was followed up by the advance of Johnson's Union cavalry division, which Chalmers and Rucker successfully held off until they learned that the little brigade of infantry on the Harding Pike, to their right, had been driven away and that the enemy was already beyond Belle Meade, and so two miles in their rear. Chalmers, thus cut off from communication with the main army, gathered his forces, broke off contact with the troops in his front and, on his own motion, set out on a wide swing to the rear and right to regain touch with the rest of Hood's command.[25]

During this day of December fifteenth the Confederate right under

Cheatham held its own and Lee's center was not seriously engaged, but the left, under Stewart, on which were concentrated the weight of front and flank attacks by a force which considerably exceeded in strength the whole of Hood's army, was driven back from the Hillsboro Pike to the Granny White, and there pushed back southward for a mile or more. During the night, while Chalmers and Rucker still were on their wide swinging march to rejoin the Confederate left flank, Hood rearranged and shortened his lines. The whole line was drawn back from the valley of Brown's Creek to a new position just north of the Brentwood Hills, a knobby ridge rising from 500 to 600 feet above the surrounding country. Cheatham was switched from right to left during the night, leaving Lee's corps covering the Franklin Pike as the right of the new line, with Stewart's corps as the center and Cheatham's disposed across and along the Granny White Pike as the left. Chalmers, coming up before daylight, joined the left wing, extending the line to the Hillsboro Pike some miles south of the position held by the Confederates the day before.[26]

It was not until noon that the skirmishers of the Federal infantry had re-established contact with the new Confederate line, averaging about two miles south of the line held the day before. Then, with the new position developed, Thomas resumed his attack. Two divisions of Union cavalry drove Chalmers' force off the Hillsboro Pike and back through the hills across the Granny White toward Brentwood, while there was increasing pressure by both infantry and dismounted cavalry against the Confederate infantry positions.

Disaster came about four o'clock in the afternoon of December sixteenth, when overwhelming force, front and flank, poured through and over the position held by T. B. Smith's brigade of Bate's division—a weak salient in the line where it bent back along the Granny White Pike, where Lieutenant Colonel William Shy, commanding a consolidation of the Twentieth, Thirty-seventh, Tenth and Second Tennessee regiments, died fighting, to leave his name to Shy's Hill.[27]

From Hood's position there were but three roads passing through the high, rugged Brentwood Hills to the south, the Franklin and the Granny White Pikes and a country road angling through the hills between them. These were the ways for the inevitable Confederate retreat—if, indeed, a way could be kept open for retreat. Lee's corps, which had been less heavily engaged than the other flank of the line, covered the Franklin Pike. To Chalmers and Rucker, driven back earlier in the afternoon, went an agonized message from Hood at 4:30 P.M. to "hold the Granny White pike at all hazards."[28] A copy of the message was captured by the victorious and elated Union troopers but Chalmers received the message and, with Rucker, returned to the Granny White Pike. At the early dark of a rainy, misty December afternoon, they began to throw up rail barricades, but before the work could be completed, Hatch's and Johnson's divisions of Wilson's cavalry were upon Rucker and his men. In the melee Rucker, conspicuous on a white horse in the darkness, engaged in a saber fight with Colonel George Spalding of the Twelfth Tennessee (Union) Cavalry and Captain Joseph C. Boyer of the same regiment. In the fight, in some fashion, Rucker lost his saber but took one from one of his antagonists, and continued the fight with the exchanged weapon. Finally, when a chance pistol shot broke his arm, he was compelled to yield.[29]

While Confederate commands were fighting to hold open the roads to the rear, the army as a whole gave way in the only rout of a major Confederate force during the entire war—"flying to the rear in wildest confusion," as Stephen Lee put it in his report.[30] "The men then, one by one, climbed over the rugged hills in our rear," Major General Bate reported, "and passed down a short valley which debouched into the Franklin turnpike. The whole army on this thoroughfare seemed to be one heterogeneous mass, moving back without organization or government. Strenuous efforts were made by officers of all grades to rally and form line of battle, but in vain. The disorganized masses swept in confusion down the Franklin turnpike, amid the approaching darkness and drenching rain, until beyond Brentwood, when the fragments of commands were, in some measure, united, and bivouacked in groups for the night."[31]

The night before, Wilson had advised Thomas on the basis of prisoners' reports that Forrest "was at Murfreesborough." It was not until the close of the fighting of the second day, however, that he became convinced that Forrest was not with Hood, through noting that all stragglers picked up and examined during the two days had been from Chalmers' cavalry or Hood's infantry and none from the cavalry of Buford or Jackson. "Besides," Wilson wrote, "nothing was seen of the redoubtable Forrest himself. He was not on the field or we should certainly have known it before. . . . While it cannot be said with certainty that, had Forrest been present with his force united with that of Chalmers on the left of Hood's line he would have been able to hold it, it may well be claimed that he could have made a better and more stubborn defense than was made by Chalmers and Ector alone. . . . We should doubtless have broken through, but with Forrest also resisting us we should have had much more difficult work and could hardly have pushed our turning movement far enough to reach, drive back, and take in reverse Hood's main line of defense for a mile and a half as we did."[32]

409

Since this turning movement of Wilson's which put him into the rear of Hood's line, more than any other one thing, caused the break and rout of the Army of Tennessee, the diversion of Forrest's force to Murfreesborough was not only futile but in the end frightfully costly to Hood's army.

As the wounded Rucker was captured, at the close of the fighting of the sixteenth, he was taken before Brigadier General Edward Hatch, whom he promptly informed that "Forrest has just arrived with all the cavalry, and will give you hell tonight. Mark what I tell you."[33] Just then, one of Rucker's regiments, the Seventh Alabama, which included a cadet company from the University at Tuscaloosa, made a flank attack in the darkness and drove Hatch's men back along the Granny White Pike. The conjunction of Rucker's remark and the renewed attack, the Confederates believed, influenced Wilson in halting pursuit for the night. There were great opportunities for pursuing cavalry then, but also unknown risks and, more important still, a vast weariness of men and of animals which could not be denied. "Night having closed in the enemy was enabled to make his escape," Wilson reported. "The pursuit was necessarily discontinued, men and horses being worn out and hungry."[34]

Chalmers' cavalry, to which was joined Biffle, who had crossed the rear of the retreating infantry from the right of the army where he had been posted during the two-days' battle, encamped with the rear guard forming on the Franklin Pike. Lieutenant Colonel Raleigh White of the Fourteenth Tennessee, senior remaining officer of Rucker's brigade, was left on picket to watch the Federal cavalry on the left. And so the rest of the dreadful night was passed, with the two lines of picket fires in sight of each other.[35]

Forrest was not at hand, as Rucker had claimed to his captors, but neither had he been "killed certainly at Murfreesborough," as Schofield had that day advised Thomas on the basis of reports of citizens, or as Rousseau reported.[36] He was on his way. Word that the Battle of Nashville had begun reached him in his camp before Murfreesborough late in the afternoon of December fifteenth. By nine o'clock that night he had issued orders for the concentration of his command at daylight of the sixteenth.[37] On that day he had his entire command, except Buford who was away to the north picketing the Cumberland River, on the Wilkinson turnpike six miles from Murfreesborough, ready to march. That night, with further news from Nashville, he sent word to Buford to move south by way of La Vergne so as to reach the pike from Nashville south to Franklin and Columbia, "for the purpose of protecting the rear of General Hood's retreating army." Forrest's own orders

410

from Hood were to retreat by way of Shelbyville and Pulaski. On his own initiative he changed them, sending Armstrong's brigade to join the rear guard of the army and moving himself, with the rest of the cavalry, with the infantry under his command, with his sick and wounded, with 400 prisoners, with his wagon trains and a great drove of cattle and hogs which he had collected, to intercept the main army at its crossing of Duck River, thirty miles north of Pulaski.[38]

During the night of the sixteenth a firm rear guard was formed under command of Lieutenant General Lee at Hollowtree Gap, four miles south of Brentwood. At daylight of the seventeenth the Federal cavalry resumed a "most vigorous pursuit, charging at every opportunity and in the most daring manner," Lee reported. But as Wilson wrote, "Chalmers made a gallant stand and compelled us to develop a full front, thus gaining precious time."[39] Delay was all that could be gained, but delay was precious, enabling the rear guard to reach Franklin and get across the Harpeth. There Abe Buford and his Kentuckians reported, and were added to Chalmers' cavalry command to help fend off the pressing pursuit. A stand was made below Franklin at the crossing of the West Harpeth from which, after hard fighting, the rear guard was flanked out. In one of the desperate cavalry melees on the flanks Buford found himself engaged with three Union horsemen. One he shot, the second he clubbed with his empty pistol, the third he grabbed by the hair and dragged from his saddle, indicative of the desperate, hand-to-hand fighting required to hold off the determined pursuit of Wilson's troopers.[40]

But days are short in December and dark comes early for pursuers and pursued. That night the Confederates camped between Thompson's Station and Spring Hill, with bitter memories of the opportunities lost there two weeks before. There Stephen Lee, who had been wounded early in the afternoon, turned over command of the rear guard to Major General Carter L. Stevenson.[41]

"The enemy, having nothing to cook, lit out by daylight" of the eighteenth, Wilson wrote. That day the Confederates fell back across Rutherford Creek, bankfull and unfordable, destroying the bridge on which they had crossed. That day also Armstrong's brigade of cavalry, sent ahead by Forrest from Murfreesborough, joined, with news that Forrest was close behind, while Lee's corps was replaced by Cheatham's as the rear guard. "The enemy did not press us, and we had no fighting beyond a little skirmishing," was Chalmers' report of the day. The fact was that Wilson, having outrun his supplies and being in a country which armies passing and repassing had "eaten out," was compelled to wait for rations to come up.[42]

411

On this same day, the eighteenth, in a message curiously compounded of congratulations and "lecturing," Grant announced to Thomas that "the armies operating against Richmond have fired 200 guns in honor of your great victory," but showed his anxiety by the admonition, "In all your operations we hear nothing of Forrest. Great precautions should be taken to prevent him crossing the Cumberland or Tennessee below Eastport."[43] Forrest, however, was not thinking of any such raiding operation. He was making his way to Columbia, where he arrived that afternoon, still hanging onto his prisoners, his wagons and his droves of cattle and hogs. At nightfall of the following day, December nineteenth, the Confederate force was withdrawn south of Duck River, running bankfull with the waters from the chill rains and melted sleet and snow of a December forever memorable in Tennessee.[44] All bridges for miles up and down the stream, meanwhile, had been effectually destroyed.

"After the fight at Nashville" it had been General Hood's hope "to be able to remain in Tennessee, on the line of Duck River" for the winter.[45] After getting to Columbia, however, Hood realized, as he had not before, that his defeat had been so crushing, his losses so heavy and the demoralization of his command so great that nothing less than the broad Tennessee would protect the shattered fragments from the implacable winter pursuit of Thomas. The retreat must be continued for eighty miles more.

On December twentieth, therefore, General Hood started south with the army but before starting he designated a permanent rear guard under Forrest—Forrest's cavalry and the fragments of eight brigades of infantry organized as a division under Edward C. Walthall, the thirty-three-year-old Mississippian who had risen from lieutenant to major general in the Western armies. From the same Warfield house where, less than four weeks before, the advance from Duck River to Nashville had been planned, Forrest that afternoon issued his orders for covering the retreat to the Tennessee River.[46]

Forrest's cavalry had been reduced in the campaign to few, if any, more than 3,000 men. To these were added Smith's and Palmer's brigades, temporarily consolidated under Colonel J. B. Palmer; Quarles's and Featherston's, under Brigadier General W. S. Featherston; Maney's and Strahl's, under Colonel Hume R. Feild; and Ector's and Reynolds', under Brigadier General Daniel H. Reynolds—an imposing-sounding array but totaling all together not more than 1,850 men, fully 400 of whom were without shoes.[47]

On December twentieth, the day on which Forrest and Walthall organized the devoted band with which they were to hold off the pursuit of an army, Wilson's pursuing forces got across Rutherford Creek on

412

a floating bridge constructed from the ruins of the railroad bridge. Hatch, in the lead, pressed on the few miles to Duck River but there was to be no crossing of that swollen and booming stream until the Federal pontoons should arrive. And here fortune favored Forrest for, by some error never explained, the wagons bearing the Federal pontoons had been sent lumbering down the pike from Nashville toward Murfreesborough instead of Columbia. By the time the error was found and the pontoons brought back, forty-eight hours had been lost to the Union pursuers[48]—hours of which Forrest took full advantage.

From the opposite bank of the river which they could not cross Hatch's advance began shelling Columbia in the afternoon of December twentieth. Appearing on the bank under flag of truce, Forrest held parley across the booming current with his old antagonist, Hatch, explaining to him that there were no Confederate troops in the town and that the shelling could only result in injury to the several hundred wounded of both sides who were there, and to the inhabitants. By agreement the shelling was discontinued, but Hatch, acting under orders, declined to exchange or receive on parole any of the 2,000 or so Union prisoners captured during the campaign, whom Forrest was holding.[49] During the two days in which the pursuing forces were held on the north bank of the Duck for lack of their pontoons, the main body of the Confederate army, with trains and artillery, was plodding south through freezing rains from a winter sky and freezing mud underfoot. The best of the animals were taken to double-team the Confederate pontoon train, without which there could be no escape to the comparative safety of the south bank of the Tennessee. The wagons stripped to provide the animals for this most essential service were moved with oxen impressed from the countryside in some cases, or left behind with the idea that as teams reached the Tennessee they could be turned back light to pick up what could not be pulled on the first trip. In all these arrangements for the movement and management of the defeated army was seen the hand of Forrest, who had at the same time to command the fighting rear guard.

On the twenty-second the Federal pontoons arrived on the north bank of the Duck. An infantry brigade, commanded by Forrest's old antagonist, Colonel Abel D. Streight, was put to work to lay the bridge and, although new to the work, did it with "commendable celerity"—perhaps because Colonel Streight had in mind how the tables had turned since he was pursued by Forrest. The bridge was laid and the troops of the Fourth Corps began to cross in time to make camp that night two miles south of Columbia.[50]

Thomas was not depending entirely upon direct pursuit by his cavalry and infantry to head off and destroy Hood. At the same time he was sending a force under Major General Steedman from Murfreesborough by rail through Stevenson, Alabama, to Decatur to block any attempt of the Confederates to cross the Tennessee there, while at his request Rear Admiral Lee was sending a gunboat flotilla up the Tennessee River, to get above the Muscle Shoals and prevent a crossing below Decatur.[51]

As Thomas' pursuing forces came across their bridge at Duck River, Forrest's rear guard was falling back toward Pulaski, turning savagely to fight off pursuit when it grew too close and insistent. The pursuing force on the twenty-third was infantry, which first forced Forrest's retirement and then, in the hills some five miles south of Columbia, was held in check. That night Forrest halted in the vicinity of Lynnville, sixteen miles south of Columbia, "to prevent any pressure upon my wagon train and the stock then being driven out."[52]

The real pursuit below Columbia did not begin until the twenty-fourth, when Wilson's cavalry passed to the front of the column. That day was one of "constant skirmishing," with a strong stand by the rear guard on Richland Creek near Buford's Station in which General Buford was wounded. Chalmers took over the command of Buford's division along with his own—the strength of the two being now no more than a good-sized brigade. That night the rear guard camped in Pulaski.[53]

Pulaski was the end of the turnpike which, worn as it was by the repeated passage of armies, was far better than the "almost impassable" road beyond to Bainbridge on the Tennessee. At Pulaski, therefore, on Christmas morning Forrest destroyed the ammunition which General Hood had not been able to carry off, burned the two railroad trains which had been captured at Spring Hill four weeks earlier, to keep the Yankees from retaking them, and started south. Jackson was left behind to destroy the covered bridge across Richland Creek just south of the town "after everything had passed over." In his eagerness to inflict all the delay possible upon the pursuers Jackson held on in Pulaski so long that finally he had to leave "very rapidly"—so rapidly, in fact, that some of his rear troopers singed off their hair and eyebrows as they dashed away through the burning tunnel formed by the old-fashioned covered bridge.[54] The pursuing Federals, moreover, promptly put out the fire, saved the bridge and passed on in pursuit.[55]

Seven miles beyond Pulaski, where the road to Bainbridge ran between high hills, Forrest laid an ambuscade for his pursuers at the head of a V-shaped ravine, with infantry, cavalry and artillery disposed to put fire upon an approaching column from front and flanks. One of the infantry soldiers in a regiment placed to support Morton's battery has

414

told how Forrest passed his position on foot, going to the front in a half-bent position, watched the advance of the enemy up the winding road between hills for a few minutes and hurried to the rear. "In a moment we hear the clatter of a horse's feet . . ." he continued, "and Forrest dashes by at half speed, riding magnificently, his martial figure as straight as an arrow and looking six inches taller than was his wont, a very god of war, yelling as he reaches the waiting ranks: 'Charge! *Charge!* CHARGE!' "[56]

"Before this overpowering force," reported the commander of the leading Federal brigade, "my men were obliged to fall back. . . ." Hatch, the division commander, reported that the leading Federal elements were "driven back in confusion" in "a flying mass," although all agree that as support came up the Federal forces countercharged and outflanked the Confederate position, and drove them off—not, however, until the Confederates had captured and carried away one field gun, as the sole artillery trophy of the Tennessee campaign in which Hood lost more than half a hundred guns.[57]

In this flash of fight Forrest might have thought back over the four Christmas days he had spent in the army—in 1861, making ready to march out on the next day toward his first fight at Sacramento, Kentucky; in 1862, in the midst of the success of his first great independent raid in West Tennessee; in 1863, again in West Tennessee, bringing out with him the troops, armed and unarmed, who were to form a large part of the force with which he had accomplished so much in twelve months; and now, in 1864, in the rear guard of a forlorn hope.

And yet, "ragged, barefoot, bloody, without food and without hope,"[58] the rear guard fought on. "Defeated and broken as we were," one of them wrote, men in that rear guard were "determined to do their duty to the last. . . ." Their conversation and demeanor, however, was that of men "without hope, who felt that they must gather strength even from despair," but General Forrest "alone, whatever he may have felt (and he was not blind to the dangers of our position) spoke in his usual cheerful and defiant tone. . . . Not a man was brought in contact with him who did not feel strengthened and invigorated, as if he had heard of a reinforcement coming to our relief."[59]

And so even the barefoot infantry whom he had placed in wagons to save their poor feet from the cutting of the frozen and rutted roads would dismount and hobble into action when he called for a stand to be made. And they did it all with a sort of grim cheerfulness. They were "making tracks for the Tennessee River," as one of them wrote, "at a quickstep known to Confederate tactics as 'double distance on half rations,'" and some were the bloody steps of the barefooted. They

415

knew that they were falling back from their homes for the last time; that their chances of escape beyond the Tennessee were slight, and yet they were "able to appropriate to themselves a strange and reckless pleasure wrung from hard and desperate conditions,"[59a] with flashes of banter and high spirits, and even the touch of sardonic humor. "Ain't we in a hell of a fix," one Tennessee soldier observed as he rose from a fall in the mud, "ain't we in a hell of a fix, a one-eyed President, a one-legged General and a one-hoss Confederacy!" But he, like the rest, tramped on through the cold and mud and darkness, walking, as one of his comrades put it, "not by sight but by faith"[60]—faith in the man under whose command they struggled on and fought back.

On the day after Christmas, with the pontoon bridge up at Bainbridge, the main army began to cross the Tennessee. That day, also, at Sugar Creek, Forrest's men turned again on the enemy, in the last flash of fight in the retreat, to hold off the pursuers from the army ordnance train which had been left at Sugar Creek while its mules were used to help haul the pontoons to the river. The Sugar Creek affair was fought in a dense fog which concealed the Confederate line—all except a few men purposely left in sight in front as decoys—until it rose up and blasted its pursuers at short range, drove them into the creek, and captured prisoners and horses. The ordance train having gained distance by that time, Forrest and Walthall fell back in the fog from Sugar Creek, to camp that night only sixteen miles from the river.[61]

On December twenty-seventh Forrest marched to the pontoon bridge, unmolested by the enemy, and that evening crossed over. On the same day Admiral Lee's gunboats came up through the Shoals, with apparent intent to break and destroy the floating bridge, but failed to get in reach—a result which Wilson ascribed to "the independence of the navy and the natural timidity of a deep-water sailor in a shoal-water river."[62] That night Walthall and the infantry held the light field entrenchments about the north end of the bridge, though there were no further Federal attacks that day. On the morning of December twenty-eighth, with the army or what was left of it across the river, the guns and wagons across, even the drove of cattle and hogs with which Forrest had left Murfreesborough across, Walthall's valiant rear guard marched across, leaving a detail of 200 men to help take up the bridge—a task accomplished just as the advance of the Federal pursuit appeared on the north bank.[63]

There was in the whole war no pursuit which compares with that after Nashville, whether in the length of time and the space of country over which it extended, or the vigor with which it was pressed or the conditions under which it was carried on. And yet it failed to bring Hood's broken army to bay, or to prevent its crossing of the Tennessee. It failed,

416

Ordered by the President

I hereby authorize and direct the Secretary of State to affix the Seal of the United States to a Warrant (form N° 3) for the pardon of N. B. Forrest,

dated this day, and signed by me and for so doing this shall be his warrant.

Andrew Johnson

Washington 17ᵗʰ July, 1868

Executive Mansion

July 21/68

A PARDON FROM THE PRESIDENT

From the collection of Monroe Cockrell

FORREST IN POLITICAL CARTOON

In this cartoon, typical of the campaign of that year, R. E. Lee and N. B. Forrest are included with Seymour and Blair, the nominees for President and Vice-President, Andrew Johnson, Vallandigham and others, to connect the Democratic ticket of 1868 with the Confederate cause and the Copperhead movement.

in part, because it was carried on in a memorably cold and wet winter season. But these handicaps of darkness, rain, snow, sleep, frozen mud and rising rivers were handicaps to the pursued no less than to the pursuers. The pursuit failed of its purpose of capturing Hood's broken army because, as General Thomas himself reported:

"With the exception of his rearguard, [Hood's] army had become a disheartened and disorganized rabble of half-armed and barefooted men. . . . The rearguard, however, was undaunted and firm, and did its work bravely to the last."[64]

CHAPTER XXVI

THE LAST CAMPAIGN AND SURRENDER

December 29, 1864-May 9, 1865

FROM the Tennessee River the remnant of the defeated and all but ruined Army of Tennessee was drawn off southward to Tupelo, Mississippi, lacking "guns, small arms and accoutrements . . . shoes and blankets, and this in a winter of unusual severity for that latitude." There, General Hood having retired from the command, Lieutenant General Richard Taylor devoted himself energetically to reorganization and such refitment of the command as was possible before sending it off on the longest march of that far-marching army, to the Carolinas to oppose Sherman's anticipated march northward from Savannah.[1]

Forrest in Corinth, Mississippi, found himself "left to defend as well as can be done this section of the country," with little resources other than the command, which, as he put it, he had been "compelled almost to sacrifice to save the Army in its retreat from Nashville."[2] The command was so greatly in need of men, mounts, arms, equipment, clothing, supplies, everything save fortitude and devotion to its leader that on New Year's Day, 1865, Forrest ordered the men from the near-by sections in Tennessee, Alabama and Mississippi sent home for twenty days "to collect absentees, procure clothing and remount themselves," with an offer of a twenty-day furlough within the next twelvemonth to every man who brought in with him a deserter or a well-mounted recruit.[3]

Weariness of man and horse was forgotten in the "rush and hurry of that ride for home, through the blinding snow storm, which would never be forgotten by the participants," as one of them afterward wrote. Many rode fifty to sixty miles a day, "so as not to lose an hour of precious time."[4] Most of them—in some regiments, all—returned in accordance with their promise, many bringing in the dismounted men who had been absent during the Nashville campaign. During the wholesale furlough Ross's brigade of Texans—too far from home to go and return—remained on picket and outpost duty.

But even with the touch of home which the furlough gave most of his men, and with what little added strength they were able to bring back, in every material way the command was still deplorably weak as compared

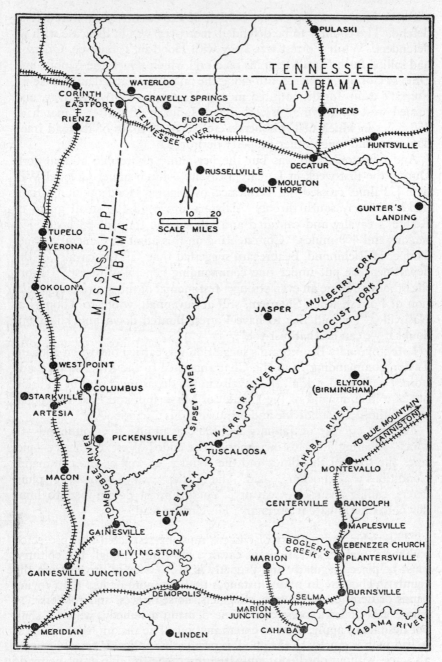

THE SELMA CAMPAIGN—1865

with the forces massing on the borders of the country they were left to defend. The country to be defended, moreover, was in like case with its defenders. While Forrest was away with Hood in Tennessee, Grierson had sallied forth from Memphis on a raid which struck the Mobile and Ohio at Corinth, turned south along the railroad, attacked and broke up Forrest's camp for dismounted men at Verona on Christmas Day, and turned west to arrive at Vicksburg on January fifth after a march of 450 miles in which 600 prisoners were taken, 80 miles of railroad track damaged, and much other property destroyed.[5]

And Grierson's raid was but the beginning of trouble of that sort. During the first week in January a cavalry column under Colonel William J. Palmer crossed the Tennessee, overhauled Hood's pontoon train making its way south through Alabama, drove off the small guard of Roddey's cavalry and captured and burned the train of 83 boats, 150 wagons and 400 mules.[6] Commenting on this affair to General Samuel Cooper in Richmond, Beauregard suggested that "all the cavalry of the department be put under one commanding general—Forrest."[7] From the other side came an even stronger testimonial of the growing appreciation of Forrest, when Sherman, still at Savannah, wrote to Thomas at Nashville, "I would like to have Forrest hunted down and killed but doubt if we can do that just yet."[8]

Late in January Beauregard's suggestion was carried out when Richard Taylor, commanding from the Chattahoochee to the Mississippi, made Forrest commander of all the cavalry in the department and in addition put him in command of the District of Mississippi and East Louisiana, with authority to subdivide and organize at his discretion.[9]

Forrest's circular of January 24, 1865, assuming the command—to which, apparently on his own motion, he added West Tennessee—pictures the state of the times and the country, as well as the command. Conditions were shockingly bad. The district was full of bands of plunderers, calling themselves cavalry. These Forrest determined to hunt down, to exterminate if necessary. His circular read:

"The rights and propery of citizens must be respected and protected and the illegal organizations of cavalry, prowling through the country, must be placed regularly and properly in the service or driven from the country. They are in many instances nothing more or less than roving bands of deserters, absentees, stragglers, horse-thieves, and robbers . . . whose acts of lawlessness and crime demand a remedy, which I shall not hesitate to apply, even to extermination. The maxim 'that kindness to bad men is cruelty to the good' is peculiarly applicable to soldiers; for all agree, without obedience and strict discipline troops cannot be made effective, and kindness to a bad soldier does great injustice to those who are faithful and true; and it is but justice to those who discharge their duties with promptness and fidelity that others who are disobedient, turbulent and mutinous, or who desert or straggle from their commands, should be promptly and effectively dealt with, as the law directs."[10]

Nor was Forrest content with orders and circulars on the subject. His brother Jesse, recovered from the wound suffered at Athens, Alabama, in September, was sent through the no-man's land between the picket lines in northern Mississippi to arrest and send to their commands the large numbers of deserters "infesting the country, robbing friend and foe indiscriminately," as they were described by one of General Cooper's assistants on inspection duty. "The condition of the citizen is pitiable in the extreme," the inspector wrote. "Dismounted Confederate cavalry steal his horses, while a dastard foe robs him of food and clothing. Grain cannot be grown and food cannot be purchased." But, he added, "General Forrest, with that energy and ability which always characterize his actions . . . and with the aid of his brother, Colonel Jesse Forrest, has lately arrested and sent to their commands many of these deserters"— 600 as appears in another report.[11]

And all the while Forrest was busy with the immediate problem of making ready his command, insofar as it was in his power to do so, to meet the irruptions of Federal force which were bound to come. The war was to be carried to the country. To Major General E. R. S. Canby, commanding the Federal forces operating against Mobile, Grant wrote: "It is important to prevent, as far as possible, the planting of a crop this year, and to destroy their railroads, machine shops, etc."[12] Expeditions against the territory entrusted to Forrest were in the making in the Federal posts at Memphis, at Vicksburg, at Baton Rouge and at Pensacola.

Far more serious than these threats from the Mississippi River or the Gulf Coast, however, was the threat poised on the north bank of the Tennessee—young James H. Wilson's new cavalry corps in its fine cantonments at Gravelly Springs and Waterloo, in the northwestern corner of the state of Alabama, where it could be readily supplied with all things needful by steamers on the Tennessee, and whence it could at discretion strike south through either Alabama or Mississippi. By February Wilson had there assembled 22,000 men organized in five divisions. Sixteen thousand of his men were mounted, despite the fact that, in the terrible pursuit from Nashville, Wilson had broken down and used up 5,000 animals. Thirteen thousand of his force were armed with the Spencer repeating carbine, using metallic cartridges, and concededly the best military arm of its time.[13] Never before, and never since,

421

was such a cavalry command assembled in the Western hemisphere.

Upon taking over command of his new district Forrest once more re-organized and reassigned his forces in an attempt to create a more compact and effective body of troops. The Tennessee troops, Bell's brigade and Rucker's—subsequently commanded by Brigadier General Alexander W. Campbell, who had been on the staff of Leonidas Polk—were brought together with Ross's Texans in one division under the command of William H. Jackson. The Mississippi troops, three brigades commanded by Brigadier Generals Frank Armstrong, Wirt Adams and Peter B. Starke, were assigned to a division commanded by Chalmers. Buford was sent with the remnant of his Kentuckians to take command of the cavalry in the district of Alabama, where Brigadier General Dan W. Adams was district commander. That other gallant remnant of a command from a state in the enemy hands, the Second Missouri and its Colonel McCulloch, were assigned to Forrest's immediate and personal command for special duty.[14] The total strength of the command, with all the territory it had to cover, did not exceed 10,000 men.

On February 9, 1865, too late to be of any real effect upon the war, there came a great change in the whole Confederate organization with the appointment of General Robert E. Lee as commander of all the forces. The failing state of those forces by that time is indicated by Lee's General Order No. 2, issued two days later, offering amnesty to deserters returning within thirty days. The slowness and difficulty of communications within the South is indicated by the fact that the thirty days already had expired before the notice of amnesty began to be published in the newspapers in Selma and in Mississippi. Taylor extended the time of amnesty in his territory, therefore, until April fifteenth—by which time there was no longer a Confederacy.[15]

Before the end of February Taylor and Forrest had begun the movement of forces toward Selma, rightly judging that the most vital blow which could be struck to Confederate resources in the West would be there. Selma, connected with the coal and iron region of Alabama by a railroad built just before the war, and with Meridian and the state of Mississippi by another completed during the war, had communication also by steamboat with Mobile and with Montgomery, where connection was made with the railroads running to the Eastern South. At Selma there were located the most considerable ironworking plants and shops, arsenals and navy yards in the Western South. There was small doubt that a blow would be attempted against Selma, therefore, but considerable uncertainty as to whether it would come from the Gulf Coast below, where Canby's major army was operating against Mobile, and where the Union had held Pensacola since early in the war, or from

Wilson's gathering force on the Tennessee River. And all the while, being upon the enforced defensive, Taylor and Forrest had to keep in mind the possibilities of raids from the line of the Mississippi River as well.[16]

In this state of affairs each side was anxious, as always, for even scraps of information as to the other. On February seventeenth, therefore, Thomas sent Colonel John G. Parkhurst, his provost marshal general, to meet Forrest under flag of truce and discuss his proposal of an exchange of prisoners, or at least of supplying shoes, clothing and blankets to the 7,000 Federal prisoners whom Forrest was holding in the interior of Mississippi. With Colonel Parkhurst, Wilson sent along one of his most observant officers, Captain Lewis M. Hosea, recent graduate of West Point, to "keep his eyes open" and gather information as to the country, its food supplies and military resources, and especially to learn what he could as to Forrest's state of mind and general intentions.[17]

The party left Eastport, Mississippi, on February twenty-first with an escort of twenty men, carrying ten days' food and forage, and proceeded well below Corinth before they met the first rebel outpost. Their flag being accepted, they passed on to Rienzi where, on the twenty-second, their presence was telegraphed to Forrest, who came up by train from Verona, his headquarters, to meet them, accompanied by Major Anderson and by Judge Robert L. Caruthers, the Confederate Governor-elect of Tennessee, who like Governor Harris had his "capital" where there were Tennessee troops.

The meeting between the two groups began about 9·00 P.M. of February twenty-third and, by the mellow glow of lamplight, went on until four in the morning, after which Forrest went south to Meridian to confer with Taylor, while the Parkhurst party remained at Rienzi to await word of Taylor's decision on the arrangements proposed. In the course of the all-night conversation, Forrest "remarked that he was as anxious to rid the country of guerrillas as was any officer in the U. S. Army, and that he would esteem it a favor if General Thomas would hang every one caught."[18] The greater interest attaches now, however, to the personal report which the observant young Captain Hosea wrote home and the military report made to his chief, General Wilson.

In his letter home, written while he waited at Rienzi, Captain Hosea, with the fondness of his generation for Napoleonic allusion, gave a "word picture of the great Confederate Murat." He wrote:

"The general effect [of Forrest] is suggestive of notables of Revolutionary times, with powdered hair as we see them in the portraits of that day; and to our unaccustomed eyes the rich gray uniform with its embroidered collar (a wreath of gold on black ground enclosing three silver stars) added much to the effect produced. [Evidently Forrest was determined that, so far as appearances could prevent, Wilson should not learn the plight of his forces.] His habitual expression seemed rather subdued and thoughtful, but when his face lighted up with a smile, which ripples all over his features, the effect is really charming. . . . His language indicates a very limited education, but his impressive manner conceals many otherwise notable defects. . . . He invariably omits the final 'g' in the termination 'ing,' and many words are inexcusably mispronounced, and he always uses the past participle in place of the past tense in such words as 'see' (as 'I seen' instead of 'I saw' and 'holp tote,' meaning to 'help carry') etc. . . . In a very short time, however, these pass unnoticed. He speaks of his success with a soldierly vanity, and expresses the kindliest feelings toward prisoners and wounded."[19]

He did not mention it in his letter, but to General Wilson, Captain Hosea reported the interest shown by Forrest in the history and personality of the new Federal cavalry commander. Hearing that Wilson was a West Point graduate and a former engineer officer, Forrest remarked that "he knew nothing of military tactics, except what he had learned in actual campaigning. Then he added, reflectively, 'But I always make it a rule to get there first with the most men.'" Significantly, Hosea did not mention "fustest" or "mostest." Had such words been used there is hardly a chance that this young man with his keen ear and critical interest in speech would not have mentioned it. Forrest sent a message to Wilson by the Captain, also, that he preferred revolvers to sabers, and "would give more for fifteen minutes of the bulge on him than for three days of tactics."[20]

On February twenty-seventh, after delays due to washouts on the railroad and breaks in the telegraph, word came from Forrest closing the arrangement for the exchange of prisoners at Iuka, Mississippi, on March third or fourth, and also confirming a proposal he had made to run relief trains on the railroads in the vicinity of Corinth to supply food to the inhabitants of that repeatedly devastated area, Forrest undertaking that no military use would be made of them.[21]

While the Parkhurst party waited, the rains came, the small streams rose, the railroad washed out above and below them, and they were marooned at Reinzi for a "week of rain and seven-up." When the water had sufficiently subsided for them to leave, Captain Hosea, mindful of his evening with Forrest, astonished the telegraph operator at Rienzi by sending a message in Latin to Judge Caruthers—assuming, and probably rightly, that of Forrest's party the Judge would best get the import of the line from the *Aeneid*, "Haec olim meminisse juvabit tetegisse dextrano tyranni," the Captain's translation being, "Hereafter it will rejoice me to remember that I have touched the right hand of your leader."[22]

The waters which detained the flag of truce party at Rienzi were precursors of the great floods of the spring of 1865 in that section. By March second Forrest had to send word to Parkhurst that he could not get to Iuka with the prisoners before the tenth on account of high water, and by the tenth the waters were still higher. Railroad bridges were washed out and at Eastport, the steamboat landing for Iuka, everything was under water or floated off, so that arrangements were made for the exchange of prisoners at Vicksburg and Mobile instead of along the Tennessee River.[23]

The floods had the effect, also, of delaying the start of Wilson's expedition. On March thirteenth, to Sherman, impatient for him to be gone to the South, Wilson wrote that the Tennessee was higher than it had ever been known to be and that it was impossible to put his troops across.[24] Forrest, meanwhile, with a sense of terrible urgency, was driving forward in the work of preparing his command to do all that it could do when the blow should come.

Since February 28, 1865, he had been a lieutenant general, a rank more in keeping with the size and difficulties of his problems and responsibilities than with the strength of the force and resources available to do what was expected of him. On the same date Tyree Bell was at last commissioned a brigadier general, but McCulloch's promotion to that rank, though long since recommended by Forrest, did not come through.[25]

As early as February twenty-second Forrest had started shifting his troops toward what he conceived to be the threatened point of Selma. Courier lines were established, connecting Forrest's headquarters at West Point, Mississippi, with other headquarters and also with Henderson's company of scouts pushed out toward Eastport, and with various points in Alabama. A bridge was put across "Bigbee" at Waverly, and a pontoon bridge was laid across the Warrior at Finch's Ferry. Ration dumps were established on the roads to the east, and the roads themselves were marked with signboards and distinctive blazes and chops on the trees, indicating the way to Tuscaloosa and to Selma. Through it all, Forrest was pressing his subordinates—"spare no time," "we have no time to lose," "be in readiness," "not a moment should be lost."[26]

But while their General and his subordinate commanders might strain to make ready for the coming storm, the soldiers in the camps in Mississippi had, as soldiers so frequently do, a lot of inactive waiting time on their hands There were no recreational or morale services in those days but the old soldiers remember that during the two months or so they were at Verona and West Point a great wave of interest in the games of checkers and shooting marbles swept the camps. The General had no objection to those sports but he did issue orders against promiscuous shooting-off of guns, which wasted ammunition, and the practice of horse racing about the camps, which wore out horseflesh. In a defiant mood, there was a good deal of firing in the camps that night, while on the next day the backers of rival horses in two outfits ostentatiously staked off a quarter-course before Forrest's headquarters and there staged a race. Forrest, coming to the door, watched the proceedings, joined in the joking and even in the betting, and was heartily cheered by the young men—who, on the way back to their camps, were met by a strong provost guard, put in arrest and put on punishment fatigue for their fun. Willie Forrest, the General's son, was one of those who remembered that he had to carry rails until his shoulders were sore.[27]

And always there was the problem of "deserters, absentees and stragglers." Jesse Forrest was sent forth again into the debatable land on March thirteenth, to round up all he could catch, to be "dismounted, disarmed and forwarded," in irons if necessary, to Brigadier General Marcus J. Wright, commanding the post at Grenada, with intent to break up entirely the companies of irregular "scouts" who were, rather, "regular banditti, preying upon friends and foes."[28] One band of deserters, indeed, about this time killed Colonel W. W. Faulkner, of the Twelfth Kentucky Cavalry, near Dresden, Tennessee.[29]

This condition against which he strove so hard was in Forrest's opinion, in no small degree due to the policies of the Confederate War Department. On March eighteenth, therefore, he addressed to the department a very earnest communication on the subject, which Taylor forwarded with approval. The immediate occasion for the letter was a proposal to send officers into Kentucky to get out recruits from within the enemy's lines. That had been tried, Forrest pointed out, by men as capable as Brigadier Generals Adam Johnson and Hylan Lyon, who had done all that men could do with success so scant as to make the effort not worth while. Passing on to the general practice, he bitingly observed:

"The authorities given to would-be colonels, and by them delegated to would-be captains and lieutenants, have created squads of men who are dodging from pillar to post, preying upon the people, robbing them of their horses and other property, to the manifest injury of the country and our cause. . . . The country is filled with deserters and stragglers who run away and attach themselves to the commands of those who have the authorities referred to. They never organize, report to nobody, are responsible to no one, and exist by plunder and robbery. . . . Roving bands of guerrillas, jayhawkers and plunderers are the natural offspring of authorities given to parties to raise troops within the enemy's lines."[30]

426

"I speak truly," he said in a second communication on the subject, "when I say that whenever a paper of the kind is presented to me I can but regard it as an exemption from duty for the war, a license to plunder, and a nest-egg of desertion."[31]

Long before Forrest's protests reached Richmond, however, he was engaged in a more deadly business—for on March eighteenth, the Tennessee having somewhat subsided, Wilson began crossing to the south bank. One of his five divisions, Knipe's, had been sent to Canby for use in the campaign against Mobile. Another, Hatch's, had to be left behind because of the nonarrival of the horses to mount it. But between the eighteenth and the twenty-second Wilson put across the river, ready to march, the three divisions commanded by Brigadier Generals Eli Long, E. McCook, and Emory Upton—the same whose subsequent study, *The Military Policy of the United States*, was so profoundly to affect for the better the whole military thought and organization of the nation. Wilson had on the south bank of the Tennessee 12,500 mounted men, armed with Spencer repeating carbines; three batteries of horse artillery; a light pontoon train of 30 canvas boats and a supply train of 250 wagons, the trains being guarded by 1,500 dismounted men for whom it was planned to capture horses.[32] The command, in Wilson's words, was "in magnificent condition, well armed, splendidly mounted, perfectly clad and equipped"[33]—and, he might justly have added, exceedingly well led at all levels of command.

On March twenty-second he left the south bank of the river, marching on three roads, partly to spread out for the better foraging of the country, partly to promote uncertainty as to his real destination. The first eighty miles or so of his march being through a mountainous country, agriculturally poor at best and now devastated, Wilson carried rations for five days, with supplies of such items as coffee and sugar for as much as sixty days, the whole intended period of his expedition. This was to be no more hit-and-run raid but a sustained invasion. On the fifth day out the several columns began to cross the upper forks of the Black Warrior River near Jasper, and on March thirtieth were closed up and concentrated at the hamlet of Elyton where, a few years later, there would begin to grow the Southern iron and steel center of Birmingham.[34]

Before Wilson started, Forrest had already shifted Chalmers eastward into Alabama, at Pickensville. On the twenty-second, the day Wilson started south from the river, Chalmers was ordered to hold his command ready to move, while a day later at Taylor's direction he was ordered to move on Selma—not, however, so much on account of Wilson's advance as of one reported to be under way from the Gulf Coast.[35] Chalmers led off with Armstrong's brigade, to be followed a day later by Starke's—his third brigade under Wirt Adams having been left behind to guard the railroad line in Mississippi.

On March twenty-fifth Wilson's column, by that time three days' march below the Tennessee, began to enter into the Confederate calculations. That night Forrest sent word to Chalmers to hasten on to Selma, while the next morning he ordered Jackson to Tuscaloosa, eighty miles north of Selma, where it appeared that he would be on the flank of Wilson's line of march, with instructions that it was "important to strike him as soon as possible."[36]

Chalmers was going to Selma to help the local commander Dan Adams, but it was Taylor's expressed intention, "in view of movements from Moulton and Russellville [Wilson's]" that "Jackson, with his own and Lyon's command, should meet, whip and get rid of that column of the enemy as soon as possible."[37] As late as March twenty-eighth Taylor expressed the hope that he could "whip the large raids from North Alabama" in "three or four days" and then turn to the aid of besieged Mobile.[38] None of the Confederate commanders seems to have realized as yet that this "raid from above" was not the cavalry raid to which they were accustomed. It was something new in the war—as new in its way as the German "panzers" in 1940—a mounted invasion with all the speed and mobility the times afforded backed by power enough to fight its way wherever it was called upon to go.

Having started his columns, Forrest himself with his escort followed on March twenty-seventh heading toward Finch's Ferry across the Warrior, near Eutaw.[39] On the way, at the bridge over the Sipsey between Carter's and Colter's Ferries, the advance of Forrest's force took into custody two men, or rather a man and a boy, accused of desertion. They were immediately tried before a drumhead courtmartial and, in spite of protestations of innocence which Dr. Wyeth was informed were afterward found to be true, were condemned to death, and executed forthwith. Their bodies were laid out by the side of the road along which the troops were to pass, beneath a tree to which was nailed a large sign, SHOT FOR DESERTION. As the column passed, General Jackson was ordered to leave behind an officer and twenty men to guard the bridge and ferries "until day after tomorrow morning, when they will bury the two men who have been shot here at the bridge today, then follow on and report to their commands . . . Should the officer left behind catch other deserters he will take them to the bridge and execute them." And so for two days these pitiful victims lay almost under the hoofs of the horses, as examples to the men and witnesses of the savage determination with which Forrest was waging his last campaign against desertion and absenteeism in his own army as well as against the forces of the advancing enemy.[40]

On the night of March thirtieth, Forrest was at Scottsville, twenty-five miles southeast of Tuscaloosa and within five miles of the bridge over the Cahaba at Centerville—a bridge which was soon to become crucial in the campaign. The whole campaign, in fact, was conditioned by the pattern of the considerable streams in that part of Alabama, the Tombigbee, the Sipsey, the Black Warrior and the Cahaba, all of them in flood at the time, and all of them running athwart the necessary line of march of the Confederates, if they were to come at Wilson. Wilson, on the other hand, marching from north to south in the same general direction as the flow of the streams, had but one of consequence to cross—a fork of the Cahaba, well up toward its headwaters.

On this day, at Elyton, Wilson detached John Croxton's brigade, 1,100 strong, to march seventy miles southwest to Tuscaloosa to destroy the University of Alabama, looked upon as a "military college" because of its cadet corps, and the public works and government stores, after which he was to march south by the road through Centerville to rejoin the main column before Selma.[41] With the rest of his force Wilson pushed on with good speed southward for Montevallo, on the railroad connecting Selma with the coal and iron regions. With Upton's division leading, the Cahaba was crossed at Hillsboro, early in the morning of March thirtieth, by planking over the 900-foot-long railroad bridge. That night and the next morning the four iron furnaces, a rolling mill and five coal mines located at Montevallo were destroyed.[42]

On the morning of the last day of March, as Wilson himself was approaching Montevallo from the north, Forrest was coming from the west. From Scottsville Forrest sent orders that morning to Jackson at Tuscaloosa, to "move on tonight to Centerville," the critical crossing of the Cahaba, and by all means to hold the bridge there.[43]

At 1:00 P.M. of March thirty-first, Wilson himself reached Montevallo, to learn that Confederate forces had been encountered below the town. The forces were no more than Roddey with his cavalry, Crossland's fragment of a brigade and Dan Adams, commanding a handful of infantry who had come up from Selma, but Wilson believed that "Forrest was in our front. We were face to face at last. True to his own rule, he was striving . . . to strike the first blow"—which Wilson in no wise intended to allow him to do.[44]

The last battle had begun—a running fight which was to last forty-eight hours, almost without intermission, and to stretch from Six Mile Creek, below Montevallo, back to Selma, fifty miles away, in which Wilson's men went at their work with a dash and a power that knew no stopping. As their commander gleefully commented, they "had the bulge on Forrest and held it to the end . . . fairly turning his own rules of war against himself."[45]

Forrest himself was not in front of Wilson at the opening fight at Six Mile Creek but, having crossed the Cahaba at the Centerville bridge, was coming in from the west when he heard the fighting. Dashing forward with his escort—the only troops with him—he struck into the advancing Federal column behind the front of the fight, cut it in two, drove one segment northward, changed direction and fought the segment to the south, captured enough prisoners and found enough wounded Confederates on the ground to learn something of the earlier fight, swung off to the east, circled around Wilson's advance, and at ten o'clock that night came into the Confederate camp below Randolph, sixteen miles south of Montevallo—so rapidly had the fight moved that afternoon. It was this afternoon's fight and one of the next day which led one of Crossland's Kentuckians to write admiringly after the war that great as Forrest was as a commander, he was a "greater close-quarters fighter."[46]

Forrest, however, had no intention of doing more with the troops in front of Wilson than to delay him until his other columns could come up—Chalmers, marching for Selma and presumed to be then in the neighborhood of Plantersville, and Jackson, whom he had ordered down from Tuscaloosa and who was presumed to be approaching the bridge over the Cahaba at Centerville. To Jackson, Forrest sent a message at 6:00 P.M. of March thirty-first: "Enemy moving right down the railroad . . . follow down after them, taking the road behind them from Montevallo down . . . [avoiding a general engagement] unless you find balance of our forces in supporting distance of you." To Chalmers, who had been delayed by high water, flooded swamps, unbridged streams and changes in orders, likewise went a message outlining the position and urging him forward for the combination which Forrest was seeking to make against Wilson—front, flank and rear.[47]

To good planning and good management Wilson had added in this campaign surpassing good fortune. The courier carrying Forrest's messages was captured that night, the message found, and from that time on the whole game was in Wilson's hands. McCook, with La Grange's brigade, was sent forthwith to seize and burn the Cahaba bridge at Centerville, while the rest of the command, still numbering 9,000 men, pushed on with assurance that their rear was protected.[48] Forrest took up his position on April first at Ebenezer Church, or Bogler's Creek, six miles north of Plantersville. Chalmers was not there, having been delayed by high water and bad roads which had caused him to deflect his march to the northward toward Randolph. Part of Armstrong's brigade, which was marching one day in advance of the rest of Chalmers' division and which had come up by a forced march on hearing of the fight,

430

were on hand and were put into the short battle line. The rest of the line was made up of Crossland's little band of Kentuckians, Roddey's Alabama cavalry, and some 300 infantry whom Dan Adams had sent out from Selma—no more than 1,500 men altogether. Against them came the divisions of Long and Upton, five times their number and, with their repeating rifles, many times greater in fire power. "In less than an hour," Wilson reported, "although the resistance was determined, the position was carried by a gallant charge, and the rebels completely routed."[49]

The most desperate fighting of the day centered around Forrest himself, his escort company commanded by Captain Nathan Boone, and two companies of Kentuckians under the intrepid Captain H. A. Tyler. It was a hand-to-hand affair, with six-shooter against saber. One gallant young Indiana captain, J. D. Taylor, choosing Forrest for his own opponent, succeeding in inflicting upon him his fourth wound of the war before Forrest was able to draw his pistol and kill his assailant. "If that boy had known enough to give me the point of his saber instead of the edge," Forrest said to Wilson afterward, "I should not have been here to tell you about it."[50]

Forrest's force, the General himself covered with blood from the saber hacks on his arm, halted that night after a running fight of twenty-four miles during the day "without pause or rest" at Plantersville, only nineteen miles north of Selma itself. And that night, too, fortune favored Wilson in finding Millington, the English civil engineer who had laid out the defense works of Selma, and who was quite willing to draw for his captors the full detail of those works. It resulted that on the following day, when they assaulted the works, the Federal forces were far better informed as to their location and features than was Forrest.[51]

Forrest, who had spent the night of April first in search of his troops, came into Selma, horse and rider covered with blood from his wounded arm, about ten in the morning of Sunday, April second—just about the same hour, as it happened, when word came that another and more famous center of Confederate resistance, Richmond, must be evacuated. Selma seethed with excitement and with efforts to get out the stores and the prisoners, either by train to Demopolis to the west or by river steamer.

To defend the three-and-one-half-mile trace of entrenchments about the town, Forrest had only the 1,400 men of Armstrong's brigade, of Chalmers' division, which had got his word to hasten and had come in by a forced march; what was left of the men who had fought at Ebenezer Church the day before; Dan Adams' militia, and a few old men and boys impressed from the city for its defense—altogether barely more than

431

3,000 men of all sorts and descriptions.[52] Chalmers, with the rest of his force, was west of the Cahaba; Jackson to the northwest of that stream. The defense would have to be made with what was available—for Wilson was coming swiftly and implacably on. As he had marched from Plantersville at daylight, his skirmishers were about the Confederate lines by 2:00 P.M. Knowing the Confederate situation from the captured dispatches, he threw out one brigade to watch for the possible approach of Chalmers from the west, and with the rest of his troops lined up for the assault.

The assault came after five o'clock and not long before dark. Nearly 9,000 men charged forward, admirably arranged and capably led, against a force little more than one-third their number, spread thin in an attempt to hold a system of fortifications built for a garrison much larger. Nevertheless, the improvised garrison "fought with considerable coolness and skill," as one Federal writer puts it, but from the beginning it was a hopeless defense. Just about dark, when the militia which made up the center of the Confederate line broke back into the town, the end came, and with a rush. Armstrong and Roddey, holding the flanks, were borne back, as were Forrest and the escort company, posted behind the center. Nevertheless, Forrest, with the ever-faithful escort, and Armstrong and Roddey, with small bands of their troopers, managed to cut their way out in the darkness and confusion, and make their escape from the captured city on the Burnsville road to the east.[53]

And even on that last desperate night, as he and the escort picked their way around the town through unfamiliar country byways illuminated by the glare on the sky from buildings burning in Selma, Forrest retained the aggressive spirit. Surprising and capturing a picket of the Fourth United States Cavalry, he learned that a larger body was at the near-by home of Mr. Godwin. Forrest decided to surround and capture them, but his men refused to make the attack unless he would stay with the horse-holders a quarter of a mile in the rear, which he did. The attack was led by Lieutenant George Cowan, who had succeeded to command of the escort after the wounding of Captain Boone at Ebenezer Church the day before.

The affair that follows appears in Federal accounts as an unprovoked attack upon men asleep, who were killed and wounded in spite of "their cries for surrender." One account, indeed, says that "Forrest fell upon the party with the ferocity of a wild Indian and killed every man of it." Cowan, who himself was wounded in the fight, and the other Confederate officers involved, insist that the first shot was fired by Lieutenant Royce's Union detachment which resisted with great courage and almost with success until a squad detached to charge them in the rear came into action, and that "not a single man was killed after he surrendered." Both sides were hard and veteran fighters and there was every circumstance that would lead to a bitter battle in the dark, but it is unlikely that there was such a thing as a planned massacre. If there was, the plans were not carried out, for the Confederates took a number of prisoners. On the next day, however, Mr. Godwin's house was burned by a reprisal squad.[54]

Circling to the north, Forrest reached Plantersville on the morning of April third, and there turned to the west toward Marion. A mile out he met the advance of McCook's Union force, returning from its expedition against the Centerville bridge. Aggressive to the last, Forrest's handful charged first. While McCook was throwing his men into line of battle to resist this unexpected attack, Forrest drew off into the woods, and continued his march that day and that night—the third consecutive all-night ride and all-day fight for Forrest and the men who followed him. The Cahaba was crossed by dawn of April fourth and Marion was reached in midmorning. There Forrest found Chalmers with Starke's brigade and Jackson who, unable to get across the Cahaba at Centerville as ordered, had moved down the west side of that stream. There he found, too, the train and the artillery, which had come up from Mississippi. He was wise enough, however, not to attempt a renewal of the fight with Wilson, who now held Selma with all his force except Croxton's detached brigade.[55]

That brigade had been deflected from its direct march to Tuscaloosa by news of the presence there of Jackson, and had crossed the Warrior forty miles above, and approached the town by way of Northport, the hamlet on the opposite side of the Warrior, only on the night of April third. There they rushed the bridge in the darkness, captured its guards, and were across and in possession of the town before the garrison of local militia and the cadet company from the University—young soldiers in neat, trim uniforms whom the worn, ill-clad Confederates of Jackson's division had nicknamed "Katydids," to the intense indignation of the cadets—was able to assemble and offer effective resistance. By 1:00 A.M. of April fourth Croxton had received the formal surrender of the place. That day the college and other public works and stores were burned.[56]

On April fifth Croxton left Tuscaloosa, recrossed the Warrior, burned the bridge and turned southwest toward Eutaw. On the sixth he met Wirt Adams' brigade in a late afternoon fight, in rain, thunder and lightning, and mud, which resulted in Croxton's turning back north by way of Jasper and so back to Elyton, which he reached twenty days after he had left there.[57]

None of this, of course, was known to Wilson at Selma. Anxious to

433

learn what he could of the brigade which he had detached at Tuscaloosa, he proposed a conference with Forrest under flag of truce, osten-
sibly to discuss arrangements about the parole and exchange of the considerable number of prisoners which each side held. The meeting was
held at the old town of Cahaba, at noon of April eighth—the day before Appomattox. As to prisoners, it was agreed that officers and men
paroled by the enemy were to be declared exchanged and returned to
duty,[58] while in the course of the conversation Wilson gathered that
Croxton still was safe—his main point of concern.

The real point of interest in the conference, now, is in the personal
impression made. After a bountiful dinner at the home of Colonel
Matthews, Wilson writes, he and Forrest retired to the parlor alone, and
soon were "treating each other like old acquaintances, if not old friends."
He found Forrest, with his arm in a sling, somewhat depressed but
nevertheless exhibiting the "great firmness, excellent judgment, inflexible
will" which Wilson had come to expect of him. "I came to know him
well, if not intimately, after the war, when we were both engaged in building railroads," Wilson added. "I found him in civil life a modest, un-
assuming and trustworthy man of affairs."[59]

Captain Hosea, however, was not so favorably impressed with Forrest
this time. His second interview with the Confederate leader, he wrote,
"quite removed the favorable impression of the first. The first was in a
respite of the war. . . . I next saw him in the midst of turmoil and strife,
wounded, defeated, savage and unkempt." Accepting as true the current stories of the affair at Godwin's house, he went on to say in his letter
home that Forrest had "surprised and pistoled a lieutenant, Royce of
the 4th Regular Cavalry, and 38 men who had been detached in observation toward the Cahaba River at our right rear" and had killed them in
a manner "cold-blooded and dastardly." Believing the story, as he naturally did, it was equally natural that he should say that "all the brutal
instincts of the slave driver stood out unconcealed; and to these was
added a sulky and guilty consciousness that we regarded him as the mur-
derer of Royce and his party."[60]

Meanwhile, having completed the thorough destruction of the important Confederate works at Selma, mounted his dismounted men, shot
the 500 surplus horses left over to keep them from falling into rebel
hands,[61] and laid a pontoon bridge across the Alabama River, Wilson
started east from Selma on April tenth, the day after Appomattox. Two
days later, on the fourth anniversary of the firing on Fort Sumter, his
men raised the flag of the United States above the original Capitol of
the Confederate States at Montgomery. Thence Wilson passed on east
to Columbus and Macon, Georgia, where, well into May, he was joined
by Croxton with the lost brigade which for six weeks had wandered

almost at will through the hollow shell of the decayed Confederate defenses in north Alabama and Georgia.[62]

Wisely and fortunately, Forrest made no effort to follow Wilson on his great and destructive march. On April twelfth, the day on which Wilson entered Montgomery and Maury's Confederate garrison at last evacuated Mobile, Forrest was at Gainesville, Alabama, a pleasant village situated on a forested bluff on the western side of the Tombigbee, and at that time also reached by a branch line of railroad. A day later Taylor issued orders for a concentration of troops and of steamboat transportation, seemingly looking to active operations "on either river," the Tombigbee or the Alabama. On the fifteenth, however, orders were changed and Forrest began to gather his troops in camps in the vicinity of Gainesville, although because of difficulties in getting across the flooded Tombigbee it was not until April twenty-fourth that the concentration was complete.[63]

The country and the command boiled with rumors, especially when a flag of truce went from Taylor to Canby, whose Federal troops now occupied Mobile. The rumor of Appomattox had reached interior Alabama, but the Confederate government still was in existence, even though in flight, and there had been no orders for surrender or even the cessation of hostilities which common sense had brought about. On April twenty-fifth, therefore, Forrest issued an address to his troops, declaring that the rumors running through camp "should not control actions or influence feelings, sentiments or conduct." After giving his command several wildly favorable rumors "from Southerners" and therefore presumably the more reliable, the General closed with the admonition, "At this time above all others it is the duty of every man to stand firm at his post and true to his colors. A few days more will determine the truth or falsity of all the reports now in circulation."[64]

Four days later, on April twenty-ninth, General Taylor boarded a railroad handcar at Meridian and was "pumped" down the road to Magee's Farm, twelve miles north of Mobile, where he met General Canby who, like Taylor, had charge of all things military on his side between Georgia and the Mississippi River. When the Generals met, Canby's band outside struck up "Hail Columbia." Canby, the considerate host, stepped out and had the tune changed to "Dixie," whereupon Taylor, not to be outdone, asked that the original air be continued since it appeared that all could once more "hail Columbia."[65]

The convention entered into that day between the two tactful and considerate officers followed the terms already agreed upon between Sherman and Joe Johnston at their first meeting in North Carolina. Forrest was notified on the last day of April that hostilities had ceased, subject to renewal on forty-eight hours' notice if the terms were disavowed by either government.[66]

The United States Government having disavowed the terms of the Sherman-Johnston convention, notice was given of the resumption of hostilities within forty-eight hours. Taylor, having no slightest intention of resuming war, again journeyed down the railroad, this time to Citronelle, forty miles north of Mobile, and there on May 4, 1865, surrendered the last Confederate forces in arms east of the Mississippi—chiefly Maury's garrison out of Mobile and Forrest's men at Gainesville. In promulgating the order of surrender from his headquarters at Meridian on May sixth Taylor praised the "liberality and fairness" of the terms granted by Canby, and urged "an honest adherence" to them as a matter touching the honor of all.[67]

Uncertainty and speculation as to what Forrest and his command would do in the event of surrender runs through all the story of those dying days of the Confederacy. His old arch-antagonist Sherman wrote to Grant, on April twenty-fifth:

"I now apprehend that the rebel armies will disperse and . . . we will have to deal with numberless bands of desperadoes, headed by such men as Mosby, Forrest, Red Jackson, and others, who know not and care not for danger and its consequences."[68]

To his wife Sherman wrote in like vein:

"There is great danger of the Confederate armies breaking up into guerrillas, and that is what I most fear. Such men as Wade Hampton, Forrest, Wirt Adams, etc., never will work and nothing is left for them but death or highway robbery. They will not work and their negroes are all gone, plantations destroyed, etc."[69]

There was some basis for his fear, too, as is indicated by the correspondence of Lieutenant General Wade Hampton and President Jefferson Davis. To the President, Hampton wrote, "If you will allow me to do so, I can bring to your support many strong arms and brave hearts—Men who will fight to Texas & will seek refuge in Mexico, rather than the Union. . . . My plan is to call the men who stick to their colors and to get to Texas. I can carry with me quite a number and *I can get there*."[70]

To his wife, fleeing ahead of him with their children, President Davis wrote, "For myself, it may be that a devoted band of Cavalry will cling to me, and that I can force my way across the Mississippi, and if nothing can be done there which it will be proper to do, then I can go to Mexico. . . ."[71]

436

When President Davis received word of the final intention of General Johnston to surrender to the overwhelming force of Sherman, he started southwest from Charlotte, North Carolina, to make his way to Alabama to the troops commanded by his brother-in-law, Richard Taylor, and Forrest. At the last Confederate council of war, held at Abbeville, South Carolina, the President once more urged prosecution of the war, and it was only when the five brigadiers present, commanding the five fragmentary brigades which constituted the President's escort—one of them was the remnant of Forrest's Old Brigade under Dibrell—set their faces against such a plan that the President abandoned it.[72]

Through it all, however, Forrest gave no indication of what he would do, other than his appeal of April twenty-fifth to stand firm until rumors could be resolved. He was busy, as always, no longer with plans for combat but with the administration of his command—for men, even or perhaps especially, defeated men waiting for the end, must eat, animals must be fed and groomed, the work of the camps must go on, order must be maintained. And for all these things the commanding general still was responsible.

"General Forrest is a hard worker," young George Cable wrote to his mother at this time from "Hq Qr Gainsville [sic], Ala.," from which he could look out and see the pontoon bridge laid across the Tombigbee to connect camps on both sides of the river, and the two steamboats unloading at the landing below the bluff. "Everybody about him must be busy. I think he calls for 'them clerks' a dozen times a day. He attends to everything himself, sits and talks to everyone, knows everyone by name, tells everything he intends to do, and tells the same instructions over fifty times in half an hour. His brain, however, is as clear as crystal and he seems to think of a dozen things at once."[73]

As Colonel Kelley wrote, in those days at Gainesville "all was gloom, broken only by wild rumors."[74] And then came the surrender order of May sixth. Talk of "going to Mexico" filled the air. The "younger element revolted against surrender"[75] and Forrest himself was not oblivious of the possibility. Taking Anderson with him as a companion, he started on a long night ride, silent and thinking. At a fork in the road Anderson interrupted with the query:

"Which way, General?"

"Either. If one road led to hell and the other to Mexico, I would be indifferent as to which to take."

The talk began. The levelheaded Anderson argued with him. Finally he reminded the General of the duty he owed to lead into the ways of peace the young men who had followed him in war.

"That settles it," Forrest answered, and turned back to camp.[76]

In the camps there was seething and rebellious unrest, with a strong

437

movement on foot to head for Texas, maybe for Mexico. Lieutenant "Pap" Nichols was carrying the crowd with him in a fiery and eloquent address of protest, despite the calmer counsel of older officers, including General Bell. And "then General Forrest came," and with the homely eloquence of which he was master brought them back to reason.[77]

On the next night the General had another long ride with Anderson, talking to him the ideas which, on May 9, 1865, became Forrest's farewell address to his troops.[78] He said:

"That we are beaten is a self-evident fact, and any further resistance on our part would be justly regarded as the very height of folly and rashness. The armies of Generals Lee and Johnston having surrendered, you are the last of all the troops of the Confederate States Army east of the Mississippi River to lay down your arms. The cause for which you have so long and manfully struggled, and for which you have braved dangers, endured privations and sufferings, and made so many sacrifices, is today hopeless. The government which we sought to establish and perpetuate is at an end. Reason dictates and humanity demands that no more blood be shed. . . . It is your duty and mine to lay down our arms, submit to the 'powers that be,' and to aid in restoring peace and establishing law and order throughout the land. The terms upon which you surrendered are favorable to all. They manifest a spirit of magnanimity and liberality on the part of the Federal authorities which should be met on our part by a faithful compliance with all the stipulations and conditions therein expressed. . . .

"Civil War, such as you have just passed through, naturally engenders feelings of animosity, hatred and revenge. It is our duty to divest ourselves of all such feelings, and, so far as it is in our power to do so, to cultivate friendly feelings toward those with whom we have so long contested, and heretofore so widely but honestly differed. . . . The attempt made to establish a separate and independent confederation has failed, but the consciousness of having done your duty faithfully and to the end will in some measure repay you for the hardships you have undergone. . . . I have never on the field of battle sent you where I was unwilling to go myself, nor would I now advise you to a course which I felt myself unwilling to pursue. You have been good soldiers, you can be good citizens. Obey the laws, preserve your honor, and the government to which you have surrendered can afford to be and will be magnanimous.
"N. B. FORREST, Lieutenant-General."

On this high note ended the career of Forrest as a soldier and the history of Forrest's cavalry. Ahead was the new and in many ways more difficult world of peace and reconstruction.

438

CHAPTER XXVII

THE GRAND WIZARD OF THE INVISIBLE EMPIRE

1865-1869

THERE was, of course, much speculation as to Forrest's course after the surrender. Men of all faiths and factions seemed to find it hard to believe that the man whose fighting had become—and remains—the epic of the Confederacy in the West would be content to accept the new order of things; would, in fact, become one of the strongest forces for peace and genuine reconstruction.

The first public note of the new attitude of Forrest and the new attitude toward him was the reprinting by the Memphis *Bulletin* of his farewell address to his soldiers. The same paper on May 30th, 1865, printed a dispatch from Grenada, Mississippi, stating that:

"Gen. N. B. Forrest was at Grenada till the middle of last week. He acted honestly and fairly in his negotiations with the Federal authorities. He turned over all the property in his possession. He remarked that he was now as good a Union man as anybody—that the South was whipped and he was going to support the Federal government as heartily as any one could. . . . When Genl. Forrest left Grenada for his plantation on the Mississippi River about 20 of his former slaves started with him."

General Forrest was on his way to Sunflower Landing in Coahoma County, Mississippi. Four years before, he had been worth, according to his own estimate, "a million and a half of dollars." When the Confederacy fell he and his wife found themselves, so far as wealth was concerned, not greatly better off than they had been at the beginning of their married life twenty years before. "I came out of the war pretty well wrecked," Forrest said afterward, ". . . completely used up, shot all to pieces, crippled up . . . a beggar."[1] Mary Montgomery Forrest, described by a writer in the Memphis *Avalanche-Appeal* as "apparently delicate, but with great reserve force and powers of endurance," had "survived the privations, inconveniences and exposures of four years, moving about from place to place as the scenes of war shifted, like a true soldier,"[2]

439

but now she had entered upon a new struggle, working with her husband in the remaking of their broken fortune.

On July 1, 1865, having gone to Jackson, the capital of Mississippi, to "make application to the President for a pardon"—which he was not to receive for yet another three years—Forrest wrote from there to his old department commander, Lieutenant General Stephen D. Lee, that he had taken the necessary amnesty oath, to be attached to his application which Governor Sharkey had agreed to forward to the President with his approval. "I would advise if you will allow me to do so," he continued, "that you make and send yours forward as early as practicable."

With this matter of public business out of the way, Forrest turned to more personal matters. "I have settled for the present at my plantation in Coahoma Co., Miss.," he wrote, using as he always did the old-fashioned long "s" so that the abbreviated name of the state appeared as "Mifs," and "have gone to work—have a fine crop of corn—if the seasons hit will make a fine crop. Mrs. F. is making butter and raising chickens, so come to see us and bring Mrs. Lee with you."[3]

"I carried seven Federal officers home with me, after the war was over," Forrest told the Congressional committee investigating the "Ku Klux Conspiracy" in 1871, "and I rented them plantations, some of my own lands, and some of my neighbors'. In 1866 these seven officers made a crop in my neighborhood. . . . These men were all young men, and they made my house their home on Sundays."[4]

One of the Federal officers, Major Diffenbocker of Minnesota, went into partnership with Forrest in his planting. Commenting on this in January 1866, before the first of the Reconstruction Committees of Congress, Major General Edward Hatch, under whom the Major had fought against Forrest, testified that "there is no more popular man in West Tennessee today than the late rebel General Forrest." The former Federal officer told him, Hatch added, that he went into partnership with Forrest "because he is popular, and will take care of him and his interests."[5]

The war was over, so far as Forrest's associations were concerned. He was on friendly terms with numerous Union soldiers against whom he had fought, and who remained in the South or returned there after being mustered out. One of these was Frank P. Blair, as much as any one man responsible for keeping Missouri in the Union in 1861, and subsequently a major general commanding one of Sherman's army corps, who met Forrest in Memphis shortly after the war. He had shared the common prejudice against "Forrest of Fort Pillow" but found a hardworking and useful citizen. When in the fall of 1866 it appeared that

Forrest's business would make it necessary for him to apply for an enlargement of his parole, he wrote President Johnson for the necessary extension. Frank Blair, forwarding the letter to his brother Montgomery, Lincoln's Postmaster General, who was to present it to the President, wrote that it breathed "the spirit of moderation and accommodation." General Forrest's "influence, more powerful than that of any man in West Tennessee," he added, "has been wielded invariably in the maintenance of peace and amicable feelings. . . . I have conceived a very great personal attachment for Forrest. He was one of the finest soldiers of the Confederacy. . . . His noble bearing since the war in accepting without complaint the result and using his powerful influence to make others accept it in the same spirit, have inspired me with a respect and admiration I have not felt for any other man"—and Frank P. Blair, be it remembered, had associated from boyhood with the nation's great, civil and military.[6]

Besides managing a plantation along the big river, where farmhouses were five or six miles apart, the General "made a full hand" in the long-neglected work of repairing fences, houses and barns. In August a troop of Federal cavalry was riding by Forrest's place, as much out of curiosity to see him as for any more definite reason. The war horse King Philip was grazing in the front lot. As the blue-clad cavalry filed into the lot on the way up to the house, King Philip's training in many a melee reasserted itself, and he rushed at the bluecoats, teeth bared and front feet flailing. When some of the soldiers, astonished at his onslaught, struck at him, Forrest's wartime body servant Jerry—whom the other Negroes in the Forrest command had referred to, and obeyed, as "the Gin'ral"[7]—rushed out to defend the horse. After Forrest himself had come out and the horse was back in his stable and things had quieted down, the Federal captain observed, "General, now I can account for your success. Your negroes fight for you, and your horses fight for you."[8]

Life was not always simply pastoral at Sunflower Landing. There was the time when some 200 colored former Union soldiers, employed as hands on Forrest's and adjoining plantations, and forming the local company of militia, advanced against his house, armed and with intent to violence. But an hour or two before, Forrest had heard from the Negro quarters the screams of a woman. Entering the cabin he found a man beating his wife to death with a stick of stovewood. When the General kicked and knocked him off the woman, the enraged man attacked him with a wicked knife. Forrest, unarmed, backed away toward the door, keeping his face to his assailant. Reaching behind him to find the latch on the cabin door his fingers closed over the handle of an

441

ax. As the Negro rushed, Forrest swung the ax up and brought it down, splitting his skull.

The story, or at least the fact that Forrest had killed a Negro, ran through the fields. The hands put down their tools, got their guns, gathered together and advanced in military array across the wide lawn in front of the plantation home. In the house were only the General and Mrs. Forrest. Willie, who had come out of the war at nineteen a veteran soldier but lacking the education his father wished him to have, was away as a student at the University of Mississippi. Hearing the disturbance outside, Forrest stepped to the veranda. Mrs. Forrest, against orders, followed him outside. As the militia drew up to the steps Forrest, in his compelling voice, gave the command, "Halt!" The company halted. "Order arms! Ground arms!" were obeyed. "Now get out of here and get back to work!" he added—and again he was obeyed. The aftermath was a trial before a Negro magistrate at which Forrest was completely exonerated and freed.[9]

During all this time there still hung over Forrest the indictment for treason returned against him by the Federal grand jury after his raid on Memphis in August 1864. There began, in some of the Northern papers, moreover, an agitation for severe measures against Admiral Raphael Semmes, the "pirate of the *Alabama*," which soon was enlarged to include "Forrest of Fort Pillow." Friends in Memphis, conceiving that Forrest was in danger of molestation, sent word to him in Mississippi to escape to Europe, and at the same time sent a letter of credit to supply him with the necessary funds. Convinced that he was covered and protected by his parole, as were other surrendered Confederates, he went instead to Memphis, told the commandant there that he was quietly at work observing the terms of his parole and intended to keep on doing so, and that he expected that the government on its side would do likewise—in which position the military commandant agreed with him.[10]

The indictment for treason, however, presented another question. Forrest, therefore, appeared in the office of the clerk of the United States Circuit Court for the District of West Tennessee on March 13, 1866, and made bond in the sum of $10,000, with R. C. Brinkley and Frazer Titus as sureties. Subsequently, on September 3, 1866, the bond was renewed in the same amount with Landon C. Haynes and Samuel P. Walker as sureties. Apparently no further steps were taken under the indictment.[11]

In the spring of 1867 in all probability—though it is not a matter of record, and no man who of his own knowledge could have known the fact has ever publicly revealed it even unto this day—Forrest was called to a new service as head of the Ku Klux Klan.

Forrest did not originate the Ku Klux Klan. The order was born early in 1866, when half a dozen young ex-Confederate soldiers got together in the little Middle Tennessee town of Pulaski to form a secret society solely for their amusement. The mysterious name, all the more mysterious because meaningless, was a corruption of the Greek *kuklos,* circle, with Klan added for the alliterative rhythm it gave. The ritual, so far as it has been preserved, and the cipher and code words, were as meaningless to the outsider as the name. The whole thing was got up "just for fun."

The new order began to hold its meetings in a ruined house on a lonely hill in the outskirts of Pulaski—the sort of house which in the South is apt to become known as "haunted." It became noised abroad among the Negroes that the "ha'nts" of dead Confederate soldiers were meeting in the old house and marching about the country. That was enough. The Klan had stumbled upon a power mightier than that of the law, superstitious terror, which was soon recognized, carefully cultivated and preserved.

It was natural that the use of the new-found weapon should spread, not only over Tennessee but neighboring states. A sort of vague authority in the Grand Cyclops of the original Den at Pulaski was recognized but there was no real central organization. There was already throughout the south an organization of "Loyal Leagues," semimilitary in character, the membership including Negroes and whites of the persuasions hated by the ex-Confederates as "scalawags" and "carpetbaggers." The Leagues, of course, were recognized, protected and encouraged by the government, civil and military. Against them and against the rising tide of depredation and lawlessness, against the almost total lack of protection by law for ex-Confederates and their families, against the gnawing fear of a war of races, it was decided to oppose the force of the terrors excited by the pranks of the Pulaski Den and its successors.

In April of 1867 a secret convention met at Nashville. It adopted the "Prescript" which became the basis of the organization and government of the Klan, and—in all probability—it elected as its chief officer, or Grand Wizard, Nathan Bedford Forrest. There is a large literature on the Ku Klux movement—thirteen weighty volumes of Congressional testimony and reports, much of it worthless because of its intense partisanship; much romancing; some history.[12] To their dying days, however, no actual Klansman ever directly named the Grand Wizard in public print.

John C. Lester, one of the six founders of the original Den, of course, knew his identity, but writing in 1884 the first authentic history of the

443

Klan from inside sources, he refers to him merely as a "citizen of Tennessee."[13] John W. Morton, confessedly a staff officer of the Grand Wizard, knew, but the nearest he comes to naming his chief is in an appendix to his story of Forrest's artillery, in which he quotes with approval an address by T. W. Gregory, subsequently Attorney General in President Wilson's Cabinet, in which the Wizard is referred to again just as a "citizen of Tennessee." In the same appendix, however, Captain Morton quotes from a magazine article by Thomas Dixon, Jr., the facts of which could have been received from no one but Morton himself, the story of Forrest's initiation into the Klan at his own request. Forrest, according to the story, realized the potentialities of the new movement, and came from Memphis to Nashville to get into it. Morton, Grand Cyclops of the Nashville Den, took him to the woods outside Nashville, gave him the preliminary oath and directed him to report to Room 10 in the old Maxwell House that night for the final initiation.[14]

Major James R. Crowe of Sheffield, Alabama, one of the original six of the Pulaski Den, in a letter written in 1908, but not published until 1914, after his death, stated the case succinctly and no doubt correctly: "After the order grew to large numbers we found it necessary to have someone of large experience to command. We chose General N. B. Forrest."[15]

The official record of Forrest's connection with the Klan, if it may be called a record, is found in Volume 13 of the testimony taken in 1871 by the Joint Select Committee of Congress to inquire into the condition of affairs in the late insurrectionary states, the so-called Ku Klux Investigation. Examined before this committee in Washington on June 27, 1871, Forrest displayed a considerable acquaintance with the purposes of the Klan but astonishing infirmities of memory as to details and the sources of his knowledge—or perhaps not so astonishing, either, when it is considered that at that time connection with the Klan was a serious criminal offense and that even if Forrest had been willing to expose himself to prosecution, he had to think of others whom he could not so expose.

In maintaining his attitude before the committee Forrest was hampered and hindered by an interview with him published in the Cincinnati *Commercial* on September 1, 1868, professing considerable familiarity with the Klan, its membership and its operations. Nor was this his greatest embarrassment. The interview he could treat as inaccurate and a campaign-year misrepresentation of what he had said, particularly since the reporter had found him with a violent sick headache and had insisted upon interviewing him as he walked the ninety yards or so to his home and sat on his front doorstep, occasionally vomiting. The greater stumbling block in the General's testimony was that

444

three days after the interview he had written a letter of correction which neither corrected nor denied all the statements which he now wished to deny—an omission which he explained by saying that he was unaccustomed to being questioned by reporters or to writing letters to newspapers.[16]

As to the Klan, the General "could not speak of anything personally" and his only "knowledge of the existence of any such order as the Ku Klux" was "information from others." To inquiry as to the identity of these others, Forrest recalled that one was a "gentleman by the name of Saunders," resident of Mississippi, but Mr. Saunders, it seemed, was now dead—poisoned by his wife at Asheville, North Carolina. Then there were others, whose names he could not remember at first. He did succeed in recalling, afterward, that one was named Jones, first name not given, but Mr. Jones had gone to Brazil. There was still another informant who was doubly in oblivion, being both dead and having had his name forgotten—and that was as far as Forrest could recall specifically the sources of his information about the Ku Klux.[17]

He thought, nevertheless, that "the organization did exist in 1866 and 1867," although he wasn't just sure what it was named. "Some called them Pale Faces; some called them Ku Klux." He had, in fact, joined the Pale Faces in Memphis in 1867, but "that was a different order from this. . . . Something like Odd Fellowship, Masonry, orders of that sort. . . ." It developed in the questioning about the Pale Faces, however, that he was "never in the organization but once or twice," knew little of its tests for membership, took no oath, could not recall its passwords, grips or signs, if it had any, and could remember the names of no one present at the meetings he had attended. He did remember, though, that the meetings were in a building on Second Street, which may have been significant since the traditional location of Klan headquarters in Memphis was the Irving Block on that street. And that was all he could remember about the Pale Faces. As to the Knights of the White Camellia, he admitted first that he had heard of them but later said that was a mistake, and he knew nothing about them.[18]

Yes, he had seen and had had a copy of the constitution of the order under investigation. Some party unknown had sent it to him in a letter "from some place in Tennessee" which he could not then recollect. No, he had it no longer. He had burned it.

"What was the name of that organization given in that constitution?"

"Ku Klux."

"It was called Ku Klux?"

"No, sir; it was not called Ku Klux. I do not think there was any name given to it."

"No name given to it?"

445

"No sir; I do not think there was. As well as I recollect, there were three stars in place of a name. I do not think there was any name given to it," but Forrest let slip a moment later, that the constitution he had received and burned was called by the odd name of a "Prescript."[19]

What, then, was the purpose of this organization which had for a constitution a prescript, and for a name, three stars? On that question, the General was a great deal better informed and more communicative. It was for self-protection. The people of Southern sympathies were "very much alarmed" at what they saw going on around them. They were apprehensive about the Loyal Leagues, organized among the Negroes by Northern men of the sort called "carpetbaggers"—though by no means were all Northern men who came South of that persuasion, the General explained—and Southern men called "scalawags." There was "great fear" that there would be a war of races, and a "revolution something like San Domingo." And finally, said the witness, there was alarm at Governor Brownlow's proclamation of martial law in Tennessee, which was looked upon as an invitation to violence and, indeed, a "kind of amnesty in advance for future depredations" upon the Southern people.[20]

And who were the people who had formed this organization for self-protection? Forrest's "information was that they admitted no man who was not a gentleman and a man who could be relied upon to act discreetly; not men who were in the habit of drinking, boisterous men, or men liable to commit error or wrong, or anything of that sort; that is what I understood. . . ."

"Were they rowdy or rough men?"

"No, sir; worthy men who belonged to the Southern army; the others are not to be trusted; they would not fight when the war was on them, and of course they would not do anything when it was over."[21]

But why did not these people appeal to the protection of the laws?

"The very name of Brownlow at that time was a terror to the people of Tennessee. . . . They were very much frightened. . . . A large portion of the people were disfranchised."[22]

And how did General Forrest come to be concerned with this organization for self-protection?

"I was getting at that time from fifty to one hundred letters a day and had a private secretary writing all the time. I was receiving letters from all the Southern States, men complaining, being dissatisfied, persons whose friends had been killed, or their families insulted, and they were writing to me to know what they ought to do."

No, he had none of the letters. "Most of them, I burned up, for I did not want to get them into trouble. I suppose they were excited at the time; there was a great deal of excitement in 1866 and 1867, immediately after the war."

"Were all of these people personal acquaintances who wrote to you?"

"A great many of them I never saw."

"How came they to write to you?"

"I do not know;"—and then, proudly—"I suppose they thought I was a man who would do to counsel with."[23]

Well, what had he done about this organization he had heard about? The Ku Klux Klan, he thought, was "disorganized in the early part of the year 1868," though maybe it was "the latter part of 1867." He wasn't sure of the exact date but "it was understood among the Southern people that this organization had disbanded about the time of the nomination of candidates for President of the United States," although upon further questioning and thought the time of disbandment was extended to "the latter part of 1868, I reckon." The General's efforts, he said, "were addressed to stop it, disband it and prevent it."

"Were you trying to suppress the organization, or the outrages you speak of?"

"I was trying to suppress the outrages."

"Outrages committed by colored men?"

"By all people; my object was to keep peace."

"Did you want to suppress that organization?"

"Yes, sir; *I did suppress it.*" (Italics supplied.)

The cat was out of the bag but for no more than a moment.

"How?"

"Had it broken up and disbanded," he said, by talking with different people and writing letters to them. Since 1868, he did "not think there has been any organization together; if there has been, it has been by irresponsible parties, without any organization at all." . . .

"Then you at least had the confidence of the organization?"

Proudly, again, "I had the confidence of the Southern people, I think."[24] And again, summing up his position:

"I am disposed to do all I can to try and fetch these troubles to an end. . . . I tried to do my duty as a soldier, and since I have been out of the war I have tried to do my duty as a citizen. I have done more probably than any other man in the South to suppress these difficulties and keep them down. . . . I want our country quiet once more, and I want to see our people united and working together harmoniously."[25]

And there the matter rested after the General's uncomfortable day on the witness stand in an examination which covers nearly forty large pages of exceedingly small type. At its end the committee officially was no wiser than when it started, but every member, in all probability, came away convinced that if the actual Grand Wizard of the Invisible Empire had not been the witness before them, he had had a lot more to do with it than receiving and writing letters. And, under all the circumstances and the obligations upon him toward the membership, it is likely that no member of the committee inwardly blamed him for his palpable evasions—to use the mildest term possible.

The committee in its report did not formally find that Forrest was an officer or even a member of the Klan. The majority did, however, repeat some eight pages of his testimony, setting forth much of it in parallel columns with the Prescript of the ***. "This contrast might be pursued further," the committee continued, "but our design is not to connect General Forrest with this order, (the reader may form his own conclusions upon this question), but to trace its development. . . ." The minority of the committee likewise quoted at length from Forrest's testimony, "as illustrative of the origin, objects, and dissolution" of the Ku Klux, with the comment that all he said "about the alarm which prevailed in Tennessee during the administration of Governor Brownlow was strictly true. No State was ever reduced to such humiliation and degradation as that unhappy commonwealth during the years Brownlow ruled over her."[26]

While there is no real doubt that Forrest was the Grand Wizard of the Klan and that, as he told the committee, he "did suppress" it, there is much uncertainty as to when he did so and why. In his testimony he placed the date all the way from late 1867 to late 1868. Others place it still later. There is extant an "order of dissolution," dated in the Ku Klux cipher in January 1869, but this may have been no more than an order to prohibit masking and going in disguise, including the' destruction of regalia, rather than a complete dissolution of the organization.[27] Lester and Wilson, in their work published in 1884, give the date as the spring of 1869. Judge J. P. Young, who was secretary of the Memphis Den and one of the last survivors of those intimately associated with its officers, dated the dissolution still later, in the summer of 1869.[28]

Judge Young's recollection is the more credible because he did not attempt to recall a date but placed the event with reference to another publicly recorded event, the date of which is certain. De Witt C. Senter, a conservative Republican who became governor by automatic succession when "Parson" Brownlow, the Reconstruction Governor of Tennessee, resigned on February 20, 1869, to go to the United States Senate, stood for re-election by the people in August of that year. In a contest of great strife and bitterness the Conservative Republicans and those Demo-

448

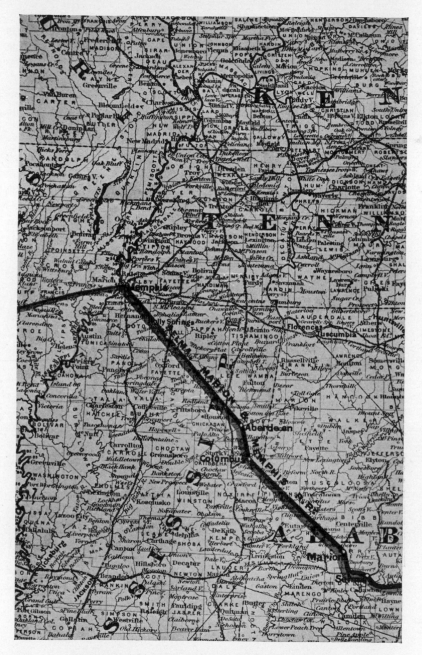

THE RAILROAD FORREST TRIED TO BUILD

Map of the proposed Selma, Marion and Memphis Railroad, from an 1869 circular of Henry Clews & Co., New York, its fiscal agents. Parts of the uncompleted railroad are now included in the Southern and the Frisco systems.

FORREST STILL RIDES

The equestrian statue in Forrest Park, Memphis, beneath which the General
and Mrs. Forrest are buried.

crats who could vote, powerfully aided by the Klan, most of whose members could not, managed to re-elect Senter, and overthrow Radical rule[29] in Tennessee, for good.

Within ten days after the election, said Judge Young, the Memphis Den, holding its regular noon session in the Irving Block, received orders from the Grand Wizard, then at Nashville, to disband, destroy records and regalia—simply blot itself out. The order was delivered by messenger and also, in cipher, by telegraph. The latter excited apprehension and criticism among the members, who feared for leaks and a discovery, which, however, did not come.

And so, sometime between the fall of 1867 and the fall of 1869, the Ku Klux Klan, as an organization, was officially dissolved by the Grand Wizard, acting under the absolute powers granted him in the Prescript adopted at the Nashville convention in 1867.

The reasons for his action are equally clouded in mystery. One view is that Governor Brownlow's proclamation of martial law in certain strong Klan counties in Tennessee early in 1869 brought it about—a view that takes no account of the character of the Klan. It is hardly likely that proclamation of martial law in a few counties in one state would have caused it, at the height of its power, to go out of existence.

Certainly that had not been the earlier reaction of the ex-Confederate part of the population of Tennessee when the legislature created the "Brownlow Militia" and the Governor threatened to call them out against the Ku Klux in the summer of 1868. Forrest was called to Nashville where, on August 1, 1868, he met with thirteen other general officers of the Confederate army and about thirty leading citizens in what came to be known as the "Council of Peace." The conferees protested that they did not believe there was an organization in the state seeking the overthrow of the government, and their conviction that there was no need for calling armed forces into action, to which they added their pledge to see that peace and order were maintained if the causes of friction and discord were removed by the legislature. The offer was dismissed with scant consideration as an impudent assertion of extralegal power.[30]

Forrest, who acted as a sort of unofficial spokesman for the would-be peacemakers, was entirely conciliatory in presenting their proposition. Ten days later, however, in a speech at Brownsville, Tennessee, he spoke out. Governor Brownlow, he said, threatened to declare Ku Klux, by which he meant ex-Confederates, to be outlaws, who might be shot down by the militia without fear of prosecution. "I for one do not want any more war," he went on. "I have seen all the war and all the bloodshed I want. . . . I wish you to do nothing that will give the Radical party any

449

pretext to bring on a war. . . . They would like nothing better . . . but if they bring this war upon us, there is one thing I will tell you—that I shall not shoot any negroes so long as I can see a white Radical to shoot, for it is the Radicals who will be to blame for bringing on this war. . . ."[31]

Another, and no more likely, reason offered for the disbandment order and perpetuated in local tradition at Pulaski, is that Forrest and General Grant had a secret meeting in Washington immediately after Grant's inauguration as President, at which it was agreed that efforts would be made to restore civil government in the South, and that the Klan, in recognition of this fact, would disband its "invisible empire" and go out of existence.[32]

The more likely reason for its dissolution is to be found in the Klan itself. Its purposes, as expressed in the Prescript which was not intended to be and was not made public, were high—to protect the weak and the innocent from the lawless and violent; to protect and defend the Constitution of the United States, to assist in the execution of all constitutional laws, and to protect the people from oppression. But the Klan, even with its high purposes, was a desperate venture, meeting privileged oppression and lawlessness with organized and secret lawlessness. Where its operations were in capable and high-minded hands, it worked; where its local officers did not measure up to that difficult standard, it failed to greater or less degree.

And there was another even more serious weakness in the very nature of the Klan. In the vital matter of protecting itself from imitation by the low and vicious, it was foredoomed to failure by the very necessities of its situation—a secret membership, operating in disguise and without the law. There simply was no way to keep others from using the same disguises and the same methods. The Klan tried, and tried hard, to judge from what is known of its real history. In fact its later history, so far as it is to be found, was largely taken up with strenuous and sometimes violent efforts to protect its name and reputation from others who used its disguises and methods for vicious ends, but it failed, as it was bound to do. The Klan method, in short, could not be made to work.

For that, or some, reason, the Grand Wizard dissolved it. The authorized and organized Ku Klux, so far as they got the decree, disbanded according to its terms. Laws had been passed forbidding the publication or distribution of Klan notices, however, and some Dens probably never received the order. New Dens were formed after the dissolution, also, by individual members without authority. The imperfect Prescripts of some such dens, evidently written from memory, have been preserved. Moreover, totally unauthorized persons, many of them the so-called "loyal" men, had found the Klan disguise an effective cover

450

for crime or personal vengeance, and continued to use it. So it was that the movement in various ways kept on until the last of the dread days of Reconstruction in the last state of the South, a dozen years after the surrender, despite the dissolution decreed by the Grand Wizard of the original and authorized Ku Klux Klan.

The original Klan was a desperate device of a people defeated and all but despairing. It was his reputed leadership in this effort, as much as in the war, which adds point to the statement that "what Robert Bruce was to the Scots, Scanderbeg to the Albanians, Markos Bozzaris to the Greeks," Forrest was to the South.[33]

CHAPTER XXVIII

THE HARDER WAR
1865-1877

BESIDES his labors as Grand Wizard of the Invisible Empire—assuming that he was that officer—Forrest, with health impaired[1] by the hardships, privations and tremendous exertions of the four years of war, faced the difficult and discouraging task of making a living.

In 1866 he "planted" again in Mississippi but in 1867 returned to Memphis, where he became president of a fire-insurance company, and was interested in the organization of a company for life insurance as well[2]—the same lines of endeavor, incidentally, in which another distinguished ex-Confederate, Jefferson Davis, was to engage in the same city of Memphis, and with the same lack of success.

Forrest's discouragement at this period is shown in a letter written by him as president of the Planters' Insurance Company to a young Confederate Colonel, Garnett Andrews, Jr., of Yazoo City, Mississippi, who had asked about prospects of employment in Memphis. "I have no business nor do I no of any by which you could find employment in this City at any price. I have sold out all the contracts I have had on hand and am now settling up my affairs as rapidly as possible, believing as I do that Every thing under the laws that will be inaugurated by the military authority will result in ruin to our people."[3]

His pessimism was well-founded, certainly as to his own affairs, for on February 5, 1868, Forrest, who before the war had counted himself worth more than a million dollars, filed his petition in bankruptcy in the United States District Court at Memphis, giving up his property for the benefit of his creditors and applying for discharge from his debts. No creditors appearing in opposition, this discharge was granted in the spring of 1869.[4]

How profound was Forrest's despondency in this period may be gathered from a conversation he had in Chattanooga, reported by Norman Farrell, late of the Confederate army and a friend of Brigadier General Thomas Benton Smith. "On Sunday afternoon General Smith and I had a long talk with General Forrest," Farrell wrote on February 25, 1868, to his fiancée in Nashville. He continued:

452

"He told us of a scheme of his for conquering Mexico, asked Tom if he could raise a regiment, and wanted to know if I would go with him: Now I have no idea of trying such a desperate venture. . . . Smith, however, seemed willing enough to go, indeed he says he likes a soldier's life better than any other. Forrest said that he had been promised 20,000 muskets and that he would want 30,000 men, he could conquer the country in six months; that he would then confiscate the mines and the church property; that is about ⅓ of all the real estate of the country; hold possession of each state, as he advanced, by leaving four or five thousand men in each; take possession of all the offices for himself and his men, among which, of course, N.B. would get the lion's share with the title of King or President; while the private would get his in bullets; and then he concluded: 'I would open up the country to immigration, after I had given it a free government, and would get at least 200,000 people from the southern states, besides many from Europe and the north.' He said there are at least 50,000 young men in the south who won't plow, but who would fight or dig for gold. I asked him if he did not think the United States would interfere with his little arrangement, but he said they would be glad to get rid of him.

"From the appearance of things at Washington if Mr. Forrest would just keep quiet a little while he can get enough fighting in this country. I will send you N. B.'s autograph soon."[5]

So far as now appears, this interesting instance of the once prevalent American custom of casting a filibustering eye to the southward did not get beyond the stage of Sunday afternoon conversation. At any rate, that summer Forrest was a delegate from Tennessee to the first Democratic National Convention after the war, which met in New York on July 4. He became a delegate, he said in an open letter published in Tennessee newspapers and reprinted in the New York *Times* of May 24, 1868, not from any "desire to take part in politics or to hold any political position whatever" but because he did not wish to see his "state represented by men whose only claim to public favor is the dexterity with which they took either side in the late war as interest dictated."

The Tennessee and Kentucky delegates, Basil Duke relates in his reminiscences, traveled together to New York in the same coach. The presence of Forrest in the group attracted attention, and was telegraphed ahead. As the train approached one point north of the Ohio, the conductor, a former Union soldier, came in to tell the delegates that he had had word that the town bully was waiting at the station with a crowd threatening to thrash Forrest. No one wanting trouble, Forrest agreed to remain quietly in the coach but when the train stopped, the truculent bully burst in upon him.

453

"Where's that damned butcher Forrest?" he called out. "I want him."

Forrest bounded to his feet, with such a transformation in appearance as he had never seen in a man, Duke wrote. Erect, eyes blazing, face the color of heated bronze, he strode toward the approaching assailant, saying:

"I am Forrest. What do you want?"

Whereupon the assailant turned tail and ran. Forrest, following him for a moment in accordance with his battle rule to "keep the skeer on him," burst out in a "tremendous shout of laughter," in which the crowd joined. In the few more minutes which the train remained, many pressed forward to shake him by the hand.[6]

His presence in New York attracted the attention of the newspapers, who took notice in items ranging all the way from the rigidly Republican *Tribune*'s reference to "Gen. N. B. Forrest of Fort Pillow notoriety" to the descriptions in the *Herald* of "General Napoleon Bonaparte Forrest" who was stopping with the Tennessee delegation at the Astor House— "looking as bold and erect as ever, standing over six feet high, and presenting the finest physical type of the belligerent element in the Southwest . . . and a man of a good deal more common sense than he has ever been given credit for. Forrest is one of the best reconstructed rebels in this city today and his career in the convention will vindicate this assertion. . . ."[7]

Forrest took a keen interest, though by no means a prominent speaking part, in the convention. His support for the nomination for President, and that of the Tennessee delegation, went to President Andrew Johnson, who had but a little while before passed through the impeachment trial in which the Radicals sought his removal from office. After a dozen or so ballots, it being apparent that Johnson could not be nominated, the Tennessee delegation began dividing its votes among other candidates until, finally, on the twenty-first ballot, it joined in the unanimous nomination of Governor Horatio Seymour of New York and Forrest's friend, Major General Frank P. Blair of Missouri, for President and Vice-President.

Forrest became something of an issue in the campaign of 1868 and a favorite topic of Republican editorial writers and cartoonists in the development of the Bloody Shirt theme, his name being always good for a round of denunciation. Forrest said three years later, "there were a great many things said in regard to myself that I looked upon as gotten up merely to affect the elections in the North."[8]

One speaker who continually assailed him, however, seems to have aroused Forrest's special anger. On October twenty-eighth, from Memphis, Forrest wrote General H. R. Shackelford of New Haven, Connecticut, who had called his attention to a speech made there by General Judson Kilpatrick, commander of Sherman's cavalry on the March to the Sea, in which he had savagely attacked Forrest for having "nailed negroes to the fences, set fire to the fences and burned the negroes to death," at Fort Pillow.

"All such reports," Forrest wrote Shackelford, ". . . . are utterly untrue. . . . I am not prone to obtrude matters of this kind upon the public notice, and would have been glad to have met Kilpatrick and settled this affair in a less public and more emphatic manner. . . . I am ready to meet him in any way that he may choose and while I am averse to personal conflict, I would much prefer to gratify any wish he may cherish in that way to being the further object of . . . defamation and . . . misrepresentation." Denouncing "General Judson Kilpatrick as a blackguard, a liar, a scoundrel and poltroon," Forrest closed by saying, "If he is the heroic figure he would have the Northern people believe him, my friend, Gen. Basil W. Duke, at Louisville, Ky., is authorized to receive, on my behalf, any communication he may choose to make."

Here General Duke takes up the story. Forrest's open letter was reprinted in Louisville. "I was flattered by Forrest's selection of me as his friend in this affair," Duke wrote afterward in his *Reminiscences*, "and at one time would have acted with alacrity and even a certain degree of pleasure. But just then the thought of having to act as either second or principal in a duel in Kentucky was not at all agreeable," because of constitutional provisions which, among other penalties, would have disbarred him from the practice of law for such an offense. "I had come out of the war . . . and begun the practice of law in Louisville. My prospects in that line were not brilliant, it is true, but they were all that I had, and I was exceedingly loath to relinquish even that small chance of making a living." Duke thought of transferring the meeting to some other state but he was afraid that Forrest might not get fair play north of the Ohio, while the South was still under military rule and the authorities, on account of the prominence of the parties and the attention which the challenge was arousing, might "feel obliged to interfere." In Kentucky, however, "both men would have friends and sympathizers," Duke felt, "and the general sentiment would be that they should fight 'in peace,' without partisan or impertinent interference." Despite his own difficulty, therefore, Duke enlisted the aid of friends in making arrangements for the affair, which are described in inimitable detail by General Duke, at whose hands no story ever suffered in the telling.

On October thirtieth a Connecticut friend of General Kilpatrick wrote to General Shackelford, who had sent the account of the original speech to Forrest, that since officers of the army had investigated Fort Pillow, "hundreds of witnesses" had been examined, and a Committee of Congress had "not only confirmed his [Kilpatrick's] statements on the subject but had given additional and more shocking details of Forrest's inhuman conduct at Fort Pillow, Gen. Kilpatrick has nothing to communicate to either Forrest or Basil Duke, except to reiterate his denunciation of Forrest's unparalleled atrocities"—which was the last of what might have been one of the most celebrated of American duels, especially if the combatants had acceded to one suggestion made, that they fight with sabers on horseback.[9]

In that campaign summer of 1868 Forrest's mother died. After the war, like so many other Southerners of the time, her younger Luxton sons had moved to Texas, where one son, Matthew, afterward became sheriff of Uvalde County. Another son, Jim, fell ill at the roadside inn of Ira Camp in Grimes County, Texas, and his mother was summoned to him. In alighting from a buggy before the inn she stepped upon a nail, the wound received resulting in blood poisoning. In her delirium the staunch old matriarch kept calling and calling for her first-born Bedford, and could be quieted and comforted only by the assurance that he was on his way to her. There Mariam Beck died, and there she was buried in the private burying ground of the Camp family, three miles northeast of Navasota, Texas.[10]

Before the summer was over, Forrest received from President Johnson his pardon, issued on July 17, 1868, "for which," he told a Tennessee audience a few days later, "I am truly thankful."[11] He was once more a citizen of the United States, although under the Tennessee state law disfranchising Confederates for a period of fifteen years, he was not yet a voting citizen.

The Seymour-Blair ticket lost the Presidential election, as was foredoomed from the beginning, but the result does not seem to have added greatly to Forrest's depression, for in the same fall of 1868 he found a new field for his endeavors, a new outlet for his energies and renewed hope for the future, when he turned to railroad building.

Forrest believed in the destiny of Memphis as a center of railroads, a belief which events have justified. While still head of the Klan, probably, he undertook the enterprise of connecting his city by rail with the country in Mississippi over which he had fought so much and which he knew so well, and beyond that with the coal and iron regions of Alabama, the importance of which he sensed and pressed upon the attention of the commercial world of Memphis.

The result of his efforts was the organization of two companies—the Selma, Marion and Memphis Railroad, chartered in Alabama on December 31, 1868, to take over the franchises and properties of the

Cahaba, Marion and Greensboro Railroad, which before the war had built thirteen miles from Marion Junction, on the railroad between Selma and Demopolis, to the town of Marion; and another Selma, Marion and Memphis company, chartered in Mississippi and Tennessee, to take over the Memphis, Holly Springs, Okolona and Selma Railroad, the charter of which dated back to 1859, but which had built no railroad. The two new companies of similar name were consolidated on March 17, 1871, for the building and operation of a through line from Memphis to Selma, where it was proposed to connect with another new railroad to be built to the Atlantic seaport of Brunswick, Georgia.

Forrest's new railroad was enthusiastically described in a circular issued to investors by Henry Clews and Company, New York bankers, in September 1869. It was to run 280 miles, through a territory from which it was expected there would be shipped 1,000,000 bales of cotton a year when the country became fully developed, and would also reach the growing iron and coal developments in Alabama. The cost of the road was estimated at $25,000 a mile. Bonds, secured by a first mortgage on the line, limited in amount to $16,000 a mile, and to be endorsed by the State of Alabama only as sections of the line should be "finished, equipped and completed" as a "first class road," were offered and recommended to investors.[12]

In addition to the bonds the road was to be financed mainly through subscriptions to its capital stock by the counties through which it was to run. The most populous and important of these was Shelby County, Tennessee, in which Memphis was located, where both the county and the city, by public election, voted to take stock in the enterprise. Forrest himself, and his associates, canvassed the eight counties in Mississippi and the five in Alabama through which the line was to run, presenting the proposition to meetings of citizens and to "railroad conventions." In some counties, at least, Forrest made speeches in every civil district. "I said when I started out that railroads had no politics," he told a Committee of Congress; "that I wanted the assistance of everybody; that railroads were for the general good of the whole country."[13]

At the Alabama end the original thirteen miles of line taken over from the ante-bellum company were extended twenty-two miles from Marion to Greensboro and a farther extension in the direction of Eutaw was put under way. At the Memphis end the roadbed was partially graded as far out as Holly Springs, Mississippi, and ties were placed along the grade.

The road, like so many others of the period, was being built chiefly on hopes and prospects. And then, with the new company in its most vulnerable position, its financing incomplete, its line under construction,

457

and its traffic still to be developed, twin disasters struck—the money stringency of late 1872, prelude to the great national and international panic of 1873, and, in the latter year, the appalling local disaster of yellow fever in Memphis. The Selma, Marion and Memphis had no chance to earn the money to pay the interest on its bonds, guaranteed by the state of Alabama. Receivers were appointed, after default, by Federal courts both at Memphis and in Alabama, and both receivers undertook to sell the entire property at foreclosure, to satisfy claims against it, thereby creating a conflict of title which was finally resolved only by dividing the two ends of the line in separate ownerships. The road in Alabama, afterward extended to a connection with the Alabama Great Southern at Akron, finally became and is now operated as a branch line of the Southern Railway System. The road in Tennessee and Mississippi, completed during the 1880's, became part of the main line of the St. Louis-San Francisco Railway between Memphis and Birmingham.[14]

While Forrest was president of the road—he resigned in 1874—he made a gift of $5,000, payable in its stock, to the fund of $200,000 then being raised in Tennessee to meet the conditions of a gift of $500,000 offered by Cornelius Vanderbilt for the founding at Nashville of the University which now bears his name. The default and bankruptcy of the company rendered Forrest's subscription of no value, as things turned out, other than as an expression of his interest in the education which he himself did not have.[15]

Forrest's railroad was never built as projected, but finally much of it was, adding its part to the development and wealth of the South. To Forrest himself, however, it brought labor, vexation, litigation and finally financial disaster. One of its unhappy consequences was a breach with his friend Minor Meriwether, civil engineer and Confederate engineer officer who was superintendent and chief engineer of the road. It was Meriwether's responsibility to certify the completion of sections of the road so as to secure the payment of the subscriptions to its securities. Forrest, as the story was subsequently told by Meriwether's son, asked for certificate of completion of certain mileage before, in Meriwether's opinion, it could properly be certified; Meriwether refused the certificate and "at a directors' meeting . . . stated that he would discuss the matter that night at a mass meeting in the Greenlaw Opera House." Forrest, objecting that such a speech would be an attack on him, threatened that if the speech were made "one of us will not leave the Greenlaw alive." To friends who went to Forrest to urge that he keep the peace, "the General listened courteously but gave no sign what impression the appeal made upon him." That night at the Opera House, with Forrest present and the audience, having heard rumors of conflict, sitting tense on the edges of their chairs, Colonel Meriwether stepped to the table in the center of the stage, pulled out a pistol, and laid it down carefully with the remark, "I understand that some persons object to my speaking here tonight. If that is true, let the objections be made now. I do not wish to be interrupted after I begin my speech." And then, after a breathless moment, the audience sank back in their chairs with an almost audible sigh—for Forrest said nothing and did nothing, and the speech went on. Subsequently, at a Confederate memorial meeting, the two comrades were reconciled and, as Forrest lay dying, Meriwether took his son—the same who tells the story above—to see him.

"Don't be afraid, Lee," said the gaunt man on the bed. "Your father is my friend. Come closer. Let me look at you——."

"As we walked away from that house," the junior Meriwether wrote many years later, "my father's eyes dimmed with tears as he said to me: "Lee, the man you just saw dying will never die. He will live in the memory of men who love patriotism, and who admire genius and daring."[16]

Forrest's last years were a struggle with debt, arising from his railroad ventures, and with sickness, a wasting chronic dysentery, arising no doubt from his Confederate service—for dysentery might, indeed, almost have been called the "Confederate disease," so common it was in the armies.

To make a living he went back to planting. His Mississippi plantations having been sold long before to satisfy his debts, he leased land on President Island in the Mississippi River just below Memphis. For labor he leased the city's prisoners, this being before the day of proper workhouses and prisons in the South, when the common way of dealing with convicts was to lease their labor. Some degree of success seems to have attended his planting, to judge from his remark just before his death that he was in a "fair way to discharge every obligation I owe to man."[17]

In these latter years of tribulation the prayers of Mary Montgomery Forrest were answered when Bedford turned to the religion which always had been so large a part of her life. On the streets of Memphis one day in 1875 Forrest met the Reverend Raleigh White, the same who as a lieutenant colonel had long commanded the old Fourteenth Tennessee Cavalry, and who now, as he told his general, was in Texas "preaching the word of God." After a short conversation the two stepped into the quiet of the parlor of a bank near by, to kneel together in prayer.[18] Not long afterward, on November 14, 1875, a calm Sabbath evening, the General walked into the Court Street Cumberland Presbyterian Church, Mrs. Forrest on his arm, and told the minister, the Reverend G. T. Stainback, that he had decided to accept the Christian faith.[19]

"There was no half way of doing things with Forrest," the minister said afterward in a lecture, "and this is the way he entered the religious faith. . . . The news of his conversion had gone abroad and the church was filled the following Sunday morning. When I called for new members he folded his arms and deliberately walked down the aisle to the altar. I thought then that I had never seen such a magnificent man as General Forrest that day!"[20]

In preaching Forrest's funeral sermon nearly two years after his conversion, the minister observed that "General Forrest has said a good many things that didn't look much like a Christian"—the language habits of a lifetime are strong—but he was assured that in essentials the old warrior had kept the faith.[21]

In these last years Mrs. Forrest's influence over the General, always quieting, soothing, gentling, grew. It was upon her that the doctors relied to see that Forrest followed their orders, as is related by Major Anderson, who in the late summer of 1877 joined his old chief and Mrs. Forrest at Hurricane Springs, in the Middle Tennessee highlands where, it was hoped, the water would improve the General's health. Anderson wrote:

"There was a new gentleness in him. At first I thought it must be his illness, and then I remembered that in the old days when he was sick or wounded he was the most restless and impatient man I ever saw. I mentioned the change to the General. He smiled toward his wife. ' "Old Mistess" is responsible,' he said. The next morning we came in and sat down at the table. One of the symptoms of his illness was an abnormal appetite. He picked up knife and fork and started to go after the substantial breakfast before us. 'Please don't eat that,' she remonstrated, 'Your breakfast has been prepared and will be here in a few minutes.' 'Major,' said Forrest, 'I know that Mary is the best friend I have on earth, but sometimes it does seem that she is determined to starve me to death.' "[22]

Six weeks before his death, coming back from the "springs" a mere shadow, his giant frame shrunken until he weighed little more than a hundred pounds, supporting himself on the shoulders of two friends, Forrest dragged his way from the train to a carriage, to be taken to his residence on President Island.[23] There he remained until Sunday, October twenty-eighth, when his condition became so hopeless that he was brought back to the residence of his only surviving brother, Jesse, on Union Street to die. During that day and the next he recognized a few old friends, and roused up to speak to Jefferson Davis, when the ex-President of the Confederacy came to his bedside. At half past seven

460

o'clock in the evening of October 29, 1877, in the fifty-sixth year of his age, Forrest died.[24]

On Wednesday, the last day of October 1877, they buried him in accordance with arrangements made by his Confederate comrades in arms at a memorial meeting held the afternoon before. The funeral procession moved from the home of Jesse Forrest to the church on Court Square, and on south to Elmwood Cemetery—a line of march of three miles, lined by 20,000 people, white and black.[25]

From a hotel window on Main Street, Lafcadio Hearn, an unknown reporter making his way by stages down the river from Cincinnati to New Orleans, watched the procession pass. Hearn, not long in America, "half hoped to see Confederate uniforms in the troop. But," he added, "there was only one Confederate uniform in the procession, and that was worn by the occupant of the hearse."[26]

The Confederates were there, however, even though the time had not yet come when the Confederate uniform should once more be worn in public procession. The Escort Company, led by its commander in its final fight, Lieutenant George L. Cowan, came down from Nashville to join "All Mounted Confederates" in heading the procession. The pallbearers included members of Forrest's staff, among others, and President Davis. Behind the hearse marched the lodge of the Independent Order of Odd Fellows, of which Forrest was a member, and the several local military companies, as well as Confederates on foot, civic and public bodies, the Fire Department, and "Citizens Generally on Foot." As the procession marched, fire bells and church bells tolled and minute guns were fired by local artillery, in charge of Major J. C. Thrall, who had for so long commanded one of Forrest's batteries in more deadly firing.[27]

As bells tolled and minute guns crashed, while Forrest was being carried to his place of rest in Elmwood Cemetery, the Anglo-Ionian stranger, Hearn, watched and noted what he saw and what he heard—that here was a man of mixed report, idolized by some, by others feared and disliked; a man whose violence of temper led him occasionally into outbursts for which he would, at times, "apologize . . . as humbly and sincerely as any human being could apologize"; a man "tough as hickory, his vitality of that kind which never requires the stimulus of alcohol"; a man by nature imperious and arbitrary, but one to whom "at last there came . . . the fantastic Rider of the Pale Horse, whose ways were much more arbitrary and whose will was much stronger than even the ways and the will of Nathan Bedford Forrest."

To Hearn, "who saw and heard these things only as a stranger in a strange city may observe the last of a long chain of unfamiliar events," it "seemed a strange coincidence that the funeral procession down

461

mourning Main Street by the Gayoso House . . . was passing down the very street along which Forrest's Cavalry had made their desperate charge one gray morning, thirteen years before."

And so Forrest's comrades in arms laid him away in Elmwood where, fifteen years later, they were to lay Mary Montgomery by his side—to remove them both, in 1905, to their final resting place beneath the equestrian statue of the General in Forrest Park, Memphis.

But, as the observant Hearn noted in Memphis in 1877, "soldiers who served under him never seem to tire of talking about Forrest." From that day to this they have talked and have handed on the talk to spread wide in time and space till Forrest's name has become known through the world.

The soldiers who followed Forrest, the generals under whom he served and those against whom he fought, the distinguished soldiers across the seas who knew him only by his record—all are agreed that here was no common man and no common commander. In an intimate after-the-war conversation General Joseph E. Johnston, who had better opportunities than any other of the high commanders of the Confederate forces to see and judge his work, "pronounced General Forrest the greatest soldier the Civil War produced," even though "according to Lee and Jackson the full measure of their fame."[28]

Robert E. Lee himself has been quoted, also, as having rated Forrest as the "greatest soldier," or the "greatest general," of the Southern armies, but such expressions, resting upon hearsay or possibly imperfect understanding and recollection, hardly accord with Lee's habitual reticence in expressing opinions as to the comparative merits of Confederate commanders.[29]

It is not necessary, however, to enter upon any scheme of comparative rating of Confederate commanders to accept the idea that Forrest was an original and effective force in warfare.

As Stonewall Jackson's men were called "foot cavalry," so were Forrest's men described as "winged infantry"—that being, of course, long before the plane and the parachute made such soldiers into an actuality.[30] The idea of troops who could combine the mobility in maneuver of cavalry with the striking power in battle of infantry, did not originate with Forrest, of course, even in the Confederate service,[31] but there is truth, nevertheless, in Viscount Wolseley's statement that "Forrest was the first general who in modern days taught us what Turenne and Montecuculli knew so well, namely the use of the true dragoon, the rifleman on horseback, who from being mounted has all the mobility of the horse soldier."[32]

There is no evidence that Forrest ever read Colonel Lucius Davis' manual for Mounted Riflemen in the Confederate service, and even less reason to believe that he ever heard of the European masters of horse to whom Wolseley referred, but through his own great common sense he worked out for himself, and applied in practice, surprisingly "modern" methods in dealing with time, space, men and materials—methods by which he was enabled with meager resources to accomplish in his field major results.

It was this quality of making the most of what he had, as much as any other one thing, which led Viscount Wolseley to say, as he did in 1892, that

"If ever England has to fight for her existence . . . may we have at the head of our government as wise and far-seeing a patriot as Mr. Lincoln, and to lead our mounted forces as able a soldier as General Forrest!"[33]

Another quarter of a century and, in 1914, England was indeed fighting for her life. On a morning in late November of that year there chanced to meet, upon the balcony of a rare book shop in Piccadilly, a British officer and Colonel Granville Sevier, one of a group of United States officers in London at the time. The British officer remarked that he was looking for a copy of Wyeth's life of Forrest. Having just noticed a copy in one of the cases, Colonel Sevier pointed it out. A brief conversation followed, in which the American remarked that he had known Dr. Wyeth and that General Forrest had seated him on his first horse. The British officer was at once interested.

"And were you old enough to have known General Forrest?" he asked.

Colonel Sevier explained the circumstances—that his father, a staff officer in the Confederate armies in the West, had become a close friend of Forrest's; that after the war and in the last year of his life the General had come to Sewanee, Tennessee, to visit the elder Colonel Sevier who was teaching there at the University of the South; that the General seemed to weary of the conversation of the elders, mostly about the then late war, and would come out and spend long periods talking with the children; that, learning that young Sevier had not been taught to ride, he had called up his father's old war horse, then retired, had sent for a bridle and saddle, and then and there had instructed the seven-year-old boy in how to approach a horse, how to bridle him, how to put on the saddle and how to mount and sit, going over the whole thing several times in great detail and with great patience.

In the conversation which developed, Colonel Sevier explained that from the time he was old enough to know anything he had known many of Forrest's men mentioned in Wyeth—Bell, Dibrell and the rest, and that he had grown up in the Forrest atmosphere.

463

The British officer began eagerly questioning him as to his views of certain campaigns and battles, with such an evident thorough and detailed knowledge of the subject as compelled the American to admit that he was abashed at not knowing more.

"You know much more about General Forrest and his campaigns than I, or than most of us in America," he said.

"Officers of our British cavalry service study his campaigns and his methods," was the answer. "We regard him as one of the greatest, if not the greatest, of English-speaking commanders of mounted troops."

The British officer, with his copy of Dr. Wyeth's book, left. Shortly afterward Colonel Sevier returned to the main floor of the store. Mr. Buchanan, of the book shop, asked him how he had enjoyed his conversation. Colonel Sevier expressed his great pleasure, and also his chagrin that the British officer should have known so much more about General Forrest and his record than he.

"Who was he?" he asked Mr. Buchanan.

"You don't know?"

"No. Somewhere before I've seen his face. Perhaps met him in France," said the Colonel.

"Is this he?" asked Mr. Buchanan, holding up a full-page newspaper picture, with his hand over the caption.

"Yes," answered the Colonel.

Mr. Buchanan uncovered the name—Sir Douglas Haig, whose First Corps of the British Expeditionary Force had just fought and won the first Battle of Ypres.[34]

This professional appreciation of Forrest's place in warfare, which began with Wolseley's study and estimate in 1892, would have pleased Forrest's old soldiers, but would in no wise have astonished them. They could have told the professionals about it themselves, long before.

They knew that no book had to teach Forrest that a commander must know what his enemy is up to; must guard his own troops from surprise; must so mask his plans as to sow doubt and indecision in his enemy's mind; must always and forever look to his necessary supplies and communications; must fight, not merely to be fighting, but must fight for something, and that something reasonably attainable by first-class fighting men. As Forrest once said of himself, he "fought by ear" but he seemed to know by instinct, and to appreciate at their full value, the factors in warfare taught by the campaigns of the greatest masters—mobility, secrecy, security, surprise, concentrated striking power and, above all, the incalculable value of that imponderable, the fighting heart of the soldier.

Because these soldiers of his believed in him—in his devotion to his cause and to his soldiers, in his courage which took account of dangers but was not daunted, in his immense common sense that spent effort and men only with reason—because the men who marched along "aching weary, staggering sleepy, starving hungry"[35] believed in him, they would march for him a little farther and a little faster, and fight for him a little harder. His was the power, as one of his young soldiers said more than sixty years after, to "make heroes out of common mortals"— the true power of the handful of the truly great captains.

A NOTE ON GEOGRAPHICAL CHANGES

In the years since 1865 there have been material changes in the geography of the country over which Forrest marched and fought, not only in the growth of towns and cities, and the opening up of highways and railroads, but in the names of places and political subdivisions and in the very shape of the land.

The most profound change, by far, has been the creation by the Tennessee Valley Authority of a series of lakes whose waters have covered, or soon will cover, the scenes of most of Forrest's exploits along and across the Tennessee River.

That part of Bedford County, Tennessee, in which Forrest was born and from which he took his middle name, is now Marshall County. That part of Tippah County, Mississippi, to which he removed at the age of thirteen, is now Benton County. The hamlet of Salem, his boyhood home in Mississippi, is no longer in existence, its site being known as Old Salem. The nearest town now is Ashland, Mississippi, county seat of Benton County. Chapel Hill, Tennessee, where Forrest was born, is a thriving village, however, marked with an obelisk erected on the site of his birthplace.

Another town which figures in Forrest's operations, Estenaula, Tennessee, once a famous inn and stage crossing of the Hatchie between Memphis and Jackson, Tennessee, is no longer in existence, although the brick foundations of the old inn are still discoverable. The nearest point is Hatchie Station on the Nashville, Chattanooga & St. Louis Railroad.

Several places which figured in Forrest's operations are still in existence but under different names. Brice's Cross Roads is now the post office of Bethany, Lee County, Mississippi. Panola, Mississippi, is now Batesville. La Fayette, Tennessee, is now Rossville. Crawfish Springs is now Chickamauga, Georgia.

Spelling of place names is as they were spelled in the time of the War between the States. Thus Murfreesboro, Tennessee, as it is now spelled, appears herein in its spelling of the sixties as Murfreesborough.

The railroad lines which played so large a part in the operations of Forrest appéar under the names by which they were then known. The following table relates them to present-day lines, the 1860 designation being shown in italics:

Southern, now the Yazoo & Mississippi Valley connecting **Meridian,** Jackson and Vicksburg, Mississippi.

Mississippi Central, now the Illinois Central between Canton, Mississippi, and Jackson, Tennessee, via Grand Junction.

Mississippi and Tennessee, now the Illinois Central between Grenada, Mississippi, and Memphis.

Mobile & Ohio, now the line of the Gulf, Mobile & Ohio between Mobile, via Meridian, Corinth, Mississippi, and Jackson, Tennessee, and Columbus, Kentucky.

Memphis & Charleston, now the line of the Southern Railway between Memphis and Stevenson, Alabama.

Blue Mountain, or *Alabama & Tennessee River,* now the line of the Southern Railway between Selma, Alabama, and Anniston, Alabama.

Selma & Meridian, now the line of the Southern Railway between those cities.

Louisville & Nashville, now the same, between the cities whose names it bears, and also between Bowling Green and State Line (now Guthrie), Kentucky.

Tennessee & Alabama, Central Southern and *Tennessee & Alabama Central,* now the Nashville and Decatur line of the Louisville & Nashville, via Columbia, Tennessee.

Edgefield & Kentucky, now that part of the line of the Louisville & Nashville between Guthrie, Kentucky, and Amqui Junction, Tennessee.

Memphis & Ohio, now that part of the line of the Louisville and Nashville between Memphis and Paris, Tennessee.

Memphis, Clarksville & Louisville, now the line of the Louisville & Nashville between Paris, Tennessee, and Guthrie, Kentucky.

Nashville & Chattanooga, that part of the Nashville, Chattanooga & St. Louis between the cities named.

Nashville & Northwestern, that part of the Nashville, Chattanooga & St. Louis between Nashville and Johnsonville, Tennessee, and between McKenzie, Tennessee, and Hickman, Kentucky.

Western & Atlantic, that part of the Nashville, Chattanooga & St. Louis between Chattanooga and Atlanta.

East Tennessee & Georgia, that part of the Southern Railway between Knoxville and Chattanooga, Tennessee, and Dalton, Georgia.

NOTES, BIBLIOGRAPHY AND INDEX

NOTES

CHAPTER I

A MEASURE OF A MAN

[1] "I went into the army worth a million and a half dollars, and came out a beggar." N. B. Forrest testimony, "Ku Klux Report" of 1872, 2nd Session, 42nd Congress, Senate Document No. 41, Vol. 13, p. 24.

[2] Twenty-four men in the Confederate service attained the rank of lieutenant general or higher. When Forrest enlisted, all the others were already officers in the Confederate service. Twenty of the twenty-four were graduates of the United States Military Academy and had been officers in the Regular Army. The others were Sterling Price, former Governor of Missouri who had served with distinction in the Mexican War and, in June 1861, was in command of the Missouri state forces; and three who were with the army in Virginia in June 1861—Richard Taylor, son of General and President Zachary Taylor, colonel of the Ninth Louisiana; and Wade Hampton, colonel of Hampton's South Carolina Legion. John B. Gordon, frequently listed among the Lieutenant-Generals, did not actually receive that rank although at the end of the war he exercised a command appropriate to it, that of a Corps of the Army of Northern Virginia. At the time of Forrest's enlistment he was a major in the Sixth Alabama.

[3] In a postwar letter to the Union General James Grant Wilson, Forrest's second-in-command, Chalmers, wrote that he had seen this classic and often quoted bit of "indorsement hereon." Captain J. Harvey Mathes, *General Forrest* (New York, 1902), p. 383. It appears to be no longer in existence, despite occasional published reports of its being in the Confederate Museum at Richmond, or elsewhere. The indorsement as quoted by Chalmers spells "No" as "Know." This may have been an exaggeration by General Chalmers who seems to have delighted somewhat in shocking his Northern friends with stories of Forrest's unorthodox spelling.

[4] Lafcadio Hearn, *Occidental Gleanings,* edited by Albert Mordell (New York, 1925), p. 148. Hearn, on his way from Cincinnati to work in New Orleans, was in Memphis at the time of Forrest's death, saw his funeral, interviewed citizens of the town and reported what he saw and heard in the first of the series of letters signed "Ozias Midwinter." This letter, entitled "Notes on Forrest's Funeral," appeared in the Cincinnati *Commercial,* Nov. 6, 1877.

[5] "Ku Klux Report" of 1872, Vol. 13, p. 24.

[6] Lucy Leffingwell Cable Bikle, *George W. Cable: His Life and Letters* (New York, 1928), p. 20.

[7] Hearn, p. 145.

[8] Thomas F. Gailor, Bishop of Tennessee, in the *Sewanee Review,* January 1901; reprinted in *Southern Historical Society Papers* (Richmond, 1876), Vol. 29, pp. 337-339.

[9] John Milton Hubbard, *Notes of a Private* (Memphis, 1909), p. 133.

[10] Sergt. Frank T. Reid, in John Berrien Lindsley, *Military Annals of Tennessee* (Nashville, 1886), p. 851. Sergeant Reid of Morton's artillery became a prominent businessman of Seattle after the war.

[11] J. P. Young, Seventh Tennessee Cavalry, in Memphis *News-Scimitar*, May 16, 1905; *Confederate Veteran*, Vol. XIII, p. 389.

[12] Hearn, p. 149.

[13] Lieut. Col. George T. Denison, *A History of Cavalry* (London, 1877), p. 529. In this work, published while Forrest was yet living, Colonel Denison traced the development of the mounted infantryman back to Alexander the Great.

[14] Rev. W. H. Whitsitt, Fourth Tennessee Cavalry, before the Richmond, Virginia, Camp, United Confederate Veterans, reported in the *Confederate Veteran*, Vol. XXV, pp. 361-362.

[15] *Personal Memoirs of U. S. Grant* (New York, 1885), Vol. II, p. 346.

[16] U. S. War Department, *The War of the Rebellion—A Compilation of the Official Records of the Union and Confederate Armies* (Washington, 1889), Serial No. 78, pp. 121, 142. (This work is hereinafter referred to as *O.R.*)

[17] Adam R. Johnson, *The Partisan Rangers of the Confederate States Army* (Louisville, 1904), p. 72. Johnson served afterward under Morgan and in independent command as a brigade general. His military service ended when both eyes were shot out at the skirmish of Grubb's Crossroads, Kentucky, Aug. 21, 1864.

[18] Manuscript of Lecture by Tully Brown, Adjutant General of Tennessee and formerly lieutenant under Forrest, in the Tennessee State Library, Nashville.

[19] Lindsley, p. 851.

[20] Walter A. Clark, *Under the Stars and Bars, or Memories of Four Years Service with the Oglethorpes of Augusta, Georgia* (Augusta, 1900), pp. 157, 161. The Oglethorpes were part of the Sixty-third Georgia Infantry, Featherston's brigade, assigned temporarily only to Forrest as commander of the rear guard in Hood's retreat from Tennessee.

[21] Conversation under flag of truce with Capt. Lewis M. Hosea, U. S. A., *Sketches of War History* (Ohio Commandery of the Loyal Legion, Cincinnati, 1888), Vol. I, p. 81.

[22] John A. Wyeth, *Life of General N. B. Forrest* (New York, 1899), quoting President Jefferson Davis, p. 634.

[23] Dabney H. Maury, Maj. Gen., C. S. A., *Recollections of a Virginian* (New York, 1894), p. 224.

[24] Personal communication from Brig. Gen. Frank C. Armstrong, C. S. A., reporting postwar conversation with General Sherman. Wyeth, p. 635. Dr. Wyeth, eminent New York surgeon, served in his youth as a Confederate soldier. He was never himself under Forrest's command, but was in the Fourth Alabama Cavalry, which previously had served under Forrest. "The enthusiastic devotion to General Forrest of these veterans . . . who seemed never to tire of speaking of his kind treatment of them, his sympathetic nature as a man, his great personal daring, and especially his wonderful achievements as a commander," led Dr. Wyeth to an interest which caused him to collect the vast amount of Forrest lore which went into the writing of his truly invaluable biography.

[25] *Reminiscences of General Basil W. Duke* (New York, 1911), p. 346.

[26] Richard Taylor, *Destruction and Reconstruction* (New York, 1879), p. 200.

[27] Donn Piatt and H. V. Boynton, *General George H. Thomas: A Critical Biography* (Cincinnati, 1893), p. 599. The meeting mentioned in this work is the same described in much more detail in the contemporary home letters of Capt. Lewis M. Hosea, U. S. A., afterward embodied in *Some Sidelights on the War for the Union*, a paper read before the Ohio Commandery of the Military Order of the Loyal Legion at Cleveland, Ohio, on October 9, 1912. Although Captain Hosea's

letter devotes much attention to Forrest's pronunciation and use of words, it does not mention "fustest with the mostest," which a young man of Captain Hosea's interest in and sensitivity to oddities of expression would most certainly have noticed and mentioned, especially as he reported the remark "first with the most" to his chief, General Wilson. James H. Wilson, *Under the Old Flag* (New York, 1912), Vol. II, p. 184.

[28] In the Memphis *Commercial-Appeal*, May 14, 1905. Captain John W. Morton, Forrest's Chief of Artillery in the last year of the war, in writing his memoirs, published in 1909, noted with scorn the statement in its transitional state of "fust with the mostest," as a travesty on what Forrest said. John W. Morton, *The Artillery of Nathan Bedford Forrest's Cavalry* (Nashville, 1909), p. 198. Nevertheless, the phrase "fustest with the mostest" has come into wider and wider use, especially since the outbreak of the Second World War, when it has been used in dispatches, books, articles, advertisements and objurations of sundry sorts as an antidote to the policy of "too little, too late." There remain, however, doughty defenders of the truth as to what Forrest said, notably the Baltimore *Evening Sun's* "Antiquarian Correspondent" and Dr. John N. Ware of Shorter College, writing in the Atlanta *Journal*.

[29] New York *Tribune*, May 27, 1918.

[30] New York *Times*, May 28, 1918.

[31] Maj. Gen. Sir Frederick B. Maurice, *Robert E. Lee, the Soldier* (New York, 1925), p. 21.

[32] Joel Chandler Harris, *The Shadow Between His Shoulder Blades* (Cambridge, 1909), p. 62.

[33] Hearn, p. 145.

[34] In a series of articles, "General Forrest," by General Viscount Garnet Wolseley, in the *United Service Magazine*, Vol. V, New Series (London, 1892), p. 119. Extracts were published in the New Orleans *Picayune* of April 10, 1892, from which they were quoted in the *S.H.S.P.*, Vol. 20, pp. 325-335. Dr. Wyeth quoted extensively from the parts of the Wolseley articles republished in America but not from those parts of the original articles which were not so republished. The passage here quoted is from the original London articles.

[35] Maury, pp. 150 (quoting Gen. Joseph E. Johnston), 205.

CHAPTER II

THE FIRST FORTY YEARS

1821-1861

[1] Will D. Muse, Memphis *Commercial Appeal*, May 14, 1905. But, wrote Wolseley, "a man with such a record needs no ancestry." *United Service Magazine*, Vol. V, New Series, p. 123.

[2] The most complete account of the Forrest ancestry is in *General Forrest* (of the "Great Commanders" series) by Capt. J. Harvey Mathes of Memphis, pp. 1-3. Loss of the Forrest family Bible in the fire which destroyed the General's temporary home on President Island about a month before his death in 1877 is responsible for much of the lack of precise information about family matters. Captain Mathes never served under Forrest, but as a Memphis newspaperman of many

years' experience, and as a friend of many of the survivors of the Forrest cavalry, he had an unusual knowledge.

[3] By that time the name of Forrest or anything associated with him had become such a power in West Tennessee that one Watson, a guerrilla, sought to capitalize on it by impersonating Joseph Luxton, Forrest's young half brother. Watson was captured by Federal forces when he raided and burned steamers collecting cotton up the Hatchie River, near Brownsville, Tennessee, and was hanged on April 22, 1865, and left hanging. *O.R.* (Naval), Vol. 27, pp. 148-149.

[4] Benton County was organized in 1870, with Ashland as the county seat. Salem Post Office was discontinued April 30, 1901. Post Office Records; letter from A. A. Autry, Chancery Clerk, Benton County, Mississippi.

[5] Upon one occasion a panther attacked Mrs. Forrest. The story of the attack illustrates the character of both mother and son. The panther was after a basket of young chickens which Mrs. Forrest was bringing home at nightfall. She could have thrown the chickens to the panther and, being mounted, could have escaped. But declaring that she was not "going to let any varmint have her chickens," she made for the cabin and reached it with the fowls, even though the panther actually leaped upon her and lacerated both her and the horse she rode.

Equally characteristic was the son's reaction. As soon as he had carried his wounded mother into the cabin where she could be cared for, he called his dogs and set out, after nightfall, in pursuit of the animal. The pursuit lasted all night but in the morning Bedford brought back to the cabin the scalp and ears of the panther.

[6] Mathes, p. 4.

[7] Gen. George W. Gordon, Memphis *News-Scimitar,* May 16, 1905.

[8] Gen. James R. Chalmers, *S. H. S. P.,* Vol. 7, p. 455.

[9] Miss Hall, afterward Mrs. Joel Jones of Nashville, was visiting in Hernando at the time and remained for the wedding, in which she was her schoolmate's bridesmaid. Nashville *Banner,* July 7, 1935. "Cussing and gambling," interestingly, were the two practices against which General Forrest most earnestly warned his only son in a letter of advice written at Gainesville, Alabama, on April 15, 1865, in the anxious period between Appomattox and his own final surrender. H. J. Eckenrode, *Life of N. B. Forrest* (Richmond, 1905), p. 169.

To judge from the story told to James R. Randall, author of "Maryland, My Maryland," by Capt. John W. Morton, Forrest's Chief of Artillery, the General himself was not through with gambling. "Forrest liked occasionally to play cards for money," Randall quoted Morton as saying. "After the war, when very needy, he won $3,000 gambling, although his wife, to whom he was very devoted, tried to persuade him to live on half rations rather than play cards. One night at Nashville, he said to me: 'John, can you tell me where I can find a gambling saloon?' I answered in the negative but inquired why he asked. 'Well,' he replied dryly, 'I found one tonight, broke the bank and have $2,500 of their money. I thought I had time to tackle another before I went to bed.'" Sunday *News,* Charleston, South Carolina, Sept. 27, 1903, reprinted from *The Catholic Columbian,* Columbus, Ohio. In Morton Scrapbooks.

[10] *Confederate Veteran,* Vol. XX, p. 210.

[11] Same, Vol. XII, p. 279.

[12] Hearn, pp. 145, 148.

[13] Hubbard, p. 133.

[14] This entire story of the rescue of Able from a mob by Forrest is dismissed by

Frederic Bancroft in his study of the slave traders of the Old South as an invention of "Forrest's hero-worshipping biographers." Bancroft does not believe that he played so prominent or dramatic a part in the affair because it is not mentioned in the contemporary newspaper accounts but only in the subsequent biographies of Jordan and Pryor, Wyeth and Mathes, and in J. P. Young's *Standard History of Memphis,* and because there are discrepancies in detail in these four accounts. Mr. Bancroft's assumption is that the story was invented, or at least embellished, to give respectability to Forrest as a former slave trader. Elsewhere in his study he points out that, despite the tradition to the contrary, "when [slave] traders prospered, were honest, thrifty, and bought plantations, like Forrest . . . and many others, they enjoyed the essentials of respectability." Frederic Bancroft, *Slave Trading in the Old South* (Baltimore, 1931), pp. 259-268, 378. Chapter XII of this work is devoted to the slave trade as practiced in Memphis.

[15] Don C. Seitz, *Uncommon Americans* (Indianapolis, 1925), pp. 127-128.

[16] Memphis *Appeal,* May 19, 1861; June 22, 1861; Sept. 25, 1861.

[17] John C. Cooke, Nashville *Banner,* Jan. 2, 1932.

[18] Memphis newspapers, May 19, 1861.

[19] Memphis *Appeal,* June 1, 1861.

[20] Dinkins, Sunday *Republic,* St. Louis, August 22, 1899, preserved in scrapbook by Capt. John W. Morton, Forrest's Chief of Artillery; Interview with Forrest by LEO, dispatch of June 17, 1868, from Memphis to the Louisville *Journal,* reprinted in the New York *Times,* June 22, 1868.

[21] *O.R.,* Serial No. 4, pp. 402, 431, 436.

[22] Memphis *Appeal,* Aug. 2, 1861.

[23] Same.

[24] Same, Aug. 4, 1861.

[25] Same, July 17, 1861.

[26] Irvin S. Cobb, *Exit Laughing* (Indianapolis, 1941), p. 219.

[27] The company, with three others, became Logwood's battalion, which in the spring of 1862 became the Seventh Tennessee Cavalry, Colonel William H. Jackson. The regiment, then commanded by Colonel W. L. Duckworth, became part of Forrest's force in January 1864, and served under him until the surrender.

[28] Hubbard, p. 15.

[29] *S. H. S. P.,* Vol. 7, p. 455.

CHAPTER III

THE FIRST COMMAND AND THE FIRST FIGHT
July 10, 1861-December 28, 1861

[1] *Confederate Veteran,* Vol. V, p. 478; General Thomas Jordan and J. P. Pryor, *The Campaigns of Lieut.-Gen. N. B. Forrest* (New Orleans, Memphis and New York, 1868), pp. 41-42. This, the earliest of the four American and one British full-length biographies of Forrest, was written without the advantages of perspective of time or access to the records, but with the inestimable advantage of personal contact with Forrest himself and with many of his men. In an introductory note dated October 3, 1867, Forrest says: "For the greater part of the statements of the narrative I am responsible."

[2] Jordan and Pryor, pp. 42-43.

[3] Wyeth, p. 26.

[4] D. C. Kelley, *The Methodist Review* (Nashville), Vol. 49 (March-April, 1900), p. 221.

[5] *O.R.*, Serial No. 4, p. 177.

[6] *O.R.*, Serial No. 110, pp. 100-101.

[7] *O.R.*, Serial No. 3, pp. 141-142.

[8] These arrangements are fully discussed in Arndt M. Stickles, *Simon Bolivar Buckner* (Chapel Hill, 1940), Chapters V and VI. The general subject of Kentucky neutrality is treated in E. Merton Coulter, *The Civil War and Readjustment in Kentucky* (Chapel Hill, 1926), Chapters III-VII inclusive.

[9] *O.R.*, Serial No. 4, pp. 179-192.

[10] Same, pp. 196-198.

[11] Same, p. 257.

[12] Same, pp. 404-405.

[13] *Jefferson Davis, Constitutionalist*, Dunbar Rowland, editor (Jackson, Mississippi, 1923), Vol. VIII, pp. 231-232.

[14] *O.R.*, Serial No. 4, p. 193-194.

[15] Same, pp. 194, 408, 410, 417-418, 421-423, 431-434, 452, 474.

[16] Same, pp. 452-453, 459, 468.

[17] Same, pp. 457, 459-462.

[18] Same, pp. 480, 501. The whole of Kelley's command, he wrote afterward, was "fed and foraged by the generous Kentuckians . . . without cost to the Confederate government" while on this work. Lindsley, p. 762.

[19] *O.R.*, Serial No. 4, pp. 297-298.

[20] Same, p. 465.

[21] Same, p. 467. General Alcorn became, after the war, a Reconstruction Governor and United States Senator from Mississippi.

[22] Same, pp. 485-486, 500.

[23] Same, p. 495.

[24] He was reported by the commander at Fort Donelson as having been there on Nov. 5. *O.R.*, Serial No. 4, p. 519.

[25] Same, p. 551.

[26] There is, however, an earlier dispatch in the records *about* Forrest. In a postscript to a communication about guns and artillery and ammunition, and the prospects of supplying them, Sam Tate of Memphis, president of the Memphis & Charleston Railroad, wrote General Johnston: "Colonel Forrest's regiment of cavalry, as fine a body of men as ever went to the field, has gone to Dover or Fort Donelson. Give Forrest a chance and he will distinguish himself." *O.R.*, Serial No. 4, p. 512.

[27] Same, p. 549.

[28] Jordan and Pryor, pp. 44-45.

[29] Same, p. 46.

[30] *O.R.*, Serial No. 7, pp. 4-6.

[31] Same, pp. 4-6. General Clark, reporting to headquarters Forrest's return, added that he had "brought in two prisoners of war. Where shall I send them?" *O.R.*, Serial No. 110, p. 229.

[32] Johnson, *The Partisan Rangers*, p. 40.

[33] "The enemy threaten an immediate move on Hopkinsville from Calhoun, on Green River (on road from Owensboro to Hopkinsville). If defeated Clark can

fall back to Clarksville." A. S. Johnston to Benjamin, Dec. 21, 1861. *O.R.*, Serial No. 7, pp. 781-782.

[34] Same, p. 65.

[35] A nearly contemporary account of this startling battle transformation which came over Forrest, taken from manuscript notes of Major Kelley, appears in Jordan and Pryor, p. 53. Another of Forrest's soldiers described this transformation in his appearance and voice as a "singular exaltation which, however, appeared to leave him in absolute control of his faculties. He was never more sane nor more cool nor more terrible than in the moment of doubtful issue." *Confederate Veteran*, Vol. XXV, p. 358.

[36] The cause of the rout as reported by the Union commander was that "some dastard unknown shouted, 'Retreat to Sacramento!'" *O.R.*, Serial No. 7, pp. 62-63.

[37] From Adam Johnson's lively eyewitness account in *The Partisan Rangers*, pp. 42-43. Johnson and Robert M. Martin, afterward colonels under John Morgan, were the scouts who reported the Federal crossing at Rumsey.

[38] *O.R.*, Serial No. 7, p. 64.

[39] Wyeth, p. 35.

CHAPTER IV

OUT OF THE FALL OF FORT DONELSON
December 28, 1861-February 16, 1862

[1] *O.R.*, Serial No. 7, pp. 444-445, 451, 458, 464, 473, 487-488, 521, 526, 532.

[2] Same, pp. 698-700, 711, 719, 737, 744-745. A large part of the population of the region about the forts was engaged as wood choppers for the charcoal iron furnaces of the Cumberland Iron Works, six miles above Fort Donelson. Since these works were "the only ones which can now supply the requisite material for the manufacture of small-arms and other munitions," Polk ordered Tilghman that "all operatives and wood choppers, white and black," must be exempted from military duty or labor.

[3] *O.R.*, Serial No. 7, pp. 561, 572-573.

[4] Same, pp. 844-845.

[5] Same, pp. 120-122.

[6] Same, pp. 122-126, 136-145.

[7] Same, pp. 153-156, 870. Commander S. L. Phelps, in his report of this successful foray, expressed his astonishment at the extent and depth of the sentiment of loyalty to the Union which he found among the people living along the Tennessee River. His observations were correct. The section was one of strong Union sentiment and after the war became and remained predominantly Republican in politics.

[8] Same, p. 124.

[9] Same, pp. 861-864, 130-131.

[10] Same, p. 859.

[11] Same, pp. 278, 867-868.

[12] Same, p. 383.

[13] Same, p. 383.

[14] Same, p. 328.

[15] Same, p. 272.

[16] Same.

[17] Same, p. 379.

[18] Same, Oglesby's report, pp. 183-187; Forrest's report, pp. 383-384.

[19] Same, p. 384.

[20] Same, pp. 384-387. The story of the Confederate command at Fort Donelson is spread through reports and investigations extending from page 254 to page 418, and from page 859 to page 883 of Vol. 7 of the *Official Records,* as well as in articles and memoirs by or about many of the participants. The confusion of the time is reflected in many of the subsequent accounts.

[21] Same, p. 282. "Colonel Forrest's cavalry gallantly charged a large body of infantry supporting the battery, driving it and forcing the battery to retire, and taking six pieces of artillery." Pillow's Report.

[22] Forrest's own report is silent on the matter of horses shot under him. See Mathes, p. 38. Nor does he mention the fifteen bullet holes found in his overcoat. Jordan and Pryor, p. 83.

[23] Johnson, pp. 65-66. The "young Baptist preacher" who gave up his horse to Forrest was soon supplied with another. In after years he became the revered and beloved pastor of the First Baptist Church in Nashville.

[24] *O.R.,* Serial No. 7, p. 283.

[25] Same, p. 333.

[26] Same, p. 255.

[27] Same, p. 295; Johnson, pp. 66-69.

[28] *O.R.,* Serial No. 7, pp. 256, 269-270.

[29] Robert M. Hughes, in *Harper's Weekly,* May 11, 1912; *Virginia Historical Magazine,* Vol. 43 (October, 1935), p. 316; and *Confederate Veteran,* Vol. XXX, No. 11 (November 1930), p. 417.

[30] *O.R.,* Serial No. 7, p. 288.

[31] Same, p. 334.

[32] Same, p. 295.

[33] Same, p. 297.

[34] Forrest did not take notice of the fact that Captain Frank Overton, commanding the Boone Rangers, the first company formed in his regiment, and six lieutenants were in some way overlooked, and failed to come out with the command. They were included in the surrender. Bushrod Johnson's Report, *O.R.,* Serial No. 7, p. 364.

[35] E. W. Gantt. Before the end of 1863 he was active in the Unionist movement in Arkansas, helping to organize a new state government under President Lincoln's "ten percent" proclamation of Dec. 8, 1863. Thomas S. Staples, *Reconstruction in Arkansas* (New York, 1923).

[36] *O.R.,* Serial No. 7, p. 295.

[37] Jordan and Pryor, pp. 92-93.

[38] *O.R.,* Serial No. 7, p. 386.

[39] Same, pp. 415-416.

[40] Same, p. 386.

[41] Same, p. 296.

[42] Same, p. 387.

[43] Same, pp. 364-365.

CHAPTER V

PURPOSE IN THE MIDST OF PANIC
February 17, 1862-March 16, 1862

[1] Jordan and Pryor, pp. 99-101.

[2] *O.R.*, Serial No. 7, pp. 739, 741, 757.

[3] *The Great Panic*, Being Incidents Connected With Two Weeks of the War in Tennessee. By an Eye-Witness (Nashville, 1862), pp. 7-8. This pamphlet, published anonymously and almost contemporaneously with the event, was reproduced in serial form in the *Annals of the Army of Tennessee*, Vol. I (Nashville, 1878), under the name of its author, John Miller M'Kee, who was in 1861-1862 editor of the Nashville *Union & American*.

[4] Same, p. 11.

[5] Same, p. 9.

[6] Same, p. 10. The usual route from Nashville to Memphis at that time was southeast to Stevenson by the Nashville & Chattanooga R. R., thence west by the Memphis & Charleston R. R.

[7] Edd Winfield Parks, *Charles Egbert Craddock* (Chapel Hill, 1941), p. 24. The future famous novelist was a pupil of the school.

[8] Same, pp. 12-13.

[9] *O.R.*, Serial No. 7, pp. 430-431.

[10] Same, p. 428; *Great Panic*, p. 9.

[11] Same, p. 15.

[12] *O.R.*, Serial No. 7, p. 428.

[13] *Great Panic*, p. 19.

[14] Same, pp. 20-21.

[15] Jordan and Pryor, pp. 101-102.

[16] *O.R.*, Serial No. 7, pp. 386, 429.

[17] *Great Panic*, p. 21.

[18] Same, p. 24.

[19] Same, pp. 2-3; *O.R.*, Serial No. 7, p. 428. The railroad bridge, only two years old, contained, according to the Nashville City Directory of the time, the "longest railroad draw span in the world," being four feet longer than the one in the Mississippi River bridge at Rock Island, Illinois. The suspension roadway bridge, designed by Colonel A. Heiman, captured at Fort Donelson, had been constructed by D. M. Field, brother of the subsequently famous layer of the first Atlantic cable. The destruction of the bridges did delay Buell's advance from Nashville in pursuit of Johnston's retreating army by about one week. *O.R.*, Serial No. 20, p. 28.

[20] Mathes, p. 52.

[21] *O.R.* In his responses to the interrogatories of Congress, Forrest says (p. 429) that he was ordered to take command of the city "on Tuesday morning." In his earlier official report (p. 386) he says he was placed in command of the city on Thursday. Comparison with Jordan and Pryor shows that the latter is correct.

[22] Jordan and Pryor, p. 103; *Great Panic*, p. 25.

[23] *O.R.*, Serial No. 7, p. 430.

[24] *Great Panic*, p. 28.

[25] *O.R.*, Serial No. 7, p. 431. Capt. Charles W. Anderson, afterward to become a member of Forrest's staff but in February 1862 a quartermaster of transportation at Chattanooga, received telegraphic orders to receive and care for 1,000 to 1,200 of these unfortunate wounded. There was at the time no hospital organization in Chattanooga, and no funds with which to improvise one. With the help of local citizens, Anderson set up a crude canteen service to give the men coffee and bread on arrival, and cleared out and cleaned up three large buildings in which to house them. Of 300 men on the first train, three arrived dead and two more died before they could be taken to the buildings provided. The rooms were warmed but there were no beds until several days later. One of the "refugee" ladies who helped in the work was Mrs. Emily Todd Helm, sister of Mrs. Abraham Lincoln and wife of the Confederate General Ben Hardin Helm. *Confederate Veteran,* Vol. IV, pp. 289-291.

[26] *O.R.*, Serial No. 7, pp. 904-905.

[27] Same, pp. 900-901.

[28] Same, pp. 425, 668.

[29] Same, p. 632.

[30] Same, p. 628.

[31] Same, pp. 668, 670.

[32] Same, p. 674.

[33] Same, pp. 679-680.

[34] Same, p. 682.

[35] Jordan and Pryor, p. 106. The state of the new command is indicated by the field return of the Central army of Kentucky for March 31, 1862 (*O.R.*, Serial No. 11, p. 377), which shows an aggregate of 863 men, of whom 785 were present and 679 "for duty." Nine percent of Forrest's regiment were absent, as compared with 20 percent for the army as a whole. Of those present, Forrest had 86 percent "for duty"; the army as a whole, 57 percent.

CHAPTER VI

BATTLE AT THE PLACE OF PEACE

March 16, 1862-May 30, 1862

[1] *O.R.*, Serial No. 7, pp. 914-915.

[2] *O.R.*, Serial No. 10, pp. 24-27.

[3] Gilbert Vincent Rambaut, *Forrest at Shiloh,* a paper read before the Confederate Historical Association of Memphis on Jan. 14, 1896, and published in the *Commercial Appeal,* Jan. 19. Rambaut, in civil life manager of the Worsham House, subsequently the Arlington Hotel, in Memphis, enlisted in the Forrest regiment. He became Forrest's Chief Commissary, with the rank of Captain, later Major, on July 21, 1862.

[4] *O.R.*, Serial No. 10, pp. 83-84.

[5] Same, pp. 385-395.

[6] Same, p. 614.

[7] Jordan and Pryor, p. 113. Forrest made no official report of the operations of his regiment at Shiloh, presumably because of the severe wound he suffered on the third day. The work of Jordan and Pryor, which he saw in manuscript, is the closest approach to such a report.

[8] *O.R.*, Serial No. 10, p. 567.

[9] Jordan and Pryor, p. 113; *O.R.*, Serial No. 10, p. 89.

[10] Rambaut paper.

[11] *O.R.*, Serial No. 10, p. 89.

[12] *Battles and Leaders of the Civil War*, edited by Robert Underwood Johnson and Clarence Clough Buel (New York, 1884), Vol. I, p. 555.

[13] Rambaut paper; *O.R.*, Serial No. 10, p. 454.

[14] Mathes, p. 56; Jordan and Pryor, pp. 127-128; Rambaut paper. Here, as almost everywhere in the story of Shiloh, it is difficult to determine from a maze of varying, indefinite and sometimes conflicting reports the exact course of events. The difficulty is not lessened by the lack of any report from Forrest himself.

[15] *O.R.*, Serial No. 10, p. 279.

[16] Part of the Forrest regiment conveyed a portion of the Hornet's Nest prisoners to the rear. Lt. Col. D. C. Kelley, in Nashville *American*, October 2, 1905.

[17] *O.R.*, Serial No. 10, pp. 550-551.

[18] *Confederate Veteran*, Vol. XVI, pp. 192+xxvi-xxvii.

[19] Jordan and Pryor, p. 135.

[20] *O.R.*, Serial No. 10, p. 355. Ambrose Bierce, a junior officer in an Indiana regiment in the relieving forces, noted thousands of men huddled under the bluff when the transports came up. When the boat landed, the regiment disembarking had to beat them back with rifle stocks to clear a way to get off the boat. Ambrose Bierce, *Collected Works of Ambrose Bierce* (New York and Washington, 1909), Vol. I, pp. 244-246.

[21] Brig. Gen. James R. Chalmers, before the Southern Historical Society, at its meeting of Aug. 15, 1879, at the White Sulphur Springs, West Virginia, *S. H. S. P.*, Vol. VII, No. 10, p. 458.

[22] Jordan and Pryor, p. 137.

[23] Same, pp. 139, 143-144.

[24] By one of the coincidences of the war the Confederate fortress on Island No. 10, in the Mississippi River, 120 miles away to the northwest, surrendered on the same day in which the Confederates fell back from the Tennessee River at Shiloh.

[25] Jordan and Pryor, pp. 144-146.

[26] Based on Sherman's report, *O.R.*, Serial No. 10, pp. 639-641; the report of Maj. Thomas Harrison, commanding Wharton's Texas Rangers after that officer was wounded, Vol. X, p. 923-924; the Rambaut paper; and Jordan and Pryor, pp. 145-148.

[27] Jordan and Pryor, pp. 148-149.

[28] Dr. Cowan was a first cousin of Mrs. Forrest.

CHAPTER VII

FROM MISSISSIPPI TO KENTUCKY

June 1, 1862-September 25, 1862

[1] Alfred Roman, *Military Operations of General Beauregard* (New York, 1884), Vol. I, p. 402. The work of Colonel Roman, son-in-law and staff officer to General Beauregard, is generally regarded as almost autobiographical.

[2] *O.R.*, Serial No. 11, p. 402.

[3] *O.R.*, Serial No. 22, pp. 30-33.

[4] Captain George P. Winton, "Nathan Bedford Forrest," *The Infantry Journal*, Vol. 37 (August 1930), p. 125.

[5] *O.R.*, Serial No. 23, pp. 722-723.

[6] *O.R.*, Serial No. 22, p. 33.

7 Same, p. 810.

8 Jordan and Pryor, pp. 166-167.

9 Jordan and Pryor, pp. 166-167. Nearly forty years later, when funds were being raised for the erection of the Forrest monument in Memphis, one of the prisoners held in the Murfreesborough jail, Elder William B. Owens, minister of the Primitive Baptist Church at Walter Hill, Tennessee, contributed fifty dollars as an "expression of gratitude and appreciation." "There was a Federal soldier killed in two miles and a half of my home," he wrote, "and I was one of five Southern men who were taken up under the order of the Military Governor of Tennessee and held as hostages for the killing. I am the only one of the five now living. We were sentenced to be hung Monday morning, but the Confederates released us. I am an old man now . . . [and] expect never to see the monument you erect. . . ." Original letter of Elder Owens, October 31, 1900, in Morton Scrapbooks. Elder Owens may have been the prisoner thus referred to in a novel of life in Murfreesborough during the war: "It was said that among the incarcerated citizens there was one, a worthy old Baptist preacher, intensely pious, and with great faith in prayer . . . who knelt in the midst of his fellow prisoners, prayed to be delivered from the hands of the Philistines, and continued to pray until he heard the tramp of Forrest's cavalry, and then he jumped up and shouted." Mrs. L. D. Whitson, *Gilbert St. Maurice* (Louisville, 1875), p. 90.

10 *O.R.*, Serial No. 22, pp. 794-795, 797. There had been warning of Forrest's coming from a source that would never have been credited—John Hunt Morgan, the raider, who was in Kentucky on a raid when, on July 10, he played one of his telegraphic practical jokes by having "Lightning" George Elsworth, his operator, tap the lines and send a fake message from Stanley Matthews, Provost Marshal at Nashville, telling the Provost Marshal at Louisville that "General Forrest, commanding brigade, attacked Murfreesborough, routing our forces, and is now moving on Nashville." Three days later the first part of the message came true; ten days later the whole of it! *O.R.*, Serial No. 22, p. 775.

11 Charles W. Bennett, Pvt. Co. G, *Diary of Life in Murfreesborough*, in "Historical Sketches of Ninth Michigan Infantry," (Nashville *Banner*, July 13, 1937.)

12 Wyeth, pp. 90-92.

13 "Tradition hath it thus—softly, softly—that, coatless and shoeless, when the thunder of Forrest's guns reached your ears, you crouched . . . on the floor, under the bed, in the house of a citizen!" Mrs. Whitson, pp. 77, 97-98.

14 There is confusion in Forrest's report as to the identity of the troops in the several parts of the day's fighting. He refers to Morrison's First Georgia and Lawton's Second Georgia but also speaks of "Colonel Morrison . . . with the Second Georgia" and "Colonel Lawton with the First Georgia." *O.R.*, Serial No. 22, p. 810.

15 *O.R.*, Serial No. 22, p. 805.

16 From Forrest's report, *O.R.*, Serial No. 22, pp. 809-811; the reports of Crittenden and subordinate officers, pp. 792-809; and the findings of a Court of Inquiry, pp. 796-798. Forrest's report shows that he expected to make a more complete statement after receipt of reports from his subordinate officers. The activities of the campaign, plus the fact that this brigade was soon transferred from his command, presumably prevented this from being done.

17 Jordan and Pryor, p. 175. Captain Christopher C. Andrews (afterward Brevet Major General) recalls that the prisoners were "treated with politeness." The officers sent on to Knoxville were "fed with the best the country could supply." "Once," he added, "when the table was not very large, our captors, like

true gentlemen, waited until we had first eaten." The prisoners were lodged at the best hotel in Knoxville and sent on by first-class railroad cars to their place of imprisonment at Madison, Georgia. Christopher C. Andrews, *Recollections: 1829-1922*, edited by his daughter, Alice E. Andrews (Cleveland, 1928), pp. 161-163.

[18] Wolseley, *United Service Magazine*, Vol. V (New Series), p. 115.

[19] Don C. Seitz, *Braxton Bragg, General of the Confederacy* (Columbia, South Carolina, 1924), p. 148.

[20] *O.R.*, Serial No. 22, p. 268.

[21] *O.R.*, Serial No. 23, p. 729.

[22] Same, pp. 716, 721, 731.

[23] Seitz, *Braxton Bragg*, p. 150.

[24] *O.R.*, Serial No. 22, pp. 818-819.

[25] The adjutant of the Union regiment stationed at Gallatin testified afterward that the Lebanon garrison "burned their camp equipage and baggage and retreated to Nashville. Thus we were left at Gallatin with four companies . . . and Forrest, with a force supposed to be about 3,000, at Lebanon, 17 miles distant." To meet the situation, he continued, they "burned all the ferry boats [on the Cumberland River] from Hartsville down below Gallatin, and waited for Forrest in the court house. . . ." All that saved him, he believed, was a sudden rise in the river that night. *O.R.*, Serial No. 22, pp. 852-853.

[26] *O.R.*, Serial No. 22, p. 818; Jordan and Pryor, p. 176.

[27] *O.R.*, Serial No. 23, p. 190.

[28] Jordan and Pryor, pp. 176-177.

[29] *O.R.*, Serial No. 22, pp. 818-819.

[30] *O.R.*, Serial No. 23, p. 198.

[31] Jordan and Pryor, pp. 177-178.

[32] *O.R.*, Serial No. 22, p. 816.

[33] *O.R.*, Serial No. 23, p. 734.

[34] *O.R.*, Serial No. 22, p. 35.

[35] *O.R.*, Serial No. 23, p. 266.

[36] Same, pp. 217-219.

[37] Same, p. 226.

[38] Same, p. 234.

[39] Same, p. 255.

[40] Same, pp. 270-271.

[41] Same, p. 304.

[42] Same, p. 293.

[43] Same, pp. 743-744.

[44] Same, p. 749.

[45] The most damaging consequence of this raid was the burning of the timber-lined twin tunnels on the Louisville & Nashville Railroad above Gallatin on August 12, with resulting rock falls which kept this principal supply line of the Union forces in Tennessee out of commission for several months.

[46] *O.R.*, Serial No. 23, p. 335.

[47] Same, p. 357.

[48] Same, pp. 758-759.

[49] Same, p. 761.

[50] Same, pp. 365, 371, 378.

[51] Same, p. 407.

[52] Same, pp. 425-426.

[53] Same, p. 429.

[54] *O.R.*, Serial No. 22, p. 887.
[55] *O.R.*, Serial No. 23, p. 770.
[56] Jordan and Pryor, pp. 179-181.
[57] *O.R.*, Serial No. 22, pp. 802-804.
[58] Jordan and Pryor, p. 181, footnote, refers to "the Federal report of this affair as an amusing instance of the sheer falsehood by which petty transactions were magnified into victories."
[59] *O.R.*, Serial No. 22, pp. 900-902, 904-906.
[60] *O.R.*, Serial No. 23, p. 462.
[61] Same, p. 754.
[62] Same, p. 489. General McCook's dispatch reveals a high degree of exasperation with his cavalry. "If my cavalry do not fight," he wrote, "you will never hear from them. I have given my infantry orders to shoot every one of them that runs to the rear."
[63] Same, p. 490; Jordan and Pryor, p. 182.
[64] *O.R.*, Serial No. 110, p. 338.
[65] *O.R.*, Serial No. 23, pp. 485-487.
[66] Same, p. 500.
[67] *O.R.*, Serial No. 110, pp. 348-349.
[68] Same, p. 508.
[69] Same, p. 824.
[70] Same, p. 833.
[71] Same, p. 848.
[72] Same, pp. 863-864. The nature of Forrest's disability does not appear.
[73] Same, pp. 865-866.
[74] Same, p. 868.
[75] Same, pp. 876-877.

CHAPTER VIII

THE FIRST WEST TENNESSEE CAMPAIGN
September 25, 1862-January 3, 1863

[1] *O.R.*, Serial No. 30, p. 415.
[2] *O.R.*, Serial No. 25, p. 876.
[3] *O.R.*, Serial No. 30, p. 422. This impression that Forrest's men were "loosely organized" and mere "bands of partisan rangers" who "roamed almost at will" persists to this day even in so careful a study as that of Doctor Lonn. Ella Lonn, *Desertion During the Civil War* (New York, 1928), pp. 15, 32.
[4] *O.R.*, Serial No. 25, p. 988.
[5] *O.R.*, Serial No. 30, p. 399.
[6] *O.R.*, Serial No. 24, p. 258; Jordan and Pryor, pp. 187-188; Lindsley, p. 795.
[7] *Confederate Veteran*, Vol. XVI, p. 192+xxvi-xxvii.
[8] Young Morton had a hard time achieving his ambition to join Forrest's new command. Returning from Camp Chase as an exchanged prisoner, he reported at Murfreesborough with ten men of his old battery to Maj. R. E. Graves, Bragg's chief of artillery. Armed with an order to take charge of Forrest's artillery, he was sent on to Columbia, where Forrest was readying his brigade for its next operation. Reporting confidently, the young officer was sharply rejected by Forrest, who did not propose "to have Captain Freeman interfered with." On the next day

Forrest relented so far as to agree that Morton might join the command if he could get orders to that effect from the chief of cavalry, General Wheeler. Morton rode to La Vergne, where Wheeler was, got his order and returned to Columbia, a ride of 104 miles accomplished in twenty-three hours without change of horses. Forrest permitted him and his squad of artillerists to go along on the expedition, with the idea that guns might be found for them later. Morton, pp. 45-46.

[9] *O.R.*, Serial No. 25, p. 971.

[10] *S.H.S.P.*, Vol. 37, p. 364.

[11] Lindsley, p. 651.

[12] *O.R.*, Serial No. 25, pp. 980-981.

[13] *O.R.*, Serial No. 29, p. 6. References to the Union forces as "Abolitionists" in this report may have been due to the fact that it was the first made by Forrest after the issuance of the preliminary Emancipation Proclamation.

[14] Same, p. 6. The editors of the *Official Records* amended this dispatch of Forrest's to make it appear that the Morgan attacking in Edgefield was "John T.," rather than "John H." Colonel John T. Morgan, afterward for many years the distinguished Senator from Alabama, fought on the south side of the Cumberland that day, under Forrest, commanding the column which drove in on the Lebanon Pike.

[15] The statement of Forrest's disappointment at being compelled to withdraw without attempting to press home his attack appeared first in Jordan and Pryor, pp. 189-191. Since statements of fact in this biography were reviewed by Forrest himself, it may be that there were oral orders from Breckinridge on direction of Bragg, as there stated.

[16] *O.R.*, Serial No. 29, pp. 3-5.

[17] *O.R.*, Serial No. 30, p. 41.

[18] Same, p. 402.

[19] Same, p. 420.

[20] Basil Duke, whose general opinion of Federal commanders was that "we were rarely afraid of their Generals," rated Buell as the best of them, except that he "lacked one quality . . . he could not advertise himself." *S.H.S.P.*, Vol. 6, pp. 136-137.

[21] *O.R.*, Serial No. 24, p. 755.

[22] *O.R.*, Serial No. 30, p. 422.

[23] Lt. Col. William Waller Edwards, "The Invincible Raider," *The Cavalry Journal*, Vol. 37 (October, 1928), p. 513.

[24] Same, p. 386.

[25] Jordan and Pryor, p. 194.

[26] There is a tradition in West Tennessee that the citizen who performed so well this hazardous and difficult service was the famous Confederate scout, Lamar Fontaine. Fontaine's own memoirs, however, do not mention it, and from them it appears that he was at the time with the Army of Northern Virginia. A few months later he did perform a somewhat similar service by taking a supply of caps into besieged Vicksburg.

[27] *O.R.*, Serial No. 30, p. 150.

[28] Same, p. 184.

[29] *O.R.*, Serial No. 24, p. 477; No. 25, pp. 404-405, 426; No. 30, pp. 150, 184.

[30] *O.R.*, Serial No. 24, p. 554.

[31] *S.H.S.P.*, Vol. 37, p. 305. One of Ingersoll's biographers says that his first remark upon surrender was "Hell, what a mess!" Cameron Rogers, *Colonel Bob Ingersoll* (New York, 1927), pp. 162-164.

³² *O.R.*, Serial No. 24, pp. 554-555, 593. The other two guns of the battery were added ten days later, when Maj. T. A. Napier's battalion joined Forrest at Union City, bringing with it a section of artillery under Lieutenant A. Wills Gould. Morton, pp. 61-62. These guns had been acquired when Napier led his men in a mounted charge against three Federal transports grounded on a sand bar in the Tennessee River at the mouth of the Duck. Lindsley, p. 687.

³³ *Confederate Veteran*, Vol. XV, p. 54. The account is given by V. Y. Cook, who was a fourteen-year-old run-away-from-home soldier with Forrest.

³⁴ Morton, p. 58. Morton notes merely that Ingersoll became quite "chummy" with Dr. Cowan and borrowed $100 from him; that years later, while in Nashville on a lecture tour, he met Cowan, whom he had sought in vain to locate so that he might repay the debt, which he sought to do with interest. The latter, Dr. Cowan would not take.

Other angles of the story are supplied by Louis J. Brooks, in a paper read before the United Confederate Veterans and the Sons and Daughters of the Confederacy of St. Louis, on February 14, and published in the Nashville *Banner* of February 21, 1932. Brooks, as a boy of nine, saw the little battle of Lexington, and helped his mother and other ladies there care for the wounded of both sides, without distinction. Thirty years later, while editor of the Jackson, Tennessee, *Whig,* he met in the Maxwell House at Nashville "an ex-Confederate soldier" who told him of the capture of Ingersoll, of his popularity with his captors, and of his taking a hand in a friendly game of poker. As he played, the story went, "his cash diminished and he proposed withdrawing, when one of the Confederates staked him with a roll of Confederate bills. When the charming Colonel quit the game, he was $50 short, which, said the ex-Confederate with a merry chuckle, he has never repaid."

Although Mr. Brooks did not mention the name of the ex-Confederate who made the poker loan in his St. Louis address, he did in his contemporary story in the Jackson *Whig.* The story was reprinted in a Chicago paper, where Ingersoll saw it and immediately forwarded his check to square the debt—which, observes Mr. Brooks, shows that whatever his religious beliefs may have been, his "poker ethics were absolutely sound."

³⁵ *O.R.*, Serial No. 24, p. 555.

³⁶ *O.R.*, Serial No. 25, p. 436.

³⁷ *S.H.S.P.*, Vol. 37, p. 305.

³⁸ *O.R.*, Serial No. 24, p. 551; No. 25, pp. 481, 495.

³⁹ *O.R.*, Serial No. 24, pp. 300-301.

⁴⁰ Same, p. 482.

⁴¹ Same, p. 593.

⁴² Same, p. 556.

⁴³ Same, p. 598.

⁴⁴ Same, pp. 551, 593.

⁴⁵ Same, p. 568; No. 25, p. 436.

⁴⁶ *O.R.*, Serial No. 24, pp. 551, 559.

⁴⁷ *O.R.*, Serial No. 25, p. 463.

⁴⁸ Col. George E. Waring, Jr. (Colonel, Fourth Missouri Cavalry, U. S. A.), *Whip and Spur* (Boston, 1875), consisting mostly of articles first printed in the *Atlantic Monthly.*

⁴⁹ *O.R.*, Serial No. 24, pp. 562-566, 594, 598.

⁵⁰ Same, pp. 593-594.

[51] Same, pp. 560-562.

[52] *S.H.S.P.*, Vol. 37, p. 306.

[53] Morton, pp. 59-60; Mathes, p. 95, footnote, citing Captain William M. Forrest, Major J. B. Cowan and others. Dr. Wyeth's statement to the contrary, p. 50, apparently is in error.

[54] Morton, p. 59.

[55] *S.H.S.P.*, Vol. 37, p. 306.

[56] *O.R.*, Serial No. 24, pp. 593-595.

[57] *O.R.*, Serial No. 25, pp. 467, 481-482.

[58] *O.R.*, Serial No. 24, p. 548; No. 25, pp. 481, 486.

[59] Same, p. 549.

[60] Same, p. 495. General Fisk, who became Commissioner of the Freedmen's Bureau for Tennessee and Kentucky after the war and for whom Fisk University at Nashville is named, also advised his chief that he was using for his headquarters "the best secesh house in town, formerly occupied by the Right Rev. Maj. Gen. Bishop Polk, C. S. Army."

[61] Same, p. 491.

[62] Same, p. 505.

[63] *O.R.*, Serial No. 24, p. 595; Jordan and Pryor, pp. 206-208.

[64] *O.R.*, Serial No. 25, p. 504.

[65] The reports of Colonel Dunham and his subordinates appear in *O.R.*, Serial No. 24, pp. 579-590.

[66] The reports of Colonel Fuller and his subordinates appear in *O.R.*, Serial No. 24, pp. 568-579.

[67] Forrest's official report is in *O.R.*, Serial No. 24, pp. 595-597; Dibrell's on pp. 598-599. No other subordinate commanders made reports which have been preserved. Other details of the fight, from contemporary and nearly contemporary Confederate sources, are in Jordan and Pryor, 209-219, and in Morton, pp. 64-69.

The explanation of the failure of the companies sent out to observe the approach of Fuller's column from Huntingdon, given in Jordan and Pryor, pp. 217-218, is another evidence of the necessity of clear and explicit orders. Captain William Forrest with one company was out toward Huntingdon. On the morning of the thirty-first Captain McLemore was sent with three companies of the Fourth Tennessee, under orders given secondhand, which indicated no other object than joining Captain Forrest at Clarksburg, and returning with him to the main body. Arriving at Clarksburg after moving across country some seven miles, McLemore found that Captain Forrest had been obliged to fall back, while the road gave evidence that a considerable body of troops had passed. Hearing artillery firing from the direction of Parker's Cross Roads, and having no further specific orders, Captain McLemore marched toward the sound of the firing, detouring to the right to avoid the Federal force assumed to be on the road. Had the purpose of his mission been made clear to him, he would doubtless have got word to Forrest that a column was approaching his rear.

[68] "On the morning after crossing the river [i.e., upon the return from West Tennessee] Gen. Forrest came to the camp of the battery, and calling for Baxter, complimented him for gallantry on the field at Parker's Cross Roads." Lindsley, p. 797. Baxter is quoted by S. A. Steele, of Mansfield, Louisiana, in an article on file in the Tennessee State Library, as having said that he was "cussed out" by the General for wheeling the teams and caissons of his section out of the line of fire and sending them to a sheltered place, which, to the General, looked like "running

away." The spunky young officer convinced the General that there was sound reason for handling the teams and caissons as he did, whereupon Forrest, before the assembled battery, made his apologies.

[69] *O.R.*, Serial No. 24, pp. 552-553.

[70] Jordan and Pryor, pp. 216-217.

[71] *O.R.*, Serial No. 24, pp. 590-591, 599.

[72] Same, p. 552.

[73] Same, p. 572.

[74] Forrest turned in valid paroles for a total of 1,439 Federal prisoners, *O.R.* Serial No. 119, p. 431. General Chalmers, who had not yet become part of Forrest's force and was not on this expedition, said afterward that Forrest recrossed the Tennessee "with a command stronger in numbers than when he started, thoroughly equipped with blankets and oil cloths, their shot guns replaced with Enfield rifles and with a surplus of five hundred rifles and eighteen hundred blankets and knapsacks." *S.H.S.P.*, Vol. 7, p. 460.

[75] *O.R.*, Serial No. 24, p. 577.

[76] *O.R.*, Serial No. 30, p. 476.

[77] *O.R.*, Serial No. 29, p. 672.

CHAPTER IX

MIDDLE TENNESSEE: THRUST AND PARRY
January 3, 1863-April 10, 1863

[1] On the days on which Stones River was fought, Forrest was marching to and crossing the Tennessee River. In an interesting example of the persistence of a fixed idea, once it has been established, Bragg's biographer remarks that Forrest "proved of no value either at Stones River or Chickamauga. The open road, not the battle ground, was his field." (Seitz, *Braxton Bragg*, p. 387.) Forrest wasn't at Stones River. He was 150 miles away at the time, on a mission upon which he had been dispatched by Bragg. What Forrest did at Chickamauga, and what Bragg might have done there had he followed the aggressive course urged upon him by Forrest, will appear in Chapter XII.

[2] *O.R.*, Serial No. 110, pp. 404-405.

[3] *O.R.*, Serial No. 30, pp. 339-341. This confusion of identity between Wheeler's exploit on the Cumberland in January 1863, and Forrest's more famous one on the Tennessee in the following year, persists to this day. In Mrs. Cornelia McDonald's interesting *Diary with Reminiscences of the War* (Nashville, 1934), admirably edited and annotated by her son Hunter McDonald, the editor corrected two references to Wheeler's capture of gunboats to show that she meant Forrest's (pp. 125, 147 n.) Mrs. McDonald's diary is correct as written.

[4] *O.R.*, Serial No. 34, pp. 39-40.

[5] Jordan and Pryor, pp. 224-225.

[6] *O.R.*, Serial No. 34, p. 34; Serial No. 35, pp. 35, 967.

[7] Wyeth, pp. 146-147.

[8] *O.R.*, Serial No. 34, pp. 34-35.

[9] Same, p. 39.

[10] Forrest made no official report of the action at Dover. In Jordan and Pryor, p. 227, it is said that an hour was agreed upon for a simultaneous charge by Forrest and Wharton and that "at the hour designated, Forrest charged."

[11] O.R., Serial No. 34, pp. 40-41.

[12] Wyeth, pp. 150-152; Mathes, pp. 99-100

[13] O.R., Serial No. 34, p. 32. Forrest, who had captured more than fifty men in the Dover operation, sent a flag of truce to General Davis making a special effort to exchange Captain Von Minden for Captain Rambaut. General Davis replied that he was without power to make such exchanges, and it was several months before Rambaut returned to the command. O.R., Serial No. 118, pp. 262, 264.

[14] O.R., Serial No. 35, pp. 637-638.

[15] Lindsley, pp. 596, 690-691, 717; O.R., Serial No. 35, p. 650.

[16] Same, pp. 636-637.

[17] O.R., Serial No. 30, pp. 503.

[18] O.R., Serial No. 35, pp. 637-638, 641.

[19] Same, p. 718.

[20] O.R., Serial No. 34, p. 86.

[21] Same, pp. 126-131, 142-144.

[22] Same, p. 78.

[23] Same, pp. 90, 109.

[24] Same, pp. 88-89.

[25] Jordan and Pryor, p. 247.

[26] Bromfield L. Ridley, Battles and Sketches, Army of Tennessee (Mexico, Mo., 1906), pp. 177-179.

[27] Jordan and Pryor, pp. 234-235; Wyeth, p. 161. Details of the death of Roderick appear in The Annals of the Army of Tennessee, Vol. I, pp. 429-430.

[28] O.R., Serial No. 34, pp. 89, 117.

[29] Same, p. 120.

[30] Jordan and Pryor, p. 235 n.

[31] O.R., Serial No. 34, p. 78.

[32] O.R., Serial No. 35, pp. 665, 669-672.

[33] O.R., Serial No. 34, pp. 130-135; Serial No. 35, pp. 677, 679, 681-687; Jordan and Pryor, pp. 239-240. In connection with this series of movements, Col. P. D. Roddey, commanding the cavalry outpost in front of Chapel Hill, was criticized for not having given more timely warning of Sheridan's advance, and ordered to send in reports at six-hour intervals, which he did until he had to report: "My paper will soon all be gone, and I don't know where I can get supplies in this country."

[34] O.R., Serial No. 34, pp. 150-151; Serial No. 35, p. 721.

[35] O.R., Serial No. 34, p. 193.

[36] Same, p. 191. This regiment, organized after Shiloh as the First Tennessee Cavalry, is also referred to in the records as the Sixth. At Brentwood it captured a fine set of twenty-four silver band instruments, which it used for the rest of the war. Lindsley, p. 887.

[37] Same, p. 188; Wyeth, p. 170.

[38] O.R., Serial No. 34, p. 190.

[39] Same, p. 192.

[40] Same, pp. 179-181.

[41] Same, pp. 193-194.

[42] Confederate Veteran, Vol. XXVII, p. 416. Lieutenant Hanson of Armstrong's staff, in another account of how Forrest seized a guidon and rallied the forces for a charge, adds that he "never saw Forrest more hilarious over an achievement, a victory, than he was over this." G. A. Hanson, Minor Incidents of the Late War (Bartow, Florida, 1887), p. 37.

[43] *O.R.*, Serial No. 34, p. 189. See Chapter X, p. 139.

[44] *O.R.*, Serial No. 35, p. 732.

[45] *O.R.*, Serial No. 34, pp. 222-227.

[46] Same, p. 230.

[47] Same, pp. 230-234.

[48] Jordan and Pryor, pp. 245-247; Wyeth, pp. 179-184. There are no Confederate official reports of this affair, other than a return of casualties compiled from a nominal list, showing a total loss of 3 killed, 32 wounded and 33 missing. Freeman's battery suffered the heaviest loss—Captain Freeman killed, 1 man wounded, 29 missing. *O.R.*, Serial No. 34, p. 239. According to other prisoners, including a member of the Union forces afterward captured, Freeman had struck his knee against some obstruction and lamed himself. When he failed to keep up he was shot in the face, at such close range that he was powder-burned. *The Annals of the Army of Tennessee*, Vol. I, pp. 23-26.

Lt. A. L. Huggins, of Freeman's battery, who was captured at the same time, and who afterward was to succeed to the command of the battery, said no more than that "Captain Freeman was killed after he became a prisoner. The Fourth U. S. Regulars were the capturing party but whether he was killed by them or by a stray shot is not known." Lindsley, p. 798.

[49] Wolseley, *United Service Magazine*, Vol. V (New Series), p. 121.

[50] *O.R.*, Serial No. 34, p. 237; Serial No. 35, p. 236.

[51] *O.R.*, Serial No. 34, p. 240.

[52] *O.R.*, Serial No. 35, pp. 224-225, 232.

CHAPTER X

THE PURSUIT AND CAPTURE OF STREIGHT
April 10, 1863-May 5, 1863

[1] *The Prisoner of War*, Lt. A. C. Roach, Aide to Colonel Streight (Indianapolis, 1865), pp. 15-16.

[2] Same, p. 13.

[3] *O.R.*, Serial No. 34, pp. 246, 281, 286.

[4] Same, p. 286. In Wyeth, pp. 189-190, it is stated that the stampede of the mules at Eastport was caused by scouts of Roddey's creeping up to their corral, firing guns and pistols and hooting and yelling. Neither Streight's report nor Lt. Roach's book mentions this as a cause of the stampede. No official report was made by Roddey.

[5] *O.R.*, Serial No. 35, p. 778. Could the scout who reported to Roddey the landing at Eastport have been one of those supposed to have stampeded the mules?

[6] *A Soldier's Honor*, By His Comrades (New York, 1902), pp. 276-279. In this memoir of General Van Dorn by his comrades there are two other somewhat different accounts, pp. 283-285 and pp. 297-300. The last account appears also in *S.H.S.P.*, Vol. 7, pp. 144-146, in the form of a letter from Colonel Edward Dillon to General Dabney Maury, dated June 16, 1877. Still another version, from another member of General Van Dorn's staff, appears in Wyeth, pp. 176-177.

[7] *O.R.*, Serial No. 35, p. 788; Ridley, pp. 171-176. The latter sketch of the Streight raid was prepared by Maj. M. H. Clift, a Confederate participant, and read at the Louisiana Soldiers' Home by Lt. Gen. A. P. Stewart.

[8] Jordan and Pryor, pp. 249-255. The only published official report of the Streight affair from Confederate sources is in two brief telegrams from General Bragg to Richmond, dated May 5 and 7, O.R., Serial No. 34, p. 294.

[9] Same, pp. 245, 287.

[10] Same, p. 287; Jordan and Pryor, p. 253.

[11] The Prisoner of War, p. 21.

[12] O.R., Serial No. 34, pp. 289-290.

[13] Same, p. 288.

[14] Same, p. 289; Wyeth, p. 204.

[15] O.R., Serial No. 34, pp. 289-290.

[16] Jordan and Pryor, p. 264.

[17] O.R., Serial No. 34, p. 290; Wyeth, p. 207.

[18] The Prisoner of War, p. 30.

[19] Jordan and Pryor, pp. 267-269.

[20] Wyeth, p. 212. At its session in 1863 the Legislature of Alabama granted to Miss Sanson, in recognition of her courage and her service, a section of 640 acres of the public lands of the state, which was revoked by the first Reconstruction Legislature of the state. Miss Sanson married C. B. Johnson, a Confederate soldier, in 1864, and removed with him to Calloway, Texas, in 1876. There her husband died in 1887, leaving her with a family of seven children. In February 1899 the Legislature of Alabama restored the act of 1863, by the almost unanimous passage of a bill granting Mrs. Johnson a section of land to be selected by her from the public lands of the state, in token of "admiration and gratitude." Newspaper dispatch from Montgomery, Alabama, in Morton Scrapbooks.

[21] The Prisoner of War, p. 32.

[22] O.R., Serial No. 34, pp. 290-291.

[23] Same, p. 291.

[24] George Magruder Battey, Jr., A History of Rome and Floyd County (Atanta, 1922), pp. 162, 164; The Prisoner of War, pp. 36-37.

[25] O.R., Serial No. 34, p. 292; Jordan and Pryor, pp. 272, 277. The precincts, or militia districts of Cherokee County must have been named with an eye to picturesque pioneer humor in place nomenclature. They included such names as Possum Snout, Blue Gizzard, Pop Skull, Wolf Skin, Buzzard Roost, Panhandle, Tangle Leg, Lick Skillet and Shake Rag. Chattanooga Daily Rebel (published at Selma, Alabama), Mar. 15, 1865.

[26] Wyeth, p. 215.

[27] Gadsden, Alabama, Times-News, July 29, 1909, reprinted in Battey, pp. 171, 173. In gratitude to Mr. Wisdom, the citizens of Rome presented him with a $400 silver service, and also sent a like sum in money to the Widow Hanks in appreciation of her letting him use her lame pony.

[28] Rome, Georgia, Tri-Weekly Courier, May 9, 1863, reprinted in Battey, p. 164.

[29] Report of the Committee of the Senate Upon the Relations Between Labor and Capital, Washington. Government Printing Office, 1885, Vol. IV—Testimony, p. 335. The testimony is that of Margaret Ketcham Ward (Mrs. George R.), a resident of Rome in 1863 but in 1883 residing at Birmingham, Alabama, as it was given to Senator Henry W. Blair of New Hampshire, chairman of the committee, at an evening session held in the old Relay House in Birmingham. The story of what happened in Rome is but one incident of the many which enliven Mrs. Ward's sparkling testimony, covering more than thirty-five pages of the committee print. The testimony has been privately reprinted, under the title War Memories—

Margaret Ketcham Ward, for a copy of which I am indebted to Mrs. John R. Marsh of Atlanta.

[30] Atlanta, Georgia, *Southern Confederacy,* reprinted in Battey, pp. 166-168. "Bill Arp's" remark at the end of four years of war, "I've killed as many of them as they have of me. I'm going home," became one of the most widely known of postwar sentiments.

[31] Mrs. Ward, pp. 334-335.

[32] Battey, p. 167.

[33] The crew of the Rome Railroad train, lying over that night at Kingston, the junction with the Western & Atlantic Railroad of the state of Georgia, ran the train the eighteen miles to Rome, picking up a total of 700 volunteers for defense of the place. Atlanta, *Southern Confederacy,* May 4, 1863, reprinted in *The Prisoner of War,* pp. 40-41.

[34] Battey, p. 173.

[35] Same, p. 173; *The Prisoner of War,* pp. 37-39; Jordan and Pryor, p. 276.

[36] Jordan and Pryor, p. 272; Wyeth, pp. 216-217.

[37] *O.R.,* Serial No. 34, p. 292.

[38] Jordan and Pryor, p. 273.

[39] *O.R.,* Serial No. 34, p. 292.

[40] Jordan and Pryor, p. 272, footnote; Ridley, pp. 175, 178-179. The latter account is from Maj. McLemore, Haynes's commanding officer.

[41] Maury, p. 209.

[42] *O.R.,* Serial No. 34, p. 292; Jordan and Pryor, pp. 273-274.

Both of these stipulations afterward became the subject of extended correspondence. The first was of importance because of the presence in Streight's command of the two companies of Alabamians listed as the First Middle Tennessee Cavalry, virtually all of whom were subject to the Confederate conscription and some of whom, doubtless, were deserters from the Confederate service. Within five days of the capture, on May 8, Governor John Gill Shorter of Alabama wrote to Secretary of War Seddon, declaring that these men were traitors to Alabama and the Confederate States, offering to waive the state's jurisdiction over them, but requesting that they be tried for "their treasonable acts" either by the Confederate or the Alabama authorities. After correspondence between Seddon and General Bragg, Seddon advised Governor Shorter on June 8 that "it does not appear . . . that any slaves were associated as soldiers with the enemy's troops and if there were any Alabamians enlisted among them they made their escape before capture." *O.R.,* Serial No. 118, pp. 946-947, 952, 955-956, 960, 969. Forrest reported that he "found no negroes in arms" among the prisoners surrendered by Streight. *O.R.,* Serial No. 119, p. 415.

Among the property was the remainder of a sum of $5,000 in Southern bank notes and U. S. Treasury notes, with which Streight had left Nashville, and which he claimed as his own personal property. At the time of the surrender Forrest's quartermaster, it seems, purchased the horses of Streight's surgeons (private property), paying for them in Confederate money. Colonel Streight thereupon purchased this money from his surgeons, paying for it with United States Treasury notes at the rate of twenty cents on the dollar, and thereafter exchanged the Confederate money thus obtained with Forrest himself for United States money, at even exchange, dollar for dollar. The status of the money taken from Streight and receipted for when he entered Libby Prison, whether public funds or private property, and especially the status of the $850 which he purchased from Forrest, was the subject of correspondence between Streight and the Confederate authorities and among the latter, resulting in the conclusion that (1) the bulk of the money carried by Streight was government property and not his own, as claimed, and therefore was subject to confiscation; and (2) the $850 bought from his surgeons and exchanged with Forrest were his personal funds, and should be returned to him, which was done.

In his report on the transaction Forrest states that at the time he exchanged U. S. money for the Confederate which Streight had, he was of the impression that the latter was the property of the surgeons. *O.R.*, Serial No. 119, pp. 82, 241-242, 267-268, 275, 414-415, 469-470, 507-509.

[43] Jordan and Pryor, p. 275-6.

[44] Kate Cumming, *A Journal of Hospital Life in the Confederate Army of Tennessee* (Louisville, 1866), p. 79.

[45] Mrs. Ward, p. 336.

[46] Battey, p. 171.

[47] Mrs. Ward, p. 336.

[48] Battey, p. 174.

[49] Mrs. Ward, p. 336.

[50] *The Prisoner of War*, p. 43. This expression takes on more meaning in the light of the rest of the book, which is concerned almost entirely with complaint and criticism of the treatment of prisoners of war by the Confederates, on the theme, "While our men in Southern prisons were dying from starvation and exposure, the rebels in Northern prisons fared sumptuously every day." (P. 67.)

[51] Jordan and Pryor, 279-280.

[52] Battey, p. 169. This splendid horse, bearing the name of Highlander, was not to serve the General long. He was killed four months later at Chickamauga. Morton, p. 119; Hanson, p. 54.

[53] Same, p. 162.

[54] Jordan and Pryor, p. 280.

CHAPTER XI

RETREAT WITH THE ARMY OF TENNESSEE
May 5, 1863-July 6, 1863

[1] These scouts of Forrest's were a little-known but important part of his organization and method. Their work was intensely individual and often desperately dangerous. By its very nature, it is little recorded, except in its results. A sense of what manner of men they were and how they did their work may be got from Caroline Gordon's novel, *None Shall Look Back* (New York, 1937).

[2] Jordan and Pryor, pp. 280-281.

[3] The assassin was Dr. George B. Peters; the reason alleged, excessive intimacy between General Van Dorn and Mrs. Peters—an allegation wholly and indignantly denied by friends of Van Dorn. *A Soldier's Honor*, pp. 249-250, 254-255, 349-354.

[4] Morton (p. 283) identifies this animal as the most famous of all Forrest's war horses, King Philip. According to other accounts King Philip was the gift of citizens of Columbus, Mississippi, in the following year.

[5] The wartime travel conditions on the railroad used by Forrest may be judged from the report of Lieutenant Colonel Fremantle of the Coldstream Guards, who

traveled the same way in the same month. "The train was crammed to repletion with soldiers rejoining their regiments," he wrote, "so I am constrained to sit in the aisle on the floor of one of the cars. . . . From my position in the tobacco juice I was unable to do justice to the scenery. I saw stockades at intervals all along the railroad, which were constructed by the Federals who occupied this country last year." Lt. Col. A. J. L. Fremantle, *Three Months in the Southern States* (Edinburgh, 1863), pp. 136-137.

[6] Referring to uneasiness in Richmond about the "persistency" with which small parties of Stoneman's Union raiders were "hanging about the city," Rebel War Clerk Jones added, "But the raids in the West don't seem to flourish so well. We have an official dispatch from Gen. Bragg, stating that Gen. Forrest has captured 1600 of the enemy's cavalry in a body, near Rome, Georgia." J. B. Jones, *A Rebel War Clerk's Diary,* edited and annotated by Howard Swiggett (New York, 1935), Vol. I, p. 313.

[7] Jordan and Pryor, p. 281.

[8] General Pillow's letter, dated Huntsville, Alabama, May 9, 1863, relates that he met Forrest in Columbia, as the latter was passing south two weeks earlier, and that Forrest "applied to me and urged me to get myself assigned to the command of the cavalry, and asked to be placed under my orders; so did General (W. H.) Jackson. I did not like that service; greatly preferred the infantry; but though I had declined Forrest's and Jackson's applications, yet the command suddenly being rendered vacant, and having no command, and being tired of my present position, I concluded I would accept that duty. Since, however, Forrest is assigned to the command, I am gratified at the result. He deserves the position, though I had not thought he would be assigned to it." *O.R.,* Serial No. 35, pp. 827-828.

[9] Jordan and Pryor, p. 284.

[10] Lindsley, p. 798.

[11] On May 8 a "delegation of Mississippians" called upon President Davis to ask that General Forrest with his brigade be assigned to duty in northern Mississippi. When the matter was put up to Bragg, he reported "Forrest's command not in condition. Jackson's division, Van Dorn's command, ordered to General Johnston." *O.R.,* Serial No. 110, pp. 470, 472.

[12] Jordan and Pryor, pp. 286-287.

[13] Morton, p. 102.

[14] *History of a War Battery* (Morton's) by "T. C.," Nashville *Rural Sun,* May 22, 1879. This battery history, published as a serial in May-July 1879, is preserved in the scrapbooks of Captain Morton, with pencil interlineations and corrections. In the account of the Gould affair there given, it is related that Forrest told Morton, after his return to duty with the battery, that when ordered to "take his guns to the top of the hill at Franklin," Gould "seemed to keep them behind the hill." Upon inquiry Morton learned that when the guns were fired, they were driven back from the crest by the recoil, and were then loaded and pushed to the crest again by hand for the next round. Riding up and noticing this handling, Forrest angrily asked, "Why in the hell, Lieutenant, don't you push your guns on top of the hill? Are you afraid?" to which Gould answered, "No, General, I am only protecting my men from the sharpshooters." In his own memoirs, published thirty years later and more than forty-five years after the event, Morton makes no reference to this story.

[15] Nashville *Banner,* April 29, 1911. The account there given is by Frank A. Smith, one of the four boys, who was for nearly half a century an honored edu-

cator at the Columbia Atheneum, and Secretary of the Maury County Historical Society.

16 *O.R.*, Serial No. 34, pp. 459-461.

17 Jordan and Pryor, p. 290.

18 *O.R.*, Serial No. 34, pp. 586 ff.

19 Same, pp. 618-619.

20 Same, pp. 533, 539.

21 Jordan and Pryor, pp. 290-291.

22 Wyeth, p. 231; W. C. Dodson, *Campaigns of Wheeler and His Cavalry* (Atlanta, 1899), pp. 88-89. "The charge of Stanley's ten thousand horsemen was . . . made in column of fours. It was seven miles to Shelbyville, and they were unable to make a stand and only fired a few shots from their artillery. More than once on this long charge they were compelled to move their artillery rapidly to the rear to prevent capture." W. B. Carter, *History of First Regiment of Tennessee Volunteer Cavalry (U. S. A.)* (Knoxville, 1902), p. 77.

23 While it is not so stated in the work, the vivid account of this affair in Wyeth, pp. 231-233, is that of an eyewitness and participant. Wyeth, *With Sabre and Scalpel* (New York, 1914), Chapter XVI; also article in *Harper's Weekly*, June 18, 1898.

24 Dodson, pp. 89-94; John P. Dyer, *"Fightin' Joe" Wheeler* (Baton Rouge, 1941), pp. 106-107. In the Dodson account there is a distinct undertone critical of Forrest's conduct on this day.

25 Jordan and Pryor, p. 291.

26 *O.R.*, Serial No. 34, pp. 534-541.

27 Same, p. 620; Jordan and Pryor, p. 291.

28 Wyeth, *With Sabre and Scalpel*, Chapter XVI. One of Hardee's staff officers, asked at this time about the derivation of the unusual name "Tullahoma," explained that it was from two Greek words—*tulla*, meaning "mud" and *homa* meaning "more mud." Irving A. Buck, *Cleburne and His Command* (New York and Washington, 1908), p. 108.

29 Jordan and Pryor, pp. 291-292.

30 *O.R.*, Serial No. 34, pp. 621-624.

31 Same, pp. 624-625.

32 Morton, p. 110.

33 *O.R.*, Serial No. 34, p. 584.

CHAPTER XII

VICTORY WITHOUT FRUITS

July 6, 1863-September 20, 1863

1 Morton, pp. 111-112.

2 *O.R.*, Serial No. 53, pp. 507-510. In explaining his confidence in the possibilities of his plan, Forrest remarked, "I have resided on the Mississippi River for over twenty years. Was for many years engaged in buying and selling negroes, and know the country perfectly from Memphis to Vicksburg on both sides of the river; and am also well acquainted with all prominent planters in that region, as well as above Memphis. I also have officers in my command and on my staff who have

rafted timber out of the bottom, and know every foot of ground from Commerce to Vicksburg."

3 Lindsley, p. 787.

4 Same, p. 784. The remark quoted is by Austin Peay of Garrettsburg, Kentucky.

5 *O.R.*, Serial No. 53, p. 508.

6 Same, pp. 527-528. To someone who must have doubted the completeness of his victory, Minty wrote, on August 11, "Of course I whipped Dibrell. . . . His men were scattered about the country like blackberries." *O.R.*, Serial No. 109, p. 437.

7 *O.R.*, Serial No. 53, pp. 546-547.

8 *O.R.*, Serial No. 51, p. 137. D. H. Hill says, in this report, that news of the crossing was not brought in by the Confederate cavalry outposts on this flank but by a vigilant citizen.

9 *O.R.*, Serial No. 53, p. 569.

10 Same, p. 591.

11 Johnson, pp. 157-158. Morgan's men would have lost their cherished identity, Johnson believed, but for the "resolute action of Forrest, who positively refused to execute orders" to dismount them, and "ran the risk of trial by court martial by refusing to carry out this policy of Bragg's." This, in Johnson's opinion, was the "real cause of the breach between Forrest and Bragg."

12 *O.R.*, Serial No. 53, p. 594.

13 Same, pp. 610-611.

14 Same, p. 622.

15 Same, p. 615.

16 Same, pp. 613, 621.

17 *O.R.*, Serial No. 51, p. 71.

18 *O.R.*, Serial No. 53, p. 628.

19 Same, p. 627; Jordan and Pryor, pp. 305-306.

20 *O.R.*, Serial No. 51, p. 28; No. 53, p. 627.

21 *O.R.*, Serial No. 51, pp. 523-524.

22 Same, p. 528; Mathes, p. 136-137.

23 *O.R.*, Serial No. 50, p. 466; No. 51, p. 530; Jordan and Pryor, pp. 307-308.

24 *O.R.*, Serial No. 50, p. 466.

25 Wyeth, *Forrest*, p. 240, quoting Major Anderson.

26 *O.R.*, Serial No. 51, p. 26.

27 Same, pp. 30, 49.

28 Same, p. 31.

29 *O.R.*, Serial No. 52, p. 691.

30 *O.R.*, Serial No. 51, p. 31.

31 Same, pp. 31, 451.

32 Same, pp. 451, 524.

33 Same, p. 524.

34 H. V. Boynton, *The Chickamauga National Military Park*, An Historical Guide (Cincinnati, 1895), p. 34.

35 *O.R.*, Serial No. 51, p. 524.

36 Wyeth, *Forrest*, p. 252. The conversation was between General Hill and Major Anderson, on the second day of the battle.

37 *O.R.*, Serial No. 51, p. 528.

38 The veteran W. H. T. Walker's estimate of the fight, as given in his official report, is that "the unequal contest of four brigades [Pegram's, Dibrell's, Wilson's

and Ector's] against such overwhelming odds is unparalleled in this revolution, and the troops deserve immortal honor for the part borne in the action." *O.R.*, Serial No. 51, p. 240.

[39] Wyeth, *Forrest*, p. 250; Morton, p. 119.

[40] The battle of the morning and early afternoon on the Confederate right is covered in the Confederate reports in *O.R.*, Serial No. 51, as follows: Forrest's report, pp. 524-525; Pegram's, pp. 528-529; Walker's, p. 240; Wilson's, pp. 248-249; Liddell's, pp. 251-253; Govan's, pp. 258-259; Walthall's, pp. 272-274; and regimental and battery commanders on pp. 255-257, 261-271, 276-287. Among the Union reports dealing with this part of the battle are the following in *O.R.*, Serial No. 50; Thomas', pp. 249-250; Baird's, pp. 274-276, and his brigade commanders, Scribner, pp. 285-287, Starkweather, pp. 299-300, and King, p. 309; Brannan's, pp. 400-401, and his brigade commanders, Connell, p. 408, Chapman, pp. 415-416, Van Derveer, pp. 427-429; together with regimental and artillery commanders. Croxton, one of Brannan's brigade commanders, made no report, but the activity of his brigade is dealt with in the report of Chapman, who commanded the left portion of the brigade during part of the battle.

[41] Hanson, p. 55.

[42] Liddell's report, *O.R.*, Serial No. 51, p. 252. Major General Walker reported that he "had no watch," p. 240.

[43] Walthall estimated that the "engagement lasted about an hour," *O.R.*, Serial No. 51, p. 273; Govan, that it "lasted nearly two hours," p. 258.

[44] Piatt and Boynton, p. 396. General Boynton, then Lieutenant Colonel of the Thirty-fifth Ohio, who commanded the extreme left of Van Derveer's line, spoke from personal observation. This passage is erroneously cited by Dr. Wyeth in connection with the battle of the afternoon of the twentieth, instead of the nineteenth.

[45] Forrest warmly praised the conduct of Maj. John Rawle, chief of artillery, and the old Freeman battery (now Huggins'). Another of Forrest's battery commanders and a future chief of artillery, John Morton, celebrated his coming of age on this bloody day by the loss of a new artillery uniform eaten out of a wagon by a hungry mule and the loss of his rations when his colored servant, quite understandably and excusably, ran off with them to the rear. Morton, p. 119.

[46] Morton, p. 118; Wyeth, *Forrest*, pp. 248-249.

[47] *O.R.*, Serial No. 51, pp. 256, 270.

[48] Same, p. 525. Most of the secondary accounts of this day's battle refer to Armstrong coming up in the afternoon but it does not so appear in the contemporary records.

[49] Jordan and Pryor, p. 330.

[50] *O.R.*, Serial No. 51, p. 525; No. 50, pp. 854-856.

[51] *O.R.*, Serial No. 51, p. 525.

[52] *McClure's Magazine*, February, 1898.

CHAPTER XIII

TO NEW FIELDS

September 21, 1863-November 14, 1863

[1] Hanson, p. 60.

[2] Jordan and Pryor, p. 350.

[3] Wyeth, *Forrest*, p. 259. The story was told to Dr. Wyeth by Gen. Armstrong.

[4] *O.R.*, Serial No. 53, p. 681. The dispatch is reproduced in facsimile in Wyeth, *Forrest*, p. 260.

[5] Wyeth, *Forrest*, p. 260; *S.H.S.P.*, Vol. 24, p. 94. The article in the *Papers* is based on an item in the Washington *Star* of Jan. 15, 1897, by "Holland," New York correspondent of the Philadelphia *Press*, who quotes the Union soldier and writer, Gen. H. V. Boynton, to the effect that Forrest was in error in his conclusions as to the movements and intentions of "General Rosencranz," and that Bragg's information was more nearly correct.

[6] *O.R.*, Serial No. 10, p. 470.

[7] *O.R.*, Serial No. 53, p. 675.

[8] *O.R.*, Serial No. 51, pp. 525-526, 531; Jordan and Pryor, pp. 351-352.

[9] *O.R.*, Serial No. 53, p. 679.

[10] Hanson, p. 61.

[11] Manuscript lecture of Lt. Tully Brown, Morton's battery, afterward Adjutant General of Tennessee, in Tennessee State Library.

[12] *S.H.S.P.*, Vol. 12, p. 223.

[13] Samuel R. Watkins, *Company "Aytch" (Maury Grays) First Tennessee Regiment*, pp. 39, 93, 100. Reference is to the second edition, published by the Chattanooga *Times* in 1900, not to the original edition published in 1882 by the Columbia *Herald*.

[14] *O.R.*, Serial No. 51, pp. 526, 529-531; Jordan and Pryor, p. 353.

[15] *O.R.*, Serial No. 51, p. 526 (Forrest's report).

[16] *O.R.*, Serial No. 53, pp. 711, 719-720.

[17] *O.R.*, Serial No. 51, p. 526.

[18] Lindsley, p. 801.

[18a] Mathes, Capt. J. Harvey, *The Old Guard in Gray* (Memphis, 1897), p. 78.

[19] Conversation with the late Nat Baxter of Nashville, Tennessee. Lieutenant Baxter became, after the war, a major figure in the development of iron and other industries in the South.

[20] *O.R.*, Serial No. 53, pp. 705-706.

[21] *O.R.*, Serial No. 51, p. 37.

[22] *O.R.*, Serial No. 53, p. 710.

[23] Same, p. 711.

[24] Same, p. 715.

[25] Same, p. 719.

[26] Same, pp. 719-720.

[27] *O.R.*, Serial No. 51, p. 723.

[28] Lindsley, pp. 785, 801.

[29] Hanson, p. 65.

[30] Wyeth, *Forrest*, p. 264.

[31] Jordan and Pryor, p. 357.

[32] Same, p. 358. There is no reference to any resignation by Forrest nor to a letter from President Davis in either the *Official Records* or the President's published correspondence.

[33] Wyeth, *Forrest*, pp. 264-266; Mathes, p. 155. There was no publication of this strange encounter between Bragg and Forrest until these biographies appeared. The story got about, however, by word of mouth, and when General and Mrs. Forrest visited Chattanooga a few years after the war Major M. H. Clift asked him about the reported story, which was confirmed substantially by Forrest. Morton, p. 131.

[34] *O.R.*, Serial No. 51, pp. 54-70, as to Polk; pp. 148-153, as to Hill; pp. 292-313, as to Hindman.

[35] *O.R.*, Serial No. 53, pp. 705-706, 708.

[36] *O.R.*, Serial No. 51, pp. 65-66.

[37] The story of the dissensions between Bragg and his officers, as it is developed in the memoirs of various participants as well as in the *Official Records,* is well told in Stanley F. Horn, *The Army of Tennessee* (Indianapolis, 1941), Chapter XV.

[38] *O.R.*, Serial No. 53, pp. 744-745.

[39] *O.R.*, Serial No. 56, p. 604. The President's attention may have been directed to Forrest at this time, also, because of a telegram of September 24 from Isham G. Harris, Governor of Tennessee, recommending his promotion. To this telegram the President replied on September 25 that Forrest's "services have heretofore attracted my favorable attention" but that "other questions than that of individual merit enter into the selections for appointment of generals," such as the organization of the army, vacancies, etc. *Jefferson Davis, Constitutionalist,* Vol. VI, pp. 49-50. Also, *O.R.*, Serial No. 110, p. 529.

[40] *O.R.*, Serial No. 56, pp. 603-604.

[41] Same, p. 645. The report was sent from Atlanta on November 7, as Forrest was on his way to Mississippi.

[42] Same, p. 646. To President Davis, who was at Savannah, Georgia, at the time, General Bragg wrote on October 31: "General Forrest's requests are all granted and he has left for his new field, apparently well satisfied." *O.R.*, Serial No. 110, p. 557.

[43] *O.R.*, Serial No. 56, pp. 618-619.

[44] Jordan and Pryor, p. 359.

[45] *O.R.*, Serial No. 56, p. 694.

[46] Same, p. 31.

CHAPTER XIV

A GENERAL FINDS—AND MAKES—HIS ARMY
November 15, 1863-February 12, 1864

[1] *O.R.*, Serial No. 56, pp. 730-732.

[2] Same, p. 641.

[3] Same, p. 646.

[4] *S.H.S.P.*, Vol. 7, p. 463. The quotation is from General Chalmers.

[5] *O.R.*, Serial No. 56, p. 766.

[6] Maury, p. 150.

[7] *O.R.*, Serial No. 54, pp. 588-589; No. 56, pp. 816-817, 829. President Davis replied that Hampton could not be spared, that Forrest was promoted to major general "to supply your wants in West Tennessee and North Mississippi so as to enable you to draw Major-General Lee to the southern part of your department," and that Lee remained the senior officer of cavalry in the department. See also *O.R.*, Serial No. 110, p. 572.

[8] *O.R.*, Serial No. 54, pp. 576-577, 588-589.

[9] *O.R.*, Serial No. 56, pp. 336, 343.

[10] Same, pp. 242-243.

[11] Same, p. 187.

[12] Lindsley, p. 776.

[13] O.R., Serial No. 56, pp. 789-790. Forrest asked, also, for the assignment of Brig. Gen. Frank C. Armstrong, from the Army of Tennessee, to help in the work of gathering and organizing the new army. (P. 798.) His request was not granted.

[14] William Witherspoon, *Tishomingo Creek, or Brice's Cross Roads As I Saw It* (Jackson, Tennessee, 1906).

[15] O.R., Serial No. 56, p. 789.

[16] Same, pp. 411-412. Sherman professed, at this time, no great interest in what Forrest was doing. From Nashville he wrote to Admiral D. D. Porter, commanding naval forces on the western waters, on December 21: "Forrest (at Jackson, Tenn.) is not hurting us. We are not interested in the fate of the people he is harassing. I propose to strike at large armies and large interests and let the smaller ones work out their salvation." His plan was to send an expedition up the Yazoo to Grenada, to destroy the railroad there; then one across into Louisiana, to Monroe and the Ouachita, to levy contribution to pay for damages to boats on the river; then to collect everything at Memphis and Vicksburg and "go up the Red River as high as Shreveport and make that rich country pay in gold and cotton for all the depredations on our river commerce." O.R. (Naval), Vol. 25, p. 645.

[17] O.R., Serial No. 56, pp. 431, 436.

[18] Same, p. 445.

[19] Same, pp. 443-446, 449-451, 456, 473.

[20] Same, pp. 844-845.

[21] Same, pp. 853-854.

[22] Same, pp. 858-859.

[23] O.R., Serial No. 54, pp. 607, 612-613.

[24] Same, pp. 612-613; Jordan and Pryor, pp. 366-367.

[25] Same, pp. 367-369.

[26] Same, p. 368.

[27] Wyeth, *Forrest*, pp. 283-284.

[28] O.R., Serial No. 54, p. 613.

[29] Memorandum of conversation with Pvt. Mack Watson, Forrest's Escort, of Nashville, Tennessee.

[30] O.R., Serial No. 54, pp. 607-608; No. 56, pp. 492-493, 501, 517, 518. So persistent was this belief that both Grierson and Hurlbut sent messages as late as the morning of December 27, when Forrest's advance was approaching La Fayette Station, expressing the opinion that he would move out to the east of La Grange.

[31] O.R., Serial No. 54, p. 494; No. 56, pp. 607, 610-612.

[32] Same, p. 494.

[33] Same, p. 614.

[34] O.R., Serial No. 56, p. 500.

[35] Jordan and Pryor, p. 374.

[36] Same, pp. 375-376.

[37] Same, pp. 376-377; O.R., Serial No. 54, pp. 608-611, 614-618.

[38] O.R., Serial No. 56, p. 524.

[39] O.R., Serial No. 54, pp. 618-619.

[40] O.R., Serial No. 56, p. 515.

[41] Jordan and Pryor, p. 377.

[42] O.R., Serial No. 56, p. 534.

[43] To an inspector who reported him as "inefficient" because of his failure to intercept Forrest at La Fayette Station (O.R., Serial No. 54, p. 610) Colonel Mor-

gan angrily retorted, with a lengthy recital and explanation, including the statement, "It affords me pleasure to be able to state that we here parted company with the distinguished (?) acting assistant inspector-general of the Cavalry Division. Taking the train upon which was the battery attached to this brigade, he returned, we believe, to La Grange the same night, there to regale his commanding and superior officers with his exploits, and to assure them of his superior military talent by criticising the operations of this brigade and by speaking disparagingly of it and its commander." (P. 618.)

General Grierson's comment in his report was, "If Colonel Morgan had evinced as much enterprise in pursuing and attacking the enemy as he has in making excuses for his tardy movements, success would undoubtedly have attended our efforts." (P. 609.)

Forrest had a way of making the commanders opposed to him dissatisfied with one another.

[44] *O.R.*, Serial No. 54, p. 621.

[45] *O.R.*, Serial No. 56, p. 533.

[46] *O.R.*, Serial No. 54, pp. 620-621.

[47] *O.R.*, Serial No. 56, pp. 876-877.

[48] Captain James Dinkins, *Personal Recollections and Experiences in the Confederate Army* (Cincinnati, 1897), p. 123. The diarist of the Second Tennessee Cavalry recalled that "this memorable night, in which the old year stepped out and the new stepped in, was the coldest night of the war." R. R. Hancock, *Hancock's Diary, or a History of the Second Tennessee Confederate Cavalry* (Nashville, 1887), p. 298.

[49] *O.R.*, Serial No. 58, pp. 512-513.

[50] *O.R.*, Serial No. 119, pp. 800, 806, 811, 813, 816, 839. One prisoner in Federal hands, described on the lists for the proposed exchange as a second lieutenant in McDonald's battalion, "is not and never was an officer," Forrest wrote. "He is a private, a deserter and a thief." Nevertheless, he added, "in order to get him will give a man for him."

[51] *O.R.*, Serial No. 58, p. 529; Jordan and Pryor, p. 382.

[52] *O.R.*, Serial No. 58, p. 617.

[53] Same, p. 614.

[54] Hancock, pp. 301-303; *The Old Guard in Gray*, p. 33.

[55] This description is from a letter from Achilles V. Clark, Sergeant and afterward Lieutenant and Captain, Company K, Twentieth Tennessee Cavalry, to his sisters, Mrs. Josiah Horton Porter and Mrs. Samuel Ray, whose husbands were also Confederate soldiers. The letters were seen through the kindness of his daughter, Mrs. Sydney S. Crockett, of Nashville.

[56] Forrest was notified upon his return from West Tennessee that 2,000 stand of arms and accouterments to go with them which he had requested before going in had been received, and were in depot at Demopolis, Alabama, while the funds for pay of troops, subsistence and quartermaster's stores were being sent to him through Lee's headquarters at Grenada. *O.R.*, Serial No. 56, pp. 868, 876. They lacked considerably being enough to meet the necessities of his command.

[57] Hancock, pp. 309-310.

[58] Dinkins, p. 131. Many persons throughout the South, according to Captain Dinkins' account, heard of the sentencing to death but did not hear of the reprieve, and believing that the men were executed, "censured General Forrest greatly and . . . have never forgotten."

501

CHAPTER XV

OKOLONA: DEBUT IN VICTORY
January 8, 1864-February 26, 1864

[1] *O.R.*, Serial No. 58, p. 75.

[2] Same, p. 49.

[3] Same, pp. 75-76.

[4] "The Sixteenth Corps had become so domiciled at Memphis and along the railroad that it is like pulling teeth to get them started," Sherman wrote Grant. *O.R.*, Serial No. 58, p. 201.

[5] *O.R.*, Serial No. 57, pp. 181-182.

[6] *O.R.*, Serial No. 58, p. 123.

[7] Same, pp. 252-253.

[8] *O.R.*, Serial No. 57, p. 182.

[9] *O.R.*, Serial No. 58, p. 251.

[10] Over the Missouri River, for the Alton Railroad, at Glasgow, Missouri, in 1879.

[11] For information as to General Grierson I am indebted to Dr. Paul M. Angle, Secretary of the Illinois Historical Society, for the loan of the notes of a lecture presented to the Chicago Civil War Round Table. General Grierson remained in the regular army after the war, rising to the permanent rank of brigadier general, with a fine record in the Indian wars. He retired in 1890 and died in 1911, in his eighty-fifth year.

[12] Dinkins, pp. 129, 146-147.

[13] *O.R.*, Serial No. 58, p. 557, notes the receipt of the dispatch by Polk on the fourteenth.

[14] Same, p. 567.

[15] Governor Clark of Mississippi was the same General Clark under whom Forrest had had his first active service, while he was in command of the post of Hopkinsville, Kentucky. General Clark had been wounded at Shiloh, and wounded and captured at Baton Rouge. After his exchange, he was elected Governor of Mississippi.

[16] *O.R.*, Serial No. 58, pp. 639, 648.

[17] George W. Adair of Atlanta, who served as a volunteer aide to Forrest at this time, has left a circumstantial account of one measure taken to acquaint General Polk with the state of affairs. At Forrest's headquarters at this time, also, was Governor Isham G. Harris, of Tennessee, the same who had brought about Forrest's discharge as a private and his authorization to raise a battalion of cavalry. After telegraphing Polk briefly, Forrest decided that it would be better for him to have more detailed information, whereupon he asked Adair and Governor Harris to take a message to him at his headquarters at Demopolis. The two messengers traveled eastward across country to Tupelo, on the Mobile & Ohio Railroad, where they planned to take train to Meridian. There were no trains—all withdrawn to the south to escape the anticipated Federal raid. The distance, nearly 200 miles, was too great to cover on horseback but an idle handcar was borrowed from the section foreman, together with two hands to work it, and on this the two volunteer

aides started, both of them helping to get the car up the heavy grades, and "jolting, jouncing, bouncing" as they let her run downhill. Two days of such travel brought them to a point where trains were running, but after a short journey on this more conventional vehicle, they came to the broken end of track. The final stages of the journey were made by horseback. George W. Adair tells the story in good-humored detail in the Atlanta *Constitution* of Aug. 1, 1897. For the citation I am indebted to Miss Alma Jamison of the Carnegie Library and Mrs. John R. Marsh, of Atlanta.

[18] *O.R.*, Serial No. 58, pp. 616, 662-663, 673.

[19] Same, pp. 673, 680-681, 693.

[20] Same, pp. 685, 687.

[21] Same, pp. 315-316.

[22] Same, pp. 316-317.

[23] *O.R.*, Serial No. 57, p. 176.

[24] *O.R.*, Serial No. 58, p. 493.

[25] Same, p. 363.

[26] *Memoirs of General William T. Sherman* (New York, 1875), Vol. I, pp. 389-390.

[27] *O.R.*, Serial No. 57, pp. 347-348; No. 58, pp. 703, 706, 720.

[28] *O.R.*, Serial No. 57, p. 349.

[29] Waring, pp. 109-110.

[30] *O.R.*, Serial No. 58, pp. 755, 758.

[31] *O.R.*, Serial No. 57, p. 252.

[32] *O.R.*, Serial No. 58, pp. 317, 431.

[33] *O.R.*, Serial No. 57, p. 257.

[34] Waring, pp. 112-113.

[35] *O.R.*, Serial No. 58, p. 431.

[36] *O.R.*, Serial No. 57, pp. 252, 256.

[37] *O.R.*, Serial No. 58, p. 784.

[38] Same, p. 498.

[39] *O.R.*, Serial No. 57, pp. 252, 256-257.

[40] *S.H.S.P.*, Vol. 7, p. 465; Wyeth, *Forrest*, pp. 299-301, quoting Chalmers.

[41] Hancock, p. 323.

[42] Memorandum of conversation with J. P. Young, Seventh Tennessee Cavalry, Nov. 10, 1930.

[43] Wolseley, *United Service Magazine*, May 1892, p. 120. Wolseley's informane as to many personal details about Forrest was an unnamed "general officer who rode with Forrest for the last year and a half of the war"—perhaps W. H. Jackson or Frank C. Armstrong.

[44] *O.R.*, Serial No. 57, p. 300. Report of Major Datus E. Coon, Second Iowa Cavalry.

[45] *O.R.*, Serial No. 58, pp. 787-788.

[46] *O.R.*, Serial No. 57, p. 350.

[47] Waring, p. 117.

[48] J. P. Young, *The Seventh Tennessee Cavalry (Confederate)* (Nashville, 1890), p. 77.

[49] Jordan and Pryor, p. 392.

[50] *O.R.*, Serial No. 57, p. 353.

[51] Young, p. 77.

[52] *O.R.*, Serial No. 57, p. 283.

[53] Same, p. 353.

[54] The boyhood incident is described in a dispatch from Lewisburg, Tennessee, in the Memphis *Commercial-Appeal*, as having occurred on the farm of John Patterson, two miles west of Chapel Hill. Item in Morton Scrapbooks. Forrest's remark to General Pillow is quoted in the Memphis *Appeal* of Nov. 1, 1877.

[55] Hancock, p. 322-323.

[56] *O.R.*, Serial No. 57, p. 304.

[57] Same, p. 302.

[58] Same, p. 268. Col. W. P. Hepburn, Union brigade commander, settled for several years after the war in Memphis, where he joined with his old Confederate enemies in business enterprises before returning to his native Iowa to enter upon a distinguished career in Congress, in the course of which he became Chairman of the Committee on Interstate and Foreign Commerce of the House of Representatives.

[59] Jordan and Pryor, pp. 395-396. "The loss of my brother, Col. J. E. Forrest, is deeply felt by his brigade as well as by myself and it is but just to say that for sobriety, ability, prudence and bravery he had no superior of his age." Forrest Report, *O.R.*, Serial No. 57, pp. 354-355.

[60] *O.R.*, Serial No. 57, p. 268.

[61] Wyeth, *Forrest*, p. 316.

[62] Jordan and Pryor, p. 398. King Philip, the only one of Forrest's war horses to survive the war, was a great favorite with the soldiers, and has become part of the Forrest tradition. His first military service was at the siege of Vicksburg, which he survived. Later he was presented by citizens of Columbus, Mississippi, to Forrest. He was a big gelding, iron-gray, twelve years old and ordinarily a quiet, almost a sluggish animal, who "became superbly excited in battle." He learned that blue was the color of the enemy's uniform and was ready to fight bluecoats with bared teeth and flashing forefeet. Mathes, p. 185.

[63] Jordan and Pryor, p. 398.

[64] Wyeth, *Forrest*, p. 316.

[65] *O.R.*, Serial No. 57, p. 354. Colonel Waring states that the charge which so impressed Forrest was made by the Fourth Missouri Cavalry (Union). *Battles and Leaders*, Vol. IV, p. 417.

[66] William Witherspoon, *Reminiscences of a Scout, Spy and Soldier of Forrest's Cavalry* (Jackson, Tennessee, 1910), pp. 34-36.

[67] Waring, p. 125.

[68] *O.R.*, Serial No. 57, p. 289.

[69] Same, p. 252.

[70] Same, pp. 276-315.

[71] *Battles and Leaders*, Vol. IV, p. 418.

[72] Testimony before a Sub-Committee of the Committee on the Conduct of the War, published as Report No. 65, House of Representatives, 38th Congress, 1st Session, under the title *Fort Pillow Massacre* (Washington, 1864), p. 64.

[73] Sherman, *Memoirs*, Vol. I, pp. 394-395.

[74] Grant, *Memoirs*, Vol. II, pp. 108-110.

[75] *O.R.*, Serial No. 57, p. 356.

[76] Same, pp. 346-347.

THE "OCCUPATION" OF WEST TENNESSEE AND KENTUCKY

February 26, 1864-April 10, 1864

[1] *O.R.*, Serial No. 110, p. 632.

[2] *O.R.*, Serial No. 59, pp. 578-579.

[3] Same, p. 586. The young soldiers of Forrest's command paid particular attention to the young ladies of Columbus and Starkville. John Morton, who was left behind with the artillery when Forrest went back into West Tennessee, says that at Columbus "sometimes there were as many as three parties in a single night, and frequently all-night parties were turned into all-day picnics on the following day." Morton, pp. 159-160. "General Forrest was fond of company, and spent the time there [at Columbus] most pleasantly," wrote Captain Dinkins, while at near-by Starkville, Chalmers and his staff had a "most pleasant halt and rest." Dinkins, pp. 138-139.

[4] *O.R.*, Serial No. 59, pp. 593-594.

[5] Same, p. 602.

[6] Same, p. 616.

[7] Same, pp. 609-610.

[8] Same, pp. 622, 644, 648, 677.

[9] Bell Irvin Wiley, *The Life of Johnny Reb* (Indianapolis, 1943), p. 338.

[10] *O.R.*, Serial No. 57, p. 611.

[11] *O.R.*, Serial No. 59, pp. 616-617, 621.

[12] Same, pp. 663-664.

[13] Young, p. 83; Witherspoon, *Reminiscences of a Scout, Spy and Soldier of Forrest's Cavalry*, pp. 40-45.

[14] *O.R.*, Serial No. 59, pp. 117-119, 664-665.

[15] Young, pp. 83-85.

[16] *O.R.*, Serial No. 59, pp. 127-129.

[17] *O.R.*, Serial No. 57, pp. 502-503, 540-541.

[18] Same, pp. 540-546, 607; Young, pp. 85-86.

[19] *O.R.*, Serial No. 59, pp. 135-136.

[20] Same, pp. 165-168, 175.

[21] Jordan and Pryor, p. 412.

[22] *O.R.*, Serial No. 57, pp. 607, 612. The report of Colonel Hicks, commanding the defense, is on p. 547.

[23] *O.R.* (Naval), Vol. 26, pp. 198-201.

[24] Same, p. 199.

[25] *O.R.*, Serial No. 57, p. 505.

[26] *O.R.*, Serial No. 59, pp. 157, 167, 173, 181, 185-188, 191, 196.

[27] Jordan and Pryor, pp. 415-416.

[28] *O.R.*, Serial No. 59, p. 155.

[29] *O.R.*, Serial No. 63, p. 184.

[30] *O.R.*, Serial No. 57, p. 607.

[31] *O.R.*, Serial No. 110, p. 653. The immediate purpose of Forrest's letter to Johnston was to request the transfer to his command of Col. T. G. Woodward for assignment to his Kentucky brigade. While leaving the matter of the advisability

of the transfer entirely to General Johnston's judgment, Forrest proposed that "if the transfer be made I will send to your army from the conscripts and deserters in this portion of the State at least two men for every one of Colonel Woodward's command that may be sent to me."

[32] O.R., Serial No. 59, p. 165.

[33] Same, pp. 145-146, 196.

[34] O.R., Serial No. 57, pp. 585, 607, 623; Serial No. 59, p. 733.

[35] O.R., Serial No. 57, pp. 547-581.

[36] O.R., Serial No. 59, pp. 710, 718.

[37] O.R., Serial No. 57, p. 581; Serial No. 59, pp. 227, 230.

[38] O.R., Serial No. 37, p. 512; Serial No. 59, pp. 216, 233-234, 242; O.R. (Naval), Vol. 26, p. 198.

[39] O.R., Serial No. 63, p. 184.

[40] O.R., Serial No. 57, pp. 581-583, 608; Serial No. 59, pp. 253-254; Jordan and Pryor, pp. 420-421.

[41] O.R., Serial No. 59, pp. 244-245, 448-449, 255.

[42] O.R., Serial No. 59, p. 261.

[43] O.R., Serial No. 57, p. 608; Serial No. 59, p. 328.

[44] Same, p. 751.

[45] Same, pp. 284-286.

[46] Same, pp. 308-310.

[47] Same, p. 305.

[48] Same, pp. 267, 299, 329, 336.

[49] O.R., Serial No. 57, pp. 552-553; Mathes, pp. 208-212; Jordan and Pryor, pp. 416-417.

[50] O.R., Serial No. 57, pp. 549-550.

[51] Jordan and Pryor, pp. 417-418.

[52] O.R., Serial No. 57, p. 620; Serial No. 59, pp. 310, 754, 758.

[53] Same, pp. 759, 770.

CHAPTER XVII

"FORREST OF FORT PILLOW"

April 10, 1864-April 13, 1864

[1] See Laura A. White, "Atrocity Charges of the Civil War," The World Tomorrow (February 1929), a condensation of which appeared in The Reader's Digest, March, 1929 (Vol. VII), p. 649.

[2] O.R., Serial No. 57, p. 618.

[3] Same, p. 617.

[4] Two such dispatches widely quoted are one referring to Fort Pillow, reading, "We busted the fort at ninerclock and scattered the niggers. The men is still a cillanem in the woods;" and another, referring to prisoners, "Them as was cotch with spoons and brestpins and sich was cilled and the rest of the lot was payrold and told to git."

The alleged originals of these dispatches were submitted to Gen. James Grant Wilson, one of the editors of Appleton's Cyclopedia of American Biography, in 1887, were accepted by him as genuine, and were used in his sketch of Forrest in the first edition of that work (1888), Vol. II, p. 506.

As editor of the Great Commander Series, which includes Mathes' *General Forrest*, General Wilson learned of doubts as to the genuineness of the dispatches. To an inquiry on the subject, General Chalmers replied: "I do not believe that General Forrest wrote the Fort Pillow telegraphic dispatch, because the statements are not altogether in accordance with the facts. As to the second, I have no knowledge."

"The two doubtful dispatches," General Wilson wrote, "were omitted from the second, and succeeding editions of the *Cyclopedia of American Biography*." (Mathes, pp. 382-383—Appendix.)

The alleged dispatch, nevertheless, had been thrown into the stream of "history," from which it is occasionally fished out and re-used even yet. Perhaps the latest instance is its use in Lloyd Lewis' *Sherman, Fighting Prophet* (New York, 1932), p. 353, as proof of Forrest's insincerity in saying that "he had tried to halt the horror" of killing "many while trying to surrender," as well as "an example of his subliterate spelling." The slightest acquaintance with the facts of Fort Pillow shows that the alleged dispatch could not have been sent by Forrest. The fort was not "busted at ninerclock."

[5] *Fort Pillow Massacre Report,* p. 66.

[6] Same, p. 65.

[7] *O.R.,* Serial No. 57, p. 556.

[8] Same, p. 609.

[9] Same, p. 620; Hancock, pp. 351-352.

[10] *O.R.,* Serial No. 57, p. 559.

[11] Same, p. 557.

[12] Same, pp. 559-560.

[13] *Fort Pillow Report,* pp. 3, 4.

[14] Same, p. 86.

[15] Wyeth, *Forrest,* p. 342.

[16] *O.R.,* Serial No. 57, pp. 585-586.

[17] Same, p. 560; Wyeth, *Forrest,* p. 344.

[18] *O.R.,* Serial No. 57, pp. 560-561, 614.

[19] Same, pp. 572-573. Brig. Gen. George F. Shepley, who had been Military Governor of Louisiana and was on his way back north on the *Olive Branch,* gives very complete details.

[20] *O.R.,* Serial No. 57, p. 561.

[21] Same, p. 614.

[22] Same, p. 561.

[23] Same.

[24] *Fort Pillow Report,* p. 39. Similar testimony is given by other witnesses on pp. 36, 106 and 112.

[25] Same, p. 92.

[26] Same, p. 86.

[27] *O.R.,* Serial No. 57, p. 597.

[28] Same, pp. 561-562.

[29] Same, p. 570.

[30] Hancock, p. 368.

[31] *O.R.,* Serial No. 57, pp. 597-598.

[32] *Fort Pillow Report,* p. 86.

[33] *O.R.,* Serial No. 57, p. 598.

[34] *O.R.,* Serial No. 59, p. 777.

[35] *O.R.*, Serial No. 57, p. 571; *O.R.* (Naval), Vol. 26, p. 222.

[36] Same, p. 225.

[37] *O.R.*, Serial No. 57, p. 562.

[38] Same, p. 565.

[39] *O.R.*, Serial No. 59, p. 797.

[40] Jordan and Pryor, p. 437.

[41] *O.R.*, Serial No. 57, pp. 598-599.

[42] Same, p. 610.

[43] Same, p. 571.

[44] *O.R.* (Naval), Vol. 26, pp. 224, 234.

[45] Same, p. 222.

[46] *Fort Pillow Report*, p. 60.

[47] *O.R.* (Naval), Vol. 26, p. 231.

[48] Same, p. 220.

[49] Same, pp. 218-219.

[50] *Fort Pillow Report*, p. 41.

[51] Same, p. 93.

[52] Same, pp. 1-7.

[53] *O.R.*, Serial No. 57, p. 572.

[54] *Fort Pillow Report*, pp. 75-76. In a letter to Gen. Chalmers, then a member of Congress, the surgeon of the garrison at Fort Pillow, Dr. C. Fitch, referred thus to charges of the murder of "babes": "I don't believe there was a babe there for any one to kill, as early in the morning all of the women and all of the noncombatants were ordered on to some barges, and were towed up the river to an island by a gunboat before anyone was hurt. I fail to see how you could have gotten on that island to kill that babe." *S.H.S.P.*, Vol. 7, pp. 440-441.

[55] *Fort Pillow Report*, p. 15.

[56] Same, p. 40.

[57] Same, p. 94.

[58] Same, p. 95.

[59] Same, p. 30. The apparent influence of the idea of crucifixion upon the imagination of this witness is matched by the *Uncle Tom's Cabin* touches in the testimony of another witness, Edward B. Benton of Vermont and Missouri, who was putting in a cotton crop of 100 acres just outside the fortifications, who took a musket and, as he testified, "fired forty-eight shots in all." That night he escaped and made his way to "Pass No. 2, leading out of the fort, inside of it, where I could see all, where I laid until the next day about two o'clock. I heard fifty-one or fifty-two shots fired singly at different times within the fort during that time, and screams and cheers. About two o'clock the dogs were getting so close to me that I knew they were on my track."

"What do you mean by dogs?"

"Hunting out people everywhere. They have dogs."

"They had bloodhounds?"

"Yes, sir." ...

"You say they had bloodhounds; did you see any of them?"

"Yes, sir; and not only I but others saw them. One other, Mr. Jones, was treed by them, and staid there a long time."

"What Mr. Jones was that?"

"I don't know his given name. He lives on Island 34. He is not any too good a

Union man, but is rather southern in his feelings." (*Fort Pillow Report*, pp. 121-122.)

60 *Fort Pillow Report*, p. 18.

61 Same, p. 21.

62 Same, p. 47.

63 Sergeant (afterward Captain) Clark's letter was made available through the kindness of his daughter, Mrs. Sydney S. Crockett, of Nashville, Tennessee.

64 Wyeth, *Forrest*, p. 386. Anderson's affidavit.

65 Same, pp. 386-389.

66 Same, p. 389.

67 *S.H.S.P.*, Vol. 7, pp. 439-441.

68 Wyeth, *Forrest*, pp. 383-390.

69 Jordan and Pryor, p. 443.

70 *Fort Pillow Report*, pp. 31-32.

71 Same, pp. 39-40.

72 Same, pp. 91-92.

73 Wyeth, *Forrest*, p. 387.

74 *Fort Pillow Report*, p. 86. As Dr. Wyeth wrote in his letter to Gen. Chalmers, "what was done was done very quickly."

75 *O.R.*, Serial No. 59, p. 381.

76 Same, p. 464.

77 Same, p. 381; *O.R.*, Serial No. 57, pp. 518-540; *Fort Pillow Report*, pp. 104-123.

78 Sherman, *Memoirs*, Vol. II, pp. 12-13.

79 *O.R.*, Serial No. 59, p. 366.

CHAPTER XVIII

A SWORD AGAINST SHERMAN'S LIFE LINE
April 14, 1864-July 9, 1864

1 *O.R.* (Naval), Vol. 26, pp. 215-216, 238, 240, 246. The gunboats ordered to Fort Pillow from the rivers above were the *Hastings, Moose* and *Volunteer;* from the Mississippi and Red Rivers, below, the *Benton* (flagship), *Choctaw, Lafayette, Avenger, Ouachita, New National.*

2 Same, p. 264. The White River boats ordered to Memphis were the *Tyler* and *Queen City.*

3 *O.R.*, Serial No. 57, pp. 777-778. Forrest's orders to Chalmers were to move back with his entire command "between the Hatchie and the Forked Deer, so as to sweep the country, bringing in every man between the ages of eighteen and forty-five to Jackson. . . . Take no excuse, neither allow conscripts to go home for clothes or anything else; their friends can send them to Jackson."

4 *O.R.*, Serial No. 57, p. 592.

5 Same, pp. 612-613.

6 Same, p. 616.

7 Same, p. 778.

8 *O.R.*, Serial No. 59, pp. 348, 367.

9 *O.R.*, Serial No. 57, p. 609.

10 Same, p. 349; Serial No. 59, p. 374.

11 Same, p. 798.

[12] Same, pp. 482, 822. The "system" is described in the Chattanooga *Daily Rebel* (published at Selma), Mar. 26, 1865.

[13] *O.R.*, Serial No. 59, pp. 798-799, 809.

[14] Same, p. 800.

[15] Same, p. 367.

[16] Same, pp. 381-382, 397.

[17] Besides changing commanders at Memphis, Sherman ordered McPherson, who was assembling the troops for the right wing of the great advance into Georgia, to halt some of those coming by transport up the Tennessee River at Clifton, and to send them, with other units gathered in Middle Tennessee or north Alabama, to "strike Forrest inland," so as to cut off his retreat. Same, pp. 382-383, 399, 400.

[18] Same, p. 402. Upon Sturgis' arrival to take command of the cavalry at Memphis, Grierson asked to be relieved of duty, thinking that there was no need for more than one brigadier general for the cavalry there. His request to return to Illinois and Iowa for the purpose of "reorganizing, arming, mounting and equipping the regiments of my old division" was not granted. Same, p. 502.

[19] Same, pp. 411, 415, 430, 441.

[20] Same, pp. 462-463.

[21] From the diary of J. Pugh Cannon, entry of April 12, 1864, p. 196. Mr. Cannon's diary, printed for his family, was furnished me by his grandson, Pugh Moore of the Associated Press.

[22] *O.R.*, Serial No. 59, p. 485.

[23] Same, pp. 516-517.

[24] Same, pp. 521, 527.

[25] *O.R.*, Serial No. 63, p. 275.

[26] *O.R.*, Serial No. 59, p. 490.

[27] Same, p. 536.

[28] Same, pp. 809, 819, 821-822.

[29] Jordan and Pryor, pp. 456-457.

[30] *O.R.*, Serial No. 57, pp. 693, 696, 698-699.

[31] Jordan and Pryor, pp. 457-458; *O.R.*, Serial No. 57, pp. 696, 699, 700, 702. "Four of Company E," the historian of the Seventh Tennessee Cavalry wrote afterward, "had been on a lark that day, and the whole party were feeling strongly the inspiration of bold John Barleycorn. When the command retreated through Bolivar these four youngsters 'made a stand' in front of the residence of a well-known citizen, and quickly came in collision with the head of the Federal column at not more than fifty yards' distance. The first volley sent the four horses rolling in the dust, when they quickly recovered their feet, but two of the youngsters, being topheavy, could not remount their wounded steeds. They were lifted into the saddles by the other two, and the whole party rode off unhurt by the storm of bullets sent after them by the Federals, who were annoyed beyond measure at the contemptuous indifference of the youngsters and the ineffectiveness of their own fire. They afterward declared that 'the boys were bullet proof.' " (Young, p. 87.)

[32] *O.R.*, Serial No. 57, pp. 693, 695-697, 700.

[33] Same, p. 697.

[34] Same, p. 698.

[35] *O.R.*, Serial No. 75, p. 685.

[36] Sherman, *Memoirs*, Vol. II, p. 399.

[37] *O.R.*, Serial No. 74, p. 625.

[38] *O.R.*, Serial No. 75, p. 689.

[39] Same, pp. 197-198.
[40] *O.R.*, Serial No. 78, pp. 594-596, 610, 624.
[41] Same, p. 603.
[42] Same, pp. 596-597.
[43] Same, pp. 628, 643.
[44] Same, pp. 640-642.
[45] Same, pp. 601, 608.
[46] Same, p. 614.
[47] Same, p. 618.
[48] Same, p. 627.
[49] Same, pp. 605, 608.
[50] Same, p. 606; *O.R.*, Serial No. 75, p. 723.
[51] Dinkins, p. 146.
[52] *O.R.*, Serial No. 78, p. 37.
[53] Same, pp. 23, 595, 602, 609.
[54] *O.R.*, Serial No. 75, pp. 723-724.
[55] *O.R.*, Serial No. 78, p. 729.
[56] *O.R.*, Serial No. 110, p. 672; Jones, entry of May 25, 1864.
[57] *O.R.*, Serial No. 75, pp. 734, 740-741, 752-754. Chalmers, on account of the state of his health, went on this expedition riding in an ambulance. The surgeons had suggested an operation but Chalmers would not apply for leave of absence. Forrest prompted Lee to write him that Armstrong or some other officer be put in his stead until he could be operated upon and recover. Chalmers declined to be relieved.
[58] Same, pp. 294-295.
[59] *O.R.*, Serial No. 78, pp. 41, 44, 48-49.
[60] Same, p. 625.
[61] Same, p. 628; *O.R.*, Serial No. 75, p. 747.
[62] Same, p. 748.
[63] Same, pp. 750-751.
[64] *O.R.*, Serial No. 78, p. 73.
[65] *O.R.*, Serial No. 77, pp. 85-86. There is a discrepancy in the number of field guns taken on the expedition, which is variously reported as 16, 18, 20 and 22. The count here given is secured by adding the number of pieces reported with each subordinate command. See pp. 89, 90, 156, 158, 175, 196, 202, 217.
[66] In a letter to Forrest, *O.R.*, Serial No. 57, pp. 586-589.
[67] *O.R.*, Serial No. 57, p. 555.
[68] *O.R.*, Serial No. 77, pp. 87, 90. Forrest reported that the damage done at Rienzi consisted chiefly of burning the depot. (P. 222.)
[69] Same, pp. 91, 162, 200, 207. Colonel McMillen told the board which investigated the rout at Brice's Cross Roads that he remarked that he "would rather go on and meet the enemy, even if we should be whipped, than to return again to Memphis without having met them." Same, p. 207.
[70] Same, pp. 221-222.
[71] Lindsley, p. 853 (quoted in Morton, pp. 173-174); Hanson, p. 76.
[72] *O.R.*, Serial No. 77, p. 222.
[73] *O.R.*, Serial No. 75, p. 442.
[74] Wyeth, *Forrest*, pp. 398-399.
[75] Wolseley, *United Service Magazine*, Vol. V (New Series), p. 118.
[76] Mitchell, Lt. Col. William A., United States Military Academy, *Outlines of the World's Military History*, published for the *Infantry Journal*, Washington, 1931, pp. 460-461.

CHAPTER XIX

BRICE'S CROSS ROADS: HIGH-WATER MARK OF VICTORY
June 10, 1864-June 13, 1864

1 Wyeth, *Forrest*, p. 400.

2 *O.R.*, Serial No. 77, p. 222. Forrest's was the only Confederate report made on the battle. The Union reports are numerous and complete, covering, with the testimony taken by the Sturgis Board of Investigation, 137 pages.

3 Brice's Cross Roads is now the post office of Bethany, Lee County, Miss. An excellent treatment of the country about the Cross Roads, and of the battle as it appeared to a young boy of the neighborhood, is given in an account by the Reverend Samuel Agnew, son of Dr. Agnew, whose house was one of the battle landmarks, first published in the *Southern Sentinel* of Ripley, Miss., of March 28, 1895, and subsequently reprinted in a series of Historical Sketches by Andrew Brown in the same paper in June and July 1935.

4 *O.R.*, Serial No. 77, p. 222.

5 Same, p. 132.

6 Same, pp. 129, 132, 200.

7 Same, p. 153.

8 Wyeth, *Forrest*, p. 400.

9 Captain Gartrell was a newspaper publisher and former Mayor of Rome, Georgia, whose nephew Henry W. Grady afterward became the editor of the Atlanta *Constitution*. He may have been the source of the information about Forrest which another member of the *Constitution* staff, Joel Chandler Harris, used in his realistic picture of the General in the story, "The Shadow Between His Shoulder Blades."

10 *O.R.*, Serial No. 77, p. 223.

11 Same, pp. 132, 190-191.

12 Same, p. 223.

13 Same.

14 Wyeth, *Forrest*, p. 409.

15 *O.R.*, Serial No. 77, p. 223.

16 Same, pp. 129-130, 200-201.

17 Same, pp. 153-154, 201; William Forse Scott, *Story of a Cavalry Regiment*, 4th Iowa Veteran Volunteers (New York, 1893), pp. 245, 270-272.

18 *O.R.*, Serial No. 77, p. 93.

19 Hubbard, p. 110.

20 *O.R.*, Serial No. 77, pp. 153, 157.

21 Same, pp. 107, 111, 114, 119, 124, 125, 144, 146, 157, 163, 165, 169, 173, 175, 197, 205, 208, 210.

22 Same, p. 119.

23 Same, p. 208.

24 Same, pp. 92, 132, 154.

25 Same, pp. 92, 104, 107, 124.

26 Same, p. 135.

27 Same, pp. 92, 187.

28 Same, p. 223.

29 Same.

30 Hubbard, pp. 110-111.

[31] Witherspoon, *Tishomingo Creek*, p. 61.

[32] Lindsley, p. 643; Young, p. 92.

[33] Memorandum of conversation with Mack Watson, private, Forrest's Escort.

[34] In the sketches of Samuel Agnew it is stated that Barteau's regiment, moving from Old Carrollville, "entered the Ripley Road in the rear of Sturgis, on the top of the hill west of Camp Creek, five and a half miles from the Cross Roads and moving down the road a mile and a half, they deployed into the enemy, who were beginning to fall back." *Southern Sentinel*, Ripley, Miss., June 27, 1935.

[35] Lindsley, p. 617; Hancock's *Diary*, pp. 391-392.

[36] O.R., Serial No. 77, p. 224.

[37] Same, p. 93.

[38] Same, p. 155.

[39] Same, p. 137.

[40] Same, pp. 106, 138, 145. Among the first pieces captured were two fine 3-inch steel Rodmans, to match the two captured from Colonel Ingersoll at Lexington, Tennessee, in December 1862, and so to complete the equipping of Morton's battery with this superior type of ordnance. Morton and his men were "greatly gratified." Morton, p. 176.

[41] O.R., Serial No. 77, pp. 126, 213-214. Other commanders also report their efforts to stem the rush of the rout. Same, pp. 93, 94, 105, 108.

[42] Same, pp. 178, 180.

[43] Same, pp. 138, 205.

[44] To young Morton, riding by his side at the front of the pursuit at three o'clock in the morning, Forrest discoursed upon his philosophy of winning battles. "Get 'em skeered," he said, "and then keep the skeer on 'em." Riding back from the pursuit, a day or so later, he expanded his dictum. "In any fight, it's the first blow that counts; and if you keep it up hot enough, you can whip 'em as fast as they can come up." That, Morton adds, is as near as he ever heard Forrest come to saying "git thar fust with the mostest men"—that being the form in which the remark was being quoted at the time Morton's memoirs were written. Morton, pp. 181, 198.

[45] O.R., Serial No. 77, pp. 106, 170, 182, 211, 218.

[46] Same, p. 224.

[47] Witherspoon, *Tishomingo Creek*, p. 68.

[48] O.R., Serial No. 77, p. 224.

[49] Witherspoon, *Tishomingo Creek*, p. 67.

[50] Hanson, p. 74.

[51] O.R., Serial No. 77, p. 186.

[52] Same, p. 214.

[53] Same, p. 224. "Further along, I counted ninety-five wagons laden with supplies strung along the narrow road. The wheels of some had been locked by trees and evidently abandoned in hot haste by those who had ridden the teams away." Hubbard, p. 116.

[54] Witherspoon, *Tishomingo Creek*, p. 69.

[55] Same, p. 70.

[56] O.R., Serial No. 77, pp. 93, 95, 104, 127, 129, 135, 159, 160, 211.

[57] Same, p. 171. Mrs. Faulkner's husband, Colonel Faulkner, became after the war a builder of railroads and also the author of the successful novel *The White Rose of Memphis*. William Faulkner, distinguished Mississippi novelist, is their grandson.

[58] Waring, pp. 131-132.

[59] *O.R.*, Serial No. 77, p. 224.

[60] Jordan and Pryor, p. 479.

[61] *O.R.*, Serial No. 77, p. 224.

[62] Same, p. 171.

[63] Same, pp. 145-146.

[64] Same, p. 116.

[65] Same, p. 112.

[66] Same, p. 224.

[67] Waring, p. 132.

[68] *O.R.*, Serial No. 77, pp. 106, 139.

[69] Same, pp. 116, 139, 203, 206.

[70] Memorandum of conversation with Mack Watson of Nashville, Tennessee, Private in Forrest's Escort. In most accounts of Forrest's fall from his horse, it is stated that he fainted and lay unconscious for a spell, overcome by exhaustion. Jordan and Pryor, p. 481. His fall took place almost within sight of his boyhood home at Salem, and that night (the eleventh) he passed in the home of his mother's brother, Orrin Beck.

[71] Conversation with Private Mack Watson.

[72] *O.R.*, Serial No. 77, p. 95. The losses appear to be understated in Sturgis' report, since the total of losses separately reported by the subordinate commanders exceeds 2,600.

[73] The inventories of captured men and matériel are in *O.R.*, Serial No. 77, pp. 226-228, 230-231. Included in the matériel were five fine ambulances which were loaded with captured medical supplies, of such great value to the Confederacy and dispatched across country to General Johnson's Army of Tennessee, in north Georgia. Mathes, p. 249.

[74] *O.R.*, Serial No. 77, p. 95.

[75] *O.R.*, Serial No. 57, pp. 586-591.

[76] *Battles and Leaders*, Vol. IV, p. 421.

[77] Waring, pp. 126, 130.

[78] *O.R.*, Serial No. 77, pp. 98, 101, 167, 179, 181, 196, 202.

[79] Same, pp. 172, 179, 198. The criticism of Winslow by Sturgis in his official reports was attributed by Winslow's adjutant to the fact that he had refused to write a letter of exculpation to Sturgis when requested to do so. Scott, p. 280.

[80] *O.R.*, Serial No. 75, p. 480.

[81] *O.R.*, Serial No. 77, p. 217.

[82] George W. Cullum, *Biographical Register, United States Military Academy,* 1867, Vol. II, pp. 159-160.

In 1882 General Sturgis published a defense of his conduct of the campaign under the title, *The Other Side.*

[83] *O.R.*, Serial No. 77, pp. 85, 86. General Washburn, obviously apprehensive of General Sherman's displeasure at the result of the expedition, points out that although Sherman had telegraphed him to send 6,000 troops after Forrest, he had sent 8,000 "of our best troops," and that he "felt that he had no alternative" but to put Sturgis in command, as he had been sent to Memphis for the purpose and was the ranking general present.

[84] *Home Letters of General Sherman,* edited by M. A. DeWolfe Howe (New York, 1909), p. 297.

[85] *O.R.*, Serial No. 75, p. 474.

[86] Same, p. 480.

[87] Same, p. 462.

[88] Same, pp. 478-479.

[89] *O.R.*, Serial No. 78, pp. 115, 123, 124; Serial No. 75, p. 474.

[90] The effect of the recital of the incredible events of Brice's Cross Roads, or Tishomingo Creek, upon one military inquirer is told by Basil Duke in his *Reminiscences*. Some years after the war two French cavalry officers called upon Duke in Louisville, to inquire about Morgan's operations. While there they asked him also about Forrest. Duke, not being intimately acquainted with the latter's operations, nevertheless gave them a plain story of the fight at Brice's. "I did not try to embellish the story—that could scarcely be done—but I certainly tried to do it justice," he wrote. The younger of the two French officers, Captain de La Cher, translated for the elder, Colonel Kerbrecht of the Chasseurs d'Afrique. As the story unfolded, the old chasseur inched forward in his chair until, as it was finished, he "rose to his feet, stretched both arms above his head, and with, perhaps, the only two words of our language that he knew, testified to the prowess of Bedford Forrest: 'Sapristi! God damn!' " Duke, pp. 133-134.

CHAPTER XX

HARRISBURG: AN INVASION REPELLED BY VICTORY

June 14, 1864-July 23, 1864

[1] *Home Letters of General Sherman,* p. 296.

[2] *O.R.*, Serial No. 75, p. 542.

[3] *O.R.*, Serial No. 78, p. 503.

[4] *O.R.*, Serial No. 76, p. 123.

[5] *O.R.*, Serial No. 78, pp. 123-125; No. 75, p. 474.

[6] *O.R.*, Serial No. 78, p. 121.

[7] Same, p. 123.

[8] Same, p. 124.

[9] Same, p. 130.

[10] Same, p. 142.

[11] *O.R.*, Serial No. 75, p. 689.

[12] Joseph E. Johnston, *Narrative of Military Operations* (New York, 1874), p. 359. See also *O.R.*, Serial No. 75, pp. 756, 769, 770, 772, 792, 805; Serial No. 76, pp. 869, 874-875; Serial No. 110, pp. 678-679, 692.

[13] *O.R.*, Serial No. 75, p. 774.

[14] *Battles and Leaders,* Vol. IV, p. 276.

[15] *O.R.*, Serial No. 110, p. 680.

[16] Same, pp. 704-706.

[17] *O.R.*, Serial No. 76, p. 858.

[18] *O.R.*, Serial No. 75, p. 805.

[19] *O.R.*, Serial No. 110, p. 691.

[20] *O.R.*, Serial No. 78, p. 688.

[21] Same, p. 688.

[22] *O.R.*, Serial No. 110, p. 687.

[23] Maury, p. 205.

[24] *Battles and Leaders,* Vol. IV, p. 276.

[25] *O.R.*, Serial No. 78, pp. 657, 666, 671-672; Jordan and Pryor, pp. 493-494, 497.

[26] Part of Forrest's knowledge, no doubt, was due to the work of spies in the city itself. In his lecture on Forrest before the Southern Historical Society, General Chalmers tells the story of one such spy who reported that during the time A. J. Smith was getting ready to go after Forrest, Sturgis, who was in Memphis attending the investigation of his expedition, was heard sitting in a hotel soliloquizing, "It can't be done, sir!" and when asked what it was that could not be done, replied "They c-a-n-'t whip old Forrest!" *S.H.S.P.*, Vol. 7, p. 474.

[27] *O.R.*, Serial No. 78, pp. 645-648. During the two weeks in which this correspondence was passing, General Pillow had under his command one of Forrest's brigades, Neely's of Chalmers' division, which he used in an attempt to cut Sherman's railroad in north Georgia. He got as far as LaFayette, Georgia, about twenty-five miles from the rail line. There an attempt to surprise and capture the Union garrison failed, partly because a party of Union officers happened to be playing poker at 3:00 A.M. with local citizens, the Union garrison putting up money and the citizens, having no money, putting up tobacco. *Sketches of War History,* Papers of Ohio Commandery, Military Order of the Loyal Legion (Cincinnati, 1890), Vol. III, p. 331. See also, *O.R.*, Serial No. 73, pp. 777-778, 795-800; No. 74, pp. 994-1008, for official reports, Federal and Confederate, of this expedition.

[28] *O.R.*, Serial No. 78, pp. 683-684.

[29] Same, p. 682; Jordan and Pryor, p. 496.

[30] *O.R.*, Serial No. 78, p. 652; Jordan and Pryor, p. 496.

[31] Hubbard, p. 122.

[32] *O.R.*, Serial No. 78, p. 142.

[33] *O.R.*, Serial No. 64, p. 587.

[34] *O.R.*, Serial No. 78, pp. 147, 149-150. Sturgis' loss of field artillery had been so great that General Rosecrans, commanding at St. Louis, was called upon to send guns to Memphis to supply the lack. He sent twenty-six pieces. *O.R.*, Serial No. 78, pp. 207, 209.

[35] Same, pp. 150, 670.

[36] Same, p. 671.

[37] Morton, p. 203.

[38] *O.R.*, Serial No. 78, pp. 674-677.

[39] Same, pp. 163, 168.

[40] Same, p. 694.

[41] *O.R.*, Serial No. 77, pp. 250, 318.

[42] A detailed account of the burning of Ripley is given by Andrew Brown in his Historical Sketches, *Southern Sentinel,* Ripley, Miss., Sept. 30, 1934.

[43] Dinkins, p. 166; Jordan and Pryor, p. 498.

[44] *O.R.*, Serial No. 77, p. 250.

[45] Same, pp. 320, 329.

[46] Same, p. 324; *O.R.*, Serial No. 78, p. 696.

[47] *O.R.*, Serial No. 77, pp. 320, 325.

[48] Same, p. 325.

[49] Same, pp. 250-251.

[50] Same, p. 325.

[51] *O.R.*, Serial No. 78, pp. 700, 702.

[52] *O.R.*, Serial No. 77, pp. 251, 301.

[53] Same, pp. 325-326.

[54] Same, p. 330.

[55] Same, pp. 251, 257, 259.

[56] Same, pp. 302, 304, 316-317, 319.

[57] Same, pp. 251, 259.

[58] Jordan and Pryor, p. 505.

[59] Morton, pp. 204-205.

[60] *O.R.*, Serial No. 77, p. 322.

[61] Same.

[62] In an unpublished memorandum of eight typewritten pages, preserved in Captain Morton's Scrapbooks. The memorandum was prepared in answer to General Lee's presentation before the Mississippi Historical Society.

[63] From a letter of Feb. 18, 1902, to Captain Morton, published in the Memphis *Commercial-Appeal.* Morton's Scrapbooks.

[64] *S.H.S.P.*, Vol. 7, pp. 476-477.

[65] Stephen D. Lee, "Battle of Harrisburg, or Tupelo," *Publications* of the Mississippi Historical Society, Vol. VI, pp. 38-52; also printed as a pamphlet, *Gen. Stephen D. Lee's Account of the Battle of Harrisburg, Read Before the Mississippi State Historical Society, Differing in Many Respects from the Version Generally Accepted.*

[66] Memoirs of John N. Johnson of Dublin, Virginia, and Morgan's command, prepared for his son, unpublished manuscript in Tennessee State Library. The fighting quality of the Morgan "remnant," as it is described in the reports, is attested by their division and brigade commanders on the day of Harrisburg. *O.R.*, Serial No. 77, pp. 333, 341.

Hearing of the part played by this detachment of his men, General Morgan wrote from Abingdon, Virginia, to Forrest, "I never learn of your successes that they do not arouse the most pleasurable feeling of friendly satisfaction. I was truly glad to learn that in your late engagement with the enemy at Tupelo some 300 men of my command arrived on the field in time to afford you assistance, and am highly pleased with your acknowledgment of their service. I send Major Cassell of my brigade, to take command of the men referred to and march them back to this point." *O.R.*, Serial No. 78, p. 727.

[67] *O.R.*, Serial No. 77, p. 326.

[68] Morton, pp. 207-208.

[69] *O.R.*, Serial No. 77, p. 322.

[70] Same, p. 336.

[71] Same, p. 322.

[72] Same, p. 326.

[73] Same, p. 322.

[74] Same, p. 252. General Smith's reference to the "yelling and howling" of the charge refers, no doubt, to the rebel yell. This yell, John N. Johnson explained to his son, was "impossible unless made in a dead run in full charge against the enemy. . . . It cannot be imitated standing still . . . it is worse than folly to try to imitate it, especially with a stomach full of food and a mouth full of false teeth" —after a dinner served by the Daughters of the Confederacy to the Veterans. Johnson Memoir, Tennessee State Library.

[75] *O.R.*, Serial No. 77, pp. 264, 280, 282, 285.

[76] Same, p. 252.

[77] Same, p. 257.

[78] Same, p. 327.

[79] Same, pp. 281, 293.
[80] Same, pp. 328, 333, 335.
[81] Lindsley, p. 619.
[82] Same, p. 854.
[83] Jordan and Pryor, p. 510.
[84] Mathes, p. 259.
[85] Jordan and Pryor, p. 508.
[86] Mississippi Valley Historical Society, *Publications*, Vol. VI, pp. 45-47.
[87] Letters from Generals Lyon, Rucker and Bell, published in the Memphis *Commercial-Appeal*, undated clipping in the Morton Scrapbooks. Colonel Kelley's reply to General Lee, submitted to and approved by the three brigade commanders named above, together with all surviving members of Forrest's staff—Anderson, Morton and Cowan—was published in the *Commercial-Appeal* of March 16, 1902. General Lee's exchange of correspondence with Colonel Kelley—three letters from Lee to Kelley, two from Kelley to Lee—appears in the Nashville *Daily News* of March 27, 1902. In addition to these published statements, the Morton Scrapbooks contain manuscript memoranda from Captain H. A. Tyler, Major Charles W. Anderson and Captain Morton himself, and an undated clipping giving in full a letter of Lieutenant Samuel Donelson, of Forrest's staff, to General Lee, dated January 31, 1902.
[88] *O.R.*, Serial No. 77, p. 252.
[89] Same, pp. 259-260, 263, 323, 348.
[90] Same, pp. 327, 333.
[91] Same, pp. 323-324, 327.
[92] Same, p. 328.
[93] Same, p. 179.
[94] *O.R.*, Serial No. 78, p. 184.
[95] *O.R.*, Serial No. 76, pp. 194-195.
[96] *O.R.*, Serial No. 78, p. 201.

CHAPTER XXI

MEMPHIS: THE RAID THAT RECALLED AN INVADING ARMY
July 24, 1864-August 25, 1864

[1] *O.R.*, Serial No. 78, pp. 202, 204.
[2] Same, pp. 207-208.
[3] Same, p. 219.
[4] Same, p. 233.
[5] *O.R.*, Serial No. 76, p. 471.
[6] *O.R.*, Serial No. 78, pp. 743-744.
[7] The description of Forrest in his buggy is given by a character in Joel Chandler Harris' story, "The Shadow Between His Shoulder Blades," p. 45.
[8] *O.R.*, Serial No. 78, p. 748.
[9] Same, p. 756.
[10] Same, pp. 752-753, 756, 758, 763, 765.
[11] Same, pp. 760-761.
[12] Same, pp. 762-763.
[13] *O.R.*, Serial No. 77, pp. 372, 375-376, 381, 394; Serial No. 78, p. 765.

[14] Same, pp. 765-766.

[15] Jordan and Pryor, p. 530, from the manuscript notes of Colonel T. H. Logwood.

[16] Hubbard, pp. 136-137.

[17] O.R., Serial No. 78, p. 242.

[18] O.R., Serial No. 77, pp. 396-399.

[19] Same, pp. 372, 373, 376-377, 380-381; Serial No. 78, p. 261.

[20] Manuscript notes of lecture by Lt. Tully Brown, Morton's battery, afterward Adjutant General of Tennessee, in Tennessee State Library.

[21] Hubbard, p. 139.

[22] O.R., Serial No. 78, p. 783; Jordan and Pryor, p. 534. That the idea of the march to Memphis was not one suddenly conceived is indicated by a message sent by Forrest on August eighth, while still at Okolona, asking, "What facilities for crossing the river at Panola? How many boats are there?" O.R., Serial No. 78, p. 765.

[23] Dinkins, pp. 179-180; Jordan and Pryor, pp. 535-536; S.H.S.P., Vol. 36, p. 187; Hancock, pp. 446-447.

[24] Hubbard, p. 141.

[25] Dinkins, p. 180.

[26] Captain Forrest's unceremonious equestrian entrance into the Gayoso is often attributed to his brother, the General. One who professed to have seen the General there was a Negro soldier who assured those who would listen that he was standing in the alley "when I seed him come up. He rid his hoss right up to de hotel, and I'm tellin' you the Gord's truf, he hitched his horse right to the second-story bannisters." Dinkins, p. 193.

[27] O.R., Serial No. 77, p. 472.

[28] Same, p. 469.

[29] O.R., Serial No. 77, pp. 473-474; O.R. (Naval), Vol. 26, p. 517.

[30] Dinkins, pp. 187-188.

[31] Confederate Veteran, Vol. XI, p. 503.

[32] This account of events in Memphis in the early morning of August twenty-first is condensed from the several accounts by Jordan and Pryor, Wyeth, Mathes, Hubbard, Dinkins and Hancock. Forrest made no report of the affair, other than a brief telegraphic dispatch.

[33] O.R., Serial No. 77, pp. 480-481; Jordan and Pryor, pp. 545-546.

[34] Wyeth, Forrest, pp. 474-475. A variant of the story, given in Mathes, p. 272, is that Washburn sent out the cloth with buttons and braid to make full uniforms for Forrest and his staff. See also Chalmers' account, S.H.S.P., Vol. 7, p. 477.

[35] O.R., Serial No. 78, p. 282.

[36] O.R., Serial No. 77, pp. 178, 293, 481.

[37] Same, pp. 469-470; Serial No. 78, p. 297.

[38] O.R., Serial No. 77, p. 471; Serial No. 78, pp. 297, 301-302, 310.

[39] O.R., Serial No. 77, p. 470.

[40] Same, pp. 787-788.

[41] Same, p. 387; S.H.S.P., Vol. 7, p. 478.

[42] O.R., Serial No. 77, pp. 372-373, 376-377, 379, 393.

[43] Quoted in Jordan and Pryor, pp. 550-551. See also S.H.S.P., Vol. 36, pp. 192-195.

[44] O.R., Serial No. 78, p. 302.

[45] Same, p. 792.

[46] *O.R.*, Serial No. 77, pp. 471-472, 474; Serial No. 78, p. 302.

[47] Same, p. 296.

[48] *O.R.*, Serial No. 77, p. 484.

[49] *O.R.* (Naval), Vol. 26, p. 517.

[50] Gaillard Hunt, *Israel, Elihu and Cadwallader Washburn* (New York, 1925), p. 347.

[51] *O.R.*, Serial No. 126, p. 366; *S.H.S.P.*, Vol. 36, p. 195.

[52] *O.R.*, Serial No. 78, p. 796.

[53] Quoting W. M. Lea, Company A, Eleventh Mississippi Regiment, Army of Northern Virginia. Maud Murrow Brown, *The University Greys* (Richmond, 1940), p. 54.

[54] For a photostatic copy of the indictment of Forrest for treason, I am indebted to Messrs. Thomas B. Collier of Memphis and Monroe Cockrell of Chicago. The indictment covers four legal-size pages. Mr. Collier appeared in open court at Memphis and received permission to have the document photographed.

[55] The Marshal's return was made in March 1865. Memphis *Commercial-Appeal*, March 12, 1939.

CHAPTER XXII

TO TENNESSEE—TOO LATE

August 25, 1864-October 10, 1864

[1] *O.R.*, Serial No. 78, p. 806.

[2] Same, pp. 797-804.

[3] Same, pp. 805-806.

[4] Young, *The Seventh Tennessee Cavalry*, p. 100.

[5] *O.R.*, Serial No. 78, pp. 831-832.

[6] Young, *The Seventh Tennessee Cavalry*, p. 101; Mathes, p. 283; *Confederate Veteran*, Vol. XVI, pp. 501, 560-561.

[7] *O.R.*, Serial No. 78, pp. 806, 813, 818-819.

[8] *O.R.*, Serial No. 79, pp. 640, 807, 810, 846, 868, 909-910.

[9] Douglas S. Freeman, editor, *Lee's Dispatches* (New York, 1915), p. 283.

[10] *O.R.*, Serial No. 110, p. 731.

[11] Same, p. 729.

[12] Maury, p. 215. About this time Grant at City Point, Virginia, wrote to Sherman at Atlanta: "Petersburg paper of the 9th contains a dispatch from Mobile of the 7th announcing the arrival of Generals Forrest and Taylor. It is to be hoped that the enemy have found it necessary to call in Forrest's forces." *O.R.*, Serial No. 78, p. 355.

[13] Same, pp. 818-819.

[14] *O.R.*, Serial No. 110, p. 732.

[15] Taylor, pp. 198-199.

[16] *O.R.*, Serial No. 78, p. 831.

[17] Same, p. 356.

[18] *O.R.*, Serial No. 76, p. 652.

[19] *O.R.*, Serial No. 78, p. 830.

[20] Memorandum of conversation with Judge J. P. Young, Memphis, Tennessee, a soldier in and historian of the Seventh Tennessee Cavalry, Nov. 10, 1930.

[21] *O.R.*, Serial No. 78, pp. 835, 839; Jordan and Pryor, p. 557.

[22] Dinkins, p. 198.

[23] *O.R.*, Serial No. 78, pp. 839-840.

[24] Same, p. 845; Jordan and Pryor, p. 557.

[25] *O.R.*, Serial No. 78, p. 849.

[26] Same, p. 859.

[27] Same, p. 873.

[28] *United Service Magazine*, Vol. V, New Series, p. 118; *S.H.S.P.*, Vol. 20, p. 331.

[29] *O.R.*, Serial No. 77, p. 542; Jordan and Pryor, p. 560.

[30] Hubbard, pp. 159-160.

[31] *O.R.*, Serial No. 77, p. 542.

[32] Same, p. 513.

[33] Same, pp. 523-524.

[34] Same, p. 521.

[35] "Barteau deployed his men in line (with about two men to a cross-tie) along the railroad, and when the command 'All together' was given, a portion of the road the length of the regiment was lifted from its bed. Then moving on to another place the same process was repeated, and so on, thus swapping sides with a considerable portion of the track." Hancock, p. 465. The method was not effective for destruction of track but it was sufficient for the immediate purpose of preventing the arrival of reinforcements by train from the north.

[36] *O.R.*, Serial No. 77, pp. 542-543; Jordan and Pryor, p. 561.

[37] *O.R.*, Serial No. 77, pp. 521-522, 543.

[38] Same, pp. 522, 543; Jordan and Pryor, pp. 561-563.

[39] *O.R.*, Serial No. 77, p. 524.

[40] Same, p. 523.

[41] Same, pp. 519, 544.

[42] Jordan and Pryor, pp. 564-565.

[43] *O.R.*, Serial No. 77, p. 544.

[44] Same, pp. 520, 544.

[45] Lt. Col. W. E. Merrill, "Block-Houses for Railroad Defense," a paper prepared for the Ohio Commandery of the Military Order of the Loyal Legion of the United States, and published in *Sketches of War History* (Cincinnati, 1890), Vol. III, p. 410.

[46] These are the dimensions given in Forrest's report, *O.R.*, Serial No. 77, p. 545. Brig. Gen. Daniel C. McCallum, Director General and Manager of U. S. Military Railroads, gives the dimensions of this "most formidable trestle" on the line as "1,100 feet long and about 90 feet high." Serial No. 77, p. 507.

[47] Same, pp. 514, 520, 533, 544-545; Jordan and Pryor, pp. 567-569.

[48] *O.R.*, Serial No. 78, pp. 876-877, 882, 884.

[49] Jordan and Pryor, p. 570.

[50] *O.R.*, Serial No. 77, p. 537.

[51] Same, pp. 537-538, 545; Jordan and Pryor, p. 571.

[52] *O.R.*, Serial No. 77, pp. 545, 548.

[53] Same, pp. 505, 532.

[54] In this fight Col. William A. Johnson was wounded and the command of Roddey's troops devolved upon Col. J. R. B. Burtwell. Jacob Gaus, Forrest's bugler, had his bugle put out of commission, with three bullets through it. Hancock, pp. 477-478.

[55] *O.R.*, Serial No. 77, p. 585.

[56] *O.R.*, Serial No. 79, pp. 517, 541, 631.

[57] Hubbard, p. 167.

[58] Morton, pp. 239-240.

[59] *O.R.*, Serial No. 77, pp. 512, 546, 585.

[60] Same, p. 546; *O.R.*, Serial No. 78, p. 829.

[61] *O.R.*, Serial No. 77, p. 585; Serial No. 78, pp. 454-455, 464-466, 468, 479, 484-485, 488-489, 494, 504, 524, 528, 540; Serial No. 79, p. 42.

[62] *O.R.*, Serial No. 78, p. 517.

[63] *O.R.*, Serial No. 77, p. 546.

[64] Same, pp. 516-517.

[65] Mrs. Adelia C. Lyon, compiler, *Reminiscences of the Civil War*, from the War Correspondence of Col. William P. Lyon, published by William P. Lyon, Jr. (San Jose, California, 1907), p. 168.

[66] *O.R.*, Serial No. 77, pp. 621, 633, 636.

[67] Same, pp. 509-510, 517, 546.

[68] Same, p. 546; Hancock, p. 480.

[69] Jordan and Pryor, p. 561.

[70] Merrill, "Block-Houses for Railroad Defense," p. 413.

[71] *O.R.*, Serial No. 77, pp. 507-508, 546-547.

[72] *O.R.*, Serial No. 79, p. 39.

[73] *Confederate Veteran*, Vol. XXVIII, p. 373.

[74] *O.R.*, Serial No. 77, pp. 585-587; No. 79, pp. 20, 28, 40, 57-60, 79.

[75] Same, p. 82; No. 78, p. 533.

[76] *O.R.*, Serial No. 79, pp. 81-82.

[77] *O.R.*, Serial No. 77, p. 547.

[78] Jordan and Pryor, p. 580.

[79] *O.R.*, Serial No. 77, p. 547.

[80] Wyeth, *Forrest*, pp. 507-508, from manuscript notes of Dr. Z. T. Bundy of Texas.

[81] *O.R.*, Serial No. 77, p. 548; Jordan and Pryor, p. 581; Young, pp. 111-112; Hancock, pp. 487-491.

[82] *O.R.*, Serial No. 79, pp. 140, 157, 170, 175, 190.

[83] *O.R.* (Naval), Vol. 26, pp. 582-587; *O.R.*, Serial No. 77, pp. 539-541; Jordan and Pryor, pp. 584-586.

[84] *O.R.*, Serial No. 79, p. 79.

[85] Same, p. 395.

[86] Same, p. 358.

[87] Same, p. 162.

[88] Mrs. Lyon, p. 168.

CHAPTER XXIII

AMPHIBIOUS OPERATIONS, 1864 STYLE

October 10, 1864-November 13, 1864

[1] *O.R.*, Serial No. 79, p. 807.

[2] John Forrest, next to Bedford in age, lived at the Worsham House in Memphis, where his connection with a brother of growing fame combined with his

own apparently strong will and tempestuous temper to produce trouble with the Federal authorities at times. Under the headline JOHN FORREST HELD, the Memphis *Appeal* (published at Grenada, Mississippi, after the fall of Memphis) on June 15, 1862, said: "John Forrest, who shot the master's mate of the Federal gunboat *Carondelet* at Puss Pettus' harem on Wednesday night, was yesterday taken aboard that boat to wait the result of the wounds. It is understood that if the wounded man dies it will go very hard with Forrest." (Reprinted in Memphis *Commercial-Appeal*, Jan. 1, 1940.)

Apparently no action was taken against Forrest, other than his detention on the gunboat, at this time. Upon another occasion, a Union officer with a detachment of men visited the place of his mother, Mrs. Luxton, and acted in such a manner as aroused her ire. All her other adult sons being in the army, she came to town the next day and told her crippled son John what had occurred. When the officer in question next came by the Worsham House, John Forrest taxed him with misconduct. High words followed, with Forrest threatening to break his crutch over the Federal officer's head, and the officer denouncing the whole Forrest family and, as the altercation grew more heated, kicking John's crutches from under him. Lying on the ground, John Forrest drew his pistol and severely wounded the Federal officer. He was afterward acquitted and lived in Memphis for several years after the war. Mathes, p. 8.

3 Lt. Tully Brown, manuscript notes in Tennessee State Library.

4 Memphis *Appeal-Avalanche*, Jan. 23, 1893. The story, upon the occasion of the death of Mrs. Forrest upon the preceding day, is not signed but probably was written by Captain Gallaway himself.

The practice of the wives of officers remaining close to their husbands during inactive periods was quite common during the war, on both sides. For example, Mrs. Grant was with General Grant at Holly Springs, Miss., during the winter of 1862-1863. Rumors were published, during the Presidential campaign of 1868, that the Grants had taken and carried away furniture, including a piano, from the house in which they were quartered. Forrest investigated the rumor, found it totally false, and denounced those responsible for it. "I talked with the people with whom he and his lady lived . . ." he said, "and they say their conduct was everything which could be expected of a gentleman and lady, and deserving the highest praise." Cincinnati *Commercial*, Aug. 28, 1868, interview with Forrest, corrected by Forrest on Sept. 3, 1868. See Testimony of N. B. Forrest before the Joint Select Committee to Inquire into the Condition of Affairs in the Late Insurrectionary States (Washington, 1872), Vol. 13, p. 14.

5 *O.R.*, Serial No. 79, p. 807. The actual number of guns captured by Forrest in 1864 up to this date was thirty-nine.

6 Same, p. 811.

7 Dinkins, pp. 197-198. The General, as Captain Dinkins tells the story, fed the Colonel of the Mississippi state troops on the best he had—dough made up in a bucket, stuffed into saturated corn shucks and placed in the embers to cook, and bacon broiled over the coals on the end of a stick—and then told him and some of his men the story of Travis at the Alamo, after all hope of successful resistance to Santa Anna had passed, drawing a line on the floor with his sword, and calling upon those willing to keep up the fight for freedom to cross it. "And do you know," said Chalmers, "they all crossed the line to Travis but one"—whereupon the Mississippi state troops crossed the line into Tennessee.

8 *O.R.*, Serial No. 79, p. 221.

[9] Same, pp. 815-819.

[10] To facilitate communication Forrest ordered the repair of the telegraph lines from Corinth to Grand Junction and to Jackson, Tenn., but the order could not be carried out because all the wire "had been used up by the citizens along the line for the purpose of baling cotton," and there was no more available. Same, p. 838.

[11] Same, pp. 817, 819, 821.

[12] O.R., Serial No. 126, p. 989. Report of Brigadier General McCallum on operations of United States Military Railroads.

[13] O.R., Serial No. 78, pp. 198, 210, 439, 447.

[14] Same, pp. 526-527; Serial No. 79, pp. 59-60, 86-87.

[15] O.R., Serial No. 77, p. 549; Jordan and Pryor, p. 590.

[16] Jordan and Pryor, p. 591.

[17] O.R., Serial No. 78, pp. 811-813.

[18] O.R., Serial No. 79, p. 162.

[19] Same, p. 356.

[20] Same, pp. 837-838.

[21] Same, pp. 265, 323, 345, 378-379, 404, 407; Serial No. 86, pp. 5, 34, 70-72, 106, 327.

[22] Same, pp. 427-428, 431, 452, 469.

[23] O.R., Serial No. 79, pp. 282, 302-303, 343, 345, 357, 379, 383, 385-386, 407, 458-459, 472-473, 475, 491, 525, 549, 625. In one of his appeals for "more assistance," General Meredith said, "Give me a sufficient force and I will drive him [Forrest] out of the country." O.R., Serial No. 77, p. 867.

[24] Same, p. 870; Jordan and Pryor, p. 591.

[25] O.R., Serial No. 77, p. 870; Jordan and Pryor, pp. 591-592.

[26] Hancock, p. 495.

[27] O.R., Serial No. 77, pp. 860-861, 863, 869-870; Jordan and Pryor, pp. 592-593. There is disagreement among the diarists and historians as to the identity of the soldier who swam or paddled across the river to take possession of the *Mazeppa*. In Jordan and Pryor his identity is given as Captain Frank Gracey of the Third Kentucky. Morton, Young and Hancock name Private Claib West of the Second Tennessee Cavalry, while Dinkins identifies him as Private Dick Clinton of Walton's (Hudson's) Battery.

[28] Hancock, p. 496; Dinkins, p. 201; Morton, p. 247; S.H.S.P., Vol. 10, p. 263.

[29] O.R., Serial No. 77, p. 870; Serial No. 109, p. 121. Viewing the captured stores, Buford's soldiers remarked that they were "much obliged to Uncle Abe for the supplies that he sent us by the *Mazeppa*," to which another replied that it would be better to "return thanks to General Buford for making the requisition, and to Captain Morton for enforcing it." Hancock, p. 497. This is almost the last entry made in Sergeant Hancock's diary. On the next day he received a wound in the spine which kept him bedridden for eighteen months, and until long after the close of the war.

[30] O.R., Serial No. 77, p. 870; Serial No. 79, p. 550; Jordan and Pryor, p. 593.

[31] O.R. (Naval), Vol. 26, pp. 602-603. Publication of the Naval Records throws new light on the Johnsonville affair, and corrects erroneous impressions and statements in both the Confederate and Union army accounts, in both of which, for example, it appears that the *Venus* and the *Cheeseman* came down the river under convoy of the *Undine*.

32 *O.R.* (Naval), Vol. 26, p. 603; *O.R.*, Serial No. 77, pp. 860, 870, 872-874.

33 Same, p. 873.

34 "Neither Delmonico nor Mme. Begue ever prepared a spread that gave as much pleasure as the men had that night" with the "pickles, hams, coffee" and other good things they took off the *Cheeseman.* Dinkins, pp. 203-204.

35 Jordan and Pryor, p. 597; Morton, pp. 248-249. Captain Gracey told the Southern Historical Society that several members of the crew of the *Undine,* who had been with him at the siege of Vicksburg, had there served on the Confederate ram *Arkansas* in its great running fight with the Union fleet in the Mississippi. *S.H.S.P.,* Vol. 10, p. 476.

36 Same, p. 249.

37 *O.R.,* Serial No. 77, pp. 870, 874; Serial No. 79, p. 617; *O.R.* (Naval), Vol. 26, pp. 606-607.

38 *O.R.* (Naval), Vol. 26, pp. 610, 615, 624; *O.R.,* Serial No. 77, pp. 861, 870, 874; Serial No. 79, pp. 601-602, 608; Serial No. 109, p. 121.

39 *O.R.* (Naval), Vol. 26, pp. 624-625; *O.R.,* Serial No. 77, pp. 861, 874.

40 Manuscript notes, unsigned, preserved in Morton Scrapbooks, give the details of the abandonment and destruction of the *Undine.*

41 *O.R.* (Naval), Vol. 26, pp. 611-614, 622, 630 and map; *O.R.,* Serial No. 77, p. 866; Serial No. 109, p. 123.

42 Morton, pp. 252-253.

43 *O.R.,* Serial No. 77, p. 871; Morton, p. 253; Dinkins, pp. 206-207.

44 *O.R.,* Serial No. 109, p. 124.

45 *O.R.,* Serial No. 77, pp. 861-862, 864-867, 871, 875.

46 Morton, pp. 256, 262-264; *S.H.S.P.,* Vol. 10, p. 484; *O.R.,* Serial No. 109, p. 656.

47 Manuscript notes, unsigned, preserved in Morton Scrapbooks.

48 *O.R.,* Serial No. 77, p. 862.

49 Same, p. 871; Serial No. 110, p. 777.

50 *O.R.,* Serial No. 77, pp. 862, 871; Serial No. 109, p. 683.

51 *O.R.,* Serial No. 77, pp. 853, 856, 858. On this march, the Army of Tennessee passed the Sanson home near Gadsden, Alabama. "Out of compliment to Miss Sanson, and in recognition of the aid given Forrest on the Streight raid," Major General Samuel G. French had one of the army bands play a serenade at their home. "While we were honoring Miss Sanson," he wrote in his diary, "a hungry soldier was skinning one of the Madam's hogs. I had the skin secured to the soldier's back, and thus he was marched about camp, a warning to others not to plunder." Samuel G. French, *Two Wars: An Autobiography* (Nashville, 1901), p. 288.

52 *O.R.,* Serial No. 93, p. 751.

53 *O.R.,* Serial No. 77, pp. 800, 802-803; Serial No. 110, p. 774.

54 Dinkins, p. 221.

55 Hanson, p. 78.

56 Jordan and Pryor, p. 607.

57 *O.R.,* Serial No. 79, pp. 630, 653.

58 Same, pp. 674, 685, 691-692.

59 Same, pp. 694-697, 709-710.

60 Same, p. 659.

CHAPTER XXIV

ADVANCE: SPRING HILL AND FRANKLIN
November 14, 1864-November 30, 1864

[1] *O.R.*, Serial No. 77, p. 808. From the journal kept by Brig. Gen. Francis A. Shoup, Chief of Staff.

[2] The soldiers of the Army of Tennessee, one of them wrote, "loved Joe Johnston because he made us love ourselves." Samuel R. Watkins, *Co. Aytch, First Tennessee Regiment: A Side Show of the Big Show*, p. 150. The reference is to the second edition of the work published by the Chattanooga *Times* in 1900. The first edition was published in 1882 by the Columbia, Tenn., *Herald*.

[3] *O.R.*, Serial No. 77, p. 802.

[4] *O.R.*, Serial No. 79, p. 576; Serial No. 93, p. 647.

[5] Same, p. 657.

[6] *O.R.*, Serial No. 79, p. 747. Grant, however, from the beginning of the discussion felt that "Hood would probably strike for Nashville." Same, p. 202.

[7] *O.R.*, Serial No. 93, pp. 752, 1211.

[8] Sherman, *Memoirs*, Vol. 2, p. 179.

[9] Beauregard, who left Hood to hasten to Georgia when news came of Sherman's advance, received a request from President Davis that Forrest be sent to Georgia to impede Sherman's march. From Macon, Georgia, on November twenty-eighth, Beauregard replied that "Forrest's cavalry cannot now be spared from the Army of Tennessee; moreover, it could not reach here in time." *O.R.*, Serial No. 92, p. 881; Serial No. 93, p. 1254.

[10] *O.R.*, Serial No. 93, pp. 575, 585.

[11] Same, pp. 557, 752.

[12] Same, pp. 752, 763; Jordan and Pryor, pp. 614-616.

[13] *O.R.*, Serial No. 93, p. 576; Jordan and Pryor, pp. 617-618.

[14] *O.R.*, Serial No. 93, pp. 70, 144, 400, 763; Jordan and Pryor, pp. 616-617.

[15] *O.R.*, Serial No. 93, pp. 752, 763.

[16] Same, pp. 145, 147.

[17] Jordan and Pryor, p. 619.

[18] *O.R.*, Serial No. 93, pp. 752-753; Jordan and Pryor, pp. 619-620.

[19] *O.R.*, Serial No. 79, pp. 414-417; Wilson, *Under the Old Flag*, Vol. II, Chapter 1.

[20] *O.R.*, Serial No. 93, p. 1014.

[21] Same, p. 443.

[22] Same, p. 557.

[23] Same, p. 1118.

[24] Same, p. 1143.

[25] Same, p. 341.

[26] Same, pp. 113, 148, 341-342.

[27] Same, pp. 550, 557, 1145-1146.

[28] Same, pp. 343, 1138.

[29] Same, pp. 753, 769.

[30] Same, pp. 113, 148, 342.

[31] J. P. Young, in the *Confederate Veteran*, Vol. XVI, p. 25. This study by Judge Young, embodying both close study of everything published on the subject

and wide correspondence with surviving participants, will remain the most complete and accurate analysis of the affair at Spring Hill.

[32] *O.R.*, Serial No. 93, pp. 113, 148, 342, 753.

[33] Same, p. 753.

[34] Young, *Confederate Veteran*, Vol. XVI, p. 31; Irving A. Buck, *Cleburne and His Command* (New York, 1908), p. 320; *O.R.*, Serial No. 93, p. 753.

[35] John K. Shellenberger, *The Battle of Spring Hill*, a paper read before the Missouri Commandery of the Military Order of the Loyal Legion, Feb. 2, 1907, pp. 13-14.

[36] *O.R.*, Serial No. 93, p. 1138. In General Schofield's *Forty-Six Years in the Army* (New York, 1897), pp. 170-175, there is no such note of urgency.

[37] Young, *Confederate Veteran*, Vol. XVI, p. 38; Buck, p. 314.

[38] *O.R.*, Serial No. 93, p. 742.

[39] *S.H.S.P.*, Vol. 9, p. 538.

[40] Young, *Confederate Veteran*, Vol. XVI, p. 38 (Letter from Stewart).

[41] *S.H.S.P.*, Vol. 9, p. 526.

[42] *O.R.*, Serial No. 93, pp. 712-713.

[43] Same; Jordan and Pryor, pp. 622-624.

[44] *S.H.S.P.*, Vol. 9, p. 541.

[45] *O.R.*, Serial No. 93, pp. 769-770; Jordan and Pryor, p. 524.

[46] *O.R.*, Serial No. 93, pp. 148-149, 342; Schofield, pp. 173-175.

[47] *O.R.*, Serial No. 93, p. 770.

[48] Shellenberger, *The Battle of Spring Hill*, p. 23. Ambrose Bierce, who was with one of the rear units, wrote that the Union forces "sneaked by" the Confederate campfires with "hearts in our throats." Bierce, Vol. I, p. 318.

[49] Few small affairs during the war—although Spring Hill had in it the possibilities of an affair by no means small—have been more written about than this. Among the Confederate participants there is General Hood's own book, *Advance and Retreat* (New Orleans, 1880), to which reply was promptly made by Cheatham, Brown, Bate and, to some extent, Stewart, in Volume 9 of the *S.H.S.P.*, published in 1881. In a series of articles in Volumes 3 and 4 of the *Southern Bivouac* (Louisville, 1884-1885) Maj. D. W. Sanders, Adjutant General of French's division, Stewart's corps, published an analytical account of the whole campaign. Judge Young's close study of Spring Hill, in which he participated, was published in the *Confederate Veteran* in 1907, and Major Buck's account of Cleburne's part in 1908.

In addition to published accounts by Confederate participants there is an unpublished memorandum of a "remarkable conversation with Gov. Isham G. Harris" (who was with Hood at Spring Hill), written out by Maj. Campbell Brown of Spring Hill on May 5, 1868, "about ten days or two weeks" after the conversation itself. Major Brown was not in Spring Hill at the time of the fight, being with Lt. Gen. Richard Ewell in the Army of Northern Virginia. For the opportunity to examine Major Brown's account I am indebted to the late Mr. Lucius P. Brown of Spring Hill.

On the Union side, there are four major accounts—Schofield's *Forty Six Years*, published in 1897; David S. Stanley's *Memoirs*, published in 1916; Jacob Cox's *Franklin and Nashville* (Vol. 10 of *Campaigns of the Civil War*, New York, 1882) and the same author's *Battle of Franklin*, 1897; and Capt. John K. Shellenberger's *Fighting at Spring Hill*, *Confederate Veteran*, Vol. XXXVI, pp. 100-103, 140-143, 188.

Two unified studies of the campaign and of the affair at Spring Hill, both of great value, have been made in recent years—Thomas Robson Hay's *Hood's Tennessee Campaign* (New York, 1929), an admirable monographic study, and Chapters 18 and 19 of Stanley F. Horn's *The Army of Tennessee*.

[50] Young, *Confederate Veteran*, Vol. XVI, p. 42.

[51] John B. Hood, *Advance and Retreat* (New Orleans, 1880), p. 290.

[52] By Captain James Dinkins, in the New Orleans *Picayune*, Nov. 30, 1902.

[53] *O.R.*, Serial No. 93, pp. 753, 764; Jordan and Pryor, pp. 624-625.

[54] Jacob D. Cox, *The Battle of Franklin, A Monograph* (New York, 1897), pp. 85-86.

[55] *O.R.*, Serial No. 93, p. 550.

[56] Cox, pp. 62, 67; French, p. 298, quoting Maj. Gen. T. J. Wood, who took over command of the Fourth Corps (Union) after the wounding of Stanley.

[57] *O.R.*, Serial No. 93, pp. 1169-1170.

[58] Jordan and Pryor, pp. 625-626; Wyeth, *Forrest*, p. 544, citing personal letter of Col. D. C. Kelley.

[59] Buck, p. 327.

[60] *O.R.*, Serial No. 93, pp. 559-560, 754, 770.

[61] Same, p. 343.

[62] In his article, *The Battle of Franklin*, in the New Orleans *Picayune*, Nov. 30, 1902, Captain Dinkins draws interesting parallels and contrasts between the great charge at Franklin and Pickett's charge at Gettysburg.

Pickett charged, Captain Dinkins points out, with 15,511 men; the five divisions which made the charge at Franklin, with 15,551 men. Pickett charged after a lengthy artillery preparation by more than 100 guns, the Confederates at Franklin without artillery preparation or support. Pickett's charge had the shorter distance to go, nearly half, and had to go against no more than a stone wall, while the Confederates at Franklin went against regular entrenchments, with ditch, parapet, head logs and all the military engineering protection of the day. Pickett's charge barely reached its objective and fell back; the Army of Tennessee penetrated the Union works and held its position along their face. Pickett's losses, killed, wounded and missing, were slightly more than one-fifth; the losses at Franklin, considerably more than one-third of those engaged.

All of which and other considerations led Captain Dinkins to write in 1902 that the charge at Franklin was "the greatest drama in American history."

[63] *O.R.*, Serial No. 93, pp. 684-686.

[64] Cox, p. 15. General Cox, citing Colonel Maurice's figures, mentions also that the Confederate loss in killed at Franklin was almost exactly the same as that of the British at Waterloo.

[65] French, p. 296.

CHAPTER XXV

THE REAR GUARD OF RETREAT FROM TENNESSEE

December 1, 1864-December 28, 1864

[1] *O.R.*, Serial No. 93, p. 731. In a keen and vivid boy's-eye account of the Battle of Franklin by H. P. Figuers of Columbia, Tennessee, there is described the way in which the women of the little town helped to care for the thousands of wounded, both Federal and Confederate, who filled not only all the rooms of the "Female

College," but also the Court House, every church in the town and most of the private homes.

[2] *O.R.*, Serial No. 93, pp. 35, 344, 560, 576, 754.

[3] Same, pp. 754, 764. The turnpikes which played so prominent a part in the operations around Nashville are, in order beginning with the Cumberland River east of or above the town and going clockwise to the river below, as follows: Lebanon, Murfreesborough, Nolensville, Franklin, Granny White, Hillsboro, Harding, Charlotte. With two exceptions they bear the names of the towns to which they extended. The Granny White Pike took its name from the tavern in the gap of the Brentwood Hills kept by "Granny" White. The Harding took its name from the Harding family, whose home "Belle Meade," southwest of Nashville, was the headquarters for Chalmers' cavalry during the operations about the city. Another of Forrest's division commanders, W. H. Jackson, afterward married the daughter of General Harding and continued the development of Belle Meade as one of the most famous of all American thoroughbred racing farms and centers of hospitality. Still another of Forrest's division commanders, Buford, engaged in the breeding and raising of thoroughbred racing stock in Kentucky, after the war.

[4] The fortifications of Nashville included seven major forts and twenty separate batteries, connected by rifle pits, arranged in a double line. The inner line was seven miles long with an outer line one to two miles beyond it on the southwest and west of the city. *O.R.*, Serial No. 104, pp. 775-781.

[5] *O.R.*, Serial No. 93, pp. 34-35. From fighting against his West Point classmate Schofield at Franklin, Hood marched to Nashville to fight his onetime immediate commander in the old army, Thomas. Hood had been a captain in the Second Cavalry, of which regiment Thomas was major, Robert E. Lee lieutenant colonel, and Albert Sidney Johnston colonel.

[6] Same, pp. 654, 658, 660, 744, 754.

[7] Jordan and Pryor, p. 639.

[8] *O.R.*, Serial No. 93, pp. 754, 764.

[9] Same, p. 764; Serial No. 94, pp. 44, 51; *O.R.* (Naval), Vol. 26, pp. 640-664. Rear Admiral Lee, the Union naval commander on the Cumberland and other western waters, was a cousin of Robert E. Lee.

[10] *O.R.*, Serial No. 93, pp. 631-635, 744-745, 754-755; Serial No. 94, p. 652.

[11] *O.R.*, Serial No. 104, pp. 502-503.

[12] *O.R.*, Serial No. 93, pp. 617-618, 745, 755; Jordan and Pryor, p. 632.

[13] Park Marshall, *A Life of William B. Bate* (Nashville, 1908), p. 150.

[14] *O.R.*, Serial No. 93, p. 613; Memorandum of conversation with Judge J. P. Young, Nov. 10, 1930.

[15] *O.R.*, Serial No. 93, pp. 613, 746-747, 755.

[16] Same, p. 755.

[17] Memorandum of conversation with Judge J. P. Young. Another story, as given in Wyeth, *Forrest*, p. 522, is that Forrest shot down a color-bearer and took the flag from him. Judge Young was positive that he did not do so. In this fight, also, Jacob Gaus had another bugle riddled and ruined. Gaus's bugles were seemingly as expendable as horses ridden by Forrest.

[18] *O.R.*, Serial No. 93, p. 755.

[19] Same, pp. 613, 618, 756; Morton, pp. 281-282.

[20] *O.R.*, Serial No. 93, pp. 740, 756, 771. Brigadier General Ross of Jackson's division, the only Confederate commander immediately concerned who made a report of this capture, says that the train carried 200,000 rations.

21 Same, p. 756.

22 Same, p. 654; Hood, *Advance and Retreat,* p. 300.

23 *O.R.,* Serial No. 94, p. 18.

24 The whole subject is interestingly discussed in Thomas R. Hay, *Hood's Tennessee Campaign,* pp. 141-147, and in Wilson, Vol. II, Chapter 3. The legend of Thomas' "slowness" is of a piece with the legend of Forrest as a "guerrilla," and equally indestructible.

25 *O.R.,* Serial No. 93, pp. 562-564, 765.

26 Same, p. 765.

27 In dealing with the general outlines of the Battle of Nashville, I have followed the admirable brief work of William E. Beard, *The Battle of Nashville* (Nashville, 1913). No attempt is made to treat details of movements other than those in which Forrest's troops were engaged.

28 *O.R.,* Serial No. 93, pp. 765-766.

29 Same, p. 654; Jordan and Pryor, pp. 640-643; Wyeth, *Forrest,* pp. 556-557; Wilson, Vol. II, p. 123.

30 *O.R.,* Serial No. 93, p. 689.

31 Same, p. 750.

32 *O.R.,* Serial No. 94, p. 202; Wilson, Vol. II, pp. 119-120.

33 Jordan and Pryor, pp. 642-643; Wyeth, *Forrest,* p. 559. That night, Rucker, Wilson and Hatch occupied the same room in a near-by house. Hatch gave up his bed to Rucker and slept on the floor, arising frequently in the night to bring water to his wounded captive, whose arm had to be amputated above the elbow. Rucker, who did not sleep during the night, remembers that Wilson sat cross-legged, tailor-fashion, in the other bed in the room all through the night, receiving dispatches and writing orders for the next day's work.

34 *O.R.,* Serial No. 93, pp. 564-565.

35 Same, p. 766. Biffle had been sent to the right by order of Hood, to picket from the infantry positions to the river, on December tenth. *O.R.,* Serial No. 94, p. 673.

36 *O.R.,* Serial No. 94, pp. 233, 252.

37 Same, p. 693.

38 *O.R.,* Serial No. 93, p. 756.

39 Same, p. 689; Wilson, Vol. II, p. 128.

40 Jordan and Pryor, p. 644; Col. H. A. Tyler in *Confederate Veteran,* Vol. XII, p. 436.

41 *O.R.,* Serial No. 93, p. 690.

42 Same, pp. 566, 766; Wilson, Vol. II, p. 133.

43 *O.R.,* Serial No. 94, p. 248.

44 *O.R.,* Serial No. 93, pp. 731, 756; Serial No. 94, p. 710.

45 *O.R.,* Serial No. 93, p. 655.

46 *O.R.,* Serial No. 94, pp. 714-715.

47 *O.R.,* Serial No. 93, pp. 728-730, 757.

48 Same, pp. 42, 566, 592-593.

49 Same, p. 757; Jordan and Pryor, p. 646.

50 *O.R.,* Serial No. 93, pp. 136, 296.

51 Same, pp. 43, 506; Serial No. 94, pp. 249, 308, 329, 345; *O.R.* (Naval), Vol. 26, pp. 670-673, 675-677.

52 *O.R.,* Serial No. 93, p. 757.

[53] Same, pp. 567, 757-758.
[54] Memorandum of conversation with Judge J. P. Young.
[55] *O.R.*, Serial No. 93, pp. 567, 603, 727, 758.
[56] Clark, pp. 159-160.
[57] *O.R.*, Serial No. 93, pp. 567, 578-579, 603, 727, 758.
[58] Tully Brown, manuscript lecture, Tennessee State Library.
[59] Jordan and Pryor, p. 647.
[60] *The Old Guard in Gray*, p. 171.
[61] Clark, p. 155.
[62] *O.R.*, Serial No. 93, pp. 727-728, 758.
[63] Wilson, Vol. II, p. 142.
[64] *O.R.*, Serial No. 93, pp. 567, 579, 728.
[65] Same, p. 42.

CHAPTER XXVI

THE LAST CAMPAIGN AND SURRENDER

December 29, 1864-May 9, 1865

[1] *S.H.S.P.*, Vol. 3, p. 156.
[2] *O.R.*, Serial No. 94, p. 756.
[3] Same, pp. 751-752.
[4] Young, *Seventh Tennessee Cavalry*, pp. 130-131.
[5] *O.R.*, Serial No. 94, pp. 552-553, 556.
[6] *O.R.*, Serial No. 93, pp. 142-144. The Union commander on this operation afterward achieved fame as the founder of Colorado Springs, and the builder of the Denver & Rio Grande railroad.
[7] *O.R.*, Serial No. 94, p. 804.
[8] Same, p. 622.
[9] *O.R.*, Serial No. 103, p. 938.
[10] Same, p. 930.
[11] Same, pp. 950, 1032.
[12] Same, p. 781.
[13] Same, p. 354.
[14] Same, pp. 933, 952, 971-972, 1005; Jordan and Pryor, pp. 657-658.
[15] *O.R.*, Serial No. 104, pp. 1182, 1203; Chattanooga *Daily Rebel* (published at Selma), March 14, 1865. The method of securing the publication of this G. O. No. 2 in the Southern newspapers is an interesting sidelight on the workings of what, to anticipate modern usage, might be called the Public Relations Office of the Confederate command. "All newspapers in the Confederate States," ran a notice repeated in each advertisement giving the text of the order, "are requested to copy six times the above and send bills (with a copy of the paper) to the Richmond *Enquirer* for payment."
[16] *O.R.*, Serial No. 103, pp. 1005, 1040-1041. To Brig. Gen. Dan Adams' request for 7,500 additional infantry for the defense of Alabama, Taylor's adjutant replied that "if the lieutenant general commanding had 7,500 infantry he would consider himself in condition to assume the offensive and would never think of dividing them into several garrisons." Same, pp. 1012-1013.

[17] Same, pp. 689-690, 710-711, 725-727; Serial No. 121, pp. 238, 244; Lewis M. Hosea, Brevet Major, U. S. A., *Some Side Lights on the War for the Union,* Paper read before the Ohio Commandery of the Loyal Legion (Cleveland, Ohio, Oct. 9, 1912), p. 8; Piatt and Boynton, p. 598. This was not Colonel Parkhurst's first meeting with Forrest, as he had been in command of one of the camps at Murfreesborough which Forrest surrounded and captured in July 1862.

[18] *O.R.,* Serial No. 121, p. 325.

[19] Hosea, p. 11.

[20] Wilson, Vol. II, pp. 184-185; Piatt and Boynton, p. 599.

[21] *O. R.,* Serial No. 121, pp. 326-328.

[22] Hosea, p. 15.

[23] *O.R.,* Serial No. 121, pp. 335, 354, 402; Serial No. 103, p. 869.

[24] Same, p. 909.

[25] Marcus J. Wright, *Tennessee in the War* (New York, 1908), p. 33.

[26] *O.R.,* Serial No. 103, pp. 996, 1005, 1032, 1051, 1057, 1060; Serial No. 104, pp. 1122-1123, 1126-1127, 1139.

[27] Mathes, p. 364.

[28] *O.R.,* Serial No. 103, pp. 1011, 1057-1058. The General Wright referred to is the same who afterward rendered such notable service as one of the Confederate editors in the preparation of the *Official Records.*

[29] Lindsley, p. 781.

[30] *O.R.,* Serial No. 104, pp. 1124-1125.

[31] Same, pp. 1125-1126.

[32] *O.R.,* Serial No. 103, p. 356.

[33] Wilson, Vol. II, p. 189.

[34] *O.R.,* Serial No. 103, p. 383.

[35] *O.R.,* Serial No. 104, pp. 1146-1147.

[36] Same, p. 1158.

[37] Same, pp. 1160, 1165.

[38] Same, p. 1167.

[39] Same, p. 1170. From "camp near West Point," young Cable wrote his mother on March thirtieth, "Gen'l Forrest is not here. He left here for some unknown region three days ago," the letter being signed "George W. Cable, Brig. Genl Comdg Cuisine [!]," which sounds as if it might have been New Orleans French for "kitchen police." Bikle, p. 22.

[40] *O.R.,* Serial No. 104, p. 1172; Wyeth, *Forrest,* pp. 588-589.

[41] *O.R.,* Serial No. 103, pp. 343, 357, 419; Bvt. Maj. Gen. C. C. Andrews, *The Campaign of Mobile, including the Cooperating Operations of Gen. Wilson's Cavalry in Alabama* (New York, 1867), p. 246.

[42] *O.R.,* Serial No. 103, pp. 383-384; Scott, pp. 432-433.

[43] *O.R.,* Serial No. 104, p. 1181.

[44] Wilson, Vol. II, p. 207.

[45] Same, pp. 209, 218.

[46] Jordan and Pryor, pp. 663-664; *Confederate Veteran,* Vol. XXV, p. 491. The story as given by Jordan and Pryor was "impossible," according to Major Scott's Union account. Nevertheless, there was some such flank attack. Scott, pp. 438-439.

[47] *O.R.,* Serial No. 104, pp. 173, 1182; *S.H.S.P.,* Vol. 7, p. 485.

[48] *O.R.,* Serial No. 103, p. 359.

[49] Same, p. 359. In Major Scott's Union account it is said that the "infantry on

the rebel extreme right soon broke and fell back" but that the "veteran dismounted cavalry held on for half an hour." (P. 443.)

50 Wilson, Vol. II, pp. 214, 244.

51 *O.R.*, Serial No. 103, p. 351; Andrews, p. 252; Scott, pp. 434-435.

52 Taylor, pp. 219-220; Jordan and Pryor, p. 672; Mathes, p. 346. Federal estimates of the number of the Selma garrison are about double this figure. Scott, pp. 448-449.

53 *O.R.*, Serial No. 103, pp. 351, 359-361; Jordan and Pryor, pp. 673-676.

54 Wyeth, *Forrest*, pp. 608-610.

55 Mathes, pp. 349-350.

56 *O.R.*, Serial No. 103, pp. 421-422; Andrews, pp. 261-262; *Confederate Veteran*, Vol. II, p. 504. Col. L. C. Garland, of the University faculty (afterward first Chancellor of Vanderbilt University), had previously been unable to persuade General Jackson's Confederates not to impress all the cadet horses. *O.R.*, Serial No. 104, pp. 1177-1178, 1182.

57 *O.R.*, Serial No. 103, pp. 422-423; Andrews, pp. 263-264.

58 *O.R.*, Serial No. 104, p. 271.

59 Wilson, Vol. II, pp. 240-245. During the same years in which Forrest was building a line in Alabama and Mississippi, Generals Wilson and Edward F. Winslow, another of Forrest's old opponents, joined in building the St. Louis & Southeastern Railroad between St. Louis and Evansville, now part of the Louisville & Nashville Railroad.

60 Hosea, pp. 17-18.

61 Twenty-five of these surplus horses Wilson sent to Forrest for the use of the Confederate surgeons, reciprocating like courtesies extended by Forrest to the Union surgeons whom he had gathered up from time to time. *O.R.*, Serial No. 104, p. 272. Wilson states, in his memoir, that the rest of the surplus horses were shot and thrown into the Alabama River. But see *Confederate Veteran*, Vol. XIX, p. 67, for a description of the stench that overwhelmed Selma from the carcasses left in the streets.

62 *O.R.*, Serial No. 103, pp. 363-365, 424; Andrews, pp. 258-259, 266.

63 *O.R.*, Serial No. 104, pp. 1224-1225, 1229, 1235-1236, 1239, 1244, 1256, 1259, 1261.

64 Same, pp. 1263-1264.

65 *S.H.S.P.*, Vol. 3, p. 155.

66 *O.R.*, Serial No. 104, p. 1270.

67 *O.R.*, Serial No. 104, pp. 1283-1284; *S.H.S.P.*, Vol. 3, pp. 155-158.

68 *O.R.*, Serial No. 100, p. 303.

69 *Home Letters of General Sherman*, p. 346.

70 *Jefferson Davis, Constitutionalist*, Vol. VI, pp. 553-554.

71 Same, p. 561.

72 Duke, p. 385; also in *Southern Bivouac*, August 1886, condensed in *Battles and Leaders*, IV, 764.

73 Bikle, p. 23.

74 *Confederate Veteran*, Vol. XVI, pp. 192+xxvi.

75 *Confederate Veteran*, Vol. XXIII, p. 317.

76 Unidentified newspaper clipping in Morton Scrapbooks. See also *Confederate Veteran*, Vol. XVI, pp. 192+xxvii.

77 *Confederate Veteran*, Vol XXIII, p. 317.

78 *O.R.*, Serial No. 104, pp. 1289-1290.

CHAPTER XXVII

THE GRAND WIZARD OF THE INVISIBLE EMPIRE
1865-1869

1 *Testimony Taken by the Joint Select Committee to Inquire into the Condition of Affairs in the Late Insurrectionary States* (Washington, Government Printing Office, 1872), Vol. 13, p. 24. Hereafter cited as "Ku Klux Investigation, 1872."

2 Memphis *Avalanche-Appeal,* Jan. 23, 1893.

3 Mathes, pp. 336-337 (in facsimile). Mrs. Lee was a bride, she and the General having been married at Columbus, Miss., on Feb. 9, 1865.

4 Ku Klux Investigation, 1872, Vol. 13, p. 24.

5 *Report of the Joint Committee on Reconstruction,* 1st Session, 39th Congress (Washington: Government Printing Office, 1866), Part I, p. 106.

6 Atlanta *Constitution,* Oct. 31, 1870, reprinted in Memphis *Appeal,* Nov. 3, 1870.

7 Hanson, p. 59.

8 Dinkins, pp. 264-267.

9 Mathes, pp. 359-360.

10 Same, pp. 360-361; Wyeth, *Forrest,* pp. 616-617.

11 Memphis *Commercial-Appeal,* March 12, 1939.

12 The most complete and accurate history of the Ku Klux is to be found in Stanley F. Horn, *Invisible Empire* (Boston, 1939). The relation of the Klan movement to the Reconstruction period is treated in Robert S. Henry, *The Story of Reconstruction* (Indianapolis, 1938).

13 J. C. Lester and D. L. Wilson, *The Ku Klux Klan: Its Origin, Growth and Disbandment* (Nashville, 1884), with an introduction by Walter L. Fleming (New York, 1905), p. 30.

14 *Metropolitan Magazine,* September 1905; Morton, Appendix, pp. 339-346.

15 The letter was addressed to the United Daughters of the Confederacy chapter in Sheffield.

16 Ku Klux Investigation, 1872, Vol. 13, pp. 4, 5, 6, 19, 21.

17 Same, pp. 6, 12, 29, 30.

18 Same, pp. 6, 22-24.

19 Same, pp. 8-10.

20 Same, pp. 6, 7, 14, 15, 24, 28, 29.

21 Same, pp. 22, 29.

22 Same, p. 15.

23 Same, pp. 9, 27.

24 Same, p. 12.

25 Same, p. 30. Forrest's activities in this direction, he explained to the committee, had brought upon him the condemnation of some of the Southern people and their newspapers, who felt that he had gone over to the Radicals, while at the same time he was being "vilified and abused" in Northern papers for things he "never did in the army, and since." Testimony, pp. 18, 30. Forrest, it seems, was suffering the traditional troubles of the peacemaker.

26 *Report of the Joint Select Committee to Inquire into the Affairs in the Late Insurrectionary States,* made to the two Houses of Congress, February 19, 1872. Senate Document, 42nd Congress, 2nd Session, Report No. 41, Part I, pp. 6-14, 449-454.

[27] Horn, *Invisible Empire*, pp. 356-357. This reputed "dissolution" of the Klan is dated in the organization's cipher "Dismal Era, Fourth Green Day, Last Hour, C. A. R. N.," which, being interpreted, is January, fourth Monday, twelve o'clock, 1869.

[28] Lester and Wilson, p. 128. Memorandum of conversation with Judge J. P. Young, Nov. 10, 1930.

[29] It is perhaps not necessary to note that "Radical" is here used in the sense in which it was employed in the Reconstruction period, 1865-1877, to denote a "root-and-branch" Republican of the strictest sect.

[30] Hilary A. Herbert, *Why the Solid South?* (Baltimore, 1890), pp. 205-206; Horn, *Invisible Empire*, pp. 101-105.

[31] New York *Times*, Aug. 17, 1868 (reprinted from Memphis *Avalanche*).

[32] Mr. and Mrs. William Bethel Romine, *A Story of the Original Ku Klux Klan* (Pulaski, 1924, 1936), p. 25. Forrest's movements just after Grant's inauguration, so far as they can be checked from publications, are as follows: On March 4, 1869, he addressed the Chamber of Commerce at Memphis on the advantages of the railroad of which he was then President. On March 8 he attended a "railroad convention" at Selma, Alabama. On the following day, on a train going north from Jackson, Mississippi, he was interviewed by "J. W. R.," a correspondent of the Louisville *Courier-Journal,* to whom he said, "I would not have one of my negroes enslaved if I could." His next appearance noted in the press was at Columbus, Mississippi, in the interest of his railroad project on March 23. On April 2 he was back at home in Memphis. Between March 9 and 23 he *could* have gone to Washington to see President Grant but there is no real evidence that he did. If he did, and made the agreement which this tradition says he did, Forrest was badly worsted in the trade.

[33] George Creel, *Sons of the Eagle* (Indianapolis, 1927), p. 251.

CHAPTER XXVIII

THE HARDER WAR
1865-1877

[1] Ku Klux Investigation, 1872, Vol. 13, p. 21.

[2] Same, p. 25.

[3] From the original letter, in the possession of Mr. Garnett Andrews of Chattanooga, Tenn., which was published in the Chattanooga *Times* of May 21, 1944.

[4] Original records on file in the office of the Clerk of the District Court of the United States, District of West Tennessee, Memphis. The first suggestion of the existence of this record came from Mr. Garland S. Moore, attorney, of Nashville, who noted reference to a plea of discharge in bankruptcy made on behalf of Forrest in a case in the Tennessee courts, reported in 56 Tennessee, p. 563. Through the interest of Mr. Monroe Cockrell, of Chicago, others were interested in pursuing the inquiry, which resulted in the finding of the long-lost record in the attic of the Federal building at Memphis. There being no index to such papers, finding it was somewhat on the order of turning up the needle in a haystack.

[5] From the original letter of Feb. 26, 1868, now in possession of Mr. Farrell's son, Mr. Norman Farrell of Nashville.

[6] Duke, pp. 348-349.

[7] New York *Tribune*, July 4, 1878; New York *Herald*, July 3 and 4, 1898.

8 Ku Klux Investigation, 1872, Vol. 13, p. 13.

9 New York *Times,* Nov. 3 and Nov. 12, 1868; Duke, pp. 350-355.

10 Mathes, p. 10; Letter of Mrs. J. Wallace Broseg, president of the Hannibal Boone chapter, United Daughters of the Confederacy, Navasota, Tex., July 3, 1943. The Daughters of the Confederacy chapter placed a monument over Mrs. Luxton's grave, which was unveiled on May 23, 1925.

11 New York *Times,* Aug. 17, 1868.

12 Original circular in possession of author.

13 Ku Klux Investigation, 1872, Vol. 13, p. 25.

14 Interstate Commerce Commission Valuation Dockets No. 556, Southern Railway, et al., pp. 212-213, 221, 584-586, and No. 400, St. Louis-San Francisco Railway, et al., pp. 394-395, 693.

15 Nashville *Christian Advocate,* Jan. 9, 1875. For knowledge of this interesting light on the range of Forrest's interests I am indebted to Professor Edwin Mims, who unearthed it in his researches for the history of Vanderbilt University, now in preparation.

16 Lee Meriwether, *My Yesteryears* (Webster Groves, Missouri, 1942), pp. 59-64. Colonel Meriwether, among other works, had been the engineer for the Cumberland Mountain tunnel of the Nashville & Chattanooga Railroad at Cowan, Tenn., one of the earliest long tunnels bored in the United States.

17 The Reverend G. T. Stainback, in Forrest's funeral sermon, as reported in Memphis *Appeal,* Nov. 1, 1877.

18 Mathes, pp. 368-370.

19 Memphis *Appeal,* Nov. 1, 1877.

20 Unidentified clipping in Morton Scrapbooks.

21 Memphis *Appeal,* Nov. 1, 1877.

22 *Confederate Veteran,* Vol. IV, p. 387.

23 Memphis *Avalanche,* Oct. 30, 1877. The island, twelve miles long and 32,000 acres in area, is the largest in the Mississippi River. It takes its name from the fact that at one time Andrew Jackson owned a small farm on the island. During, and immediately after, the war the Freedmen's Bureau maintained on the island an asylum for refugee Negroes, caring for more than 1,500 of them at the close of the war. This work had been closed out in 1869. Memphis *Commercial-Appeal,* Jan. 1, 1940.

24 Memphis *Appeal,* Oct. 30, 1877.

25 Same, Nov. 1, 1877.

26 Hearn, Vol. II, pp. 144-154, "Notes on Forrest's Funeral," from which this and subsequent quotations are taken.

27 Memphis *Appeal,* Nov. 1, 1877.

28 Maury, p. 150.

29 In *Bedford Forrest and His Critter Company,* by Andrew Nelson Lytle (New York, 1931), p. 357, General Lee is quoted as having said at Appomattox, in answer to a question as to who was the greatest soldier under his command, "A man I have never seen, sir. His name is Forrest."

In an item in the *Confederate Veteran,* Vol. XXV, p. 362, quoting a Cincinnati newspaper, the same remark is attributed to General Lee as having been made in conversation with George Alfred Townsend, the well-known correspondent "Gath."

Almost the same remark appears again in *General Robert E. Lee After Appomattox,* edited by Franklin L. Riley of Washington and Lee University (New York, 1922). The story as given in a commemorative sketch of General Lee at the Uni-

536

versity, written by J. W. Ewing of Rome, Georgia, is that young Ewing and his student roommate, John M. Graham, had to report to the office of the General to explain an explosion in the stove of one of the Professors of a stick of firewood which Graham had plugged with gunpowder in an effort to detect the person who was stealing the student's firewood. While waiting in an anteroom, the two young students heard General Lee talking with "Lord Wolseley, the commander of the English armies." The visitor, as Mr. Ewing recorded the conversation more than half a century later, "asked General Lee whom he thought the greatest military genius developed by the war, to which General Lee answered without hesitation, 'General N. B. Forrest of Tennessee, whom I have never met. He accomplished more with fewer troops than any other officer on either side.'"

The date of the stovewood incident is located exactly through an entry in a professor's diary as Dec. 4, 1866. Colonel Wolseley, as he was then, was not in Virginia at that time, but was on duty in Manitoba. A check of local newspaper files kindly made by Col. William Couper does not reveal any other English officer visiting Lexington at the time.

[30] *S.H.S.P.*, Vol. 7, p. 455.

[31] See *The Trooper's Manual: or Tactics for Light Dragoons and Mounted Riflemen*, Col. J. Lucius Davis (Richmond, 1861).

[32] *United Service Magazine*, Vol. V (New Series), p. 4.

[33] Same, p. 119.

[34] Memorandum of conversation with the late Col. Granville Sevier, U. S. A. (Retired), at "Idlewild," Nashville, Tenn., July 26, 1933.

[35] From a letter of George W. Cable, published in Bikle, p. 19.

ACKNOWLEDGMENTS

DURING the nearly twenty years in which this book has been in the making, I have received so much help from so many friends, acquaintances and strangers, as well as from published works and manuscript sources, that I despair of making suitable acknowledgment.

To the late Colonel John W. Thomason, Jr., United States Marine Corps—biographer and storyteller extraordinary, splendid soldier, great gentleman and fine friend—I am deeply grateful for his gracious offer to illustrate the volume with his own inimitable drawings of the Confederate soldier. Circumstances prevented his doing more than one drawing, which appears on the jacket of the volume and, since jackets are so frequently lost or defaced, as the frontispiece as well.

Mrs. West H. Morton of Nashville generously turned over to me the scrapbooks kept over many years by Captain John W. Morton, in which there are preserved many things of interest about Forrest which otherwise would have been hopelessly scattered and lost. The books, which have been of the greatest assistance, will be placed in the Tennessee State Library so that they may be available to all who are interested.

Special acknwledgment should be made also to Messrs. Monroe Cockrell and Ray D. Smith of Chicago and Evanston, Illinois. Mr. Smith has not only put at my disposal his remarkable collection of regimental histories and memoirs, but has also called to my attention numerous indirect and collateral references to Forrest and his operations. Mr. Cockrell has been of assistance in many ways, starting with the use of his admirable map of Forrest's war movements day by day, and the notes from which he prepared it, and continuing to the discovery of documents of the greatest interest. He has been, indeed, a veritable one-man research staff.

I am grateful also for assistance graciously rendered by Mrs. John Trotwood Moore of the Tennessee State Library, Mrs. Sydney Crockett, Miss Alice Eloise Stockell, Professor Edwin Mims, Judge R. B. C. Howell, Colonel James L. Jordan, U. S. A., retired, and Messrs. William E. Beard, Stanley F. Horn, Norman Farrell and Garland S. Moore of Nashville, Tennessee; by Messrs. Garnett Andrews and Gilbert E. Govan, of Chattanooga, Tennessee; Mr. Roy Black of Bolivar, Tennessee; Mr. Alfred Alexander Bell of Jackson, Tennessee; Judge Robert M. Hughes of Norfolk, Virginia; Miss Alma Jamison and Mrs. John R. Marsh of Atlanta, Georgia; Judge R. E. Sparkman of Italy, Texas; Mrs. J. Wallace Broseg of Navasota, Texas; Mr. Pugh Moore of Oklahoma City, Oklahoma; Mr. Lee Lyles of Chicago, Illinois; Messrs. Willard Teague, Pierre Martineau, Gilmer Richardson, J. A. Osoinach and Thomas B. Collier, of Memphis, Tennessee; the Reverend Parker C. Webb of Bennington, Vermont; and Messrs. Carlton J. Corliss, David Chambers Mearns, and Major Cecil F. Holland, author of that fine biography of another Confederate cavalryman, *Morgan and His Raiders,* of Washington, D. C.

ROBERT S. HENRY.

September 3, 1944.

For convenient reference, works cited more than once in the chapter footnotes are indexed below according to the short titles under which they appear:

Andrews. *The Campaign of Mobile, including the Cooperative Operations of Gen. Wilson's Cavalry in Alabama,* by Maj. Gen. C. C. Andrews, New York, 1867.

Annals of the Army of Tennessee, The. Edited by Dr. Edwin L. Drake, Lieutenant Colonel, C.S.A., Nashville, 1878.

Battey. *A History of Rome and Floyd County,* by George Magruder Battey, Jr., Atlanta, 1922.

Battles and Leaders of the Civil War, based upon the "Century War Series," edited by Robert Underwood Johnson and Clarence Clough Buell, four volumes, New York, 1884-1887.

Bierce. *Collected Works of Ambrose Bierce,* Vol. I, New York and Washington, 1909.

Bikle. *George W. Cable: His Life and Letters,* by Lucy Leffingwell Cable Bikle, New York, 1928.

Brown. Manuscript of Lieutenant Tully Brown, Morton's Battery, subsequently Adjutant General, State of Tennessee, in Tennessee State Library.

Buck. *Cleburne and His Command,* by Major Irving A. Buck, New York and Washington, 1908.

Confederate Veteran, The, edited by S. A. Cunningham and Miss Edith Pope, 40 volumes, Nashville, 1893-1932.

Denison. *A History of Cavalry,* by Lieutenant Colonel George T. Denison, London, 1877.

Dinkins. *Personal Recollections and Experiences in the Confederate Army,* by Captain James Dinkins, Cincinnati, 1897.

Dodson. *Campaigns of Wheeler and His Cavalry,* by W. C. Dodson, Atlanta, 1899.

Duke. *Reminiscences of General Basil W. Duke, C.S.A.,* New York, 1911.

Dyer. *"Fightin' Joe" Wheeler,* by John P. Dyer, Baton Rouge, 1941.

Eckenrode. *Life of N. B. Forrest,* by H. J. Eckenrode, Richmond, 1918.

Fort Pillow Report. *Reports of the Committee on the Conduct of The War: Fort Pillow Massacre,* 38th Congress, 1st Session, House of Representatives Report No. 65, Washington, 1864.

French. *Two wars: An Autobiography,* by Major General Samuel G. French, Nashville, 1901.

Great Panic, The. Pamphlet published anonymously, Nashville, 1862.

Hancock. *Hancock's Diary, or a History of the Second Tennessee Cavalry, C.S.A.,* by Sergeant R. R. Hancock, Nashville, 1887.

Hanson. *Minor Incidents of the Late War,* by Lieutenant G. A. Hanson, Bartow, Florida, 1887.

Hay. *Hood's Tennessee Campaign,* by Thomas Robson Hay, New York, 1929.

Hearn. *Occidental Gleanings,* by Lafcadio Hearn, edited by Albert Mordell, two volumes, New York, 1925.

Home Letters of General Sherman, edited by M. A. DeWolfe Howe, New York, 1909.

Horn. *Invisible Empire: The Story of the Ku Klux Klan, 1866-1871,* by Stanley F. Horn, Boston, 1939.

Hosea. *Some Side Lights on the War for the Union,* by Brevet Major Lewis M. Hosea, Cleveland, 1912.

Hubbard. *Notes of a Private,* by John Milton Hubbard, St. Louis, 1909, 1913.

Johnson. Manuscript of John N. Johnson, of Dublin, Virginia, in Tennessee State Library.

Johnson. *The Partisan Rangers of the Confederate States Army,* by Brigadier General Adam R. Johnson, Louisville, 1904.

Jordan and Pryor. *The Campaigns of Lieutenant General N. B. Forrest and of Forrest's Cavalry,* by Brigadier General Thomas Jordan and J. P. Pryor, New Orleans and New York, 1868.

Ku Klux Report, 1872. *Ku Klux Conspiracy: Report of the Joint Select Committee to Inquire into the Condition of Affairs in the Late Insurrectionary States,* made to the two Houses of Congress February 19, 1872, 42nd Congress, 2nd Session, Senate Report No. 41, 13 volumes.

Lester and Wilson. *The Ku Klux Klan,* by J. C. Lester and D. L. Wilson, New York, 1884 and (with an introduction by Walter L. Fleming) 1905.

Lindsley. *The Military Annals of Tennessee, Confederate,* edited by John Berrien Lindsley, Nashville, 1886.

Lyon, Mrs. *Reminiscences of the Civil War,* compiled by Mrs. Adelia C. Lyon from the War Correspondence of Colonel William P. Lyon, San Jose, California, 1907.

Lytle. *Bedford Forrest and His Critter Company,* by Andrew Nelson Lytle, New York, 1931.

Mathes. *Bedford Forrest,* by Captain J. Harvey Mathes, New York, 1902. In the "Great Commanders" Series.

Mathes. *Old Guard in Gray, The,* by Captain J. Harvey Mathes, Memphis, 1897.

Maury. *Recollections of a Virginian,* by Major General Dabney H. Maury, New York, 1894.

Merrill. "Block Houses for Railroad Refense," by Colonel William E. Merrill, in *Sketches of War History,* Vol. III, Cincinnati, 1890.

Morton. *The Artillery of Nathan Bedford Forrest's Cavalry,* by John W. Morton, Chief of Artillery, Nashville, 1909.

Morton Scrapbooks. A collection kept by Captain John W. Morton, five volumes.

O.R. *The War of the Rebellion: A Compilation of the Official Records of the Union and Confederate Armies,* 128 volumes plus atlas, Washington, 1881-1901. Citations are to Serial Numbers in accordance with the table on pages iv and v of the General Index Volume (Serial No. 130), rather than to the separate series, volumes and parts.

O.R. (Naval). *Official Records of the Union and Confederate Navies in the War of the Rebellion,* 30 volumes, Washington, 1894-1922.

Piatt and Boynton. *General George H. Thomas,* by Donn Piatt and H. V. Boynton, Cincinnati, 1893.

Prisoner of War and How Treated, Containing a History of Colonel Streight's Expedition to the Rear of Bragg's Army in the Spring of 1863, etc., by Lieutenant A. C. Roach, published by the Railroad City Publishing House, A. D. Streight, proprietor, Indianapolis, 1865.

Ridley. *Battles and Sketches of the Army of Tennessee,* by Lieutenant Bromfield L. Ridley, Mexico, Missouri, 1906.

Scott. *Story of a Cavalry Regiment, 4th Iowa, Veteran Volunteers,* by William Forse Scott, New York, 1893.

Seitz. *Braxton Bragg, General of the Confederacy,* by Don C. Seitz, Columbia, South Carolina, 1924.

Sheppard. *Bedford Forrest, the Confederacy's Greatest Cavalryman,* by Captain Eric William Sheppard, O.B.E., M.C., London and New York, 1930.

Sherman. *Memoirs of General William T. Sherman,* two volumes, New York, 1875.

S. H. S. P. *Southern Historical Society Papers,* 44 volumes, published at Richmond by the Society, 1876—.

Soldier's Honor, A. Memoir of Major General Earl Van Dorn, by His Comrades, New York, 1902.

Southern Bivouac, The. A Literary and Historical Magazine Conducted by Basil W. Duke and R. W. Knott, Louisville, Kentucky, 1882-1887.

Taylor. *Destruction and Reconstruction,* by Lieutenant General Richard Taylor, New York, 1879.

Ward, Mrs. *War Memories—Margaret Ketcham Ward,* reprinted from testimony contained in the *Report of the Committee of the Senate Upon the Relations Between Labor and Capital,* Vol. IV, Washington, Government Printing Office, 1885.

Waring. *Whip and Spur,* by Colonel George E. Waring, Jr., Boston, 1875.

Watkins. *"Co. Aytch," Maury Grays, First Tennessee Regiment;* or, *A Side Show of the Big Show,* by Sam R. Watkins, Columbia, Tennessee, 1882, and Chattanooga, 1900.

Whitson, Mrs. *Gilbert St. Maurice* (a novel), by Mrs. L. D. Whitson, Louisville, 1875.

Wilson. *Under the Old Flag,* by Major General James Harrison Wilson, two volumes, New York, 1912.

Witherspoon. *Reminiscences of a Scout, Spy and Soldier of Forrest's Cavalry,* by William Witherspoon, Jackson, Tennessee, 1910, in which is included the same author's *Tishomingo Creek, or the Battle of Brice's Cross Roads as I Saw It* (Jackson, 1906).

Wolseley. "General Forrest," articles in *United Service Magazine,* Vol. V (New Series), London, 1892, by Field Marshal Viscount Garnet Wolseley, reprinted in part in New Orleans *Picayune* of April 1, 1892, and in *S. H. S. P.,* Vol. 20, pages 325-335.

Wyeth. *Life of General N. B. Forrest,* by John Allan Wyeth, New York, 1899.

Young. *The Seventh Tennessee Cavalry (Confederate): A History,* by J. P. Young, Nashville, 1890.

INDEX

Abbeville, Miss., 310, 330, 343
Abbeville, S. C., 437
Aberdeen, Miss., 224-225
Acworth, Ga., 284
Adams, Dan W., 422, 428, 429, 431
Adams, John, 400
Adams, Wirt, 80, 311, 345, 422, 428, 433
Advance and Retreat, John B. Hood, 395
Agnew, Dr., 295
Akron, Ala., 458
Alabama Great Southern Railroad, 458
Alabama River, 434, 435
Alabama Union Cavalry, 147
Alcorn, James L., 40, 41, 104
Alfaretta, the, 154
Allin, Philip T., 347
Alpine, Ala., 177, 179, 180
Altamont, Tenn., 97
Anderson, Charles W., becomes Forrest's assistant adjutant and inspector general, 104; Forrest confides misgivings about Dover to, 124; Forrest's dispatch to Polk, Sept. 21, 1863, 191; writes to Burford, 197; mentioned, 252; at Fort Pillow, 253, 254, 256; mentioned, 283, 292; Harrisburg, 317, 323; Memphis battle, 340; Middle Tennessee, 352; with Forrest at Rienzi, 423; surrender of South, 437, 438; quoted on Forrest's last illness, 460
Anderson, Patton, 131
Anderson, Ransom, 265
Anderson, Robert, 37, 40
Andrews, Garnett, Jr., 452
Anna, the, 372-373
Anniston (Blue Mountain), Ala., 370
Appomattox, 434, 435
Armstrong, Frank C., Middle Tennessee, 132, 137; Rome, Ga., 156; reorganization of command, 161; Shelbyville, Tenn., 165; at LaFayette, Ga., 178; at Chickamauga, 183, 187; pursuit of Confederates, 191; joins Wheeler, 196, 197, 201; Spring Hill, 390; Nashville, 405, 411; assigned Chalmers, 422; Selma, Ala., 427, 430, 431, 432
Army of Northern Virginia, 47, 180-181, 349
Army of Tennessee, surrender, 47; first West Tennessee campaign, 107, 122; retreat, 164-168; march toward Rome,

Army of Tennessee—*Cont.*
176; Chickamauga, 189, 190, 193; dislike of Bragg, 193; Wheeler assigned to cavalry, 197; visited by Jefferson Davis, 200; Forrest leaves, 201, 203; Forrest uses absentees and deserters from, 207, 279; Johnston becomes commander, 212; in northern Georgia, 240, 276, 281; commanded by Hood, 329; Wheeler's cavalry detached, 347; recalled, 332; supply line, 370; Forrest joins, 379, 382; Nov. 1863-Nov. 1864, 382; Hood's Tennessee campaign, 382-417; Spring Hill, 389-396; Franklin, 396-400; Nashville, 401-412; pursuit by Confederates, 412-417
Army of the Cumberland, 172, 181, 355
"Arp, Bill," *see* Smith, Charles H.
Asheville, N. C., 445
Astor House, 454
Athens, Ala., 353-355, 360, 361, 421
Athens, Tenn., 195
Atlanta, Ga., 347, 365, 370, 382, 384
Aurora, the, 364

Bacot, W. C., 98, 100
Bailey's Ferry, Tenn., 49
Bainbridge (Crossing), Ala., 379, 414, 416
Baird, 184, 186
Baker, John, 153
Baldwyn, Miss., 284, 286-288
Baltimore *Sun,* 20
Bangs, Eli A., 266
Banks, N. P., 244-245, 274
Bardstown, Ky., 100, 319
Barrow, Sen., 64
Barteau, C. R., 214, 224, 228, 254, 256, 265, 291, 293, 354
Bate, William B., 390, 391-392, 393, 400, 402, 403, 404, 405, 409
Batesville, Miss., *see* Panola
Baton Rouge, 421
Baxter, Nat, 118, 195
Bayou Gayoso, Tenn., 371
Beard, Dan, 113
Beauregard, Pierre G. T., 29, 50, 70, 75-81, 82, 379, 383, 420
Bedford County, Tenn., 22
Beech Creek, 109
Bell, Tyree H., West Tennessee, 205, 208, 209, 210-211; commands brigade, 214;

545

546

Duff, 289, 291-292
Duffield, William, 86, 87, 89
Duke, Basil, 19, 201, 453-456
Dunham, Cyrus L., 116-119
Dykes' Bridge, 153, 155

Eagleville, Tenn., 164
Earle, Samuel G., 130
East Lynne, 335
Eastport, Miss., 141, 142, 364, 365, 368, 370, 412, 423, 425
Eastport, the, 50
Eaton, Colonel, 298
Eaton, Tenn., 250
Ebenezer Church (Bogler's Creek), 430, 431, 432
Ector, 184-185, 409, 412
Eddy, Col., 338
Edgefield, Tenn., 57, 64, 68, 106
Edmondson, James H., 127, 145, 148
Eighteenth Mississippi cavalry (Confederate), 337
Eighth Kentucky (Confederate), 236
Eighth Tennessee (Confederate), 104, 144, 172, 201
Eighth Texas (Confederate), 85
Eleventh Tennessee Cavalry (Confederate), 127, 130, 145
Eleventh Tennessee Infantry (Union), 342
Elfin, the, 375
Elizabethtown, 100
Elk River, 356
Elkton, 357
Elliott, Dr., 25
Elliott, Jonas, 355
Ellis, Powhatan, 324
Ellis' Bridge, 225-226
Elmwood Cemetery, 461, 462
Elyton, Ala., 159, 427, 429, 433
Enfield rifles, 345
Enrolled Militia (Memphis), 338
Enterprise, Miss., 354
Erie, the, 338
Estenaula, Tenn., 207-208
Etowah River, 276, 281
Eutaw, Ala., 428, 433, 457

Fairplay, the, 402
Fairy, the, 375
Farmington, Tenn., 201
Farragut, David Glasgow, 107, 305
Farrell, Norman, 452-453
Faulkner, W. W., 205, 210, 212, 214, 236, 246, 278, 288, 298, 426
Faulkner, Mrs. W. W., 297
Fayette County, Tenn., 71
Fayetteville, Tenn., 358
Featherston, W. S., 412
Feild, Hume R., 412
Ferguson, Capt., 258-259, 263
Ferrell's Georgia battery, 145, 155-156, 319

Fifteenth Tennessee Cavalry (Confederate), 337, 347, 386
Fifth Tennessee (Confederate), 201
Finch's Ferry, 425, 428
First Corps of the British Expeditionary Force, 464
First Georgia Cavalry (Confederate), 85
First Missouri Infantry, 65
First Tennessee (Confederate), 77, 133
Fisk, Clinton B., 115, 116
Fitch, C., 264
Fitch, LeRoy, 258-259, 375, 376
Fithian, W., 380
Fleming, railway superintendent, 349
Florence, Ala., 144, 273-274, 303, 352, 360, 362, 368, 379, 382, 384, 385, 402
Floyd, John B., 52f., 65-68
Foote, Andrew H., 49
Forked Deer River, 208, 250
Forrest, Aaron, 22, 271
Forrest, Fanny (sister), 23
Forrest, Jeffrey E. (brother), 22, 23, 31, 55, 59f., 104, 201, 203, 214, 225, 229-230
Forrest, Jesse (brother), 23, 71, 298, 310, 314, 337, 338, 353, 354, 355, 421, 426, 460, 461
Forrest, John (brother), 23, 366
Forrest, Jonathan (uncle), 24
Forrest, Mariam Beck, 22, 23, 367, 456
Forrest, Mary Ann Montgomery (Mrs. N. B. Forrest), 24-25, 366, 367, 439-440, 442, 459, 460, 462
Forrest, Moreau, 362
Forrest, Thomas, 22
Forrest, Nathan (grandfather), 22
Forrest, Nathan Bedford, birth and early life, 13-14, 22; business of, 14, 25-27; characteristics, 14-15; becomes Confederate soldier, 15; soldierly gifts of, 16-18; epigram of, 18-20; second public career, 20-21; goes to aid of Texas, 24; marriage, 24-25; slaves of, 26; moves to Memphis, 26-27; alderman, 27; cotton grower, 27; member of Company D, 31; recruits Mounted Rangers, 31; lieutenant colonel, 39; earliest dispatch, 41; first fight, 42; engagement at Sacramento, 44-45; at Donelson, 51-62; Great Panic at Nashville, 66-69; furloughs men at Huntsville, 71; elected colonel, 71; at Shiloh, 77-80; wounded, 81; recruiting, 82; organizes new brigade, 83-86; raids Murfreesborough, 86-90; gains time for Bragg, 91; at Lebanon, 92; "threatens" Nashville, 92-93; strikes at Manchester, 94; brigadier general, 95; Kentucky campaign, 95-101; demonstrates against Nashville, 106; sent to operate against Grant's rear, 108ff.; captures Trenton, 113; captures men at Rutherford Station, Kenton, and Union

Forrest, Nathan Bedford—*Cont.*

City, 114; at Parker's Cross Roads, 116-119; at Columbia, 122; attack on Dover, 124-126; at Columbia, 127; captures Thompson's Station, 131; captures men at Brentwood, 132-136; thrust against Franklin, 136-138; capture of Streight, 139-159; relations with Van Dorn, 142-143; joins Roddey, 144; at Moulton, 145-146; note to Emma Sanson, 151; praised by Bragg, 160; retreat with the Army of Tennessee, 160-168; takes over Van Dorn's command, 161; and signal flag at Franklin, 161; wounded by Gould, 161-163; at Tullahoma, 167; feared, 171; plan to destroy boats on the Mississippi, 171-172; joins Buckner at Loudon, 174; ordered to Charleston, Tenn., 174; in command of all cavalry east of Chattanooga, 174; Bragg's estimate of, 175; impatience with Bragg, 175; march toward Rome, 176; at Dalton, 178; at Ringgold, 179; wounded at Tunnel Hill, 179; at Chickamauga, 182-189; pursuit of enemy after Chickamauga, 191; letters to Polk, 191-193; interview with Bragg, 193; at Charleston, 195; under Wheeler, 196; protest to Bragg, 198; quarrel with Bragg, 199-200; visit of President Davis, 200; transfer to Mississippi, 200; assigned to command of West Tennessee, 202; under Stephen Lee, 203-204; Johnston's opinion of, 204; recruiting in West Tennessee, 204-207; fight with Prince's men, 208; made major general, 209; at Como, 212; letter to Cooper, 213; organization of army, 215, 220; desertions, 215; absentees, 220; Sherman on, 222; to aid Stephen Lee, 223; at Starkville, 224; at Ellis' Bridge, 225-226; at West Point, 227; value of the offensive, 228; at Okolona, 228-232; praises his men, 231; comments on, 233; letter to President Davis, 233; reorganization of command, 236; and Chalmers, 236; West Tennessee-Kentucky expedition, 237-247; at Paducah, 240; conference at Jackson, 245; Fort Pillow, 248-268; question of "massacre," 248, 256-268; dispatch to Polk quoted, 258; into Middle Tennessee, 270; at Jackson, 273-274; against Sturgis, 275; in Mississippi, 277; troops inspected, 278-279; to Middle Tennessee, 286; Tupelo, 284; defeat of Sturgis at Brice's Cross Roads, 286-304; threat to Sherman's supply line, 307, 309; reorganizing command, 310-312; Union preparations against, 314-315; Harrisburg, 315-327; wounded, 325; turns over command to Chalmers,

Forrest, Nathan Bedford—*Cont.*

325; Union measures to stop, 328-329; rumor of death, 328-329; Maury letter to, 329-330; resumes command, 330; controversy over election of field officers, 330-331; at Oxford, 332-333; march to Memphis, 333-335; raid on Memphis, 338, 341, 342, 343; withdrawal, 339; pursuit by Federals, 339-340; flag of truce, 340; summoned to aid Mobile, 343, 345, 347; indicted for treason, 343-344; reorganizes command, 345-347; ordered to operate against Sherman's communications in Tennessee, 348-349; Maury's description of, 349-350; rail movement, 351; Athens, Ala., 353-355; Middle Tennessee raids, 355-365; requests furlough, 366, 367; neglect of personal affairs, 366-367; organizes command for West Tennessee expedition, 367-369; at Jackson, 369-371; amphibious operations at Paris Landing, 372-374; attack on Johnsonville, 375-379; rumored in Chicago, 380-381; rejoins Army of Tennessee, 382, 384; Spring Hill, 389-396; Franklin, 396-400; at Murfreesborough, 403-405; absence from battle of Nashville, 409-410; joins Nashville battle, 410-411; at Columbia, 413, 414; pursuit by Federals, 414-416; in Corinth, Miss., 418; made commander of cavalry, put in command of District of Mississippi and East Louisiana, 420; circular quoted, 420-421; reorganization, 422; movement toward Selma, 422-423, 425; Hosea's descriptions of, 423-424, 434; opinion of Wilson, 424; need for recruits, 426-427; Alabama campaign, 429-436; Sherman predicts Forrest's lawlessness after surrender, 436; reaction to surrender, 437-438; farewell to troops, 438; financial condition, 439-440; settles on plantation, 440, 441; Blair's opinion of, 441; trial for killing Negro, 442; indictment for treason dropped, 442; believed head of Ku Klux Klan, 442, 443-444; testimony before Ku Klux Investigation, 444-448; "Council of Peace," 449; speech quoted, 449-450; secret meeting with Grant, 450; pessimism about business affairs, 452; delegate to Democratic National Convention, 453-454; issue in campaign of 1868, 454-456; death of mother, 456; receives pardon, 456; organizes railroads, 456-457; accepts Christian faith, 459-460; influence of wife, 460; failing health, 460; death, 461; funeral, 461-462; soldiers' devotion to, 462, 464-465; as cavalry commander, 463, 464; acquaintance with Colonel Sevier, 463-464

548

549

555

Silvey's Ford, 194
Sipsey River, 428, 429
Six Mile Creek, 429, 430
Sixteenth Army Corps, 205, 217, 318, 338, 383, 402
Sixteenth Tennessee, 297-298, 363
Sixth Illinois Cavalry, 339
Sloan, A. M., 159
Smith, A. J., 205-207, 217, 221-227, 229, 232-233, 244-245, 274, 303, 307, 313-326, 328-334, 340-341, 343, 383, 402, 405
Smith, Baxter, 86, 90
Smith, C. F., 56, 71, 73, 76
Smith, Charles H. ("Bill Arp"), 154
Smith, D. D., 146
Smith, Green Clay, 134, 136
Smith, John E., 303
Smith, Kirby, 83, 85, 91, 99, 280, 301
Smith, Morgan L., 368, 371
Smith, Preston, 186
Smith, Thomas Benton, 404, 408, 412, 452, 453
Smith, William Sooy, 94, 206, 217, 219-220, 244, 272, 303, 314, 315, 321, 322, 326, 387
Somerville, Tenn., 209-210, 242, 275
Sons of Liberty, 29
Southern Historical Society, 317
Southern Railway System, 458
Southrons, 29
Spalding, George, 356-357
Sparta, 98, 172
Spaulding, Zephoniah, 117
Spencer repeating carbine, 421, 427
Spring Garden, Ala., 153
Spring Hill, 142, 144, 160, 361, 388, 389-396, 397, 401, 411, 414
Springfield, Ill., 380
Stainback, G. T., 459, 460
Stanley, David S., 136, 137, 164, 165, 383, 389, 390, 394, 395
Stanton, Edwin M., 267, 302, 406
Starke, H. F., 143
Starke, Peter B., 422, 427, 433
Starkville, Miss., 224-225, 235
Starnes, J. W., 43, 44, 95, 106, 111, 118ff., 130, 132-135, 136, 145, 147, 161, 167, 201, 351
Starr, Matthew H., 339-340
State Female College (Memphis), 339
Steedman, James B., 137, 359, 402, 414
Stevens' Gap, 175, 177, 179
Stevenson, Ala., 160, 173, 305, 414
Stevenson, Carter L., 411
Stevenson, V. K., 65
Stewart, Alexander P., 189, 388, 390, 392, 393, 395, 396, 397, 408
Stewart, F. M., 337, 347
Stones River, 122, 400, 403, 404. *See also* Murfreesborough
Strahl, Otho, 186, 399, 412

Straightneck Precinct, Ala., 153
Strange, John P., 71, 119
Strange, Maj., 275, 351, 405
Streight, Abel D., 139-159, 413
Stubbs' Farm, Miss., 287, 295-296
Sturgis, Samuel D., 272, 275-277, 282-287, 289-290, 294, 296-298, 300, 302-303, 307, 326, 387
Sugar Creek, 416
Sullivan, Jere C., 109, 111-113, 114-119, 120
Sulphur Branch, Tenn., 355
Sulphur Trestle, Tenn., 356
Summerville, Ga., 176
Sumner County, Tenn., 22
Sunflower Landing, Miss., 439, 441
Susan Hopley, or the Trials and Vicissitudes of a Servant Girl, 335
Sweeden's Cave, Tenn., 168
Sweet, 380
Sweetwater, Tenn., 195

Tallahatchie River, 212-213, 223, 232, 314, 328, 330, 331, 333, 334, 341, 343
Tate, Thomas, 298
Tawah (No. 29), the, 375
Taylor, J. D., 431
Taylor, Richard, 19, 175, 348-350, 351-352, 356, 358, 366, 367, 368, 370, 378, 383, 418, 420, 422-423, 426, 427, 435-436, 437
Taylor, Zachary, 349
Tennessee and Alabama Railroad, 68
Tennessee Mounted Rangers, 13
Tennessee Mounted Rifles, 30
Tennessee Provisional Army, 29-30, 39
Tennessee River, 39, 49, 305, 352, 360, 362, 363, 364, 365, 368, 369, 373-378, 383-384, 403, 412, 413, 414, 415-416. *See also* Fort Henry, Fort Donelson
Tenth Tennessee, 39, 110, 134, 201, 408
Third Arkansas Cavalry, 130
Third Kentucky, 236
Third Minnesota Infantry, 86
Third Tennessee (Union), 229, 354
Thirteenth Tennessee Cavalry (Union), 249
Thirty-second Alabama Infantry, 102
Thirty-seventh Tennessee Regiment, 408
Thomas, DeWitt, 297
Thomas, George H., commands Union recruits at Camp Robinson, 37; commands at McMinnville, 95; dispatch to Buell, 98; considers sending expedition after Forrest, 99; Chickamauga, 173-174, 177-180, 182, 186, 188-90; reinforced by Sherman, 204, 205; quoted, 357; sent to dispose of Forrest, 359, 362; Forrest escapes, 363-364; commands in Tennessee, 370, 382; garrisons and troops of, 383; overwhelms Hood, 385; instructs Schofield to delay Hood, 387; warned

557